PRICE
THEORY
AND
APPLICATIONS

JACK
HIRSHLEIFER
University of California, Los Angeles

PRICE
THEORY
AND
APPLICATIONS

THIRD EDITION

Prentice-Hall, Inc., Englewood Cliffs, N.J. 07632

Library of Congress Cataloging in Publication Data

HIRSHLEIFER, JACK.
   Price theory and applications.

   Includes bibliographical references and index.
   1. Microeconomics.   I.   Title.
HB172.H55   1984   338.5   83-21165
ISBN   0-13-699736-8

Editorial/production supervision: Barbara Grasso
Interior and cover design: Anne T. Bonanno
Manufacturing buyer: Ed O'Dougherty

Printed in the United States of America

10   9   8   7   6   5   4   3

ISBN 0-13-699736-8

Prentice-Hall International, Inc., *London*
Prentice-Hall of Australia Pty. Limited, *Sydney*
Editora Prentice-Hall do Brasil, Ltda., *Rio de Janeiro*
Prentice-Hall Canada Inc., *Toronto*
Prentice-Hall of India Private Limited, *New Delhi*
Prentice-Hall of Japan, Inc., *Tokyo*
Prentice-Hall of Southeast Asia Pte. Ltd., *Singapore*
Whitehall Books Limited, *Wellington, New Zealand*

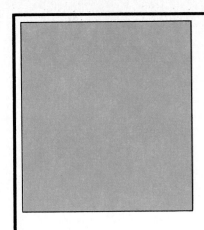

CONTENTS

PART TWO: PREFERENCE, CONSUMPTION, AND DEMAND

PART THREE: THE FIRM AND THE INDUSTRY

CONTENTS   ix

PART SEVEN: POLITICAL ECONOMY

PREFACE

Economics is a science designed to explain the real world. So it is not only dull but fundamentally misleading to present "theory" in the absence of "applications." I have provided dozens of boxed Examples throughout this book to indicate specific ways—and, of course, specifics are essential here—in which microeconomic theory does indeed illuminate the real world. These discussions, based as they usually are upon recent research reported in scholarly books or journals, also help the student gain some idea as to the scientific work that economists actually do. (This is a story that needs telling. Judging from the media picture, the economics profession is nothing but a squabbling band of rival soothsayers. That there are actual scientific results in economics may be a surprise to most students.) In addition to these brief Examples, many applied topics—among them the negative income tax, rationing of consumption goods, monopolistic suppression of inventions, and minimum-wage laws—are discussed in more extended fashion at appropriate places in the text.

Two other methodological points warrant mentioning. First, I try to emphasize that economics is a way of thinking, something over and above a body of facts or propositions to be memorized. How often have we heard a student say, "Prof, tell me what pages you want me to learn and I guarantee I'll know every word." Such a student is always chagrined to hear that memorization is not enough. On the other hand, not everything can be left to inspiration; there is no blinking the fact that some hard slogging work is required. In economics, as elsewhere, there is no easy royal road to true understanding. Only by working through actual models can a sound base for understanding be built.

Second, traditional economics has been narrow in its conception of man, and insular in ignoring the problems addressed and results achieved elsewhere in the social sciences. (The opposite side of the coin is the very true proposition that economics has much to contribute to these other disciplines.) I have therefore made use of materials from scientific work in anthropology, psychology, political science, social biology, etc., wherever economic principles or methods could be illuminated thereby. To cite but one instance, students frequently complain that a businessman can hardly be expected to engage in anything as subtle and complex as marginal analysis. But biologists have discovered numerous instances where marginal analysis correctly predicts animal behavior (see "Birds Do It! Bees Do It!" in Chapter 2), and we know that birds and bees are dumber than businessmen. On the side of technique, only recently has the classical scientific method of *experiment* begun to play an important role in economic research. This is a very exciting development. Accordingly, I have devoted quite a few of the Examples to reports of experimental studies. One important instance: while the conditions of perfect competition are never fully satisfied in the real world, we have learned from experiments that even highly imperfect markets may generate results close to the theoretical ideal (see "Experiments in Perfect and Imperfect Markets" in Chapter 13).

As to coverage and level of difficulty, *this is not a minimal book.* Partly to meet the needs of a range of users, partly to build in growth potential (so that the text can serve as reference and guide for later self-study or coursework), or perhaps just because there's so much fascinating material I couldn't bear to exclude, there is more here than can usually be covered in briefer (one term or less) intermediate-theory courses. To meet the needs of instructors and students in briefer or less demanding courses, a shorter book-within-the-book exists in the series of *Core Chapters* (Chapters 1-8 and 11-13). Also, if time pressures so dictate, certain more advanced or tangential discussions (set apart in specially marked sections or sub-sections within the chapters) can be omitted. A two-term undergraduate course, I have found, however, can cover all or almost all the material in the text.

A special effort has been made to provide aids to understanding, which now include the following: (1) Explanatory descriptive legends accompany the diagrams; a student often can efficiently review a chapter by reading these legends in sequence. (2) Each chapter is followed by a Summary and two groups of Questions—a first group for review, and a second for further thought and discussion. Answers to about half the questions are provided in the back of the book. (3) As an innovation for this edition, a good many numerical exercises have been introduced (with worked answers) right into the main text.

Users of the preceding edition will find substantial organizational changes in the text. Condensation has permitted elimination of two chapters, and the order of topics has also been modified. Part One ("Introduction") and Part Two ("Preference, Consumption, and Demand") continue as before. Part III now moves directly to "The Firm and the Industry," viewed in terms of product-market prices and outputs. The more difficult factor-market aspects (production, factor demand, etc.) are covered together with the individual's factor-supply decisions in a separate Part IV ("Factor Markets and Income Distribution"). Part V takes up "Exchange," Part VI "Intertemporal Analysis," and Part VII "Political Economy."

A number of features of this book are, I claim, improvements upon conventional textual coverage. Among them I will mention:

1. Traditional intermediate texts offer no price-theoretic explanation for *money*. In Part V the analysis of exchange as a costly economic activity provides the foundation for understanding how a monetary commodity works. And even earlier, in Part III, it will have been indicated that the existence of business firms is also a consequence of the costliness of exchange.

2. "Monopolistic competition" is covered in Part III under a more general heading—variation of product. The topics under this heading also include equilibrium of product *quality* and of product *assortment*.

3. Saving and investment are tied to the underlying theory of intertemporal choice and equilibrium in Part VI. The coverage here provides a bridge to macroeconomics, and to the business-finance literature.

4. In Part VII on "Political Economy," after a treatment of the traditional normative issues of welfare economics in Chapter 15, the final Chapter 16 moves on to a *positive* analysis of government. Two views of the state, a voluntarist or public choice model versus an exploitative or conflict model, are contrasted. The novel theory of conflict interactions offered here represents, I believe, the first time this overwhelmingly important topic has been addressed in an intermediate economics text.

As to the mathematics required, as in previous editions calculus techniques are employed only in marked mathematical footnotes. But the delta (Δ) notation used in defining marginal concepts will be naturally translated into derivative or differential terms by the student equipped with calculus. The instructor should, of course, warn students that further command of college math will be necessary in order to study economics beyond the intermediate level.

Whether a proper balance has been struck between coverage and simplicity, between theory and application, between technical accuracy and intuitive suggestion, only the reader can judge. I will be grateful for guidance on this point from instructors and students, as well as for specific corrections where errors appear.

As in past editions, a Teacher's Manual for this third edition of *Price Theory and Applications* is available to instructors, upon request, from the publisher. For the first time with this edition, a Study Guide to accompany the text will be available for purchase by students. The Study Guide has been prepared by Professor Michael Sproul of Loyola Marymount University of Los Angeles.

ACKNOWLEDGMENTS

In its several editions this book has had the advantage of helpful reviews by many colleagues, including Professors Daniel S. Christiansen, Robert Dorfman, Ross Eckert, David L. McNicol, Edwin Mills, R. Charles Moyer, Allen R. Sanderson, and Lloyd M. Valentine. I am particularly grateful to the faculty members, students, and other readers who independently took the trouble to send me valuable corrections and comments. Thanks are due to my research assistants over the years, who have worked mainly on the Examples used in the text and on the questions and answers at the end of each chapter: Charles Knoeber for the first edition; for the second edition Ralph Cole, Gary Galles, David A. Hirshleifer, Carroll Shelor, M. Holly Crawford, Shirley Svorny, and Richard Tontz; and for this third edition Michael Sproul and Laurel Clark. As in the previous edition, typing and editorial assistance of an exceptional order was provided by Lorraine Grams, nobly assisted by Carole Wilbur.

PRICE
THEORY
AND
APPLICATIONS

1

THE NATURE AND SCOPE OF ECONOMICS

CORE CHAPTER

Economics concerns decisions—choosing among actions. The first thing to appreciate about decisions is that every possible course of action has its pros and cons, benefits and costs. Tennis may trim your figure and improve your disposition, but take time from your studies and damage your joints. If you drop out of college you can start earning an income right away, but completing your degree might lead to a more rewarding lifetime career. And similarly in business and government: every conceivable decision—whether it be the corner grocer putting a price-tag on potatoes or the Congress of the United States voting on a declaration of war—will encounter arguments for and against. How then can we ever decide? Economics develops methods for determining the *best* action through a systematic assessment of all the relevant pros and cons.

Economics also studies what happens when different people's decisions *interact*, as they usually will. If the grocer raises the price of potatoes, customers are likely to reduce their purchases—so that the higher price may not, after all, yield the grocer any bigger profit. And similarly when it comes to social problems: once the likely responses of other people are taken into account, the outcome often turns out to be much less attractive than first appears. Take a scheme that might seem at first glance to alleviate some social anguish, for example a law requiring all grocers to cut food prices in half so that the poor can afford to buy more to eat. Before concluding that this is a good idea we would surely have to allow for the reactions of the grocers and of their suppliers—will they be able and willing to provide grocery products at the lower prices?(A law forcing sellers to cut prices in half may seem like something unlikely ever to happen. But when, for example, apartment rents are frozen during a generally inflationary period, in *real* terms the suppliers of housing services are being compelled to accept a sharp price reduction.)

Economics has been called the dismal science because economists are so often the ones who have to bring the bad news: to wit, that a superficially appealing project or scheme may turn out not to be such a great idea once the responses of *all* the affected individuals are properly taken into account.

Let's look at some other examples. The following Table lists a number of social problems with possible "solutions." (Notice that sometimes the same problem has diametrically opposed "solutions.") Take a moment yourself to think of possible objections to each solution listed. Then note the "hidden" adverse consequences mentioned for each.

SOCIAL PROBLEMS	"SOLUTIONS"

1. Our country's steel producers are threatened by competition from imports.

Impose a tariff on imported steel.

Possible "hidden" consequences: (a) Our country's steel consumers will have to pay more for steel and so will consume less. (b) Foreigners, once they sell fewer goods to us, will buy less of our country's exports.

2. Apartment rentals have gotten very high.

Freeze apartment rents.

Possible "hidden" consequences: (a) Landlords will skimp on upkeep and repair of apartments. (b) In the longer run, fewer rental units will be constructed.

3. Women who are "mere housewives" are living unfulfilled lives, not contributing their talents to society at large.

Encourage females to leave the home and find market employment.

Possible "hidden" consequences: (a) Women's wages in market employment will tend to fall. (b) Husbands, having more household chores, will be less productive at work.

4. Commercial fishing for tuna kills large numbers of dolphins.

Require our nation's fishermen to use special nets that permit dolphins to escape.

Possible "hidden" consequences: (a) Consumers will have to pay more for tuna. (b) Foreign fishermen will take over more of the tuna trade.

5. Medical costs are very high.

Have government pay a share of medical bills, especially for the poor.

Possible "hidden" consequences: (a) Doctor's bills and hospital charges will rise even more than they had previously. (b) Taxes will have to go up.

6. Huge numbers of people are becoming addicted to drugs.

Toughen enforcement of narcotics laws.

Possible "hidden" consequences: (a) Street prices of narcotics will rise, forcing addicts to engage in more anti-social behavior to feed the habit. (b) Huge financial stakes in the narcotics trade will lead to more corruption of the police and judiciary.

7. Same as number 6.

Abandon enforcement of narcotics laws.

Possible "hidden" consequences: Increased availability and lower prices of narcotics will widen usage and addiction.

How many of these "hidden" consequences did you think of yourself? [If you got them all, perhaps you don't need to study this book.] Are they all valid, do you think? Are there others that should be added? Finally, why is it that such consequences are so often overlooked? [*Probable answer:* Because they involve something not directly visible here and now, *changes* in people's behavior as they react to the imposed "solution."]

Discovering undesirable consequences does not necessarily imply that a proposal should be rejected. *All* the consequences, favorable and unfavorable, must be considered and weighed. But when people become committed to one side of the question they generally don't want to listen to contrary arguments. So learning to think like an economist may not make you very popular, although it will make your private decisions more effective and your views on social issues more balanced.

The economist is thus the opposite of the *advocate*, someone who looks only for arguments favoring his or her side of the question. Of course, there is a time and a place for advocacy. If you were on trial for murder you'd probably not want your lawyer to present the evidence for your guilt with the same enthusiasm as the evidence for your innocence. And we all know of people who can never stop saying "But, on the other hand . . . ," who are incapable of needed action. ("The native hue of resolution is sicklied o'er by the pale cast of thought"— *Hamlet*.) Nor can the economist replace the *prophet* and *poet* who inspire us to aim at ideal goals. Economics does not give us our goals, but only weighs the consequences of trying to achieve them. Prophets and poets, men and women of action, and even advocates are needed elements in society. But so are economists.

1.A
ECONOMICS AS A SOCIAL SCIENCE

It may have struck you that the outlook attributed to the economist is essentially the same as that of the *scientist*. And indeed this book is an introduction to economics as a science: as a body of analytical models (theories) that yield verifiable implications about the real world. More specifically, economics is a *social* science; it aims to explain how human beings interact with one another in the world of affairs.

1.A.1 ☐ Is Economics a Science?

Is economics really a science? Let's first hear from a cynic: "Anyone who reads the papers knows that economists are always disagreeing with one another—that doesn't give me much confidence that economics has arrived at scientific truth. Furthermore, if economics can scientifically predict financial and commercial events, why aren't all economists rich?"

Differences among economists do not necessarily mean that economics is unscientific. All sciences advance through disagreement, as new theories challenge established ideas. In astronomy the geocentric model of Ptolemy was opposed by the new heliocentric model of Copernicus; in chemistry Priestley supported the phlogiston theory of combustion while Lavoisier propounded the oxidation theory; and in biology the creationism of earlier naturalists was countered by Darwin's theory of evolution. It is not universal agreement but rather the willingness to consider evidence that signals the scientific approach. For Galileo's opponents to disagree with him about Jupiter's moons was not unscientific of itself; what was unscientific was their refusal to look through his telescope and see. An inspection of economics texts and journals will reveal that current great issues, whether it be the monetarist versus fiscalist hypotheses in macroeconomics, or the determinants of labor's share in distribution theory, or the effectiveness of centralized planning for achieving economic growth, are under continuous scientific evaluation. Failure to arrive at a general scientific consensus[1] may be due to the complexity of the problem or the incompetence of the investigators, but there will always be unresolved issues in any living science.

---

[1]*Scientific* consensus need not imply general agreement as to *policy*, however. See the discussion of "Normative versus Positive Analysis" in Section 1.A.3 below.

Are there, however, any *resolved* issues in economics? This book will highlight a great many, in the area of price theory or microeconomics. (For some comments on *macro*economics, see Section 1.D below.) There is little remaining disagreement on essentials of such topics as the impact of taxes or subsidies on prices and outputs, the implications for consumers of competitive versus monopolistic market structures, the effects of reducing tariffs, etc.

Observers often exaggerate not only the extent of disagreement among economists, but also the degree to which the natural sciences (sometimes miscalled the "exact" sciences) have mastered their respective fields of inquiry. Few topics have been so well studied as strength of materials in applied physics. Yet engineers, after going through their calculations, commonly add on a huge safety factor (50% or even 100%) before undertaking construction of a bridge or a dam. And even so, bridges still collapse and dams wash away. If economists predicting the rate of inflation were permitted as wide a safety factor as engineers, they would rarely go astray.

EXAMPLE 1.1
Hydrology versus Economics

In 1955 the Board of Water Supply of New York City projected that the city's future rate of water use would reach 1320 MGD (million gallons per day) as of 1960, rising further to 1500 MGD by 1970. "Safe yield" (a hydrologic concept supposedly representing a reliable minimum supply) from existing water sources was pegged at 1550 MGD throughout. With only a thin safety margin (1550 − 1500 = 50 MGD) anticipated as remaining by 1970, the Board of Water Supply decided to acquire a new water source to come into service before that date.

A team of economists reviewed this decision in 1960. They concluded that the Board's projections of water use were much too high; the economists' prediction was that actual water use in New York City would surely not reach 1500 MGD by 1970, if ever. Since the "safe yield" supposedly guaranteed by hydrologic science already equaled 1550 MGD, the economists concluded that an enormously expensive new supply was not warranted.

After 1960, the economists' prediction about actual use was borne out. Water consumption in New York City stabilized well below 1300 MGD, far under the Board's projected rate of 1500 MGD, and never came anywhere near the supposed "safe yield" of 1550 MGD. So all should have been well. Instead, the city was hit by a catastrophic water shortage. What had happened? Throughout the early 1960s the *actual* yield of water sources was far, far below the hydrologists' alleged "safe yield." In the four successive years 1962 through 1965, the *highest* actual water yield was only 1204 MGD. Economics, one of the social sciences, thus proved to be immensely more reliable than one of the vaunted natural sciences.[a]

[a]For a discussion, see J. Hirshleifer and J. W. Milliman, "Urban Water Supply: A Second Look," *American Economic Review*, v. 47 (May 1967), pp. 169–78.

What about the charge that if economics were truly a science, economists would all be rich? To this several answers, not all mutually consistent, are commonly offered. It is sometimes argued that a scientific knowledge of economics ought *not* to be expected to lead to financial success. If Henry Aaron had studied the aerodynamic equations governing the motion of spheroidal missiles, would that have helped him beat Babe Ruth's home-run record? This argument should not be pressed too far, however. After all, what is the use of economics (or of aerodynamic knowledge, for that matter) if it does not lead to *some* practical result? In the case of economics this usefulness is surely in understanding market phenomena, which ought to be convertible, at least to some extent, into higher cash income. While the general run of people can hardly be expected to match the achievements of geniuses like Henry Aaron in his field or J. Paul Getty in his, there ought to be some observable effect of economics training on income. And indeed, it seems, to some degree there is!

EXAMPLE 1.2
Salaries

The Table below shows salaries for college instructors in a number of selected fields.

Salaries of University or College Instructors with Ph.D.'s (1975)

FIELD	MEDIAN SALARY
Engineers	$18,900
Medical scientists	18,700
Economists	18,400
Agricultural scientists	18,200
Oceanographers	18,100
Computer specialists	18,000
Statisticians	17,800
Physicists	17,700
Earth scientists	16,900
Psychologists	16,900
Mathematicians	16,800
Sociologists/anthropologists	16,800
Social scientists, other than economists or sociologists	16,800
Chemists	16,600
Biological scientists	16,200

Source: National Science Foundation, *Characteristics of Doctoral Scientists and Engineers in the United States.* 1975 Surveys of Science Resources Series, pp. 112–13.

Nevertheless, the data in Example 1.2 do not prove that it is *the economics training* that leads to the higher incomes reported. There are other possible explanations of income differentials. It might be that economics is so unpleasant that its practitioners must be offered added financial compensation—rather like sewage workers or hangmen. Or perhaps the higher salaries that economists earn are only normal rewards for those exceptional talents necessary to understand economics in the first place.

The following quotation from Aristotle (384–322 B.C.) is also of some relevance. Aristotle is discussing his predecessor Thales (approx. 636–546 B.C.), considered to be the first Greek philosopher and scientist.

> Thales . . . was reproached for his poverty, which was supposed to show the uselessness of philosophy; but observing from his knowledge of meteorology (so the story goes) that there was likely to be a heavy crop of olives, and having a small sum at his command, he paid down earnest-money, early in the year, for the hire of all the olive presses in Miletus and Chios; and he managed, in the absence of any higher offer, to secure them at a low rate. When the season came, and there was a sudden and simultaneous demand for a number of presses, he let out the stock he had collected at any rate he chose to fix, and making a considerable fortune he succeeded in proving that it is easy for philosophers to become rich if they so desire, though it is not the business which they are really about. (Aristotle, *Politics,* I.)

Thales was renowned not only as a meteorologist but as an astronomer, mathematician, and statesman. Still, we may doubt Aristotle's assertion that "it is easy for philosophers to become rich if they so desire"—unless, like Thales, a philosopher happens to be a pretty good economist as well.

1.A.2 □ The Scope of Economics

Economics is not the only social science. Sociology, anthropology, political science, social psychology, and even social biology have much to contribute to our understanding of how human beings behave in relation to their fellows. No absolute boundaries can be drawn between the topics covered by economics and those addressed by her sister social sciences. That the boundaries are indistinct is actually a healthy intellectual situation, since the modes of attack of different disciplines can then compete over the bordering territories. It is useful to think of economics as having a central nucleus, plus outlying extensions into the domains more usually associated with other disciplines. The nucleus of economics covers a limited range of human activity: *rational behavior,* on the part of individuals who relate to one another through a particular social mechanism, the *market.*

What is "rational behavior"? At least two meanings are in common use (and are often confused). The first meaning refers to *method,* the second to *result.* In terms of method, rational behavior is action selected on the basis of considered thought rather than habit, prejudice, or emotion. In terms of result, rational behavior is action that does in fact achieve your goals. The two are not the same. In the first place, good method can lead to bad result: "The best laid schemes o' mice and men/Gang aft a-gley" (Robert Burns). And Nature shows us that the seemingly inferior methods available to creatures with very limited capacity for thought often work very well. Anyone who has chased a fly with a swatter knows that the insect, despite its tiny brain, may defeat us and achieve its goal of survival. But in general, on the human level we expect that considered thought will (at least on average) lead to better action.

Everyone behaves irrationally to some extent—out of passion, thoughtlessness, mental defect, or just plain perverseness. Some do so to such a degree that they are institutionalized for their own or others' protection. In view of the prevalence of human irrationality, how can rationality be postulated in economics? Clearly, only to the extent that the assumption works in providing usable predictions of social phenomena. Rational behavior is systematic and purposive, whereas irrational behavior tends to be unpredictable and erratic. Since it is the aggregate behavior of a great number of individuals that determines social results, the cumulative effect of even a limited degree of rationality tends to dominate over the unsystematic irrational elements. Predictions of social phenomena in terms of rational responses do tend to work, often in surprising ways (see "Rational Psychotics?", Example 1.3 below). And yet economics as a science is not irrevocably wedded to the rationality postulate. When an alternative that proves more usable for predictive purposes comes along, it will be adopted instead.

EXAMPLE 1.3
Rational Psychotics?[a]

With 44 female psychotics (primarily schizophrenics) as experimental subjects, the psychologists T. Ayllon and N. H. Azrin studied responsiveness of patients in a mental institution to changes in systems of reward for services. Prior to the beginning of the experiment patients were allowed to choose among a variety of tasks (laundry service, dietary service, etc.) for which they were to be rewarded. The reward took the form of tokens, which were con-

[a]Discussion based upon T. Ayllon and N. H. Azrin, "The Measurement and Reinforcement of Behavior of Psychotics," *Journal of the Experimental Analysis of Behavior,* v. 8 (Nov. 1965).

vertible into commissary articles (clothing, toiletries, cigarettes, etc.) or into hospital privileges (e.g., privacy, leave from the ward).

During the first 20 days patients were rewarded with tokens only upon completion of their tasks—a system the psychologists term "contingent reinforcement." After 20 days it was announced that the same number of tokens as before would henceforth be paid each patient automatically, *whether or not the tasks were performed*—in psychological jargon, a shift to a system of "non-contingent reinforcement." On an average day in the first period of "contingent reinforcement" (that is, where wages were paid for services rendered), the 44 patients worked 45 hours in total, just a bit over one hour per patient per day. After the shift to "non-contingent reinforcement" (i.e., to the free gift of tokens) the total number of hours worked by the 44 patients declined to 35 on the first day and to 20 hours on the third. Shortly afterward the bottom dropped out, and close to zero hours were worked thereafter.

Then, at the end of a second period of 20 days, the earlier system of "contingent reinforcement" was reinstated. The total number of hours worked jumped immediately to 45 hours per day, and remained near that level to the end of the experiment 20 days later.

CONCLUSION: The experimental subjects may have been psychotic, but they were not stupid. They showed an ability to adapt to systems of rewards in their society. If working was necessary to earn these rewards, they worked; if the rewards came without working, they chose not to work.

Rationality is an instrumental concept. It requires the prior existence of goals. The economist regards the process whereby individuals somehow become pointed toward particular desired ends as outside his sphere of competence. He is interested only in the net result of this process, the patterns that he calls *tastes* or *wants* or *preferences*. These are, from his point of view, arbitrary. In one society individuals may protect children but eat cattle; another society may protect cattle but expose unwanted infants. Either way, the scientific economist is prepared to make predictions about the social consequences of the given preferences.

This undoubtedly leaves a great territory, including what are perhaps the most important aspects of social phenomena, for other sciences to study. Goals and preferences are not determined randomly. Psychologists explain them in terms of primitive instincts, as reinforced or suppressed by socialization processes. Anthropologists analyze the relevance of culture for goal formation, and sociologists the relevance of class or other group identification. Social biologists have shown that human goals must have tended over evolutionary time to promote the survival of the individuals concerned and their offspring, since otherwise the process of natural selection would have eliminated them in the long period of development of the human species. The economist has allowed this division of intellectual labor to operate, leaving the explanation of the formation of tastes and goals as a task for other social sciences.

The economist's mode of procedure inclines him to suppose that preferences are generally quite *stable*, only rarely constituting the dynamic element in social changes. If a tax on liquor is imposed, his analysis will almost automatically assume that the desire to drink is just as great—only that the tax makes it more expensive to indulge that desire. This represents a possible blind spot. Take liquor: the temperance campaign of Father Mathew around 1850 in Ireland reduced that country's consumption of spirits from 12,000,000 to 5,000,000 gallons per annum (but only temporarily). And if there is a higher tax on liquor, its imposition may itself reflect a change of tastes in the form of increased revulsion against drinking. Nor is the assumption of unchanging tastes very helpful for analyzing the element of fashion and style in consumption. Far more important, many of the really great social changes in human history have clearly stemmed from shifts in people's goals for living. Indeed, the economist is in danger of trivializing these fundamental values and goals by suggesting that they are merely arbitrary "tastes." From the prophets of ancient Israel to the ministry of Jesus to the recent decline in effective belief in God, the changes in the kinds of rewards that people seek from life have had an enormous effect upon the shape of the social system of the West. The ethical messages of Buddha and Confucius have perhaps had similar impacts upon the civilization of the East. The areas the economist fails to explain are therefore at least as important as those he feels equipped to examine.

It is sometimes charged that economics also postulates that people's preferences are completely selfish. This is an uninformed criticism. It is true that, observing facts as they really are, the economist ordinarily operates on the premise that individuals seek their own advantage. "It is not from the benevolence of the butcher, the brewer, or the baker, that we expect our dinner, but from their regard to their own interest."[2] That this is a main truth about human activity it would be absurd to deny. Nevertheless, charity is an important feature of economic life; people have, in a sense, a taste for benevolence. Even so, the economist is likely to say, if benevolence were made less costly (for example, if the Internal Revenue Service permitted more ample tax deductions for charitable giving) we would see more of it. As another example, the economist can hardly explain the aid that parents give children in terms of complete selfishness. But again, if we want to elicit a higher degree of love and care on the part of parents, a financial inducement would help.

In addition to the postulate of rational choice, the sensible selection of means for achieving given ends, the nucleus of economics has also specified something about the ways in which people's rational decisions interact. If consumer A wants bread from baker B, it may seem like rational behavior for A to get a job and earn the price of a loaf. But it may also be rational, in certain circumstances, for A to simply steal the bread from B. Alternatively, A might organize a political party with the object of passing laws dictating that B must give bread to A. Or, A might attempt to persuade B that it is the latter's charitable duty to help out hungry A's. Economics concentrates upon the first of these forms of interaction: the integration of individuals' separate goal-seeking activ-

[2]Adam Smith, *The Wealth of Nations,* Book I, Chap. 2.

ities *through the market.* For the most part crime has been left to sociology, the uses of state power to political science, and techniques of persuasion to psychology. But the vigor and rigor of economic science are proving increasingly useful in these related areas. Economics has tended, therefore, to overflow these boundaries, as the following example shows.

EXAMPLE 1.4 _____
Rational Criminals?

Crime may well be, in certain circumstances, an effective way of achieving one's goals without using the market. (That is, without bothering to offer something in exchange for what one wants to get.) The dominant opinion in modern criminology (a field of study which, up to quite recently, made no use of economic analysis) had been that criminals were best thought of as individuals with "deviant" motivations. The solution to crime, it was therefore inferred, should be sought on the psychological level—for example, by improving the mental health of potential criminals, or providing them with better role models to follow. Economic analysis, without necessarily denying that criminals are psychologically "deviant" in some ways, suggests nevertheless that they may still (like the psychotics in Example 1.3 above) respond to changes in incentives in a way that could be regarded as rational.

A study by Isaac Ehrlich asked whether commission of major felonies was affected by the punishments and rewards for crime in the different states of the United States.[a] As economists would expect, the crime rate tended to be lower the more effective the punishment. The rate of commission of robberies, for example, decreased about 1.3% in response to each 1% increase in the proportionate *probability* of punishment and also decreased about 0.4% for each 1% increase in the *severity* of punishment (length of imprisonment). Another seemingly rational response was that the property crime rate in a state tended to be higher where average income and inequality of income were both high. Presumably, in those states criminals were relatively poor individuals living in an environment containing many attractive targets.

The most controversial of Ehrlich's results concerned the effect of capital punishment in deterring murder. Concentrating emphasis on the abnormal psychology of murderers, the standard view in criminology had been that murderers are surely too "deviant" to be deterred by the threat of execution. Yet Ehrlich's investigation indicated very big deterrent effects: according to one set of data each execution was associated with 7 to 8 fewer murders, according to another set 20 to 24 fewer murders.[b]

[a]I. Ehrlich, "Participation in Illegitimate Activities: A Theoretical and Empirical Investigation," *Journal of Political Economy,* v. 81 (May/June 1973).
[b]I. Ehrlich, "The Deterrent Effect of Capital Punishment: A Question of Life and Death," *American Economic Review,* v. 65 (June 1975), p. 414; "Capital Punishment and Deterrence: Some Further Thoughts and Additional Evidence," *Journal of Political Economy,* v. 85 (Aug. 1977), p. 779.

These inferences were, however, based upon complex statistical manipulations, to which a number of more or less serious reservations or objections were raised by critics. A panel of the National Academy of Sciences, mainly consisting of non-economists, was set up to review the conclusions of Ehrlich and the broadly similar results reached by other economists studying crime. The panel, while conceding that the evidence tended to support the deterrence hypothesis, nevertheless regarded it as still unproven.[c] As more data are accumulated and more accurate analytical techniques are devised, we can expect this scientific disagreement ultimately to be resolved.

[c]Panel on Research in Deterrent and Incapacitative Effects, *Deterrence and Incapacitation: Estimating the Effects of Criminal Sanctions on Crime Rates* (Washington, D.C.: National Academy of Sciences, 1978).

These results suggest that economic analysis is applicable also to non-market interactions. And indeed, even the social inter-relationships of animals (which do not ordinarily engage in anything recognizably like exchange) are beginning to be analyzed by biologists in economic terms.[3] One important human non-market form of interaction is *politics*, a topic that will be examined from the economic point of view in Part Seven of this book.

Returning to market interactions, these have distinctive characteristics that set them apart from other forms of human transactions. *The market relation is mutual and voluntary.* Theft, a non-market interaction, is clearly *involuntary* on one side. The gift relation, another non-market interaction, is voluntary but not *mutual.* Two different objections can immediately be raised on this score. First, if A is hungry and B has bread, can their relation really be voluntary? Must not the A's of this world be "wage slaves" of the B's? Then how does the market differ from coercive dominance? Second, suppose some highwayman declares to his victim, "Your money or your life!" Isn't he offering a voluntary deal? Then how can criminal transfers be distinguished from market exchange?

The explanation of these puzzles turns on the legal concept of *property*. To take up the highwayman first, he is indeed proposing a market deal: to "sell" the victim back his or her own life, in exchange for money. But under our legal system each person has property in his or her own life. The seemingly voluntary transaction proposed by the highwayman is premised upon his seizing power over something he has no right to—his victim's life. As for the "wage slave" contention, it is of course true that those endowed with more valuable property will be better off in the market than those possessing little in the way of resources. But there is a vast difference between laborers possessing property rights in their own labor power, in a position to bargain with alternative employers for the best

[3]Martin L. Cody, "Optimization in Ecology," *Science*, v. 183 (March 22, 1974): David J. Rapport and James E. Turner, "Economic Models in Ecology," *Science*, v. 195 (Jan. 18, 1977).

available terms, and slaves. The latter have no property; indeed, they are property. They cannot market or trade their labor power, for it is not legally theirs to dispose of.

1.A.3 ☐ Normative versus Positive Analysis: "Is" versus "Ought"

In its scientific aspect economics is strictly *positive*. It answers the question "What is reality like?" But *normative* issues in public policy, turning upon the question "What ought to be done?", also require economic analysis. Given the social objective aimed at, scientific economists can use their knowledge of reality to analyze the problem and suggest efficient means for attaining the desired end. This book will touch upon many policy issues, always emphasizing the positive point of view.

When economists disagree on policy issues, it may be because they are seeking divergent goals; one may be more concerned with achieving social equality, another with promoting individual freedom. Where the divergence is on such a philosophical plane even the most complete scientific understanding of economic reality will not resolve the conflict. But it is often the case that variance of opinion among economists is over *means* rather than *goals*. Further scientific progress in positive economics will, over time, tend to eliminate this source of disagreement.

1.B
THE INVISIBLE HAND

As astronomy has Newton's principle of universal gravitation, and biology Darwin's principle of evolution through natural selection, economics also has a great unifying scientific conception. Its discovery was, like Newton's and Darwin's, one of the important intellectual achievements of humanity.

Adam Smith's *The Wealth of Nations* appeared in 1776. The key idea is suggested by the following quotation:

> But it is only for the sake of profit that any man employs his capital. . . . he will always, therefore, endeavour to employ it in the support of that industry of which the produce is likely to be of the greatest value, or to exchange for the greatest quantity either of money or of other goods. . . . he is in this, as in many other cases, led by an invisible hand to promote an end which was no part of his intention. Nor is it always the worse for the society that it was no part of it. By pursuing his own interest he frequently promotes that of the society more effectually than when he really intends to promote it.[4]

In more modern language we might reformulate this as follows. A person will be motivated by self-interest to employ the resources under his or her control

[4]Book IV, Chap. 2.

wherever they command the highest return. But if your "capital" (or any other resource you might own, like land or labor) commands a high return in a particular employment, that is because the resource must be very scarce there relative to the intensity of consumer demand for it. Consequently, seeking your own advantage in the way of highest return automatically leads you to direct your resources to the employments that best suit consumers' desires.

Does this seem obvious? Two centuries ago people commonly believed (and a great many today still do believe) that one can only help others by benevolently intending to help them—by "doing good." More sophisticated individuals know, with Adam Smith, that you often help others more by trade than by direct aid. Nevertheless, it is a little difficult to understand just why an economic system of untrammeled selfishness does not lead to mutual harm, or even to total chaos. How is that the city of New York can be regularly fed by converging food shipments from all corners of the earth—without any governing plan to make sure that the Kansas farmer, the New England fisherman, and the Florida orange-grower actually deliver to the hungry city? Yet the city is fed, although none of its suppliers need be motivated by any particular love and concern for New Yorkers. Kansas farmers simply find it more profitable to ship to New York than to eat their own wheat, and similarly for the others.

To quote *The Wealth of Nations* still once more: "In civilized society [man] stands at all times in need of the cooperation and assistance of great multitudes, while his whole life is scarce sufficient to gain the friendship of a few persons."[5] The Invisible Hand is what leads an individual to work for the good of other persons, practically all unknown to him, in a vast interlocking network of *spontaneous order* that has arisen without anyone's planning it that way.

Adam Smith's object in composing *The Wealth of Nations* was largely policy-oriented or *normative;* he opposed the then politically dominant "mercantilists,"[6] arguing instead in favor of a policy of "natural liberty."[7] But it is not his policy recommendations that will mainly concern us. His key conception is that *the economy is an integrated system whose behavior follows scientifically determinable laws.* In early times, the motion of the planets was so incomprehensible that it was thought they were pushed in their courses by angels. The development of astronomy eventually led to the scientific idea of gravitation to explain these motions. Similarly today, all too many people find it utterly incomprehensible why (for example) water is cheap and diamonds expensive, a strange situation that they are all too likely to attribute to the actions of angels or devils. We owe to Smith the scientific idea of the market economy as a mechanism, harnessing as motive power the self-interest of participants, yet so integrating their activities that *each is led to serve the desires of the others.* How this leads to water being cheap and diamonds expensive we shall see in the pages to come.

---

[5]Book I, Chap. 2.

[6]The mercantilists believed that a nation's well-being could best be furthered by accumulation of gold and silver, to be achieved by systematic government interventions designed to encourage exports and restrain imports.

[7]Smith recommended free trade among nations and *laissez faire* within.

ELEMENTS OF THE ECONOMIC SYSTEM, AND THE CIRCULAR FLOW OF ECONOMIC ACTIVITY

That *there is an economic system*—that there are laws of economics—is the first message to learn. We can now survey some of the necessary elements going into the makeup of the economic system.

1.C.1   ☐ Decision-making Agents in the Economy

We shall deal in this book with three main categories of decision-making units: individuals, firms, and governments.

Individuals are the ultimate active members of social systems, the only agents said to have goals or *preferences* and to engage in the process of *consumption* (to be discussed in Part Two). Actually, recognizing the mutual support and cohesiveness of the family, some economists prefer to consider the "household" to be the effective consumptive unit. Except where otherwise specified, the individual here will be understood as making decisions for his or her family or household.

The business firm is an artificial unit; it is ultimately owned by or operated for the benefit of one or more individuals. Surprisingly, this fact is often not appreciated. It is sometimes argued, for example, that "soul-less corporations" can be taxed without cost to the people. But of course taxing a corporation will hurt some people: the company's owners will suffer reduced profits, its workers may find it harder to get wage increases, its customers are likely to find that prices of its products have been increased. (At the same time, the taxes paid will allow government to provide assistance to other people—as usual, every choice of policy involves both costs and benefits.) The economist finds it convenient to think of firms as distinct agents specialized in the process of *production,* the conversion of resource inputs into desired goods as outputs. Firms will be the center of attention in Part Three of the text. In point of fact, however, much production actually takes place within the household; cooking, gardening, and home maintenance are examples.

Individuals and firms are not the only economic decision-making agents. A third category, government, is of great and growing importance. Governments, like firms, are artificial groupings. They differ from firms in not being owned by individuals, and also by having powers to take property without consent, yet legally (as by taxation). From the economic point of view governments are agencies engaging in a number of collective productive and consumptive activities, the scope of which is determined by a political rather than a market process. Perhaps even more important, governments establish the legal framework within which the entire economy works. Just as ownership of valuable resources (economic power) leads some individuals to superior outcomes through the market mechanism, similarly possession of influence over government policies (political power) can be expected to lead others to superior outcomes through the political mechanism. (The role of government is examined specifically in Part Seven.)

In complex modern economies there are still other "collective" decision-making units. Trade unions and cartels are of particular interest as representing organizations of buyers or sellers in markets, and will be discussed in the text below. Of lesser economic importance are voluntary associations like clubs, foundations, and religious institutions, which can be regarded as instruments whereby individuals combine for certain collective consumption choices.

1.C.2 ☐ Scarcity, Objects of Choice, and Economic Activities

The all-pervasive economic problem is that of *scarcity*. Not all desired things are available to individuals, the ultimate decision-making agents, when and as desired. Even if all desired physical commodities were present in unlimited quantities, we would not have enough *time* to enjoy them all. And, in addition, we all desire things other than material commodities: power, love, prestige. There can never be enough of these. It is the fact of scarcity that forces us to make economic decisions, that is, to organize our efforts for production and/or to engage in trade with a view toward obtaining desired objects.

Setting aside the desire for social relations and distinctions like affection or prestige, the entities that we usually think of as the objects of economic choice are called *commodities,* or *goods and services.* Goods as distinguished from services are physical things (wares or merchandise). Services represent a flow of benefits over a period of time, derived either from physical goods (like the shelter service provided by a house) or from human activities (like the entertainment service provided by concert performers). The distinction between wares and services will not be essential for us until the discussion of resources and production in Part Four. For the present, therefore, we will think of commodities or goods as synonymous words covering also desired consumption services.

Consumption of commodities or goods represents one of the main economic activities. In their consumption decisions, individuals pick out assortments within their means that best accord with their given tastes. We shall say that goods are the *objects of choice* for the consumption decision.

Production is another main economic activity. We shall sometimes find it convenient to regard it as engaged in by individuals, and sometimes by firms. We usually think of production as the physical conversion of inputs into outputs, of resources (or the services of resources) into consumable goods. More fundamentally, production is any transformation adding to the social totals of some desired goods at the expense of a reduction in the amount of others. Production might represent a transformation *of physical form,* as in the conversion of leather and human labor into shoes, but not necessarily so. Transformations would still be regarded as productive if they took place *over space* (shipment of oranges from Florida to Maine) or *over time* (storing of potatoes after harvest so as to distribute consumption over the year).

Of course, to be economically rational, production should represent a conversion from a less desired to a more desired configuration. To burn an antique Chippendale chair for heat is a kind of production, but ill-advised under ordinary conditions. (On the other hand, a person on the point of freezing to death might find the conversion from chair to warmth exceedingly advantageous.)

The third main economic activity is *exchange* (to be discussed in Part Five). For the individual, exchange is also a kind of conversion—he or she trades away some objects for others. But from the social point of view, exchange is distinguished from production in that the totals of commodities are unaffected; goods and services are reshuffled in trade, but wherever one person has less someone else must have more. Thus, exchange is a kind of transfer. But it is a mutual and voluntary transfer; *all* parties involved are satisfied. The objects of choice in exchange activities may be either consumption goods and services or production goods and services.

1.C.3 ☐ The Circular Flow

In a simplified world with only two types of economic agents, individuals and business firms, the relations between them can be pictured as in Figure 1.1. Individuals and firms have dual aspects, and thus transact with one another in two distinct ways. Individuals are in one aspect *consumers of goods*, while firms are *producers of goods*. Thus, the diagram shows a "real" flow of consumption goods (solid upper channel) from firms to individuals. But the goods must be produced. To permit this there must be a "real" flow of productive services (solid lower channel), from the individuals in their second aspect as *owners of resources* to the firms as *employers of resource services*.

In a socialist command economy these flows of goods and resources might be directly ordered by a dictator. But in a private-enterprise economy the relations are based on exchange and so must be mutual and voluntary. Hence, offsetting the "real" flows are reverse "financial" flows of claims that in a modern economy normally take the form of money payments. The consumers' financial expenditures on goods (dashed upper channel) become the receipts or revenues of the firms. The exchange of consumption goods between individuals and producing firms, and the balancing financial payments, take place in what is abstractly termed "the product market." (Actually, there will of course be a host of separate product markets, one for each distinct consumption good.)

The revenues from sales to consumers provide the firms with the wherewithal to buy productive services from resource-owners (dashed lower channel). This closes the circle; the firms' payments for productive services become income to the individuals, available once more for consumption expenditures to begin the next cycle. The purchase and sale of productive services take place in what is abstractly called "the factor market," again, really a number of distinct markets for the various types of productive services.

Looking within the box representing the firms as economic agents, what takes place there is the process of *production*, i.e., the physical transformation of resources into products. Within the box representing individuals, *consumption* of the produced goods takes place. Here again, the circle is closed by the fact that

FIGURE 1.1 The circular flow of economic activity.

consumption is necessary to recreate the main productive resource—labor power—for the next cycle.

MICROECONOMICS AND MACROECONOMICS

A distinguished professor of logic, deploring the division of his subject between deductive reasoning and inductive reasoning, once declared: "In our textbooks on deduction we explain all about logical fallacies; in our textbooks on induction, we then commit them." In economic theory as well, we have an as yet unresolved split of the subject—microeconomics versus macroeconomics. In microeconomics we see how and why the Invisible Hand operates (how and why self-interest leads toward a spontaneous system of productive cooperation); in macroeconomics we examine the consequences of the Invisible Hand failing to do so!

An easy explanation of this unsatisfactory state of affairs is not available. For our purposes here, we can notice that microeconomics concentrates mainly upon equilibrium states of particular markets, presuming an equilibrium of the market system as a whole. But it seems to be the case that the equilibrium of the market system as a whole is not as robust as might be hoped. The *overall* circular flow of economic activity may become disorganized, to greater or lesser degree. Some types of disturbance may generate self-reinforcing aggregate movements (e.g., the Keynesian "multiplier") likely, at least for a time, to lead the system of the circular flow away from rather than back to an equilibrium condition. It is these disequilibria of the system as a whole that macroeconomics studies.

For some period of time, starting in the 1930s, macroeconomists attempted to develop modes of reasoning largely independent of any microeconomic foundation; some theorists went so far as to dismiss classical microeconomics as obsolete or irrelevant. It is now generally recognized that this attempt has failed. Significant recent progress in macroeconomics has been made precisely by improving the logical connection of the subject with the microeconomic theories of production, consumption, and exchange. So if we cannot solve the key questions of macroeconomics here, we can still promise that the study of microeconomics will also promote understanding of the former subject.

☐ SUMMARY OF CHAPTER 1

Economics is a social science, whose nucleus is the study of the *rational behavior* of economic agents interacting through *market exchange*. Rational behavior is the appropriate choice of means for achieving given ends—always involving comparison of benefits and costs, the advantages and disadvantages of alternative courses of action. Economists do not ordinarily attempt to go behind the ends sought by individuals, their tastes or wants or desires, but take these as facts which are to be explained (if at all) by the other social sciences. Individuals can achieve their desires in human society in a number of ways, among them persuasion, force, theft, or government power. But economics mainly studies interaction through market relations—voluntary exchange.

Adam Smith's principle of the Invisible Hand indicates how individuals interacting through markets are led to cooperate, simply in their own self-interest. The Invisible Hand is what makes the economy a system of spontaneous order, an integrated arrangement whose behavior follows scientifically determinable laws.

The main agents (acting units) in the economic system are individuals (possibly acting on behalf of their families or households), firms, and governments. Individuals are the only agents who consume. Individuals may also produce goods and services. But, in modern economies, production takes place primarily through business firms—artificial agents created by individuals for that purpose. The activity of production must be distinguished from exchange: *pro-*

duction transforms the physical shape or location or time-availability of commodities, whereas *exchange* merely reshuffles the existing goods and services among the economic agents.

The circular flow of economic activity summarizes the interactions among economic agents. In *the product market,* individuals in their capacity as consumers purchase consumption goods from firms; in *the factor market,* individuals in their capacity as resource-owners supply productive services to firms. The "real" circular flow has resources moving from individual owners to firms, being converted by firms into consumption goods, and in that form returning to the individuals so as to complete the circle. The "financial" circuit has funds paid out by firms to individual resource-suppliers, thus providing the latter with an income for purchase of consumption goods; these purchases circulate the funds back once again to the firms, allowing the next cycle to begin.

☐ QUESTIONS FOR CHAPTER 1

MAINLY FOR REVIEW

*R1. In what respects can it be said that economics is a science? Give an example of a prediction that modern economic science can confidently make. Are there predictions that economic science has not yet shown itself competent to make?

*R2. What is rational behavior? Give examples of rational and of irrational behavior. Can the economist's postulate of rationality be useful even when irrational elements strongly influence behavior?

R3. Does the economist assume stable preferences? Give an example of a change in preferences that has had important economic effects.

R4. Does the economist assume that everyone is selfish? Give an example of an area where unselfish behavior has important economic consequences.

R5. Market transactions or exchanges are said to be both *mutual* and *voluntary.* Give an example of a non-market interpersonal transaction that is not voluntary. Of one that is voluntary but not mutual.

R6. What are positive issues in economics? Normative issues? Give an example of each.

*R7. How does the "Invisible Hand" lead individuals in a market economy to cooperate for mutual advantage even without any definite intention on their part to do so? Would self-interested behavior lead to mutual advantage in a monastic economy where all income is equally divided? In a dictatorship where the political authorities confiscate the lion's share? In an economy with no property, so that any person could take what he needs from any other person?

R8. What are the most important classes of decision-making units in a modern economy? In what types of activity do they engage? In what sense are firms and governments "artificial" units?

*R9. In the circular flow of economic activity, distinguish between the "real" and "financial" circuits of flow. What is the relation between the two? Distinguish between the "product market" and the "factor market." How are these connected?

*The answers to asterisked questions appear at the end of the book.

R10. "The principle of the Invisible Hand asserts that self-interested behavior on the part of resource-owners leads inevitably to chaos." True or false, and why?

R11. What is the difference between production and exchange?

FOR FURTHER THOUGHT AND DISCUSSION

*T1. Other things being equal, would you expect the murder rate to be lower in jurisdictions applying capital punishment? If the income-tax exemption granted for each child were increased, would you expect the birth rate to rise?

*T2. The psychiatrist T. S. Szasz argues that what is called "mental illness" is the result of rewarding people for disability. Not only is the patient motivated to become "ill," but there is a financial advantage to the healing professions in declaring personal problems to be "illnesses." How could mental illness be made less "rewarding"? Would doing this result in less mental illness?

T3. If government were to increase relief payments to the unemployed, would you expect unemployment to rise?

T4. In terms of the circular flow of economic activity, explain what determines the fact that some individuals are wealthy (in a position to consume a great deal in the product market) and others are poor.

*T5. If the Invisible Hand leads individuals to serve their own interests by serving others, why are some people led to a life of crime? Why do some corrupt politicians find it advantageous to serve themselves at the expense of their constituents? Why are dictators motivated to seize power? [*Hint:* Does the principle of the Invisible Hand apply to all kinds of social interactions, or does it hold only when individuals interact in a particular way?]

*T6. Would an effectively enforced law requiring drivers to wear seat belts tend to reduce driver deaths? Pedestrian deaths?

*T7. Dr. Samuel Johnson: "There are few ways in which a man can be more innocently employed than in getting money." Charles Baudelaire: "Commerce is satanic, because it is the basest and vilest form of egoism." What do you think each had in mind?

T8. Classify each of the following statements or propositions as either *positive* or *normative*. (Does the classification "positive versus normative" have any bearing upon truth or falsity?)
   a. Smoking in enclosed public spaces should be banned.
   b. Prohibiting smoking in public places would reduce the demand for cigarettes.
   c. Proposed legislation to limit the places in which smokers may indulge in their habit would elicit opposition from the tobacco industry.
   d. Non-smokers' rights to breathe clean air are more important than smokers' rights to pollute the air.
   e. Anti-smoking laws will have no effect on sales of cigarettes because smokers will light up just as much as before but confine their puffing to legal areas.

T9. It may soon become possible to predict the place and time of earthquakes, weeks or even months before their occurrence. Some influential writers have argued that such predictions should be kept secret, or even that investigations leading to such predictions should be banned. Allegedly, the panic caused by predicting an earthquake would be more damaging than the earthquake itself. What does this view imply as to individual rationality? Would you be for or against banning earthquake prediction?

2 WORKING TOOLS

CORE CHAPTER

Let's start with some good news. It is a remarkable fact that practically all the analysis in this book, and even throughout economics generally, makes use of only two analytical techniques. The two techniques are: (1) *finding an optimum* and (2) *finding an equilibrium.* Facing any question, the student who asks himself or herself, "Is this an optimization problem or an equilibrium problem?", will seldom go astray.

What's the difference between the two sorts of problems? The lists below will give you the main idea.

OPTIMIZATION PROBLEMS	*EQUILIBRIUM PROBLEMS*
1. Would I do better to buy a new car, or stick a while longer with my old one?	1. Are new-car prices likely to be cheaper next year?
2. Will I be happier working, or should I drop out of the rat-race and be supported by "welfare" on a commune?	2. Would generous "welfare" provision for the unemployed raise the unemployment rate?
3. Is it more profitable to buy or to lease?	3. What determines the ratio between the annual rental of a building and its purchase price?
4. To counter drug abuse, should narcotics laws be made stricter or more lenient?	4. If all narcotics laws were abolished, would drug usage increase?
5. Is now the time to go out on strike, or had we better accept management's offer?	5. Do strikes raise the wages of workers?

We need not go into the answers here, although a good number of these questions (or others like them) will be answered later in the book. The main point is to grasp the essential difference between the two types of problems. The first type, the optimization problems, always are of the form: "Is it better for me (or my business, or my group, or the nation) to take this action or that action?" The second type, the equilibrium problems, are of the form: "What would be observed about prices and/or quantities in markets if some event like imposition of a tariff or of price controls were to take place?"

Each of these two techniques, finding an optimum and finding an equilibrium, employs a characteristic working tool. To solve optimization problems, to find the best choice for a decision-making agent, the student must have an understanding of *the relations among total, average, and marginal magnitudes.* To solve equilibrium problems, to find the condition of balance in the market when all individual decisions interact together, the student must be able to use *supply–demand analysis.* Almost all readers of this book will already have had some exposure, in introductory economics courses or elsewhere, to these working tools. What this chapter provides is therefore mainly a review, plus illustrative applications of these tools.

2.A
EQUILIBRIUM: SUPPLY–DEMAND ANALYSIS

2.A.1 ☐ Equilibrium of Supply and Demand

The supply–demand diagram of Figure 2.1 should be familiar, but let's go over some of the details. The horizontal axis represents the quantity Q of some good G—to be specific, let's say grain (in tons).[1] The vertical axis of the diagram represents price P per ton of grain. *A price is a ratio of quantities*: it signifies the amount of some other commodity that must be given up to obtain a unit of the desired good G. Thus, we might speak of the price in cigarettes of a hat, or the price in labor-hours of a loaf of bread. However, in modern societies prices are normally quoted in terms of *money.* While money is a very peculiar "good" whose nature and role will not be examined until much later in the book, for the present we can speak in terms of money prices: the number of monetary units that must be given up per unit of the desired good. Consequently, the dimensionality of the vertical axis (price axis) of Figure 2.1 is the ratio $\$/Q$—dollars per ton of grain.

The demand curve DD shows, for each price P, the quantity that purchasers choose to take from the market. Its negative slope is to be accepted for the moment as an empirical fact: buyers are willing to purchase more, the lower the price. [*Verification*: We often observe sellers trying to win more customers by claiming to be offering unusually low prices. Do sellers ever try to attract customers by asserting that their prices are exceptionally high?] Similarly, the positive slope of the supply curve SS asserts as an empirical fact that sellers will offer more the higher the price. (In later chapters, further light will be cast upon the normal shapes of supply and demand curves.)

In Figure 2.1 market equilibrium is represented by the intersection point E, whose coordinates are the quantity Q^* and price P^*.[2] Suppose the market price were momentarily at any price higher than P^*, such as P' in the diagram. At that price the quantity along the demand curve, the number of units Q'_d that consumers are willing to purchase, is less than Q'_s, the number of units that suppliers

---

[1]In accordance with the idea that the economy represents a continuing *circular flow* of activity, it is sometimes important to think of quantity as a rate per unit time: tons per month, or per week, etc. That quantities represent flows over time will be taken as understood throughout this book.

[2]In this text we will generally follow the convention of designating *solution values* (values of the variables associated with equilibrium or optimum positions, as the case may be) by asterisks.

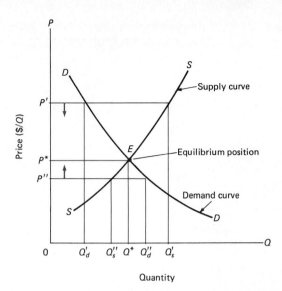

FIGURE 2.1 Demand and Supply. The equilibrium at point E determines the price P^* and quantity Q^* where supply and demand are in balance.

offer on the market. Not all the suppliers can find customers. What will then happen? It is reasonable to suppose that some suppliers will quote lower prices rather than be left with undesired stocks of goods. Thus, the excess of the supply-quantity Q'_s over the demand-quantity Q'_d generates *downward* pressure on price, indicated in the diagram by the arrow pointing downward from the horizontal line representing the price P'.

What if market price were momentarily at some level lower than P^*, such as P'' in Figure 2.1? Then the quantity demanded would be Q''_d, in excess of the supply-quantity Q''_s offered on the market. Not all demanders would be able to find the number of units they desire to purchase, and hence some of them will start to bid up the price. Here there is *upward* pressure on price, indicated in the diagram by the arrow pointing upward from the horizontal line representing the price P''.

Clearly, one or the other process will always be at work so long as price is not at the equilibrium P^*. Only at P^* are the demand-quantity Q_d and the supply-quantity Q_s equal to one another, so as to rule out any upward or downward pressure on price. When Q_d equals Q_s, we have the market equilibrium quantity Q^*.

How realistic is this picture? What we are dealing with here is a *model* of reality, not reality itself. It is a model (as will be explained later) of perfect competition among individuals interacting in a perfect market. The question of scientific interest is not the literal truth of the model but rather its usability for understanding reality and predicting the consequences of change. This is the subject of the next section.

CONCLUSION: The intersection of demand and supply curves determines the equilibrium values of price and quantity exchanged.

2.A.2 ☐ Comparative Statics of Supply and Demand: Shift of Equilibrium

Equilibrium was determined, in the picture of Figure 2.1, by the intersection of *given* supply and demand curves. But the concepts of supply and demand are mainly used to analyze the consequences of *changes* in economic data. Such changes can be interpreted as shifts or displacements of either the supply curve of the good, of its demand curve, or both at once.

Suppose, for example, that buyers suddenly wanted to consume more of the commodity in question, perhaps as a result of altered preferences. Then more of the good would be purchased at each possible price. This is called an *increase of demand*. As shown in Figure 2.2, the demand curve shifts *to the right* (from a position like D_1D_1 to D_2D_2). Where the old equilibrium price was P_1^* and quantity Q_1^*, the new equilibrium price and quantity are P_2^* and Q_2^*.

How does the revision of the equilibrium position actually come about? Suppose the price remained unchanged at P_1^* after the demand curve shifted to D_2D_2 in Figure 2.2. Then consumers would want to purchase the quantity Q_d' which exceeds Q_1^*. But at price P_1^* suppliers would still be offering only the quantity Q_1^*. There is an excess of quantity demanded over quantity supplied, leading to upward pressure on price. In a free market, price will respond to this pressure and continue to move upward until Q_d equals Q_s at the new equilibrium price P_2^*.

While this description of the process of price–quantity adjustment to change is plausible, it is not entirely free of problems. For example, some transactions might actually take place at "wrong" prices (before P_2^* is reached), and these "wrong" transactions might in turn affect the supply or demand curves.

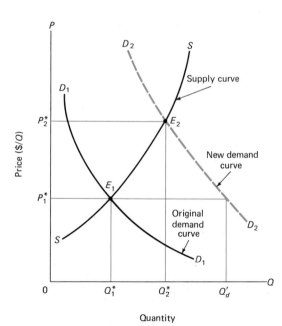

FIGURE 2.2 Increase of Demand. When consumers' preferences change in such a way that they desire to purchase more at each price, the demand curve shifts to the right from D_1D_1 to D_2D_2. Equilibrium price and equilibrium quantity both increase.

That is, the final equilibrium reached might conceivably depend upon the path for getting there. Issues of this kind are studied in the branch of economics called *dynamics*. We will, except where the contrary is indicated, omit consideration of dynamics and instead only compare the initial and the final equilibrium situations. This is called *the method of comparative statics*. While some aspects of reality cannot be successfully modeled without use of dynamics, the relatively simple tools of comparative statics can still tell us a great deal about real-world phenomena.

Our basic technique, then, in analyzing the consequences of some change in market circumstances will be to ask: Is the change reflected in a shift of supply, or a shift of demand (or, possibly, of both)? It will be immediately evident from Figure 2.2 that *an increase in demand alone leads to an increase in both equilibrium price and equilibrium quantity.* An increase in *supply* (see Figure 2.3) is to be interpreted as a *rightward* displacement of the supply curve (from S_1S_1 to S_2S_2), since at each price a larger quantity is offered. (WARNING: A common slip is to think of an "increase" of demand or supply as an *upward* shift of the corresponding curve; this is correct for the demand curve but incorrect for the supply curve. To avoid error, interpret an "increase" always as a *rightward* shift of the corresponding curve.) *An increase in supply thus leads to an increase in equilibrium quantity, but to a decrease in equilibrium price.* [*Question:* What can be said if both supply and demand increase together?]

> PROPOSITION: If demand increases, equilibrium price and quantity *both* rise. If supply increases, equilibrium quantity rises but equilibrium price falls.

Any change in economic data affecting market equilibrium can be expressed as a shift in demand or in supply (or both). But what are the sources of these shifts? It is sometimes useful to distinguish between those sources of change

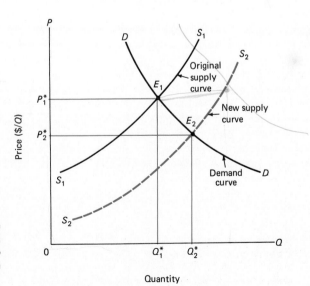

FIGURE 2.3 Increase of Supply. When a change in conditions induces sellers to offer more at each price, the supply curve shifts to the right from S_1S_1 to S_2S_2. Equilibrium quantity increases, but equilibrium price falls.

originating "outside" and those originating "inside" the economic system. The "outside" sources of variation include: (1) *Changes in tastes*: A temperance campaign may alter a population's willingness to consume hard liquor. (2) *Changes in technology*: Eli Whitney's invention of the cotton gin vastly increased the market availability of cotton. (3) *Changes in resources*: An important oil discovery will enlarge the world's supply of petroleum. (4) *Changes in the political–legal system*: "Decriminalization" of the trade in marijuana can be expected to increase both the market supply and the market demand for that substance. All these changes can be regarded, in some degree at least, as originating autonomously rather than in response to economic factors.

Displacement of equilibrium in a particular market may, however, also stem from movements "inside" the economic system as a whole. Such "inside" variations might include: (1) *Changes in prices (or quantities) of goods related in demand*. An increase in the price of butter (however caused in terms of the ultimate or "outside" sources of variation) will tend to raise the demand for margarine. (2) *Changes in prices (or quantities) of goods related in supply*. A rise in the production of wool will almost necessarily increase the supply of mutton on the market. (3) *Changes in levels of income*. The higher incomes recently received by petroleum-exporting countries would be expected to raise their demands for a variety of consumption goods.[3]

It is of considerable importance for the student to develop his or her intuition by analyzing a number of situations in which the price–quantity equilibrium of particular markets varies over space or time.

[3]There is no hard-and-fast rule as to what elements lie "outside" and what "inside" the economic system. While the text speaks of changes in resources as an "outside" source of variation, prospecting for mineral resources would surely be affected by mineral prices, tax policies, and so forth. Even population, regarded as a resource, is likely to respond to economic incentives—for example, if governments subsidize large families. The pace and direction of technological change also will vary with the financial attractiveness of possible inventions. (When the British government in the eighteenth century offered a prize for an accurate chronometer, significant advances in time-keeping were made by inventors.)

EXAMPLE 2.1
Catholics and Fish

For over a thousand years, the Roman Catholic Church required believers to abstain from consuming meat on Fridays. But a liberalization of the regulations of the Church abolished this requirement for American Catholics as of December 1966 (except for Fridays falling within Lent).

Frederick W. Bell studied the impact of the liberalization upon the price of fish in New England (population approximately 45% Catholic). The study compared a ten-year period before the liberalization with the nine-month period just after (excluding Lenten months). In estimating the shift of the demand curve (price paid for given quantities of fish landed by New England fishermen), it was necessary to adjust for a number of economic factors: imports of fish, prices of closely competitive foods (poultry and meat), cold storage holdings, and personal income among them. Having made these adjustments, the effect of the liberalization on fish prices can be seen in the Table.

Prices of Fish, Monthly Data, 1957–1967

SPECIES	PERCENT CHANGE DUE TO LIBERALIZATION
Sea scallops	−17
Yellowtail flounder	−14
Large haddock	−21
Small haddock (scrod)	− 2
Cod	−10
Ocean perch	−10
Whiting	−20

Source: F. W. Bell, "The Pope and the Price of Fish," *American Economic Review*, v. 58 (Dec. 1968), p. 1348.

The results show that, for any given quantity of fish landings (and after adjusting for the other variables mentioned above), the prices received for fish of all seven species were lower after the liberalization than before.

The "Catholics and Fish" example clearly represents a *decrease* in the demand for fish. (The demand curve for fish shifted leftward, rather than rightward as in Figure 2.2.) The source of the variation would seem to lie clearly "outside" the economic system, since the modification in Church regulations was not in any evident way a response to market factors.

EXAMPLE 2.2
Potatoes

That vegetables are cheap at harvest time may well have been the first law of economics observed in primitive society. In the case of potatoes there is some production throughout the year, but the major crop is harvested in the fall. The Table shows the average U.S. prices and production of potatoes in the various seasons of the year during the period from 1968 to 1970.

Prices and Production of Potatoes, 1968–1970

SEASON	AVERAGE PRODUCTION (CWT.)	AVERAGE PRICE RECEIVED BY FARMERS ($/CWT.)
Fall	237,391	1.90
Winter	3,765	2.09
Early spring	5,154	2.48
Late spring	20,977	2.71
Early summer	13,483	2.73
Late summer	29,790	2.07

Source: Data from U.S. Dept. of Agriculture, *Agricultural Prices, 1970 Annual Summary*, p. 22; *Crop Production*, July 9, 1971, p. A2, July 10, 1969, p. 2.

What we see here is obviously an *increase in supply* (rightward shift of the supply curve as in Figure 2.3) in the main fall harvest season. Quantity is biggest, and price is lowest, in that season. It is perhaps surprising that the price variation is so small, given the enormous production swings over the year. The main reason is that potatoes are *stored* from harvest on. Therefore, price is still relatively low in the winter season just after the fall harvest, even though production is at a minimum in the winter. As stored holdings are gradually consumed, price rises steadily over the year until the new crop begins to arrive in the late summer season.

The original source of agricultural supply variation over the year is the "outside" element of God-given seasonal climate. But note that the "inside" element of storage activity greatly modifies the force of the external factors. Other economic activities like improvements in transportation, changes in agricultural practices, and development of new seed varieties may also be at work to minimize the impact of seasonal variation of supply.

EXAMPLE 2.3
Heating Oil

The supply of petroleum is relatively constant over the year, but there is substantial seasonal variation in demand. Gasoline purchases tend to be highest in the summer months, and of course heating oil is most required during the winter.

The first column of the Table is an index of monthly consumption of heating oil during the period 1960–66. (The index figure of 100 represents average consumption over the entire year.) A slight adjustment has been made in the data to account for the differing numbers of days in the months. The second column is a similar index of the monthly prices per gallon of heating oil at retail. Here an adjustment has been made in the data to eliminate the effect of continuing inflation, which tends to make all end-of-year prices higher than beginning-of-year prices.

Indexes of Retail Sales and Prices, Fuel Oil No. 2, in the United States, 1960–1966

MONTH	INDEX OF AVERAGE CONSUMPTION (MILLIONS OF BBLS, ADJUSTED FOR NUMBER OF DAYS IN MONTH)	INDEX OF AVERAGE PRICE (PER GALLON, RETAIL, ADJUSTED FOR INFLATION)
January	153	102.3
February	143	102.5
March	121	101.8
April	90	100.5
May	74	99.2
June	68	98.3
July	64	98.2
August	68	98.2
September	76	98.5
October	83	99.4
November	111	99.9
December	149	101.1

Source: Indexes calculated from data in American Petroleum Institute, *Petroleum Facts and Figures, 1971 Ed.,* p. 452, and U.S. Dept. of Commerce, *Survey of Current Business,* March 1961 through April 1967.

Consumption of fuel oil varies widely over the year, with December and January by far the highest months. Evidently, the demand curve is greatest (farthest to the right) in those months. Increased demand is also accompanied by higher prices, as would be expected. On the other hand, it is surprising that the price swings are so small. Here once again, the explanation is that *storage* over the year permits a buildup of stocks to meet the peak winter demand. As another factor in the situation, refineries in winter months can produce larger fractions of heating oil and smaller fractions of gasoline from their petroleum input, since demand for gasoline is less in those months. So a rightward shift of heating oil *supply* partially offsets the increase in demand. The storage feature is also reflected by the way the price index lags slightly behind the quantity index. In early winter, December is a high-consumption month, but price is still moderate because stocks tend to be ample. By February consumption has begun to decline; nevertheless, prices are high in February since inventories have been drawn down to their lowest levels.

EXAMPLE 2.4
Brides

Among the Sebei in Uganda, husbands obtain wives by purchase. The anthropologist Walter Goldschmidt secured data on bride-prices paid by husbands in two communities: the cattle-herding district of Kapsirika and the farming district of Sasur.

The Kapsirika herders pay higher prices for brides than the Sasur farmers, even though the herders are not generally wealthier. The rate of polygyny (plural wives) is also higher among the Kapsirika; their wife/husband ratio is 1.52, whereas among the Sasur farmers it is only 1.17.[a] There is a substantial intermarriage rate, but it takes entirely the form of herder husbands buying farmers' daughters. Thus, the herders' demand curve for brides seems to be higher; they pay more, and so they get more.

[a]Walter Goldschmidt, "The Brideprice of the Sebei," *Scientific American*, v. 229 (July 1973), pp. 74–85.

The "Brides" example shows how supply–demand analysis can be used to interpret changes over space or across communities as well as over time within a given community. In the example, the herders' demand curve for brides can be regarded as greater than (lying to the right of) the farmers' demand curve. The *source* of the difference might seem to be just the "outside" factor of differential preferences for brides on the part of the males in the two communities. An alternative "inside" explanation is that wives are better productive assets for herders than for farmers among the Sebei. One interesting question is why any bride-price difference persists: if Kapsirika herders and Sasur farmers compete to buy wives, why don't they end up paying about the same? The answer appears to be that intermarriage takes only the form of the Kapsirika "importing" wives; it seems that the "importers" must pay some kind of premium in order to overcome unwillingness of brides to move from one community to the other.

EXAMPLE 2.5
Computing Power

An outstanding instance of technological advance in recent decades has been the development of the computer. It is difficult to directly show changes in computer prices (actually, large computers are usually rented, so the "price" is an annual or monthly rental) over time because quality has improved so drastically. Gregory C. Chow developed an index for the quantity of *computing power* represented by the physical stock of computers in existence at any moment of time. Taking account of the improvements in quality variables like multiplication time, memory size, and access time, he expressed this quantity in terms of 1960 rental equivalents. Associating the quantity index with the current prices of computing power for each year led to the results shown in the Table.

Quantity and Price of Computing Power

YEAR	QUANTITY (THOUSANDS OF 1960 RENTALS)	ABSOLUTE PRICE INDEX
1954	370.26	3.2554
1955	991.67	2.9610
1956	2,389.9	2.5336
1957	5,087.6	2.3168
1958	8,362.	2.0342
1959	12,549.	1.5884
1960	19,072.	1.0716
1961	38,264.	0.9042
1962	64,349.	0.6873
1963	95,815.	0.5712
1964	136,845.	0.4186
1965	194,136.	0.3416

Source: Gregory C. Chow, "Technological Change and the Demand for Computers," *American Economic Review,* v. 57 (Dec. 1967), p. 1124.

Between 1954 and 1965 the quantity of computing power rose over fiftyfold, while the unit price fell to around 10.5% of its original level. Since the rise in the general price level due to inflation between 1954 and 1965 was some 20%, in real terms the fall in the price of computing power was even greater.

In the "Computing Power" example, technological advances brought about an increase in supply, a rightward shift of the supply curve, leading to an increase in quantity and fall in price. At the same time, business firms were in the process of learning about what computers could do, and so the demand curve was surely also shifting to the right. This makes the drastic reduction in price all the more remarkable, since the demand shift considered separately was placing *upward* pressure on price. The increase in supply due to technological advances in the computer industry was therefore the dominant element in the picture.

2.A.3 ☐ Algebra of Supply–Demand Analysis

We have seen that equilibrium in supply–demand analysis is found geometrically at the point of intersection of the supply curve and the demand curve. It is also useful for the student to be able to solve the equivalent problem algebraically. This is not at all difficult if the demand and supply curves are straight lines, as pictured in Figure 2.4.

Let the equation of the demand curve take the linear form $P = A - BQ_d$, where Q_d is the quantity demanded and A and B are positive constants. Geometrically, A corresponds to the intercept of the demand curve with the vertical price axis (the price so high that purchases are zero); $-B$ is the negative demand-curve slope (as suggested by the little right triangle, with base 1 and altitude B, drawn along the demand curve). The supply curve has the equation $P = C + DQ_s$, where Q_s is the quantity supplied. Here the positive constant C is the intercept of the supply curve on the vertical axis (the price so low that none of the good will be supplied), and the positive constant D represents the supply-curve slope. It is useful to think of the intercept A as the "choke price for demand" while C is the "choke price for supply."

The condition of equilibrium is that the quantity demanded must equal the quantity supplied:

(2.1) $$Q_s = Q_d$$

Using the symbol Q for the equalized quantities, we have a system of two simultaneous equations:

(2.2)
$$\begin{cases} P = A - BQ \\ P = C + DQ \end{cases}$$

Exercise 2.1: Suppose that in a certain market the demand schedule is given by the linear equation $P = 300 - Q_d$ and the supply schedule by $P = 60 + 2Q_s$. Find the solution values for price and quantity.

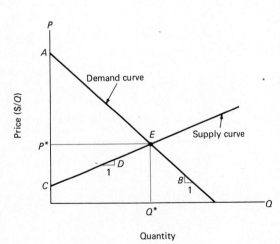

FIGURE 2.4 Linear Supply and Demand Curves.
The linear demand curve has equation $P = A - BQ_d$, while the linear supply curve has equation $P = C + DQ_s$. At the equilibrium point E, $Q_d = Q_s$.

Answer: Setting the right-hand sides of equations (2.2) equal, after substituting the numerical values for A, B, C, and D, we have $300 - Q = 60 + 2Q$. The solution is $Q^* = 80$, $P^* = 220$.

More generally, equations (2.2) can be solved algebraically to yield the following expressions for the solution values:

$$(2.3) \qquad\qquad Q^* = \frac{A - C}{B + D} \quad \text{and} \quad P^* = \frac{AD + BC}{B + D}$$

Substituting the numerical values in the example above for A, B, C, and D in these equations provides a check on the answers obtained for P and Q.

What about the comparative-statics analysis of *changes* in equilibrium? If an increase in demand takes place (rightward shift of the demand curve), it is elementary to verify that the numerical value of A must rise in the demand-curve equation $P = A - BQ_d$. The solution equations (2.3) then tell us that equilibrium quantity Q^* and price P^* both increase (compare Figure 2.2). On the other hand, if an increase in supply takes place (rightward shift of the supply curve), the numerical value of C in the supply-curve equation $P = C + DQ_s$ falls! (You should satisfy yourself that this is the case, if necessary by drawing a sketch.) The solutions in (2.3) then tell us that equilibrium quantity Q^* rises but equilibrium price P^* is lower (compare Figure 2.3). [*Question:* What happens to the solution values if A, the choke price for demand, remains unchanged but the demand curve becomes flatter?]

Exercise 2.2: Starting from the data of Exercise 2.1, suppose the supply-curve slope D rises from $D = 2$ to $D = 3$. (That is, with the same vertical intercept the supply curve has become steeper.) Find the new solution.

Answer: The demand-curve equation remains $P = 300 - Q_d$, but the supply-curve equation becomes $P = 60 + 3Q_s$. Setting the right-hand sides equal we have $300 - Q = 60 + 3Q$. The numerical solution is $P^* = 240$ and $Q^* = 60$; price has risen, but quantity has fallen.

2.A.4 ☐ An Application: Introduction of a New Supply Source

Suppose that a certain country, having previously barred imports of grain, now permits imports. Figure 2.5 pictures the situation, using linear supply and demand curves for simplicity. The demand curve is D, the "home" supply curve is S^h, and the "import" supply curve is S^i. Initially, in the absence of imports, the equilibrium E_0 is at the intersection of the D and S^h curves. When imports are allowed to enter, the new equilibrium E_1 must represent the intersection of the demand curve with the aggregate or *summed* supply curve. In the diagram, the curve labeled ΣS (read this as "sigma-S") is the *horizontal* summation of the S^h and S^i curves. [*Note the slightly tricky feature:* Below the import choke price F the ΣS curve is identical with S^h; only for prices high enough for imports to enter does ΣS diverge to the right of S^h.] If, as in the diagram, the initial equilibrium price

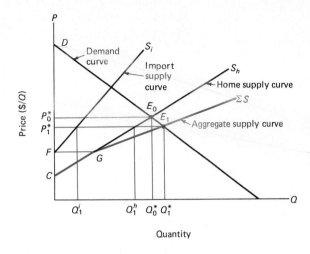

FIGURE 2.5 Introduction of an Import Supply. In the absence of imports the equilibrium E_0 is at the intersection of the demand curve D and the home supply curve S_h. When the import supply S_i also becomes available, the new equilibrium is E_1. The aggregate supply curve ΣS represents the horizontal summation of S_h and S_i, within the positive range of each supply curve.

P_0^* was high enough to induce some imports, then allowing imports to enter will clearly reduce the equilibrium price ($P_1^* < P_0^*$) and raise the equilibrium aggregate quantity purchased and sold ($Q_1^* > Q_0^*$). However, the amount supplied from "home" sources alone will clearly fall ($Q_1^h < Q_0^*$). [*Question:* What would happen if the initial equilibrium price P_0^* were less than the import choke price F?]

Exercise 2.3:   Assume that the demand curve $P = 300 - Q_d$ of Exercise 2.1 is still applicable. Assume also that the "home" supply curve is numerically the same as the supply curve of Exercise 2.1, so that $P = 60 + 2Q_s^h$. Then the initial equilibrium E_0 has $P_0^* = 220$ and $Q_0^* = 80$ as before. Let the new "import" supply curve be $P = 80 + 4Q_s^i$. Find the new equilibrium, E_1.

Answer: Note first that the import choke price, 80, is below the original equilibrium price, $P_0^* = 220$. So imports will surely enter, and we must calculate the aggregate supply curve ΣS. This is done by summing the quantities at each price. Rewriting the home supply curve we have $Q^h = (P - 60)/2$. Doing the same for imports, we have $Q^i = (P - 80)/4$. Then the summation-curve equation is $Q = Q^h + Q^i = 3P/4 - 50$. Solving this simultaneously with the demand curve leads to the numerical solution $P_1^* = 200$ and $Q_1^* = 100$ (of which $Q^h = 70$, $Q^i = 30$).

2.A.5   ☐ An Application: Effects of a Tax on Transactions

The familiar sales tax is an example of a tax on transactions. Consider an "excise tax" levied upon *sellers,* in the form of a fixed dollar charge per unit of commodity exchanged, say, $\$T$ per unit. The situation is portrayed in Figure 2.6 where, for simplicity, the supply and demand curves are all shown as straight lines. We can think of the tax as shifting the original supply curve SS *upward* (recall that an upward shift of the supply curve is *not* an "increase of supply") by the amount T, to the position $S'S'$. Why? The original SS curve specifies the number of units that suppliers were willing to provide at any price P. They still

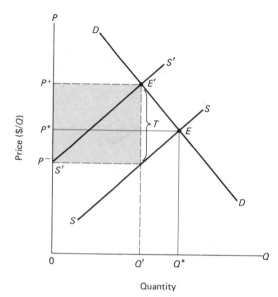

FIGURE 2.6 A Tax upon Sales. A tax of $\$T$ per unit sold shifts the supply curve (*gross* of tax) upward to $S'S'$. The original *SS* is the *net* supply curve. The new equilibrium quantity Q' is less than the pre-tax equilibrium quantity Q^*. The equilibrium gross price P^+ (inclusive of tax) is higher than the pre-tax price P^*, but net price P^- (exclusive of tax) is lower than P^*.

must be paid the same *net* "supply price" if they are to supply the same number of units. But if the *net* price is P dollars along *SS*, the *gross* price per unit ("demand price") must be $P + T$ dollars along $S'S'$ if the tax is $\$T$ per unit. Using the symbols P^+ for the gross price and P^- for the net price, we have:

$$P^+ = P^- + T$$

The new equilibrium quantity is determined by the intersection of the shifted supply curve $S'S'$ with the original demand curve *DD*. Evidently, the equilibrium quantity Q' bought and sold is less as a result of the tax. What about price? Carelessness can cause confusion here, because the new *gross* price P^+ is higher than the previous equilibrium P^*, but the new *net* price P^- is lower than P^*. One must state *which* price, gross or net, in asking whether price has risen or fallen.

> *PROPOSITION:* A tax on transactions lowers the equilibrium quantity exchanged in the market. The new price *gross* of the tax (the demand price paid by buyers) is more than before; the new price *net* of the tax (the supply price received by sellers) is less than before.

It may seem arbitrary that our analysis here took the form of shifting the supply curve rather than the demand curve. This seems logical if the tax were, legally, levied upon sellers. What if it were levied on buyers instead? It is left for the student to determine, as an exercise, that a shift of the *demand curve* (downward from *DD* by the vertical distance T) would lead to exactly the same solution as before for quantity and for gross and net prices. So the supply–demand analysis leads to a possibly surprising conclusion: *It makes no difference whether a tax on transactions is formally levied upon buyers or upon sellers.*

For the algebraic solution we can start again with equations (2.2), but now must distinguish between the price *gross of tax* (P^+) and the price *net of tax* (P^-), using the relation $P^+ = P^- + T$. The consumers must of course pay the gross price, while the suppliers receive only the net price. Here we have three simultaneous equations:

$$\begin{cases} P^+ = A - BQ \\ P^- = C + DQ \\ P^+ = P^- + T \end{cases}$$

In Figure 2.6 the geometrical solution was found at the intersection of the demand curve with the supply curve, the latter having been shifted upward by the amount of the tax. This corresponds algebraically to re-writing the second equation in terms of P^+, making use of the third equation in doing so. The revised second (supply) equation becomes $P^+ = (C + T) + DQ$. Having reduced the three equations to two, we can use the usual algebraic procedures to obtain the solution values:

$$Q^* = \frac{A - (C + T)}{B + D} \qquad P^+ = \frac{AD + B(C + T)}{B + D} \qquad P^- = \frac{(A - T)D + BC}{B + D}$$

Since T is necessarily positive, Q^* here is surely less than Q^* in the solution in equation (2.3)—the tax has reduced the volume of transactions. The new gross price P^+ is greater than and the new net price P^- is less than the old solution price P^*, thus confirming the geometrical result.

Exercise 2.4: Starting from the supply curve and demand curve of Exercise 2.1, suppose an excise tax $T = 15$ is imposed. Find the new equilibrium.

Answer: The three simultaneous equation of the text become, numerically: $P^+ = 300 - Q$, $P^- = 60 + 2Q$, and $P^+ = P^- + 15$. Substituting from the third equation, the second equation can be rewritten as $(P^+ - 15) = 60 + 2Q$. We now have the first and second equations in terms of two variables P^+ and Q, and so can easily solve to obtain the solution values $Q^* = 75$ and $P^+ = 225$, from which it follows that $P^- = 210$. As expected, imposition of the tax has reduced quantity exchanged (from 80 to 75), and raised the *gross* price to 225 but lowered the *net* price to 210 (in comparison with the previous no-tax price of 220).

2.A.6 ☐ Interferences with Equilibrium

Government policy, as in the case of a tax or a subsidy, may cause a shift from one equilibrium position to another. Government action may also be directed to improving the perfection of the market process. For example, the judicial system may enforce private contracts, reducing the need for individuals to make costly private enforcement arrangements. This facilitates the process whereby markets attain equilibrium.

Government interventions may, however, be designed to *prevent* markets from reaching equilibrium. It is not our purpose to make normative judgments as to the wisdom of such interventions. Rather, we seek only to show how the tool of supply–demand analysis enables the economist to understand and predict the consequences.

In the current inflationary period, we are all familiar with attempts to hold down inflation by "freezes" or other forms of maximum wage–price controls. In the deflationary period of the 1930s there were similar attempts to prevent a feared downward spiral of prices by *minimum* wage–price controls under the NRA (National Recovery Administration). The extent to which such "price ceilings" or "price floors" can actually cure a general inflation or a general deflation, as the case may be, remains a controversial issue in macroeconomics. We shall not be concerned with the macroeconomic problem, but only with the impacts of control policies upon particular markets.

Apart from the macroeconomic motivation, government may interfere with the equilibrium of markets in order to promote the interests of particular economic groups perceived as particularly deserving of aid (or, perhaps, merely as wielding enough political clout).

Figure 2.7 pictures a "meaningful" ceiling price P'. (To be meaningful, the ceiling must be *below* the equilibrium price $P*$.) At the ceiling price, the quantity demanded Q'_d exceeds the quantity supplied Q'_s, so there is upward pressure on price, indicated by the upward-pointing arrow. However, the arrow is blocked by the fixed ceiling price P', which remains in effect regardless of the upward pressure. (We do not consider here the possibility of illegal trading at higher prices—black markets.)

What about the actual quantity traded? There is a fundamental maxim of markets, "It takes two to tango." That is, exchange requires willing buyers *and* willing sellers. At the fixed ceiling price P' the sellers are willing to offer only Q'_s.

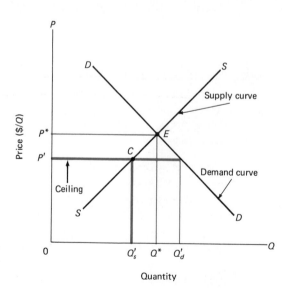

FIGURE 2.7   A Price Ceiling. Imposition of an effective ceiling at the level $P' < P*$ reduces the quantity traded from $Q*$ to Q'_s.

The buyers would be delighted to take this much and any larger quantity up to Q'_d, but they can only find trading partners to the extent of the smaller magnitude. Thus, the position denoted C is the actual price–quantity situation. So the effective price is lower than the unregulated equilibrium P^*, but the effective quantity is also lower than the equilibrium Q^*. This sometimes surprises students, as they expect the quantity traded to be some compromise between the larger quantity demanded Q'_d and the smaller quantity offered Q'_s. But the result is no compromise; *it is the smaller of the desired transaction magnitudes that governs.* This is emphasized in Figure 2.7 by the bold vertical drawn through the point C.

EXAMPLE 2.6
Repressed Inflation and Trekking

During and after World War II all the major belligerent powers were troubled by severe inflationary pressures. Wartime and postwar needs led to enormous government deficits, covered largely by increased monetary issues. And yet consumer prices were frozen at low ceiling levels. Since the necessities of life were scarce, there was strong upward pressure on prices. Indeed, often the absolutely minimal needs of life were not legitimately available. In postwar Germany, for example, the official daily ration at one point was down to the incredibly low figure of 1180 calories.

In these circumstances the curious institution of "trekking" developed in a number of different countries. City-dwellers would leave town for a day and scour the nearby countryside for food, making private black-market deals with farmers or, indeed, often simply stealing. The more the governments succeeded in controlling prices in the legitimate means of food distribution, the more the abnormal system of trekking flourished. On one single day, it was reported, over 900,000 persons trekked from Tokyo into the countryside.[a] In Germany, the "Erhard reforms" of 1948 abolished price freezes and thus eliminated trekking. But a curious and unexpected consequence was a financial crisis for the State railroads. Shorthaul railroad passenger traffic dropped immediately to less than 40% of its pre-reform volume, evidencing the massive volume of trekking that had previously been going on.[b]

[a]Jerome B. Cohen, *Japan's Economy in War and Reconstruction* (Minneapolis: University of Minnesota Press, 1949), p. 378.
[b]Lucius D. Clay, *Decision in Germany* (Garden City, N.Y.: Doubleday, 1950), p. 191.

A meaningful price *floor* is pictured in Figure 2.8. At the legal floor P'' the quantity offered by sellers Q''_s exceeds the quantity desired by buyers Q''_d. There is downward pressure on price. Here the effective price is higher than the unregulated equilibrium P^*, but the effective quantity is again *lower* than the equilibrium Q^*, as indicated by the bold vertical drawn through the point F. Once more, "It takes two to tango." We see, therefore, that although price ceilings and price floors have opposite effects on price they have similar effects upon the real volume of transactions; *in either case, the quantity exchanged is less than*

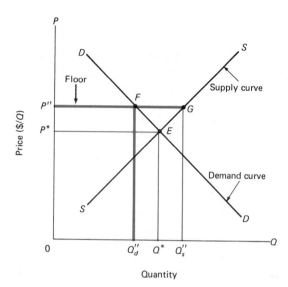

FIGURE 2.8 A Price Floor. Imposition of an effective price floor at the level $P'' > P^*$ reduces the quantity traded from Q^* to Q_d''. However, if the floor is "supported" by government purchases, the amount Q_s'' will actually be supplied. The difference between Q_s'' and Q_d'' will be accumulated as a "surplus."

in the unregulated market. (Again, a kind of black market may come into existence, permitting the trading of somewhat larger quantities at illegally low prices.)

Floors hold up better when they are *supported.* The supply–demand analysis of supported floors shows results drastically different from those of unsupported floors. Support takes the form of a "buyer of last resort"—Uncle Sam in the case of agricultural price supports in the United States. Going back to Figure 2.8, private buyers are only willing to take Q_d'' at the high floor price P''. But now suppose the government as buyer of last resort is available as trading partner for unrequited suppliers. Then the latter *can* actually dispose of their supply-quantity Q_s''; the actual situation is represented by the position G in the diagram. There is no black market problem with a supported floor, as no supplier would let units of the good go for less than the floor price. Instead there is a "surplus" problem. The buyer of last resort finds himself accumulating larger and larger unwanted stocks of the supported commodity.

> *CONCLUSION:* Meaningful ceilings hold down prices; meaningful floors keep them up. In either case, the quantity exchanged is *less* than in unregulated equilibrium. If, however, the floor is *supported*, quantity will be greater than equilibrium, but the "buyer of last resort" must accumulate inventories.

EXAMPLE 2.7
Agricultural Parity Prices

The U.S. government has attempted since the 1930s to maintain parity prices for agricultural products. "Parity" is interpreted to mean the relationship between agricultural and non-agricultural prices that obtained during the years 1910–14, a period of farm prosperity. Throughout the 1950s and 1960s the primary method employed to achieve parity was price support of farm products: a federal agency called the Commodity Credit Corporation (CCC) stood always ready to buy any unsold fractions of supported crops at 90% of the parity price.

The "surpluses" purchased by the CCC were for the most part kept in storage, the intention being to release them to the market in years of deficient crops. But as parity corresponded to an unusually favorable price relationship from the farmers' point of view, in most years the government had to purchase sizable shares of the supported crops. By 1960 the CCC held in storage as much wheat as the entire 1960 crop (not to mention amounts that had previously been disposed of).

With the burden of maintaining such huge stores becoming increasingly intolerable, other methods were turned to. Food stamps and school lunch programs subsidized market demand. More important, under a system of acreage limitations farmers were paid *not* to produce. The consequent increase in demand and decrease in supply cooperated to raise the market prices received by farmers. In addition, the price support levels were adjusted downward. The Table shows the resulting reduction of CCC purchases in the 1960s.

Yearly Acquisitions of Three Supported Crops by the Commodity Credit Corporation, Selected Years

| | MILLIONS OF BUSHELS | | |
	Grain Sorghum	*Corn*	*Wheat*
1953	40.9	422.3	486.1
54	110.1	250.6	391.6
55	92.6	408.9	276.7
56	32.5	477.4	148.4
57	279.5	268.1	193.5
58	258.0	266.6	511.0
1963	125.1	17.9	85.1
64	66.8	29.1	86.9
65	85.0	11.2	17.4
66	0.3	12.4	12.4
67	9.1	191.0	90.0
68	13.7	34.4	182.9

Source: Commodity Credit Corporation charts, Nov. 1972, pp. 49, 75, 115.

2.B

THE OPTIMIZATION PROCEDURE: TOTAL, AVERAGE, AND MARGINAL MAGNITUDES

The second major category of economic problems is *optimization,* finding a best situation or outcome. Economists have devised a process of solving optimization questions that does the work of the mathematical calculus without

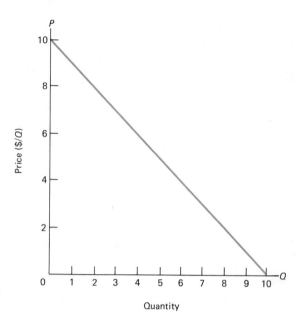

FIGURE 2.9 A Demand Curve. The demand curve, which shows price as a function of quantity, can also be regarded as an Average Revenue curve, since $P \equiv R/Q \equiv AR$.

requiring any formal knowledge of calculus techniques. The key to this process is understanding the relationships among total, average, and marginal magnitudes.

It is important to appreciate that these relations are ones of fundamental logic. The principles remain the same regardless of whether we are thinking of Total, Average, and Marginal *Cost* or of Total, Average, and Marginal *Revenue* or of Total, Average, and Marginal *Utility* (to mention only a few of the variables to which these concepts will be applied in the pages to come). The purpose of this section is to illustrate and review these general logical principles.

Consider Figure 2.9, which represents an assumed straight-line market demand curve for some good. Numerical data for this demand curve are tabulated in the first two columns of Table 2.1, representing Quantity (Q) and Price (P) of the good.

If we multiply Price times Quantity, we obtain definitionally the magnitude economists call Total Revenue or sometimes simply Revenue (R). Thus[4]

(2.4) $$R \equiv PQ$$

Total Revenue is tabulated in the third column of Table 2.1, and the corresponding data are plotted in the upper diagram of Figure 2.10.

Revenue R is a *total* magnitude or function of Quantity. And Price P can be regarded as an *average* magnitude. In Table 2.1, for example, at quantity $Q = 2$ Total Revenue R equals 16. If we ask what is the Average Revenue received per unit of quantity when $Q = 2$, the answer is obviously 8, which is, of course,

[4]The triple equality sign $\equiv$ represents *mathematical identity*. This symbol will be used in the text where it is desired to emphasize that both sides of the equality are definitionally equivalent.

TABLE 2.1

Total, Average, and Marginal Revenue

QUANTITY (Q)	PRICE—OR AVERAGE REVENUE (P OR AR)	TOTAL REVENUE (R ≡ PQ)	MARGINAL REVENUE— BETTER APPROXIMATION (MR)	MARGINAL REVENUE— POORER APPROXIMATION (MR)
0	10	0		—
			9	
1	9	9	8	9
			7	
2	8	16	6	7
			5	
3	7	21	4	5
			3	
4	6	24	2	3
			1	
5	5	25	0	1
			-1	
6	4	24	-2	-1
			-3	
7	3	21	-4	-3
			-5	
8	2	16	-6	-5
			-7	
9	1	9	-8	-7
			-9	
10	0	0		-9

nothing but the price along the demand curve associated with that quantity. Formally, equation (2.5) defining Average Revenue (AR) follows immediately from equation (2.4):

$$(2.5) \qquad\qquad AR \equiv \frac{R}{Q} \equiv P$$

Dimensionally, Price is measured in terms of *dollars per unit quantity* ($/Q$), whereas Revenue is simply scaled in dollars.

To understand the geometrical relation between total and average magnitudes, it is best to take the *total* measure as the fundamental or primitive concept. In the upper diagram of Figure 2.10, for any level of Q, say $Q = 4$, consider the line *OK* from the origin to the curve. The slope of this line is the ratio R/Q at $Q = 4$—the height R reached along the curve, divided by the horizontal length represented by the distance Q. By equation (2.5), R/Q equals Price P or Average Revenue AR. Numerically, at $Q = 4$ we have $AR = 24/4 = 6$. Consequently, in the lower diagram of Figure 2.10 the Average Revenue AR at $Q = 4$ is shown as equal to 6. By repeating the procedure for all levels of Q, the entire AR curve in the lower diagram can be derived. [*Warning*: The vertical axis of the upper or "total" diagram is scaled in terms of R—in dollars. The vertical axis of the lower diagram is scaled in terms of R/Q—dollars *per unit of quantity*.

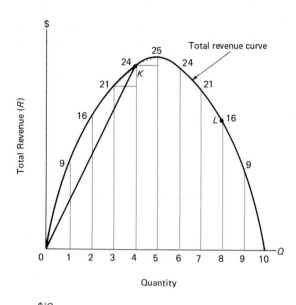

FIGURE 2.10 **Derivation of Average and Marginal Magnitudes from Total Function: Revenue.**
The upper diagram illustrates the derivation of the magnitudes of AR and MR when $Q = 4$ and $R = 24$. The height of the AR curve in the lower diagram at $Q = 4$ corresponds to the slope of the bold line in the upper diagram, so that $AR = 24/4 = 6$. The height of the MR curve in the lower diagram equals the slope *along* the R function in the upper diagram. At $Q = 4$, it is found by averaging the slopes of the dotted hypotenuses of the two small triangles. Thus $MR = (1/2)[(25 - 24) + (24 - 21)] = 2$.

Total and average magnitudes should never be plotted in the same diagram, since the dimensionality conflicts. Confusion is almost certain to result when this warning is overlooked.]

For the particular numbers assumed in Table 2.1, the Average Revenue AR is declining throughout (negatively sloped demand curve). Geometrically, we can see that AR must be falling since, in the "total" diagram of Figure 2.10, the slope of the line connecting the origin to points on the Total Revenue curve diminishes in moving to the right along the humped shape of the function. Thus, the slope of the line OL, showing Average Revenue at $Q = 8$, is less than the slope of the line OK.

The straight-line demand curve or AR function implied by the data of Table 2.1 has the specific algebraic form:

$$P = 10 - Q$$

Since $R = PQ$, the Total Revenue curve satisfies the equation:

$$R = (10 - Q)Q = 10Q - Q^2$$

So much for the connection between average and total magnitudes. The *marginal* function is akin to the average function in that both are measured, geometrically, in terms of slopes derived from a total magnitude. Consequently, marginal and average curves are scaled in the same dimensions (dollars per unit of quantity) and can, without danger of confusion, be plotted in the same diagram. The difference between average and marginal concepts is the following: the *average* function AR corresponds to the slope of a line like OK or OL connecting the origin to positions *on* the Total Revenue curve R; the *marginal* function MR, on the other hand, is defined geometrically as the slope *along* the curve R itself.

We already know that, at $Q = 4$, the slope from the origin to the Total Revenue curve is $24/4 = 6$. To approximate the slope *along* the curve at $Q = 4$, first consider what happens when Q increases by one unit (notationally, $\Delta Q = 1$) from $Q = 4$. The corresponding small vertical change in R is denoted ΔR. The ΔQ and ΔR so obtained are the horizontal and vertical legs of the small triangle shown between $Q = 4$ and $Q = 5$ in the upper diagram of Figure 2.10. The desired slope along the curve at $Q = 4$ is approximated by the slope $\Delta R / \Delta Q$ of the hypotenuse of this small triangle (dotted in the diagram). Numerically, this slope is $\Delta R / \Delta Q = (25 - 24)/1 = 1$. But this dotted slope upward of $Q = 4$ is not a very good approximation of what we want, which is the Marginal Revenue or exact slope of the Revenue curve *at* $Q = 4$. (In Table 2.1, the MR figures derived from this upward variation of Q are tabulated in the last column under the heading "Marginal Revenue—Poorer Approximation.")

Inspecting the upper diagram of Figure 2.10 makes it evident that this upward-variation method of approximation provides a better estimate of the true slope along the TR curve halfway between $Q = 4$ and $Q = 5$—rather than exactly at $Q = 4$. That is why the fourth column of Table 2.1, labeled "Marginal Revenue—Better Approximation," places the $MR = 1$ estimate derived from the upward variation halfway between the $Q = 4$ and $Q = 5$ rows—i.e., at $Q = 4\frac{1}{2}$. Similarly, the slope of the dotted hypotenuse of the lower small triangle corresponding to the downward variation from $Q = 4$ to $Q = 3$, or numerically $(24 - 21)/1 = 3$, is best regarded as estimating MR at $Q = 3\frac{1}{2}$, and is accordingly plotted in the fourth column halfway between the $Q = 3$ and the $Q = 4$ rows. To estimate the MR exactly at $Q = 4$, we simply take the average of the two estimates—the estimate of 1 for $Q = 4\frac{1}{2}$ and of 3 for $Q = 3\frac{1}{2}$—which is, of course, 2. Or, in the Table, we would linearly interpolate 2 between the MR numbers shown in the fourth column a half-line above and a half-line below $Q = 4$.

Even the "better approximation" will not in general be precisely correct. But when (as in this discussion) the underlying demand curve is linear, it can be shown mathematically that the "better approximation" will indeed be perfect. So $MR = 2$ is the *true* Marginal Revenue at $Q = 4$. More generally, the degree to which the slope represented by the hypotenuse of any small triangle (as in the upper diagram of Figure 2.10), for an upward or downward variation ΔQ, approximates the exact slope along the Total Revenue curve itself (the latter being the true Marginal Revenue) can be improved by taking a smaller and smaller variation ΔQ. This leads to the formal definition of Marginal Revenue as:

(2.6)
$$MR \equiv \lim_{(\text{as } \Delta Q \to 0)} \frac{\Delta R}{\Delta Q}$$

Even though the denominator ΔQ approaches zero in the limiting process, it will in general be the case that the ratio of ΔR to ΔQ approaches some definite number, which is the slope *along* the curve. This ratio is known as the *derivative* in the calculus.[5] In this book we will however think of Marginal Revenue as the ratio of small finite differences (symbolized as $\Delta R / \Delta Q$), which is not quite exact but generally close enough if the "better approximation" is used.

Exercise 2.5: Consider the non-linear demand curve given by the equation $P = 100 - Q^2$. To find: the better and poorer approximations for MR at $Q = 4$.

Answer: Since $R = PQ$, the Total Revenue equation is $R = 100Q - Q^3$. If $Q = 4$, then $R = 336$. Consider first the upward variation alone. At $Q = 5$, we have $R = 375$. Thus, the "poorer approximation" for the MR at $Q = 4$ is $\Delta R / \Delta Q = (375 - 336)/1 = 39$. To find the "better approximation," we must also look at the downward variation. Since, at $Q = 3$, TR is $R = 273$, we have $\Delta R / \Delta Q = (336 - 273)/1 = 63$. Averaging the two, the better approximation for MR at $Q = 4$ is $\frac{1}{2}(39 + 63) = 51$. [Calculus techniques give the true figure as $MR = 52$—note how much closer this is to the better approximation (51) in comparison with the poorer approximation (39).]

So long as the Total Revenue R is rising as Q increases, it is obvious from Figure 2.10 that the slope along the R curve must be positive; hence the Marginal Revenue MR exceeds zero. When R is decreasing in the region past the hump in the upper diagram of Figure 2.10, however, the slope along the curve and therefore the MR must be negative. Thus we have the following geometrical relations between total and marginal functions:

PROPOSITION 2.1a: *When a total function or magnitude is rising, the corresponding marginal function or magnitude is positive.*

[5]*Mathematical Footnote:* Marginal Revenue as a derivative is symbolized dR/dQ and defined as:

$$MR \equiv \frac{dR}{dQ} \equiv \lim_{\Delta Q \to 0} \frac{\Delta R}{\Delta Q}$$

PROPOSITION 2.1b: When a total magnitude is falling, the corresponding marginal magnitude is negative.

But when R reaches a maximum (or a minimum) the function is neither increasing nor decreasing, i.e., it is level. Drawing the obvious inference, we have:

PROPOSITION 2.1c: When a total magnitude reaches a maximum or a minimum, the corresponding marginal magnitude is zero.[6,7]

Verifying in Table 2.1 we see that at $Q = 4$ where the Total Revenue function R is rising, $MR = 2$ (the better approximation) is positive. At $Q = 8$, R is in its falling range and $MR = -6$ (again, using the better approximation) is negative. Where does the Total Revenue function reach a maximum? In the upper diagram of Figure 2.10, we see that the true maximum of $R = 25$ is reached at $Q = 5$.[8] This is correctly indicated by the interpolated $MR = 0$ for $Q = 5$ in the "better approximation" column. Note that the "poorer approximation" column incorrectly suggests that MR equals zero at $Q = 5\frac{1}{2}$ where the Total Revenue function is already beyond its maximum.

In the lower diagram in Figure 2.10, we also see a geometrical relation between average and marginal functions:

PROPOSITION 2.2a: When the average magnitude is falling, the marginal magnitude must lie below it.

This can be intuitively appreciated: If adding one more unit to a previous collection reduces the average of some measure, the additional unit or newcomer must have been below average. In Figure 2.10 the Average Revenue AR is always falling, hence the Marginal Revenue MR lies always below it.

What if the average magnitude is not falling but rising? Then we have the analogous proposition:

PROPOSITION 2.2b: When the average magnitude is rising, the marginal magnitude must lie above it.

And, of course, Propositions 2.2a and 2.2b together imply:

---

[6]*Mathematical Footnote:* When $dR/dQ > 0$, the Total Revenue function R is increasing; when $dR/dQ < 0$ it is decreasing; and when $dR/dQ = 0$, we have a stationary value of the function.

[7]Some technical qualifications should be made to these assertions. Not all minima or maxima are "flat." In the upper diagram of Figure 2.10, Total Revenue R has an interior maximum at $Q = 5$, for which $MR = 0$. But it also has *minima* at $Q = 0$ and $Q = 10$ (since revenue R can never be less than zero). But the curve is not flat at those points. In this book we will be dealing almost always with flat minima or maxima, so that Proposition 2.1c holds.

[8]*Mathematical Footnote:* If $R = 10Q - Q^2$, then $dR/dQ = 10 - 2Q$. Setting $dR/dQ = 0$ (first-order condition for a maximum), we have $Q = 5$.

PROPOSITION 2.2c: *When an average magnitude is neither rising nor falling (at a minimum or maximum, or other stationary point), the marginal magnitude must be equal to it.*[9]

[9]*Mathematical Footnote*: Let us verify Proposition 2.2a of the text, and specifically that *MR* is below *AR* when the latter is falling (a declining function of *Q*). For *AR* to be falling:

$$0 > \frac{d(AR)}{dQ} = \frac{d(R/Q)}{dQ} = \frac{Q(dR/dQ) - R}{Q^2}$$

This directly implies $dR/dQ < R/Q$, or $MR < AR$. Similar proofs for Propositions 2.2b and 2.2c can easily be shown.

EXAMPLE 2.8
Birds Do It! Bees Do It!

Critics of academic economics often argue that the theoretical reasoning required to solve optimization problems involves concepts too subtle to be employed in actual decision-making. The *marginal* concept has been an object of particular attack; it has been contended, for example, that businessmen can hardly be expected to compute and employ marginal concepts of revenue or cost in choosing price or output.

Biologists, in contrast, have recently discovered that the adaptive decisions of animals can often be best interpreted in marginal terms. Consider a bird foraging for seeds or insects that are distributed in patches over the environment. The bird must decide when to leave its current patch and fly off to look for another. As it continues to exploit the current patch, food becomes sparser and sparser there—the marginal "revenue" (energy intake) the bird receives per unit of time spent is falling. But if the bird abandons its current patch, it must suffer an entire loss of energy intake in the dead time before it locates a fresh patch. Bioeconomic reasoning in this situation says that the bird should continue to exploit its current patch until the *marginal* "revenue" per unit of time spent there falls to equality with the *average* "revenue" it can attain elsewhere, allowing for the dead time between patches.[a]

Field studies have tended to confirm that foraging birds do indeed behave as if they can solve this economic problem. Under more controlled laboratory conditions, Richard Cowie[b] was able to study in more detail the foraging behavior of the great tit (*Parus major*). His results indicate that these birds are able to estimate quite precisely the marginal and average "revenue" (energy intake) of time spent in different patches of the environment.

And what the birds can do, the bees can too. C. M. Hodges and L. L. Wolfe[c]

[a]Eric L. Charnov, "Optimal Foraging, the Marginal Value Theorem," *Theoretical Population Biology*, v. 9 (April 1976).
[b]Richard J. Cowie, "Optimal Foraging in Great Tits (*Parus major*)," *Nature*, v. 268 (July 14, 1977).
[c]Clayton M. Hodges and Larry L. Wolfe, "Optimal Foraging in Bumblebees: Why Is Nectar Left Behind in Flowers?" *Behavioral Ecology and Sociobiology* (Spring 1981), p. 41.

studied nectar consumption of bumblebees feeding on flowers containing, on average, 6.09 microliters of nectar. If the bees obeyed correct marginal principles, they calculated, a flower would be abandoned when its remaining nectar fell to 1.0 microliters. The actual measured amount of nectar left behind was 1.24 microliters, the difference of 0.24 being small enough to be attributed to sampling and measurement error.

The lower diagram of Figure 2.10, with its falling AR curve, illustrates Proposition 2.2a. To illustrate Propositions 2.2b and 2.2c, we need to look at an average magnitude that has both a rising and a falling range, as in the lower diagram of Figure 2.11. Figure 2.11 shows, in the upper diagram, a different

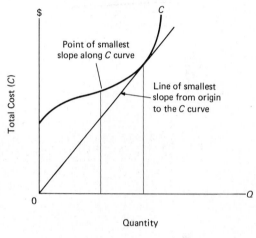

FIGURE 2.11 Derivation of Average and Marginal Magnitudes from Total Function: Cost. The lower diagram sketches the average and marginal functions AC and MC derived from the Total Cost function C in the upper diagram. Where the slope along the *Total Cost* function is least, MC is at a minimum. Where the slope of the line drawn from the origin to the curve is least (tangent line in the upper diagram), AC is at a minimum. Where AC is falling MC lies below it; where AC is rising, MC lies above it.

total function to be frequently employed in this book: a firm's Total Cost C as a function of Quantity Q. The Total Cost function shown is positive even for $Q = 0$, and rises throughout. The initial positive intercept of the C function is called the "fixed cost." This fixed positive quantity dictates that, at $Q = 0$, the average cost $AC \equiv C/Q$ is infinite. Using the technique of determining the average function as the slope of a line connecting the origin with a point on the curve, we can see that as Q increases this slope will first fall (become flatter) but then rise (become steeper). Hence in the lower diagram of Figure 2.11 the AC curve has at first a declining, and then a rising range—so that it must have a minimum in between. The MC curve is of course below AC in the latter's declining range, and above AC in the latter's rising range. Therefore, MC must cut AC at the latter's minimum as asserted in Proposition 2.2c. Note also that the minimum of the MC curve in the lower diagram corresponds to where the slope *along* the C curve is least in the upper diagram; the minimum of the AC curve in the lower diagram corresponds to where the slope of a line drawn from the origin *to* points on the C curve is least in the upper diagram (tangent line out of origin).

EXAMPLE 2.9
The Oil Entitlements Program

In the period 1973-1974 the Organization of Petroleum Exporting Countries (OPEC) was able to effect a startling increase in the world price of crude oil from about \$2 to almost \$12 per barrel (see the example, "The OPEC," in Chapter 8). The U.S. government, concerned about its balance of payments, immediately began efforts to reduce oil imports. But another aspect of the situation was that the enormous jump in the world price of crude, if allowed to become effective in domestic transactions, would have led to huge profits for American producers of crude oil. United States policy-makers, regarding such profits as inequitable, also wanted to eliminate such "windfall" gains. Unfortunately, the way chosen to achieve the second objective tended to defeat the first,[a] because of the impact upon oil importers' calculations of marginal and average costs.

To prevent domestic producers from reaping windfall gains, the U.S. government froze the price of domestic crude. This immediately caused a problem, because some refiners did and others did not have access to the limited supply of artificially cheap domestic crude. Again in the interests of "equity," the Entitlements Program was undertaken. The basic idea was that every refiner was entitled to buy, at the low frozen price, the nationwide average fraction of cheap domestic oil. This program forced those refiners having more-than-average access to cheap domestic crude to compensate those

[a]This is necessarily a very simplified discussion of the enormously complicated and ever-changing details of U.S. oil policy. In particular the legal distinction between so-called "new domestic oil" and "old domestic oil" has been omitted here.

refiners making more-than-average use of expensive imported crude. The unanticipated effect was to *encourage* rather than discourage imports.

From the point of view of the nation as a whole, the Marginal Cost of crude oil was a rising function, the highest-cost step being the imported crude at $12 per barrel. Had refiners using imported crude been required to pay this full world price, they would have had an incentive to reduce imports. But, under the Entitlements Program, each barrel imported entitled the importer to a great bargain: a certain amount of domestic crude at the cheap frozen price. In effect, all refiners were "equitably" treated by being able to obtain crude at the nationwide Average Cost, no matter what their source of crude. But, as a result, no refiners were discouraged from using imported crude even though that source represented the highest Marginal Cost for the nation as a whole.[b]

[b]Many discussions of the oil entitlements program are available. See, for example, C. E. Phelps and R. T. Smith, *Petroleum Regulation: The False Dilemma of Decontrol* (Santa Monica, Calif.: The Rand Corporation, 1977).

The unintended effects of government policy illustrated in Example 2.9 may have stemmed from a failure to distinguish properly between Average and Marginal Cost. Confusion may sometimes exist between marginal and total concepts, as indicated below.

EXAMPLE 2.10
Taxes

The Table below shows the personal income-tax schedule for single tax-payers in the tax year 1982. For any "Taxable Income"[a] bracket on the left-hand side of the table, the right-hand side shows the Total Tax at the bottom of the bracket and the Marginal Tax for increments of income within the bracket. In the $15,000–$18,200 income bracket, for example, the Tax Due is stated as $2330 + 27%. Therefore, $2330 is the Total Tax for someone earning exactly $15,000, and $0.27 (or 27 cents) is the Marginal Tax per dollar of income thereafter (up to the top of the bracket).

The following fallacy is sometimes encountered. An employee is making an annual income of $14,999 and paying a Total Tax just under $2330. His employer offers him a raise of $1000, which the worker refuses on the ground that it would put him in a higher tax bracket. The worker may think that, in moving up to a higher *marginal* tax rate (27% instead of 23%) he will be taxed more heavily on his $14,999 in addition to whatever tax he must pay on the $1000 raise. This is incorrect. The worker's additional tax would be a trifle under 27% of $1000, or $270. Had he accepted the raise he would be better

[a]"Taxable Income" is earned income minus the amount of exemptions, deductions, etc., as provided in the tax law.

off by $1000 − $270. His net loss of $630 is one of the costs of being unable to comprehend the marginal concept of economics.

TAXABLE INCOME		TAX DUE	
Over	But Not Over	Amount	Of Excess Over
$ 2,300	$ 3,400	$ 12%	$ 2,300
3,400	4,400	132 + 14%	3,400
4,400	6,500	272 + 16%	4,400
6,500	8,500	608 + 17%	6,500
8,500	10,800	948 + 19%	8,500
10,800	12,900	1,385 + 22%	10,800
12,900	15,000	1,847 + 23%	12,900
15,000	18,200	2,330 + 27%	15,000
18,200	23,500	3,194 + 31%	18,200
23,500	28,800	4,837 + 35%	23,500
28,800	34,100	6,692 + 40%	28,800
34,100	41,500	8,812 + 44%	34,100
41,500		12,068 + 50%	41,500

Source: Internal Revenue Service, Department of the Treasury, *1982 Federal Income Tax Forms*, p. 29.

☐ SUMMARY OF CHAPTER 2

This chapter covers two main topics: supply–demand analysis, and the relations among total, average, and marginal magnitudes.

Supply–demand analysis is the main working tool for solving problems of *equilibrium*. Equilibrium price and quantity are determined by the intersection of a supply curve and a demand curve. Changes in demand or in supply conditions are represented by shifts in the positions or shapes of one or both of these curves. An increase in demand (rightward shift of the demand curve) raises both equilibrium price and equilibrium quantity in the market; an increase in supply (rightward shift of the supply curve) raises equilibrium quantity but lowers equilibrium price. A tax on transactions will reduce the quantity exchanged; it raises the *gross price* (the price paid by buyers) but lowers the *net price* (price received by sellers).

Price ceilings or floors, if effective, prevent markets from reaching equilibrium. In such cases the quantity exchanged is always the *smaller* of the differing amounts demanded and supplied—except in the case of a *supported* price floor.

The relations among total, average, and marginal magnitudes are essential for understanding problems of *optimization*. Regardless of the variable involved (whether Revenue, or Cost, or Utility, or other), the marginal magnitude is positive, zero, or negative depending on whether the total magnitude is rising, level, or falling. And the marginal magnitude is below, equal to, or above the average magnitude depending on whether the latter is falling, level, or rising.

☐ QUESTIONS FOR CHAPTER 2

*R1. Which of the following are optimization problems? Which are equilibrium problems? [*Note:* You're not asked for the *answers,* but you might think about them.]

   a. As a businessman, should I have occasional sales at reduced prices, or would I do better to stick with moderate prices all year round? O
   b. If gold were discovered in Hawaii, would apartment rents rise on the island? E
   c. If the punishment for murder were made more severe, would there be fewer murders? E
   d. As a general, should I attack now when the enemy doesn't expect it—or wait for my reinforcements, even though the enemy will then be alerted? O
   e. Over the year, why is the price of strawberries more variable than the price of potatoes? E
   f. If my spouse and I have had three girl babies in a row, should we give up or try again for a boy? O

R2. Supply–demand analysis is the key tool for which of the two main analytical techniques of economics? For what class of problem is the relation among total, average, and marginal quantities the key tool?

*R3. In what sense is price a "ratio of quantities"?

R4. Explain why market equilibrium is determined by the *intersection* of the supply curve and the demand curve.

R5. How does an "increase in demand" shift the demand curve? How does an "increase in supply" shift the supply curve? Do the effects upon equilibrium price and equilibrium quantity go in the same direction in the case of an increase in demand? In the case of an increase in supply?

*R6. In the analysis of a $T per unit tax described in the text, the supply curve was shifted upward by $T to find the new equilibrium. Would the same result have been achieved if instead the demand curve were shifted downward by $T? Explain.

*R7. In each of the following cases, state whether an excise tax will raise the (gross) price *paid* by consumers, or lower the (net) price *received* by sellers, or both.
   a. Supply curve upward-sloping, demand curve downward-sloping.
   b. Supply curve horizontal, demand curve downward-sloping.
   c. Supply curve vertical, demand curve downward-sloping.
   d. Supply curve vertical, demand curve horizontal.

R8. Suppose that an $S per unit *subsidy* upon sales of a particular commodity is put into effect. What would the implications be for the quantity exchanged? For the gross and the net price?

*R9. What is a "meaningful" price ceiling or price floor? Why is it that meaningful floors and meaningful ceilings both *decrease* the quantity traded? What happens, however, if a price floor is "supported"?

R10. Starting from a given Total Revenue function R, show how the Average Revenue function AR is derived. Show how the Marginal Revenue function MR is derived.

R11. Starting from a given Total Cost function C, show how the Average Cost function AC and the Marginal Cost function MC are derived.

*The answers to asterisked questions appear at the end of the book.

*R12.   In terms of the general relations among total, average, and marginal quantities, which of the following statements are necessarily true, and which are not?
a. When the total function is rising, the marginal function is rising.
b. When the total function is rising, the marginal function is positive.
c. When the total function is rising, the marginal function lies above it.
d. When the marginal function is rising, the average function is also rising.
e. When the average function is falling, the marginal function lies below it.
f. When the marginal function is neither rising nor falling, the average function is constant.

*R13.   For a Total Revenue function given at integer quantities as in Table 2.1, explain the nature of the "better approximation" of Marginal Revenue that provides a greater degree of accuracy.

FOR FURTHER THOUGHT AND DISCUSSION

*T1.   For a particular commodity, suppose that the supply curve is very steep (positively sloped, but almost vertical). Would a $T tax tend to have a relatively large or a relatively small effect on quantity exchanged in the market? Would there tend to be a relatively large or a relatively small effect on the gross price paid by buyers? Upon the net price received by sellers? In terms of the underlying economic meaning, why would these consequences be anticipated?

T2.   Analyze correspondingly the case where the demand curve is very steep (negatively sloped, but almost vertical).

*T3.   If the price of gasoline rises as a result of a reduction in petroleum supplies, what effect would you anticipate upon the price of automobiles? Upon the relative price of small, light cars versus large, heavy cars?

*T4.   What assumptions underlie "the method of comparative statics"? Will these assumptions ever be met in the real world?

T5.   During World War II in Great Britain, a ceiling was imposed to hold down the market price of bread. Explain why there was upward pressure upon the price of bread. What consequences of the upward pressure would you anticipate, given continuing enforcement of the ceiling? To help reduce this upward pressure, the British government took fresh bread off the market—all bread sold had to be at least one day old. Would you expect this regulation to achieve the desired effect?

*T6.   In the year A.D. 302, the Roman emperor Diocletian "commanded that there should be cheapness." His edict declared:

> Unprincipled greed appears wherever our armies, following the commands of the public weal, march, not only in villages and cities but also upon all highways, with the result that prices of foodstuffs mount not only fourfold and eightfold, but transcend all measure. Our law shall fix a measure and a limit to this greed.

Why do you think Diocletian found food prices higher wherever he marched with his armies? What result would you anticipate from the command that "there should be cheapness"?

*T7.   From the tax-schedule data in the text, graph the Total Tax ("tax due") as a function of Taxable Income in the range from $0 to $10,000 of income. Also graph the corresponding Average Tax and Marginal Tax functions. Note that Average Tax and Marginal Tax are percentages. Why?

*T8. Suppose that you were given a partial tabulation of a demand function, as indicated here. Estimate Marginal Revenue at $Q = 3$.

QUANTITY	PRICE
0	30
3	20
6	12

[handwritten annotations:] $R = QP$ MR   0 — 20, 60 —, 72 — 4, —12 MR at q=3   36, 2√72, 12*

T9. The following is part of a price schedule, showing the quantity discounts offered by a printing shop.

Does something peculiar happen as the size of your order approaches the upper limit in a given price range? Explain in terms of Marginal Revenue to the printing shop. How does this price-bracketing scheme differ from the way the tax brackets in the Income Tax example affect your marginal tax?

SIZE OF YOUR ORDER	YOUR PRICE
1–10 units	50¢ each
11–20 units	40¢ each
21–50 units	35¢ each
Over 50 units	30¢ each

UTILITY
AND
PREFERENCE

CORE CHAPTER

The two basic techniques of analysis over which the student must gain command, we saw in the preceding chapter, are *finding an optimum* and *finding an equilibrium*. Here in Part Two of the book we will concentrate upon the optimum of the consumer—the choice of a best combination of consumer goods.

3.A
THE DECISION PROBLEM OF THE INDIVIDUAL

As the circular flow of economic activity (Figure 1.1) shows, the individual must make two types of optimizing choices. Facing the product market, everyone must decide how best to spend his or her income on consumable goods and services. (A person can also save, as will be explained more fully later; however, saving is indirect purchase of *future* consumable goods.) But a consumer's income is not heaven-sent: it must be *earned,* an activity that also involves a decision-making process. Facing the factor market, each person seeks the best employments for his or her owned resources (brains, brawn, rental property, etc.). The earnings obtained from such employment become the consumer's income for spending on consumption goods.

Part Two of this book considers the individual as consumer, taking as given the income resulting from whatever decisions may have been made as resource-owner. But it should be kept in mind that in *both* of these aspects, consumer and resource-owner, the rational individual will be optimizing—attempting to make the decision that is best in terms of his or her existing tastes and preferences.

The economist describes the process of choosing the best decision as the *maximization of utility.* Utility as a hypothetical magnitude serving as an index for preference will be the central topic of this chapter.

3.B
LAWS OF PREFERENCE

Scientific analysis always involves simplified pictures of reality. These pictures are called *theories* or *models*; they are idealizations in which irrelevant or unsystematic peculiarities are stripped away to permit us to concentrate upon the essentials.

As an idealization or theory, then, we will assert that the individual's preferences for consumption commodities follow two laws:

1. *Axiom of Comparison*: Any two distinct baskets *A* and *B* of commodities can be compared in preference by the individual. Each such comparison must lead to one of the three following results: (1) Basket *A* is preferred to basket *B*, or (2) *B* is preferred to *A*, or (3) *A* and *B* are indifferent.

The Axiom of Comparison is an idealization of reality, in that we suppose that the individual never says "I simply can't compare *A* and *B*." Nor is he supposed ever to say "Two-thirds of the time I prefer *A*, but the other one-third of the time *B*."[1]

2. *Axiom of Transitivity*: Consider any three baskets *A*, *B*, and *C*. If *A* is preferred to *B*, and *B* is preferred to *C*, then *A* must be preferred to *C*. Similarly, if *A* is indifferent to *B*, and *B* to *C*, then *A* is indifferent to *C*.

The Axiom of Transitivity is also an idealization, for violations of it no doubt take place. But if an individual were to tell you, "I prefer Apples to Bananas and Bananas to Cherries," and were then to add, "But I'll always take Cherries over Apples!" you'd regard that person as rather odd.

[1]There are more advanced theories in economics that allow for individuals' limited ability to make comparisons. Such theories, dealing with less idealized decision-makers, are more realistic but also more complex to analyze.

EXAMPLE 3.1
Transitivity and Age

Arnold A. Weinstein administered a questionnaire to experimental subjects asking them for preference rankings over ten commodity bundles, offered as pairs in random order. Among the bundles, all having a market value of around $3 at the time, were items such as: (1) $3 in cash; (2) the three latest Beatles 45-rpm phonograph records; (3) three men's clip-on bow ties, all with red polka dots, one brown, one blue, one gray; (4) a brush-stroke print of El Greco's "View of Toledo"; (5) a vanilla malted milk (two glasses) per day for ten days; and so forth.

The intent of the experiment was to detect possible intransitivities of preference over *triads* of offerings, in the course of the subjects' successive *pairwise* comparisons. An intransitivity would occur if, for example, a particular subject were observed to choose cash over malted milk, malted milk over bow ties, but bow ties over cash. The great majority of the triads showed consistent transitive preferences. An interesting result obtained was that transitivity tended to increase with age, as indicated in the Table:

PART 2   PREFERENCE, CONSUMPTION, AND DEMAND

Transitivity Experiment Results

| | PROPORTION OF |
GROUP	TRANSITIVE RESPONSES (%)
52 children aged 9–12	79.2
36 teenagers aged 14–16	83.3
46 high-school seniors aged 17–18	88.0
18 mature adults (mostly teachers)	93.5

Source: Table compiled from data reported in Arnold A. Weinstein, "Transitivity of Preference: A Comparison among Age Groups," *Journal of Political Economy*, v. 76 (March/April 1968), p. 310.

The experimenter's interpretation was that consistency in preference ordering is an acquired skill, hence more difficult for younger people to achieve. More arguably, he concluded that his results lent some support for the legal restrictions and protections placed on youth in our society.

> COMMENT: As an alternative explanation, younger persons are more likely to engage in choices that seem inconsistent only because they are really *exploratory* in nature. "Don't knock it until you've tried it" is a dangerous maxim, but one with some appeal. If *all* possibilities are to be tried by actual consumption, some seeming intransitivities of choice are inevitable. Consider the three possibilities: cash, malted milk, and bow ties. If cash is chosen over malted milk and malted milk over bow ties, the only way to try out the bow ties is to choose them when offered next—even over cash. So the Laws of Preference presume an already well-settled pattern of consumer desires.

The Axiom of Comparison and the Axiom of Transitivity taken together lead to the:

PROPOSITION OF RANK ORDERING OF PREFERENCES: All conceivable baskets of commodities can be consistently ranked in order of preference by the individual. This ranking is called "the preference function."

Exercise 3.1: John prefers the mixed consumption basket one beer + one taco to either two beers alone or two tacos alone—but as between the latter baskets, he would rather have the two beers. Do the facts just stated, absent any other information, indicate that the Axiom of Comparison and the Axiom of Transitivity apply for John—at least among the three combinations described? If they do apply, what is his rank ordering of preferences?

Answer: As to the Axiom of Comparison, yes, the stated facts show John's preferences in all possible pairwise choices among the three consumption baskets. As to the Axiom of Transitivity, the answer again is yes. Transitivity would tell us that if John prefers the mixed basket over two beers, and two beers over two tacos, he should prefer the mixed basket over two tacos—and, we are told, in fact he does. His rank ordering is, clearly: first the mixture, then the two beers, then the two tacos.

For simplicity, consider the individual choosing between only two commodities, X and Y. Amounts x and y are scaled[2] along the horizontal and vertical axes of Figure 3.1. Four possible combinations of X and Y are being considered by the consumer: the baskets represented by the points A, B, C, and D in the diagram. Notice that basket A represents more of both commodities than basket D. Also, basket A has as much of commodity Y as has basket B, and more of commodity X; in comparison with basket C, basket A has as much of X and more of commodity Y. What do the Laws of Preference tell us about this situation? Only two things: (1) that the individual is capable of ranking all four combinations; and (2) that if, for example, A is preferred to B and B to D, then (by transitivity) A must be preferred to D.

It may seem plausible to assert that the combination A—containing at least as much of either commodity as any other basket, and exceeding every other basket in quantity of X or of Y or both—must be preferred to all the others shown in Figure 3.1. This plausibility is sometimes erected into a principle known as: *More is preferred to less.* But "More is preferred to less" is not an inviolable law of preference. Rather, it can be regarded as defining what we mean by *goods*. Undesired commodities, *bads*, also surely exist; household garbage is a homely example. Some commodities, like tapioca pudding, may be goods for some individuals and bads for others. And even for a great many (all?) undoubted goods, beyond a certain point of satiation they would become bads. (See Example 3.5, "Ball-Point Pens and French Pastries.") If disposal of undesired objects were always free, it would do no harm to assume that all commodities were goods. Any

[2]Capital letters X and Y here designate the commodities; lowercase letters x and y indicate particular quantities of each.

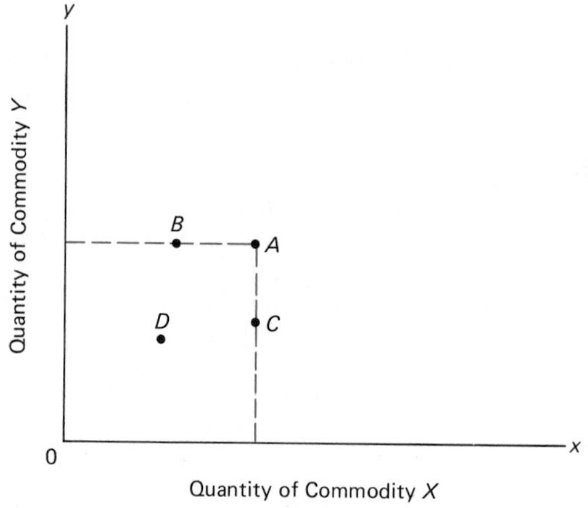

FIGURE 3.1 **Alternative Consumption Baskets.** A point like A, B, C, or D represents a combination or basket containing amounts of commodity X and commodity Y. If X and Y are both *goods*, then A is preferred to any of the other marked points.

bads would be immediately and costlessly discarded. But as a practical matter, disposal is a costly economic activity; more is *not* always better than less.

DEFINITION: A *good* is a commodity for which more is preferred to less.

3.C
UTILITY, PREFERENCE, AND RATIONAL CHOICE

The term "utility" was introduced by the British philosopher Jeremy Bentham. Bentham declared:

> Nature has placed mankind under the governance of two sovereign masters, *pain* and *pleasure*. . . . The *principle of utility* recognizes this subjection. . . . By the principle of utility is meant that principle which approves or disapproves of every action whatsoever, according to the tendency which it appears to have to augment or diminish the happiness of the party whose interest is in question. . . .[3]

For Bentham, then, the maximization of utility is an assertedly true psychological principle—that men avoid pain and seek pleasure or happiness.

The modern economic theory of choice is not based upon this arguable psychological premise, that man's goals are nothing but seeking pleasure and avoiding pain. Economists today simply say that individuals tend to make consistent choices: that the Laws of Preference of the preceding section, while undoubtedly idealized, are a good approximation of actual behavior observed in the world. Since the Laws of Preference are really rules of rational choice, this reduces to the postulate of rationality discussed in Chapter 1.

What modern economists call "utility" reflects nothing more than rank ordering of preference. The statement "Basket *A* is preferred to basket *B*" and the statement "Basket *A* has higher utility than basket *B*" mean the same thing. They both lead to the empirical prediction: "Basket *A* will be chosen over basket *B*."

CONCLUSION: Utility is the variable whose relative magnitude indicates direction of preference. In finding the most preferred position, the individual maximizes utility.

3.D
UTILITY: CARDINAL OR ORDINAL MAGNITUDE?

Early writers had no doubt that utility was a quantitatively measurable entity like length or temperature. They would have regarded it as perfectly reasonable to employ a construction like the upper diagram of Figure 3.2 in which any individual's utility (scaled in "utils" according to the vertical column of numbers

---

[3]J. Bentham, *An Introduction to the Principles of Morals and Legislation* (1823 edition), Chap. 1.

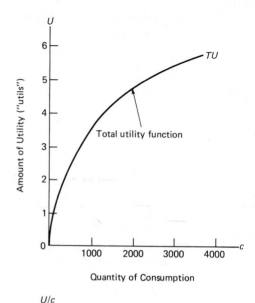

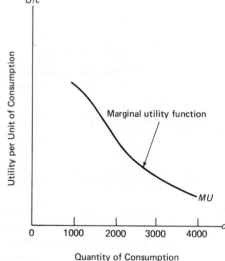

FIGURE 3.2 Cardinal Utility: Total and Marginal. If utility is "cardinally measurable," Total Utility U can be represented quantitatively as in the upper diagram. Marginal Utility in the lower diagram can be derived from Total Utility as explained in Chapter 2. Since Total Utility increases but at a decreasing rate as consumption rises, Marginal Utility is positive but declining.

U in the diagram) is shown as a function of the quantity taken of some generalized consumption good C. Some even believed it possible to add up these "util" numbers interpersonally: that 5 of John Doe's utils could be added to 7 of Richard Roe's so as to make a total of 12 utils for the pair. Jeremy Bentham apparently believed that public policies—for example, whether the state should punish crime more or less severely, whether the rich should be taxed more or less heavily in comparison with the poor—could be determined by summing the utils of everyone involved. This seems to be what Bentham meant in recommending public policies designed to achieve "the greatest good of the greatest number," a mystifying though noble-sounding expression. Economists today generally believe that summation of the utilities of different people is meaningless, and cannot be used as a basis for economic policy.

3.D.1 ☐ Cardinal Magnitudes

What do we mean when we say that a variable is "quantitatively measurable"? We do not necessarily mean that there is only a *single* way of measuring or scaling it. Temperature is certainly quantitatively measurable, but there are alternative ways of doing so. For example, 32° Fahrenheit is 0° Celsius, and each degree up or down of Celsius corresponds to 1.8 degrees up or down of Fahrenheit. The two scales differ, but only in *zero-point* and *unit interval*. Similarly, altitude could be measured from sea level or from the center of the earth (shift of zero-point) and in feet or meters (shift of unit interval). Both temperature and altitude are more technically called *cardinal* magnitudes, variables which have the following property: that, regardless of shift of zero-point and unit interval, the relative magnitudes of *differences* remain the same. In the case of altitude, for example, there's a bigger difference between the heights of the base and crest of Mount Everest than between the ground floor and roof of even the tallest man-made building. The difference remains bigger whether we scale altitude in feet or in meters, or measure from sea-level or from the center of the earth.

In plotting utility as in the upper diagram of Figure 3.2, we are assuming it is a cardinally measurable variable. In doing so it does not matter where we place the zero-point and what the unit interval is for the vertical U scale. What is really being asserted is that it is possible to compare the *relative magnitudes of utility differences*. For example, regardless of how we might shift the zero-point and the unit interval of the U scale along the vertical axis in the diagram, it remains true that moving from 1000 to 2000 consumption units yields a bigger utility improvement than moving from 2000 to 3000 units.[4]

Exercise 3.2: In the upper panel of Figure 3.2, verify that the utility difference between $c = 2000$ and $c = 1000$ remains greater than the utility difference between $c = 3000$ and $c = 2000$—even if an alternative "new-util" scale were adopted such that the "old-util" zero-point shown in the diagram is assigned the "new-util" value 10, and each unit up or down on the old scale would be 2 units on the new.

---

[4]*Mathematical Footnote:* Two utility scales U and U' are cardinally equivalent if measurements along the two scales are related by the linear equation:

$$U' = a + bU \quad \text{(for } b > 0\text{)}$$

The constant a here represents the shift of zero-point, and the constant b the change in unit interval. Consider three quantities U_1, U_2, and U_3 along the U scale, where the difference $U_3 - U_2$ exceeds the difference $U_2 - U_1$. Then $U_3' - U_2'$ also exceeds $U_2' - U_1'$, as can be verified by direct substitutions. So the *ranking of differences* is preserved for all cardinally equivalent scales.

Answer: A visual estimate indicates that the "old-util" difference between $c = 2000$ and $c = 1000$ is around $(4.8 - 3.6) = 1.2$, while the corresponding difference between $c = 3000$ and $c = 2000$ is about $(5.4 - 4.8) = 0.6$. So the first utility difference is the larger, in fact about twice as big. On the "new-util" scale the first difference would be around $(19.6 - 17.2) = 2.4$ while the second difference would be about $(20.8 - 19.6) = 1.2$. Evidently, the first difference remains the larger, in fact remains approximately twice as big.

Utility in the upper diagram of Figure 3.2 is a *total* function of consumption C. The corresponding *Marginal Utility* function, defined (as described in Chapter 2) as the slope or rate of change of the Total Utility function, is shown in the lower diagram of Figure 3.2. Since Total Utility is shown as rising throughout, by Proposition 2.1a Marginal Utility MU is always positive. But since Total Utility in the upper diagram is increasing *at a steadily decreasing rate,* the MU curve in the lower diagram declines as consumption increases. This property, called *diminishing Marginal Utility,* is unaffected if we change the zero-point or unit interval of the utility scale.[5] Putting it more generally: If the underlying total variable is a cardinal magnitude, it is possible to say when the corresponding marginal variable is an increasing or decreasing function. This is so because marginal quantities are of the nature of differences of total quantities, and the comparison of differences is unaffected by shift of zero-point or unit interval.

The assertion that people experience diminishing Marginal Utility, as consumption income rises, is an empirical one. This assertion was and is widely believed, despite the absence of a generally accepted measuring rod for utilities. It corresponds to our commonsense notion that more income makes us happier, but we usually get more of a thrill from our first million than from our tenth.

[5] *Mathematical Footnote*: Since $U' = a + bU$, and b is positive, positive Marginal Utility according to the U scale ($dU/dc > 0$) implies positive Marginal Utility according to the U' scale ($dU'/dc = bdU/dc > 0$). Note that a change in zero-point a does not affect MU at all, and a change in unit interval b changes it only by the same positive multiplicative constant everywhere. *Diminishing* Marginal Utility according to the U scale ($d^2U/dc^2 < 0$) similarly implies diminishing Marginal Utility according to the U' scale ($d^2U'/dc^2 < 0$).

EXAMPLE 3.2
Does Money Buy Happiness?

While most economists do not believe that there is a valid cardinal scale for utilities, the economist Julian Simon disagrees. He has proposed to measure utility, among other ways, by asking people, "Are you happy?"[a] Psychologists have carried out questionnaire surveys asking people to classify themselves as very happy, pretty happy, or not too happy. The percentage results in the Table were obtained from a survey of residents in four small Illinois towns reported in 1965.

[a] One of the "other ways" he proposes is to look at the suicide rate. See Julian L. Simon, "Interpersonal Welfare Comparison Can Be Made—And Used for Redistribution Decisions," *Kyklos,* v. 27 (1974).

PART 2   PREFERENCE, CONSUMPTION, AND DEMAND

Income and Happiness

| | | | PERCENT RESPONDING | |
INCOME	Very Happy	Pretty Happy	Not Too Happy	SCORE*
Less than $3000	14	55	31	−0.17
$3000–3999	21	63	16	+0.05
$4000–4999	27	61	12	+0.15
$5000–5999	26	64	10	+0.16
$6000–6999	24	65	10	+0.14
$7000–7999	30	60	10	+0.20
$8000–9999	29	63	7	+0.22
$10,000 or more	38	54	8	+0.30

Source: N. M. Bradburn and D. Caplovitz, *Reports on Happiness* (Chicago, Aldine, 1965), p. 9.

*Method for computing "Score" is described in text.

In interpreting these data, we still need a numerical utility (happiness) scale. Let us count "very happy" as +1, "pretty happy" as 0, and "not too happy" as −1. The average for each income group is then shown by the column headed "Score." If plotted, the Score data would show (despite some irregularities) a picture not too different from Figure 3.2.

EXAMPLE 3.3
The Weber-Fechner Law

An empirical generalization was developed by the psychologists E. H. Weber (1846) and G. T. Fechner (1860) concerning the relation between degree of stimulus and subjective sensitivity. The assertion is that subjective ability to discriminate is a function of *proportionate* change in the magnitude of stimulus.

Applying this to utility, subjective satisfaction can be regarded as sensitive to *proportionate* changes of income (or material well-being) regarded as stimulus. For example, if an increase in income from $10,000 to $12,000 (i.e., by 20%) is valued as a "one-util" improvement, then a further 20% increase from $12,000 to $14,400 would add a second util and still another 20% increase from $14,400 to $17,280 would provide a third util. If this is the case, utility would be a *logarithmic* function of income. Such a function would accord with the general picture of Figure 3.2, and in particular would imply diminishing Marginal Utility.

The idea of diminishing Marginal Utility, therefore, has both intuitive appeal and some evidential basis. It might also seem to explain the fact that people *save* more (i.e., buy more *future* consumption) as their wealth increases. If current consumption yields diminishing Marginal Utility, it is reasonable to respond to increments of income by arranging for part of the increment to be spent on *future* consumption. Unfortunately, this argument is far from iron-clad. For, in general, we would expect the quantity of the one type of consumption to affect the utility of the other. It may be that an extra unit of current consumption *raises* its Marginal Utility but raises the Marginal Utility of future consumption *even more*. So the evidence that people save more as income rises is not conclusive as to diminishing Marginal Utility. What we need is a way of considering utility as depending simultaneously upon the amounts of *all* the different goods consumed. That is the topic of the next section.

3.D.2 ☐ Utility of Commodity Baskets

Usually in economics we think of a person's utility as a function of several variables, as depending upon the quantities he or she consumes of a number of different commodities. (It may also depend upon the amount of factor-services like labor effort provided, but the resource-supply decision is not being considered here.) Suppose we take, for simplicity, a world of two goods X and Y. Here, if the utility scale $U(x, y)$ were cardinal, the total of "utils" would depend upon the quantities consumed x and y. There is likely to be some interdependence in the satisfactions derived from each of the goods. The Marginal Utility a consumer derives from another pound of butter normally depends also upon the person's current rate of consumption of other commodities like margarine (a "substitute") or bread (a "complement").[6]

Figure 3.3 pictures a possible cardinal utility function $U(x, y)$. The quantities x and y are measured along the horizontal axes. Utility is measured in the upward direction, as the height of the surface above the base plane. When $x = x_1$ and $y = y_2$, for example, utility is the height $T'T$. If the quantity of Y is held constant at $y = y_1$, we can see how utility varies with x. This is shown by the curve PQR lying on the utility surface; note that Total Utility rises steadily as X increases. If Y is held constant at $y = y_2$ instead, we obtain a similar curve STU; or if Y is held constant at $y = y_3$, we observe the curve BVG. In each case the curves are rising (Total Utility is increasing) as x increases, and so (in accordance with Proposition 2.1a) the Marginal Utility of X is positive. Similar statements can be made about the Marginal Utility of the other commodity Y. But, in general, the Marginal Utility for *either* commodity depends upon the specific amounts of *both* commodities. For example, the Marginal Utility of X at the point T (i.e., when $x = x_1$ and $y = y_2$), given by the slope at point T in the x-direction along the curve STU, is not necessarily the same as the Marginal Utility of X at the point V (where $x = x_1$ but $y = y_3$), given by the slope at V along BVG. So we see that Marginal Utility of X may depend upon the quantity of Y, and vice versa.

Figure 3.4 is another representation of the same utility surface as Figure 3.3. But, in contrast with the preceding diagram, the curves drawn here on the surface (CC, DD, and EE) are *contours* connecting points of equal altitude on the

---

[6]*Mathematical Footnote*: Where Utility $U(x, y)$ is a function of amounts consumed of both X and Y, the Marginal Utilities are defined as *partial derivatives*: $MU_x \equiv \partial U / \partial x$ and $MU_y \equiv \partial U / \partial y$. In general, each Marginal Utility will be a function of both x and y, that is, the cross-derivative $\partial^2 U / \partial x \, \partial y$ will not ordinarily be zero.

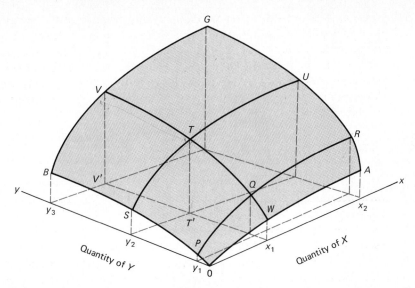

FIGURE 3.3 A Cardinal Total-Utility Function of Two Goods. Utility is measured vertically, and the horizontal axes *x* and *y* represent quantities consumed of commodities *X* and *Y*. The curves *OA*, *PR*, *SU*, and *BG* along the surface show how Total Utility changes as *x* rises, holding *y* constant (at a different level for each curve). Similarly the curves *OB*, *WV*, and *AG* show how Total Utility changes as *y* increases, holding *x* constant.

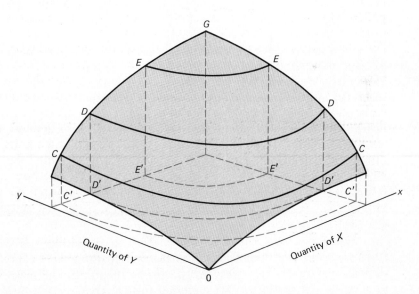

FIGURE 3.4 Cardinal Utility and Indifference Curves. The surface here is the same as the preceding diagram, but the curves *along* the surface (*CC*, *DD*, *EE*) are contours connecting equal heights (levels of utility). The projections of these curves onto the base plane (*C'C'*, *D'D'*, *E'E'*) are the indifference curves.

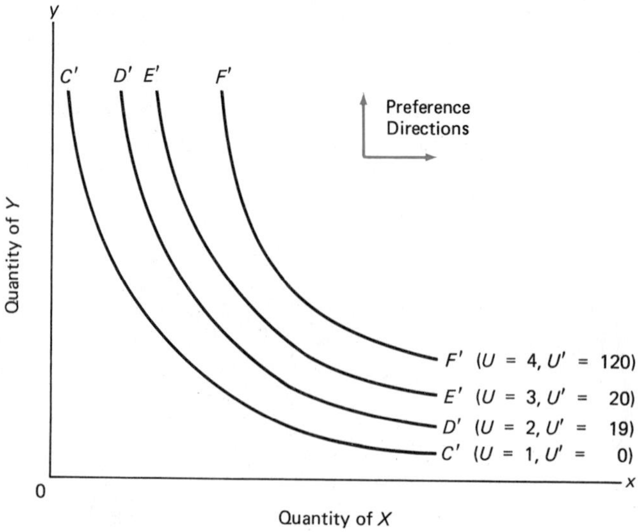

FIGURE 3.5 Indifference Curves and Preference Directions: Ordinal Utility. Here the cardinal scaling of utility has been stripped away, and we are left with the indifference curves. These indifference curves, together with the preference directions, give us all the information needed to compare (to rank) alternative consumption baskets in terms of *ordinal* utility.

"utility hill"; in effect, they show slices into the hill at fixed heights parallel to the base plane. These contours therefore are *curves of constant utility*. They were first employed by Edgeworth (1881)[7] who called them *indifference curves*. Any contour such as *CC* represents the equal level of utility yielded by a set of alternative consumption baskets (combinations of X and Y) that the consumer therefore regards as *indifferent* to one another. In Figure 3.4, looking through the transparent utility surface we can see on the base plane the *projections* $C'C', D'D', E'E'$ of the various indifference contours.

Next, suppose we simply deleted the vertical dimension of Figure 3.4, so as to leave *only* the base plane. We are left with the pure projection map shown in Figure 3.5. We can now think of the projections of the contours as being themselves the indifference curves; this step was taken by Pareto (1906).[8] Since X and Y are both goods, "More is preferred to less." Hence the *preference directions* are north and east as indicated by the arrows on the diagram. Thus, as between any two indifference curves, the one that can be reached moving northeast of the other is "higher up" on the invisible utility hill. Apart from the indifference curves, the preference directions are all we need to know for evaluating the *relative* preference status of alternative consumption combinations. So long as we know which of two baskets is on the higher indifference curve, we will choose that one over the other.

But if the contour map of indifference curves (with preference directions) fully describes preference, it is unnecessary to think of the invisible vertical dimension—utility—as having any particular quantification (other than *direction* of increase up or down). We describe this by saying that utility need *not* be regarded as a "cardinal" but only as an "ordinal" magnitude. For an ordinal

[7]Francis Y. Edgeworth, British economist, 1845–1926.
[8]Vilfredo Pareto, Italian economist and sociologist, 1848–1923.

PART 2   PREFERENCE, CONSUMPTION, AND DEMAND

magnitude the only meaningful comparisons are equality or else ranking (*direction* of difference.)[9] In ordinal terms the two radically disparate numerical preference scales U and U' attached to the indifference curves of Figure 3.5 are equally satisfactory, since *they give the same answers as to which baskets are equal in utility* (lie along the same indifference curve) *and as to how baskets that are unequal in utility should be ranked* (direction of preference). This is all we need to know.

3.E
CHARACTERISTICS OF INDIFFERENCE CURVES FOR GOODS

If we are dealing only with *goods*, indifference curves have four crucial properties: (1) Indifference curves are negatively sloped; (2) indifference curves cannot intersect; (3) one indifference curve passes through each point in commodity space; (4) indifference curves are "convex" with respect to the origin (i.e., they bulge toward the origin).

1. *Slopes of indifference curves*: For simplicity assume there are only two goods X and Y. We plot their quantities as before in the x, y-plane (the *commodity space*). Then if we consider some initial point like A in Figure 3.6, all points northeast of A (within the upper-right quadrant formed by the vertical and horizontal lines through A) in commodity space represent larger quantities of *both* goods. But for goods, "More is preferred to less." Hence, moving northeast is moving up the invisible utility hill. By a corresponding argument, moving southwest from A is moving down the utility hill to lower levels of satisfaction. It follows that all points *indifferent* to A must lie either to the southeast like points R or Q or to the northwest like points S or T. And so the indifference curve must have a negative slope more or less like U_1 or U_2 in the diagram.[10]

---

[9]*Mathematical Footnote*: If the two utility scales are only ordinally equivalent, all we can say is that $U' = F(U)$ and $dU'/dU = F'(U)$, where $F'(U) > 0$. The positive derivative dU'/dU always preserves rankings of *magnitudes*: If $U_1 > U_2$, the associated $U'_1 > U'_2$. Since the second derivative $d^2U'/dU^2 = F''(U)$ has indeterminate sign, however, the ranking of *differences* according to the U' scale need no longer correspond with their ranking on the U scale.

[10]*Mathematical Footnote*: In terms of calculus, along any indifference curve utility $U(x, y)$ is constant. So:

$$0 = dU \equiv \frac{\partial U}{\partial x}\, dx + \frac{\partial U}{\partial y}\, dy$$

Then the slope along the indifference curve is:

$$\left.\frac{dy}{dx}\right|_U = -\frac{\partial U/\partial x}{\partial U/\partial y}$$

Since $\partial U/\partial x$ and $\partial U/\partial y$ are both positive (X and Y are both *goods* with positive Marginal Utilities), the slope is negative.

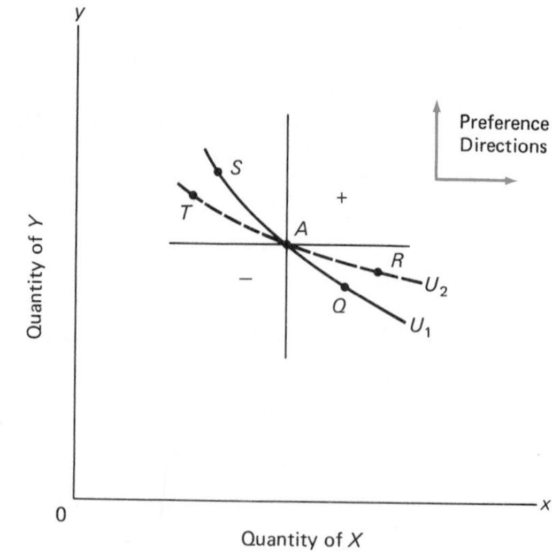

FIGURE 3.6 **Properties of Indifference Curves.** The preference directions indicate that every point in the + region is preferred to A, while A is preferred over every point in the − region. So any indifference curves through A must have negative slope. There can be only one indifference curve through A, since intersecting indifference curves violate transitivity of preference.

2. *Non-intersection of indifference curves*: Employing Figure 3.6 again, suppose we use the indirect method of proof and tentatively assume that two indifference curves like U_1 and U_2 can actually intersect as in the diagram. According to indifference curve U_1, points A and Q are indifferent. According to indifference curve U_2, points A and R are indifferent. By transitivity, Q and R must be indifferent. But R lies northeast of Q, and "More is preferred to less," so R and Q cannot be indifferent. This logical contradiction disproves the premise that indifference curves can intersect. Hence the intersecting indifference curves in Figure 3.6 cannot be a valid representation of preference.

3. *Coverage of indifference curves*: The proposition that one indifference curve passes through each point in commodity space is expressed in compact language as "Indifference curves cover the space." It follows that between any two indifference curves another can always be drawn. A corresponding property is possessed by the real number system. For example, between any two numbers like 17.4398 and 17.4399 we can always find another number like 17.43986 larger than the first and smaller than the second. The coverage property is implied by the first law of preference in Section 3.B above, the Axiom of Comparison. It is assumed *always possible to compare* the preference levels of any baskets of commodities whatsoever. Hence, any describable basket must lie on some indifference curve. Empirically, as already mentioned, this is to be regarded as an idealization rather than a literal description of reality.[11]

[11]Psychological experiments indicate that there is a minimum "threshold" below which sensations cannot be distinguished from one another. This suggests that indifference curves have some "width" in actuality, which would not fit very conveniently into our picture. But this is no more disturbing than the fact that Euclid's "lines" (straight curves with no breadth) cannot actually be observed in the world, since the best we can do in line-drawing still leaves some crookedness and some breadth. (Nevertheless, some economists in the interests of a more powerfully predictive theory are currently attempting to construct models of choice that incorporate perception thresholds.)

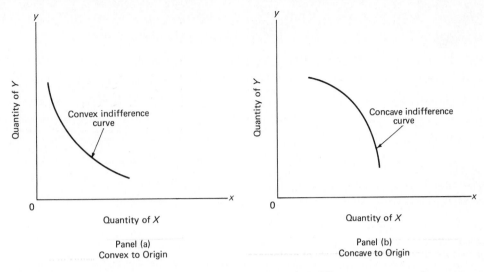

Panel (a)
Convex to Origin

Panel (b)
Concave to Origin

FIGURE 3.7 Convexity and Concavity.   Between two goods, indifference curves must have negative slope. Curvature may be "convex to origin" as in Panel (a), or "concave to origin" as in Panel (b). The convex case is the normally observed situation, even though concavity would not necessarily violate the axioms of rational choice.

4. *Indifference curves convex to origin*: In the two panels of Figure 3.7 we see the curvatures defined as "convex" and "concave" to the origin. It is the convex curve of Panel (a) that corresponds to the picture of Figure 3.5 and represents the standard assumption applicable to indifference curves between two goods. In contrast with the previous three properties (negative slope, non-intersection, and coverage), *convexity cannot be proved from the postulates of rational choice*. Rather, it is based upon a well-established empirical generalization about the world called "the principle of diversity in consumption" (to be discussed in Chapter 4).

The following commonsense explanation of convexity may be convincing, however. Suppose that an individual is to be held on an indifference curve (constant utility level) between two commodities like food X and entertainment Y.[12] If his initial position is far to the southeast or lower right on the indifference curve, he is consuming a great deal of food (x is great) but is bored for lack of entertainment (y is very small). Then it is reasonable to expect him to be willing to give up a relatively large amount of his very ample food for even a small amount of fun. So starting at an extreme position toward the southeast, we would expect to be able to find an indifferent point along the same curve that is well to the left (considerably less X) but only a little higher (a bit more Y). This implies relatively flat indifference curves in the southeast sector of the preference map. By a corresponding argument, toward the northwest the indifference curves are

[12]Food and entertainment are aggregations, rather than simple commodities, but this does not affect the point at issue.

likely to be steep. Thus the picture of Panel (a) of Figure 3.7, and not of Panel (b), seems to fit our normal patterns of preference.

Exercise 3.3: (a) Someone claims that the two equations $xy = 100$ and $x + y = 20$ can both be valid indifference curves for some single individual. Is this correct? (b) What about the curves corresponding to the equations $xy = 100$ and $xy = 200$?

Answer: (a) No, algebraically it may be determined that the curves corresponding to these two equations intersect at $x = 10, y = 10$. This violates indifference-curve property 2 of the text. (b) As these curves never intersect, property 2 is satisfied. But we should also check the other properties. By algebra or by plotting, the reader should be able to satisfy himself that the curves are negatively sloped (property 1) and are convex toward the origin (property 4). So these two curves could both be valid indifference curves for some person.

Example 3.4 below suggests something about the shape of parents' indifference curves between numbers of sons and daughters, regarded as "goods." (These goods happen to be of a kind ordinarily produced at home rather than purchased in the market, but that is quite apart from the preferences that parents might have.)

EXAMPLE 3.4
Preferences for Children: Number and Sex

The Table shows the results of a survey of white families who had two or more children as of 1970. The intention was to determine the proportion of parents who chose to have *more* children, given an initial number of children distributed between boys and girls.

Here the two "goods" are boy children and girl children. The proportion of families who decide to have *more* children can be interpreted as the proportion for whom additional children are still goods, so that the preference directions remain north and east as in Figure 3.5. (Actually, this is a serious underestimate, because some parents might regard additional children as desirable but be unwilling to pay the heavy monetary and psychic costs of having more offspring.)

The Table shows that the fraction of parents planning on *more* children is on the whole greatest for those families initially having only two children (regardless of the sex distribution) and least for those families who already have four. But the essential point for our purposes is the somewhat subtler one that, for any given total number of children, the *families with more balanced sex distributions are notably less interested in having more children.*

Going on, or planning to go on, to have more children evidently signifies dissatisfaction with the present situation. For two-child families 56% of those with unbalanced sex distributions (two boys or two girls) were dissatisfied but only 51% of those with one boy and one girl were dissatisfied. While this difference is perhaps not very large, balanced sex distributions remain pre-

Fraction of Families Who Had Another Child—by Number and Sex of Children

NUMBER OF CHILDREN	NUMBER OF BOYS	NUMBER OF FAMILIES	FRACTION WHO HAD ANOTHER CHILD
2	2	35,674	0.56
	1	64,585	0.51
	0	31,607	0.56
3	3	10,431	0.47
	2	26,497	0.44
	1	24,897	0.45
	0	8,948	0.48
4	4	2,619	0.40
	3	8,260	0.40
	2	11,489	0.38
	1	7,527	0.40
	0	2,241	0.41

Source: 1970 Census data reported in Yoram Ben-Porath and Finis Welch, *Do Sex Preferences Really Matter?* The Rand Corporation Paper Series, P-5560 (Dec. 1975), p. 7.

ferred over unbalanced distributions for three-child and four-child families as well.

This pattern of choices can be interpreted as showing that indifference curves are *convex* as in Figure 3.5. Recall that a high fraction in the righthand column of the table expresses dissatisfaction. For any given number of children, the dissatisfaction tends to be greater at the unbalanced positions than toward the middle. With two children, for example, the position $(1, 1)$ is preferred to (on a higher indifference curve than) either $(0, 2)$ or $(2, 0)$. Such a pattern of preferences implies that the indifference curves bulge toward the origin, as in Panel (a) of Figure 3.7.

3.F
GOODS, BADS, AND NEUTERS

As has been suggested above, not all commodities of economic significance are *goods*, i.e., desired objects. Consider pollution. Our society has to choose a combination of industrial production (a *good*) in association with an amount of undesired by-products in the form of contamination of the environment (a *bad*).

One very important application of utility theory in recent years has been to the problem of *portfolio selection*, the balancing of an individual's wealth over assets like stocks, bonds, real estate, and so forth. Portfolio analysts construct utility functions into which M, the *mean* asset return (average percent yield of the portfolio) enters as a desired feature or good, while the *riskiness* S of the return enters as an undesired feature or bad—since investors seem to behave as if they want high average returns and low risk. Figure 3.8 illustrates the indifference map of such an investor. Note that the preference directions here are north and

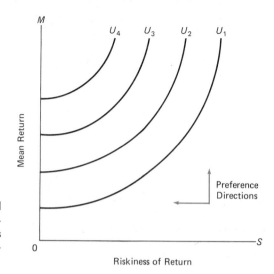

FIGURE 3.8 Indifference Curves between a Good and a Bad. Mean Return M (on assets) is a good, but Riskiness of Return S is a "bad." The preference directions are therefore north and *west*, implying that the indifference curves have *positive* slope.

west. For the "good" commodity M, more is preferred to less. But for the "bad" commodity S, less is preferred to more. These preference directions imply that the indifference curves have *positive* slopes, as shown in the diagram.

Our everyday experience also tells us that a commodity can be a good up to a point of satiation, and then become a bad if we are forced to increase our consumption beyond that point.

EXAMPLE 3.5
Ball-Point Pens and French Pastries

K. R. MacCrimmon and M. Toda[a] conducted an experimental study of indifference-curve patterns. The subjects were college students. The first choice offered was between money (which we may interpret here as the equivalent of a generalized consumption commodity) and ball-point pens. The subjects' indifference-curve patterns all showed negative slope. The next choice offered was between money and French pastries, with the proviso that the pastries had to be actually eaten on the spot. Not surprisingly, French pastries became a bad after the first one or two; the subjects would eat more only if paid more money for doing so. Consequently, these indifference curves had normal negative slope only in the region marked as Zone 1 in Figure 3.9, west of the curve drawn through the lowest points of the successive indifference curves. In Zone 1 the preference directions are north and east as usual. In Zone 2, to the right of the dividing curve, French pastries have become a bad; the preference directions are north and west, and the indifference curves take on a positive slope.

[a]Kenneth R. MacCrimmon and Maseo Toda, "The Experimental Determination of Indifference Curves," *Review of Economic Studies*, v. 37 (Oct. 1969).

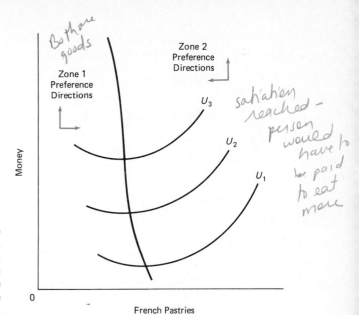

FIGURE 3.9 Satiation. In Zone 1 both commodities, money and French pastries, are goods so that the indifference curves have negative slope. Zone 2 is the region of satiation for French pastries; in this region the preference directions are north and *west,* and the indifference curves have positive slope. In this region an individual would have to be paid to eat another pastry.

So long as commodities are definitely goods or definitely bads, there is no problem with the properties of indifference curves. Making the obvious changes where called for by the reversal of preference direction leads to a correct description, whether we are dealing with two goods, two bads, or a bad and a good. What if there were a commodity that was a *neuter,* neither adding to nor detracting from utility? Then the indifference-curve picture will be as in Figure 3.10.

Exercise 3.4:   For each of the following algebraic utility functions, and assuming that x and y are always positive, indicate whether each commodity is a good, a bad, or a neuter: (a) $U = xy$. (b) $U = x/y$. (c) $U = 2xy/y$.

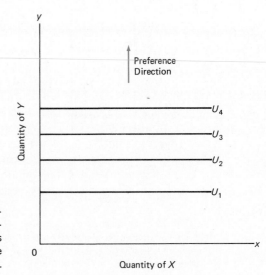

FIGURE 3.10   A Neuter Commodity.   Here X is a neuter commodity. Regardless of the amount of Y purchased, the consumer does not care whether he has more or less of X. Since Y is a good, the only preference direction is north. The indifference curves are horizontal.

Answer: (a) Since utility U rises as x and y grow, both X and Y are goods. (b) Here U rises with x but falls as y increases, so X is a good while Y is a bad. (c) Note here that y cancels out, to leave the function simply $U = 2x$. So X is a good, but Y is a neuter (since utility does not depend at all upon y).

3.F.1 ☐ An Application: The Economics of Charity

The following observations, among others, can be made about charity: (1) Not everyone makes charitable contributions. (2) But some people do. (3) Those who give charity almost always give to persons poorer than themselves. The problem is to construct an indifference-curve picture or pictures consistent with these observations.

One approach is as follows. Figure 3.11 has as axes "My Income" (measured horizontally to the right) and "His Income" (measured vertically upward)—assuming for convenience that the recipient is one male person. We are thinking solely of "my" preferences, so the feelings of the other individual are in no way involved in the picture. Imagine first that I am completely uninterested in whether he has any income or not. Then "His Income" is a neuter commodity for me; I do not care at all about movements north or south. This is the situation pictured in Panel (a) of Figure 3.11. Since "My Income" is surely a good for me, the only preference direction shown is *east*, and my indifference curves are vertical.

If my preferences were as pictured in Panel (a), would I give charity to the other individual? That is the same as asking whether I would be willing to move

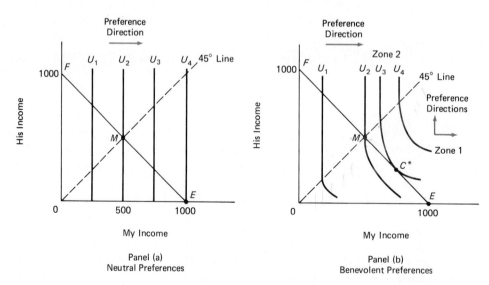

FIGURE 3.11 Preference and Charity. If my preferences are as pictured in Panel (a), "His Income" is a neuter commodity for me. I would never give charity. But if Panel (b) pictures my preferences, I may give charity to people poorer than myself but never to people richer. ("His Income" is a good for me below the 45° line, but is a neuter commodity for me above the 45° line.)

-

from my initial situation to another involving less income for me but more income for him. If the initial situation were at E in Panel (a), I have 1000 units of income and he has zero. Suppose that I could transfer income to him, on a one-for-one basis. In the diagram, this means that I could attain any point along the line EF. But any such movement from point E puts me on a lower indifference curve. So I would not give charity. Notice that I am in no way *malevolent* to the other individual here, simply that I am not *benevolent* either.

Panel (b) of Figure 3.11 is a more interesting case, as it pictures a degree of benevolence. But suppose that observation (3) above applies, that I am benevolent only to people poorer than myself. The positions where he is poorer than me are those lying *below the 45° line* (Zone 1 in the diagram). Only in Zone 1 am I benevolent, so that "His Income" and "My Income" are both goods for me and the indifference curves have their usual negative slopes. In this range, if my initial situation were at E my optimal solution, in the light of my benevolent preferences, is to transfer just enough income to attain point C^*. (Why? Because C^* is a point on indifference curve U_3, my highest attainable level of utility.) If on the other hand my initial situation were at a point like M, any charity on my part *would make him richer than me* (would put me above the 45° line, in Zone 2). But I do not give charity under these circumstances, according to observation (3). Therefore, my indifference curves in this range must be vertical.

3.G
THE SOURCES AND CONTENT OF PREFERENCES

Why do people want some things, and not others? Why are our desires for some goods easily satiated, for others not? Can anything be said about how preferences vary among people of different ages, with different ethnic origins, in different circumstances?

As indicated in Chapter 1, individuals' goals and preferences are taken as given in economics; their nature and formation are regarded as falling within the province of our sister social sciences. Yet in some cases the forces involved are clear enough. It is not hard to predict that iced drinks will be more popular in Georgia than in Alaska; that diapers are not a big merchandising item in retirement communities; that bagels sell better in Jewish neighborhoods, and soul food in Harlem. But what are the bases for these commonsense judgments? The economist who intends to apply his discipline should have some knowledge of the deeper forces determining preferences.

On a very primitive level, human beings as organisms choose (and so can be said to have preferences for) objects that will promote their own survival or comfort. We need to keep our skins intact, our body parts connected up nicely, and our blood temperatures not very far from 98.6° Fahrenheit. Physical considerations like these broadly explain the desires for food, for shelter, for protection against injury. But cultural and personal elements are clearly involved in whether these very general desires are translated, more specifically, into preferences for commodities like three-piece suits or Levi's, pizza pies or *pâté de foie gras,* split-level houses or mobile homes.

Beyond meeting physiological needs, as people grow richer they can afford to indulge their tastes for esthetics, for social distinction, for novelty. These non-material "goods" therefore become more significant as society becomes more affluent. If economics is to retain its validity for explaining behavior, it will increasingly have to address the question of these non-material tastes and drives.

A very essential element in human society is the extent of help that individuals are willing to give one another, as in the charity behavior discussed above. One observation was already made as to the nature of the "taste" for providing this kind of help: that people will often give charity to those poorer than themselves, only rarely to those richer than themselves. Another fact about the taste for helping others is even more obvious: that people are inclined to help their own children in preference to almost anyone else. This last fact suggests a biological evolutionary explanation. Organisms that choose to help their own offspring in preference to the offspring of others have tended to leave more descendants over the generations.[13]

The degree to which biology, or ethnic culture, or idiosyncrasies of individual psychology determine the tastes of individuals remains an important topic about which very little is yet known.

☐ SUMMARY OF CHAPTER 3

The individual, in solving his problem of optimization in consumption, is said to maximize utility. We postulate that preferences follow the Axiom of Comparison (a person can compare all possible pairs of consumption baskets) and the Axiom of Transitivity (if someone prefers basket A to B, and B to C, then he prefers A to C). These together imply that he can rank all conceivable consumption baskets in order of preference.

If utility is quantifiable in the sense of being "cardinally" measurable, statements can be made about the shape of the Marginal Utility curve. But for most purposes in modern economics it suffices if utility is only "ordinally" measurable. If one basket is preferred to another we need only say that the utility of the former is greater—how much greater does not matter.

In choosing baskets of two (or more) commodities, cardinal utility would be represented by a quantifiable "utility hill" defined over amounts of the commodities. The ordinal utility interpretation lets us suppress the utility dimension and portray preferences in terms of *indifference curves*—contours connecting consumption baskets yielding equal utility—together with an indication of the *preference directions* (which way is up on the invisible utility hill). For a *good*, utility increases as the amount consumed increases. For a *bad*, utility decreases with the amount consumed. For a *neuter*, utility is unaffected by the amount consumed.

Indifference curves have three properties that follow from the laws of rational choice: negative slope, non-intersection, and coverage. There is also a

[13]W. D. Hamilton, "The Genetical Evolution of Social Behavior," *Journal of Theoretical Biology*, v. 7 (1964).

fourth property, convexity to the origin, that is based upon the observation that individuals tend to diversify the commodities they consume.

Although economics takes tastes as given, actual applications of economics often require us to have some understanding of the nature and determinants of human preferences. As yet very little is known on this subject.

☐ QUESTIONS FOR CHAPTER 3

MAINLY FOR REVIEW

*R1. An individual is offered a choice between a ski trip to Aspen and four cases of Cutty Sark whiskey. Which of the following possible responses violate the laws of preference?
   a. "They're so different, I can't choose." *violates Ax. of Comparison*
   b. "I don't care, you choose for me." — *doesn't break a law— shows indiff.*
   c. "Whichever I choose, I know I'll be sorry." → *inconsistency— violates Ax. of comp.*

R2. Name a commodity which is a good for many people, but is a bad for you. Name a commodity which is a good for you, but only up to a point; after that it becomes a bad.

R3. Draw possible indifference maps between:
   a. Two goods.
   b. A good and a bad.
   c. A good and a neuter.
   d. A good and a commodity which is a good up to a point, but then becomes a bad.

*R4. What do modern economists mean by the term "utility"? *preference ranking*

R5. From a "cardinal" (quantitatively measurable) Total Utility function, show how a corresponding Marginal Utility function is derived.

*R6. What can be said about the Marginal Utility function if Total Utility is given only in "ordinal" terms? *just the signs— not the quant. increments*

R7. What are the four essential properties of indifference curves between two goods? Explain the justification for each of the four properties.

*R8. Which of the following requires only *ordinal* utility, which requires *cardinal* utility, and which requires *interpersonal comparability* of cardinal utilities?
   a. Indifference curves can be drawn. — *ordinal* ✓
   b. A Marginal Utility function can be used to see numerically how Total Utility changes as consumption of a good increases. *cardinal* ✓
   c. It can be determined which person in a group is most desirous of receiving a particular prize. *interpersonal comp of card util* ✓

FOR FURTHER THOUGHT AND DISCUSSION

*T1. Is it possible to give an exact meaning in utility terms to the expression "greatest good of the greatest number"? *NO*

T2. In suppressing the "cardinal" dimension of the utility hill so as to picture prefer-

*The answers to asterisked questions appear at the end of the book.

ences only in terms of indifference curves, why is it necessary also to indicate the preference directions?

*T3. An example of an ordinal measure is the military rank system. A sergeant has more authority than a private, a lieutenant more than a sergeant, and so on. Give another example of an ordinal scale of magnitude.

T4. Since you probably would not want to eat pickles and ice cream out of the same bowl, does it follow that your indifference curves between these two goods are concave rather than convex?

*T5. For "His Income" and "My Income" regarded as goods, what shape for the indifference curves would correspond to The Golden Rule ("Love thy neighbor as thyself")?

*T6. In surveys of income and happiness (see Example 3.2), a puzzling discrepancy has been noted. While there is higher reported happiness with higher income *at a moment of time,* this conclusion does not seem to hold for comparisons *over time.* Even though wealth has risen over the years in the United States all across the scale so that both rich and poor have higher incomes than before, reports on happiness do not average higher than before.[14] The most natural explanation of this paradox is that happiness is more powerfully affected by *relative* income status than by actual consuming power represented by income. The poor are richer than before, but are still on the bottom of the heap in the comparative sense; therefore they may still feel just as unhappy as before. Is this preference pattern consistent with either panel of Figure 3.11? If not, how would you draw the preference map?

[14]See R. A. Easterlin, "Does Economic Growth Improve the Human Lot? Some Empirical Evidence," in P. David and M. Reder, eds., *Nations and Households in Economic Growth; Essays in Honor of M. Abramovitz* (New York: Academic Press, 1974).

[handwritten notes:]

T5) any shape symmetrical across the 45° line —

my income = 1,000   ≡   my income = 2,000
his   " = 2,000   his   " = 1,000

T6) No

preference map — rays out of the origin along any single ray, representing a fixed RATIO of 'my income' to 'his income', the individual would be equally happy

preference directions? 'my income' = a good "his income" = a bad

4

CONSUMPTION AND DEMAND

CORE CHAPTER

In this chapter we get down to the specifics of the optimizing decision of the consumer. We will see how the individual's choices among consumption goods depend upon (1) his or her preferences (as discussed in the preceding chapter) together with (2) his or her market opportunities. Opportunities depend, in turn, upon the amount of *income* available and, of course, upon the market prices of goods. We will also learn how these considerations enable the economist to predict what will happen to consumption plans in the event of changes in people's tastes, in their incomes, or in the prices they face.

4.A
THE OPTIMUM OF THE CONSUMER[1]

4.A.1 □Optimum of the Consumer: Geometry

Preferences and opportunities are brought together, for a particular individual, in Figure 4.1. Here there are just two commodities, X and Y, both assumed to be goods (rather than bads or neuters). Consequently, the indifference curves U_1, U_2, . . . are negatively sloped (as in Figure 3.5). This is equivalent to saying that the *preference directions* are north and east. In addition, the indifference curves are shown as *convex* to the origin.

Since preferences are defined for all conceivable combinations (baskets) of commodities, the indifference curves should be regarded as covering the entire positive quadrant between the X- and Y-axes. But the individual's range of opportunities or *opportunity set,* representing all the baskets he is able to achieve in the market, includes only a limited portion of the positive quadrant. In fact, as we will see shortly, the market opportunity set takes the form of the shaded triangle in Figure 4.1.[2]

---

[1]The optimum of the consumer is sometimes carelessly called the "equilibrium" of the consumer. Such wording blurs the distinction between the two key analytical concepts—equilibrium and optimum—that the student must learn to handle, each in its proper place. An *optimum* is the result of goal-oriented choice on the part of an economic decision-maker. An *equilibrium* represents simply a balance of forces. Here we are dealing with an optimizing decision.

[2]Other types of consumption opportunity sets can also exist. Robinson Crusoe, for example, could be regarded as having an opportunity set as between combinations of commodities like fish and bananas available on his island. Crusoe's consumption opportunity set would depend entirely upon his own isolated efforts, and in no way upon the possibility of transactions in markets.

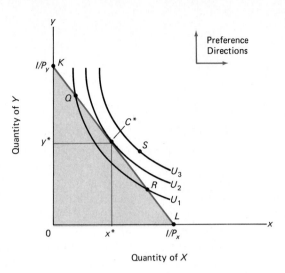

FIGURE 4.1 **Optimum of the Consumer.** The shaded region *OKL* represents the consumer's market opportunity set, bounded by the horizontal and vertical axes and by the budget line *KL*. The position of the budget line is determined by the individual's income *I* and the market prices P_x and P_y. The optimum is the point where the line *KL* touches the highest attainable indifference curve (point C^* on indifference curve U_2); this is the consumption basket yielding the greatest achievable utility.

The amount of *income, I,* available for spending on consumption is one determinant of an individual's market opportunity set. The *prices* of consumer goods, specifically here the prices P_x and P_y of commodities X and Y, respectively, constitute the other determinants. The consumer will ordinarily have obtained income, of course, by selling productive services to business firms.

In a modern economy prices are generally quoted in money terms. And income is also measured as a money flow of earnings from resource services, per unit time. How money functions as a *medium of exchange,* i.e., as a counter whose universal acceptability facilitates the process of trade, will be examined later on. For our purposes here we want to "pierce the veil" of money and deal only with the underlying *real* magnitudes. Consequently, we will think of prices and income as measured in terms of some standard real good called a *"numéraire."* Then P_x, the price of X, is the amount of the standard good that must be paid for a unit of X; P_y is the amount that must be paid for a unit of good Y; and income I is the amount available for spending, all in units of the standard *numéraire* good.

Suppose that expenditures on commodities X and Y exactly exhaust income. Then we have the equation:

(4.1) $$P_x x + P_y y = I$$

This equation is plotted as the straight line *KL* in Figure 4.1. Note that it is the northeast boundary of the shaded region. The horizontal intercept of the line equals I/P_x, which is the number of units of X purchasable if the individual were to spend all his income I on commodity X. Similarly, the vertical intercept of the line is I/P_y, representing the number of units of Y obtained by spending all income on Y. Any mixed basket containing positive quantities of both X and Y will lie somewhere along the line between the two intercepts. The shaded opportunity set in Figure 4.1 is also bounded by the horizontal and vertical axes, since quantities purchased of X and of Y can never be negative.

Alternatively, suppose that we wanted to allow for the possibility of not expending all of income on X and Y. This would be expressed algebraically by the condition:

$$(4.1') \qquad P_x x + P_y y \leqq I$$

The more general expression $(4.1')$, together with the non-negativity assumptions, describe the entire shaded opportunity region of Figure 4.1.

The northeast boundary KL of the opportunity set, corresponding to the exact equality of equation (4.1), is called the *budget line* of the consumer. Since X and Y are the only desired goods, and since the preference directions are north and east, in a market situation only this budget line or northeast boundary is of concern to the consumer.[3] (He can get to any position in the *interior* of the shaded region, starting from a point on the budget line, simply by throwing away some X or some Y or both. But since X and Y are goods, he would never want to do so.)

We will very frequently be referring to the *slope* of curves or lines drawn on x, y-axes. The slope will by symbolized as $\Delta y / \Delta x$, the change in y per unit change in x along the curve. In the case of a line, the slope is constant throughout its length. The slope of the budget line specifically, symbolized $\left. \dfrac{\Delta y}{\Delta x} \right|_I$, can be expressed as the ratio of the vertical intercept I / P_y to the horizontal intercept I / P_x.

$$(4.2) \qquad \left. \frac{\Delta y}{\Delta x} \right|_I = - \frac{I / P_y}{I / P_x} = - \frac{P_x}{P_y}$$

This slope carries a negative sign since, along the budget line, an *increase* in x is associated with a *decrease* of y.[4]

Algebraically, equation (4.2) tells us that the slope of the budget line is equal to the negative of the price ratio P_x / P_y. This has a natural economic interpretation. Giving up one unit of X is equivalent to moving up to the left along the budget line. How far up? The unit of X foregone makes available the amount P_x for spending on Y, so that the number of units of Y obtainable in exchange is just P_x / P_y. If P_x were 10 and P_y were 2, giving up one unit of X would permit purchase of $10/2 = 5$ units of Y, so that -5 would be the slope of the budget line.

Exercise 4.1: Suppose that prices are $P_x = 10$ and $P_y = 2$, while income is $I = 100$. (a) What is the equation of the budget line, and what are the intercepts on the two axes?

---

[3]This statement is valid if there are no *other* imposed constraints upon the consumption decision. It may be that the consumer, while having enough income to purchase certain consumption baskets at currently ruling prices, is barred from doing so on other grounds. One example would be a ration limit upon purchases (discussed in Chapter 5 below).

[4]*Mathematical Footnote:* With the equation of the budget line as $P_x x + P_y y = I$, the slope is found as the derivative:

$$\left. \frac{dy}{dx} \right|_I = - \frac{P_x}{P_y}$$

Since this derivative is a constant, it equals the ratio of finite increments $\left. \dfrac{\Delta y}{\Delta x} \right|_I$ in equation (4.2).

What is the slope? (b) Describe what happens if, with I unchanged, the price P_x were to be cut in half. (c) Describe what happens if, with the original prices unchanged, income I were to double.

Answer: (a) The equation of the budget line $P_x x + P_y y = I$ becomes, after substituting the given numerical prices, $10x + 2y = 100$. The x-intercept is $100/10 = 10$ while the y-intercept is $100/2 = 50$. The slope is $-50/10 = -5$. (b) If P_x were cut in half, the new equation would be $5x + 2y = 100$. The x-intercept becomes 20 instead of 10, while the y-intercept is unchanged. So the budget line, after swinging around to the right, has a new, flatter slope equal to $-50/20 = -2\frac{1}{2}$. (c) If, with the original prices, I were to double, then the equation becomes $10x + 2y = 200$. Both intercepts double. So the budget line retains the same slope as before: $-100/20 = -5$. In this case the line has moved outward, parallel to itself, doubling its distance from the origin in both the x-direction and the y-direction.

We have now seen how the market opportunity set depends upon the commodity prices P_x and P_y (whose ratio determines the *slope* of the budget line), and upon income I (whose magnitude determines the distances of the intercepts I/P_x and I/P_y from the origin and therefore the *position* of the budget line). With the data both as to preferences and opportunities in hand, we can proceed to the optimum of the consumer.

From inspection of Figure 4.1, it is evident that the consumer's best attainable position along the budget line KL (and, therefore, the best position attainable within the shaded market opportunity set) is the point C^*—the consumption combination containing x^* of commodity X and y^* of commodity Y. At C^* the indifference curve U_2 is just *tangent* to the budget line. The geometrical relationships are such that the optimum must be at a tangency, if a tangency position exists (as discussed below). Non-tangency points like Q and R in the diagram, both lying on indifference curve U_1 at the points where U_1 cuts the budget line, must necessarily be inferior in terms of preference to the tangency point C^* on indifference curve U_2. In terms of the invisible "utility hill" of Chapter 3, Q and R lie along a lower contour than C^*; the highest contour attainable is the one that can just barely be reached at the single tangency point C^*. It is true that a point like S on indifference curve U_3 would be even superior to C^*—but the combination S is not attainable since indifference curve U_3 never lies within the opportunity set.

> CONCLUSION: The optimum of the consumer is found at the tangency between the budget line and a convex indifference curve (if such a tangency exists).

In Chapter 3, convexity of indifference curves was asserted to follow not from the logic of the Laws of Preference but rather from observation of behavior in the world. This point can now be demonstrated. Imagine hypothetically that curves of indifference between goods X and Y have negative slope but the opposite concave curvature. Such a situation is pictured in Figure 4.2, where the preference directions, shaded opportunity set, and budget line KL remain as in the previous diagram. Here there is again a tangency, the point T. But T is not the optimum. Indeed, T is the *least* preferred point on the budget line, lying as

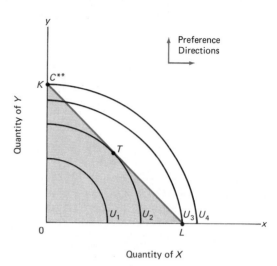

FIGURE 4.2 Concave Indifference Curves and Corner Solution. If the indifference curves were negatively sloped but concave to the origin, the best attainable position along the budget line *KL* must be a *corner solution,* lying along one or the other axis. In this case the corner solution is at *C*** on the *y*-axis.

it does on U_2, the *lowest* indifference curve reached along *KL*. With concave indifference curves, the highest level of preference along a budget line will necessarily be found at the intersection of the budget line with one or the other axis. This means that the best use of income would always be to devote expenditure exclusively to the purchase of one commodity—to consume only one of the two goods available. In Figure 4.2 the optimum position is denoted C^{**} on indifference curve U_4, at point *K* on the *Y*-axis. Such an outcome is called a *corner solution,* as opposed to the ordinary *interior solution* as at C^* in Figure 4.1.

Now in the actual world individuals are observed to *diversify* their consumption, to purchase a *mixture* of many different commodities. Only a convex indifference-curve map like Figure 4.1 can lead to interior solutions and thereby explain this observation.

There is one difficulty with the explanation, however. Let us drop the limiting assumption of exactly two commodities and recognize that the typical individual makes consumption choices among many thousands of alternative goods. (We are really dealing with a multi-dimensional preference function, with a separate axis for each commodity available. For three commodities there would be three axes. Then the three-dimensional indifference contours would be *shells,* nested like the skins of an onion. Beyond three dimensions we cannot picture any geometrical representation, but can still imagine the generalization to more commodities.) Now in point of fact we actually do observe "corner solutions" with respect to many or even most goods; the typical individual buys positive quantities of only a small number of the distinct commodities that might conceivably be purchased. In some cases this may be because a commodity that is a *good* for some people is a *bad* for others (tapioca pudding). But even among the vast numbers of commodities that consumers recognize as goods, many are not actually purchased. The reason is, of course, that the price is regarded as too high relative to the consumer's desires. You may enjoy the flavor of Beluga caviar, be able to afford at least a small quantity of it, and yet not be willing to pay the steep

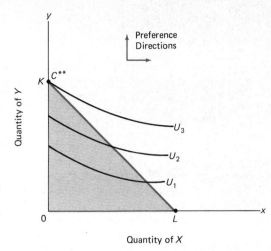

FIGURE 4.3   Convex Indifference Curves and Corner Solution.   If indifference curves are convex to the origin, a corner solution is not inevitable, but remains possible. Here the consumer optimum along the budget line *KL* is at point *C*** on the *y*-axis.

price required. Thus, you are at a corner solution with regard to the "caviar axis" of your multicommodity utility function.

Observation of actual corner solutions for *some* goods does not, however, require us to abandon convexity to the origin as a property of indifference curves. Figure 4.3 shows in two dimensions how a corner solution can be perfectly consistent with convexity. The most preferred position (highest indifference curve attainable in the market opportunity set) is at *C***, reached along the vertical axis at *K*, where only *Y* and no *X* is consumed. We do not have a tangency, but the optimum is the *closest to tangency* (equality of slopes) that the consumer can achieve along the budget line *KL*. Convex indifference curves are thus capable of explaining *both* the observation of interior solutions in some cases and corner solutions in other cases.

> *GEOMETRICAL OPTIMUM PRINCIPLE:*   The optimum of the consumer, the position where he maximizes utility or satisfaction subject to his limited income, is the point on the budget line touching his highest attainable indifference curve. With convex indifference curves, the consumer optimum may be an *interior solution* at a tangency between the budget line and the best attainable indifference curve. Or, it may be a *corner solution* where the budget line reaches the highest attainable indifference curve along an axis.

4.A.2   ☐ Optimum of the Consumer: Analysis

Setting aside geometry, let us now reconsider the problem of consumer choice in terms of underlying concepts. The consumer is seeking to maximize satisfaction, to distribute his given income *I* optimally over the different commodities he might conceivably purchase—in our example, over the two goods *X* and *Y*.

Suppose that we were allowed to think in terms of a "cardinal" preference function, measured in units of utils. Then it would be meaningful to speak of the magnitude of Marginal Utility. The older economists postulated "diminishing Marginal Utility" with respect to additional units consumed of goods like X or Y. Given diminishing Marginal Utility for each of the two goods, the consumer will be at an (interior) optimum when the following Consumption Balance Equation is satisfied:

$$(4.3) \quad \frac{\text{Marginal Utility of } X}{\text{Price of } X} = \frac{\text{Marginal Utility of } Y}{\text{Price of } Y} \qquad \begin{array}{l}\text{Consumption} \\ \text{Balance Equation} \\ \text{(Interior Solution)}^5\end{array}$$

The explanation is immediate. For any commodity, Marginal Utility divided by price is *Marginal Utility per dollar* spent on that commodity. For the consumer not to want to change his purchase rate of X relative to Y, the Marginal Utility per dollar of X and Y must be equal. The last dollar must yield equivalent satisfaction, whether spent on X or spent on Y. If this were not the case, the consumer would buy more of the commodity for which Marginal Utility per dollar was high, and less of the one whose Marginal Utility per dollar was low. He would continue to reallocate his spending in this way until Marginal Utilities per dollar become equal over all commodities purchased.

What about the possibility of a corner solution? Suppose that, for some commodity like Beluga caviar, the Marginal Utility per dollar remains lower than that of the other commodity even when zero units of caviar are purchased. Then we would have a corner optimum, which can be expressed (letting X represent caviar) as the inequality:

---

[5]*Mathematical Footnote:* In optimization problems in economics, a very neat technique called "the method of Lagrangian multipliers" is generally used. Specifically, in the present case we seek to maximize a cardinal utility function $U(x, y)$ subject to the constraint $P_x x + P_y y = I$ (where P_x, P_y, and I are constants). The technique involves setting up an artificial maximand in the following form:

$$\underset{(x, y, \lambda)}{\text{Max }} L = U(x, y) + \lambda(P_x x + P_y y - I)$$

The first-order conditions for a maximum are:

$$\frac{\partial L}{\partial x} = \frac{\partial U}{\partial x} + \lambda P_x = 0$$

$$\frac{\partial L}{\partial y} = \frac{\partial U}{\partial y} + \lambda P_y = 0$$

$$\frac{\partial L}{\partial \lambda} = P_x x + P_y y - I = 0$$

The first two conditions imply:

$$\frac{\partial U / \partial x}{P_x} = \frac{\partial U / \partial y}{P_y}$$

This is, of course, the Consumption Balance Equation (4.3). The technique works because in taking the partial derivative with respect to λ we obtain $P_x x + P_y y - I = 0$. This guarantees that the constraint condition (the budget equation) is always met, and also assures that the maximum of the artificial variable L is the same as the desired maximum of U.

PART 2   PREFERENCE, CONSUMPTION, AND DEMAND

$(4.3')$ $$\frac{MU_x(x=0)}{P_x} < \frac{MU_y(y>0)}{P_y}$$ Consumption
Balance Inequality[6]
(Corner Solution)[7]

So, at the optimum of the consumer either the Consumption Balance Equation (for an interior solution) or the Consumption Balance Inequality (for a corner solution) will be applicable. In addition, the consumer will also have to meet the budget-line condition (4.1) that constrains his expenditure to equal his income.

Exercise 4.2:   Suppose that commodity X is bread, and commodity Y is wine. Imagine that the Marginal Utility of bread, MU_x, is given algebraically by the expression $MU_x = 40 - 5x$. Similarly, let $MU_y = 20 - 3y$. [Note the special assumption that MU_x depends only on the quantity x, and MU_y on the quantity y; this property, called "absence of complementarity," will be discussed shortly below.] Let the prices be $P_x = 5$ and $P_y = 1$, and the consumer's income be $I = 20$. To find: the optimum of the consumer.

Answer: The budget equation (4.1) is $5x + 1y = 20$. Trying first for an interior solution, the Consumption Balance Equation is:

$$\frac{40 - 5x}{5} = \frac{20 - 3y}{1}$$

Solving the two equations, we obtain $x^* = 3$, $y^* = 5$ (verifying that we indeed have an interior solution).

This is very direct and simple. But, we saw in Chapter 3, it is only with "cardinal" utility that quantitative comparisons of Marginal Utility are possible. (With "ordinal" utility, we can do no more than determine when Marginal Utility is positive, zero, or negative.) Can we re-work our analytic solution above, dispensing with cardinality and so with quantitative Marginal Utility comparisons? The answer is yes.

Instead of thinking in terms of the Marginal Utility of X and of Y, think now of the ratio at which the individual is *just willing to substitute a small amount of Y for a small amount of X* in his consumption basket. This ratio is termed the Marginal Rate of Substitution in Consumption, denoted MRS_C . The expression "just willing to make small substitutions" means the same as "indifferent between small

---

[6]If there were many commodities, there might be corner solutions as between some pairs of goods and interior solutions for others. In the case of just three goods, the solution might take the form:

$$\frac{MU_x(x=0)}{P_x} < \frac{MU_y(y>0)}{P_y} = \frac{MU_z(z>0)}{P_z}$$

Here positive amounts of commodities Y and Z, but not of commodity X, are being purchased.

[7]*Mathematical Footnote:* Since a corner solution is generally not at a tangency, calculus techniques involving equality of derivatives are not applicable; the optimum is not at a point where the indifference-curve slope equals the budget-line slope. Corner solutions arise because of non-negativity constraints. Where such constraints exist, as in our standard assumption that consumption cannot be negative, the calculus must be used with caution.

substitutions." More specifically, we can write:

$$MRS_C \equiv - \frac{\Delta y}{\Delta x} \bigg|_U$$

where the expression on the right refers to the absolute value of the indifference-curve slope for small changes Δx and Δy.[8]

Consider Figure 4.4. At position A the individual is initially holding the consumption basket (x°, y°); he is contemplating a small move to position B representing the basket (x', y'). Evidently, baskets A and B are indifferent for him, both being on indifference curve U. As the triangle ADB indicates, the ratio at which he is just willing to substitute small amounts of good X for good Y is 5:2, and this is approximately the numerical slope of his indifference curve U in this range. (The smaller the move considered, the better will MRS_C approximate the exact slope at a point along U.)

We now have a concept explaining the terms according to which the individual is *willing* to make small substitutions of Y for X in his consumption basket. The next question is, at what ratio does the market *enable* him to make such substitutions? This second ratio is termed the Marginal Rate of Substitution in Exchange, denoted MRS_E, and is simply equal to the price ratio: $MRS_E \equiv P_x/P_y$. In Figure 4.4, along the budget line $I = 5x + 3y$ we have $P_x = 5$ and $P_y = 3$. Then the individual is *able to* exchange 5 units of Y in the market for 3 units of X.

Clearly, the consumer cannot be at an optimum position unless the rate at which he is *willing* to make substitutions in his consumption bundle (MRS_C) equals the rate at which he *can* make substitutions via market trading (MRS_E). In

[8]*Mathematical Footnote:* In terms of derivatives:

$$MRS_C \equiv - \frac{dy}{dx} \bigg|_U$$

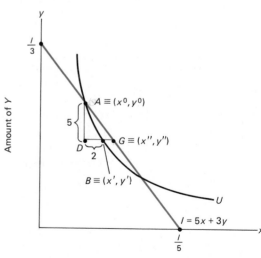

FIGURE 4.4 Marginal Rate of Substitution in Consumption (MRS_C) and Marginal Rate of Substitution in Exchange (MRS_E). MRS_C at point A is the absolute value of the slope of indifference curve U at that point. It is approximated by the ratio $AD/DB = 5/2$ in the diagram. MRS_E, which is also the price ratio P_x/P_y, is the constant absolute slope along the budget line I. In the diagram it is given by the ratio $AD/DG = 5/3$. The inequality of MRS_C and MRS_E shows that A cannot be an optimum for the consumer.

this case, starting from basket A the individual could move to point G representing basket (x'', y'')—which is preferred to both A and B. Since the individual can thus better his position, A cannot have been an optimum consumption basket.

EXAMPLE 4.1
Prisoners of War: Tea versus Coffee

The economist R. A. Radford had the unfortunate opportunity of studying, from the inside, social behavior in prisoner-of-war camps in Germany and Italy during World War II. He found that highly active economies functioned in these camps, particularly under the relatively "favorable" conditions that prevailed in the earlier war years.

Cigarettes served generally as the *numéraire* (or standard good) in terms of which prices were quoted. Coffee might go for about 2 cigarettes per cup, a shirt might cost 80, washing service 2 cigarettes per garment, and so on.

In the camp section holding English prisoners, tea was definitely preferred to coffee—and the reverse in the French section. A regular smuggling trade was conducted between the two, permitting prisoners in each section to adjust their consumption choices to the price ratio reflecting the overall supply–demand balance in the camp as a whole.[a]

COMMENT: The two panels of Figure 4.5 illustrate the situations of typical English and French prisoners. In both camp sections prices were quoted, in cigarettes, for coffee (P_c) and for tea (P_t). The efficient smuggling trade between sections prevented disparities from developing between the coffee prices or between the tea prices in the two sections. Therefore, the Marginal Rate of Substitution in Exchange, $MRS_E = P_c/P_t$, was the same for both groups of prisoners. But for the English prisoners, the tangency point C^* where $MRS_C = MRS_E$ was well over toward the tea axis, while for the French prisoners the optimum lay in the opposite direction, toward the coffee axis.

[a]R. A. Radford, "The Economic Organisation of a P.O.W. Camp," *Economica*, v. 12 (1945). In his enforced period of stay Radford made many other striking observations, some of which will be mentioned below.

We see, therefore, that (in the case of an interior solution) the optimum of the consumer occurs where the following condition, the Substitution Equivalence Equation, holds:

(4.4) $MRS_C = MRS_E$ or $-\dfrac{\Delta y}{\Delta x}\bigg|_U = \dfrac{P_x}{P_y}$ Substitution Equivalence Equation (Interior solution)

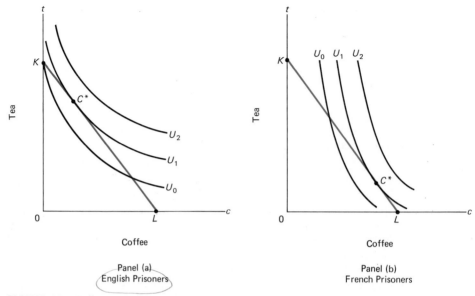

FIGURE 4.5 Coffee versus Tea in a P.O.W. Camp. English and French P.O.W.'s had different tastes for tea relative to coffee. An efficient smuggling system equalized the price ratio P_c/P_t, so both groups of prisoners faced the same MRS_E. For the French prisoners, the optimum C^* equating MRS_E to MRS_C (the indifference-curve slope) lay toward the coffee axis; for the English prisoners, the solution lay toward the tea axis.

ANALYTICAL OPTIMUM PRINCIPLE: The optimum of the consumer, the point where the consumer maximizes utility or satisfaction subject to the limitation of income, is characterized by equality between the Marginal Rate of Substitution in Consumption (MRS_C) and the Marginal Rate of Substitution in Exchange (MRS_E). In addition, the amounts spent must exhaust the consumer's budget. These conditions are the equivalent of the geometrical tangency of indifference curve and budget line, and therefore determine an interior optimum. (If MRS_C and MRS_E cannot be equated, i.e., if no tangency exists, they are to be brought as near to equality as possible by reducing the quantity taken of one of the commodities to zero. This is a corner solution.)

One important implication of this analysis is that, despite differences of tastes, *on the margin* everyone actually consuming each of two commodities X and Y places the same relative valuation upon them (has the same MRS_C). In our prisoner of war example above, French prisoners preferred coffee and English prisoners preferred tea. Nevertheless, once each group had adapted to the ruling prices, a French prisoner was no more willing than an English prisoner to give up a unit of tea for coffee. Thus, one result of trade is that the "objective" price ratios in the market measure the "subjective" marginal valuations for all the participants actually consuming the goods.

As a small digression, how is it that the Substitution Equivalence Equation (4.4), while in effect doing the same work as the Consumption Balance Equation

(4.3), allows us to dispense with any notion of cardinal utility? First, by transposing we can rewrite (4.3) as:

$$\frac{MU_x}{MU_y} = \frac{P_x}{P_y}$$

But, for small changes Δx and Δy, the Marginal Utility of X can be written $\Delta U/\Delta x$ and similarly MU_y is $\Delta U/\Delta y$. Substituting in the equation above, ΔU cancels out! After cancellation we have simply $\Delta y/\Delta x = P_x/P_y$—so equation (4.3) has become equation (4.4). If we like, we can think of MRS_C as a ratio of Marginal Utilities:

$$MRS_C \equiv \frac{MU_x}{MU_y}$$

[handwritten: $= \frac{2}{1}$ 2 units of Y for 1 unit of X]

Suppose, for example, that $MU_x/MU_y = 2$. This says that, in cardinal utility units, the individual gets twice as many utils from a small increment of X as from a small increment of Y. It then follows that the person would be *just willing* to make a small substitution of 2 units of Y for 1 unit of X in the consumption basket. But this is exactly the meaning of MRS_C, the Marginal Rate of Substitution in Consumption.[9]

More generally, however, we have shown that the "cardinal" quantification of U is not necessary to determine how a consumer should balance his consumption of X and Y. All he need do is to set the rate at which he is just *willing* to exchange X for Y—his absolute indifference-curve slope, which is an "ordinal" property of his preferences—equal to the rate at which the market *enables* him to exchange X for Y. (I.e., he sets his $MRS_C = P_x/P_y$).[10]

[handwritten: exchange X for Y P_x/P_y]

[9]*Mathematical Footnote:* Along an indifference curve,

$$0 = dU \equiv \frac{\partial U}{\partial x}\,dx + \frac{\partial U}{\partial y}\,dy$$

Then:

$$-\frac{dy}{dx}\bigg|_U \equiv \frac{\partial U/\partial x}{\partial U/\partial y}$$

i.e., MRS_C equals the ratio of the Marginal Utilities of X and Y.

[10]*Mathematical Footnote:* In ordinal-utility terms, let the consumer maximize $V = F[U(x, y)]$, where $F(U)$ is *any* monotonically increasing function of U. That is, $dF(U)/dU > 0$ for all U. Then the Lagrangian artificial maximand and the optimum conditions become:

$$\operatorname*{Max}_{(x, y, \lambda)} L = F[U(x, y)] + \lambda(P_x x + P_y y - I)$$

$$\frac{\partial L}{\partial x} = \frac{dF}{dU}\frac{\partial U}{\partial x} + \lambda P_x = 0$$

$$\frac{\partial L}{\partial y} = \frac{dF}{dU}\frac{\partial U}{\partial y} + \lambda P_y = 0$$

$$\frac{\partial L}{\partial \lambda} = P_x x + P_y y - I = 0$$

(Footnote cont. on p. 94.)

Exercise 4.3: An individual has $MU_x = 40 - 5x$, and $MU_y = 20 - 3y$. What is his MRS_C at the consumption basket $x = 3$, $y = 5$? If $P_x = 5$ and $P_y = 1$, is this basket a consumption optimum?

Answer: We can, if we like, interpret MRS_C as a ratio of marginal utilities. So, numerically,

$$MRS_C = \frac{40 - 5x}{20 - 3y} = \frac{40 - 15}{20 - 15} = 5$$

Since $P_x/P_y = 5/1$, the Substitution Equivalence Equation is satisfied, and the basket is an optimum. [Note that the answer here merely reinterprets the solution of Exercise 4.2.]

As a final qualification, we need an analytic expression to indicate that, for an optimum at a tangency, the indifference curve must be convex as in Figure 4.1 rather than concave as in Figure 4.2. Convexity means that the absolute value of the indifference-curve slope, which is MRS_C, must be numerically decreasing at the tangency point. That is, *decreasing Marginal Rate of Substitution in Consumption* is needed to guarantee that the Substitution Equivalence Equation (4.4) really determines the individual's optimum consumption basket.[11]

_____

Write the first two conditions as:

$$\frac{dF}{dU}\frac{\partial U}{\partial x} = -\lambda P_x \quad \text{and} \quad \frac{dF}{dU}\frac{\partial U}{\partial y} = -\lambda P_y$$

Dividing the first by the second, we see that dF/dU cancels out:

$$\frac{\partial U/\partial x}{\partial U/\partial y} \equiv -\frac{dy}{dx}\bigg|_U = \frac{P_x}{P_y}$$

So condition (4.4) holds for ordinal as well as cardinal utility.

[11]*Mathematical Footnote:* We are dealing here with the *second-order* conditions for a maximum. The condition for indifference-curve convexity is $d(MRS_C)/dx < 0$. Or, recalling that MRS_C is defined as the absolute value of the slope, this can also be expressed as:

$$\frac{d}{dx}\left(\frac{dy}{dx}\right) \equiv \frac{d^2y}{dx^2} > 0$$

where dy/dx is the indifference-curve slope usually expressed more explicitly as $\frac{dy}{dx}\big|_U$.

$$\frac{d^2y}{dx^2} \equiv \frac{d}{dx}\left(\frac{dy}{dx}\right) \equiv \frac{\partial}{\partial x}\left(\frac{dy}{dx}\right) + \frac{\partial}{\partial y}\left(\frac{dy}{dx}\right)\frac{dy}{dx}$$

But:

$$\frac{dy}{dx} \equiv -\frac{\partial U/\partial x}{\partial U/\partial y} \equiv -\frac{U_x}{U_y} \quad \text{(in more compact notation)}$$

COMPLEMENTS AND SUBSTITUTES

Certain commodities like bread and butter, shoes and socks, tennis racquets and tennis balls, go well together and tend to be consumed jointly. Having more of one raises the desirability of the other. Such pairs of goods are called *complements,* and are said to exhibit positive complementarity. Other commodity pairs, like butter and margarine, brown shoes and black shoes, tennis racquets and badminton racquets, go poorly together and tend to be used to the exclusion of one another. Such pairs are called *substitutes* or *anti-complements,* and are said to exhibit strong substitutability or negative complementarity. Pairs of goods that are unrelated in people's preference patterns are said to be *independent* in consumption, or to exhibit zero complementarity.

Consider two commodities that consumers regard as perfect *substitutes.* For example, a person might be completely indifferent between 2 nickels and 1 dime, or between 200 nickels and 100 dimes, or between 2000 nickels and 1000 dimes. Then the typical preference map will have the appearance of Panel (a) of Figure 4.6: all the indifference curves will be parallel straight lines. If there were two goods that approached but did not quite attain perfect substitutability, the indifference curves would show a slight degree of normally convex curvature but would be very nearly linear, as in Panel (b) of Figure 4.6. For a particular consumer, bread and rolls might perhaps be so related. The observable market characteristic of strong substitute commodities is: Small changes in price ratios, with no change in real income, will lead to large shifts in relative quantities purchased. As can be seen in Panel (b), with the steeper budget line SS' (high ratio of bread price P_b to roll price P_r) the optimum solution S^* is well over toward the northwest of the diagram. But the only slightly flatter budget line FF' (lower ratio P_b/P_r) is associated with a drastically different quantity solution F^* along the same indifference curve U_2 toward the southeast of the diagram. [*Query:* Will it be the case that, for perfect substitutes, the individual will almost always be at a corner solution—buying one good to the exclusion of the other?]

In the extreme opposite case of *perfect complementarity* there would be some

---

Then:

$$\frac{d^2y}{dx^2} \equiv -\frac{U_yU_{xx} - U_xU_{xy}}{U_y^2} - \frac{U_yU_{xy} - U_xU_{yy}}{U_y^2}\left(-\frac{U_x}{U_y}\right)$$

$$\equiv \frac{-U_y^2U_{xx} + U_xU_yU_{xy} + U_yU_xU_{xy} - U_x^2U_{yy}}{U_y^3}$$

The main significance of this result is to show that diminishing Marginal Utility (U_{xx}, $U_{yy} < 0$) does not *necessarily* imply decreasing MRS_C (positive d^2y/dx^2). For, the cross-derivative U_{xy} has indeterminate sign. So even with cardinal utility, it is indifference-curve convexity rather than diminishing Marginal Utility that should be relied on to define the proper second-order condition for a maximum.

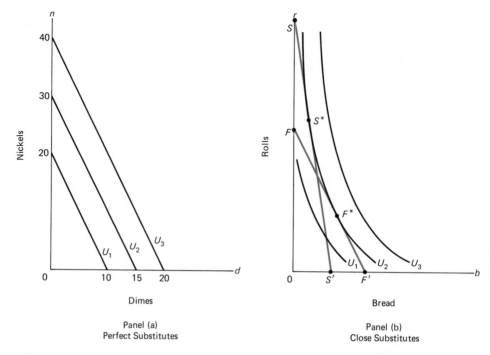

FIGURE 4.6 Substitute Commodities. The parallel straight-line indifference curves of Panel (a) indicate that the two commodities (nickels and dimes) are perfect substitutes. If the price ratio in the market $-P_d/P_n$ diverges from the indifference-curve slope, the consumer will go to a corner solution, buying whichever commodity is relatively cheaper in terms of satisfying his or her preferences. Even a small change in the price ratio, from a slope steeper than to a slope flatter than the indifference-curve slope, would flip the solution over entirely from one corner to the other. In Panel (b) the indifference curves have a slight degree of normal convex curvature, indicating that the two commodities (bread and rolls) are good though not perfect substitutes. A relatively small change in the price ratio (from slope SS' to FF') would then tend to generate a relatively large change in the quantity ratio as the consumptive optimum changes (from S^* to F^*).

fixed ratio of quantities (such as one left shoe for each right shoe) of interest to the consumer. If this ratio is departed from, the additional units of whichever commodity is in excess are completely useless. Panel (a) of Figure 4.7 shows the right-angled indifference curves implied by perfect complementarity; the slope of the dashed line through the "elbows" represents the desired ratio of the two commodities. For two goods that approach very nearly to, without quite attaining, perfect complementarity, the indifference map would be as in Panel (b) of Figure 4.7. Other examples of complementary pairs are bacon and eggs, electricity and appliances, highways and automobiles. The observable market characteristic of strong complementary commodities is: Large changes in price ratios, with no change in real income, will lead to only small shifts in relative quantities purchased. As can be seen in Panel (b) of Figure 4.7, along the steeper budget line SS' (representing a high price ratio P_e/P_a) the tangency solution S^* diverges very little from the optimum F^* along the flatter budget line FF'.

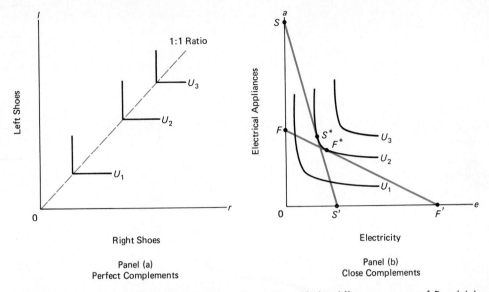

Panel (a)
Perfect Complements

Panel (b)
Close Complements

FIGURE 4.7 Complementary Commodities. The right-angled indifference curves of Panel (a) indicate that the two commodities (right shoes and left shoes) are perfect complements. A change in price ratio will have no effect upon the quantity ratio chosen, which will always be 1:1 at the best attainable "elbow" point. In Panel (b) the indifference curves are nearly but not quite right-angled: the commodities (electricity and electrical appliances) are strong though not perfect complements. Here a relatively large change in the price ratio (from slope SS' to FF') will bring about only a relatively small change in the quantity ratio as the consumption optimum changes (from S^* to F^*).

The substitutability of commodities X and Y in the preferences of a consumer is therefore indicated by the degree of response of the quantity ratio to changes in the price ratio, with real income held constant.[12]

Exercise 4.4: Suppose that for two commodities X and Y (as usual, think of Y as plotted on the vertical axis), the Marginal Rate of Substitution in Consumption is $MRS_C = y/x$.

[12]*Mathematical Footnote:* The most commonly used *measure* for this concept of substitutability is called the *elasticity of substitution* (symbolized as σ). The rationale underlying this measure can be indicated as follows. Along any indifference curve, the degree of curvature can be expressed as rate of change of the absolute indifference-curve slope (in economic terms, of the Marginal Rate of Substitution in Consumption, MRS_C) as the ratio y/x varies. Thus, curvature can be represented as $d(MRS_C)/d(y/x)$, remembering that $MRS_C \equiv -\dfrac{dy}{dx}\Big|_U$. But as the degree of substitutability is inversely related to the curvature of the indifference curves (substitutability being greater the closer these curves approach linear form), we are interested in the reciprocal derivative $d(y/x)/d(MRS_C)$. The final step is, as in all elasticity measures, to deal with *proportionate* rather than absolute changes, in both numerator and denominator. The result becomes:

$$\sigma \equiv \frac{d(y/x)/(y/x)}{d(MRS_C)/MRS_C}$$

Using the condition that at the consumer's optimum $MRS_C = P_x/P_y$, it can be verified that, if σ is large, then a small change in P_x/P_y will be associated with a large change in y/x along a given indifference curve.

For another commodity pair F and G (think of G as on the vertical axis), $MRS_C = (g/f)^2$. Which pair are better complements (poorer substitutes)?

Answer: Plotting a few points, we can determine easily that the F, G indifference curves are more tightly "curled" than the X, Y indifference curves. Thus, the F, G pair are closer complements.

EXAMPLE 4.2
Rats

A team of psychologists and economists investigated the consumptive choices of rats in response to changes in "price ratios" of desired goods.[a]

In the first experiment unlimited amounts of water and rat chow were provided, but there were two other commodities—root beer and Collins mix—that each animal could obtain only by pressing one of two levers. The total number of allowed lever presses per day was held fixed as the rat's "income." The number of presses needed per milliliter of fluid received was the "price." The price ratio was varied by increasing one price and simultaneously reducing the other, so as to hold "real income" approximately constant. Root beer and Collins mix proved to be rather good substitutes for these experimental rats; the consumption ratio changed markedly, in the expected direction, as the price ratio changed.

In a second experiment "free" food and water were no longer provided. Instead, these became the two commodities available only by paying a price (pressing the appropriate lever). When the price ratio was varied, again holding "real income" approximately constant, there was relatively little change in the ratio of quantities consumed. Food and water, it appears, were strong complements for these rats.

> COMMENT: In the second experiment, very drastic changes in the prices of food and water led to what the authors termed "disruptive" behavior. The rats failed to spend all their "income," and began to lose weight. This kind of irrational response to change may be found among humans as well, though not allowed for in standard economic theory.

[a]J. H. Kagel, H. Rachlin, L. Green, R. C. Battalio, R. L. Basmann, and W. R. Klemm, "Experimental Studies of Consumer Demand Behavior Using Laboratory Animals," *Economic Inquiry*, v. 13 (March 1975).

4.C
HOW THE CONSUMER'S OPTIMUM VARIES IN RESPONSE TO CHANGING OPPORTUNITIES

With the data as to *preferences* assumed unchanging, the optimum of the consumer can vary only in response to changes in *opportunities*. The consumer's market opportunity set, we have seen, depends upon two elements: (1) income, and (2) commodity prices. In this section we shall see how the consumer adjusts his or her preferred consumption basket in reaction to changes in these two elements governing market opportunities.

4.C.1 ☐ Income Expansion Path and Engel Curve

Suppose, to begin with, that income I increases while all prices remain unchanged. Then, in a simplified world of only two commodities X and Y, we can picture the situation as in Figure 4.8. The original optimum is at point Q, the tangency of the budget line KL with indifference curve U_0. (This position corresponds to point C^* in Figure 4.1.) Now let income rise from I to I'. Since the intercept of the original budget line KL on the Y-axis was I/P_y and the intercept on the X-axis was I/P_x, an increase in income from I to I' that leaves prices unchanged will increase both intercepts proportionately. Therefore the new budget line, $K'L'$, must be parallel to the original KL. Put another way, the slope of the budget line depends only upon the price ratio P_x/P_y and so any change in the opportunity set that leaves all prices unaffected must keep the *slope* of the budget line the same as before. The new optimum position is shown as point R, where the budget line $K'L'$ is tangent to the higher indifference curve U_1.

A further increase in income from I' to I'' leads to a further expansion of the market opportunity set, as the budget line shifts outward to $K''L''$. Here the optimum is the tangency position S on indifference curve U_2.

More generally, if I varies while prices and tastes remain unchanged, an entire curve—the Income Expansion Path (IEP)—will be traced out that connects all the different optimum positions like Q, R, and S in Figure 4.8. The Income Expansion Path indicates the response of the rational consumer to changes in income alone, prices held constant.

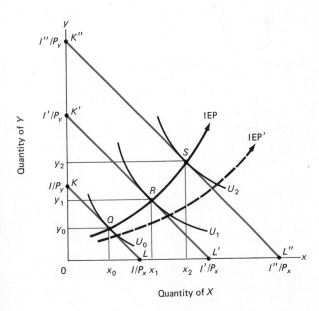

FIGURE 4.8 Derivation of the Income Expansion Path (IEP). As income increases from I to I' to I'', but with prices P_x and P_y held constant, the budget line shifts outward parallel to itself from KL to $K'L'$ to $K''L''$. The tangency defining the consumer optimum correspondingly shifts from Q to R to S. The Income Expansion Path (IEP) shows all the consumer optimum positions attained as I varies, prices remaining the same. If the price ratio P_x/P_y were to become smaller (so that the budget lines become less steep), the IEP would shift to the southeast, as indicated by the dashed IEP' curve.

Since the IEP curve reflects the effect of changing income I given some particular price ratio P_x/P_y, it follows that each different *price ratio* would dictate a different IEP *curve*. In particular, Figure 4.8 shows how a smaller ratio P_x/P_y (implying flatter budget lines KL, $K'L'$, etc.) will have the effect of displacing the entire IEP to the southeast. [*Query:* Can two IEP curves drawn for the same individual ever cross?]

Exercise 4.5: Suppose that an individual's Marginal Rate of Substitution in Consumption is given by the equation $MRS_C = y/x$. Let the market prices be $P_x = 5$ and $P_y = 1$. (a) What is the equation of the Income Expansion Path, and what does it look like? (b) How would the IEP change if P_x fell to $P_x = 4$?

Answer: (a) The Substitution Equivalence Equation (4.4) tells us that $y/x = P_x/P_y = 5/1 = 5$. So the equation for the IEP can be written $y = 5x$. It is a ray out of the origin with positive slope 5. (b) If P_x were to fall to $P_x = 4$, the IEP would rotate to the southeast, the new equation being $y = 4x$ (a flatter ray out of the origin, with slope 4).

What shapes are possible for the Income Expansion Path? Consider the three panels of Figure 4.9. In all three cases the original situation is at the point Q, a tangency with indifference curve U_0 along the budget line KL. Now let income increase, so that the budget line shifts out to the position $K'L'$. In Panel (a), the new tangency R along indifference curve U_1 is within the northeasterly quadrant formed by the vertical and horizontal dashed lines through Q. This means that the quantities purchased of X and of Y have both increased with the rise in income; in this case X and Y are called *normal* goods.

In Panel (b), the new tangency R lies to the northwest of Q, outside the normal quadrant; at the higher income, the quantity of Y purchased has increased but the quantity of X decreased. Thus in Panel (b) the IEP has negative slope through the consumptive optimum positions Q and R. A commodity like X here, whose consumption falls when income rises, is called an *inferior* good.

Unfortunately, there is no terminological agreement as to what to call the other commodity Y in this case. The term "superior good" refers to any good that is not inferior, i.e., whose consumption rises with income. Hence Y would be called superior in either the situation of Panel (a) or of Panel (b), leaving us still in need of a way to express the distinction between the two cases. Let us adopt the term *ultra-superior* for the good that is a "partner" of an inferior good. Then Y is ultra-superior in Panel (b). The defining characteristic of an ultra-superior good may be expressed as follows: Since less of an inferior good is purchased when income increases, it follows that *more than 100%* of the increase in income has been devoted to additional purchases of the associated ultra-superior good.

Finally, Panel (c) shows the opposite situation where Y is inferior and X ultra-superior. The IEP is again negatively sloped, but the new consumptive optimum position lies to the southeast (rather than northwest) as income rises.

In all three cases, the IEP curve is drawn with an arrowhead pointing in the direction of rising utility (upward on the invisible utility hill). The arrow is convenient in permitting an immediate distinction, by inspection, between the X-inferior [Panel (b)] case and the Y-inferior [Panel (c)] case.

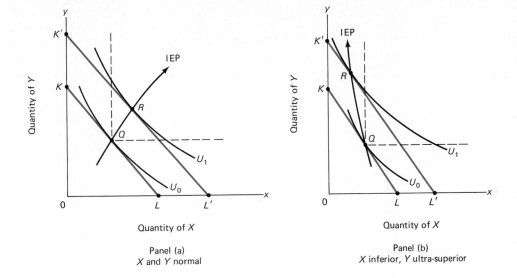

Panel (a)
X and Y normal

Panel (b)
X inferior, Y ultra-superior

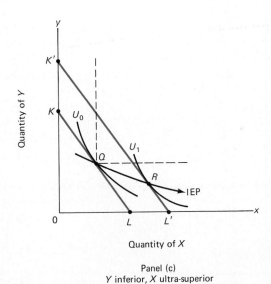

Panel (c)
Y inferior, X ultra-superior

FIGURE 4.9 Income Expansion Paths, Three Cases. In all three diagrams the outward shift of the budget line (from KL to $K'L'$) represents an increase in income I, with prices P_x and P_y held constant. In Panel (a) the upward direction of the Income Expansion Path (IEP) is northeast, so that the new consumptive optimum solution at R involves increased purchases of both commodities. Here both X and Y are normal superior goods. In Panel (b) the upward direction of the IEP is northwest; as income I increases more of Y is consumed, but less of X. X here is called an inferior good, and Y an ultra-superior good. Panel (c) is the opposite case, where the upward direction of the IEP is southeast. Here Y is inferior, X ultra-superior.

CONCLUSION: A positively sloped Income Expansion Path, for two goods X and Y, means that consumption of each rises as income grows. Then X and Y are both normal superior goods. Alternatively, if the IEP has negative slope one of the goods must be inferior. The other good must of course be superior, but more specifically may be called ultra-superior as it accounts for more than 100% of the increment of income.

Exercise 4.6: (a) Suppose, for some individual, that $MRS_C = y/x$. Are goods X and Y both normal for him, or is one of them inferior? (b) What if $MRS_C = y$?

Answer: (a) When $MRS_C = y/x$ the Substitution Equivalence Equation (4.4) is $y/x = P_x/P_y$—so that the Income Expansion Path equation can be written $y = P_x x/P_y$. Since P_x and P_y are both positive, the IEP has positive slope, implying that X and Y are both normal superior goods. (b) If instead $MRS_C = y$, the equation for the IEP by a similar development becomes simply $y = P_x/P_y$. This implies that the IEP would be a horizontal line—meaning that any increase of income is spent *entirely* on good X. So Y, while not quite inferior, is just on the borderline of being so.

EXAMPLE 4.3
Luxuries versus Necessities in a P.O.W. Camp

Goods that are predominantly purchased by relatively wealthy people are commonly called luxuries. Correspondingly, a good that accounts for a large portion of the consumption budget of poorer people is sometimes termed a "necessity." Standard items of food like bread are generally considered necessities. For, while richer people can afford to and generally do buy more loaves of bread per person than poorer people (i.e., bread is not an inferior good), the *proportion* of the budget spent on bread falls as income rises.

In the prisoner-of-war economy already mentioned in Example 4.1 above, R. A. Radford[a] also made interesting observations about necessities and luxuries. Toward the end of the war, prisoners were living in severe privation as a result of the steady deterioration of the German economy under bombing and other wartime strains. In August 1944 a further halving of real income rations, the two main items being food and cigarettes, took place. Unexpectedly, cigarettes proved to be more of a "necessity" than food (by the standard definition above). Despite the presence of many non-smokers, in the market as a whole there was a net attempt after real income fell to trade food for cigarettes. As a result, the price of food (in terms of cigarettes) became actually lower than before.

COMMENT: The implied shape of indifference curves between cigarettes C and food F at the higher income level (point Q°) and the lower income level (point Q'), for a typical prisoner, is indicated in Figure 4.10. The Marginal Rate of Substitution in Consumption,

$$MRS_C \equiv -\left.\frac{\Delta c}{\Delta f}\right|_U$$ is less (the indifference curve has flatter slope) at the lower real-income point.

[a] R. A. Radford, "The Economic Organisation of a P.O.W. Camp," *Economica*, v. 12 (1945).

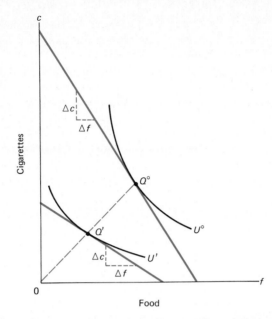

FIGURE 4.10 Food versus Cigarettes in a P.O.W. Camp. After a halving of cigarette and food rations, the typical P.O.W. was forced from an initial position like $Q°$ to a less preferred outcome Q'. Under these circumstances it was observed that P_f/P_c, the price of food in terms of cigarettes as *numéraire,* fell. Since P_f/P_c is the market ratio $\Delta c/\Delta f$ at which cigarettes and food can be exchanged, the MRS_E between cigarettes and food, and since from equation (4.4) $MRS_E = MRS_C$, we know that MRS_C (the indifference-curve slope) must have been less at lower incomes. That is, cigarettes became relatively more preferred as income fell.

The analysis to this point has shown the reaction of the consumer's optimum basket of commodities to changes in income—prices and preferences being taken as constant. For any single good such as X, the relation between income and consumption can be summarized in a convenient form for statistical determination known as the *Engel Curve.*[13] A portion of a typical Engel Curve is shown in Figure 4.11. In the case illustrated, the quantity of X consumed rises as income rises, i.e., X is a superior good.

[13]Ernst Engel (1821–1896), German statistician.

EXAMPLE 4.4
Polygyny in Maiduguri

The economist Amyra Grossbard, reviewing data compiled by anthropologists, attempted to estimate a number of the determinants of multiple wives (polygyny) in Maiduguri,[a] a region in Nigeria with an Islamic popu-

[a]Amyra Grossbard, "An Economic Analysis of Polygyny: The Case of Maiduguri," *Current Anthropology,* v. 17 (Dec. 1976).

lation. Under the primitive market conditions in that area, income and wealth could not be adequately measured in cash terms. One estimate was provided by an interviewer, who ranked the male subjects on a wealth scale from 1 to 4. It was found that each upward step in rank was associated on average with a 0.16 increase in number of wives. Several indirect or "proxy" estimates of wealth also were used. For example, it was found that males owning houses had on average 0.23 more wives than non-owners. And males whose residences had piped water had on average 0.32 more wives.

> COMMENT: No single available measure of income was fully satisfactory, but the different estimates reinforced one another to indicate that wives are a normal superior "good" for Maiduguri males. The Engel Curves would therefore be somewhat as pictured in Figure 4.11.

In practice we are almost always interested in broader categories or aggregates of consumption like food, clothing, vacation travel, and so forth, rather than in specific single commodities. There is, however, no natural or usable quantity unit for a broad commodity grouping like food or clothing. To handle this, we can replace quantity of X on the vertical axis of the Engel-Curve diagram of Figure 4.11 with consumer *expenditures* on X. If X is a single good, expenditures on the good would of course be price times quantity purchased, or $P_x x$. And if X represents an entire grouping of consumption goods $X_1, \ldots, X_G$, expenditure is $P_1 x_1 + P_2 x_2 + \cdots + P_G x_G$. The income-consumption relation in terms of expenditures may be called the *Engel Expenditure Curve*. Both the simple Engel Curve and the Engel Expenditure Curve represent the same data as the Income Expansion Paths of Figures 4.8 and 4.9, but translated onto different axes. For the former, x is plotted as a function of I; for the latter, $P_x x$ as a function of I.

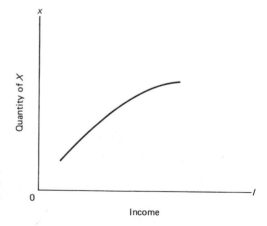

FIGURE 4.11 Engel Curve. The Engel Curve shows the quantity purchased of any good X as a function of income I. For a superior good, the Engle Curve rises with income as shown here.

DEFINITIONS: The *Engel Curve* relates consumption quantity *x* to income *I*. The *Engel Expenditure Curve* relates expenditure $P_x x$ to income *I*.

The Engel Expenditure Curve has the additional advantage (over the simple Engel Curve) of directly displaying the difference between a normal superior good and an ultra-superior good. The Engel Expenditure Curve in the three panels of Figure 4.12 correspond to the three cases of Figure 4.9. To interpret

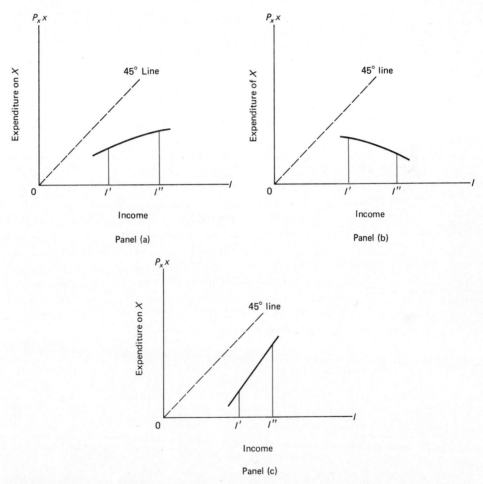

FIGURE 4.12 Engel Expenditure Curves. An Engel Expenditure Curve shows $P_x x$, the amount expended on good *X*, as a function of income *I* (where price P_x is held constant). If the curve were to touch the 45° line, at that point *all* of income would be spent on *X*. In Panel (a), the expenditure $P_x x$ rises with income but diverges from the 45° line, indicating that more is spent on *other* goods as well, as *I* rises. In Panel (b) less is spent on *X* as income rises, so *X* must be inferior. In Panel (c) more is being spent on *X* and the curve approaches the 45° line; this means that less is being spent on other goods, so that these other goods must therefore in aggregate be inferior.

Figure 4.12, first note the dashed 45° line emerging from the origin. If for any commodity (or commodity grouping) the Engel Expenditure Curve lay along this 45° line, the consumer's entire income would be devoted to purchase of that commodity or grouping. Hence the 45° line constitutes an upper limit for the Engel Expenditure Curve.

In the situation pictured in Panel (a), expenditures on X rise as income I increases. But the slope of the rising curve is less than 45°. This means that expenditures on X have risen by *less* than the rise in income, i.e., some of the increment of income must have been spent on a good or goods other than X. Hence, this corresponds to the "normal" case in Panel (a) of Figure 4.9.

Jumping to Panel (c) of Figure 4.12, in the range between I' and I'' the Engel Expenditure Curve is rising *more* sharply than the 45° line. Hence more than the total increase in income is being devoted to consumption of X. This means that X is ultra-superior, as in the Panel (c) situation of Figure 4.9. Finally, in the middle Panel (b) of Figure 4.12, expenditures on X actually decline as income rises. Since P_x is constant, the quantity of X taken must have fallen; hence X is inferior, as in the situation pictured in Panel (b) of Figure 4.9.

EXAMPLE 4.5
Engel's Laws after a Century

The nineteenth-century statistician Engel asserted that, as income increases: (1) The proportion of the budget spent on food will fall; (2) the proportions spent on lodging and clothing will remain about the same; and (3) the proportion spent on all other goods will increase.

The Table shows the proportionate expenditures on certain categories of consumer goods, for U.S. urban families in 1960–61 classified by income.

Distribution of Expenditures (%)*

| | FAMILY INCOME LEVEL, AFTER TAXES | | | |
EXPENDITURE CATEGORY	Under $2000	$2000– 2999	$3000– 3999	$4000 and Over
Food	29.5	28.4	25.9	23.7
Shelter, fuel, light, refrigeration, water	29.4	24.3	20.6	17.4
Clothing	5.9	8.2	9.0	10.8
Medical care	8.2	8.1	7.3	6.4
Automobile	3.2	6.5	11.3	13.9
All other	23.8	24.5	25.9	27.8
Total	100.0	100.0	100.0	100.0

Source: Bureau of Labor Statistics, "Consumer Expenditures and Income, with Emphasis on Low Income Families," July 1964.

*For a more complete survey, see H. Houthakker, "An International Comparison of Household Expenditure Patterns, Commemorating the Centenary of Engel's Law," *Econometrica*, v. 25 (Oct. 1957).

The data confirm Engel in showing a declining proportion spent on food as income rises. But where he predicted constant proportions spent on lodging and clothing, the twentieth-century data show a falling proportion in the former and a rising proportion in the latter category. The "All other" category also rises with income, as Engel predicted. One striking feature is the very sharp increase in the proportion spent on the *automobile* as income rises; automobile transportation is evidently a strongly superior good.

4.C.2 □ Price Expansion Path and Demand Curve

What happens when income is held constant but the other determinant of opportunities—market prices—vary? It will be convenient to let Y be the "*numéraire*" commodity, so that its price is held constant at $P_y = 1$. Then variation in prices will take the specific form of changes in P_x, the price of commodity X. Here again the change in data affects the shape of the market opportunity set. But whereas a rise in income leads to a *parallel* outward displacement of the budget line representing the northeasterly boundary of the opportunity set, a change in price leads to a *tilting* of this boundary.

In Figure 4.13, as before, the initial situation is represented by the consumer optimum at Q where the budget line KL is tangent to indifference curve U_0. Now let the price of X *fall*. Since the intercept of the budget line with the vertical Y-axis is at I/P_y, nothing has changed there; the point K remains as before. But the intercept of the budget line with the horizontal X-axis is at I/P_x, so the fall in P_x is associated with an expansion of the opportunity set taking the form of an outward tilting of the budget line to a new position like KL'. This makes sense, since the enlarged market opportunities are associated entirely with the improved terms for purchasing good X. The new optimum of the consumer is then the point R where the new budget line KL' is tangent to a higher indifference curve U_1. And a still further decline in the price P_x leads to a further outward

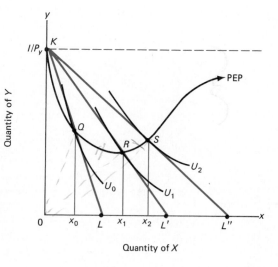

FIGURE 4.13 **Derivation of the Price Expansion Path (PEP)** As P_x falls, with income I and the price of the other good P_y held constant, the budget line tilts outward (from KL to KL' to KL''). The consumptive optimum position changes correspondingly from Q to R to S. The Price Expansion Path (PEP) connects all such consumptive optimum positions as P_x varies, the arrowhead on the PEP curve indicating the direction of utility improvement. Normally, the PEP curve moves eastward, and it can never cross above the horizontal drawn through point K. (K is the "corner solution" where, for sufficiently high P_x, none of commodity X would be purchased.)

tilting of the budget line, to the position KL''; here the associated optimum of the consumer is at S on the still higher indifference curve U_2.

A curve can now be passed through all the possible optimum positions like Q, R, and S that are generated by changes in P_x (when income I and the price P_y of the other commodity are held constant). The curve so generated can be called, in analogy with the Income Expansion Path (IEP) of the preceding section, the Price Expansion Path (PEP). The PEP curve indicates the response of the rational consumer to changes in P_x alone, income I and the price P_y being held fixed.

However, just as the IEP curve in its entirety is shifted when prices change, the entire Price Expansion Path will be displaced to a different position if income I changes. Specifically, if goods X and Y are normal, such an increase in income will tend to shift the Price Expansion Path upward and to the right. [Students should check this point to verify their understanding of the PEP curve.]

Exercise 4.7: Suppose that some individual has $MRS_C = y$, income $I = 120$, and assume that $P_y = 1$. (a) What is the equation for the Price Expansion Path (PEP) and what is its shape? (b) How would it change if income increased to $I = 150$?

Answer: (a) Here the Substitution Equivalence Equation (4.1) becomes $y = P_x/P_y$ or, even more simply (since $P_y = 1$), just $y = P_x$. The budget line equation remains $P_x x + P_y y = I$ or numerically $P_x x + y = 120$. Eliminating P_x and simplifying, we have $yx + x = 120$ or, in more convenient form, $y(x + 1) = 120$. This PEP curve has y-intercept of 120. Like the PEP curve of Figure 4.13, it slopes down from the y-intercept— but unlike that curve, it never curls up again but approaches (without ever intersecting) the horizontal axis. (b) If income increased to $I = 150$, the equation would become $y(x + 1) = 150$. The intercept on the y-axis is higher and the curve shifts generally upward and to the right.

The following additional geometrical characteristics of the Price Expansion Path (PEP) are also of considerable economic interest.

1. As the price P_x falls, the PEP curve enters regions of higher and higher levels of utility. Again, an arrowhead shows the direction of utility improvement along the PEP in Figure 4.13. The level of satisfaction increases since, with income I in numeraire terms held constant, a fall in P_x is equivalent to a rise in *real* income—in the sense of ability to purchase desired commodities.

2. If the PEP curves downward (southeasterly), as in the range between Q and R along the curve in Figure 4.13, at lower prices P_x the consumer purchases more of X but takes less of Y. If the PEP bends upward into a positive slope, as in the range between R and S in the diagram, the consumer is willing and able at the lower price P_x to obtain more X while consuming more Y as well.

3. If there is some price P_x so high that no X is purchased, at that price the optimum of the consumer is a *corner solution* on the Y-axis, as in Figure 4.3. If this condition holds, the Price Expansion Path will have a terminating point on the Y-axis as at K in Figure 4.13. On the other hand, no matter how low the price P_x falls, so long as it does not become negative, the budget line (boundary of the market opportunity set) must lie below the dashed horizontal drawn through K in the diagram. Thus, the Price Expansion Path must also lie everywhere below this horizontal.

4. Astonishing as it may seem, the PEP curve may conceivably curl back so as to be moving for a time in a northwesterly direction, as in the circled region in Figure

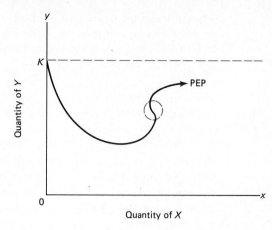

FIGURE 4.14 Price Expansion Path: Giffen Case.
The Price Expansion Path might conceivably curl back
northwest over a limited range (circled region), where
less of X is purchased as price P_x falls. In this range X
would be called a "Giffen good."

4.14. In this region, as price P_x falls the quantity of X consumed also falls! When this
condition applies, the commodity is called a "Giffen good"[14] for this consumer. But
the Giffen property can only hold over a limited range. With negatively sloped
indifference curves and positive preference directions, the PEP cannot move northwesterly very long and still be entering regions of higher and higher utility. (Giffen
goods will be discussed further below.)

Finally, we can re-plot the data summarized by the Price Expansion Path as
a relation between the quantity consumed of commodity X and the price of X, as
in the curve *dd* of Panel (a) in Figure 4.15. This is of course the individual's
demand curve for the good X.

[14]Sir Robert Giffen, British statistician and economist (1837–1910).

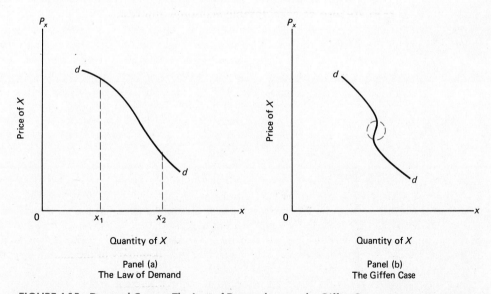

FIGURE 4.15 Demand Curves: The Law of Demand versus the Giffen Case. Panel (a) pictures a
negatively sloped individual demand curve, satisfying the Law of Demand: as the price falls, more
of X is purchased. In Panel (b) the demand curve has the exceptional "Giffen" property, more being
purchased as prices *rise,* in the small circled region (corresponding to the circled region in Figure
4.14). The Giffen property can hold, if at all, only over a limited range of prices.

Exercise 4.8: In Exercise 4.7, the Price Expansion Path $y(x + 1) = 120$ was obtained for an individual with $MRS_C = y$, income $I = 120$, and assuming that $P_y = 1$. What is the individual demand curve associated with this PEP curve?

Answer: The Substitution Equivalence Equation here, we saw in Exercise 4.7, is simply $y = P_x$. Eliminating y in the PEP equation, we have as the demand equation $P_x(x + 1) = 120$—or, after rearranging, $x = 120/P_x - 1$. [*Query*: What happens at $P_x = 120$, or any higher price? *Hint* : $P_x = 120$ is the "choke price" for good X.]

It will be evident from the discussion preceding, and also from Exercise 4.8, that so long as the PEP is moving easterly as in Figure 4.13 (whether southeasterly as in the range *KQR*, or northeasterly as in the range *RS*), the demand curve must have a normal negative slope: a lower price P_x is associated with a larger quantity of X entering into the optimum position of the consumer. But if there is a Giffen range in which the PEP curls northwesterly (the circled region in Figure 4.14), then there will be a corresponding range along the demand curve where the demand curve is positively sloped (the circled region in Panel (b) of Figure 4.15). In this range the demand curve has the "Giffen property" that at lower prices a smaller quantity is demanded.

That the Giffen demand curve is never (or almost never) observed is a principle called the *Law of Demand*. This principle, like convexity of indifference curves with respect to the origin, does *not* follow from the pure logic of choice. Its justification is empirical observation of the world.

EXAMPLE 4.6
The Law of Demand: Animals and Humans

The psychologist S.E.G. Lea reviewed in 1978[a] a number of demand studies from a wide variety of sources—including animal experiments, retailing experiments, and econometric investigations. The following is a summary showing, for each class of study, the number of instances that either support or contradict the Law of Demand, or represent mixed or uncertain results.

	LAW OF DEMAND SUPPORTED	LAW OF DEMAND CONTRADICTED	MIXED OR UNCERTAIN
Animal experiments* (18)	15	1	2
Retailing experiments† (9)	7	1	1
Selection of econometric studies‡ (25)	25	0	0

* Estimated visually from Lea, Fig. 1 (p. 447).
†Ditto, Fig. 2 (p. 448).
‡Ditto, Fig. 3 (p. 449).

[a] S. E. G. Lea, "The Psychology and Economics of Demand," *Psychological Bulletin*, v. 85 (1978).

That demand behavior can be investigated by animal experimentation is perhaps surprising. In these experiments, the commodity "purchased" (called by psychologists a *reinforcer*) was typically "paid for" by presses on a lever. Among the reinforcers used in the experiments surveyed were water, food, sucrose solution, and morphine injections! The animals included rats, mice, monkeys, guinea pigs, and Siamese fighting fish.

COMMENT: The Law of Demand is so firmly believed by economists that there is some danger of distortion of results. An econometric investigator whose data suggest a violation of the Law of Demand is likely to doubt the figures, or to reconsider the methods used, before publishing the study. That even animal experiments conducted by psychologists tend to support the Law of Demand is therefore somewhat reassuring.

Common sense tells us that the Law of Demand is consistent with the great majority of ordinary consumption decisions. But what about exceptional situations, like addicts' demand for narcotics or alcoholics' demand for liquor? Even then the income constraint imposes strong pressure in the direction of the Law of Demand. Suppose that an addict were to spend literally all of his income upon drugs, regardless of price. Then by elementary algebra he necessarily must buy less as price rises. On the other hand, in order to support his habit as price increases he might try to acquire more income—by stealing, begging, or even working. But the more income needed, the harder the effort required, and the Law of Demand still tends to hold. So we are not surprised to read, for example, that after Prohibition raised the effective price of liquor in the United States, there was indeed a decline in consumption. (Indirect evidence: the observed incidence of cirrhosis of the liver declined.)[15]

[15]H. Kalant and O. J. Kalant, *Drugs, Society, and Personal Choice* (Don Mills, Ontario, Canada: Paperjacks, 1971), p. 117.

EXAMPLE 4.7
Shocking Alcoholics

As a portion of an experiment conducted by M. B. Sobell and L. C. Sobell,[a] forty alcoholics who had voluntarily admitted themselves to Patton State Hospital in California were randomly assigned to an experimental or a control group. The twenty patients assigned to the experimental group received, in addition to conventional hospital treatment, a special sequence of sessions. In

[a]Mark B. Sobell and Linda C. Sobell, *Individualized Behavior Therapy for Alcoholics: Rationale, Procedures, Preliminary Results, and Appendix,* California Mental Health Research Monograph No. 13 (1972).

these sessions liquor was freely available, except that "inappropriate" drinking behavior was punished by an electric shock. Shocks were administered if the patient ordered a drink straight, took too large a sip, ordered drinks less than 20 minutes apart, or ordered more than three drinks in a session. During three of the thirteen sessions, however, no shocks were administered. The overall results were as follows:

SESSIONS	AVERAGE INAPPROPRIATE BEHAVIORS*
With shocks	2.2
Without shocks	18.7

*Calculated from Sobell and Sobell, p. 39.

Note that this was a case *without* a fixed constraint on purchasing power. A patient could always "earn" the right to take another drink by undergoing an electric shock. Nevertheless, when the price of drinking was high, less occurred.

COMMENT: An interesting point, touching upon the nature and stability of "tastes" (see Chapter 3, Section 3.G), was observed in follow-up studies at later dates. The experimental group seemed to have better success than the control group in remaining sober afterward. This suggests that life experiences can indeed change attitudes, not a very astonishing conclusion but one that at least superficially appears to be at odds with the standard economic assumption of unchanging preferences. One possible explanation is the following. It seems likely that admission to the hospital, which was voluntary, indicated a willingness on the part of these alcoholics to engage in *exploratory* behavior (like the children of Example 3.1), suggesting that they did not feel confident about their true preferences for being or not being an alcoholic. Seemingly, the shock treatment somehow induced more effective exploration of non-alcoholic life styles.

Since the demand curve is in effect a re-plotting of the data in the Price Expansion Path, and since the latter shifts position as income I changes, we would expect a change in income to affect the position of the demand curve for X. If X and the other commodity Y are both normal goods, the quantities consumed at any price ratio will *both* increase as income rises [Figure 4.9, Panel (a)]. Then, as has been mentioned, the entire Price Expansion Path PEP of Figure 4.11 would be displaced upward and to the right (outward from the origin). Considering the effect upon good X alone, it follows that the demand curve for X will

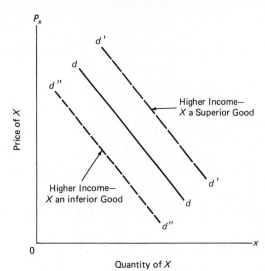

FIGURE 4.16 Effect of Income Shifts on Demand Curve. If *X* is a superior good (whether normal or ultra-superior) a rise in income implies larger purchases of *X* at any price P_x; the demand curve shifts to the right (position $d'd'$). But if *X* is an inferior good, as income increases *less* is purchased at any price P_x; the demand curve shifts to the left (position $d''d''$).

be displaced to the right as income rises— *dd* will shift to a position like $d'd'$ in Figure 4.16, showing that an increased quantity would be consumed at any price P_x. And of course if *X* is ultra-superior [Figure 4.9, Panel (c)], again *dd* will shift to the right as income rises. But if *X* is an *inferior* good [Figure 4.9, Panel (b)], the shift of *dd* as income rises will be to the left, to a position like $d''d''$ in Figure 4.16; less of *X* will be purchased at any given price P_x .

Exercise 4.9: For the individual of Exercise 4.8, what would happen to the demand curve if income rose from $I = 120$ to $I = 150$? Is *X* a superior good?

Answer: With $I = 120$ the demand equation was $P_x(x + 1) = 120$, or equivalently $x = 120/P_x - 1$. With $I = 150$, following the same technique we obtain $P_x(x + 1) = 150$ or equivalently $x = 150/P_x - 1$. The demand curve for *X* has shifted to the right at each price as a result of the increase in income. Thus, commodity *X* must be a superior good.

4.D
INCOME AND SUBSTITUTION EFFECTS OF A PRICE CHANGE

The preceding section showed how changes in the two determinants of the opportunity set, *income* and *prices*, affect the optimum of the consumer. However, this classification does not provide a clean separation of the effects of price changes versus income changes upon individual opportunities. For, if income *I* remains numerically unchanged while the price P_x falls, with the other price P_y held constant, in a sense *real* income has increased. The individual's *market opportunity set* has grown; in terms of Figure 4.13, as P_x falls with *I* and P_y held constant, we saw that the budget line *KL* shifted outward to a position like *KL'* or *KL''*. Correspondingly, of course, a *rise* in P_x, with P_y and income *I* held constant, would represent a contraction of opportunities and in that sense a fall in real income.

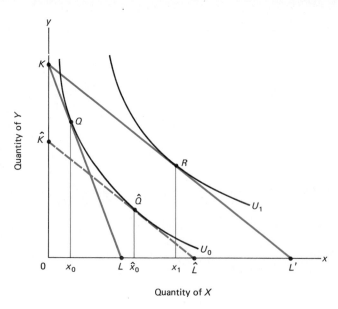

FIGURE 4.17 **Income and Substitution Effects: Hicks Decomposition.** A fall in price P_x, with I and P_y held constant, shifts the budget line from KL to KL' so that the consumptive optimum changes from Q to R. As R lies on a higher indifference curve, there has been an increase in *real* income. The "income effect" of the price change can be separated from the pure "substitution effect" by constructing an artificial budget line $\hat{K}\hat{L}$ parallel to KL' and tangent to the original indifference curve U_0 (at the position $\hat{Q}$). There is no utility improvement between Q and $\hat{Q}$, only between $\hat{Q}$ and R. The income effect of the price change upon the demand for X is therefore $x_1 - \hat{x}_0$; the pure substitution effect of the price change is $\hat{x}_0 - x_0$.

For some purposes it is desirable to correct for and thus eliminate the real-income effect of a price change upon the consumer optimum. When this is done we are left with what is called the pure *substitution effect* of the price change. The usual method of adjustment, devised by the British economist J. R. Hicks,[16] is illustrated in Figure 4.17. The budget line KL associated with the original price P_x leads to the optimum of the consumer at Q along indifference curve U_0, where the quantity taken of X is x_0. The budget line KL' reflects a lower price P_x' leading to the new optimum at R along indifference curve U_1, where $x = x_1$. Now construct an artificial budget line $\hat{K}\hat{L}$ (dashed in the diagram) *tangent to the original indifference curve U_0 but whose slope reflects the new price ratio P_x'/P_y.* The tangency of $\hat{K}\hat{L}$ with U_0 is at the point $\hat{Q}$, where $x = \hat{x}_0$.

Between the original consumer optimum Q and the artificial optimum $\hat{Q}$, real income is constant—in the sense that utility is unchanged (the individual remains on the same indifference curve as before). Thus the shift of the optimum from Q to $\hat{Q}$ (or, in terms of quantities of X, the difference $\hat{x}_0 - x_0$), is the pure "substitution effect" due to the price change. The remainder of the movement of the consumer optimum from $\hat{Q}$ to R (or, in terms of X, the difference $x_1 - \hat{x}_0$) is the "income effect." Since $\hat{Q}$ and R are tangencies along budget lines of parallel slopes, the change in the price ratio plays no role between $\hat{Q}$ and R. Thus the income effect isolates the income equivalent of the consumer's gain from the price decrease.

The usefulness of this separation turns upon the qualitatively different elements responsible for the income and the substitution effects. With negatively sloped and convex indifference curves, the substitution effect is always in the normal direction: A *fall* in P_x necessarily leads to a *rise* in the quantity of X taken.

[16]Sir John R. Hicks, contemporary British economist.

For, the fall in P_x flattens the budget line (note that $\hat{K}\hat{L}$ is less steep than KL in Figure 4.17) and so the $\hat{Q}$ tangency along U_0 must be at a point where $\hat{x}_0 > x_0$.

Turning to the income effect, we can see by comparison with the three panels of Figure 4.9 that R might lie to the northwest, northeast, or southeast of $\hat{Q}$. In the normal case [Panel (a)], or if X is ultra-superior [Panel (c)], the income effect (due to the enrichment of the consumer after the fall in P_x) *reinforces* the substitution effect so as to lead to a further increase in consumption of X. (Figure 4.17 illustrates a normal relation between X and Y, and so the income effect $x_1 - \hat{x}_0$ is positive.) But if X were *inferior* [as in Panel (b) of Figure 4.9], the income effect would tend to offset the substitution effect. And indeed it is at least a logical possibility that an abnormal (negative) income effect might outweigh a normal substitution effect. If this occurs a *fall* in price would lead to a net *fall* in quantity purchased; this is the aforementioned "Giffen case."

4.E
FROM INDIVIDUAL DEMAND TO MARKET DEMAND

The passage from demand of the individual to the aggregate demand in the market as a whole is simplicity itself. The *individual's* demand function, shown in Figure 4.18 as the curve $d_j d_j$, gives the quantities that would be purchased by a

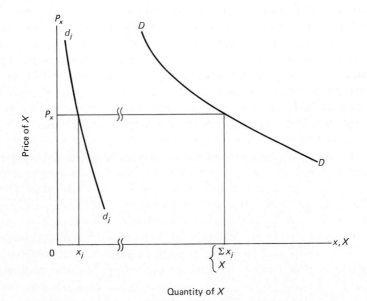

Quantity of X

FIGURE 4.18 Individual and Aggregate Demand.   To the left of the break in the horizontal axis, the curve $d_j d_j$ shows the demand curve of individual j. Every potential purchaser in the market will have such an individual demand curve. To the right of the break the aggregate demand curve DD, showing the overall quantity X purchased at any price P_x, is the horizontal summation of all the individual demand curves like $d_j d_j$. (The break indicates a considerable distance along the horizontal axis omitted in the construction.)

particular consumer (designated as j) in response to any specific price for commodity X ruling in the market. The *market* demand function, the curve DD in the diagram, shows the aggregate quantities that would be purchased by all consumers together at that price. If x_j is the quantity taken by the individual j at price P_x, then the aggregate quantity must obviously be the summation over all such individuals. Symbolically, aggregate quantities will generally be designated by uppercase letters. So we can write:

$$(4.5) \qquad\qquad\qquad X \equiv \sum_{j=1}^{J} x_j$$

This says that the aggregate quantity X (at any price along the market demand curve DD) is always the sum of the individual quantities x_j demanded at that price, where the subscript j is an index running over all of the individuals $1, 2, \ldots, J$ in the market.

Geometrically, the summation is *horizontal* (i.e., over quantities and not over prices). Note that the market demand curve in Figure 4.18 has a much flatter *slope* than the individual demand curve. This tells us that if price falls the increase in the market quantity will ordinarily be much greater than the increase in quantity consumed by any single individual. However, in terms of percentage changes, the *proportionate* increase in X along the aggregate demand curve DD as P_x falls need not be any greater than the proportionate increase along the individual demand curve $d_j d_j$. This point will be considered further when we take up the concept of "elasticity" in the next chapter.

An implicit assumption of the foregoing analysis is that the *same* price P_x is being charged to every individual in the market. Where this assumption is not appropriate, a market demand curve in the ordinary sense cannot be constructed.

> CONCLUSION: The market demand curve is the *horizontal* sum of the individual demand curves.

Exercise 4.10: If individual j has demand curve $x_j = 10 - 2P_x$ for commodity X, while individual k has demand curve $x_k = 10 - 3P_x$, and if these are the only two consumers in the market, what is the market demand curve? Compare the individual-demand slopes and the market-demand slope.

Answer: The market demand is $X = x_j + x_k = 20 - 5P_x$. The slope of j's demand curve is -2, the slope of k's demand curve is -3, while the market-demand slope is -5. Thus, as in the diagram of Figure 4.18, the market-demand slope is notably larger than any individual's demand slope.

4.F
AN APPLICATION: SUBSIDY VERSUS VOUCHER

Suppose that the government wants people to consume more of a particular good—education, let us say. One possibility might be a general *subsidy* to producers or consumers of education. (Free public education is of course an extreme kind of subsidy.) *Voucher* schemes represent a somewhat different technique.

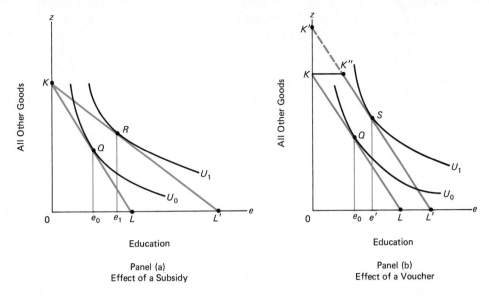

FIGURE 4.19 Subsidy versus Voucher. In Panel (a), a subsidy to consumption of education *(E)* acts like a reduction in price P_e; the budget line shifts from *KL* to *KL'*. At the new consumptive optimum, the quantity purchased of *E* will be greater (unless *E* is a Giffen good in this range, which is highly unlikely.) In Panel (b), the "voucher" pictured is a gift of income in the amount *KK'*, but spendable only on good *E*. The budget line shifts to the right, from *KL* to *K'L'*, except that the consumer is not allowed to choose an optimum in the range between *K'* and *K"* (since the full amount of the voucher would not then be spent on purchases of *E*). The new optimum at *S* will involve increased purchases of *E*, so long as *E* is not an inferior good.

In Figure 4.19, *E* represents education and *Z* "all other goods." Panel (a) shows the effect of a subsidy to education. The original (unsubsidized) tangency optimum is at *Q* on indifference curve U_0. A subsidy acts like a reduction in price; it rotates the budget line from *KL* outward to a new position *KL'*. The new optimum is at *R*, on indifference curve U_1. Apart from the unlikely possibility that *E* is a Giffen good in this range, there will be an increase in the consumer's purchases of education. In the diagram, the increase is the distance $e_1 - e_0$ on the horizontal axis.

Panel (b) of Figure 4.19 shows the effect of a voucher scheme. The initial position *Q* on indifference curve U_0 is the same as before. The "voucher" is a *gift of income spendable only on the specified commodity E*. The distance *KK'* on the vertical axis represents the amount of the gift in *Z*-units, so that the consumer's budget line shifts outward from *KL* to *K'L'*. But the gift of *KK'* is only valid to the extent that it is spent on *E*. Note the dashed portion of the new budget line between *K'* and *K"*. This range along the new budget line represents positions for which a lesser amount of income than the voucher gift *KK'* is devoted to purchases of *E*; the consumer is not permitted to move to a consumption position in this range. (If permitted to do so, the consumer would be converting some of the gift into increased purchases of "other goods" *Z*, which is what the voucher scheme is intended to prevent.) Therefore, the *effective* new budget line is only the range *K"L'* along *K'L'*. In Panel (b) of Figure 4.19 the new optimum is at *S* on indifference curve U'. The quantity purchased of commodity E will rise ($e' > e_0$) whenever E is a superior good (positive income effect).

So far it might appear that there is no great difference between the subsidy and the voucher. The former works through what is in effect a price change, the latter through what is in effect an income change. But the voucher does have a certain special power in the case of a consumer who would *otherwise take very little or none* of the commodity whose consumption it is desired to increase.

Consider Figure 4.20. Here the individual is initially at a *corner solution.* That is, at the existing prices (slope of market line KL) the optimum is the corner point K on indifference curve U_0, where the individual is consuming a zero quantity of commodity E. Even a fairly substantial subsidy, rotating the budget line outward by a considerable angle from K, might have little or no effect on consumption of E. But the voucher displaces the entire budget line upward to $K'L'$ (of which only the solid range $K''L'$ is effective). If free to spend the enlarged income, the consumer might still ideally prefer the new corner point K' on indifference curve U_2. But the farthest the consumer is permitted to go in this direction along $K'L'$ is the point K'', on indifference curve U_1. (Note that the achievable optimum K'' is *not* in general a tangency position.) Here the individual has spent the entire voucher amount on purchases of E, without spending anything further on E out of non-voucher income. A voucher will almost always be effective in increasing consumption for someone previously not consuming E at all, or previously consuming an amount less than the voucher equivalent. The only exception would be if E is not even a good (i.e., if it is actually a *bad*) from the viewpoint of the consumer. (If E were a bad for an individual, a voucher spendable only on E would simply remain unused.)

There are however at least two flaws in this analysis. First, an implicit assumption was that the market price of the good E remained unchanged throughout. This would be a reasonable assumption if the subsidy or voucher

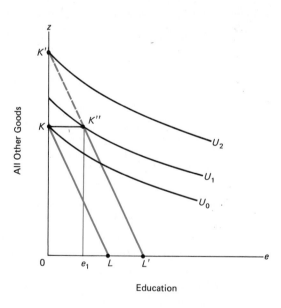

FIGURE 4.20 Corner Solution and Voucher. The initial consumptive optimum is the corner solution at K; none of commodity E is being purchased. A voucher gift of income in the amount KK' leads to a new consumptive optimum at K''. (The consumer would still prefer a corner solution at point K', but this is unavailable.) The voucher leads to increased consumption of E, compared with an initial corner solution, provided only that E is a good for this individual.

were presented only to a single individual, whose own increased consumption would almost surely not significantly affect market price. But if, as is normally the case, the benefit were available to a large class of consumers, a subsidy or voucher would tend to force the demand price upward. Such a price change would shift the *slopes* of the various budget lines in Figures 4.19 and 4.20. Second, the analysis failed to indicate the *source of the funds* needed to finance the subsidy or voucher. Collection of these funds via taxes would reduce the spendable income of some or all consumers, shifting the *positions* of the various budget lines in the diagram. So our discussion represents part of the picture, but not the whole story.

□ SUMMARY OF CHAPTER 4

The optimum for the consumer involves the interaction of *preferences* (indifference curves) with market *opportunities* (budget line). The optimum position is where the budget line bounding the opportunity set touches the highest attainable indifference curve. There are two types of optimum positions: (1) For an interior solution, the optimum occurs at a tangency point. (2) But if the geometry is such that no interior tangency exists, the highest indifference curve attainable is found at zero quantity for one of the commodities (corner solution). In the real world both situations are observed (we consume mixtures of commodities, but do not purchase positive quantities of every possible good). Convex indifference curves are consistent with the possibility of both corner and interior solutions.

Analytically, the budget equation for an individual whose income is I, with goods X and Y available at prices P_x and P_y, is:

$$P_x x + P_y y = I$$

The optimum condition (for an interior solution) can be expressed, if utility is cardinal, as the Consumption Balance Equation:

$$\frac{MU_x}{P_x} = \frac{MU_y}{P_y}$$

That is, Marginal Utility per dollar (the utility of the last dollar) spent on either commodity is the same. This implies the Substitution Equivalence Equation:

$$MRS_C = MRS_E$$

This latter form is more general, as it does not require that utility be cardinally measurable. MRS_C corresponds to the indifference-curve slope, and MRS_E to the budget-line slope. The equality of the two, together with the equation for the budget line, determine the (interior solution) optimum of the consumer.

It is useful to distinguish between pairs of goods that have positive complementarity (are poor substitutes) versus those that have negative complementarity (are good substitutes). Strong complements like bread and butter, or electricity and electrical appliances, tend to be consumed together; consequently, even a large change in the price ratio between them is likely to have only a small effect upon the ratio in which they are consumed. Close substitutes like Fords and Toyotas, or movie theaters and cable TV entertainment, tend to be consumed to the exclusion of one another. Hence, even a small price shift between them may lead to a big change in the ratio in which they are purchased.

As income I increases, with prices held constant, the budget line shifts parallel to itself and outward from the origin. The optimum positions attained as income varies, for given prices P_x and P_y, are shown by the Income Expansion Path (IEP). If both X and Y are normal superior goods, the IEP has positive slope (the upward direction in utility terms is northeast). If either good is inferior (in which case the other good can be called ultra-superior), the IEP has a negative slope; the upward direction is northwest or southeast, depending upon which good is inferior. The data in the IEP can also be plotted on I, x axes as an Engel Curve showing how the quantity of X purchased varies as income increases, or on $I, P_x x$ axes as an Engel Expenditure Curve showing how the amount $P_x x$ spent on good X varies as income increases.

As price P_x falls, with I and P_y held constant, the budget line tilts outward while retaining the same intercept on the y-axis. The optimum positions attained are represented by the Price Expansion Path (PEP). The upward direction along the PEP is (almost always) eastward. When the data represented by the PEP are plotted on x, P_x axes as a demand curve, this property corresponds to the demand curve having negative slope; more of X is purchased as P_x falls (the Law of Demand). While the Law of Demand is generally observed in the world, it is conceivable that it may be violated over a limited range of prices (the Giffen case).

A fall in P_x, with I and P_y held constant, implies an increase in *real* income (higher level of satisfaction in utility terms). It is possible to separate the "income effect of the price change" from the pure "substitution effect of the price change." The substitution effect is always in the normal direction; when P_x falls relative to P_y, more of X will be purchased. But the direction of the income effect depends upon whether X is superior or inferior. The Giffen case results when the substitution effect (which always enlarges consumption of X as P_x falls) is over-balanced by an inferior-good income effect which is not only negative in direction (tending to reduce purchases of X at higher levels of real income) but unusually large in magnitude.

Market demand is aggregated from individual demands simply by adding up, at each price, the quantities purchased by all the consumers (horizontal summation).

☐ QUESTIONS FOR CHAPTER 4

MAINLY FOR REVIEW

✓ R1. What is the meaning of the expression "the optimum of the consumer"?

R2. In a situation with just two goods X and Y, how does the amount of income I affect the shape of an individual's market opportunity set? How do the prices of the two goods affect the shape?

*R3. What is the "budget line"? What is its equation? What determines the slope of the budget line?

*R4. What is the geometrical condition for the optimum of the consumer? (Distinguish between a corner solution and an interior solution.)

R5. If indifference curves were concave, why would the consumer's optimum never be in the interior?

*R6. What is the Consumption Balance Equation that expresses the optimum of the consumer? Relate this to the Substitution Equivalence Equation. Do the equations hold for an interior solution, a corner solution, or both?

R7. Give examples of pairs of goods that are strong complements, versus pairs that are close substitutes. What is the observable market characteristic that distinguishes them?

R8. Characterize a normal good, an inferior good, and an ultra-superior good. Give examples of each. For two goods X and Y, which of the above must they be if the Income Expansion Path has positive slope? What can you say if the IEP has negative slope?

R9. Prove that if X and Y are goods, the IEP never points southwest.

*R10. A positively sloped Income Expansion Path implies what shape for the Engel Curve? For the Engel Expenditure Curve? If good X is inferior, what can you say about its Engel Curve?

R11. Show how an individual's demand curve can be derived from his Price Expansion Path.

R12. Is there a utility-increasing direction along the IEP? Along the PEP?

*R13. What does the Law of Demand say about the shape of the PEP?

R14. How does the Hicks decomposition separate the "income effect" and the "substitution effect" of a price change?

R15. Using the Hicks decomposition, show that the Giffen condition (violation of the Law of Demand) can hold only for an inferior good.

R16. How is the market demand curve derived from knowledge of individuals' separate demand curves? Can individual demand curves be determined from knowledge of the market demand curve?

*R17. "As compared with a simple subsidy, the voucher scheme is particularly effective for consumers who would otherwise have chosen little or none of the commodity." Illustrate and explain.

FOR FURTHER THOUGHT AND DISCUSSION

*T1. Could you imagine an experiment that might reveal an individual's Marginal Rate of Substitution in Consumption (MRS_C) between two goods? His Marginal Utility for either good?

T2. Why is diminishing Marginal Utility necessary if the Consumption Balance Equation is to express an optimum? Why is decreasing Marginal Rate of Substitution in Consumption necessary if the Substitution Equivalence Equation is to express an optimum?

*The answers to asterisked questions appear at the end of the book.

*T3. Why can the Giffen condition hold only over a limited range of the PEP? Could the PEP ever circle around and rejoin itself at its starting-point on the y-axis?

*T4. Would a change in P_x tend to shift the position of the IEP? Would a change in income I tend to shift the position of the PEP?

T5. If an individual's demand curve cuts the vertical price axis at some finite "choke price" P_x^o, show the equivalent situation in terms of the individual's indifference curves and budget line. Must the consumer's optimum then be a corner solution at price P_x^o?

T6. "I think I could be a good woman if I had five thousand a year"—Becky Sharp, in Thackeray's *Vanity Fair.* Here are two possible interpretations:
   a. "Being a good woman" is a good for Becky, but one she can't afford until her income gets up to five thousand a year.
   b. Becky regards "being a good woman" as an unpleasant activity (a bad, like hard labor). But for a fee (like wages for hard labor) of five thousand a year she would be a good woman.
   Which interpretation is correct? Can you imagine a test that would distinguish which of the two Becky meant?

*T7. Consider a pair of commodities like bread and butter, which are strong complements, versus another pair like butter and margarine, which are close substitutes. Which pair is more likely to have a member that is an inferior good? Explain.

*T8. Why is the income effect of a price change usually small compared to the substitution effect?

T9. "Since 1900, real income has increased tremendously, yet the average number of children per family has decreased." Consider the following possible explanations, and illustrate in terms of market opportunity sets and family indifference curves between number of children (x) and "all other goods" (y).
   a. Children are an inferior good; since we're richer now, we want fewer of them.
   b. Children are not an inferior good; however, it has become more expensive to bear and raise children.
   c. Children are not an inferior good, nor have they become relatively more expensive. What has happened is that tastes have changed; couples today want smaller families than couples did in 1900.

*T10. In the comparison of subsidy versus voucher in the text, it was assumed that in either case the market base price of the good remained unchanged. Would it be correct to anticipate some change of price? In which direction is this likely to go? Show the effect upon the market opportunity set.

T11. Still another consideration is that government expenditures on subsidies or vouchers must ordinarily be financed by taxes. Suppose that the mode of financing works out as a reduction in the typical individual's income I. Show the effect upon his market opportunity set of a tax-financed subsidy. Of a tax-financed voucher.

*T12. The following is sometimes given as an example of a Giffen-good situation. A person must make a 1000-mile train trip and has only $100 in funds available. He prefers first-class travel to coach travel, but his first priority is to complete his trip. Suppose that first-class travel costs 20 cents per mile and coach costs 5 cents per mile. Then it can be verified that he will travel $333\frac{1}{3}$ miles in first class and $666\frac{2}{3}$ miles in coach. Now let the price of coach travel rise to 10 cents per mile. Then the traveler cannot afford any first-class miles at all if he is to complete his trip, so the amount of coach travel will rise from $666\frac{2}{3}$ to 1000 even though its price has doubled! Question: Is coach travel an inferior good here? (What would happen if the travel budget were to rise above \$100?) Under what circumstances will the traveler choose a corner solution with only coach travel? With only first-class travel?

*T13. If two commodities are perfect substitutes, is it true that the consumer's optimum will almost always be a corner solution? If so, under what special conditions will it not be?

*T14. At a given price ratio, variations in income I generate an Income Expansion Path IEP. If the price ratio were different, we know that a different IEP curve would be generated. For the same individual, could these two IEP curves ever cross?

*T15. In one of the Exercises above, for a certain individual with $MRS_C = y$, income $I = 120$, and assuming that $P_y = 1$, the demand-curve equation $x = 120/P_x - 1$ was derived. What happens when $P_x = 120$? Is the equation above valid for prices $P_x > 120$, and if not, what is the correct equation in that price range?

APPLICATIONS AND EXTENSIONS OF DEMAND THEORY

CORE CHAPTER

Suppose that government wants to reduce gasoline use. Imposing a gasoline tax would be one possibility. The tax will raise prices to consumers and so (by the Law of Demand) would reduce consumption—but by how much? Similarly, a business recession would depress consumer incomes, but to what extent would that discourage gasoline usage? This chapter describes the measures used by economists to *quantify* how demand responds to changes in income, to changes in a commodity's own price, and to changes in prices of related goods. Using these tools, the chapter then takes up extensions of demand theory that illustrate its applicability to real-world problems.

5.A
THE ENGEL CURVE AND THE INCOME ELASTICITY OF DEMAND

The most direct measure of how sensitive a consumer's purchases of a good X are to changes in income I is the ratio $\Delta x / \Delta I$. For small changes Δx and ΔI, with prices held constant, this ratio can be interpreted as the slope of the Engel Curve.[1] Figure 5.1 shows portions of a number of alternative Engel Curves, assumed for simplicity to be linear. These curves indicate differing possible patterns of variations of consumption Δx in response to changes in income ΔI.

There is one serious difficulty in the use of the simple ratio $\Delta x / \Delta I$, however: it is affected by the choice of conventional *units of measurement*. If commodity X were butter, the numerical value of the ratio would vary by a factor of 16, depending upon whether we measured butter in ounces or pounds. And similarly, the numerical ratio would differ depending upon whether income I were measured in cents or dollars. This type of problem arises in many different branches of economics. To eliminate the difficulty, we make use of the concept of *elasticity*. Elasticity is a measure of relationship in which the changes in both numerator and denominator are expressed in proportionate (percentage) terms. Specifically here, the proportionate response of quantity purchased to a proportionate change in income is called "the income elasticity of demand."

---

[1]*Mathematical Footnote*: We can write this slope as $\partial x / \partial I$, symbolizing a partial derivative—since quantity purchased will also be a function of other variables such as price.

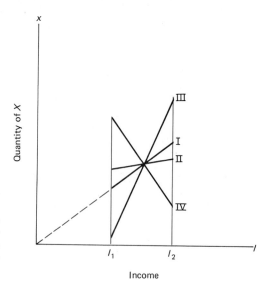

FIGURE 5.1 Engel Curves and Income Elasticity of Demand. Four possible Engel Curves relating consumption of X to income I are shown. Since income elasticity is the ratio of the slope *along* a curve to the slope of a ray drawn from the origin *to* the curve, curve I has income elasticity equal to unity, II less than unity, and III greater than unity. Curve IV has negative income elasticity.

DEFINITION: The income elasticity of demand is the proportional change in the quantity purchased divided by the proportional change in income.

Symbolizing the income elasticity of commodity X as ϵ_x, this definition is represented by the first ratio in equation (5.1) below.[2] The other two algebraic forms are also useful to remember and work with.

(5.1)
$$\epsilon_x \equiv \frac{\Delta x / x}{\Delta I / I} \equiv \frac{\Delta x / \Delta I}{x / I} \equiv \frac{\Delta x}{\Delta I} \frac{I}{x}$$

To illustrate the geometrical significance of the income elasticity of demand, consider the positively sloped Engel Curve ADB in Figure 5.2. Note that the two points A and B lie on a straight line through the origin. Then it is evident that the two variables x and I have increased in the same proportion, so that by the definition (the first ratio in equation [5.1]) income elasticity along ADB equals unity. Or, using the middle ratio of equation (5.1), the numerator fraction in this ratio, $\Delta x / \Delta I$, corresponds to the slope *along* the curve ADB. The denominator fraction, x / I, corresponds to the slope of a line drawn from the origin *to* a point on the curve. In the diagram these slopes are evidently the same and so $\epsilon_x = 1$ for the Engel Curve ADB.

Now consider the curve CDE lying above the line-segment AB but just tangent to it at the single point D. This is an Engel Curve along which the income elasticity of demand is changing. But at the specific tangency point D, we can think of *very small* changes Δx and ΔI along CDE as approximated by movement along the line AB. Thus, the Engel Curve CDE has $\epsilon_x = 1$ in the neighborhood of the point D.

[2]*Mathematical Footnote:* In terms of derivatives, $\epsilon_x \equiv \dfrac{\partial x}{\partial I} \dfrac{I}{x}$.

PART 2 PREFERENCE, CONSUMPTION, AND DEMAND

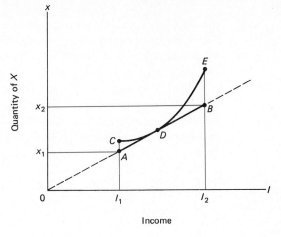

FIGURE 5.2 Engel Curve and Unitary Income Elasticity. The straight-line Engel Curve *ADB* has income elasticity of unity, since the slope *along* the curve is the same as the slope of a ray from the origin *to* any point on the curve. The non-linear Engel Curve *CDE*, tangent at point *D* to *ADB*, therefore also has unitary income elasticity for small changes in the neighborhood of point *D*. In the range *CD* the slope *along* the curve *CDE* is less than the slope of rays from the origin *to* the curve, so income elasticity is less than unity. Correspondingly, $\epsilon_x > 1$ in the range of *CDE* between *D* and *E*.

In Figure 5.1, Engel Curve I is like *ABD* in Figure 5.2; it lies on a line through the origin and so represents unitary income elasticity. Engel Curve II has positive slope, but it is flatter than curve I. It is intuitively evident that this means that x increases in a lesser proportion than I as the latter rises, i.e., $\epsilon_x < 1$. By reversing the argument, we see that the steeper Engel Curve III represents an income elasticity $\epsilon_x > 1$. What of Engel Curve IV? This differs from the others in being negatively sloped. Here x *decreases* as I rises, so X must be an inferior good. Its income elasticity is negative, i.e., $\epsilon_x < 0$.

> *PROPOSITION:* Income elasticity is greater than, equal to, or less than unity depending upon whether the slope *along* the Engel Curve is greater than, equal to, or less than the slope of a ray drawn from the origin *to* the curve. If income elasticity is negative, the Engel Curve has negative slope.

Notice that *any* positively sloped straight-line Engel Curve through the origin has income elasticity of unity, but such lines can be drawn from very nearly vertical (steep slope) to very nearly horizontal (small slope). It is not the steepness alone of an Engel Curve at a particular point that indicates elasticity, but rather the steepness *as compared with a line through the origin.*

Exercise 5.1: The following four linear equations correspond to possible Engel curves. Determine the slope and the income elasticity for each, at the point $(I, x) = (200, 25)$: (a) $x = (1/8)I$; (b) $x = 5 + (1/10)I$; (c) $x = -75 + (1/2)I$; (d) $x = 30 - (1/40)I$. In which of these cases is X an inferior good?

Answer: (a) The slope $\Delta x / \Delta I$ all along the curve is evidently 1/8. The income elasticity is the ratio of this slope to $x/I = 25/200 = 1/8$. Thus the income elasticity is $\epsilon_x = (1/8)/(1/8) = 1$. (b) The slope is 1/10, and so $\epsilon_x = (1/10)/(1/8) = 0.8$. (c) Slope is 1/2, $\epsilon_x = (1/2)/(1/8) = 4$. (d) Slope is $-1/40$, $\epsilon_x = (-1/40)/(1/8) = -0.2$. [Note that the four curves correspond generally to those pictured in Figure 5.1.] Commodity X is inferior only in case (d), where the income elasticity is negative.

In Chapter 2 a distinction was made between the slope measured *at a point* along a curve, and the slope over some finite range or *arc* along the curve. Similarly, it is sometimes important to distinguish between elasticity at a point and elasticity over some arc. The definition of income elasticity (5.1), into which the slope enters as the ratio $\Delta x/\Delta I$, is sufficiently general to cover both cases.

Suppose that we were interested in the income elasticity ϵ_x over some finite interval along the Engel Curve. Specifically, imagine that 10 units of X are purchased at an income of $5000 and 14 units at an income of $6000. Then the increments, for substitution in formula (5.1), are $\Delta x = 4$ and $\Delta I = \$1000$. The only question is what particular values for x and I within the arc to use in the formula. The natural answer is to choose the midpoints of the respective intervals, that is, $x = 12$ and $I = \$5500$. Then:

$$\epsilon_x \equiv \frac{\Delta x}{\Delta I}\frac{I}{x} = \frac{4}{1000}\frac{5500}{12} = 1.833$$

This *arc elasticity*, being greater than unity, indicates that consumption of X rises more than proportionately with income I in the interval.

Arc elasticity is a kind of average of the point elasticities along the curve, within the range of the arc considered. As the intervals Δx and ΔI shrink down toward zero, the arc elasticity approaches the point elasticity along the curve.

One simple quantitative statement can be made about income elasticities:

PROPOSITION: On the average over all goods, income elasticity must be unity.

If there is, say, a 10% increase in income, then consumption of some goods may fall and of others rise, by greater or lesser percentages. But since all of the increase in income must somehow be accounted for, those goods for which consumption rises by less than 10% must be offset by others for which consumption rises by even more than 10%. On the average, consumption must rise by the same proportion as income. If there are just two commodities X and Y, the following equation must hold:

(5.2) $$k_x\epsilon_x + k_y\epsilon_y = 1$$

Here $k_x \equiv P_x x/I$ is the proportion of the consumer's budget spent on commodity X. Similarly, $k_y \equiv P_y y/I$.

Exercise 5.2: Suppose that there are just two goods, bread X and wine Y. If bread accounts for 80% of the budget and has income elasticity $\epsilon_x = 0.9$, what can you say about the income elasticity ϵ_y of wine?

Answer: Equation (5.2) here has the form $0.8(0.9) + 0.2\epsilon_y = 1$, and so $\epsilon_y = 1.4$. [Note that a good which accounts for a very large fraction of the budget tends to have income elasticity near unity; if a good has very high income elasticity, like wine in this example, you can be pretty sure that it accounts for only a small portion of the budget.]

EXAMPLE 5.1

The Declining Public-Transit Industry

Table 5.1 illustrates the declining trend of rapid-transit ridership. Generally speaking, ridership declined sharply between 1946 and 1956, and then more slowly between 1956 and 1962. (For some cities, such as Cleveland, the trend is distorted by the opening of new transit lines.) The declining trend in riders has continued since 1962.

The major factor at work has been the different income elasticities as between transit and its close substitute—the private automobile. Example 4.5, "Engel's Laws after a Century," indicated the strong positive relationship between income and expenditures on the automobile. In the $2000–2999 income bracket, for example, 6.5% of total expenditure was devoted to the automobile; in the $3000–3999 bracket, 11.3%. Using midpoints of the brackets, the income elasticity of auto expenditures[a] over the arc can be computed as:

$$\epsilon_x = \frac{0.113(3500) - 0.065(2500)}{3500 - 2500} \cdot \frac{3000}{0.5[0.113(3500) + 0.065(2500)]}$$

$$= \frac{233}{1000} \cdot \frac{3000}{279} = 2.5 \text{ (approximately)}$$

TABLE 5.1

Rapid Transit System Ridership (1956 = 100.0)

YEAR	NEW YORK	CHICAGO	PHILADELPHIA	BOSTON	TORONTO	CLEVELAND
1946	151.8	136.8	177.8	185.1		
1950	121.9	95.2	137.3	140.2		
1951	117.5	97.1	126.3	132.3		
1952	114.1	97.0	123.0	127.0		
1953	114.0	96.1	114.8	122.8		
1954	103.9	95.8	109.2	112.1		
1955	101.0	97.2	102.8	103.6	97.0	
1956	100.0	100.0	100.0	100.0	100.0	100.0
1957	99.5	97.2	95.6	96.6	101.0	107.0
1958	96.7	92.8	92.0	94.1	99.1	105.7
1959	97.2	98.1	89.5	92.4	99.1	121.0
1960	98.7	97.6	90.1	91.2	95.7	124.7
1961	100.0	95.2	92.9	—	91.0	120.9
1962	100.5	98.9	89.4	—	91.0	117.5

Source: J. R. Meyer, J. F. Kain, and M. Wohl, *The Urban Transportation Problem* (Cambridge, Mass.: Harvard University Press, 1965), p. 96. (A number of footnotes have been deleted.)

[a]We can use auto *expenditures* $P_x x$ in the income elasticity formula since:

$$\frac{\Delta(P_x x)}{\Delta I} \cdot \frac{I}{P_x x} \equiv \frac{\Delta x}{\Delta I} \cdot \frac{I}{x}$$

In contrast, the income elasticity of public transit appears to be very low, or even negative. Using degree of housing privacy (multiple, two-family, and one-family) as a guide to or proxy for income, Table 5.2 suggests that income elasticity is indeed negative. Regardless of "workplace ring" (distance from central city), the greater the income as measured by housing privacy the less the use of transit.

TABLE 5.2

Percentage of Detroit White Workers Using Transit

| | STRUCTURE TYPE | | |
WORKPLACE RING	Multiple	Two-Family	One-Family
1	60.7	58.7	50.6
2	28.5	28.6	19.5
3	29.4	26.8	18.9
4	27.3	23.1	14.4
5	17.8	11.1	8.4
6	5.8	4.1	3.5

Source: J. R. Meyer, J. F. Kain, and M. Wohl, *The Urban Transportation Problem* (Cambridge, Mass.: Harvard University Press, 1965), p. 132.

COMMENT: There have been repeated attempts at encouraging use of public transit in place of the private automobile—in order to reduce road congestion, to counter "urban sprawl," to minimize air pollution, to save energy, etc. Despite very substantial public subsidies to transit, these efforts seem always to fail. The higher income elasticity of auto transportation, given the historical trend of rising levels of income and wealth, has defeated efforts to promote public transit.

5.B
THE DEMAND CURVE AND THE PRICE ELASTICITY OF DEMAND

In the preceding section, measures of the responsiveness of consumption to changes in *income* were obtained. Now consider the sensitivity of consumption to changes in *price*. Again the most obvious measure would be the ratio of differences $\Delta x / \Delta P_x$.[3] Recall that the demand curve represents the relationship between price P_x and the quantity x demanded. For small changes Δx and ΔP_x, therefore,

[3]*Mathematical Footnote:* In terms of derivatives, this is $\partial x / \partial P_x$.

the ratio $\Delta x / \Delta P_x$ corresponds to the *reciprocal* of the slope[4] of the demand curve. The alternative demand curves labeled I, II, III, IV in Figure 5.3 illustrate more and less steep slopes. The steeper the slope, the smaller the numerical or absolute magnitude of $\Delta x / \Delta P_x$.

As in the case of income, a slope measure like $\Delta x / \Delta P_x$ would be affected by changes in conventional units of measurement in the numerator (e.g., changes from pounds to tons) or in the denominator (e.g., changes from dollars per ton to cents per ton). To avoid this difficulty, we are led once again to an elasticity measure, a ratio of *proportionate* changes. This concept is formally known as "the price elasticity of demand." (In common use, the expression "elasticity of demand" standing alone is understood to refer to the price elasticity.)

The elasticity concept permits comparisons of price sensitivities between entirely disparate commodities. Since *slope* depends on units of measurement it would be meaningless to assert, for example, that the demand curve for wheat is steeper than the demand curve for haircuts, and therefore that the former is less responsive to price changes. The demand curve for wheat could be made to seem as steep or flat as desired, by converting from tons to pounds to ounces as quantity units, or the reverse. But it would be meaningful to say that the demand for wheat is *less elastic* than the demand for haircuts, and in that sense less responsive to price changes.

> DEFINITION: The price elasticity of demand is the proportional change in the quantity purchased divided by the proportional change in price.

[4]It is the reciprocal of the slope because economists conventionally draw demand curves with price P_x on the vertical axis.

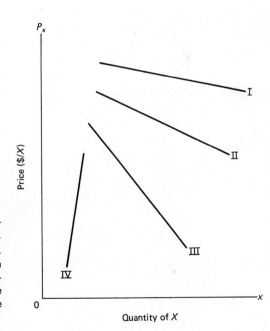

FIGURE 5.3 Alternative Demand Curve Slopes. Four demand curves, drawn as straight lines, represent different responses of quantity purchased to changes in price. Since demand curves are conventionally drawn with price on the vertical axis, a greater response is represented by a flatter demand curve. The demand-curve slope is negative (the Law of Demand), apart from the exceptional Giffen case (curve IV).

As in the case of income elasticity, there are several ways of expressing the formula for price elasticity of demand. Symbolizing price elasticity as η_x, the definition above is algebraically represented by the first ratio in expression (5.3) below.[5]

$$(5.3) \qquad \eta_x \equiv \frac{\Delta x/x}{\Delta P_x/P_x} \equiv \frac{\Delta x/\Delta P_x}{x/P_x} \equiv \frac{P_x/x}{\Delta P_x/\Delta x} \equiv \frac{\Delta x}{\Delta P_x} \cdot \frac{P_x}{x}$$

The other ratios, all identically equivalent, are also useful.

When the demand curve is negatively sloped (the Law of Demand), the changes Δx and ΔP_x have opposite signs. Thus, the price elasticity of demand η_x is normally negative. Nevertheless, when we speak of elasticity being "high" we mean large in absolute value, and "low" elasticity means small in absolute value. More specifically, the term "elastic demand" refers to an absolute value of elasticity, symbolized as $|\eta_x|$, greater than unity while "inelastic demand" means $|\eta_x| < 1$.

Exercise 5.3: The following are alternative linear equations representing an individual's possible demand for commodity X: (a) $x = 240 - 30P_x$; (b) $x = 320 - 50P_x$; (c) $x = 20 + 25P_x$. What are the associated elasticities at the point $(x, P_x) = (120, 4)$? Which, if any, is a Giffen good? Of the others, which represents the more elastic demand?

Answer: We can use, from equation (5.3), the algebraic form $\eta_x = (\Delta x/\Delta P_x)/(x/P_x)$. The denominator ratio in each case is $120/4 = 30$. Inserting the numerator ratio for each case (recall that this represents the *reciprocal* of the demand-curve slope on x, P_x axes), for (a) we have $\eta_x = -30/30 = -1$; for (b), $\eta_x = -50/30 = -5/3$; for (c), $\eta_x = 25/30 = 5/6$. Since the price elasticity is positive in the last case, the Law of Demand fails and (c) represents a Giffen good. [However, we saw in Chapter 4 that a good could have the Giffen property only over a limited range; therefore, an equation like (c) could not possibly be valid for an individual over the whole range of prices.] As between (a) and (b), the latter demand is the more elastic, i.e., shows greater responsiveness of quantity to changes in price.

For price elasticity as well as income elasticity, it is sometimes necessary to distinguish the *arc elasticity* over a finite interval of the curve from the *point elasticity* at a single point along the curve. The price elasticity formula of equation (5.3) is sufficiently general to cover both interpretations. For arc elasticity, the finite differences Δx and ΔP_x are employed in the formula, and the specific values used for x and P_x are the mid-points of their respective intervals. For point elasticity, the differences are conceived as shrinking toward zero so that their ratio $\Delta x/\Delta P_x$ approaches the reciprocal of the slope of the demand curve at that point.

Suppose that the price elasticity is unity ($|\eta_x| = 1$). What happens to ex-

[5]*Mathematical Footnote*: In terms of derivatives,

$$\eta_x \equiv \frac{\partial x/x}{\partial P_x/P_x}$$

penditure on X if there is a small decrease in price? From the first ratio in (5.3) we know that, with unitary elasticity, the proportionate *increase* in quantity $\Delta x / x$ must equal the proportionate *decrease* $\Delta P_x / P_x$ in price. But since the consumer's expenditure on good X is $P_x x$, then the proportionate increase of x just offsets the proportionate decrease of P_x—so that total expenditure remains unchanged. If the price elasticity is greater than unity ($|\eta_x|$) > 1, or "elastic demand"), the proportionate increase in quantity x is larger than the proportionate decrease in price P_x; hence total expenditure $P_x x$ increases when price falls. By a similar argument, if demand is "inelastic," a decrease in P_x leads to a less-than-offsetting rise in x—total expenditure $P_x x$ decreases.[6]

PROPOSITION: A reduction in price P_x will increase a consumer's expenditures $P_x x$ on commodity X if his demand for X is elastic, will decrease $P_x x$ if demand is inelastic, and will leave $P_x x$ unchanged if demand elasticity is unitary.

Exercise 5.4: A consumer's demand curve for good X is given by the equation $x = 100 - 2P_x$. (a) What is the elasticity of demand at the point $(x, P_x) = (20, 40)$? (b) If price were to fall from $P_x = 40$ to $P_x = 35$, what happens to total expenditure $P_x x$ and what does this imply about the elasticity of demand? (c) Verify by computing the arc elasticity of demand over the interval. (d) Compare this arc elasticity with the point elasticity obtained above.

Answer: (a) Along this linear demand curve, the ratio $\Delta x / \Delta P_x$ is a constant equal to -2. Using the second expression for η_x from equation (5.3), we have

$$\frac{\Delta x / \Delta P_x}{x / P_x} = \frac{-2}{20/40} = -4$$

(b) At $P_x = 40$ we know that $x = 20$, and so total expenditure is 800. At $P_x = 35$, the demand equation tells us that $x = 100 - 2(35) = 30$, and so total expenditure is 1050. Since expenditure is greater at the lower price, demand is elastic. (c) Over the interval, $\Delta x / \Delta P_x$ remains constant at -2. Taking the mid-point values for x and P_x, the arc elasticity is $-2/(25/37.5) = -3$, confirming that the demand is elastic over this interval. (d) The point elasticity -4 previously calculated at the quantity $x = 20$ is larger in absolute value than the arc elasticity -3 over the interval between $x = 20$ and $x = 30$. The two numbers would be much closer if the point elasticity were calculated at the mid-point of the interval. In fact, the point elasticity at the mid-point $(x, P_x) = (25, 37.5)$ is *exactly* equal to the arc elasticity over the interval—a result that always holds for linear demand curves, but not otherwise.

[6]*Mathematical Footnote*:

$$\frac{\partial (P_x x)}{\partial x} = P_x + x \frac{\partial P_x}{\partial x} = P_x + \left(\frac{x}{P_x} \frac{\partial P_x}{\partial x} \right) P_x = P_x \left(1 + \frac{1}{\eta_x} \right)$$

Recall that the sign of η_x is negative. Then the derivative on the left representing the change in expenditure is positive, zero, or negative depending on whether η_x is greater than, equal to, or less than unity in absolute terms.

THE CROSS-ELASTICITY OF DEMAND

The amount of butter demanded will depend not only upon its own price, but also to some extent upon the prices of related goods like bread or margarine. Once again, it is convenient to use a unit-free elasticity measure—called the *cross-elasticity of demand*. The definition is:[7]

$$\eta_{xy} \equiv \frac{\Delta x/x}{\Delta P_y/P_y} \equiv \frac{\Delta x}{\Delta P_y} \cdot \frac{P_y}{x}$$

Bread and butter, we know, are complements: having more of either raises the desirability of the other. Then we would expect the cross-elasticity of demand to be positive. A higher butter price tends to reduce consumption of butter (the Law of Demand), thus lowering the desirability and therefore reducing the consumption of bread. In contrast, with a higher butter price margarine will be *more* in demand; thus, between substitutes like butter and margarine the cross-elasticity of demand is surely negative.

[7]*Mathematical Footnote*: In terms of derivatives:

$$\eta_{xy} \equiv \frac{\partial x}{\partial P_y} \frac{P_y}{x}$$

EXAMPLE 5.2
Elasticities of Electricity Demand

The Table shows some results of a study of electricity demand over the period 1946–72. Among the determining variables examined were: (1) electricity price, (2) income, and (3) the price of a competing commodity—gas. It was found convenient to classify the data according to residential, commercial, and industrial use.[a]

Elasticities of Electricity Use

WITH RESPECT TO:	ELECTRICITY PRICE	INCOME	GAS PRICE
Residential	−1.3	+0.3	+0.15
Commercial	−1.5	+0.9	+0.15
Industrial	−1.7	+1.1	+0.15

Source: D. Chapman, T. Tyrrell, and T. Mount, "Electricity Demand Growth and the Energy Crisis," *Science*, v. 178 (Nov. 17, 1972), p. 705.

[a]The industrial and commercial demands are for electricity as a *factor of production* rather than as a consumer good. We have not yet come to the topic of demand for factors of production, but it is of interest to see the comparative data here.

The elasticities of electricity demand with respect to its own price are negative and in the elastic range ($|\eta_x| > 1$), showing a more than proportionate response of consumption to price change. This was the most important result of the study, running counter to the common but uninformed opinion that electricity use is some kind of absolute "requirement" independent of price. The positive elasticities with respect to income show that electricity is a normal superior good. And the positive cross-elasticities with respect to gas price show that gas and electricity are *substitutes*.

> COMMENT: The results here refute the crude techniques for projecting future electricity demands usually employed in "energy crisis" debates. Government planners, industry insiders, and outside critics have often argued as if purely mathematical extrapolations, which simply extend historically observed rates of demand growth into the indefinite future, represent valid estimates of what will happen in the absence of government intervention. This is surely mistaken; the rate of growth of electricity demand is *strongly* responsive to price. And the price of electricity is bound to increase as fuels become more expensive and as requirements for environmental protection add to cost. (Indeed, since the period of the study electricity prices *have* gone up sharply, with the anticipated discouraging effect upon electricity use.)

5.D
AN APPLICATION: FITTING A DEMAND FUNCTION

The economic statistician or econometrician, starting with the historical data, sometimes attempts to "fit" a demand curve that best explains the underlying observations of prices and quantities. Any such fitted curve is more or less artificial; the econometrician can do no more than approximate the true demand function.

5.D.1 □ Constant-Slope versus Constant-Elasticity Functions

In practice, such an approximation has to be quite simple if the statistical problems are to remain manageable. The approximations most commonly employed are the linear or *constant-slope* demand curve versus the *constant-elasticity* demand curve. Figure 5.4 compares two such curves, as fitted to hypothetical price–quantity data represented by the clusters of points. While the constant-slope demand curve is a straight line on X,P_x-axes,[8] the constant-elasticity de-

---

[8] The uppercase symbol X indicates that we are now dealing with *aggregate* consumption or demand in the market.

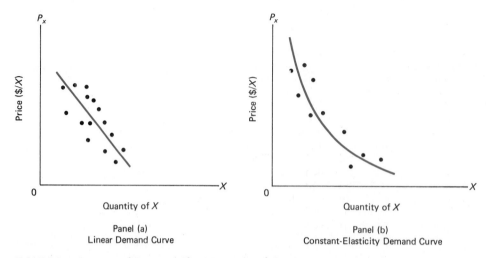

FIGURE 5.4 Linear and Constant-Elasticity Demand Curves. Simple functional forms are ordinarily assumed in attempting to estimate (to "fit") demand curves, given observed data shown as clusters of points in the diagrams. The functional forms most commonly used are linear demand as in Panel (a) and constant-elasticity demand as in Panel (b).

mand curve has a characteristic "convex" curvature: the slope changes from steep at high prices to flat at low prices. Correspondingly, along a constant-slope demand curve the elasticity must be continually changing.

Consider the straight-line demand curve DD' illustrated in Figure 5.5. First of all, from the definition of price elasticity and in particular from the relation

$$\eta_x \equiv \frac{\Delta X}{\Delta P_x} \frac{P_x}{X}$$

[corresponding to the last ratio in equations (5.3)], elasticity must be zero at the intersection D' with the horizontal axis—since at that intersection P_x is zero. Correspondingly, elasticity is infinite at the intersection D with the vertical axis where X is zero. So, evidently, elasticity rises (in absolute value) as we move upward (northwest) along a straight-line demand curve.

There are several geometrical ways of determining the numerical elasticity at any point along a linear demand curve. Perhaps the simplest is to compare (as in our earlier discussion of income elasticity and the Engel Curve) the slope *along* the curve with the slope of a ray from the origin *to* the curve. We will be using here the third algebraic relation of equations (5.3),

$$\eta_x \equiv \frac{P_x/X}{\Delta P_x/\Delta X}$$

The denominator here represents the (ordinarily negative) slope *along* the curve—the constant slope of DD' in Figure 5.5. The numerator P_x/X is the

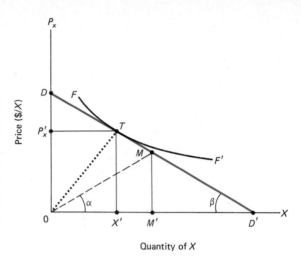

FIGURE 5.5 Graphical Measure of Elasticity.
Elasticity at a point T along a linear demand curve DD' is given numerically by the ratio of the positive slope of OT (the slope of the ray from the origin *to* the curve) to the negative slope of DD' (the slope *along* the curve). Since OT is steeper (slope is larger in absolute value) than DD', elasticity at T is greater than unity. Elasticity equals unity at the mid-point M along a linear demand curve like DD', since OMD' is an isosceles triangle (angles α and β are equal). The elasticity at a point T on the non-linear demand curve FTF' is identical, for small changes, with the elasticity at T along the tangent straight-line demand curve DD'.

(necessarily positive) slope of the ray from the origin *to* the curve—the slope of OT, if we are seeking to determine elasticity at point T. Evidently, at T the elasticity of demand is greater than unity, since OT is steeper (in absolute value terms) than DD'—the positive slope of the numerator is greater in numerical value than the negative slope of the denominator.

A direct corollary of this result is: elasticity is unitary ($\eta_x = -1$) at the *mid-point* of a linear demand curve. In Figure 5.5, at the mid-point M along DD' the positive slope of OM is equal in absolute value to the slope along DD'. That is, OMD' is an isosceles triangle, determined by the numerically equal angles α and β formed by OM and $D'M$ with the horizontal axis.

Exercise 5.5: Consider the demand curve $X = 120 - 4P_x$. What is the elasticity of demand when $P_x = 30$? When $P_x = 20$? When $P_x = 15$? When $P_x = 0$?

Answer: The reciprocal of the demand-curve slope is $\Delta x/\Delta P_x = -4$. So the elasticity is $-4/(X/P_x)$. At $P_x = 30$, $X = 0$ and the elasticity is negative infinite. At $P_x = 20$, $X = 40$ and the elasticity is -2. At $P_x = 15$, $X = 60$ and the elasticity is -1 (this is the mid-point of the demand curve). At $P_x = 0$, $X = 120$ and the elasticity is zero.

This geometrical measure of elasticity along a linear demand curve can be generalized to any demand curve whatsoever. Suppose that point T lies not on DD' but on a *non-linear* demand curve FF' in Figure 5.5. Since FF' has the same slope as DD' at point T, the denominators in the ratio

$$\eta_x \equiv \frac{P_x/X}{\Delta P_x/\Delta X}$$

are the same. And since T is on both curves the numerators P_x/X are also evidently the same. So the ratio of the slope of OT to the slope of DD' measures the point elasticity of demand at T for both DD' and FF'.

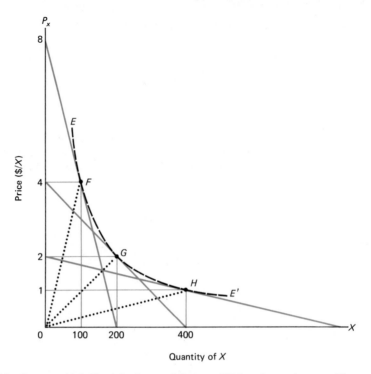

FIGURE 5.6 Constant-Unit-Elasticity Demand Curve. *EE'* is a demand curve with constant elasticity $\eta_x = -1$. Each point like *F* is the mid-point of a straight line drawn tangent to *EE'* at *F*; it is therefore the apex of an isosceles triangle with one leg along the tangent line and the other along the ray out of the origin. At all points like *F, G, H* along *EE'*, consumer expenditures $P_x X$ equal 400.

Now consider demand curves along which *elasticity* is constant. Figure 5.6 provides an example, the curve *EE'*, for which the elasticity is in fact unity throughout. Each point like *F, G,* or *H* along the curve is a mid-point of its tangent line—like point *M* in Figure 5.5. And so, everywhere along *EE'*, $\eta_x = -1$. Note also that the product of price times quantity $(P_x X)$ equals 400 for each point *F, G, H* in the diagram. This confirms the Proposition at the end of Section 5.B above, which asserted that for a demand curve of unitary elasticity the aggregate expenditures remain the same regardless of price P_x.

So a demand curve with constant elasticity equal to unity must have curvature like that of *EE'* in Figure 5.6. If the demand elasticity were constant but equal to −2 rather than −1, at any point like *F* in the diagram the ray *OF* out of the origin would have to be *twice* as steep as the line tangent to the demand curve at *F*. Such a demand curve would have a curvature generally similar to *EE'* in the diagram, but would have flatter slope throughout. And of course a demand curve with constant elasticity less than unity would be steeper than *EE'* throughout.

*5.D.2 ☐ Demand as a Function of Several Variables

A demand curve of constant slope is of course a straight line. It may be expressed in the form of a linear equation:

(5.4) $$X = A + BP_x$$

Here A and B are constants; B is normally *negative* according to the Law of Demand. When we take into account other determining variables, such as income I and the price of a related good Y, we obtain a generalized *demand function in linear form*:

(5.5) $$X = A + BP_x + CI + DP_y$$

Here A, B, C, and D are all constants. B is again normally negative. C is the slope of the Engel Curve, and is only negative when X is inferior. The sign of D would be the same as the sign of the cross-elasticity: positive if X and Y are substitutes, negative if they are complements.

A generalized demand function of this form (or, possibly, extended to take into account additional variables) could be fitted statistically to a body of data. Such a fitted function would only be expected to be a reasonable description of the true demand relation within a limited range. Indeed, pushed to extremes it must lead to logical contradictions. For example, equation (5.5) would, for some prices P_x and P_y, indicate a positive quantity X demanded even when income I is zero. This is, of course, impossible.[9]

*The section between the asterisk and the symbol ■ may contain somewhat more difficult or advanced material.

[9]But recall that our model of consumption is timeless. In a multi-period model the total of consumption expenditures in any single period *may* diverge from income of that period. The difference is accounted for by borrowing and lending between periods, or repayments of loans previously made or incurred.

EXAMPLE 5.3
Demand for Distilled Spirits

A study by T. J. Wales employed sales data for different states of the United States to estimate demand for distilled spirits.[a] It was found convenient to use a simple linear equation. Straightforward statistical regression led to the equation:

$$X_j = 0.5084 + 0.0004079I_j - 0.1771P_j$$

[a]T. J. Wales, "Distilled Spirits and Interstate Consumption Effects," *American Economic Review*, v. 58 (Sept. 1968), esp. p. 858.

Here X_j represents the number of cases of spirits per adult resident sold in state j; I_j is the disposable income per adult resident of state j; and P_j is the average liquor price, in dollars, within the state. This equation indicates that, for example, a \$1000 increase in average income leads to a consumption increase of about 0.4 case per adult resident per year. (A case consists of 12 fifths, so the increase is about 5 bottles per year.) A one-dollar increase in price leads to a decrease of around 0.18 case, or around 2 bottles per year.

But Wales suspected that the data were distorted by failure to allow for liquor sales to *non*-residents crossing state lines to take advantage of lower prices. Correcting for the estimated effect of this factor led to the revised linear equation:

$$X_{jj} = -0.4615 + 0.0004379 I_j - 0.00375 P_j$$

Here X_{jj} represents the cases sold in state j to *residents* of that state.

As may be seen, the effect of income differences remains about the same. But the effect of price is much less; demand is now highly price-inelastic. Indeed, these data suggest that the impact of price differences between states is almost entirely limited to the effect upon out-of-state purchasers.

COMMENT: The differences in prices of distilled spirits between states are mainly due to differences in liquor *taxation*. (In some states liquor is a state monopoly, in which case a high monopoly price is substantially equivalent to a high tax.) Very small sensitivity of quantity purchased to price (inelastic demand) is convenient if the purpose of the tax is simply to generate tax revenues. But if the purpose is to discourage consumption, it appears that liquor taxation is not very effective.

A demand curve of constant elasticity also has its own particular algebraic form. This form involves *logarithms*. The crucial property of logarithms for our purposes is that equal *arithmetic* steps of the logarithm represent equal *proportionate* steps of the variable. For example, as $\log_{10} X$ (the logarithm of X to the base 10) goes from 1 to 2 to 3, the variable X goes from 10 to 100 to 1000. Or, algebraically, $\Delta \log X \equiv \Delta X / X$ (for logarithms of any base).

For a demand curve of constant elasticity,

(5.6)
$$\eta_x \equiv \frac{\Delta X / X}{\Delta P_x / P_x} \equiv \frac{\Delta(\log X)}{\Delta(\log P_x)}$$

is a constant.

Equation (5.6) is equivalent to:

$$\Delta(\log X) = \eta_x \Delta(\log P_x)$$

Or, we may write this as:

(5.7)
$$\log X = \log a + b \log P_x$$

where $\log a$ is some unknown constant, and $b = \eta_x$. It is the linear equation (5.7) that would actually be fitted statistically to the observations reduced to logarithmic form.

Equation (5.7) can also be written:

$$\log X = \log (aP_x^b)$$

Taking anti-logs on both sides:

(5.8)
$$X = aP_x^b$$

This is the form of the constant-elasticity demand equation after conversion into natural units. The multiplicative constant a and the elasticity $b = \eta_x$ are the parameters estimated from the statistical data.

Generalizing (5.7), the constant-elasticity demand function (of own-price P_x, income I, and price of some other good P_y) would be expressed in logarithmic form as:

(5.9)
$$\log X = \log a + b \log P_x + c \log I + d \log P_y$$

Converting to natural units as above, this becomes:

(5.10)
$$X = aP_x^b I^c P_y^d$$

Here b is as before the price elasticity η_x, c is the income elasticity ϵ_x, and d is the cross-elasticity η_{xy}.

EXAMPLE 5.4
More on Fish

The relaxing of the fish-on-Friday rule for American Catholics led, we saw in Example 2.1 of Chapter 2 ("Catholics and Fish"), to a fall in the price of fish in New England. The same study by F. W. Bell[a] also provided estimates of a number of other parameters of the demand function for fish.

The function fitted in Bell's study was in the logarithmic form of equation (5.9), with two main differences. First, a number of determining variables other than prices and incomes were considered; among them, cold storage holdings, imports, and of course the status of the fish-on-Friday rule. We shall ignore these other variables here. Second, the equation was fitted statistically

[a]F. W. Bell, "The Pope and the Price of Fish," *American Economic Review*, v. 58 (Dec. 1968).

with the *price* of fish rather than the *quantity demanded* as the dependent variable on the left-hand side. Thus, Bell's statistically determined equation took the form:

$$\log P_i = \log \alpha + \beta \log Q_i + \gamma \log I + \delta \log P_m + \cdots$$

Here P_i is the price of fish species i (in cents per pound); Q_i is the quantity landed (in thousands of pounds); I is personal income in New England for 1957–59 (in tenths of millions of dollars); and P_m is the consumer price index for a related consumption item, meat and poultry (index based on taking the average 1957–59 price as 100). The study estimated the constants α, β, γ, and δ for each of seven fish species. A typical set of results, that for "large haddock," is: $\alpha = -0.237$, $\beta = -0.460$, $\gamma = +0.212$, and $\delta = +0.878$.

It is possible to reformulate these results in terms of the constants a, b, c, and d of equation (5.9) that relate to the desired elasticities, by rearranging the statistical equation of the study. Solving the latter for $\log Q_i$, we can write:

$$\log Q_i = -\frac{1}{\beta} \log \alpha + \frac{1}{\beta} \log P_i - \frac{\gamma}{\beta} \log I - \frac{\delta}{\beta} \log P_m$$

But equation (5.9) tells us that $\log Q_i = a + b \log P_i + c \log I + d \log P_m$. Then the desired parameters (apart from the constant term which is not needed) are $b = 1/\beta$, $c = -\gamma/\beta$, and $d = -\delta/\beta$. Remembering that the price elasticity is $b = \eta_i$, the income elasticity is $c = \epsilon_i$, and the cross-elasticity is $d = \eta_{im}$, the results imply that for large haddock:[b]

$$\eta_i = \frac{1}{\beta} = -\frac{1}{0.460} = -2.174$$

$$\epsilon_i = -\frac{\gamma}{\beta} = \frac{0.212}{0.460} = 0.461$$

$$\eta_{im} = -\frac{\delta}{\beta} = \frac{0.878}{0.460} = 1.909$$

Thus the price elasticity is in the normal negative range. The positive income elasticity indicates that large haddock is a superior good, though not very strongly superior. And the positive cross-elasticity verifies our presumption that meat and chicken on the one hand, as against fish on the other hand, are substitutes in consumption—a rise in the price of the former leads to a rise in the consumption of the latter. ■

[b]For statistical reasons that we need not explore here, these implied estimates are not *exactly* the same as would have been obtained had the equation been initially set up in the form of (5.9), with $\log Q_i$ as the dependent variable.

DETERMINANTS OF RESPONSIVENESS OF DEMAND TO PRICE

Why is it that the consumption of some commodities is highly sensitive to price, while demand for other commodities is not? Put another way, what characteristics of a commodity determine whether consumers' demand for it is highly elastic or not? Economists have discussed a number of possible explanations.

1. *Closeness of substitutes:* The contention is that demand for a commodity will be more elastic, the more numerous and the closer are the substitutes available. This argument is based upon the "substitution effect" of the price change (see Chapter 4, Section D). Panel (a) of Figure 5.7 pictures two goods that are close substitutes, like butter and margarine. Here a fall in P_x, tilting the budget line from KL to KL', leads to a relatively large change in the quantity of X demanded (x_1 is considerably greater than x_0). Panel (b) pictures two goods that are close complements, like butter and bread, and we see that at the lower price the new quantity x_1 is only a little larger than x_0.

2. *Luxuries versus necessities:* The contention here is that demand for a "luxury" will be more elastic than demand for a "necessity." (As before, a luxury is

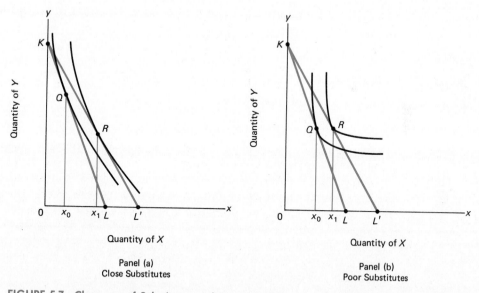

Panel (a)
Close Substitutes

Panel (b)
Poor Substitutes

FIGURE 5.7 Closeness of Substitutes and Demand Elasticity. In Panel (a) the two goods are rather close substitutes. Then a fall in P_x, with consequent shift in the budget line from KL to KL', leads to a relatively large change (from x_0 to x_1) in consumption of X. In Panel (b) the two goods are poor substitutes (strong complements), and a reduction in P_x leads to only a small change in purchase of X.

taken to be a strongly superior good, much more heavily purchased as income rises. A necessity is a good for which almost as much is consumed at low as at high incomes; or even, conceivably, more is consumed at lower incomes.) Thus the argument runs in terms of the *magnitude and direction of the "income effect"* of price change (Chapter 4, Section D). A fall in the price P_x will tend to enrich the consumer. Then if X is a strongly superior good (a luxury) the income effect will powerfully reinforce the substitution effect so as to augment the increased purchases of X. If X is only weakly superior (a necessity) there will be little reinforcement; if X is actually inferior, the income effect will tend to offset the substitution effect. So the contention is a valid inference from the income effect.

3. *Importance of the commodity:* The hypothesis here is that a commodity that is "important," that accounts for a large fraction $k_x \equiv P_x x / I$ of the consumer's budget, tends to have elastic demand. Again we are dealing with the income effect, assumed to be normal in direction (X a superior good). Then it will be evident that the real *enrichment* due to a fall in P_x will be greater, the larger is the consumer's initial expenditure $P_x x$ on commodity X. Thus, the increased purchases due to the income effect will tend to be large simply because of a large real income change as P_x falls. However, this argument is not clear-cut. There is indeed reason to expect a large *absolute* increase in purchases of X after such an enrichment. But elasticity measures *proportionate* increases of consumption. Since the amount of X being consumed may already be large, there is no reason to anticipate that the *proportionate* increase $\Delta x / x$ should be particularly great just because $k_x \equiv P_x x / I$ is large.[10] Thus, a traditional argument given for the *inelasticity* of the demand for salt—that salt accounts for only a tiny fraction of the consumer's budget—is fallacious. The true explanation is that salt is a *necessity*, and has no close substitutes.

4. *High-priced versus low-priced goods:* The contention here is that high-priced goods tend to have elastic demands, and low-priced goods inelastic demands. A "high" price can be interpreted as one for which the individual's desired quantity approaches zero, i.e., is near the vertical intercept of his demand curve.[11] As shown in Section 5.D, if the demand curve actually intercepts the vertical axis the elasticity is indeed infinite at that point. And at an intercept with the horizontal axis where P_x goes to zero, elasticity must be zero. But we also saw, in Figure 5.6, that is is perfectly possible to have a constant-elasticity demand curve, for which elasticity remains constant however closely the axes are approached. (Of course, such a demand curve cannot actually *intersect* either axis.) So the logic of the argument here is less than fully compelling.

[10]Consider the special case of an "all-important" commodity, accounting for 100% of the consumer's budget ($k = 1$). For such a commodity the price elasticity of demand is not extraordinarily large. Indeed, the elasticity must be exactly -1.

[11]A demand curve intersecting the vertical axis implies the existence of a "corner solution" at sufficiently high prices.

5.F
AN APPLICATION: GIFFEN GOOD

An interesting application of these concepts is to the Giffen case, for which the Law of Demand is violated—a lower price P_x is associated with a *smaller* quantity demanded. It follows that the elasticity η_x has reversed (positive rather than the normal negative) sign.

To have a Giffen good, the income effect must be perverse (negative) and also large enough to overcome the substitution effect, since the latter is *always* in the normal direction. Two elements tend to increase the likelihood of Giffen goods:

1. The larger the proportion of the consumer's budget accounted for by an inferior good (e.g., potatoes as the main staple of life in nineteenth-century Ireland), the weightier the perverse income effect relative to the (normal) substitution effect. If, on the other hand, a good accounts only for a small fraction of the budget, the income effect due to a change in its price will be trivial in magnitude—even if in the perverse direction.

2. The presence of a higher-quality (and dearer) substitute, such that the two are regarded as *closer equivalents at lower incomes than at higher incomes.* In the potatoes example, if the consumer is so poor as to just barely meet minimal calorie needs to stay alive, little importance is attached to the taste superiority of more expensive calorie sources—wheat bread, for example. For minimal survival, it is calorie intake that counts and the cheapest source will be purchased at a corner or near-corner solution. But under more affluent conditions potatoes and bread are not such close substitutes, and an interior solution may be obtained at which fewer potatoes are consumed.

The interaction of these conditions is illustrated in Figure 5.8. On the horizontal axis is quantity of potatoes; on the vertical axis, quantity of bread. At the original high price of potatoes represented by the steeper budget line *KL*, the consumer's nearly linear indifference curve U_1 leads him to a near-corner solution at *Q*. (Potatoes are dear, but still a cheaper source of calories than bread.) Since he is consuming practically all potatoes at *Q*, any income effect due to a change in the price of potatoes will be large. Now the price of potatoes falls, the new budget line being *KL'*. The consumer is substantially enriched. However, potatoes are inferior (as can be detected from the fact that U_2 is flatter than U_1 along any vertical line drawn in the neighborhood of the initial solution point *Q*). Thus the income effect will be both large and negative in direction. This, and the sharper curvature of U_2 (potatoes and bread are weaker substitutes at higher real incomes), constitute the forces leading to an interior solution at *R* on U_2 *northwest* of *Q*: fewer potatoes being consumed when the potato price is low than when it was high!

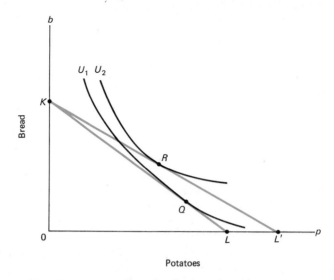

FIGURE 5.8 **Conditions for Giffen Good.** This diagram shows how potatoes might have been a Giffen good for impoverished consumers in Ireland. At the initial relatively high potato price P_p, the consumptive optimum is at Q on budget line KL. When the potato price falls, shifting the budget line to KL', the consumer is sufficiently enriched to prefer buying fewer potatoes and more wheat bread at position R. For this to occur potatoes must be strongly inferior, so that the income effect of the price change leads to reduced purchases. In order for the income effect to overcome the pure substitution effect, it is necessary to have the latter become relatively weak as the consumer is enriched. That is, the curvature of U_2 must be greater than that of U_1 (potatoes and bread are closer substitutes for poor consumers than for wealthier consumers).

5.G
MULTIPLE CONSTRAINTS

In Section 4.A the *budget line* was introduced as the upper (northeast) boundary of an individual's market opportunity set. Or, we may say, the budget line is the binding *constraint* upon the individual's choices. This constraint is due, of course, to the limited income I available for expenditure upon consumption goods.

The familiar equation of the budget line is:

(5.11)
$$P_x x + P_y y = I$$

The market opportunity set as a whole, the shaded region of Figure 5.9, is more precisely described as the area bounded by the budget line *and the coordinate axes*, the set of points satisfying the inequalities:

(5.12)
$$P_x x + P_y y \leq I$$
$$x \geq 0$$
$$y \geq 0$$

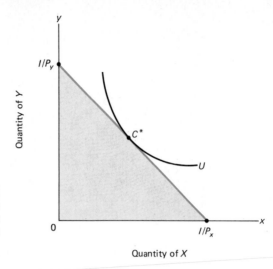

FIGURE 5.9 **Market Opportunity Set.** The normal market opportunity set is constrained only by income and non-negativity considerations. It is represented as the shaded area bounded by the budget line $P_x x + P_y y = I$ and the vertical and horizontal axes.

The latter two conditions express the physical reality that goods cannot be purchased or consumed in negative quantities.

5.G.1 ☐ Rationing

It sometimes happens, however, that the consumer faces constraints upon market decisions apart from limited income. In wartime, for example, a ration limit R_x might be placed upon consumption of commodity X. Three rationing cases of interest are shown in the three panels of Figure 5.10.

In Panel (a) the ration limit is indicated by the vertical dashed line at the quantity $x = R_x$. Here the ration is so large relative to the consumer's income as to be ineffective. In Panel (b) the ration limit R_x is *potentially* binding; it does bite into (truncate) the market opportunity set so as to reduce the size of the shaded area. However, given the individual's preferences, the ration limit is not *actually* binding; the individual does not even want to consume as much of X as the ration permits. Only in Panel (c) is the ration limit R_x actually binding; it dictates a *non-tangency* solution C^*, where, without the ration limit, the consumer would have attained the preferred tangency position T.

As an obvious implication, ration limits are less binding for poorer people, for whom spendable income already serves as a severe constraint. Note also that after imposition of a ration limit upon consumption of some commodity X, consumers' demands tend to "spill over" so that more is consumed of those commodities left unrationed.

Exercise 5.6: Suppose that an individual's preferences are represented by $MRS_C = 2y/x$, prices are $P_x = 3$ and $P_y = 1$, and income is $I = 180$. (a) What is the optimal consumption basket? (b) What happens if a ration limit $R_x = 50$ is applied to commodity X? (c) What if the ration is tightened to $R_x = 20$? (d) Returning to the original ration limit $R_x = 50$, what would happen if his income had doubled to $I = 360$?

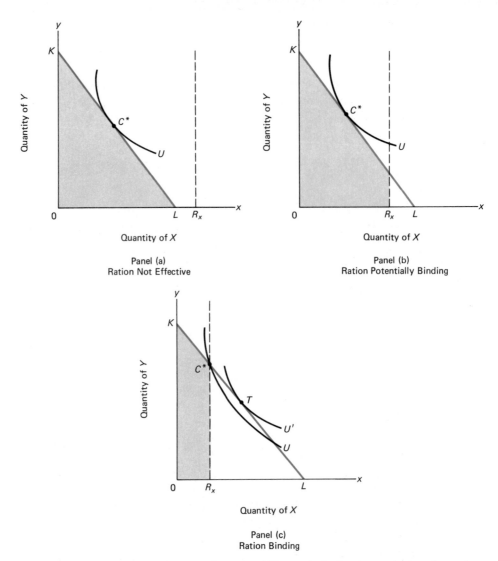

FIGURE 5.10   Rationing of One Commodity.   In addition to the budget constraint there is a ration limit R_x (vertical dashed lines) upon purchases of commodity X. In Panel (a) the ration is so large as not to constrain the consumer's choices any more than income does alone. In Panel (b) the ration truncates the market opportunity set, but the consumer's preferences are such that the limit is not actually binding. In Panel (c) the ration limit is binding; it forces a choice of less of X (and more of Y) than the consumer would have otherwise preferred.

Answer: (a) Setting $MRS_C = P_x/P_y$ as usual, we have $2y/x = P_x$ or $2y = P_xx$. Then the budget equation $P_xx + P_yy = I$ can be written $2y + y = 3y = 180$. The solution is $y = 60$, $x = 40$. (b) If $R_x = 50$ the X-ration is *potentially* binding (since the individual might have purchased as many as $I/P_x = 180/3 = 60$ units of X. But, since he preferred to buy only $x = 40$, the ration is not actually binding and his optimum is unchanged. (c) If $R_x = 20$ the ration limit is binding: he will obviously want to purchase his full allowed ration, so $x = 20$. With his remaining income $I - P_xx = 180 - 60$ he will buy $120/P_y = 120$ units of

PART 2   PREFERENCE, CONSUMPTION, AND DEMAND

commodity Y. (d) It is easy to verify that his unconstrained optimum would become $y = 120$, $x = 80$. Then the ration limit $R_x = 50$ would be binding, and he would have to choose $x = 50$, $y = 210$.

What if commodities X and Y were *both* rationed? In Figure 5.11 we see only the more interesting situations where both of the ration limits R_x and R_y are at

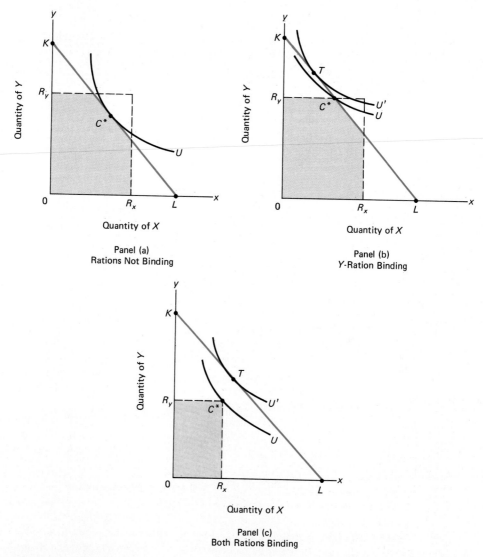

FIGURE 5.11   Physical Rationing of Two Commodities: Potentially Binding Cases.   Commodities X and Y are both subject to ration limits, R_x and R_y (vertical and horizontal dashed lines). In Panel (a) neither ration limit is binding. In Panel (b) R_y is binding, forcing the consumer to choose less of Y (and more of X) than would otherwise be the case. In Panel (c) both ration limits are binding, and the income constraint on consumption is ineffective.

least *potentially* binding, i.e., where the market opportunity set is truncated at both ends. Panel (a) shows that even when both ration limits are potentially binding, neither may *actually* be effective at the consumptive optimum position C^*. In Panel (b), only the ration limit R_y for commodity Y is actually binding; it forces the individual to a position C^* inferior to the tangency optimum T that would otherwise be chosen. (There would of course be an opposite case, not diagrammed here, in which only the ration limit R_x is binding.) In Panel (c), we see the interesting case in which *both* ration limits are actually effective. Here it is the budget constraint that is not binding. This would correspond to the situation of a rich person, well endowed with income, but unable to legally spend it all in a situation where all desired commodities are subject to severe rationing.

Let us interpret these possibilities in terms of opportunity sets. The *market* opportunity set, for which income I is the effective constraint, is the familiar triangular area bounded by the budget line and the axes in the diagrams of Figure 5.11. The *ration* opportunity set, where fixed quantitative limits on both commodities are imposed, takes the form of a rectangle. The lower bounds of the rectangle are the axes, and the upper bounds are the dashed lines $x = R_x$ and $y = R_y$. The *effective* opportunity set, shown as the shaded area in all three situations, is the intersection of the market opportunity set and the ration opportunity set; i.e., it is the collection of all points that satisfy *both* constraints. Formally, the shaded areas are determined by the inequalities:

$$(5.13) \qquad \begin{cases} P_x x + P_y y \leqq I \\ 0 \leqq x \leqq R_x \\ 0 \leqq y \leqq R_y \end{cases}$$

The objective of rationing, usually imposed under conditions of special scarcity as in wartime, is ordinarily to assure that people with modest incomes may still be able to purchase at least minimal quantities of essential goods.[12] Figure 5.11 indicates that this objective tends to be achieved. In Panel (a), representing the situation of a relatively poor person, it is only income that constrains consumption. But in Panel (c), representing the situation of a richer individual, the ration limits do force consumption of less than this person would otherwise have purchased—leaving more of goods X and Y available to others.

Nevertheless, simple quantity rationing is a relatively crude device. Suppose that tea and coffee were both rationed. Then consumers whose tastes tolerated both tea and coffee would have an advantage over those strongly preferring one over the other. Someone for whom tea was totally unpalatable, for example, would find a tea ration useless. (If sale of ration coupons is prohibited.) As a way around this objection, in the later years of World War II a number of countries introduced more sophisticated rationing systems. Instead of absolute quantity limits like R_x and R_y on specific commodities, a consumer was granted a certain amount of "point income" N that could be spent very much like ordinary income.

---

[12]This of course may not be the only purpose of rationing. In Nazi Germany, for example, smaller rations were assigned to Jews than to Aryans. Similarly, during the "war communism" period 1917–21 in revolutionary Russia, members of the former upper and middle classes were given smaller rations than individuals of proletarian origin.

Rationed commodities were then assigned "point prices" p_x and p_y in addition to money prices P_x and P_y.

Under a point rationing system, the three main possibilities for an individual's effective opportunity set are illustrated in Figure 5.12. In Panel (a)

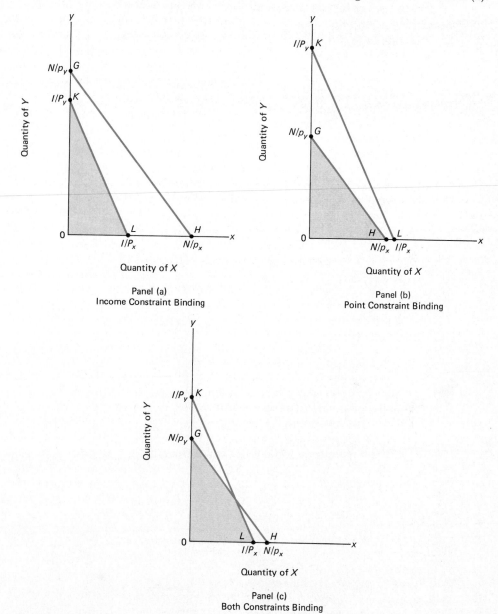

Panel (a)
Income Constraint Binding

Panel (b)
Point Constraint Binding

Panel (c)
Both Constraints Binding

FIGURE 5.12 Point Rationing. Consumption is shown as subject to an income constraint I and also a point constraint N. Commodity X is assumed to be more expensive in terms of income, and commodity Y in terms of points, so the income budget line KL is steeper than the point budget line GH. In Panel (a) "point income" is so large that only money income is binding; Panel (b) represents the opposite case. In Panel (c) each constraint is binding over a certain range.

"point income" is so large relative to ordinary income that only the latter constrains consumption. This might be the situation of a poor person. Panel (b) represents the opposite case, a rich person for whom ordinary income is so ample that only points constrain consumption. And finally, Panel (c) pictures a situation where over a certain range ordinary income is binding, but elsewhere point income is binding.

Formally, the opportunity set under point rationing is determined by the inequalities:

(5.14)
$$\begin{cases} P_x x + P_y y \leq I \\ p_x x + p_y y \leq N \\ x \geq 0, \quad y \geq 0 \end{cases}$$

In the cases illustrated in Figure 5.12, the income budget line KL is steeper than the point budget line GH. That is, $P_x/P_y > p_x/p_y$. Commodity X is therefore comparatively more expensive in terms of ordinary income, and commodity Y in terms of points. It follows that consumers extremely desirous of purchasing commodity X would tend to find the income constraint binding; those more interested in Y would tend to find the point constraint binding.

EXAMPLE 5.5
Wartime Point Rationing

Among the commodities rationed by points during World War II in the United States were cheese and canned fish. The Table compares the 1942 (pre-rationing) purchases of different income groups with the quantities purchased during 1944 when rationing was effective.

Average Weekly Purchases (lbs) by Housekeeping Families in Cities

INCOME:	$1000 OR LESS	$1000– 2000	$2000– 3000	$3000– 4000	OVER $4000
1942					
Cheese	0.26	0.57	0.64	0.81	1.03
Canned fish	0.21	0.36	0.56	0.44	0.37
1944					
Cheese	0.24	0.33	0.44	0.49	0.52
Canned fish	0.06	0.12	0.17	0.22	0.18

Source: L. A. Epstein, "Wartime Food Purchases," Monthly Labor Review, v. 60 (June 1945), pp. 1148, 1150.

This Table illustrates the overall binding power of income versus points as constraints. Looking only at the three highest income groups (last three columns), we see that their consumption patterns in 1944 were almost identical. Hence it appears that consumers in this income range were in the situation pictured in Panel (b) of Figure 5.12—consumption of cheese and canned fish was almost entirely limited by points rather than by income. An important fact about this period is that the dollar price of canned fish relative to cheese approximately doubled between 1942 and 1944. The Table indicates that the fish/cheese consumption ratio for the lowest income group consequently fell from 0.21/0.26 = 0.808 in 1942 to 0.06/0.24 = 0.25 in 1944, showing strong sensitivity to the price change (fish and cheese were evidently close substitutes). But for the highest income group the 1942 fish/cheese consumption ratio (0.37/1.03 = 0.359) remained almost unchanged (0.18/0.52 = 0.346) in 1944, since under rationing the dollar prices were simply not binding for them.

*5.G.2 ☐ Time as a Constraint

Time as well as *income* constrains consumption. Most consumption activities—playing a round of golf, watching a movie, eating a meal—require significant time inputs as well as cash. In fact, as society becomes more affluent the importance of the time constraint will grow. We will become increasingly wealthy, but increasingly harried for time to do all the things we can financially afford.

If time and income were inconvertible there would be a dual dollar-hour constraint situation like the dollar-point constraint situation pictured in Figure 5.12. Let t_x and t_y be the time inputs (assumed constant for simplicity) per unit consumed of goods X and Y, respectively. The consumer's effective opportunity set would then have to satisfy not only the income constraint $P_x x + P_y y = I$ but also a time constraint $t_x x + t_y y = T_c$, where T_c is the total time devoted to consumption activities.

But time and income are not inconvertible. Someone who engages in income-earning activities outside the home is reducing his or her consumption time T_c but raising consumable income I. The same can be said of household activities like home repairs that reduce the need to earn outside income. Since time can be sold to obtain income, the two are convertible into a single constraint upon consumption.[13] Let us suppose that the individual could work any number of hours at a given wage w.[14] Then, in effect, the total "time endowment" T is worth wT in income units. If the person has in addition an ordinary income endowment of I_0, the overall constraint upon consumption choices is given by:

(5.15) $$(P_x + wt_x)x + (P_y + wt_y)y \leqq I_0 + wT$$

---

*The section between the asterisk and the symbol ■ may contain somewhat more difficult or advanced material.

[13]In contrast, the sale of "points" for cash was definitely illegal under wartime rationing systems. For law-abiding persons, there was no convertibility.

[14]This is of course a simplification. Shifting an additional hour from consumption to work might actually yield more than the normal wage w (if, for example, overtime work at time-and-a-half is available). Alternatively, the individual might only be able to earn a lower rate of pay for additional hours because of fatigue, or because of the need to take a less desirable second "moonlighting" job. The optimum balance between time and income will be considered further when we analyze the labor-supply decision in Part Five.

The *effective price* π_x for commodity X is not the money price P_x alone but the expression $P_x + wt_x$, the money price plus the income value of the required time input. And similarly, of course, for commodity Y the effective price is $\pi_y = P_x + wt_y$.

For some purposes it is of interest to distinguish elasticity of demand with respect to the cash component of effective price, $\eta_{x \cdot P}$, from the elasticity with respect to the time component $\eta_{x \cdot wt}$. The definitions are:

$$(5.16) \qquad \eta_{x \cdot P} \equiv \frac{\Delta x/x}{\Delta P_x/P_x}$$

$$(5.17) \qquad \eta_{x \cdot wt} \equiv \frac{\Delta x/x}{\Delta wt/wt}$$

Since the wage w is assumed constant, (5.17) can be rewritten:

$$(5.17') \qquad \eta_{x \cdot wt} = \frac{\Delta x}{w \Delta t} \frac{wt}{x} = \frac{\Delta x}{\Delta t} \frac{t}{x} = \eta_{x \cdot t}$$

Thus, the wage w cancels out, and we can speak in terms of the "elasticity of demand with respect to time input."

EXAMPLE 5.6
Time-Prices of Medical Care

Jan Acton studied a number of factors determining the demand for medical care on the part of residents of two neighborhoods in Brooklyn, New York—Red Hook and Bedford-Crown. He explicitly distinguished the time input from money price. For medical services, residents of these neighborhoods made substantial use of both (1) free municipal clinics and out-patient departments, and (2) private physicians for pay. Data were obtained on the number of visits to both sources of medical care. For the private sources, both a cash payment and a time input were involved. For the free sources, *only* the time input could play a role. (The time input involves both travel time and average waiting time for service; the data in the Table below refer to travel time only, however.)

The results for the two neighborhoods are very similar. For both free and paid (private) medical care, the elasticity with respect to the time-price (travel time to the source) was negative. For Red Hook the time-elasticity for free sources was −0.958; this means that a 1% rise in travel time to free sources was associated with slightly less than a 1% fall in number of visits. The absolute value of this elasticity was much lower for private care, however; for Red Hook, −0.252 as compared with −0.958. For free sources, the time input is the sole element of effective price. Hence *all* the elasticity of effective price must show up in the time-elasticity. For private sources of medical care, the

Travel-Time Elasticities for Ambulatory Care

	RED HOOK		BEDFORD-CROWN	
	Travel Time to FSMC	Travel Time to PPO	Travel Time to FSMC	Travel Time to PPO
Visits to free sources of medical care (FSMC)	− 0.958	+ 0.332	− 0.619	+ 0.137
Visits to private physicians' offices (PPO)	+ 0.640	− 0.252	+ 0.629	− 0.337

Source: Jan P. Acton, *Demand for Health Care among the Urban Poor, with Special Emphasis on the Role of Time,* The New York City Rand Institute Report R-1151-OEO-NYC (April 1973), p. 27.

elasticity with respect to *effective* price will be divided between time-elasticity and elasticity with respect to cash price.

The positive coefficients in the Table represent cross-elasticities: the effect on usage of one source of medical care associated with increases in travel time to the other source. The positive cross-elasticities show that the two types of medical services are substitutes, as of course would be expected. ∎

5.H
THE "NEW THEORY OF CONSUMPTION"

In recent years a novel and somewhat richer theory of consumption has been developed by economists. The key idea is a distinction between *market goods* and utility-relevant qualities or *attributes*. In this new approach a market commodity like bread is no longer supposed to be desired in and of itself, but only insofar as it is capable of yielding satisfaction through its attributes: tastiness, calories, proteins, and so on. Similarly an automobile is desired only insofar as it can be the source of transportation, comfort, prestige, and the like. One interesting aspect of this approach is a recognition that often, if not always, the market commodity does not generate its satisfying attributes unaided. Rather, the consumer generally obtains satisfaction from commodities by combining his own time and effort with the market goods themselves. Utility can thus be regarded as generated by activities subject both to *income constraints* (upon the purchase of market goods) and *time constraints* (upon the hours to be allocated for their enjoyment), as discussed in the preceding section.

Here are two interesting implications:

1. Why some market goods are close substitutes, and others are not, becomes much easier to understand in this approach. Bread and potatoes (substitutes) have generally similar attributes; bread and haircuts do not. Substitutability thus, to a considerable extent, becomes an analyzable rather than a merely arbitrary fact.

2. The process whereby market commodities are combined with consumers' time and efforts can be regarded as *production within the household*, analogous to the ordinary

productive process within business firms. Indeed, production within the home often competes directly with outside production, as in home washing versus commercial laundries. It is an interesting empirical question how much of the historical advance in standards of living is due to improved methods of business production such as interchangeability of parts, more powerful energy sources, newer and better-yielding crops, and how much is due to improvements mainly in the consumption sphere such as electric light, home appliances, and new fabrics for clothing.

*5.1
INDEX NUMBERS

Suppose we want to know, in comparing two situations, whether consumers are better off in the one or the other. If the commodities involved are goods so that "more is preferred to less," this question can be reformulated as: In which situation does the individual get, on the average, a larger quantity of goods to consume? The average measure designed to answer such a question is called an *index number of quantity*. A closely related question is: In which situation does the consumer, on the average, have to pay a higher price for the goods he consumes? An average measure constructed to answer this question is called an *index number of price*.

Practical applications of index numbers of prices or quantities are almost always associated with problems involving monetary inflation or deflation, i.e., overall swings in the prices of goods measured in money terms. For example, a worker may want to know if his rising money income in an inflationary period has kept up with the rising money prices of the commodities in his consumption basket. Therefore, "income" here is to be understood as accruing to the consumer in the form of a money sum per period (symbolized as I^m). And similarly, prices are to be understood as quoted in money units.[15]

5.1.1 ☐ Index Numbers of Quantity

Consider Panel (a) of Figure 5.13. Here a person's levels of satisfaction or "standards of living" in two different time periods (period 0 and period 1) are to be compared by an observer who does *not* have knowledge of the subject's preference map. What the observer knows is that the consumer makes rational choices. He can thus infer that, in the "base year" (period 0), the consumer was at an optimum combination Q_0 (the corresponding quantities being q_x^0 and q_y^0 of commodities X and Y respectively). This optimum depends, of course, upon base-year income I_0^m and the prices P_x^0 and P_y^0 which enter into the determination of the period-0 market opportunity set and budget line K_0L_0. In the "given year" (period 1) these three determining variables will in general change to new levels I_1^m, P_x^1, and P_y^1, determining a new budget line K_1L_1 and optimum solution Q_1 (with corresponding quantities q_x^1 and q_y^1).

---

*The section between the asterisk and the symbol ∎ may contain somewhat more difficult or advanced material.

[15] An explicit rationale for the existence of money will be provided in Chapter 13.

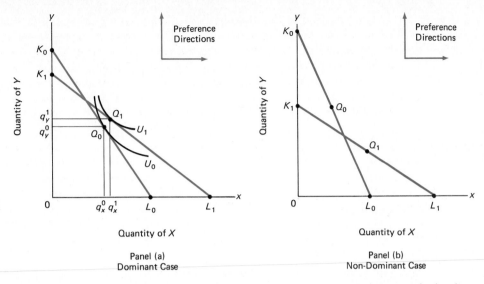

FIGURE 5.13 Standard of Living Comparisons. Here K_0L_0 represents the base-year budget line, and K_1L_1 the given-year budget line. In Panel (a) an observer, without knowing the consumer's preferences except that X and Y are both goods, would realize that the standard of living has been improved—since the consumer at Q_1 purchases more of both goods than at Q_0 (Dominant Case). In the Non-dominant Case of Panel (b), however, preference maps might be constructed for which Q_1 is preferred to Q_0 or vice versa.

Suppose prices and money income had so changed that the individual's new (given-year) budget line has greater intercepts on both the X- and Y-axes than the old (base-year) budget line. Unlike the picture in Figure 5.13, in such a case the budget line will have shifted completely outward from the origin (not necessarily strictly parallel to its initial position); the market opportunity set will have been enlarged in both the X- and the Y-directions. Since the consumer in period 1 could therefore surely do better than any position attainable along the budget line for the base year, the observer knows that the consumer must be better off in period 1. Similarly, if the budget line were entirely displaced inward, the consumer would surely be worse off. The difficult case is when income and prices change in such a way that one intercept of the budget line increases while the other decreases. In Figure 5.13, for example, in period 1 the opportunities are greater in the X-direction but poorer in the Y-direction. In other words, the new and the old budget lines intersect.

It is nevertheless possible in some cases to detect immediately an un-ambiguous improvement or an unambiguous worsening in standard of living. Since X and Y are both goods, the preference directions are north and east. Hence the situation of Panel (a) of Figure 5.13, with the new optimum at Q_1 lying northeast of the old one at Q_0, represents an unambiguous improvement. We say here that the attained consumption basket Q_1 *dominates* Q_0. Correspondingly, if Q_1 were southwest of Q_0 the new position Q_1 would be *dominated by* the old Q_0, so that an unambiguous reduction in standard of living must have occurred.

In the situation of Panel (b) of Figure 5.13, on the other hand, there is no dominance. With Q_1 lying southeast of Q_0 it would be possible to construct preference maps in which the combination Q_0 is preferred to Q_1, but equally possible to construct maps for which Q_1 is preferred to Q_0. The same would apply if Q_1 were northwest of Q_0. Since the indifference maps are not known to outside observers, no obvious conclusion could be drawn merely observing Q_0 and Q_1.

However, there is one other consideration that can be brought to bear. Consider now the situation in Panel (a) of Figure 5.14. Here Q_1 lies southeast of Q_0, so this might seem to be a doubtful case. But without knowledge of the preference map the observer can still see that *in period 0 the position Q_1 was attainable*; Q_1 lies within the shaded market opportunity set bounded by the axes and the budget line K_0L_0 that was effective at time 0. Since the basket Q_1 was attainable in period 0 but was *not* purchased and Q_0 was purchased instead, Q_0 must have been preferred to Q_1. On the assumption that preferences have not changed, the observer can infer that the standard of living must have declined between the base year and the given year as a result of the price and income changes. And he can know this even if the indifference map in the diagram were hidden from him.

Panel (b) of Figure 5.14 shows the opposite case. Since Q_1 lies northwest of Q_0, the *dominance* test in terms of preference directions does not lead to a clear conclusion. But in the given year the shaded market opportunity set, bounded by the axes and the budget line K_1L_1, includes the position Q_0. That is, in period

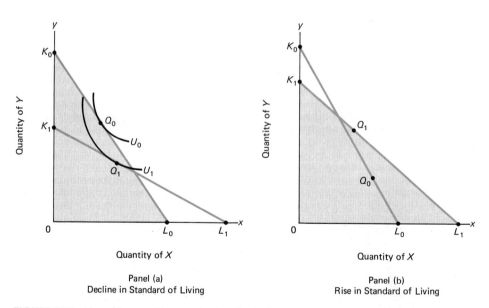

Panel (a)
Decline in Standard of Living

Panel (b)
Rise in Standard of Living

FIGURE 5.14 Unambiguous Changes in Standard of Living. Here the consumption basket Q_1 does not dominate (contain more of both goods than) Q_0, nor does Q_0 dominate Q_1. Nevertheless, in Panel (a) an observer could detect that Q_0 is preferred to Q_1 even without knowing the preference function. Since Q_1 lies within the K_0L_0 budget line it *could* have been purchased in period 0, but was not. Hence Q_0 must have been preferable. In Panel (b) we see that Q_0 lies within the K_1L_1 budget line and so could have been purchased in period 1, but was not. So here Q_1 must be preferable.

1 the combination Q_0 is attainable but is *not* being purchased. Hence Q_1 is surely preferred to Q_0, and there has been an improvement in the standard of living.

Looking back at Panel (b) of Figure 5.13, we see that the situation pictured there is not consistent with the diagrams in either Panel of Figure 5.14. This shows that in some cases we simply cannot tell, without knowing the preference function, whether the consumer is better off in period 0 or in period 1.

Let us now consider constructing an algebraic measure or index that will signify when the basket Q_1 (the consumption combination q_x^1, q_y^1) is on the average greater than—and so, in utility terms is preferred to—the basket Q_0 (the combination q_x^0, q_y^0). There are two standard ways of constructing these averages or indexes: the Laspeyres index ($\mathscr{L}$) using "base-year price weights" and the Paasche index ($\mathscr{P}$) using "given-year price weights."

The Laspeyres index of quantity is defined, where the "sigma" notation for summation provides a helpful shorthand for extending the two-good geometrical discussion to any number of commodities, as:

$$(5.18) \qquad \mathscr{L}_Q \equiv \frac{P_x^0 q_x^1 + P_y^0 q_y^1}{P_x^0 q_x^0 + P_y^0 q_y^0} \equiv \frac{\Sigma\, P^0 q^1}{\Sigma\, P^0 q^0}$$

The Laspeyres index provides an estimate as to whether quantities have increased "on the average" between period 0 and period 1, where, to make the quantity comparison a meaningful one, the same weights (in this case the base-year price weights P_x^0 and P_y^0) are used in calculating the average.

The Paasche index of quantity differs from the Laspeyres only in using given-year price weights instead:

$$(5.19) \qquad \mathscr{P}_Q \equiv \frac{P_x^1 q_x^1 + P_y^1 q_y^1}{P_x^1 q_x^0 + P_y^1 q_y^0} \equiv \frac{\Sigma\, P^1 q^1}{\Sigma\, P^1 q^0}$$

In Figure 5.15, Panel (a) represents the same situation as in Panel (a) of Figure 5.14. The indifference curves and shading have been suppressed; instead, an artificial budget line represented by the dashed line CC' parallel to the base-year budget line $K_0 L_0$ has been passed through the given-year quantity solution Q_1. The total expenditure (the income I_0^m) represented by the original solution Q_0 at the base-year prices can be written as $I_0^m = P_x^0 q_x^0 + P_y^0 q_y^0$ or $I_0^m = \Sigma\, P^0 q^0$. The new line CC' applies to the *quantities* associated with the given-year solution Q_1, but its slope represents the *base-year* prices. Hence the consumption expenditures associated with CC' can be written in summation notation as $\Sigma\, P^0 q^1$. In the situation pictured here, at the P^0 prices the basket Q_0 represents a higher expenditure level than Q_1. Hence, in Panel (a) of Figure 5.15:

$$\Sigma\, P^0 q^0 > \Sigma\, P^0 q^1 \qquad \text{or} \qquad \mathscr{L}_Q \equiv \frac{\Sigma\, P^0 q^1}{\Sigma\, P^0 q^0} < 1$$

The conclusion is that when the Laspeyres quantity index is *less* than unity, the consumer has surely become worse off in the given year. With the opportunity to buy Q_1 in place of Q_0 in period 0, the consumer chose *not* to do so. And

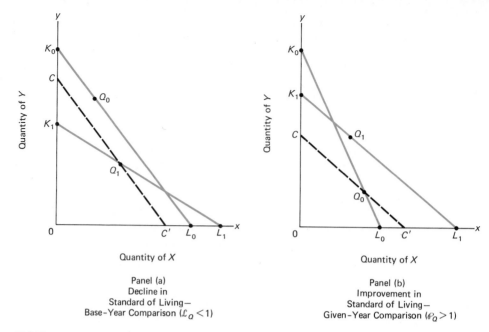

Panel (a)
Decline in
Standard of Living—
Base-Year Comparison ($\mathcal{L}_Q < 1$)

Panel (b)
Improvement in
Standard of Living—
Given-Year Comparison ($\mathcal{P}_Q > 1$)

FIGURE 5.15 Unambiguous Changes in Standard of Living: Quantity Indexes. Panel (a) represents the same situation as Panel (a) in Figure 5.14. The artificial budget line CC' has the same slope (represents the same price ratio) as K_0L_0, but is passed through the given-year consumption basket Q_1. CC' corresponds to an expenditure or income ΣP^0q^1 while K_0L_0 corresponds to ΣP^0q^0. Since CC' lies entirely within K_0L_0, the income level represented by the former is effectively lower when evaluated at the prices P^0. Any point like Q_1 along CC' must therefore be less desired than Q_0. So Q_0 must be preferred to Q_1 if the Laspeyres condition $\mathcal{L}_Q < 1$ holds. By a similar argument, the comparison in terms of given-year prices P^1 in Panel (b) shows a situation in which Q_1 must be preferred to Q_0. This is represented algebraically by the Paasche condition $\mathcal{P}_Q > 1$.

therefore, when actually observed to purchase Q_1 in period 1, he or she must have become worse off than at Q_0 in the previous period.

By a corresponding argument, Panel (b) of Figure 5.15 represents the situation where:

$$\Sigma P^1q^0 < \Sigma P^1q^1 \qquad \text{or} \qquad \mathcal{P}_Q \equiv \frac{\Sigma P^1q^1}{\Sigma P^1q^0} > 1$$

The conclusion is that when the Paasche quantity index is *greater* than unity, the consumer has surely become better off in the given year—having in the given year the opportunity of buying Q_0 in place of Q_1, and choosing not to do so.

These conclusions are in each case *sufficient* to determine the direction of improvement, but not *necessary*. If the Laspeyres quantity index is less than unity, the observer knows that the consumer must have become worse off in the given year. But the consumer *can* be worse off without this condition holding. In Figure 5.13, Panel (b), it is not the case that $\mathcal{L}_Q < 1$. Nevertheless, it would be possible to construct an indifference map for that diagram such that Q_1 is inferior to Q_0.

Similarly, if the Paasche quantity index is greater than unity the consumer must be better off in period 1—but *can* be better off without this condition holding. Again, it would be possible to show this by constructing a suitable indifference map in Panel (b) of Figure 5.13.

5.1.2 ☐ Index Numbers of Price

We now turn to index numbers of *prices*. Laspeyres and Paasche indexes of prices may be defined algebraically in the same way as for quantities. But here, as it is the prices which are being averaged, the quantities serve as weights. The definitions are:

(5.20)
$$\mathscr{L}_P \equiv \frac{\Sigma P^1 q^0}{\Sigma P^0 q^0}$$

(5.21)
$$\mathscr{P}_P \equiv \frac{\Sigma P^1 q^1}{\Sigma P^0 q^1}$$

It is useful also to define an index of money-income change as:

(5.22)
$$\mathscr{E} \equiv \frac{\Sigma P^1 q^1}{\Sigma P^0 q^0} \equiv \frac{I_1^m}{I_0^m}$$

This is of course simply the ratio of total expenditures in the two periods.

It is intuitively clear that there must be a close connection between the quantity and the price indexes. This connection turns out to involve the index of income change $\mathscr{E}$ as well.

We know from the discussion above that the consumer is surely better off in the given year if $\Sigma P^1 q^0 < \Sigma P^1 q^1$ so that the Paasche quantity index is greater than one. Dividing both sides of the inequality by $\Sigma P^0 q^0$, we have:

$$\frac{\Sigma P^1 q^1}{\Sigma P^0 q^0} > \frac{\Sigma P^1 q^0}{\Sigma P^0 q^0} \qquad \text{or} \qquad \mathscr{E} > \mathscr{L}_P$$

Thus, if the income index $\mathscr{E}$ exceeds the Laspeyres index of prices, the consumer is in an improved situation in the given year as compared to the base year. This result is implied by a Paasche index of quantity exceeding unity.

Correspondingly, of course, the consumer is worse off in the given year when the index of income $\mathscr{E}$ is less than the Paasche index of prices, or $\mathscr{E} < \mathscr{P}_P$. This is equivalent to a Laspeyres index of quantity $\mathscr{L}_Q$ that is less than unity.

The economic interpretation of the relation between the income and price indexes is quite direct. If, for example, income has risen more than in proportion to prices, on the average, then the average quantity consumed must have increased. If income has risen less than in proportion to prices, on the average, the average quantity consumed (real income) must have decreased.

CONCLUSION: If the Paasche quantity index $\mathcal{P}_Q$ is greater than unity, the consumer is surely better off in the given year. And then the income index $\mathcal{E}$ exceeds the Laspeyres price index $\mathcal{L}_P$. If the Laspeyres quantity index $\mathcal{L}_Q$ is less than unity, the consumer is surely worse off in the given year. And then the income index $\mathcal{E}$ is less than the Paasche price index $\mathcal{P}_P$.

Exploration of the theoretical niceties of Laspeyres versus Paasche indexes is helpful in forcing students to deepen their understanding of the interrelations among price and income changes. In practice, however, the really important issues do not concern these niceties. The Laspeyres and Paasche indexes will not differ very much, unless indeed an attempt is being made to compare situations so different or so far apart in time or space as to invalidate the *assumption of constant preferences* that underlies the entire analysis. In terms of common sense, the main message to be drawn is that a person whose money-income index has risen, but less than in proportion to the index of money prices (Laspeyres or Paasche makes little difference), is *not* really better off. For such a person, *real* income (index of quantity consumed) has fallen rather than risen.

But a further warning is also very much in order. Money income may have risen more than in proportion to some official price index, and even so the consumers can really be worse off! For, by accident or design, a host of devices may mask losses in real income during an inflationary period. Most, though not all, of these sources of distortion are connected with the imposition of price controls that prevent legally quoted prices from rising to a higher equilibrium level (see the discussion in Chapter 2). As a result there may be disguised price rises, not registered in the official price indexes, in such forms as: (1) Open or hidden degradation of quality (including range of varieties offered); (2) elimination of customary discounts or special sales, etc.; (3) provision of some portion of goods through illegal black-market or unofficial channels at unreported high prices; (4) forcing consumers to less-preferred combinations, at existing money prices, by such devices as coupon rationing, queue rationing, or simple unavailability of desired goods; (5) fiscal subsidies to those particular commodities appearing in the officially quoted index. (This last is akin to lowering the recorded temperature in a room by pressing an ice cube against the thermometer.)

EXAMPLE 5.7
Cost of Living in Wartime Britain

During World War II the government of Great Britain, like most of the other nations on both sides of that conflict, engaged in inflationary war finance and yet used price ceilings to hold down the prices of consumer goods. Superficially, the latter policy seems to have been successful. The official Ministry of Labor index (based on 1938 prices = 100) of the cost of living for a working-class family rose only from 127 in 1941 to 130 in 1945.

A closer look casts some doubt on this performance, however. To hold the official index down the British government subsidized just those goods whose prices were counted in the statistical averaging process. This led to a divergence between the index as calculated and what it was supposed to measure: the actual cost of maintaining the pre-war standard of living. Estimates based upon an alternative index were reported by Dudley Seers. Some of his data are summarized in the Table here.

Cost of Living Indexes

	1940	1945
Official (working class)	127	130
Alternative (working class)	130.5	149
Alternative (lower middle class)	133	154
Alternative (upper middle class)	139	170

Source: Dudley Seers, "The Cost of Living 1938–48," *Oxford Institute of Statistics Bulletin*, v. 11 (May 1949), pp. 129, 131.

As can be seen, prices rose much faster than indicated by the official index. And yet the results suggest a considerable degree of success, at least for the working class, since even the alternative index shows an increase of only about 14% for them over the four years. (The working class did relatively better, since the goods entering into the official index and therefore chosen for subsidy were predominantly those commodities entering into the consumption baskets of less affluent families.) However, this conclusion must itself be treated with reserve, since even the alternative index fails to allow for the effects of rationing, the necessity to wait in line for goods, or unavailability. As shown in the discussion of multiple constraints (Section 5.G above), such limitations on consumption tend to force individuals onto lower indifference curves representing reduced real standards of living—without showing up in any cost of living index based upon averages of price movements. ∎

*5.J
THE INCOME-COMPENSATED DEMAND CURVE

In Chapter 4 we saw that the consequences of a reduction in price P_x could be separated into an *income effect* and a pure *substitution effect*. Figure 4.17 pictured the outward tilting of the budget line (from KL to KL') as P_x falls—I and P_y still held constant—and the consequent "Hicks decomposition" of the overall effect of the price change. In this decomposition, the pure substitution effect was obtained by holding real income constant in a particular way: by hypothetically

*The section between the asterisk and the symbol ∎ may contain somewhat more difficult or advanced material.

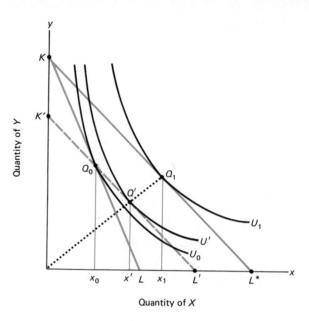

FIGURE 5.16 Income and Substitution Effects: Slutsky Decomposition. The overall effect of the price change, the shift from Q_0 to Q_1, is decomposed by drawing an artificial budget line $K'L'$ parallel to the new budget line $KL*$ but through the old optimum point Q_0. Real income is held constant between points Q_0 and Q' in the sense of the Paasche index of quantity (ability to purchase the old consumption basket at the new prices). The Slutsky pure substitution effect of the price change, in terms of purchases of X, is the distance $x'-x_0$; the income effect is the distance x_1-x'.

requiring the consumer to choose a new preferred basket along his initial indifference curve after P_x changes.

Here, however, we want to consider a different decomposition, associated with the Russian economist Slutsky.[16] In Figure 5.16 the overall effect of the price change is again represented by a shift of the optimum from Q_0 to Q_1 as the budget line tilts from KL to $KL*$ in response to a fall in P_x. But here the artificial budget line $K'L'$ parallel to the new budget line $KL*$ is drawn through the old optimum point Q_0—rather than being made tangent to the old indifference curve U_0. Thus, KL and $K'L'$ both allow the consumer to purchase the original consumption basket Q_0.

What is the advantage of the Slutsky over the Hicks decomposition of income versus substitution effects? For one thing, it permits a simple *measure* of the change in real income. For Hicks, the improvement in real income represents only attaining a higher level of utility, a magnitude that is not cardinally measurable. For Slutsky, the real-income change can be measured by the ratio of the expenditures associated with the given-year budget line $KL*$ (along which the observed Q_1 position falls) to the expenditures associated with the artificial budget line $K'L'$ (along which the observed Q_0 position falls). What is this ratio? It is nothing but the *Paasche index of quantity* defined above in equation (5.19):

$$\mathcal{P}_Q \equiv \frac{P_x^1 q_x^1 + P_y^1 q_y^1}{P_x^1 q_x^0 + P_y^1 q_y^0}$$

The comparison is of the given-year quantities (consumption combination Q_1)

[16]Eugen Slutsky, 1880–1948.

versus the base-year quantities (consumption combination Q_0), averaged in terms of the given-year price weights.

While the Paasche quantity index thus provides us with a measure of the real-income change, we do not yet have a way of separating the *real-income effect* from the *substitution effect* on the basis of the historical observations. Ideally, we would like to know the location of the hypothetical tangency optimum Q' in Figure 5.16 along the artificial budget line $K'L'$. Combination Q' would be the Slutsky analog to the artificial tangency optimum $\hat{Q}$ for the Hicks decomposition illustrated in Figure 4.17. Since the Slutsky Q' position is unknowable to an observer (as is the Hicks $\hat{Q}$ position), it must be estimated from the observations. This estimation would be based upon the statistical data and the form of the relationship fitted. Suppose, for example, that econometric analysis led to the conclusion that the income elasticity for commodity X (and, therefore, also for Y) is unity. In this case, as explained in Section 5.A, the hypothetical tangency optimum Q' along $K'L'$ in Figure 5.16 would lie on the (dashed) ray drawn from the origin to the point Q_1 along $KL*$. If the income elasticity for X were greater than unity, Q' would have to lie along $K'L'$ northwest of the intersection with this ray from the origin; if the income elasticity were less than unity, Q' would lie to the southeast along $K'L'$. But in any case, the statistical evidence would lead to a hypothetical determination of the position of Q'.

As between the points Q_0 and Q', *real income is constant in the sense of the Paasche quantity index* ($\mathcal{P}_Q = 1$). Starting with Q_0 as the initial position, the associated price–quantity combination is plotted in Figure 5.17 as point A. Holding P_y^0 constant, as P_x^0 changes to any other level P_x^1 Figure 5.17 shows the associated positions along the ordinary demand curve dd (point B) and along the Slutsky income-compensated demand curve $d*d*$ (point C). Point B shows the price and quantity associated with the consumption combination Q_1 in the preceding dia-

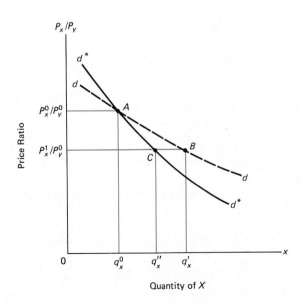

FIGURE 5.17 Income-compensated versus "Ordinary" Demand Curve. Starting from an initial optimum represented by the price–quantity point A, *dd* represents an individual's "ordinary" demand curve and *d*d** the "income-compensated" demand curve (using the Slutsky decomposition). For the ordinary demand curve, P_y and I are held constant, so that as price P_x (and therefore the price ratio P_x/P_y) falls the substitution effect and the normal income effect combine to increase purchases of X. For the income-compensated demand curve, the income effect is eliminated as P_x/P_y falls, by holding constant the ability to purchase the initial consumption basket. Consequently, if X is a normal good there will be a smaller consumption increment of X along $d*d*$ than along dd.

gram, while point C is associated with the consumption combination Q'. Q' has the same real income as the initial Q_0 (measured in terms of the Paasche quantity index) but responds to the same price ratio as the new combination Q_1.

A number of aspects of the income-compensated demand curve are of interest.

1. Since the ordinary demand curve incorporates an "income effect of the price change," which the compensated demand curve excludes, it must be that for a normal or superior good dd is flatter than d^*d^* as in Figure 5.17. When price falls the income effect is positive for a normal good; the ordinary demand, but *not* the compensated demand, reflects this (point B lies to the right of point C in the diagram). However, we saw in Chapter 4 that the income effect *may* be negative, indeed conceivably so much so that the Giffen condition obtains (positively sloped demand curve within some range). Since the compensated demand curve excludes any income effect, the Giffen possibility is also ruled out.

2. In a many-commodity world, it would be arbitrary to pick out some single other commodity Y whose price P_y would serve as the base of the price ratio P_x/P_y in measuring changes in relative prices. Instead, some general average of prices such as the Consumer Price Index would be used in actual statistical work to "deflate" the observed changes in the nominal money price of commodity X.

3. The great importance of the income-compensated demand curve stems from the fact that, as already suggested, this is the relation actually obtained from statistical studies of historical price–quantity observations. In such studies it is almost always necessary to allow for *income differences* by fitting a demand function like that of equation (5.5) to the observations. For example, it would hardly be possible to simply fit a demand curve to price–quantity data from both California and Mississippi without allowing for the real-income differences between those states. And in time-series analysis, it will similarly be necessary to allow for historical growth of real income over time. But the statistician, in making a separate allowance for differences or changes in real income, is thereby *eliminating the income effect* from the price–quantity data. This necessarily leaves the statistical result an approximation of the "pure substitution effect"—the income-compensated demand curve.

4. It is sometimes thought that the essential distinction between the ordinary and the compensated demand curves is due to money; some authors say that the ordinary demand curve dd holds *money income constant* while the compensated demand curve d^*d^* holds *real income constant*. This is incorrect; the existence of money is not the essential here. Suppose money had not been invented so that prices were quoted in terms of some real *numéraire* commodity. It would still be possible logically to distinguish the "ordinary" demand relation (which holds income endowment and other prices constant in *numéraire* units) from the "compensated" demand relation (which

employs the Hicks or the Slutsky adjustment technique to eliminate the real-income effect of price changes).

5. Nor is it true that the income-compensated demand curve is intrinsically superior to or more valid than the ordinary demand curve (along which consumers' real income rises as price P_x falls). Each has its uses. The ordinary demand curve, for example, is the function that is relevant when a business makes decisions concerning what price to charge. ∎

☐ SUMMARY OF CHAPTER 5

The *income elasticity* of demand for commodity X, denoted ϵ_x, represents the *proportionate* change in purchases of X in response to a proportionate change in income I. The first ratio below represents the definition; the others are useful alternative algebraic forms.

$$\epsilon_x \equiv \frac{\Delta x/x}{\Delta I/I} \equiv \frac{\Delta x/\Delta I}{x/I} \equiv \frac{\Delta x}{\Delta I}\frac{I}{x}$$

Income elasticity is positive for superior goods, negative for inferior goods. On the average over all goods, income elasticity must be unity (weighting each elasticity by the proportion of consumer expenditures represented by that good).

The *price elasticity* of demand for X, denoted η_x, represents the proportionate change in purchases of X in response to a proportionate change in its price P_x. The first ratio below represents this definition, and again the others are useful alternative algebraic forms.

$$\eta_x \equiv \frac{\Delta x/x}{\Delta P_x/P_x} \equiv \frac{\Delta x/\Delta P_x}{x/P_x} \equiv \frac{P_x/x}{\Delta P_x/\Delta x} \equiv \frac{\Delta x}{\Delta P_x}\cdot\frac{P_x}{x}$$

If the Law of Demand holds, price elasticity is negative. Demand is called "elastic" or "inelastic" depending on whether the absolute value of η_x is greater or less than unity. If demand is elastic, a reduction in price leads to an increase in consumer expenditures $P_x x$; if inelastic, a reduction in price leads to a fall in $P_x x$.

The *cross-elasticity* of demand η_{xy} is the proportionate change in purchases of X in response to a proportionate change in the price of *another* commodity P_y. The definition and an alternative algebraic form are:

$$\eta_{xy} \equiv \frac{\Delta x/x}{\Delta P_y/P_y} \equiv \frac{\Delta x}{\Delta P_y}\cdot\frac{P_y}{x}$$

If the cross-elasticity is positive the two goods are called *substitutes,* since a rise in the price of Y increases the purchases of X. If η_{xy} is negative the two goods are called *complements.*

Demand functions are commonly estimated from the data ("fitted") by using either linear or constant-elasticity functional forms. The price elasticity of demand increases (in absolute value) moving upward from the horizontal intercept along a linear demand curve. A constant-elasticity demand curve, correspondingly, cannot be a straight line; it must have curvature convex to the origin.

The following are often mentioned as causes of high price elasticities of demand: (1) If a commodity has *close substitutes,* the large substitution effect of the price change will lead to strongly increased consumption as its price falls. (2) If a commodity is a *"luxury"* (a strongly superior good), the large income effect of the price change will tend to enlarge its consumption as its price falls. (3) If a commodity is *important* (accounts for a large proportion of the consumer's budget), it is sometimes thought this tends to make the demand elastic. However, this argument is fallacious; even an "all-important" commodity would only have elasticity of unity. (4) At *high prices,* elasticity tends to be large if the demand curve is approximately linear. But since demand curves need not have a linear form, this generalization is not very strongly grounded.

The consumer may be subject to constraints apart from income. *Rationing* of one or more commodities, if effective, truncates the consumption opportunity set. More sophisticated schemes of "point rationing" impose a dual price scheme—money prices and point prices—upon consumers. And, even in the absence of rationing, *time* may be a serious additional constraint upon consumption.

Economists have devoted a great deal of attention to the theory of index numbers of prices and quantities, although this question is more of technical than of practical significance. The issue is to determine conditions such that an observer can detect when consumers are better or worse off, *without* knowing their preference functions. In some cases this can be done. In particular, the consumer's situation has surely improved if the Paasche quantity index (which averages consumption quantities using the new prices as weights, and therefore measures ability to buy the old consumption basket at the new prices) is greater than unity. This is equivalent to a Laspeyres price index (which averages prices using the old consumption quantities as weights) having risen by less than the index of income (ratio of new income to old income). However, in some cases the result remains indeterminate. As a matter of much greater practical importance, if (as often occurs under inflationary conditions) rationing by coupon or by points is imposed upon consumers, conventional price indexes will very seriously understate the true rise in cost of living.

In order to separate the effects of income changes and price changes upon consumption decisions, it is sometimes convenient to use an *income-compensated* demand curve—that is, a demand curve from which the "income effect" has been eliminated, leaving only the pure "substitution effect." But in statistical work it is not possible to use the substitution effect derived in Chapter 4 via the Hicksian decomposition of the overall effect of a price change, since the Hicksian decomposition requires knowledge of individual preferences. Instead, in empirical work the pure substitution effect is isolated by the Slutsky decomposition: the income effect is eliminated as prices vary along the demand curve by considering only consumption combinations such that the Paasche quantity index—ability to buy the old consumption basket at the new prices—is equal to unity. However, the income-compensated demand curve is not "superior" to the ordinary demand curve; it simply responds to a different type of question.

☐ QUESTIONS FOR CHAPTER 5

MAINLY FOR REVIEW

R1. What is the general definition of all elasticity measures? Why is the income elasticity of demand considered a more useful measure than the simple slope along an Engel Curve? Why is the price elasticity of demand considered a more useful measure than the simple slope along a demand curve? Are elasticity measures always better than the simple measures? (See the question following.)

*R2. Consider this paradox: "Income elasticity is supposed to measure the responsiveness of consumption to changes in income. But income elasticity is unity along *any* Engel Curve which is a straight line through the origin, whether very steep or very flat. Since Engel Curves of different steepness surely show different responses of consumption to income, how can they all be characterized as having the same income elasticity?"

R3. True or false: "Income elasticity is unity at any point along an Engel Curve such that the tangent at that point extends through the origin." Explain.

R4. True or false: "Since income elasticities must *average* out to unity, any commodity accounting for a very large fraction of income expenditure cannot have an income elasticity very far from unity." Explain.

*R5. What is meant by "elastic demand" and "inelastic demand"? How can elasticity at a point along a linear demand curve be determined by inspection? Along a nonlinear demand curve?

*R6. If the demand curve is $P = A - BX$, where A and B are positive constants, what is the elasticity at $X = 0$? At $X = A/B$? At $X = A/2B$?

R7. If the demand curve is $PX = 100$, what is the elasticity at $X = 10$? At $X = 50$? At $X = 100$?

R8. What is the analytical form of a demand function that is *linear* in both income and price? What is the analytical form of a demand function that has *constant elasticities* with respect to both income and price? Explain the economic meaning of each form.

*R9. If there is a single "all-important" commodity that absorbs all of the individual's income, what is its price elasticity? Income elasticity?

*R10. Gasoline rationing has been proposed as one possible remedy for the recent "energy crisis." If rations were distributed on an egalitarian basis, show the situations of a wealthy and a poor consumer in terms of their opportunity sets for gasoline consumption versus "all other goods." Show typical indifference maps if automobile usage is a luxury. Would permitting sale of coupons be a good idea?

R11. What is the difference between a Laspeyres index and a Paasche index? Show the geometrical meaning of a Laspeyres quantity index that is less than unity. Show the geometrical meaning of a Paasche quantity index that exceeds unity. Can we draw conclusions as to relative well-being in these two cases? If not, why not?

*The answers to asterisked questions appear at the end of the book.

*R12. "If the ratio of new income to old income is greater than the ratio of the new cost to the old cost of the old commodity bundle, the consumer is surely better off." What statement about indexes does this correspond to? Is the statement true?

R13. What is an income-compensated demand curve? How does it differ from the ordinary demand curve? For a normal good (positive income elasticity), which of the two curves is the more elastic?

FOR FURTHER THOUGHT AND DISCUSSION

*T1. Prove the proposition that on the average over all goods, income elasticity must be unity.

*T2. The price elasticity of demand for a given commodity is alleged to be greater:
   a. The more numerous and closer the substitutes.
   b. If it is a luxury rather than a necessity.
   c. If it accounts for a large portion of the consumption budget.
   d. At high prices rather than low prices.
   Explain the supporting argument in each case and analyze its validity.

*T3. The American economist Irving Fisher argued in 1891 that a poor community will hardly distinguish quality grades of a commodity like beef, while a rich community would.

> In the country districts of "the west" all cuts of beef sell for the same price (about 10 cts. per lb.). In the cities of the west two or three qualities are commonly distinguished, while in New York a grocer will enumerate over a dozen prices in the same beef varying from 10 to 25 cts. per lb.[17]

Construct the implied indifference curves, at low and high levels of income, between "low-quality beef" and "high-quality beef." Why should different beef qualities be better substitutes at low incomes than at high incomes? What would you anticipate about the price elasticity of demand for low-quality beef? For high-quality beef?

T4. Name some goods you expect to have elastic demands. Inelastic demands. Justify your choices.

*T5. Tickets to the King Tut exhibition are available only on a black-market basis. Professor X, calling from out-of-town, gives purchasing instructions to his secretary: "If the price is $30 each, buy one ticket for me; at $20 each, buy two; if it is $10, buy three." The secretary says: "Prof, there must be something wrong here. You're saying you'd be willing to pay more in total for two tickets than for three!" Is the secretary correct? Explain.

*T6. For a commodity with snob appeal, consumers might be willing to buy *more* at a higher price than at a lower price (violation of the Law of Demand). Is this possible or likely? Explain.

*T7. If uninformed consumers judge quality by price, they may also be willing to buy more at a higher than a lower price. Is this possible or likely? Explain.

*T8. In wartime rationing situations, purchase or sale of ration allowances for cash, or exchange of ration coupons for other goods, is generally illegal. Is there any

---

[17]Irving Fisher, *Mathematical Investigations in the Theory of Value and Prices* (New Haven, Conn.: Yale University Press, 1925), p. 74.

justification for this? Are there adverse consequences of forbidding such exchanges?

*T9. It is often thought that the wealthy must have a great deal of leisure. On the other hand, members of present-day richer societies tend to be more harried and pressed for time than were their own grandparents who lacked so many modern time-saving devices. Interpret in terms of the time constraint on consumption.

T10. Since nomadic tribes have a serious portability problem, they are somewhat reluctant to acquire heavy material possessions. Analyze in terms of nomads' income and "carrying capacity" as multiple constraints. What types of goods have high "prices" in terms of carrying capacity?

T11. In the spring of 1979 it became necessary in many areas of the United States to wait on long lines to be served with gasoline. The U.S. Department of Energy had, evidently, set gasoline prices too low to clear the market in those areas—though the problem was also in part due to the same Department's regional allocations of fuel on the basis of historical (and therefore more or less outdated) patterns of usage. If the money price of gasoline was 90 cents per gallon, if the typical consumer had to wait 30 minutes to obtain a refill of ten gallons, and if his time was worth $5 per hour, estimate what the market-clearing money price would have been. Comparing higher money prices versus long waits in line, which system is *relatively* more advantageous for rich people versus poor? For working people versus the retired and unemployed? For owners of cars with large gas tanks versus small?

T12. What would be wrong with an economic system in which everything was allocated by waiting in line rather than by charging money prices? [*Hint*: Would the Invisible Hand be able to serve its function?]

THE
BUSINESS
FIRM

CORE CHAPTER

In Part Two of this book the consuming *individual* held the center of attention. In Part Three we will be concentrating upon the *business firm,* and upon the aggregate of firms in a given market that we call the *industry.* This chapter is devoted specifically to the firm. The following chapter will develop the relationships between the competitive firm and the industry; later chapters will be devoted to firms and industries under conditions other than perfect competition.

6.A
FIRMS AND THE CIRCULAR FLOW OF ECONOMIC ACTIVITY

In Chapter 1, Figure 1.1 pictured the circular flow of economic activity. Two classes of economic agents were shown: individuals or households, and business firms. Economic analysis usually takes the existence of natural persons as a given fact determined "outside" the economic system. But actually, the size of the human population does respond to economic incentives, as has been recognized since the time of Malthus.[1] Good or bad harvests, or business conditions more generally, affect human birth rates and death rates as well as flows of immigration and emigration. And the clustering of individuals into families and households also responds to economic circumstances. Individuals or households constitute the *demand side* of the "product market," the market for consumption goods and services discussed in previous chapters.

Business firms, artificial entities which are clearly created in response to economic incentives, constitute the other pole of economic activity in Figure 1.1. Firms are the crucial *productive* agents of society, engaged in the conversion of resources into final goods. Of course, households also engage in production, but in modern economies the firm is the characteristic unit devoted to production for the market. For our purposes, then, as pictured in Figure 1.1 firms constitute the supply side of the product market and individuals the demand side.

---

[1] T. R. Malthus (1766–1834), English clergyman and economist. Malthus maintained that population would always tend to expand to the limits of subsistence. His views had an important influence upon Charles Darwin's thinking that culminated in the theory of biological evolution.

We could have production without firms. Why does a special economic agent, apart from natural individuals, emerge for this purpose? The key to the answer is twofold: (1) Production opportunities are commonly *multi-personal,* and (2) exchange through the market is not a costless process (see Chapter 13).

It is a fact of the greatest practical importance that the possibilities of multi-person or "team" production enormously expand output potentialities. The advantages of the division of labor lie not only in specialization in terms of *products* (shoemaker, butcher, baker) but also in the specialization of *tasks* in the joint production of a given end-product (clerk, assembly-line worker, inspector, foreman, etc.). Indeed, our modern economy could not exist without such specialization of tasks. But the mere fact that attractive productive opportunities are multi-personal, requiring integration of the skills and resources of a number of distinct individuals, is not enough to explain why the business firm exists. Without forming a firm, it would in principle be possible to combine resources owned by many different persons via a *multilateral contract* among all the individuals concerned. In creating a motion picture the producer, director, writer, stars, supporting actors, stagehands, cameramen, electricians, and so forth—plus the suppliers of costumes, film, sets, utilities, and the like—might all get together and agree upon a contract indicating what types and quantities of resources each party would contribute, at stated times, to the productive process. The contract must also specify, of course, each party's financial reward. Such contractual arrangements are relatively rare because of the high costs of negotiating and (what is extremely important) of *enforcing* multilateral contracts. The business firm provides a way of reaping the advantages of team production without going beyond *bilateral* contracting. Each resource-owner need not deal separately with every other participant in the productive process but instead only with a single artificial entity—the firm itself.

In actuality, however, the "firm" is an abstraction. People can really deal only with other persons. Therefore some person or group, called the "management," must be authorized to deal in the name of the abstract firm. The management may simply be the *owner or owners* of the firm, the residual claimants to the firm's profits or losses after meeting contractual obligations. But here again, especially where relatively large-scale productive operations are involved, a division of labor tends to come into existence. Management itself becomes a specialized kind of employed resource. The function of the manager is to make contractual agreements with other resource-suppliers and also to enforce or monitor performance of these contracts.

EXAMPLE 6.1
Effectiveness of Management

Using "pre-delinquent" boys in a youth home as experimental subjects, the psychologist E. L. Phillips[a] conducted experiments to evaluate the effectiveness of payment systems for the performance of various tasks. Task completion was "reinforced" by points awarded, which could be converted into desired commodities or privileges. One of the experiments involved bathroom cleaning chores.

The youths were assigned sixteen specific tasks to do in cleaning the bathroom. Among the experimental setups examined were the "group" condition and the "manager" condition. In the "group" condition, responsibility was collective. All boys received the same reward or fine, depending upon the overall group performance. In the "manager" condition, there was a weekly auction in points for the right to be responsible for the collective performance. The auction winner as manager could assign every boy to tasks, and then distribute rewards or fines based upon his judgment of the work performed. The manager himself was rewarded or fined in accordance with the overall level of achievement.

Results under the "group" condition typically showed completion of about six of the sixteen tasks. Under the "manager" condition, in contrast, about fourteen of the sixteen tasks were usually completed.

> COMMENT: Under the "group" condition each boy failing to complete any task suffered only a portion of the *overall* penalty (which was assessed upon *every* boy in the group). So the incentive to work rather than shirk was weak in the absence of a manager fully responsible for achievement. (The question of how to arrange for efficient *collective action* will be discussed in more detail in Part Five, as a problem of "political economy.")

[a]E. L. Phillips, "Achievement Place: Token Reinforcement Procedures in a Home-Style Rehabilitation Setting for 'Pre-delinquent' Boys," *Journal of Applied Behavior Analysis*, v. 1 (Fall 1968).

A manager who is not personally the owner of the firm must of course then be monitored by someone else—ultimately, by the owner or owners themselves. Hence, an inescapable decision-making aspect attaches to firm ownership; this combined function is traditionally called *entrepreneurship*. While firms are created in order to achieve certain economies in transacting among resource-suppliers, execution and enforcement of the contract *among the owners* (if there are more than one) that sets up the firm, and of the contract *between the owners and the manager* of the firm (if those two functions are not combined), both pose considerable difficulties.

A variety of devices have arisen to overcome these problems. With regard to the contract among owners that establishes the firm, the invention of the *corporate form* has greatly eased matters. By engaging in business as a corporation, large groups of people can combine their resources to exploit even very big and very risky multi-person productive opportunities. The key features of the corporation are *limited liability* and *transferable shares*. Legal and contractual obligations of the corporation, as a fictional person, cannot be brought home to the individual owner's personal account. Such a person's ownership shares may become valueless (at worst), but individual finances are otherwise safe. And an individual who is dissatisfied with the policies and procedures adopted by the other owners, or by the manager on behalf of the owners, has the option of selling out his or her shares. In consequence, the corporation is enabled to acquire and commit large amounts of resources to exploit productive opportunities, far beyond what would be achievable by a partnership without the advantages of limited liability and transferability of ownership interests. With regard to the contract between owners and management, devices like profit-sharing and stock options have emerged with the aim of linking managers' interests more closely with those of the shareholders, thus minimizing the need for detailed monitoring of managerial performance by the owners.

One interesting question is: Which classes of resource-suppliers tend to become the *entrepreneurs* or owners of the firm, whose compensation comes from residual profit and loss rather than fixed payment terms under contract of hire with the firm? In farming, the landowner may be the entrepreneur, hiring labor at a fixed contractual wage. Or, the working farmer (supplier of labor input) may be the entrepreneur instead, the land being leased at a fixed rental payment. There are also mixed "share cropping" cases, where the supplier of land and the supplier of labor share the uncertainty of residual profit and loss. In small industrial firms, *management* tends to be combined with ownership, thus avoiding the difficult problem of contracting and monitoring between the two. The owner of such a small firm will, quite commonly, also supply some labor and some of the capital required. In large industrial enterprises, on the other hand, under the corporate form the owners of the firm (stockholders) are typically only providers of capital—generalized purchasing power enabling the firm to carry on its operations. Other inputs are typically hired, including management, labor, and the remainder of the capital (through debt instruments such as corporate bonds).

6.C
THE GOAL OF THE FIRM AS OPTIMIZING AGENT

Individuals maximize utility, but what do firms maximize? In the traditional formulation the firm is said to maximize *profit*, which is the difference between *revenue* and *cost*.

Revenue consists of the receipts of the firm from sales, i.e., price times quantity sold. *Cost* is a somewhat more elusive concept. The ultimate economic cost of any activity is to be interpreted as the alternative *opportunities foregone*. The firm, in order to attract the resources or "factors" necessary to engage in production, must pay resource-owners amounts sufficient to induce them to sacrifice their best alternatives, whether these alternatives be employment elsewhere, or leisure. The payments required are, of course, the going market prices for the services of the factors of production. So *cost can be regarded as the sum, taken over all resources employed, of the factor prices times factor quantities.*

There is one tricky feature here. The owner is, as defined above, the *residual* claimant to the firm's earnings. Payment for any factor services supplied by the owner himself or herself will not ordinarily be made by explicit contract but will be mixed with the residual claim. "Profit" in the legal or accounting sense fails to distinguish these two economically distinct categories. If a small merchant works long hours in his own store, his accountant will calculate a "profit" that is likely to amount to little more than a normal wage payment for the merchant's labor services. In the case of a large corporation, "profit" as reported to the Internal Revenue Service will be confounded with a normal interest return upon the funds committed by share-owners to the firm. *Economic* or "pure" profit is arrived at by deducting the normal factor return on owner inputs, sometimes called the "normal" profit, from this accounting profit. The *value in alternative uses* of all the resources employed in production (whether explicitly hired and paid for, or only implicitly hired and not separately paid for because they are provided by the owner himself) constitutes "economic" cost. *Economic profit is thus the difference between accounting profit and normal profit, and also the difference between revenue and economic cost.* In this book, unless otherwise indicated, the word "profit" will always be used in the sense of *economic* profit.

According to the classical formulation, the aim of the firm as a decision-making agent is to maximize (economic) profit. This view has not gone un-challenged, however. Some observers maintain that the behavior of large modern corporations cannot be explained in terms of the profit-maximizing hypothesis. In such corporations the *separation of ownership and control* may be carried to an extreme degree. Where no single share-owner accounts for more than a tiny fraction of the shares outstanding, management may (it is contended) be in a position to run things without significant monitoring by nominal owners.

Of course, there are limits. If the shareholders were literally powerless, management could do whatever it wished, even dissipate the value of the firm by providing themselves enormous executive salaries and expense accounts. But no management is ever given a license to steal. Shareholders as owners have judicial recourse; they can sue for damages if they believe that management has violated the contract with the owners. Such lawsuits frequently do take place, indicating that at least some owners are actually monitoring performance of management. Perhaps a more important check is the presence of competing groups eager to take over the managerial function. Suppose a self-serving or inefficient management is in control of a corporation. Then the reduced earnings now and in prospect make the value of the corporate shares lower than they would otherwise be. An alternative management group is likely to purchase shares, at their current low prices, with the hope of obtaining enough for control. Or they may instead try to win the support of existing shareholders to vote out the current management.

The challenge to the profit-maximizing hypothesis need not, however, be so extreme. The critics might admit that management aims to achieve at least a certain minimal level of (accounting) profit, enough to placate the shareholders and avoid legal sanctions. But beyond this level, the contention is, management pursues its own goals rather than those of owners. Because of the takeover threat in the background, management's goals may take a somewhat more subtle form than crude monetary emoluments. They may involve power and growth ("empire-building"), advertising or charitable outlays to enhance a favorable "corporate image" (really a management image), amenities like luxurious offices and attractive secretaries, and a stable environment without risk of unpleasant surprises.

That forces like those just described are actually operative can hardly be doubted. But are they significant enough, restrained as they are by the ever-present takeover threat from outside contenders for managerial positions, to make the profit-maximization hypothesis unworkable? That is a question for empirical investigation. So far at least, no alternative formulation of the goal of the business firm has succeeded in displacing the classical conception of the profit-maximizing firm.

EXAMPLE 6.2
Non-profit Goals and "Technostructure Orientation"

J. K. Galbraith has given wide dissemination to the idea that the management-dominated modern American corporation does not aim to maximize profit. Among the possible competing goals, representing management desires rather than stockholder interests, he lays particular stress upon (1) *growth of sales* and (2) *stability*.[a] In Galbraith's view, those firms he calls "technostructure-oriented" are best able to achieve these goals through devices like advertising and defense contracts.

Harold Demsetz[b] attempted to test these hypotheses by converting them into quantifiable form. Demsetz used a variety of statistical criteria to interpret Galbraith's concept of "technostructure orientation," so as to be able to distinguish those firms that could be expected to adhere (on Galbraith's theory) to non-profit goals more than others. The measures of "technostructure orientation" employed by Demsetz included advertising intensity, capital intensity, and proportion of defense contracts.

With regard to sales growth as an alternative to profit-maximization, the statistical evidence was examined to see whether firms with high indexes of "technostructure orientation" tended to have high sales growth *relative to* profit rates. Had this in fact occurred, it would suggest that profit had been sacrificed for sales growth (i.e., the interests of owners for the benefit of managers) by these "technostructure-oriented" firms. But no visible effect was found in the data, except that (contradicting the tested hypothesis) high advertising intensity was found to be associated with relatively *low* sales growth relative to profit rate.

With regard to Galbraith's second stated goal, a number of alternative measures of *stability* were considered by Demsetz. But in no case was there any indication that firms with high "technostructure orientation" sacrificed profits for stability in such a way as to be distinguishable from firms of low "technostructure orientation."

[a]J. K. Galbraith, *The New Industrial State* (Boston: Houghton Mifflin, 1967), pp. 171, 199, 210, 309–10.
[b]H. Demsetz, "Where Is the New Industrial State?" *Economic Inquiry*, v. 12 (March 1974).

The book is not yet closed on possible conflict of interests between manager and owner. It may be that such conflict is more likely for *monopoly* firms and for *regulated* firms. The example following may be suggestive.

EXAMPLE 6.3
Savings and Loan Associations: Stock versus Mutual

Alfred Nicols compared the performance of savings and loan associations organized as *corporations* owned by stockholders ("stock" associations) with those organized as *cooperatives* owned by depositors ("mutual" associations). While J. K. Galbraith (see Example 6.2) had emphasized the separation of ownership and control in the modern corporation, this separation is carried to an extreme in the savings and loan "mutuals." It may be difficult to overturn management by takeover or proxy fight in a corporation, but legal provisions make it essentially impossible to do so in a "mutual" savings and loan association.

Nicols argued that managers of mutuals, practically free of owner-depositor control, would find ways of diverting association income to their own advantage. While Galbraith had maintained that a main management goal would be *growth* as an alternative to profit, Nicols' position is in sharp contrast. The diversion of association income to managers must mean that mutuals have less to offer their depositors. Hence income diversion to management, he argues, is necessarily in *conflict* with rapid growth.

The legislation of most states effectively bars stock associations, thus providing a competitive shield for the mutuals. But in California, where legislation has permitted competition between mutual and stock associations, the stock associations have indeed sharply increased their percentage of the market at the expense of the mutuals. The Table below provides comparative performance indicators for three classes of institutions: non-California institutions (overwhelmingly mutuals), California mutuals under federal charter, and California stock associations. Note that the indicators for California mutuals generally fall between those of the California stock associations and the non-California institutions. Nicols attributes this to the competitive pressure of California stock associations forcing more efficient performance upon the California mutuals.

Performance Indicators: Mutual and Stock Associations, 1963 (%)

INDICATOR	U.S. NON-CALIFORNIA	CALIFORNIA FEDERAL MUTUALS	CALIFORNIA STOCK
Gross operating income − expenses / Average assets	4.31%	4.95%	5.18%
"Dividends" / Average saving capital	4.04	4.72	4.78
New loans / Average assets	21.2	34.9	45.1

Source: Alfred Nicols, "Stock versus Mutual Savings and Loan Associations: Some Evidence of Differences in Behavior," *American Economic Review*, v. 57 (May 1967), p. 342.

These data suggest better performance by the stock associations, whether measured in terms of association net income (gross operating income minus expenses), or in terms of interest paid out to depositors (called "dividends" in savings and loan jargon), or in terms of growth (new loans divided by average assets). The "mutual" form thus does appear to permit managers to pursue goals in conflict with those of the owner-depositors.

6.D
THE OPTIMUM OF THE COMPETITIVE FIRM

According to the classical goal, the firm aims to maximize profit. Such maximization, like all behavior, is subject to constraints: in this case the constraint is the relation between *revenue* received and *costs* incurred at larger or smaller levels of output.

More specifically, we are dealing here with the *competitive* or "price-taking" firm. The market price P is assumed, for all practical purposes, to be independent of the firm's level of output. (While never literally true, this may be a usable approximation of reality.) Then Total Revenue R, which is by definition equal to the product of price P times quantity q (that is, $R \equiv Pq$), can be plotted in Panel (a) of Figure 6.1 as a ray through the origin. Since price P is constant, Total Revenue is zero when output q is zero, and increases proportionately with q. (The Total Revenue line in Panel (a) of Figure 6.1 is a special case, valid only where P is constant, of the more general Total Revenue function that was pictured in the upper panel of Figure 2.10.) The vertical axis in Panel (a) of Figure 6.1 is scaled simply in dollars, since dollars are the units in which revenue is measured.[2]

Total Cost is traditionally represented as a curve like C in Panel (a): starting from a level F of fixed costs incurred independently of any output, Total Cost rises throughout, first at a decreasing and then at an increasing rate, as output increases.

Profit is Revenue minus Cost. In symbols, $\Pi \equiv R - C$. In Panel (a), the profit-maximizing output $q*$ is the level of q such that the positive vertical difference between the R and the C curves is greatest. This maximum level of profit, $\Pi*$, is shown as the vertical bold line-segment. As is geometrically evident, the maximum difference occurs where the Total Cost curve C is parallel to (has the same slope as) the Total Revenue curve R. (The parallelism is suggested by the dashed tangent drawn along the C curve at $q = q*$.) This provides the key to the connection between the solution in "total" units as shown in Panel (a) and the solution in "average-marginal" units portrayed in Panel (b) of Figure 6.1.

The relations that logically must hold among total, average, and marginal magnitudes were expounded in Section B of Chapter 2. We saw there that (1) a *marginal* function corresponds to the rate of increase along a total function, and (2) an *average* function is simply the total function divided by the argument

---

[2]Recall that we are accepting the fact.that exchange normally takes place employing money as an intermediary or medium. The explanation for this fact will be taken up in Chapter 13.

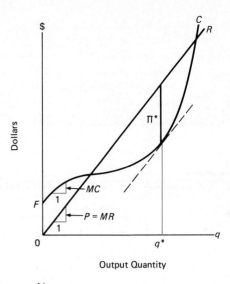

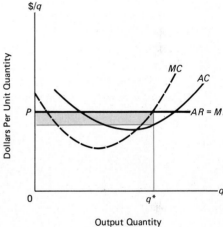

FIGURE 6.1 **Optimum of the Competitive Firm.** In Panel (a), at the optimal output q^* the vertical dollar difference between the Total Revenue curve R (a ray through the origin for a price-taking firm) and the Total Cost curve C is greatest. At output q^* the slopes along R and C are equal—implying that, in Panel (b), the horizontal Marginal Revenue curve MR must intersect the Marginal Cost curve MC at that output. The amount of the maximized profit, Π^*, is shown as the length of the vertical line-segment between the R and C curves in Panel (a), and as the shaded rectangle corresponding to the area $(AR - AC)q^*$ in Panel (b).

or choice variable. In this case, the average functions to be dealt with are R/q and C/q.

First with regard to revenue. Marginal Revenue MR was formally defined in Chapter 2 as:[3]

(6.1)
$$MR \equiv \lim_{(\text{as } \Delta q \to 0)} \frac{\Delta R}{\Delta q}$$

We will use the notation $\Delta R/\Delta q$, on the understanding that we are dealing with small increments Δ. Geometrically, MR corresponds to the *slope* along the Total Revenue curve in Panel (a) of Figure 6.1; this slope is a constant equal to the market price P. (Note the small triangle drawn along the R curve in the diagram.)

---

[3]*Mathematical Footnote:* This definition is equivalent, of course, to the derivative: $MR \equiv dR/dq$.

Since Marginal Revenue, the addition to receipts from producing one more unit of output, is constant and equal to P, it is plotted in Panel (b) as a horizontal line of height P. In terms of dimensionality, note that the vertical axis of Panel (b) is scaled in units of $\$/q$, the dimensions of price.

Average Revenue AR is defined as R/q. But since $R \equiv Pq$ necessarily, it is always definitionally true that $AR \equiv P \equiv R/q$. In this case, price P being taken as constant, the Average Revenue curve AR in Panel (b) must also be a horizontal line at the level of P. Thus, for a price-taking firm the AR and MR curves coincide in the form of a horizontal line at the level P.

Exercise 6.1: If a firm faces market price $P = 25$, independent of its own level of output q, what is the equation for its Total Revenue R? Marginal Revenue MR? Average Revenue AR?

Answer: The equation for Total Revenue is $R = 25q$. Since $\Delta R/\Delta q$—the increase in R per unit increase in q—is always 25, we know that Marginal Revenue is a constant, with equation $MR = 25$. And, since $R/q = 25$, Average Revenue is also constant with equation $AR = 25$.

For Marginal Cost MC, the formal definition is analogous:[4]

$$(6.2) \qquad MC \equiv \lim_{(as\ \Delta q \to 0)} \frac{\Delta C}{\Delta q}$$

Again, the notation $\Delta C/\Delta q$ will be used on the understanding that we are dealing with small increments Δ. MC corresponds geometrically to the (changing) slope along the Total Cost curve of Panel (a). (Note the small triangle drawn along the C curve.) MC in Panel (b) is shown as first positive but decreasing (corresponding to the region where Total Cost is rising at a decreasing rate) and then positive and increasing (corresponding to the region where Total Cost rises at an increasing rate).

Average Cost AC is C/q. For any output q, Average Cost C/q in Panel (b) corresponds to the slope of the line that could be drawn in Panel (a) from the origin to the point on the Total Cost curve at that q. At $q = 0$, Average Cost must be infinite, as can be seen directly from the definition C/q, or geometrically from the ever-steepening slope of the line from the origin to the C curve as q approaches zero. The AC curve has a falling region so long as MC lies below it (Proposition 2.2a of Chapter 2) and later a rising region where MC lies above it (Proposition 2.2b). It then follows that AC reaches a minimum (is neither rising nor falling) at the point where MC equals AC (Proposition 2.2c). Or, we may say, the MC curve cuts through the low point of the AC curve (from below).

The maximum-profit output q^*, as has already been seen, occurs in Panel (a) where the Total Revenue curve R and the Total Cost curve C have the same slope. Then at q^* in Panel (b), Marginal Revenue and Marginal Cost are equal, i.e., the MR and MC curves intersect.

---

[4]*Mathematical Footnote:* In derivative notation: $MC \equiv dC/dq$.

In terms of economic logic, if a unit increment of output will increase revenue more than it does cost ($MR > MC$) then the increment should be produced; we are not yet at the profit-maximizing output. If $MR < MC$, on the other hand, the last unit caused a decrease in profit so that output has been pushed beyond the optimum. For profit to be a maximum, then, the condition $MC = MR$ must hold. And since we are dealing with competitive (price-taking) firms for which $MR \equiv P \equiv AR$, this condition takes on the specific form:

(6.3) $MC = MR \equiv P$ Maximum-Profit Condition, Competitive Firm

The economic logic also tells us something further. For, we have just seen, if $MR > MC$ the firm should expand output, and if $MR < MC$ it should contract. This suggests that $MC = MR$ is an optimum *only if the* MC *curve cuts the* MR *curve from below.* Note that in Panel (b) of Figure 6.1 there are *two* intersections of the MC curve with the horizontal MR curve. But at the left-hand intersection, MC cuts MR *from above.* By the economic logic we see that it pays to go beyond the left-hand intersection into the range of output where $MR > MC$, until the right-hand intersection is reached[5] where MC cuts MR *from below.*[6]

> PROPOSITION: The profit-maximizing output for the firm occurs where Marginal Cost equals Marginal Revenue, provided that the MC curve cuts the MR curve from below.

Exercise 6.2:   A firm faces a price $P = 38$ that is independent of the scale of its own output q. Its Marginal Cost is given by $MC = 2 + (q - 10)^2$. (a) At what output level or levels does $MC = MR$? (b) At what levels of q does the MC curve cut the MR curve *from below*? (c) What is the most profitable level of output?

Answer: (a) Marginal Revenue here is $MR = P = 38$. Solving the equation $2 + (q - 10)^2 = 38$ leads to two solutions: $q = 16$ if we take the positive square root, $q = 4$ if we take the negative square root. The MC and MR curves intersect at both of these output levels. (b) By plotting some points we can verify that MC cuts MR from below only at the larger output, $q = 16$. (c) The most profitable level of output is $q = 16$.

The *size* of the economic profit, at the profit-maximizing output q^*, was represented in Panel (a) of Figure 6.1 as the bold vertical line-segment Π^* between the Total Revenue and the Total Cost curves. In terms of average-marginal units of measurement, we can think of profit as equal to $(AR - AC)q$. That is, profit equals the difference between *Average* Revenue and *Average* Cost, multiplied by the number of units of output. So in Panel (b), maximum profit is shown as the shaded rectangle whose area is $(P - AC)q^*$.

---

[5]The left-hand intersection of MC and MR in Panel (b) corresponds to the output in Panel (a) where the vertical difference is greatest between a *higher* Total Cost curve C and a *lower* Total Revenue curve R. This is a *minimum*-profit (or maximum-loss) output.

[6]*Mathematical Footnote:* We are maximizing $\Pi = R - C$ with respect to q. Differentiating and setting equal to zero, we have as the *first-order* condition for a maximum: $dR/dq = dC/dq$, or $MR = MC$. The *second-order* condition for a maximum is that $d^2\Pi/dq^2 < 0$, or $d^2R/dq^2 < d^2C/dq^2$. This says that MR must be falling relative to MC, i.e., that MC must be cutting MR from below to have a maximum of Π.

Table 6.1 illustrates a hypothetical set of revenue and cost data for a competitive profit-maximizing firm. Price is constant at $P = 60$, so the Total Revenue column (R) is simply $R = 60q$. The specific cost function assumed is $C = 128 + 69q - 14q^2 + q^3$. This formula was used to compute the Total Cost column C. If plotted, the Total Revenue and Total Cost functions would have the general shapes pictured in Panel (a) of Figure 6.1, and the average and marginal functions would resemble those in Panel (b).

TABLE 6.1

Hypothetical Revenue and Cost Functions: Competitive Firm

$P = 60$, or $R = 60q$
$C = q^3 - 14q^2 + 69q + 128$

q	P	R	C	MC_1	MC_2	MC	AC	VC	AVC
0	60	0	128	—	—	69	∞	0	—
					56				
1	60	60	184	56	45	44	184	56	56
					34				
2	60	120	218	34	26	25	109	90	45
					18				
3	60	180	236	18	13	12	78.7	108	36
					8				
4	60	240	244	8	6	5	61	116	29
					4				
5	60	300	248	4	5	4	49.6	120	24
					6				
6	60	360	254	6	10	9	42.3	126	21
					14				
7	60	420	268	14	21	20	38.3	140	20
					28				
8	60	480	296	28	38	37	37	168	21
					48				
9	60	540	344	48	61	60	38.2	216	24
					74				
10	60	600	418	74	—	89	41.8	290	29

Three different Marginal Cost concepts are represented by separate columns in the Table. The first two, MC_1 and MC_2, are like the "poorer approximation" and the "better approximation" discussed in Section B of Chapter 2. Suppose that we wanted to estimate the Marginal Cost at $q = 7$. The "poorer approximation," MC_1, is based upon the additional cost incurred by increasing output from $q = 6$ to $q = 7$, i.e., it is the cost of the last unit produced. Thus, $MC_1 = 268 - 254 = 14$ is taken as the Marginal Cost at $q = 7$. The "better approximation" takes this same cost increment, 14, but regards it as providing an estimate of the Marginal Cost not at $q = 7$, but halfway between $q = 7$ and $q = 6$—specifically, $MC_2 = 14$ at $q = 6\frac{1}{2}$. To obtain the better approximation MC_2 at $q = 7$, we would have to average the estimate of 14 just obtained for $q = 6\frac{1}{2}$ with a similar estimate for MC_2 at $q = 7\frac{1}{2}$—the latter based upon the cost difference $296 - 268 = 28$ incurred by increasing output from $q = 7$ to $q = 8$. Thus, the "better approximation" is the average of 14 and 28, that is, $MC_2 = 21$ at $q = 7$. (The averaged values so obtained for MC_2 at integer values of q are indicated by the bold elements in the MC_2 column.)

Finally, the *true* Marginal Cost is shown by the MC column of the Table. This was determined by calculus techniques, which yielded the equation[7] $MC = 69 - 28q + 3q^2$. As can be seen, MC_2 is indeed a much better approximation than MC_1.

With $P = 60$, setting the true $MC = P$ leads to the profit-maximizing solution $q^* = 9$. (Using MC_2 and interpolating would yield a close approximation; note that use of MC_1 and interpolating would lead to a substantial error.) At $q^* = 9$, Total Revenue is $R = 540$ and Total Cost is $C = 344$; hence the maximized profit is $\Pi^* = 196$.[8]

Exercise 6.3: Suppose that Total Revenue remains $R = 60q$ as in Table 6.1, but the Total Cost function is $C = 10 + 5q^2$. (a) How does this Total Cost function differ from that pictured in Panel (a) of Figure 6.1? (b) What is the Marginal Cost, and how does it differ from that pictured in Panel (b) of Figure 6.1? (c) What is the profit-maximizing output, and the amount of maximized profit?

Answer: (a) Plotting several points and sketching, we can see that the C curve here is always rising at an increasing rate, whereas in Figure 6.1 there is an initial range where the C curve is rising at a decreasing rate. (b) Using the "better approximation" method of the text, the points obtained fit the equation $MC = 10q$. (This is also the exact Marginal Cost that can be obtained by calculus techniques.) Unlike the MC curve in the diagram, here MC is a straight line of positive slope through the origin. (c) Since $MC = 10q$ and $MR = P = 60$, setting $MC = MR$ leads to a profit-maximizing solution at output $q^* = 6$. (The MC and MR curves intersect only once in this case.) At this output, $R = 360$ and $C = 190$, so the maximized profit is $\Pi^* = 170$.

The last two columns of Table 6.1 show *Total Variable Cost VC* and *Average Variable Cost AVC*. Total Variable Cost is simply Total Cost less Fixed Cost: $VC \equiv C - F$. Average Variable Cost is, correspondingly, $VC/q \equiv (C - F)/q$. The relations between Total Cost and Total Variable Cost are shown geometrically in Panel (a) of Figure 6.2. Evidently, the latter is everywhere lower than the former, by a constant vertical difference equal to the amount of the Fixed Cost F.

In terms of average-marginal magnitudes, the relations are as shown in Panel (b). The Average Cost AC and Average Variable Cost AVC are vertically farthest apart at the left; indeed, at $q = 0$, AC is infinite.[9] For larger q, the Average Cost $AC \equiv C/q \equiv (F + VC)/q$ approaches nearer and nearer to $AVC \equiv VC/q$, since the term F/q gets smaller and smaller as q increases. As for

[7]*Mathematical Footnote:* $C = 128 + 69q - 14q^2 + q^3$. Then $MC \equiv dC/dq = 69 - 28q + 3q^2$.

[8]There is also a false solution (where MC cuts MR *from above*) at $q = 1/3$. At this output $R \equiv Pq = 60(1/3) = 20$, while the fixed cost alone is 128.

[9]*Mathematical Footnote:* What about Average Variable Cost? At $q = 0$, $AVC = 0/0$ is indeterminate. But applying L'Hôpital's Rule, it can be seen that AVC approaches a finite limit as q approaches zero. This limit is the Marginal Cost MC at $q = 0$. So MC and AVC coincide at $q = 0$.

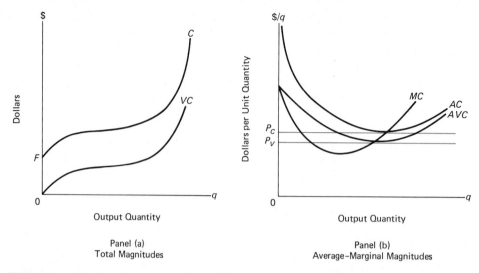

FIGURE 6.2 The Cost Function. In Panel (a), Total Cost *C* rises with output, first possibly at a decreasing rate but ultimately at an increasing rate. The curve *VC* showing Total Variable Cost lies below the curve *C* by the amount of the fixed cost *F.* In Panel (b) the *MC* curve cuts first through the low point of *AVC* and then through the low point of *AC.* P_C is the long-run shutdown price, below which the firm will not permanently stay in business; P_V is the short-run shutdown price, below which it will not produce positive output even temporarily.

the Marginal Cost curve *MC*, this is defined solely in terms of cost *differences*, and hence is in no way affected by the presence or absence of fixed costs. So there is only a single *MC* curve, reflecting the (parallel) slopes of either Total Cost *C* or Total Variable Cost *VC* at any given level of *q*. By corresponding reasoning, we see that *MC* is related qualitatively to *AVC* in the same way as it is to *AC* (Propositions 2.2a, 2.2b, and 2.2c). Specifically, *MC* cuts through the minimum point of *AVC* as well as the minimum point of *AC*, as shown in the diagram.

In the Table, the true $MC = AVC = 20$ when $q = 7$; hence this is the minimum of *AVC*. The Table indicates that $MC = AC = 37$ at $q = 8$; this is the minimum of the Average Cost *AC*.[10]

The maximum-profit condition for the competitive firm is, according to equation (6.3), $MC = MR \equiv P$ (assuming *MC* cuts *MR* from below). There are a pair of supplementary conditions, however. The maximum-profit rule of equation (6.3) is valid *provided* that the firm is actually producing positive output. But under certain circumstances the output indicated by equation (6.3) leads to a profit that, while maximized, is still actually negative. In such a case the firm has to consider the alternative of shutting down completely.

The supplementary "No-shutdown conditions" take two forms, depending upon whether a short-run or a long-run decision is being contemplated. The short-run decision is premised upon the idea that the firm will not in any case go

[10]*Mathematical Footnote:* To find the minimum of *AVC*, differentiate $AVC = q^2 - 14q + 69$ and set equal to zero. The solution is $q = 7$. To find the minimum of *AC*, differentiate $AC = q^2 - 14q + 69 + (128/q)$. A cubic equation is obtained, but the only root in the relevant range is $q = 8$.

out of business, hence will surely be incurring the fixed costs F regardless of whether it produces positive output or zero output. For the long-run decision, in contrast, the firm would sell off its fixed assets and hence recover the fixed cost F if it should decide to shut down rather than produce positive output. (The distinction between short run and long run will be discussed in more detail in Section 6.E following.)

The firm will choose zero output *in the short run* only if, at the best positive output, Total Revenue does not cover even the Total Variable Cost. While the fixed cost F runs on, the firm would do better simply incurring that fixed expense rather than generating output whose sales value falls short of the Variable Cost alone. Hence the short-run condition can be written:

(6.4a) $R > VC$ or equivalently $P > AVC$ Short-Run No-Shutdown Condition

In the long run, of course, the firm can only stay in business if its receipts cover *all* its costs. This leads to:

(6.4b) $R > TC$ or equivalently $P > AC$ Long-Run No-Shutdown Condition

In Panel (b) of Figure 6.2, the short-run condition $P > AVC$ means that the market price faced by the firm must be higher than P_V—the minimum of the AVC curve—if the firm is not to find temporary shutdown preferable to any positive output. Similarly, the long-run condition $P > AC$ indicates that the firm will go out of business and liquidate its fixed assets unless the market price is at least P_C.

Note that, if the market price is between P_C and P_V, the firm in the short run will be producing positive output—yet, were this price expected to persist so that a long-run adjustment is dictated, the firm would necessarily go out of business.

PROPOSITION: The optimal output for the price-taking firm is given by the condition $MC = MR \equiv P$, provided that $P > AVC$ in the short run and $P > AC$ in the long run. $P > AVC$

$P > AC$

6.D.1   ☐An Application: Division of Output among Plants

Sometimes a firm is faced with the problem of allocating a given total of output between two or more of its plants. Suppose there are just two plants, a and b. Then, by an obvious extension of equation (6.3), the firm's optimizing rule becomes:

(6.5) $MC_a = MC_b = MR \equiv P$

That is, the firm should so divide its production as to make the Marginal Costs of output the same in both plants; the total output, furthermore, should be such that this level of Marginal Cost equals Marginal Revenue *MR*. (In competition, of course, *MR* is identical with price *P*.)

Figure 6.3 is a geometrical representation of the division of output between two plants. The given total of output, $q_a + q_b = q$, is indicated by the horizontal distance between the two vertical axes. The output q_a of plant *a* is measured in the usual way, as the distance to the right of the left-hand axis. But q_b is, as indicated by the arrow, measured in the reversed direction as the distance to the left of the right-hand axis. This construction is convenient since the optimal division of output, where $MC_a = MC_b$, is then at the intersection of the two Marginal Cost curves (both assumed rising throughout).[11] The *total* output of the firm will be correct if the $MC_a = MC_b$ so determined is just equal to Marginal Revenue.

What if the MC_a and MC_b curves, each an increasing function of its own plant output, do not intersect? This means that for the specified total output q, one plant *always* produces less cheaply than the other. Then, regardless of fixed costs, the higher *MC* plant should not be operated at all.

Exercise 6.4: (a) Suppose that the Marginal Cost functions for the two plants are $MC_a = 5 + 2q_a$ and $MC_b = 40 + q_b$. If the total output is $q = 25$, how should the outputs be divided? (b) What if the total output were $q = 15$?

Answer: (a) Setting the Marginal Costs equal, we have $5 + 2q_a = 40 + q_b$. Making use of $q_a + q_b \equiv q = 25$ and substituting, the solution obtained is $q_a = 20$, $q_b = 5$. (b) If we try to set the Marginal Costs equal as before, a negative output would be indicated for plant *b*, which is impossible. The explanation, which can be verified by sketching, is that the Marginal Cost curves do not intersect if the total output q is only 15. For $q = 15$ it is optimal to assign all output to plant *a*, that is, to set $q_a = 15$ and $q_b = 0$. Note that at $q_a = 15$, the first plant's Marginal Cost is still only 35—while, for plant *b*, Marginal Cost is *never* less than 40.

[11]There are interesting complications if one or both of the plant *MC* curves are falling rather than rising functions of output. These topics cannot be pursued here, however.

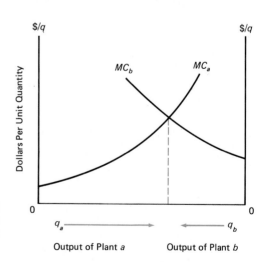

FIGURE 6.3 **Division of Output between Plants.** A firm with two plants *a* and *b* will divide any given output *q* in such a way that the two Marginal Costs MC_a and MC_b are equal.

Output of Plant *a*   Output of Plant *b*

EXAMPLE 6.4
Load Dispatching: Electrical Engineers as Economists

Electricity is typically generated by companies that operate a number of separate producing plants, with a transmission network providing connections to consumers as well as ties among the generating plants. Since electricity companies are (with some exceptions) required to meet instantaneously all demands placed upon them by consumers, the operating problem at any moment of time is to assign output most economically among the generating plants. Since the required output varies widely within the day, and even from moment to moment, the problem is both practically important and ever-present.

Fred M. Westfield[a] investigated the operating practices of a leading American electric utility. He discovered that this company employs a dispatcher to actually "assign the load" from moment to moment among the different plants. The dispatcher is guided by a Station-Loading Sliderule that shows what the economist would regard as the Marginal Cost function of each plant. By mechanically manipulating his Sliderule, the dispatcher automatically equates Marginal Cost for all plants in operation, satisfying equation (6.5) in such a way as to meet the total generation requirement. For some older plants, Marginal Cost is quite high throughout. These plants are operated only in peak-demand periods.

The company's method of division of output, and the Sliderule itself, were developed by engineers lacking the slightest acquaintance with economic theory! The company's engineers thus independently "discovered" Marginal Cost analysis—a striking intellectual achievement, though one that knowledge of intermediate economic theory would have made unnecessary.

[a]F. M. Westfield, "Marginal Analysis, Multi-plant Firms, and Business Practice: An Example," *Quarterly Journal of Economics*, v. 69 (May 1955).

6.E
SHORT RUN VERSUS LONG RUN

"In the short run some costs are fixed; in the long run they become variable." This is the fundamental difference between long run and short run. The distinction between long run and short run is not a simple dichotomy, however. The longer the run contemplated, the greater the range of costs considered as variable rather than fixed.

Consider a manufacturing firm. Toward the variable-cost end of the spectrum are the expenses of input elements like electric power, supplies of materials, and ordinary labor services; toward the fixed end are costs associated with ownership or leasing of real estate and machinery. Suppose that circumstances (e.g., an interruption of supplies, or breakdown of machinery) call for a very short, say an hour's, reduction of output. Some electric power would be saved in the slowdown, and there would be lesser usage of materials, but little else could or would be changed in the way of cost. If output were cut back over a period as long as a day, some labor might also be laid off. Over a period like a month a large fraction of the labor force might be furloughed (their wages would become a variable cost), and perhaps some leased equipment (e.g., trucks) would be dispensed with. Finally, for a permanent reduction in output the firm will sell off machinery and scale down real-estate commitments.

For simplicity, in the discussion that follows we shall treat the long-short distinction as if it were a dichotomy. The "long run" will mean that *all* costs are variable; the "short run," that some costs are fixed. The relations between *total* short-run and long-run costs, under this assumption, are shown in Panel (a) of Figure 6.4. The single Long-Run Total Cost curve $LRTC$ goes through the origin; since there are no fixed costs, if $q = 0$ then $LRTC = 0$. The $LRTC$ function shows the *lowest cost* of producing any given level of output. Why the lowest cost? Because, with all costs variable, for any output q the firm is free to choose the best (most economical) mix and proportion of all resources employed.

Three different Short-Run Total Cost functions are shown in Panel (a). First, $SRTC_1$ is associated with a low level of fixed cost F_1, adapted to a relatively small rate of output. The adaptation is optimal for the rate of output q_1 at which $SRTC_1$ is tangent to $LRTC$; this is optimal because at q_1, $SRTC_1 = LRTC$, and the latter is the *lowest* cost possible of producing output q_1. Along $SRTC_1$ the fixed

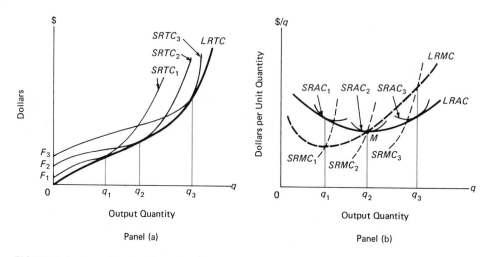

FIGURE 6.4 Short-Run and Long-Run Cost Functions. In Panel (a), *LRTC* is the Long-Run Total Cost function showing the cost of producing any output q when all factors are allowed to vary. The Short-Run Total Cost curve $SRTC_1$ applies when the fixed factor is held constant at a level appropriate for small-scale production (q_1); similarly, $SRTC_2$ and $SRTC_3$ are associated with the higher levels of fixed cost appropriate for medium-scale production (q_2) and for large-scale production (q_3). The corresponding average and marginal curves are shown in Panel (b). At output q_1, $SRAC_1 = LRAC$ (a tangency) and $SRMC_1 = LRMC$ (an intersection), and similarly for output levels q_2 and q_3. At any output, the Total Cost curves and the Average Cost curves are *never* higher in the long run than the short run. However, over certain ranges Short-Run Marginal Cost may lie below *LRMC*.

costs are small, which is fine if output is to be at a low rate. On the other hand, if the actual production should become greater than initially contemplated, $SRTC_1$ rises steeply—increments of output beyond q_1 rapidly become very costly. $SRTC_2$ is most suitable for a middling rate of output, q_2 in the diagram. The fixed cost F_2 is at a sufficiently high level to make larger output rates cheaper along $SRTC_2$ than along $SRTC_1$; on the other hand, should it turn out that only small output is desired, then it would have been better to be operating along $SRTC_1$. Finally, $SRTC_3$ represents a level of fixed cost F_3 that is optimal for the relatively large output rate q_3. It represents the best of the three situations for high output, but the worst if it should turn out that only a small output is wanted.

A common confusion runs somewhat as follows: "The short run is distinguished from the long run in that certain factors are fixed in the former but variable in the latter. Since short-run costs of expanding output involve increases in only *some* of the resources or factors, while long-run costs may involve increases in *all*, short-run costs must be less than long-run costs. Isn't it cheaper to increase output by expanding only variable costs than by expanding both variable and fixed cost?" Expressed this way, the fallacy is evident. The firm would rationally accept an increase in its fixed cost, in its long-run decision, precisely because doing so is *less costly* (involves a more economical mix or proportion of the various factors) than trying to expand output by increasing variable cost alone.

Let us now translate from the total units in Panel (a) of Figure 6.4 to average-marginal units in Panel (b). Since $SRTC_1$ lies always above $LRTC$ except at the tangency point q_1 it follows that the corresponding Short-Run Average Cost curve $SRAC_1$ will lie always above the Long-Run Average Cost curve $LRAC$ except at q_1.[12] A similar argument applies for the relation between $SRTC_2$ and $SRAC_2$, $SRTC_3$ and $SRAC_3$, etc. The upshot is that the Long-Run Average Cost curve $LRAC$ has the same "lower envelope" property relative to the Short-Run Average Cost curves that $LRTC$ has relative to the Short-Run Total Cost curves.

There is a famous conundrum reflected in the shapes of the various $SRAC$ curves relative to the $LRAC$ curve in Panel (b). Note that, while the point of contact of the middle curve $SRAC_2$ with $LRAC$ is at the minimum of the $SRAC_2$ curve itself, this is *not* true for the other two $SRAC$ curves. For $SRAC_1$, the point of contact with $LRAC$ is along the downward slope, and so the minimum of the $SRAC_1$ curve lies to the right of (at a greater output than) the tangency point q_1. For $SRAC_3$ the situation is reversed, and the minimum of $SRAC_3$ is to the left of q_3. This seems puzzling, as suggested by the question: "The point of tangency is a low-cost point. Hence shouldn't the points of tangency coincide with the low-cost points (minima) along the various $SRAC$ curves?"

Exploratory curve-bending will show that it is geometrically impossible to draw an $LRAC$ curve through the *minima* of the $SRAC$ curves, and still have it lie everywhere *below* these curves. For $LRAC$, what we really want to know is the lowest unit cost of producing any given level of output, i.e., the "lower envelope"

---

[12]$SRTC_1 > LRTC$ implies $SRTC_1/q > LRTC/q$. But $SRTC_1/q$ is simply $SRAC_1$ and $LRTC/q$ is simply $LRAC$, so $SRTC_1 > LRTC$ evidently implies $SRAC_1 > LRAC$. At the point of contact, itself, at output q_1, the equality $SRTC_1 = LRTC$ implies the equality $SRAC_1 = LRAC$.

of the *SRAC* curves. A point on this envelope is *not generally the lowest-cost output for any given level of fixed cost,* i.e., a minimum along any specific *SRAC* curve.

Consider now the short-run and long-run *Marginal* Costs. At the tangencies of the *SRTC* and *LRTC* curves in Panel (a) of Figure 6.4 not only the *levels* but also the *slopes* of the curves in contact are equal. But the marginal function is always the slope of the corresponding total function. It follows that at output q_1, the short-run $SRMC_1$ equals the long-run *LRMC*; at q_2, $SRMC_2 = LRMC$; and at q_3, $SRMC_3 = LRMC$. This leads to the relation among the various short-run and the long-run marginal curves shown in Panel (b). Note that *LRMC* has a generally less steep slope than the Short-Run Marginal Cost curves. This feature will play a role in the distinction between the short-run and long-run *supply functions of the firm,* to be discussed in the following chapter.

Exercise 6.5: A firm has a Long-Run Total Cost curve given by $LRTC = q^2$. Its Short-Run Total Cost curve is $SRTC = 2B + q^4/8B$, where B represents the level of the factor that is "fixed" in the short run, for example the number of machines. Suppose $B = 4$, so that $SRTC = 8 + q^4/32$. Then it can be shown by calculus (or approximated by tabulating) that the associated Marginal Costs are $LRMC = 2q$ and $SRMC = q^3/8$. (a) At what output are *LRTC* and *SRTC* tangent? (b) Are the Average Cost functions, *LRAC* and *SRAC*, also tangent at this output? [The answer here requires use of calculus.] (c) What can you say about the Marginal Cost functions, *LRMC* and *SRMC*, at this output? (d) Does the overall picture here differ from the cost function diagrammed in Figure 6.4, and, if so, how?

Answer: (a) For tangency, we must show that the curves touch and have equal slopes at that point. If *LRTC* and *SRTC* touch, it must be that $LRTC = SRTC$. So we can set $q^2 = 8 + q^4/32$. The solution is $q = 4$. We now must verify whether the slopes are equal at that output. Since the marginal functions correspond to the slopes of the total functions, we need to know whether $LRMC = SRMC$ at $q = 4$. Direct substitution in the *LRMC* and *SRMC* equations given above proves that this equality holds, so *LRTC* and *SRTC* (that is, the *SRTC* curve associated with $B = 4$) are indeed tangent at $q = 4$. (b) Since $LRTC = SRTC$ at $q = 4$, it is obvious that $LRTC/q \equiv LRAC$ must equal $SRAC \equiv SRTC/q$ at $q = 4$. But to show that the *slopes* are equal, we must use calculus to compare the derivatives of $LRAC = q$ and $SRAC = 8/q + q^3/32$ at $q = 4$. The comparison shows that both curves have slope of unity at $q = 4$, and so are indeed tangent. (c) We have already seen, in (a) above, that $LRMC = SRMC$ at $q = 4$. By calculus or by plotting we can show that *SRMC* is steeper; the two curves intersect, but are not tangent to one another. (d) The main difference is that the *LRTC* curve here rises throughout at an increasing rate. This implies that both *LRAC* and *LRMC* are positively sloped throughout, rather than U-shaped as in the diagram. The *short-run SRAC* curves all have the usual U-shape, however.

There is one difficulty with the concept of fixed costs that has been pushed into the background, but now ought to be faced. Common sense tells us that, for an hour's shutdown of output, a firm will not sell off its buildings and machinery with the intention of buying them back when output picks up again. But is this consistent with our analytical models? Why should a firm continue to incur any needless "fixed" costs not dictated by immediate production requirements? Why not sell off the buildings if not needed today? It is sometimes said that "fixity" is the result of previous contractual arrangements, for example, a mortgage on an owned building or a long-term lease on a rented one. But mortgages and leases on an excessive scale can always be renegotiated; any losses incurred in the process are attributable to past errors of judgment, and are in no way costs of current production.

The explanation of "fixity" is connected in part with the feature of the real world mentioned earlier in the chapter—the fact that exchange transactions are not costless. The costs of negotiating and executing complex contracts are what make absurd the idea of sale and repurchase of factory buildings for an hour's production shutdown. But there is an additional element also involved: the *specialization of resources to the firm.*

Many different types of resources may have a degree of specialization to the firm. Machinery can be made to order, buildings partitioned or remodeled, and labor can incur specific training of little or no use to other employers. The presence of such specialized resources imports a degree of irreversibility into the firm's employment decision. With only unspecialized factors, the firm can indeed, subject to the limitations of transaction costs, purchase or sell off resources as required (or enter into or cancel leases) so as to preclude any significant "fixity" as output expands or contracts. Then temporary increases or decreases in output could, to the extent permitted by transaction costs, be responded to with "appropriate" resource combinations, i.e., along the long-run cost curves. But highly specialized assets owned by the firm will be of little use to other firms and thus have little or no resale value. Hence, the firm will not be inclined to dispose of such assets to meet a reduction of output evaluated as temporary in nature. Nor will the firm very readily acquire more of such a resource merely to achieve a temporary increase in production. Even if such specialized resources are *leased* rather than *owned* (specialized labor may be placed in this category), the cost of cancellation of the lease will tend to be high. For the owner of such a resource will, before tailoring it to the needs of the firm and thereby reducing its marketability elsewhere, surely protect himself by insisting upon steep penalties in the event of cancellation.

In the absence of transaction costs, and if only unspecialized resources were employed in production, *there would then be only a single cost function*—the distinction between "long run" and "short run" would be meaningless. Continuing to neglect transaction costs, but admitting that specialized resources permit firms to produce more cheaply, there are two ways of responding to a decline in demand: (1) The "short-run" response, appropriate for a *temporary* decline in price and so in output, holds the firm's specialized resources fixed and continues to count their cost as a cost of doing business. Thus, "a loss may be incurred in the short run" (AC may exceed P), meaning that it is rational for the firm to accept a temporary loss rather than dispose of a specialized factor that would shortly have to be reacquired. (2) The "long-run" response, appropriate for a *permanent* decline in output, is to dispose of the specialized resources no longer needed for projected future production. Hence their cost is no longer "fixed," though in general not all the expenses incurred can be recovered in disposing of them. (Any accounting loss suffered in the disposition of specialized factors is a "sunk" cost, a record of a past error of judgment but not a relevant cost for any current decision.)

Corresponding considerations apply to an *increase* in demand. If regarded as temporary, it will not pay the firm to incur the cost of specializing additional resources, since the expense of doing so will not be fully recovered when the time comes to dispose of them. To the extent that the demand change is regarded as permanent, however, it will become increasingly attractive for the firm to incur additional "fixed" (specializing) costs that make it possible to produce large rates of output cheaply.

> CONCLUSION: Factors may be held fixed in the face of a temporary demand fluctuation, in order to avoid round-trip transaction costs associated with purchase and re-sale (or sale and re-purchase), and also to save the costs of specializing factors to the firm. When this occurs, the firm is making a *short-run* response to the fluctuation in demand. A *long-run* response, in which all factors are varied in amount, will be made if the demand change is regarded as permanent.

6.F
RISING COSTS AND DIMINISHING RETURNS

Throughout this chapter both Marginal Cost and Average Cost were pictured as eventually rising functions of output q. These characteristics must apply if the firm is actually operating under competitive price-taking conditions.

What if Marginal Cost were instead falling throughout? Recall that equation (6.3), $MC = MR \equiv P$, is valid as the condition for optimal output only if the MC curve cuts the MR curve *from below*. Since competitive conditions dictate a horizontal Marginal Revenue curve MR, the Marginal Cost curve MC cannot cut MR from below when MC is falling. So if MC is falling throughout, a competitive optimum cannot be found.

Exercise 6.6: What would actually happen if the firm's MC curve were falling throughout, for example if $MC = 20 + 8/(1 + q)$? Let the fixed cost be F, and suppose the market price is $P = 22$.

Answer: Setting $MC = MR \equiv P$, the algebraic solution is $q = 3$. But clearly MC exceeds $P = 22$ for all $q < 3$, so at $q = 3$ the firm is incurring a loss—even without allowing for the fixed cost F. On the other hand, as output exceeds $q = 3$ a profit is earned on each unit, and this profit increases with output forever! The firm would then try to produce an infinite output, which is obviously impossible. (If it were to try to expand output indefinitely, eventually the market price P would have to decline. This means that competitive conditions no longer apply—the market price would not be independent of the firm's own level of output.)

What if *Average* Cost were falling throughout? Then one firm with very large output could always produce more cheaply than any number of smaller firms adding up to the same output, and so the smaller competitors would be driven out of business. A falling Average Cost curve is one of the possible sources of what is called "natural monopoly," a topic to be discussed in Chapter 8. [*Query:* Was it necessary to discuss falling MC and falling AC separately? If Marginal Cost is falling everywhere, does it follow that AC must be falling? If AC is falling everywhere, must MC be falling? *Answer:* The student should verify that everywhere-falling AC does *not* dictate falling MC. On the other hand, everywhere-falling MC does dictate falling AC.]

Eventually-rising Marginal Cost and Average Cost are associated with the famous "Law of Diminishing Returns," a topic to be covered in detail when the theory of production is discussed in Chapter 11. The "law" is actually a technological principle, intended to explain why (for example) all the world's food could not be grown in a flowerpot. More formally, the principle can be stated as follows: If one or more productive factors are held constant, in order to produce additional amounts of output the other (variable) factors will have to be increased at an increasing rate. Thus, holding constant the amount of earth in the flowerpot, the attempt to generate increasing amounts of output—if successful at all—will require ever-rising increments of labor, fertilizer, etc. Of course, rising amounts of inputs imply rising levels of cost. Thus, diminishing returns (marginal and average) translate into rising costs (marginal and average).

The Law of Diminishing Returns clearly applies to the *short run,* which (we have just seen) is defined by the condition that one or more factors are being held fixed by the firm. But in Figure 6.4 not only the $SRMC$ and $SRAC$ curves are shown as eventually rising, but also the long-run $LRMC$ and $LRAC$ curves. Can this be justified? If it were literally the case that in the long run *all* relevant factors of production were variable, the Law of Diminishing Returns would not be operative. It would be possible to choose the best proportionate combination of factors, and then increase or decrease all factors together in proportion, as required to produce greater amounts of output or less. One would then expect to find the Long-Run Average Cost curve $LRAC$ to be horizontal, in which case the Long-Run Marginal Cost curve $LRMC$ would have to coincide (Proposition 2.2c). But it is not really possible to vary literally all factors together. One or more factors, and in particular *entrepreneurship,* may not be readily expandable by the firm. Also, the very nature of the firm may be associated with some unique and non-replicable productive opportunity. A mining company, for example, may be exploiting some particular body of ore; it might be able to increase use of labor and machines and other variable factors, but there's no way for the firm to duplicate the ore body itself. The existence of non-expandable factors thus explains why, in any economically possible long run, it nevertheless remains the case that the Law of Diminishing Returns continues to apply—so that even the $LRMC$ and $LRAC$ curves are eventually rising.

EXAMPLE 6.5
Diminishing Returns in Emissions Control

In 1970 the U.S. Congress enacted that a 95% reduction in certain harmful emissions from auto exhausts be achieved by 1976. Critics, especially from the automobile industry, questioned the economic rationality of such an extreme goal. They contended that it is disproportionately more costly to go to higher and higher levels of emissions control, just as it is harder and harder to squeeze the last few drops from an orange.

A later government study tended to support this objection. In the Table, note how sharply the increments of cost begin to rise after 80% emissions reduction has been achieved.

Costs of Emissions Reductions

REDUCTION IN EMISSIONS (%)	COST PER CAR
50	$ 45
55	55
60	62
65	70
70	80
75	90
80	100
85	200
90	375
95	600

Source: Cumulative Regulation Effect upon the Cost of Automotive Transportation, Office of Science and Technology RECAT Report, Feb. 28, 1972.

The fact that rising levels of emissions control are increasingly expensive does not tell us just how far society should or should not go in this direction. So the data above do not tell us that the Congress was wrong, although it might raise a question in our minds. We shall consider the problem of correct social decisions in Chapter 15, under the heading of welfare economics.

EXAMPLE 6.6
Electricity: Short-Run and Long-Run Costs

There have been a good many studies by econometricians and engineers of the *long-run* costs of electricity production. The general conclusion has been that economies of scale exist, i.e., that in the region of historical experience the Long-Run Average Cost curve *LRAC* has been a declining function of output.[a] Thus, electric power firms appear to characteristically choose levels of capacity (i.e., of "fixed" plant) so as to operate to the left of the minimum of the *LRAC* curve in the diagram of Figure 6.4. This means, in particular, that Long-Run Marginal Cost *LRMC* is less than *LRAC*.

[a] A review of recent studies is contained in D. Huettner, *Plant Size, Technological Change, and Investment Requirements* (New York: Praeger, 1974), especially pp. 29–39.

The main technological source of economies of scale is in power *generation*; almost without exception, the larger the generating plant capacity, the cheaper the power output. The main counterbalancing force is the cost of power *transmission*. The more that power generation is concentrated in a single plant of huge capacity, the higher are the transmission losses in carrying power to geographically dispersed customers.

With regard to *short-run* costs, the picture is quite different. A power system must provide for enormous variation in usage even within short periods like a single day; since electricity is non-storable, in peak hours far more power must be produced and delivered than in off-peak quiet hours. Of course, it would be absurd to expect the firm to respond by adjusting "fixed" capacity up and down within the day. And in any case, since these demand fluctuations are obviously temporary, the firm would not want to do so. Hence we would expect to find contractions and expansions of short-run output associated with *SRMC* and *SRAC* curves like $SRAC_1$ and $SRMC_1$ in Figure 6.4. In particular, with capacity held fixed, *rising* average and marginal costs should be encountered, at least at the high outputs required for meeting peak demands.

Technologically, there are two main reasons for rising short-run costs in the range of larger outputs. (1) Pieces of electrical equipment generally have a rated "capacity." This is not an absolute limit; capacity can be temporarily exceeded. But if this is done there are corresponding losses from overheating, risk of breakdown, etc. (2) Any power system has plants, and generating units within plants, of differing "technical efficiency" (output/fuel ratio). Rationality dictates that the most efficient equipment will typically be run continuously to carry the "base load." Only as required by demand will increasingly less efficient units be started up, so that average costs rise. (The less "efficient" units may simply be obsolescent equipment close to replacement, but not necessarily. It pays an electrical system to invest in units with relatively poor fuel efficiency, provided that they possess otherwise desirable properties such as low capital costs, rapid startup, etc.)

Example 6.4 ("Load Dispatching") showed that integrated power systems do take account of the rising *SRMC* curves of generating plants. If plant *SRMC* curves were not rising, there would be no need for dispatching; all the load would always be assigned to the single most efficient plant!

☐ SUMMARY OF CHAPTER 6

In the circular flow of economic activity, business firms constitute the main *productive* agents of society, engaging in the conversion of resource services into consumption goods. Firms face consumers as suppliers of goods in the product markets, and face resource-owners as demanders of resource services in the factor markets.

In principle all production could be arranged even in the absence of firms, via multilateral contracts among all the resource-owners involved. But the costs of negotiating and enforcing multilateral contracts may make it advantageous to set up a firm as an artificial entity which can contract *bilaterally* with each separate resource-supplier. The owners of firms (entrepreneurs) are those who take ultimate responsibility, by agreeing to receive only those residual rewards that remain after making contractually agreed payments to other resource-suppliers. In their own self-interest, the owners must monitor performance of these contracts, either directly or indirectly through a hired manager.

Standard economic theory postulates that the business firm can be said to maximize economic *profit*—the difference between revenue and economic cost. Economic costs include not only explicit contractual payments made to hire resources, but also implicit charges to cover the use of those resources self-supplied to the firm by owners, valued at their best alternative employments. To maximize profit, the firm chooses that output at which the excess of revenue over cost is greatest.

For a competitive ("price-taking") firm in the product market, Total Revenue R is simply proportionate to product price P (perceived as constant) as well as to output q. The constant product price itself is equal both to Average Revenue AR and to Marginal Revenue MR.

The Total Cost function C of the competitive firm is rising throughout, starting possibly from some level of positive fixed cost F. It is usually assumed to rise first at a decreasing rate (falling Marginal Cost MC) but eventually at an increasing rate (rising MC). Economic profit is the difference between Total Revenue and Total Cost ($\Pi \equiv R - C$), or equivalently it is the output quantity q multiplied by the difference between price P and Average Cost AC—$\Pi \equiv q(P - AC)$.

The output level that maximizes profit, for the competitive firm facing a constant product price P, is given by the condition:

$$MC = MR \equiv P$$

provided that the MC curve cuts the MR curve from below. (Or equivalently here, since the MR curve is horizontal, provided that MC is rising.) However, the firm will instead find zero output to be preferable: (1) In the short run, if market price is less than P_V, the minimum of the Average Variable Cost—that is, if the Total Revenue at the best positive level of output fails even to cover the Variable Costs, or (2) in the long run, if market price is less than P_C, the minimum of Average Cost—that is, if, at the best positive level of output, Total Revenue fails to cover Total Cost.

The short-run and long-run cost functions differ; in the short run, certain factors are held constant that are allowed to vary in the long run. At any level of output, Long-Run Total Cost can never exceed Short-Run Total Cost (and, similarly, Long-Run Average Cost is never greater than Short-Run Average Cost). This raises the problem of how it can be rational to respond to a demand change by moving along a short-run cost function, rather than by "unfixing" the fixed factors so as to produce the new output in the cheapest way along the long-run cost function. The answer is that, for permanent demand changes, it *will* be rational always to "unfix" the fixed factors. Short-run responses, which hold some factors fixed, are appropriate for demand changes expected to be only *temporary*. The amount of a fixed factor is not continually varied up or down with temporary demand changes because of transaction costs, together with the fact that such a factor may have been specialized to the firm so as to have comparatively little value in alternative uses.

The eventually-rising Average Cost and Marginal Cost functions that characterize the price-taking firm have their source in the Law of Diminishing Returns. If one or more factors are held constant, eventually it must be the case that increasing increments of the variable factors are needed to produce additional units of output. Since the short run is defined by the fact that one or more factors are being held constant, rising Short-Run Marginal and Average Costs are directly explained by this technological "law." But even in the long run, not all relevant factors of production can be varied: the very nature of the firm dictates that entrepreneurship, and/or the unique production opportunity exploited by the firm, cannot be expandable without limit. Therefore, even the Long-Run Average Cost and Marginal Cost curves are eventually rising.

☐ QUESTIONS FOR CHAPTER 6

MAINLY FOR REVIEW

R1. Why is most productive activity carried out by firms rather than simply by individuals who contract mutually with one another?

R2. Partnership firms are generally small and are generally managed directly by their owners. Why? How does the corporate form facilitate the organization of larger enterprises?

*R3. What is meant by economic profit? Is profit maximization an appropriate goal for owners? For managers? What tends to happen if owners are not themselves managers?

R4. What would be the effect upon the firm's decisions of a 50% tax upon economic profit?

*R5. If Marginal Cost *MC* is falling throughout, will the Average Cost curve *AC* necessarily be falling? If *AC* is falling throughout, is *MC* necessarily falling?

R6. If Marginal Cost *MC* is rising throughout, will the Average Cost curve *AC* necessarily be rising? If *AC* is rising throughout, is *MC* necessarily rising?

*R7. When will a firm respond to changes in economic conditions by a "short-run" adjustment? When by a "long-run" adjustment?

R8. Why is it that a Long-Run Average Cost curve *LRAC* cannot be drawn with both of these properties?
   a.   It shows the lowest cost at which any given output can be produced (i.e., it is a "lower envelope" of the Short-Run Average Cost curves).
   b.   It shows the lowest-cost output at any given level of the fixed factor (i.e., it goes through the minimum points of all the *SRAC* curves).
   Which of the two conditions is the correct one?

*The answers to asterisked questions appear at the end of the book.

FOR FURTHER THOUGHT AND DISCUSSION

*T1. In railroading, about two-thirds of costs are said to be "fixed" and only one-third "variable." If so, *AVC* is approximately one-third of *AC*. It would therefore always be financially advantageous for railroads, it has been argued, to take on *additional* traffic even at rates lower than Average Cost. Is this argument valid? Explain.

*T2. Why will a firm ever keep *any* factors fixed in the face of changing economic conditions? What determines which classes of factors are held fixed, and which varied?

T3. Compare the effect upon the firm's decisions of (a) a tax of $1 per unit upon output versus (b) a license fee of $200 payable each year regardless of output.

T4. Is the firm's Total Cost curve necessarily rising, or can it have a falling range? Is the firm's Average Cost curve necessarily U-shaped, or can it be rising throughout (or falling throughout)? What of the Average Variable Cost curve? For each allowable shape of the *AC* and *AVC* curves, show the implied shape of the Marginal Cost curve *MC*.

T5. Consider the problem of dividing output most economically between two plants (as in electricity load dispatching). If the Marginal Cost curves are rising, when will one of the plants not be operated? What can be said if the Marginal Cost curves are falling?

*T6. What is wrong with the following reasoning on the part of a factory manager:

> My plant is working steadily at its most efficient output. Nevertheless, I could always meet a short-run surge in demand simply by running the machines a little faster and deferring maintenance. So in the short run my Marginal Cost is practically zero.

T7. Electric utilities commonly keep their most modern and efficient generating equipment, characterized by low ratio of fuel input to power output, working around the clock. Older equipment still on hand is used only to meet periods of higher load. What does this imply about the shape of the Short-Run Marginal Cost curve for generation of electricity? Why doesn't the firm *always* use only the most modern equipment?

*T8. An urban rapid-transit line runs crowded trains (200 passengers per car) at rush hours, but very empty trains (ten passengers per car) at off hours. A management consultant makes the following argument:

> The cost of running a car for one trip on this line is about $50 regardless of the number of passengers. So the per-passenger cost is about 25 cents at rush hour but rises to $5 per passenger in off hours. Consequently, we had better discourage off-hour business.

Is there a fallacy in the consultant's argument? "Commutation tickets" sold by some transit systems (reduced-price, multiple-ride tickets) are predominantly used in rush hours. Are such tickets a good idea?

7

CORE CHAPTER

COMPETITIVE SUPPLY, EQUILIBRIUM IN THE PRODUCT MARKET, AND THE BENEFITS OF TRADE

The subject of the preceding chapter, behavior of the firm in pursuit of profit, was an instance of an *optimization* problem. In this chapter we shift emphasis to the second category of analytical problem—*determination of equilibrium*. We shall see how the optimizing decisions of the individual firms lead in aggregate to a market supply curve or supply function, which indicates how much will be offered in the market by the industry as a whole. This supply function, together with the consumers' demand function (as developed in Chapter 4), provides all the elements needed to determine the equilibrium price in the product market and the equilibrium quantity produced and consumed. Perhaps the single most important principle of economics is that market exchange is mutually beneficial to both buyers and sellers. The final topic taken up in the chapter is how to measure the benefits gained by demanders (consumers) and by suppliers (producers).

7.A
FROM FIRM SUPPLY TO MARKET SUPPLY: THE SHORT RUN

The competitive firm by definition takes market price P as independent of its own decisions. By following the maximum-profit condition of equation (6.3), $MC = MR \equiv P$, the firm establishes its own output q in response to the given market price. At a different price P the firm's q would change; the relation between P and q is the firm's *supply curve* pictured in Figure 7.1. In the diagram, point A (price P° and quantity q°) and point B (price P' and quantity q') are two points on the firm's supply curve.

Consider more specifically now the *short-run* response of the firm to changes in P. Recall the qualification expressed in inequality (6.4a): When market price is less than P_V, the minimum level of Average Variable Cost AVC, optimal short-run output for the firm is simply zero. Thus, the competitive firm's short-run supply function s_f may have a discontinuity, as illustrated in Figure 7.1. First, s_f runs along the vertical axis, from the origin up to the price P_V, indicating that at any price lower than P_V the output supplied will be zero. The supply curve then skips to the right (dotted line) and thereafter follows the rising branch of MC above the point K. The discontinuity, is associated with a minimum positive

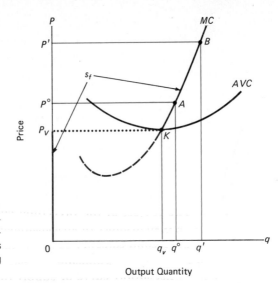

FIGURE 7.1 Competitive Firm's Supply Function: Short Run. At product prices less than P_V, the minimum level of Average Variable Cost AVC, the quantity supplied is zero (the firm's supply curve s_f runs along the vertical axis). Above this price, s_f runs along the Marginal Cost curve.

output q_V; as P rises from zero, at price P_V the firm's output response jumps suddenly from $q = 0$ to $q = q_V$. [*Query:* Why do we say that the supply function "may" have such a discontinuity? *Hint:* Is it logically necessary for the curve of Average Variable Cost, AVC, to have an initial falling range?]

Exercise 7.1: Consider the firm's cost function of Table 6.1: $C = q^3 - 14q^2 + 69q + 128$. Find the supply function of the firm, using the exact formula for Marginal Cost: $MC = 69 - 28q + 3q^2$.

Answer: The firm's supply curve is based upon the rule $MC = P$, which implies $P = 69 - 28q + 3q^2$. However, this equation is valid only for $P \geq P_V$, where P_V is the minimum of the Average Variable Cost curve AVC. We know that $AVC \equiv (C - F)/q = q^2 - 14q + 69$. The minimum of this expression could be found by calculus. Or else, making use of the rule that MC and AVC intersect at the minimum of AVC, we can write: $MC = 69 - 28q + 3q^2 = 69 - 14q + q^2 = AVC$. Solving algebraically, MC and AVC intersect at $q = 7$, where $MC = AVC = 20$. So the supply function can be written:

$$\begin{cases} P = 69 - 28q + 3q^2, & \text{for } P \geq 20 \\ q = 0, & \text{for } P < 20 \end{cases}$$

Adding up outputs of all the firms producing a particular good, the economy-wide supply curve for that commodity is obtained. (This aggregation on the supply side is of course very much like the demand aggregation in Chapter 4, in which the separate demands of the individual consumers were summed to obtain the overall market demand curve for a commodity.) Since firms tend to be somewhat specialized in production, any given good is typically produced only by a limited group of producers; this group of firms is called the *industry* associated with that good. So the economy-wide aggregate of the firm supply curves for a particular product becomes the *industry supply curve*.

Exercise 7.2: Suppose that an industry consists of 100 identical firms, each having the cost function of Exercise 7.1. What is the industry supply curve?

Answer: The industry output is $Q \equiv 100q$, where q is the output of each firm. Going directly to the supply function of Exercise 7.1 and substituting from the above, we have:

$$\begin{cases} P = 69 - 28\left(\dfrac{Q}{100}\right) + 3\left(\dfrac{Q}{100}\right)^2, & \text{for } P \geqq 20 \\[2ex] Q = 0, & \text{for } P < 20. \end{cases}$$

There are two complications to consider, however. First, the number of firms in an industry is not fixed but is itself responsive to price. If an outside firm sees a way of earning a profit in an industry, it will enter; if an inside firm faces the prospect of losses, it will exit. The aggregation of individual firms' supply curves to obtain an industry supply curve must therefore take account of a larger number of firms at high prices, a smaller number at low prices. Entry and exit of firms are considered *long-run* adaptations to changes in demand, to be discussed in the following section. Here we are discussing *short-run* adaptations and so will assume that the number of firms is fixed.

The second complication involves a point that was not emphasized in Chapter 6. The competitive firm was defined there as a price-taker with regard to *product price P*. However, it is also ordinarily true that the competitive firm can be regarded as a price-taker with regard to *factor prices* as well. That is, expansion or contraction of the output of any single firm would not significantly drive up or down the prices of factors like land or labor employed in the industry. But when *the industry as a whole* expands or contracts output in response to changes in product price *P*, there may well be an impact upon the prices of some or all of the resources used in production.

The effect of this consideration is shown in Figure 7.2. Let us suppose that an initial level of product price P' is associated with an industry aggregate output Q'; this price and quantity therefore determine one point on the industry supply curve *S*. At this initial price each firm has a Marginal Cost curve, like *MC* in Figure 7.1, which (for prices $P > P_V$) shows the supply reaction of the firm to changes in price. It might then be thought that the effect of a product price increase from P' to P'' can simply be found by moving along the curve denoted $\Sigma s_f'$ in Figure 7.2—the simple horizontal summation of the firm's supply curves—to the output level $\hat{Q}$. But, if the collective expansion of industry output affects factor prices, the industry *as a whole* cannot expand output along $\Sigma s_f'$. Normally, the consequence of increased output would be a *rise* in the prices of factors used by the industry; this would entail an *upward shift* of all the firms' Marginal Cost curves and, therefore, of their supply functions. The upshot is that with a product price rise from P' to P'', the new quantity supplied by the industry will not be $\hat{Q}$ along $\Sigma s_f'$ in Figure 7.2. The correct quantity Q'' lies along a somewhat higher summation curve $\Sigma s_f''$, which reflects the *firms'* upward-shifted *MC* curves at the higher level of *industry* output. The true supply curve, the dashed curve *S* in Figure 7.2, will therefore tend to be steeper than would be inferred from looking at the separate firms' *MC* curves. Put another way, an observer who failed

204

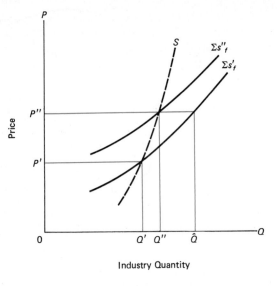

FIGURE 7.2 Industry Supply Function: Factor-Price Effect. At price P' the industry produces the quantity Q', as one point on the industry supply curve S. When actual industry output is Q', the aggregate of the supply curves *visualized by the separate firms* is $\Sigma s'_f$. But as industry output expands, in response to a product price increase to P'', factor prices tend to be driven up. This raises costs to the firms, forcing their separate supply curves upward so that the aggregate is represented by a curve like $\Sigma s''_f$. Thus, the effective industry supply curve tends to be steeper (less elastic) than the aggregate of firms' supply curves.

to take this factor-price effect into account would be led to predict too big a supply response of the industry to variations in product price P.

CONCLUSION: The short-run supply curve of a competitive firm is identical to its MC curve (above the minimum of its AVC curve). The short-run supply curve of a competitive industry is the horizontal sum of the firms' supply curves, adjusted for the factor-price effect upon firms' MC curves as the industry output expands or contracts. The factor-price effect normally operates to reduce the magnitude of the supply response to changes in demand, that is, it steepens the industry supply curve.

It is desirable to have a measure of responsiveness of quantity supplied to price, analogous to the corresponding demand measures discussed in Chapter 5. The most obvious measure of supply responsiveness would be $\Delta Q/\Delta P$, the ratio of the change in quantity per unit change in price along the supply function. But, as explained in Chapter 5, such a ratio has the disadvantage of being affected by changes of conventional units of measurement. Different values for the measure of responsiveness would be obtained if the unit of quantity were pounds instead of tons, or if price were quoted in dollars instead of in cents.

The *elasticity* concept eliminates this difficulty by expressing changes of quantity and price in terms of proportionate rather than arithmetic variation. In this case, we are interested in proportionate response of quantity supplied to proportionate change in price. This concept is called the "elasticity of supply."

DEFINITION: The elasticity of supply κ is the proportional change in the quantity supplied, $\Delta Q/Q$, divided by the proportional change in price, $\Delta P/P$.

Cross-elasticity of supply (response of supply of commodity X to changes in the price of some other commodity Y) could be symbolized as κ_{xy}. *Income* elasticity of supply could be defined as well.[1] But attention will be limited here to the direct price elasticity symbolized simply as κ.

$$\kappa \equiv \frac{\Delta Q/Q}{\Delta P/P} \equiv \frac{\Delta Q}{\Delta P} \cdot \frac{P}{Q}$$

To distinguish different commodities, appropriate subscripts would of course be used.

Aside from eliminating the problem of units of measurement, the elasticity concept permits *inter-commodity* comparisons of supply responsiveness to price. We can meaningfully say that the supply of some commodity X is more sensitive to price (X has greater elasticity of supply) than some other commodity Y. The elasticity concept also allows price-responsiveness comparisons despite wide variations in *scale;* for example, we can say that some single firm has greater supply elasticity than the industry as a whole. The relation between the firm supply curves and the industry supply curves derived in the preceding section, i.e., the relation between the shapes of the Σs_f curves and the S curve in Figure 7.2, can be expressed as follows:

> PROPOSITION: The short-run elasticity of supply of the industry is normally *less* than the separate short-run elasticities of supply of its component firms (because of the factor-price shifts that take place with industry-wide changes of output).

7.B
LONG-RUN AND SHORT-RUN SUPPLY

The supply curve of the firm just discussed and pictured in Figure 7.1 is a *short-run* supply function. The MC curve in the diagram is a *Short-Run* Marginal Cost curve $SRMC$ (like the ones in Panel (b) of Figure 6.4), associated with some given quantity of a "fixed" factor. As explained in the previous chapter, a factor may be held fixed when the firm is responding to product price changes regarded as temporary. The short-run supply curve S of the industry is derived by aggregating these short-run supply curves of the separate firms (with due allowance, of course, for the factor-price effect discussed above).

What if a change in product price P were to take place that is regarded as *permanent*? Specifically, suppose P has permanently fallen. Then the firm has clearly made a mistake in past over-expansion of the "fixed" factor. Its past planning decision that equated *Long-Run* Marginal Cost $LRMC$ to anticipated price P was based upon an over-optimistic evaluation of the price prospects. It

---

[1]The *cross-elasticity* of supply would be relevant for two goods related in production, e.g., wool and mutton. The *income elasticity* of supply might be significant if, for example, higher individual incomes led to a withdrawal of labor from the industry. (In this case, the income elasticity would be *negative*.)

now wishes to contract the scale of the "fixed" factor back to the level associated with the condition $LRMC = P$, using the more realistic value of P.[2] In the opposite case, of course, an *increase* in price regarded as permanent would be reacted to by an output adjustment setting $LRMC = P$ via an increase in the scale of the fixed factor.

The competitive firm's long-run supply function Ls_f is pictured as the broken bold curve in Figure 7.3. It has a branch along the vertical axis up to the level of P_C, the low point of the $LRAC$ curve, but above that is represented by the firm's $LRMC$ function. Suppose that a firm is initially in optimal short-run and long-run adjustment to a given level of price $P°$. In Figure 7.3, we see that at output $q°$ both $SRMC$ and $LRMC$ are equal to $P°$. Now imagine that price suddenly jumps to P'. If the price change is regarded as *temporary* by the firm, the correct reaction will be to set $SRMC = P'$ at output level q'_S; if regarded as *permanent*, the correct reaction is to set $LRMC = P'$ at output level q'_L. Of course, there will be various degrees rather than a strict dichotomy between "temporary" and "permanent" price changes. In addition, firms may differ in their estimates of the permanence of price fluctuations. In consequence, over any period of time we would expect to observe some *mixture* of "short-run" and "long-run" responses.

[2]How *rapidly* it pays to move from the over-expanded to the correct level of the fixed factor depends upon a number of features, including the durability and the resale value of the "excessive" fixed equipment specialized to the firm. If resale value is relatively high, the firm may sell off the excess equipment and move to the correct scale almost immediately. But if resale value is very low, it may pay the firm to retain the equipment until it wears out, rather than dispose of an asset of positive productivity for almost nothing. Note that it may or may not take a long period of *calendar* time to make a "long-run" scale adjustment.

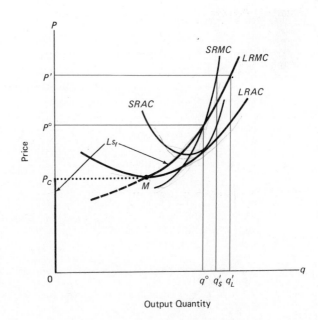

FIGURE 7.3 Firm's Long-Run Supply Function. The firm's long-run supply function Ls_f runs along the vertical axis (zero quantity supplied) up to P_C, the minimum level of the Long-Run Average Cost curve $LRAC$. Above this price, the supply function is represented by the curve of Long-Run Marginal Cost $LRMC$.

Output Quantity

Exercise 7.3: Using the information in Exercise 6.6 of the preceding chapter, let the *LRTC* curve be given by $LRTC = q^2$ and the set of *SRTC* curves by $SRTC = 2B + q^4/8B$, where B is the amount of the "fixed" factor. (a) If $B = 4$, find the short-run supply curve. (b) Find the long-run supply curve. (c) At what price and output do these supply curves intersect, and what is the significance of this intersection? (d) What would happen if price rose to $P = 27$, and were interpreted as either (1) a temporary change, or (2) a permanent change?

Answer: (a) We saw in Exercise 6.6 that the associated Marginal Cost curves are $LRMC = 2q$ and $SRMC = q^3/8$. Then the *short-run* supply curve is $P = q^3/8$. (b) The *long-run* supply curve is $P = 2q$. [*Note:* We did not have to consider here any discontinuity in the long-run or short-run supply curves. Why?] (c) The curves intersect at output $q = 4$, price $P = 8$. The significance of the intersection is that the scale of the fixed factor, $B = 4$, is optimal when $P = 8$—since the short-run supply curve and long-run supply curve dictate the same output $q = 4$. (d) If price rose to $P = 27$ and the change were regarded as temporary, the firm would respond along its short-run *SRMC* curve, setting $q^3/8 = 27$. The short-run optimal output would be $q = 6$. If the price change were regarded as permanent, the firm would make a long-run response and set $LRMC = 2q = 27$ so that output would be $13\frac{1}{2}$. Evidently, the long-run output response is greater—i.e., the long-run supply curve is less steep, or more elastic.

EXAMPLE 7.1
Cotton Spindles[a]

Cotton spinning in the United States is generally regarded as a good approximation of a competitive industry. There are two main geographical concentrations of the industry, in New England and in the South. The Table shows, for each region, the average variation (by calendar quarters over the period 1945–59) in "spindle hours." Spindles as fixed equipment are of course an essential element of spinning, so that spindle hours can be regarded as measuring output. "Changes in Hours per Spindle" may be interpreted as an index of the firms' "short-run" adjustment to the price changes taking place quarter by quarter. "Changes in Active Spindles" represents a "long-run" adjustment—variation in the amount of fixed equipment.

Changes in Cotton Spinning, per Quarter, 1945–1959

AREA	CHANGE IN HOURS PER SPINDLE (%)	CHANGE IN NUMBER OF ACTIVE SPINDLES (%)
Southern states	90.5	9.2
New England	76.5	21.8

Source: U.S. Census data cited in G. J. Stigler, *The Theory of Price*, 3rd ed. (New York: Macmillan, 1966), p. 144.

[a]Discussion based upon G. J. Stigler, *The Theory of Price*, 3rd ed. (New York: Macmillan, 1966), pp. 143–44.

Evidently, the quarterly price changes in this period were predominantly interpreted by firms as temporary, since only to a small extent did they lead to changes in the quantities of "fixed" equipment.

The difference between the two regions appears to be due to the fact that the industry, while relatively static in the South, was definitely declining in New England. In periods of low prices, the higher-cost New England firms were more likely to make long-run adjustments, gradually disposing of their fixed spindle equipment.

The *industry* long-run supply curve, like the industry short-run supply curve, is based upon the horizontal summation of the firm supply curves. As before, allowance must be made for the impact of industry-wide expansions or contractions upon factor prices, the effect of which will be as already pictured in Figure 7.2. For both short-run and long-run supply, this factor-price variation makes the industry supply curve less elastic than the separate firms' supply curves.

There is one new element that operates in the long run: *entry and exit of firms.* In long-run equilibrium, for every firm that remains in the industry, price must cover Average Cost: $P \geqq LRAC$. Or, we may say, *profit* must be non-negative. Profits are the excess of revenue (market value of output) over costs (market value of input). If this excess is negative, in the long run the resources will be freed to move to higher-valued uses elsewhere. As this applies to entrepreneurial resources as well, those firms that cannot make a profit at any achievable level of output will eventually exit or cease to exist (the entrepreneur will move to a new industry or will shift to non-entrepreneurial employments). And if a new firm (whether newly organized, or already in existence but outside the industry) can earn a profit within the industry, it will eventually enter.

Summarizing, a given price change leads to a larger supply reaction when firms in the industry adjust along $LRMC$ (i.e., when they interpret the price change as permanent) than when they adjust only along $SRMC$ (i.e., when they interpret the price change as temporary). And the entry of firms into, or exit from, the industry works in the same direction. A high price leads in the long run not only to a larger quantity response along existing firms' $LRMC$ curves, but also to an increase in the *number* of firms; a low price leads in the long run not only to output reductions along $LRMC$ curves, but to a contraction in the *number* of firms.

The effect of "length of run" upon the supply–demand equilibrium is pictured in Figure 7.4. The initial equilibrium situation is represented by price $P°$ and $Q°$ along demand curve DD. Now suppose that demand shifts upward to $D'D'$. The vertical curve labeled IS is what is sometimes called the "immediate-run" supply function. It is supposed to represent a period so momentary that production has no time to respond at all. In these circumstances the entire brunt of the equilibrating adjustment must fall upon price, which is determined by the intersection of supply curve IS with the demand curve $D'D'$ at the level P_I. In the

FIGURE 7.4 Market Response to Change in Demand. Starting from an equilibrium at point F (price $P°$ and Output $Q°$), the demand curve shifts upward from DD to $D'D'$. In the "immediate run" it is supposed that quantity $Q°$ cannot be changed at all (vertical supply curve IS); the entire impact is therefore upon price, which rises to P_I. In the "short run" (that is, if firms can vary output but evaluate the demand change as temporary), the sloping supply curve SS is relevant; there is now an increase in aggregate quantity produced to Q_S and therefore a lessened impact on price (P_S). In the "long run" (if firms evaluate the demand change as permanent), LS becomes the relevant supply curve; the change in quantity is greatest (Q_L), and the change in price is least (P_L).

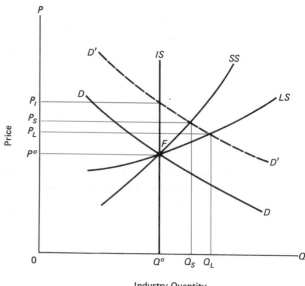

Industry Quantity

period of time allowing short-run adjustments, firms will react by varying output along their *SRMC* curves. These responses, properly aggregated, are represented by the industry's short-run supply curve *SS*. In the new short-run equilibrium, price P_S is higher than the initial $P°$ but lower than the immediate-run price P_I. Finally, in the long run a greater supply reaction is elicited, so that price declines further to the level P_L—still higher, however, than $P°$ (if the industry long-run supply curve *LS* has any positive slope).

CONCLUSION: In progressing from immediate-run to short-run to long-run industry response to changes in demand, the impact upon price is moderated while the impact upon quantity produced and exchanged becomes greater.

EXAMPLE 7.2
Preclusive Buying of Wolfram[a]

A striking example of the responsiveness of supply to price changes resulted from the Allied powers' "preclusive buying" program in World War II. In this program the United States and Great Britain attempted to cut off the flow of strategic materials from neutral countries to the Axis powers, by prior purchase in the open market.

Wolfram is an ore of tungsten, a vital alloying metal for steel. It is produced in Spain and Portugal, countries that were both neutral in the war and poten-

[a]Discussion based on D. I. Gordon and R. Dangerfield, *The Hidden Weapon* (New York: Harper & Brothers, 1947), pp. 105–16.

tial suppliers to the Axis. In August 1940, before the commencement of preclusive buying, the market price of wolfram in Portugal and Spain was $1144 per ton. Since the Allies were trying to buy up literally *all* the wolfram that would otherwise have gone to Germany and Italy, the price was rapidly driven to unprecedented levels. By October 1941 it had reached $20,000 per ton. Portugal reacted by controlling the price and allotting the wolfram supply (in a presumably "equitable" manner) between the Axis and the Allies. Spain, however, chose to let the market process operate unhindered (to the advantage of the Spanish wolfram miners).

The program "succeeded" in the sense that Germany eventually (in July 1943) quit bidding for Spanish wolfram, making do with substitutes for tungsten alloy. But before this occurred, wolfram production in Spain had increased to ten times its pre-war level. It seemed at times to Allied purchasing agents that every man, woman, and child in the country must be back in the hills, digging wolfram. In undertaking the program, the long-run supply elasticity of wolfram production had been seriously underestimated.

7.C
DETERMINANTS OF THE INDUSTRY'S SUPPLY FUNCTION

It is useful to classify the determinants of the industry supply function into: (1) elements that are *internal* to the separate firms of the industry; (2) elements that are *external* to the separate firms (but still "internal" to the industry as a whole); and (3) elements associated with entry of firms into, or exit of firms from the industry.

The first determinant of supply, reflecting elements *internal* to the firms, is the variation of cost of production as a function of each firm's *own* output. An "economy of scale" is said to exist when larger output is associated with lower Average Cost; a "diseconomy of scale," when larger output entails higher Average Cost. In the short run, as shown by the shape of the firm's supply function s_f in Figure 7.1, *diseconomies* of scale are dominant—everywhere beyond the minimum output level q_v. This is due fundamentally to the Law of Diminishing Returns studied in the previous chapter. The Law of Diminishing Returns is applicable in the short run, since in the short run one or more of the factors are being held "fixed." Hence the *internal diseconomies* of scale dictate rising short-run supply functions for the firms in an industry.

Matters are not so clear in the long run. Figure 7.3 shows that the *LRMC* curve is *less steep* than the *SRMC* curve; i.e., the individual firm's long-run supply function Ls_f is *more elastic* than its short-run supply function s_f. Indeed, it is sometimes contended that if literally *all* factors were variable in the long run, the Law of Diminishing Returns would not be operative. The firm could choose the best factor proportions, and then increase or decrease all factors together as required to produce more output or less. One would then expect to find a *horizontal* Long-Run Average Cost curve *LRAC*, in which case the Long-Run Marginal Cost curve *LRMC* would coincide with *LRAC* (Proposition 2.2c). But, as discussed in the preceding chapter, it is not really possible for the firm to vary literally all factors. Some inputs to production take forms that are not readily duplicated.[3] Realistically speaking, even in the long run the Law of Diminishing Returns will apply, so that a range of internal diseconomies will eventually be reached. Thus the competitive firm's Ls_f curve, while more elastic than its short-run supply curve s_f, will still be a rising function of output.

Even granting that a region of internal diseconomies will *eventually* be reached, for sufficiently great output, it still remains possible that this "eventual" condition will not be encountered until the firm's output is too large to be consistent with the survival of competition. If economies of scale dominate through the relevant range, one firm with very large output can always produce more cheaply than its smaller competitors, and will drive them out of business. This is the condition called "natural monopoly," to be discussed in the next chapter.

The second important determinant of industry supply consists of elements *external* to the separate firms, but nevertheless "internal to the industry." We have already encountered one such influence, illustrated in Figure 7.2—the effect of industry output upon prices of resources used by the industry. No single firm's output decision, in a competitive industry, has other than a negligible effect upon factor prices. But when the industry *as a whole* expands, the prices of factors heavily employed in that industry tend to be driven up. The factor-price effect is thus normally an *external diseconomy* of scale. As shown in Figure 7.2, it makes the supply curve of the industry less elastic than the simple horizontal sum of the separate firms' supply functions.

External economies and diseconomies can be divided into two categories: "pecuniary" and "technological." In both cases, the externality exists because changes in the *output of the industry* affect the *cost function of its component firms*. For a "pecuniary" economy or diseconomy, the interaction between industry output and firm cost function comes about solely through changes in the market prices of inputs. For a "technological" economy or diseconomy, on the other hand, industry output directly affects firms' physical possibilities of production—the firms' production functions. The factor-price effect just discussed is an external *pecuniary diseconomy*.

As an example of an *external technological economy*, consider firms in the business of farming on marshy soil. In order for farmer *A* to produce, he must drain his land. But pumping water out of his marshy soil will necessarily help to drain the lands of his neighboring competitors *B, C, D, ...* These latter find that their lands, being less marshy than before, now produce better (Average Cost and Marginal Cost are lower). Similarly, any drainage efforts by his neighbors *B, C, D, . . .* will help to shift *AC* and *MC* downward for farmer *A*. If all try to expand output together, all engaging in more drainage, the situation is as pictured in Figure 7.5. The original industry price–quantity equilibrium is at

[3]A traditional example is the following: Would it be possible, by duplicating all the components of the Paris Metro (subway), to double its output? The answer is no, unless we also duplicate Paris.

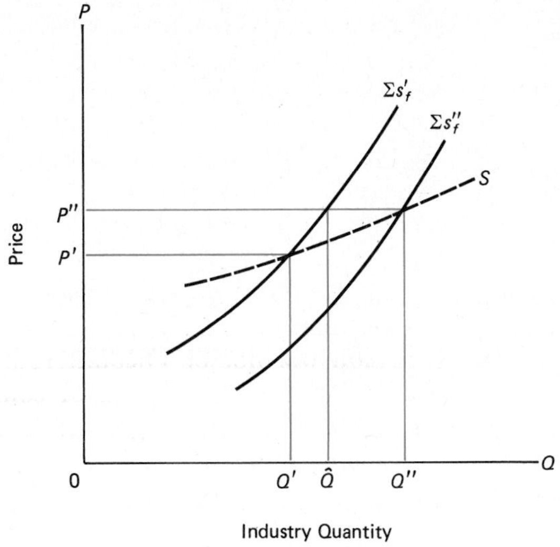

FIGURE 7.5 Industry Supply Function: External Economy. The picture here is the reverse of Figure 7.2. There, the "external diseconomy" of *rising* hire-prices of inputs, as industry output expands, raised firms' costs and so tended to steepen the industry supply curve. Here an "external economy"—*falling* costs of production incurred by firms as industry output expands—tends to flatten the industry supply curve.

P',Q'. With a rise in price to P'', the $\Sigma s_f'$ curve (the simple aggregation of the firms' s_f' curves) would indicate industry output $\hat{Q}$. But with the externality shifting the firms' MC curves downward, the curve $\Sigma s_f''$ becomes relevant so that the new equilibrium will be at $Q'' > \hat{Q}$. The industry supply curve S is thus more elastic than the separate supply curves of its component firms. It will be apparent that the direction of this external effect is the reverse of that pictured in Figure 7.2 earlier.

Now consider a *technological external diseconomy*. We can still use an example of neighboring farming firms. But suppose now that the farm lands are too dry rather than too wet. Each farmer must irrigate, pumping water up from underground wells. Doing so drains water away from neighbors' wells, thus *increasing* their Average Cost and Marginal Cost. Here the direction of the effect corresponds to Figure 7.2.

Note that the diagrams do not of themselves indicate whether the *source* of the externality is pecuniary or technological. Indeed, as a matter of *positive* analysis—for example, predicting the industry's response to price changes—it does not matter whether the "external" effect upon industry supply stems from pecuniary considerations (rising or falling factor prices as industry output expands) or from technological considerations (favorable or unfavorable impacts upon production functions of the separate firms as industry output expands). The only thing that is finally relevant is the ultimate shape of the industry supply function. The distinction between pecuniary and technological externalities is important for certain *normative* issues, for example, whether to tax or subsidize an industry, and will be discussed under the heading of "welfare economics" in Chapter 15.

Is it possible for a favorable externality, an external economy reducing costs of the separate firms as industry output expands, to be so powerful as to make the industry supply curve slope downward? That is, can the *external economies* be so great as to override the inevitable *internal diseconomies* of scale? The answer is

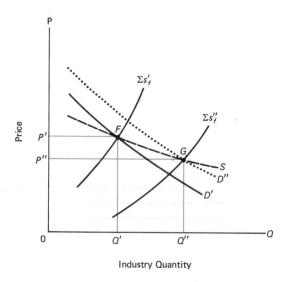

FIGURE 7.6 **Negatively Sloped Supply Function Due to External Economies.** As demand shifts upward from D' to D'', temporarily raising price, firms begin to respond along their individual supply curves whose summation is indicated by the $\Sigma s_f'$ curve through the original price–quantity equilibrium point F. But here the increased industry output sharply reduces firms' costs of production (there is a technological or pecuniary external economy), shifting the summation of the firm's supply curves downward to $\Sigma s_f''$. The new equilibrium point G represents larger quantity at lower price. Thus, the industry's supply curve S is negatively sloped.

yes. A possible instance is pictured in Figure 7.6 (which represents a more extreme version of the external-economy situation pictured in Figure 7.5). Starting from an initial equilibrium at F, we can imagine that demand shifts from D' upward to D''. At first (in the "immediate run") there must be an upward movement of price, and so firms begin to expand output along their individual supply curves whose summation is $\Sigma s_f'$. But the resulting increase of industry output sharply reduces firms' costs of production, via a technological or pecuniary external economy. Firms find they can produce more profitably than before, even after the rise in industry output has brought price back down to its old level. Point G shows the ultimate result: In response to an upward shift of demand, equilibrium quantity is larger and price lower. Thus, the industry supply curve has negative slope. At this equilibrium, however, the *firm* supply curves must still be positively sloped; we know that, for an optimum, the firm's Marginal Cost curve MC must cut the horizontal $MR \equiv P$ from below (see Figure 7.1). What has happened is that, at the new equilibrium, the new summation curve $\Sigma s_f''$ is so much *lower* than the previous $\Sigma s_f'$, while remaining positively sloped, that equilibrium price is less at the greater output.

Exercise 7.4: An industry consists of 100 identical firms, each with Marginal Cost equal to $MC = 10 + 8q - Q/10$, where q is the firm's own output and Q is the industry output. (a) Is this an external economy or diseconomy? (b) What is the equation for the industry supply curve? (c) Which diagram in the text pictures this situation?

Answer: (a) Since larger Q reduces Marginal Cost, this situation represents an external economy. (b) Since the firm sets $MC = P$, its supply function is given by $P = 10 + 8q - 0.1Q$. Using $Q \equiv 100q$ and substituting, the industry supply curve is $P = 10 + 8Q/100 - 0.1Q$, or simplifying: $P = 10 - 0.02Q$. (c) The situation is like the picture in Figure 7.6, that is, the supply curve is actually negatively sloped.

The third important determinant that affects the shape of the industry supply curve is entry and exit of firms. This is a long-run phenomenon. Any firm now *inside* the industry that finds market price P to be lower than the price P_C (representing the minimum level of its Long-Run Average Cost *LRAC* in Figure 7.3) will—if it evaluates this situation as permanent—leave the industry. Any firm now *outside* the industry that can anticipate producing with a Long-Run Average Cost function whose minimum is less than the market price of the industry's product can and therefore will profitably enter.

Exit and entry make industry supply curves more elastic: the industry response to changes in price, upward or downward, will be greater than if only output adjustments by existing firms were allowed for. Indeed, if there were an indefinitely large number of essentially identical firms standing ready to enter or leave, an industry's supply curve would be effectively horizontal (infinitely elastic).[4] But this is an unlikely situation. We must suppose that some firms have a degree of cost advantage in one industry, other firms in other industries. Therefore, if demand increases so as to induce entry, we can expect that the new firms characteristically have somewhat *higher* average costs of production than those firms already in the industry. (This need not mean that the new firms are more "inefficient"; it may only be that their alternatives elsewhere are relatively more attractive.)

CONCLUSION: In a competitive industry, the *internal* determinants (effects of firms' own outputs upon costs) tend to be diseconomies— making the industry supply curve more upward-sloping (more inelastic), though less so in the long run than in the short run. The *external pecuniary* effects of industry output upon firms' cost functions, which work through changes in factor hire-prices, also are normally diseconomies. But *external technological* effects upon cost functions, which work through changes in production functions, can be either economies or diseconomies. *Exit and entry* of firms, a long-run phenomenon, tend to make the industry supply curve more elastic, increasing the quantity response to an upward or downward shift of demand.

7.D
FIRM SURVIVAL AND THE "ZERO-PROFIT THEOREM"

Under competitive conditions there is always pressure on economic profit. Wherever profit exists output tends to expand, forcing product prices downward (lowering firms' revenue functions) and resource prices upward (raising firms' cost functions). Profit is thus squeezed from above and from below.

Returning to Figure 7.4, suppose that starting from a position of supply–demand equilibrium at price $P°$ and industry output $Q°$, an un-

---

[4]*Qualification:* For this to hold, there must also be no external economies or diseconomies, as discussed above.

anticipated increase in demand from DD to $D'D'$ takes place. As we saw in Section 7.B, in the *immediate run* the full impact is on product price, which shifts upward to P_I; every firm in the industry will then (momentarily) be receiving increased profit. Moving from the immediate period to the *short run*, the firms in the industry will increase output. The consequence will not only be a fall of product price to P_S, a partial return toward the previous equilibrium price $P°$, but also a tendency for *factor prices* to rise in response to the industry's expansion of output. Firms will still be predominantly better off at price P_S than at the previous equilibrium $P°$ (although it is conceivable that a few who are especially vulnerable to factor-price increases might actually end up worse off). The opportunity of earning an economic profit—revenues greater than economic costs—leads in the *long run* to still further expansion of firm output and also to the entry of new firms. Product price therefore moves still further back downward to P_L. Also, the additional output expansion tends to force factor-input prices upward still more.

Where does this process end? Entry stops (long-run equilibrium is attained) when no firm still outside the industry can see its way to earning a profit within. It follows that the "marginal firm," the one just on the borderline of entering or leaving the industry, can earn only negligibly more within the industry than outside. Thus, its *economic* profit (excess of revenues over the best alternative foregone) in the industry is essentially zero.

Does it follow that the "infra-marginal" firms, i.e., firms whose lower costs in the industry (or poorer alternatives elsewhere) permit them to remain in the industry even at lower prices than P_L, are earning positive economic profits in long-run equilibrium? No, because if they were there would still be upward pressure on *factor* prices. The reasoning goes as follows. If an "infra-marginal" firm is earning positive economic profit, it must be that its Average Costs are lower that those of the marginal firm. Some special resource employed by the infra-marginal firm must be responsible for its unusually low cost of production. *All firms in the industry will be bidding for the right to employ that special resource*, and in the long run its hire-price must be driven upward so as to eliminate the profit.

A clear case occurs in mining. Suppose that the demand for copper rises, and the long-run equilibrium price for copper is higher than before. New firms enter to develop copper ore bodies previously too lean to work. If the marginal firm working a very thin ore just breaks even, it might be thought that an infra-marginal firm exploiting a richer ore body should be making a handsome profit. And indeed it may, in the short run. But in the long run all firms in the industry will be bidding for the right to work the richer ore. Consequently, the owner of the resource, i.e., the owner of the richer body of ore, will be able to renegotiate with the user firm so as to recapture any extra profit earned.

What if the firm is itself the legal owner of the richer ore body? Here is where the distinction between *economic profit* and *accounting profit* (see Chapter 6) becomes essential. The accounting profit attributed to the firm controlling a rich ore body may indeed be high. But in principle, that firm could cease its operations and lease or sell the ore body to another firm. It should therefore charge itself, as an *economic cost* of its mining operations, the highest bid an outsider would make for the right to exploit its ore. In this way, its *economic profit* as a mining firm also becomes zero in long-run equilibrium.

PROPOSITION: In the long run, economic profit for any firm in a competitive industry is zero.

Of course, in an ever-changing world the "long run" may never actually arrive. Something almost always happens to change the conditions of long-run equilibrium before that state is achieved. But the *tendency* toward zero economic profit, due to downward pressure on product price and upward pressure on factor prices, is an important aspect of competitive industries.

EXAMPLE 7.3
Economies of Scale and the Survivor Principle: Medical Practice

The continuing pressure upon firm survival provides a source of information about *efficient scale* of production for firms in a competitive industry. Those firms having chosen inappropriately small or inappropriately large levels of "fixed" factors will have high Average Costs of production. In the long run, if they are to survive in the industry, such firms must shift to a more appropriate scale. "The survivor principle"[a] uses observed changes in the proportions of industry output generated by firms of different sizes as evidence concerning typical cost functions in the industry.

The survivor principle was applied to medical practice by H. E. Frech III and P. Ginsberg. They compared the market shares of physicians engaged in solo versus joint practice for the years 1965 and 1969. As can be seen from the Table, the share accounted for by solo- and two-physician practices declined, whereas all larger-sized groups gained in market share between 1965 and 1969. There is a suggestion in the data that moderate-sized groups (3–6 physicians) as well as rather large groups (26 or more physicians) may both have constituted efficient sizes in this period.

Market Share by Group Size, Medical Practice

GROUP SIZE	1965 (%)	1969 (%)	RATIO (1969/1965)
1–2	84.69	78.25	0.92
3	3.12	4.39	1.41
4	2.33	3.13	1.34
5	1.33	1.87	1.41
6	0.87	1.38	1.59
7	0.73	0.77	1.06
8–15	2.76	3.43	1.24
16–25	1.54	1.66	1.08
26–49	0.75	1.78	2.37
50–99	0.58	1.22	2.10
100+	1.31	2.12	1.62
Total	100.0	100.0	

Source: H. E. Frech III and P. Ginsberg, "Optimal Scale in Medical Practice: A Survivor Analysis," *Journal of Business*, v. 47 (Jan. 1974), p. 30.

[a]See G. J. Stigler, "The Economies of Scale," *Journal of Law and Economics*, v. 1 (Oct. 1958).

The data in the Table can be interpreted quite differently, however, depending upon whether a static or dynamic viewpoint is adopted. From the former point of view, even in 1969 the great bulk of the market was accounted for by surviving single- or two-physician groups. This strongly suggests that small size must indeed be the most efficient in medical practice. On the other hand, it is precisely this size that is declining, relative to all others. So it appears that, *on the margin,* firms of moderate and large size are the most profitable. New entrants find it advantageous to form groups of moderate or large size, while exiting firms come disproportionately from the small 1–2 physician class.

A reasonable interpretation of the data is that at any point of time there is an efficient *mixture* of firm sizes. Even though the small 1–2 physician class may on the whole be most efficient in medical practice, there may still at the present moment be relatively *too many* in this size class. So we observe proportions shifting in favor of the larger groups.

7.E
THE BENEFITS OF EXCHANGE: CONSUMER SURPLUS AND PRODUCER SURPLUS

One of the most important principles of economics is the Fundamental Theorem of Exchange:

PROPOSITION: *Voluntary trade is mutually beneficial.* (That is, it increases utility for both parties involved in the exchange.)

An alternative, mistaken view is the "exploitation theory," which claims that in exchange one party's gain is the other party's loss. The proof of the Fundamental Theorem, and disproof of the exploitation theory, hardly requires any complicated reasoning. If economic agents behave rationally, each will engage in a voluntary activity like exchange only if it is to his or her advantage.

In practical applications is it very helpful to have a measure of the benefits of trade, scaled in objective units apart from individuals' subjective utilities. *Consumer Surplus* and *Producer Surplus* are such measures. (Actually, these terms are misnomers. The benefit in question is due to the act of *trading,* rather than to the mere fact of consumption or production.)

The traditional measures of Consumer Surplus (really "buyer surplus") and Producer Surplus (really "seller surplus") are illustrated in Figure 7.7. The market supply–demand equilibrium is at price P^* and quantity Q^*. Consumer Surplus is represented by the upper shaded area, lying beneath the demand curve D but above the horizontal line P^*B. The general intention is to *show the net advantage to consumer-buyers of being able to buy all their desired units at the ruling price P^*,* even though they would have been willing to pay higher prices (as shown by the height of the demand curve) for smaller numbers of units. The Producer

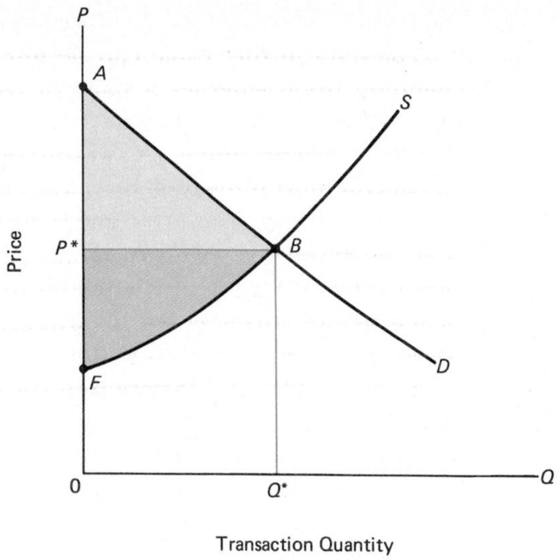

FIGURE 7.7 Consumer Surplus and Producer Surplus: Traditional Measures. At the transaction quantity Q^*, Consumer Surplus is the area lying below the demand curve D but above the equilibrium price P^*. It is the difference between the aggregate willingness to pay for the quantity Q^* (the roughly trapezoidal region $OABQ^*$) and the amount actually paid (the rectangle OP^*BQ^*). The Producer Surplus is similarly the area above the supply curve S but below the equilibrium price.

Surplus is the analogous lower shaded area, lying above the supply curve S but below the horizontal P^*B. It shows the net gain to producer-sellers of receiving a price as high as P^* for *all* units sold even though they would have been willing to supply smaller numbers of units at lower prices.[5]

The concepts of *demand price* (height of demand curve at any quantity Q) and *supply price* (corresponding height of supply curve) are useful here. For the very first unit purchased, the demand price in Figure 7.7 is OA. But the price charged is only OP^*—hence a Consumer Surplus of $OA - OP^* = AP^*$ is gained on the first unit bought. Now extend this argument to all successive units. Then, at the aggregate transaction quantity $Q = Q^*$, the sum of successive demand prices (which may be called the consumers' aggregate *willingness to pay* for quantity Q^*) is the roughly trapezoidal area $OABQ^*$ in Figure 7.7. But the aggregate amount charged is only the rectangle OP^*BQ^*. The upper shaded (roughly triangular) area AP^*B—the difference between aggregate willingness to pay and aggregate actual payments—is the Consumer Surplus. A corresponding argument applies to Producer Surplus, which can be regarded as the difference between aggregate actual receipts OP^*BQ^* and minimum aggregate *willingness to offer* $OFBQ^*$, that is, area FBP^*.

7.E.1 ☐ An Application: The Water–Diamond Paradox

Many people have found it difficult to understand why a vital commodity like water is very cheap, while diamonds—satisfying relative insignificant human needs—are so dear. Of course, comparisons like "cheaper" or "dearer" can be made only in terms of some common unit. It is rather absurd to compare the cost of gallons of water with gallons of diamonds, or carats of diamonds with carats

[5]This argument is strictly valid only under certain special assumptions that will be discussed in Chapter 13, where we go more deeply into the question of the benefits of exchange.

of water. Nevertheless, the conclusion is sometimes drawn that there is something wrong with a market system that makes the less vital commodity, diamonds, so much more expensive. This anomaly leads some people to suspect that market prices are merely arbitrary measurements, imposed in a capricious manner on goods and services.

Elementary textbooks explain the supposed "paradox" in terms of downward-sloping demand curves for both water and diamonds, together with the enormously greater supply available of the former. If water as a necessity of life were also very scarce, it would be far more valuable than diamonds. Thus, using some common physical unit (e.g., gallons) as in Figure 7.8, *for equivalent quantities* the demand curve for water, D_w, is surely far higher than the demand curve for diamonds, D_d. But at the actual tremendously disparate quantities, the market price of water is lower. A fairly typical retail price of municipal water is $100 per acre-foot, or about 3 cents per hundred gallons. At this price municipal water consumption is commonly about 150 gallons (five-eighths of a ton) per capita *per day*. Diamond quantities are measured in terms of the carat (one-fifth of a gram), and gem-quality prices run upward from $1000 per carat. At such prices (on the order of $20,000,000 per *gallon*) the number of gallons of diamonds demanded per day (or even per year or per lifetime) is small.

In terms of the benefits of trade, the Consumer Surplus in water consumption must then be enormously great, not only in comparison with the Consumer Surplus for diamonds (which is only the small hatched area under the D_d curve in Figure 7.8), but in comparison with the actual market value of water bought and sold. This market value, P_wQ_w, is represented in the diagram by the very low, flat rectangle lying just above the horizontal axis. The enormously greater area lying above this rectangle but below the demand curve D_w approximates the Consumer Surplus. Using the instructive terminology of Adam Smith, the aggregate *value in use* of water (total worth to consumers, or willingness to pay) is very, very large in comparison with its *value in exchange*—the difference between the two being the Consumer Surplus. For diamonds, on the other hand,

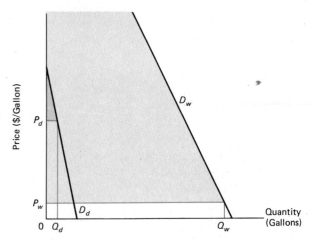

FIGURE 7.8 The Water–Diamond Paradox.
For equivalent quantities (gallons), water is "more valuable" than diamonds, in the sense that the aggregate willingness to pay (total area under the demand curve) for a necessity like water is greater. But the quantity of water available is so enormously great, in comparison to demand, that its *market value* (rectangle of width Q_w and height P_w) is small. Purchasers therefore derive a huge Consumer Surplus (shaded region). For diamonds the quantity on the market is tiny relative to the demand. Compared to the area under the demand curve, the market value of diamonds (rectangle of width Q_d and height P_d) is large and so Consumer Surplus is small.

there is comparatively little Consumer Surplus; the market value represents the great bulk of the aggregate value in use.

7.E.2 ☐ Hindrances to Trade

In Chapter 2, taxes on transactions were analyzed. The conclusion was that, regardless of whether a tax is imposed upon buyers (shifting the demand curve down) or upon sellers (shifting the supply curve up), the effects are identical. As illustrated in Figure 7.9, the quantity traded falls from a pre-tax amount $Q*$ to a post-tax $Q°$. As for price, post-tax, there are *two* prices to consider: a "gross price" P^+ inclusive of tax and a "net price" P^- exclusive of tax. Buyers would be paying the gross (demand) price, whereas sellers would be receiving only the net (supply) price; hence, it is P^+ that is relevant for transaction *demand* decisions and P^- that is relevant for transaction *supply* decisions. Figure 7.9 shows that the gross price is higher than, but the net price lower than, the pre-tax equilibrium price $P*$.

The effects of the tax upon the *gains from trade* can be analyzed in terms of the shaded and dotted areas of Figure 7.9. The entire shaded rectangle, equal to $(P^+ - P^-)Q°$, represents the aggregate tax collections. The upper shaded portion, lying above the previous equilibrium price $P*$, is at the expense of what was formerly Consumer Surplus (since the buyers now must pay the higher price P^+); the lower portion, lying below $P*$, represents a corresponding loss of Producer Surplus. However, these two losses are offset by whatever benefits stem from the uses government makes of the funds collected. And indeed, measured in dollars, the uses of funds must exactly balance the losses of surplus. Hence, the rectangular shaded area is a *transfer* from buyers and sellers to the beneficiaries of government expenditures.

FIGURE 7.9 Effects upon Consumer and Producer Surplus of a Tax on Transactions. A unit tax on transactions lowers the quantity exchanged from $Q*$ to $Q°$. The gross price paid by consumers rises from $P*$ to P^+while the net price received by sellers falls from $P*$ to P^-. The upper shaded area is a transfer from Consumer Surplus and the lower shaded area a transfer from Producer Surplus, the two transfers together constituting the amount of tax collections. The small dotted areas represent losses of Consumer Surplus and Producer Surplus that are not balanced by funds going to beneficiaries of government tax collections.

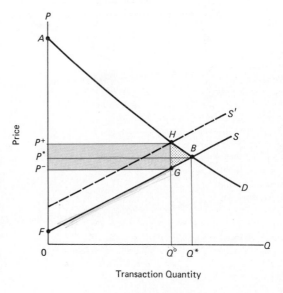

The dotted areas in Figure 7.9 represent something quite different. The triangular upper dotted area is a *net loss* of Consumer Surplus, and the corresponding lower area a *net loss* of Producer Surplus. Here there is no gain to any other party offsetting the loss to traders. The tax, by raising the effective price to buyers and lowering the effective price to sellers, *has reduced the volume of transactions* and the benefits derived from trade. The dotted areas therefore represent deadweight losses. Their aggregate magnitude constitutes the *efficiency loss* due to the tax.

But it cannot therefore be inferred that taxes should be abolished. The transfer (shaded rectangular area) represents an equivalence in *numéraire (dollar) terms* between losses in Consumer and Producer surplus on the one hand, and gains to beneficiaries of government expenditures on the other. The deadweight loss (dotted area) represents an additional loss of surplus, but it cannot be said that the "social value" (a term not defined here, and perhaps undefinable) of the government expenditures is necessarily less than the sum of the transfer and deadweight losses to traders taken together. It cannot even be proven that government revenue "should" be acquired in a way that minimizes these deadweight losses, though the analysis here is perhaps suggestive in that direction. (What economics can say about such policy issued will be examined when "welfare economics" is taken up in Chapter 15.)

> PROPOSITION: Taxes imposed on transactions reduce both Consumer Surplus and Producer Surplus. Some of the loss takes the form of a transfer of funds from consumers and producers to the beneficiaries of government expenditures. But there is also a deadweight or efficiency loss, due to the reduction in the volume of trade.

Exercise 7.5: Suppose that the market demand curve is given by $P = 300 - Q$ and the market supply curve by $P = 60 + 2Q$. The initial solution is $Q^* = 80, P^* = 220$. (a) If a per-unit tax of $T = 15$ is imposed, what is the new equilibrium? (b) What is the loss of Consumer Surplus? What is the loss of Producer Surplus? (c) What is the amount of the transfers (tax collections)? (d) How great is the efficiency loss?

Answer: (a) Using the technique of Chapter 2 (see Exercise 2.3), we can verify that the new equilibrium quantity is $Q° = 75$, the gross price (paid by purchasers) rises to $P^+ = 225$ while the net price (received by sellers) falls to $P^- = 210$. (b) The original Consumer Surplus corresponds to the area ABP^* in Figure 7.9. Since the supply and demand curves here are linear, the area is an exact triangle with size $(300 - 220) \times (80) \times (1/2) = 3200$. The new Consumer Surplus is the smaller area ADP^+ or $(300 - 225) \times (75) \times (1/2) = 2812.5$. So the loss of Consumer Surplus is 387.5. Similarly, the old Producer Surplus (the area FBP^*) was $(220 - 60) \times (80) \times (1/2) = 6400$; the new Producer Surplus (the area FGP^-) is $(210 - 60) \times (75) \times (1/2) = 5625$; and so the loss of Producer Surplus is $6400 - 5625 = 775$. (c) The transfers or tax collections (the rectangular area P^+HGP^-) are $(225 - 210) \times (75) = 1125$. (d) The remainder of the summed losses of Consumer Surplus and Producer Surplus is the efficiency loss, corresponding to the small dotted triangle HGB. Numerically it is $387.5 + 775 - 1125 = 37.5$.

Taxes hamper trade through their effect on *prices*, more specifically, by driving a "wedge" between the gross price P^+ effective for buyers and the net price P^- effective for sellers. *Quantitative* restrictions on trade, to be considered next, operate somewhat differently.

Using Figure 7.10, suppose that a *quota* equal to $Q' < Q*$ were imposed on the amount that could be supplied to the market—with no restriction upon demand. The reduced quantity Q' would then be sold at "whatever price the market will bear," determined along the demand curve D at the level P'. We want to compare this outcome with the unregulated equilibrium at price $P*$ and quantity $Q*$. The upper transfer (shaded) rectangle $(P' - P*)Q'$ is a loss of Consumer Surplus that now goes *to the suppliers* rather than to government. (And, of course, the suppliers retain the lower shaded area.) It follows that suppliers in the aggregate *may* benefit from the quantitative restriction on trading; they will do so if their transfer gain (upper shaded area) is more than their deadweight loss from the reduced volume of transactions (lower dotted area). The buyers, on the other hand, suffer *both* a transfer loss and a deadweight loss (just as in the case of a tax on transactions).

Now consider a quantitative restriction $Q'' < Q*$ on the demand side, such as *rationing*. If only those possessing ration tickets were allowed to buy, the demand curve would, as shown in Figure 7.11, in effect drop vertically from the point H representing the ration quantity Q''. The effective price would be P'' along the supply curve in Figure 7.11. An exactly corresponding analysis will show that then the buyers *may gain* on balance, though the suppliers *must lose*.

There is one important respect, however, in which these analyses of quantitative restrictions are misleading. The cases just discussed are "ideal" limiting situations; in general, the deadweight losses due to quantitative restrictions upon

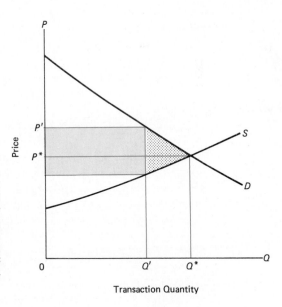

FIGURE 7.10 Effects upon Consumer and Producer Surplus of a Quota Limit on Supply. Market supply is limited to the "quota" Q', so price rises from $P*$ to P'. As before, Consumer Surplus is reduced by the upper shaded area (a transfer) plus the upper dotted area (an efficiency loss). But here the transfer is received *by the sellers*. If the transfer (upper shaded area) exceeds the sellers' efficiency loss (the lower dotted area), the sellers benefit from imposition of the quota. But buyers and sellers, considered together, lose by the amount of the dotted areas representing the combined efficiency losses.

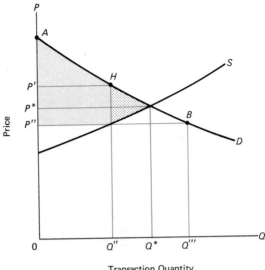

Price

Transaction Quantity

FIGURE 7.11 **Effects upon Consumer and Producer Surplus of a Ration Limit on Demand.** If a ration limit in the amount Q'' is imposed upon demand, price falls to P''. The shaded area is the Consumer Surplus under rationing which, as a result of the transfer of the lower rectangle from suppliers, may be larger than at the Q^*, P^* equilibrium. However, the dotted areas still represent an efficiency loss to consumers and producers taken together. (*Note:* The text indicates that the efficiency losses due to quota limits on supply or to ration limits on demand are generally *greater* than the dotted areas shown here and in the preceding figure.)

trade will really be *much greater* than has been indicated. Let us reconsider Figure 7.11, showing consumption rationing that limits demand to the quantity Q''. At the price P'' that suffices to elicit the desired quantity Q'' from suppliers, the shaded area in Figure 7.11 would represent the remaining Consumer Surplus in the "ideal" case just analyzed. But at a price as low as P'' the buyers are desirous of purchasing not Q'' but the much larger Q'''. Somehow or other the ration tickets must be distributed so as to validate no more than Q'' of the Q''' units demanded. Only if the validated demand units correspond exactly to the most intense demands (as measured by willingness-to-pay, or demand price) will the Consumer Surplus actually remain the shaded area in the diagram.

Consider the single most intensely demanded unit, for which some buyer is willing to pay as much as OA (where the demand curve intersects the vertical axis). It may be that the person most desiring this unit *does not obtain even a single ration ticket* and so cannot buy in the rationing situation. In contrast, consider the low-demand-price unit of demand at the point B along the demand curve, where some consumer is barely willing to offer P''. Nonetheless, this last unit may represent demand that is validated by a ration ticket, and thus effective in a rationing situation. (Note how rationing of demand, by leading to a low price P'', may induce *greater* consumption on the part of those buyers successful at obtaining ration tickets.) The upshot, of course, is that the overall efficiency loss is indeed greater than would be indicated by the previous analysis. And an exactly analogous argument holds also for quota limits on supply.

PROPOSITION: Production quotas involve a transfer of surplus from consumers to producers; rationing of demand involves a transfer from producers to consumers. In addition, both cause an efficiency loss due to the reduced volume of trade. There will generally be a further efficiency loss as a result of non-ideal assignments of rights to sell or rights to buy.

EXAMPLE 7.4

Sugar Quotas

Under the Sugar Act of 1948, the availability of sugar in the United States is limited by specific marketing quotas assigned to foreign countries and to domestic production areas. The U.S. market price for sugar is consequently at a substantial premium over the world price: for example, a 35% premium in 1960, 61% in 1968, 40% in 1970.

The effects of the U.S. quota system were studied by Ilse Mintz for the year 1970; the figures here are based upon her "low" estimates.[a] The underlying situation is pictured in Figure 7.12. Panel (a) represents a hypothetical free-market equilibrium that would have occurred in the absence of quotas. The world price is 5.5 cents per pound, and the domestic price would have to equal this. United States domestic production along the supply curve S_{US} is 2.9 million tons at this price, and imports are 8.7 million, making up a total of 11.6 million tons along the curve S_w showing world supply (inclusive of the domestic supply) to the United States. Since this is an equilibrium situation, the U.S. demand curve D intersects S_w at this price. Producer Surplus of the *domestic* producers is the small lower shaded area in Panel (a), and the U.S. Consumer Surplus is the huge upper shaded area.

The effects of the quotas are shown in Panel (b). The quota assignments (6.0 million tons of domestic supply, 5.2 million tons of imports) aggregate to only a little less than the 11.6 million tons that would have been supplied annually under free markets. But as demand is highly inelastic (price elasticity of -0.1, according to the "low" estimate), the U.S. domestic price is sharply higher at the observed 8.07 cents per pound.

The deadweight loss of Consumer Surplus [the smaller dotted triangle in Panel (b)] is estimated by assuming that the demand curve D is linear between 11.2 million and 11.6 million tons. The area of the dotted triangle is $\frac{1}{2}(8.07$ cents $-$ 5.5 cents) (.8 billion pounds) or $10,280,000 per year.

But the most obvious feature of the situation is the tremendous cost increase to consumers due to the price difference calculated upon the 11.2 million tons consumed in either case. This amounts to (22.4 billion pounds) times (8.07 cents $-$ 5.5 cents) or $575,680,000 annually.

The increased cost to U.S. consumers, all at the expense of Consumer Surplus, is broken down into four numbered areas in Panel (b). Area 1 is the transfer from domestic consumers to foreign producers, calculated on the basis of the higher price received for the 5.2 million tons they continue to

---

[a]Ilse Mintz, *U.S. Import Quotas: Costs and Consequences* (Washington, D.C.: American Enterprise Institute for Public Policy Research, Feb. 1973).

deliver to the U.S. market. This amounts to $267,280,000 per year. Area 2 is the transfer to domestic producers, calculated on the 2.9 million tons they would have delivered in either case. This amounts to $149,060,000 per year. Areas 3 and 4 are equal (assuming for simplicity that the domestic supply curve S_{US} is linear), and amount together to the remaining $159,340,000. However, they are conceptually quite different. The upper area 3, like area 2, is a transfer from Consumer Surplus to domestic Producer Surplus. But the lower area 4 is a deadweight loss. It represents increased cost of production (higher supply price) on units produced domestically that could have been obtained more cheaply from foreigners. This is the type of deadweight loss, described in the text above, that is due to a *non-ideal distribution* of quantitative restrictions upon trading. Granting that only 11.2 million tons of sugar are to be sold in the United States, there is an additional loss to the extent that quotas are assigned to high-cost domestic rather than to low-cost foreign producers. This additional deadweight loss, the larger dotted triangle in Panel (b), amounts to one-half of $159,340,000—or $79,670,000.

If we regard the transfers as canceling out, the aggregate of the deadweight losses to the United States (the "efficiency loss" due to the sugar quotas) amounts to $89,950,000 per year.

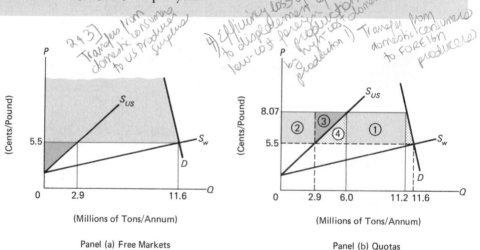

Panel (a) Free Markets   Panel (b) Quotas

FIGURE 7.12 Sugar Supply and Demand.   In Panel (a), representing the unregulated situation, the small lower shaded triangle is the annual Producer Surplus received by U.S. suppliers while the large upper shaded area is the annual Consumer Surplus of U.S. purchasers. In Panel (b), imposition of a quota slightly smaller than the equilibrium market quantity (11.2 million tons in comparison with 11.6 million) raises price quite substantially (demand is extremely inelastic). U.S. Consumer Surplus *falls* by the amount of the four numbered areas, plus the small upper dotted triangle to the right. U.S. Producer Surplus *rises* by the amount of the numbered areas 2 and 3, both being transfers from domestic consumers. Area 1 is a transfer from domestic consumers to *foreign* producers. Area 4 is an efficiency loss due to displacement of low-cost foreign production by high-cost domestic production. The small upper dotted triangle is an efficiency loss due to reduced exchange.

AN APPLICATION OF SUPPLY AND DEMAND: MANAGING A "SHORTAGE"

In a world of change the conditions determining supply and demand—preferences, productivity, and resources—are continually varying. In consequence, equilibrium or "market-clearing" prices are also ever-changing. Some of this variation does not seem to generate serious complaint. People are not disturbed that department-store sales take place after Christmas (i.e., that consumers must pay higher prices in their pre-Christmas shopping). Nor does the fact that vegetables are cheaper after harvest, or cheaper at farm roadstands than in big-city markets, seem to raise controversy. But shifts in supply or demand are sometimes both unexpected and dramatic, drastically affecting the established relations among groups in the community. In such circumstances political pressures may arise for government interventions designed to prevent or to undo some or all of the price effects of the shift to a new market-clearing solution.

Interventions designed to prevent price from adjusting to an increase in demand, or to a decrease in supply, tends to create a "shortage."[6] The standard use of the word "shortage" in economics refers not to physical scarcity, but to a supply–demand imbalance at the existing price. This does indeed seem to correspond with popular terminology. People speak of "shortages" when goods become not just expensive but *unavailable*, partially or completely, in the market. Thus, faced with a supply or demand shift dictating a higher equilibrium price, consumers are bound to lose out one way or the other—either from the higher price if the market adjustment proceeds unimpeded, or from the "shortages" that follow when interventions succeed in maintaining a lower price.

[6]In the opposite case, where interventions prevent adaptation to decreased demand or to increased supply, commodity "surpluses" are generated.

EXAMPLE 7.5
Two San Francisco Housing Crises[a]

In the 1906 earthquake and fire, the city of San Francisco lost more than half its housing facilities in three short days. Nevertheless, the first post-disaster issue of the *San Francisco Chronicle* had no report of a "housing shortage"! Indeed, the newspaper's classified advertisements carried 64 offers of houses or apartments for rent and only 5 ads for apartments or houses wanted. Of course, prices of accommodations rose sharply.

In contrast, in 1946 San Francisco was gripped by the national postwar

[a]Discussion based on M. Friedman and G. J. Stigler, *Roofs or Ceilings?* (Irvington-on-Hudson, N.Y.: The Foundation for Economic Education, Sept. 1946).

"housing shortage." In the first five days of 1946 newspapers carried only 4 ads offering houses or apartments for rent, but around 150 ads by persons wanting to rent houses or apartments. The explanation is that in 1906 the catastrophic reduction in the housing stock led to a price adjustment in the form of a sharp rise in rents to a new equilibrium level. But in 1946, rents "frozen" below the market-clearing price left an excess of quantity demanded over quantity supplied.

> COMMENT: In the physical sense, housing supply relative to popu-
> lation was clearly much more scarce after the 1906 earthquake and
> fire than in 1946. The 1946 "shortage" was an outgrowth of the
> general price freeze aimed at controlling inflation during and after
> World War II. Actually, housing supply had not decreased at all in
> the wartime period. But rising money incomes, the return of war
> veterans, and a high rate of family formation led to an upward shift
> in demand for housing. With rents frozen, a "shortage" ensued.

We shall not be concerned here with the normative question of how a shortage "should" be managed, but only with the positive consequences of alternative ways of coping with it. It is important to distinguish between short-run and long-run consequences. Figure 7.13 illustrates a "ceiling," holding price at its previous equilibrium P° after demand has shifted upward from D to D'. The *perceived* shortage is the magnitude H in the diagram—the demand–supply gap

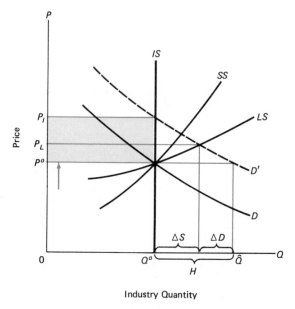

FIGURE 7.13 Effect of a Price Ceiling. An upward shift of demand in an uncontrolled market, from D to D', is met in the "immediate run" by an increase in price only (from P° to P_I). Producers benefit from a temporary "windfall" gain (shaded area) at the expense of consumers. Ultimately, an increase in supply is induced so that in long-run equilibrium price comes back down part-way to P_L. If a "ceiling" is enforced at the initial price P°, both supply and demand adjustments are blocked. H is the perceived "shortage" at the ceiling price. In uncontrolled long-run equilibrium, ΔD of the shortage amount would be the demand quantity choked off by the higher price, while ΔS would be the supply increment provided.

Industry Quantity

at price $P°$. In the unimpeded market process, price would jump in the first instance to the immediate-run level P_I, as previously discussed, but would eventually come down to the long-run equilibrium at P_L. The market would eliminate the shortage, in the short run primarily by a high price choking off demand, but in the long run increasingly via an augmentation of supply. At the price P_L in Figure 7.13, the interval ΔD is the long-run *reduction* in demand quantity while ΔS is the long-run *increment* of supply.

Exercise 7.6: Suppose that the market demand curve is given by the equation $P = 300 - Q$. The long-run supply curve is $P = 60 + 2Q$, and the short-run supply curve is $P = -180 + 5Q$. Verify that the market is in long-run and short-run equilibrium at quantity $Q° = 80$, price $P° = 220$. Now suppose that demand increases, the new equation being $P = 360 - Q$. (a) What happens in the "immediate run"? (b) What is the new short-run price–quantity equilibrium (Q'_S, P'_S)? (c) The long-run equilibrium (Q'_L, P'_L)? (d) What would be the perceived "shortage" if a price ceiling prevents price from rising?

Answer: (a) In the immediate run, quantity would be unchanged at $Q_I = 80$. The new equilibrium price would be found by using the new demand condition: $P_I = 360 - Q_I = 280$. (b) The new short-run equilibrium is $Q'_S = 90$, $P'_S = 270$. (c) The new long-run equilibrium is $Q'_L = 100$, $P'_L = 260$. Note that in the long run quantity increases more, and so price comes back down somewhat. (d) If price could not rise above $P = 220$, the quantity supplied would remain $Q = 80$ but the quantity demanded would be $Q = 360 - P = 140$. Then the perceived shortage would be $140 - 80 = 60$ units.

What about the effects upon Consumer Surplus and Producer Surplus? It might be thought at first that, *in the immediate run,* what takes place is a mere transfer between Producer Surplus and Consumer Surplus: since the same supply remains on the market, a ceiling price at $P°$ means only that producers fail to make a "windfall" gain at the expense of consumers. But this is a serious error. In the absence of a ceiling, price would have risen in the immediate run to P_I, and the supply $Q°$ on hand would have gone to those consumers willing to pay at least as much as P_I. But at the low ceiling price $P°$ there will be an *enlarged* quantity demanded—the amount $\hat{Q}$. Somehow this quantity must be distributed to consumers. Depending upon the nature of the distribution process employed, to a greater or lesser extent it may turn out that relatively low-valued demands are satisfied (some consumers willing to pay only a little above $P°$ actually acquire units of the good) while high-valued demands are not (some consumers willing to pay more than P_I do not obtain any). It may even be the case that the method employed for determining which consumers actually obtain the good is itself an additional waste of resources, for example, if acquisition of the good depends upon waiting in line (wasting the valuable resource of time). Thus, there are two distinct possible sources of loss in the immediate run: (1) the "wrong" (less highly valued) demands may be the ones satisfied, and (2) the allocation process may itself waste resources. And, of course, in the short run and increasingly in the longer run, the price ceiling reduces both Consumer Surplus and Producer Surplus by foreclosing the operation of forces that would have provided additional supplies to the market.

EXAMPLE 7.6
Gasoline Waiting Lines

Gasoline crises occurred in the United States in 1973, and again in 1979. Each crisis was precipitated by the cartel of oil-producing nations—the OPEC (Organization of Petroleum Exporting Countries)—which reduced the supplies made available to importing nations. In the United States, price ceilings on gasoline prevented the price from rising to a market-clearing level. Instead, long lines of cars waited at filling stations in the hope of getting some of the limited supplies available.

A study by H. E. Frech III and William C. Lee (1982)[a] examined the losses of Consumer Surplus during these crises. The authors employed statistical estimates of demand elasticities in the two periods in order to determine what the true equilibrium price would have been without the price ceilings. This true price still had to be paid by any consumer actually acquiring gasoline. Even though the actual dollar price was frozen below the true price, consumers were paying the difference in the form of a *waiting-time price*—the value of time wasted standing in line. The authors found that rural users tended to pay higher waiting-time prices (i.e., they waited in line longer). It may have been that rural demand is more inelastic, since in urban areas substitutes for auto travel (buses, subways, etc.) are more available. Or else, suppliers may have found it profitable to divert gasoline to the more accessible and concentrated urban markets. The Table indicates the waiting-time prices in the earlier (1973–74) crisis, in cents per gallon (adjusted to 1967 dollars). The percent of the total or true price is also indicated.

Waiting-Time Prices for Gasoline

	DEC. 1973	JAN. 1974	FEB. 1974	MAR. 1974
Urban users	3.9¢	4.2¢	13.8¢	17.7¢
(as percent of true price)	(11.1%)	(11.5%)	(29.7%)	(33.1%)
Rural users	7.5¢	7.1¢	13.8¢	29.9¢
(as percent of true price)	(19.3%)	(18.0%)	(29.7%)	(45.6%)

The authors estimated the losses in Consumer Surplus due to this waiting-time cost and also due to the reduced volume of transactions resulting from the discouragement of supply—in comparison with what would have been provided had price not been frozen. Calculated by this method, the total losses came to $369,880,000 for the December 1973–March 1974 period, and to $247,487,000 for May–June 1979.

[a] H. E. Frech III and William C. Lee, "The Welfare Cost of Rationing by Waiting across Uses: Empirical Estimates from the Gasoline Price Controls," University of California, Santa Barbara, Working Paper in Economics No. 212 (June 1982).

COMMENT: These estimates failed to allow for one additional loss of Consumer Surplus—diversion of gasoline from higher-valued to lower-valued uses. It is true that gasoline went to those consumers most willing to wait in line, but willingness to wait the longest is *not* necessarily the same as willingness to pay the most. A busy physician might have been willing to pay a very high price for gasoline, but be forced out of the waiting-line game by the high value of his or her time.

There are some less visible consequences of blocking the price rise that would adapt supply to demand. Unable to raise price openly, firms may divert energies and resources to subterfuges. They may eliminate discounts or seasonal sales, reduce quality or variety or convenience of their offerings, or concentrate production in product lines that happen to have received a better break from the price-control authorities. Supplies may be attracted into uncontrolled foreign markets that were previously unremunerative, leaving even less available for domestic consumers. And of course black markets may arise, providing a wider scope for elements of the population specializing in illegal activity. In extreme cases, the cumulative effect may be a breakdown of legitimate trade.

General price inflation, such as has been experienced in much of the world during the decade of the 1970s, is a topic in *macro*economics. But in an attempt to remedy or perhaps only to mask the inflationary process, governments may be led to impose price ceilings or "freezes" in some or all markets. Then, prices over greater or lesser reaches of the economy will no longer be free to reconcile supply and demand. While the initiating source of the disequilibrium lies in the realm of macroeconomics, the imbalances in particular markets can be analyzed by using the tools of *micro*economics. In this connection, we can learn much that is useful from a previous great inflationary episode—that associated with World War II and its aftermath.

EXAMPLE 7.7
Repressed Inflation in Post-war Germany[a]

Germany, like most of the belligerent countries in World War II, had financed her war effort by inflationary expansion of money and credit. Simultaneously, price freezes were employed to prevent this expansion from being reflected in market prices. By 1945, wartime finance had increased liquid funds in the hands of the public around tenfold, while prices were still largely at the levels frozen by the Nazi government back in 1936. And, of course, Germany faced not only the "normal" aftermath of a war that saw her cities

[a]Discussion based on J. Hirshleifer, *Disaster and Recovery: A Historical Survey*, The Rand Corporation, Memorandum RM–3079–PR (April 1963), pp. 83–112.

and industry smashed by bombing, but also the special problems of a defeated nation—divided, occupied, and subjected to punitive reparations.

In the early post-war years, the Occupation authorities directing the German economy maintained the wartime price freeze. (This was not a special attempt to punish Germany, but represented the "conventional wisdom" of the period; very much the same policies were pursued by the victorious nations in their own domestic economic programs.) But the levels of German prices were so drastically out of line with supply–demand reality that over most of the economy production for legal sale could take place only at financial loss. Industrial production in the first half of 1948 was only 45% of the 1938 amount, despite a larger population. The black market was, surprisingly, estimated to account for only 10% of transactions. This figure is extremely low because in Germany the term "black market" was given a very narrow definition: to wit, outright trading of goods for cash at illegal prices (a practice professionally engaged in by a specialized class of disreputable individuals). In contrast, *everybody* engaged without moral taint in a form of transaction known as "bilateral exchange" or "compensation trade." This trade took place at entirely legal prices in money, with one catch: No one could acquire goods or services for money alone. In addition to the money price, the purchaser had to provide "compensation" in real goods and services. Estimates are that one-third to one-half of all transactions took this form. Even the Occupation authorities engaged in it; the noon meal provided to German employees of the Occupation administration (at legal prices, of course) was often the chief attraction of such employment. Thus, the "legal" monetary transaction was a fig-leaf. What was actually taking place was the *de facto* elimination of money as a medium of exchange—regression to the inefficiencies of barter (a topic taken up in Chapter 13).

The long-standing price freeze meant that relative prices were more or less seriously out of line, but the overwhelming fact was that almost *all* money prices were too low. The Erhard policy of June 1948 was correspondingly double-barreled: (1) a drastic currency reform, exchanging new marks for old, cut down the money supply by a factor of about ten; and (2) price controls were removed. The effect was dramatic. According to one observer: "It was as if money and markets had been invented afresh as reliable media of the division of labor."[b] The German post-war economic miracle was under way.

[b]H. Mendershausen, "Prices, Money and the Distribution of Goods in Postwar Germany," *American Economic Review*, v. 39 (June 1949), p. 646.

☐ SUMMARY OF CHAPTER 7

The supply curve of the competitive firm is derived from the profit-maximizing condition $MC = P$, subject to the qualification about covering Total Variable Cost in the short run and Total Cost in the long run. As a result of these qualifications, the short-run and long-run supply curves of the firm may each have a discontinuity. For the short-run supply curve s_f, zero quantity will be offered at any price lower than P_V (the low point of the curve of Average Variable Cost AVC); above that price, s_f is identical with the Short-Run Marginal Cost curve. For the long-run supply curve Ls_f, the minimum price for non-zero output is P_C, the low point on the Average Cost curve AC; above that price, Ls_f is identical with the Long-Run Marginal Cost curve.

To find the industry supply curve, at each price the quantities offered by all firms are added (horizontal summation of the firms' supply curves). However, it is necessary to allow for the "external" effects upon firms' costs due to changes in industry-wide output. The extent of entry into or exit from the industry as demand expands or contracts must also be considered.

The "external" effects are rather complex to analyze. External *economies* reduce firms' costs as industry output rises; external *diseconomies* do the opposite. The external effects may be "pecuniary" (impact of industry-wide output changes upon hire-prices of factors) or "technological" (impact upon firms' production functions). Pecuniary external effects are normally *diseconomies,* since increases in industry output generally drive up the hire-prices of factors used in that industry; the result is to make the industry supply curve less elastic. But technological external effects can go either way. It is even possible for *external economies* to override the inevitable *internal diseconomies* of scale, so as to bring about a negatively sloped industry supply curve.

In the "immediate run," quantity produced by the industry is considered to be invariant (the *IS* supply curve is absolutely inelastic). The entire impact of any demand shift is therefore reflected by change in price. Allowing short-run adjustment of firms' outputs leads to the industry *SS* supply curve, along which positive elasticity is normal; the change in price following a demand shift is therefore moderated by a quantity response. In the long run, the industry supply curve *LS* is even more elastic. This is due to the "internal" fact that *LRMC* curves slope less steeply upward than *SRMC* curves, and also to the entry of new firms in response to price increases (or exit of old firms in response to price decreases).

Under competitive conditions there is always pressure on firms' profits. If profit exists, output expansions on the part of the industry tend to reduce product price (pressure from above) and to raise factor prices (pressure from below). In long-run equilibrium the *marginal* firm must be making zero economic profit, thus precluding either entry or exit. But even *infra-marginal* firms also achieve only zero profit in the long run. Since different firms in the industry compete for any input responsible for the low costs leading to positive profit, in the long run that factor will command a hire-price capturing the entire benefit for its owner.

Voluntary trade is mutually beneficial; this is the Fundamental Theorem of Exchange. Consumer Surplus is a measure of the benefit of trade to purchasers, and Producer Surplus a measure of the benefit to suppliers—both in terms of *numéraire* (dollar) values. Consumer Surplus is the difference between purchasers' aggregate *willingness to pay* and the aggregate total they must actually pay in the market for the good. Similarly, Producer Surplus is the difference between sellers' aggregate actual market receipts and the minimum terms at which they would have been willing to offer the marketed amount of the good. The burden of a hindrance to trade like a tax or a quota on supply can be measured in terms of losses of Consumer Surplus and Producer Surplus. Any such hindrance typically has two kinds of effects: redistributions between Consumer Surplus and Producer Surplus which are mere transfers, and uncompensated reductions of Consumer Surplus and/or Producer Surplus that represent efficiency losses to the economy.

If demand increases or supply decreases, the imposition of a price freeze creates a shortage—an excess of quantity demanded over quantity supplied. Consumers reap a transfer gain at the expense of suppliers, by not having to pay a higher price. But the supply response that would have occurred in the long run is blocked, which is a source of efficiency loss to producers and consumers together. There are also losses of Consumer Surplus and Producer Surplus due to the need for non-price methods of coping with the imbalance between demand and supply at the artificially low price.

☐ QUESTIONS FOR CHAPTER 7

MAINLY FOR REVIEW

*R1. At any rate of output, the industry *long-run* supply curve tends to be less steep than the *short-run* supply curve. Is it also necessarily more elastic? Explain.

*R2. "In the long run, a firm could always produce twice as much simply by doubling the amount of every factor employed. So in the long run there must be constant returns to scale." Evaluate.

R3. Does elasticity of supply for an industry tend to be great or small if the firms' Marginal Cost curves are sharply upward-sloping? What is the effect on elasticity of supply if higher industry output markedly drives up the prices of factors employed in the industry?

*R4. If there are N identical firms and no "external" effects on factor prices, is the *industry* supply curve more or less steep than the *firm* supply curve? More or less elastic?

R5. Explain the distinction between "internal" and "external" economies or diseconomies.

*R6. In long-run equilibrium, why does the marginal firm (the highest-cost firm in the industry) earn zero economic profit? Why do infra-marginal firms earn zero economic profit?

R7. Consider an industry with a downward-sloping supply curve. Starting from an initial equilibrium, will a decline in demand lead to a rise or a fall in price? To a rise or a fall in output? Explain.

R8. If a tax is imposed upon some commodity, indicate the areas of: loss of Consumer Surplus, loss of Producer Surplus, tax collections (transfers of Consumer Surplus and Producer Surplus to government), and efficiency losses.

*The answers to asterisked questions appear at the end of the book.

FOR FURTHER THOUGHT AND DISCUSSION

*T1. "In a competitive industry, for any firm there may be internal economies of scale over a certain range. But each firm must be actually operating in the region where internal *diseconomies* of scale dominate." True or false? Explain.

T2. Under what circumstances would you expect a rise in demand for an industry's product to be met primarily by a "short-run" output response on the part of existing firms? By a "long-run" response on the part of existing firms? By entry of new firms?

T3. Which of the following is a "pecuniary" effect, which a "technological" effect? Which is "internal" to the firm, which "external" to the firm (but internal to the industry)?
  a. As the number of films produced rises, stars' salaries go up.
  b. As fishing intensifies, each fisherman finds fish scarcer.
  c. As new shops open, existing shops find customers scarcer.
  d. Steel mills along a river use the water for cooling—but the greater the use, the warmer the water gets.

*T4. If at a certain equilibrium price every firm in the industry is earning zero economic profit, doesn't that imply that a fall in market price would mean that no firms at all could continue to survive? Explain.

T5. A number of techniques are available to cope with increased scarcity and higher world prices of petroleum. Analyze the following in terms of supply–demand responses in the short run and long run:
  a. Price freeze and "rationing by queue" (waiting in line for gasoline).
  b. Price freeze and rationing by coupon (non-salable).
  c. Rationing by coupon (non-salable) without a price freeze.
  d. A tax on all petroleum used.
  e. A tariff on *imports* of petroleum.

*T6. In policy (c) above (rationing by coupon without a price freeze), suppose consumers were permitted to sell ration coupons to one another. Would this tend to elicit more supply? Would the limited supplies be reallocated to those with higher demand prices? Explain the consequences in terms of Consumer Surplus.

T7. Suppose that, after a decline in demand for a product, a *floor* is placed under its market price. Then the problem arises of managing a "surplus." What are the disadvantages of a price floor? Would the disadvantages tend to increase over time, as in the case of managing a shortage, or would the disadvantages tend to evaporate over time in the "surplus" case? Would black markets tend to develop?

*T8. Under recent petroleum regulation in the United States, a price freeze was placed on "old oil"—defined, roughly speaking, as petroleum from existing wells. The justification was that producers had to be offered more to induce them to drill new wells, but the output from existing wells would be forthcoming even at low prices. Is this argument correct?

T9. In the longer run, the presence or even the threat of price freezes may induce firms to integrate vertically (to merge with "upstream" supplier firms or with "downstream" customer firms). Explain why.

*T10. Analyze the effects upon Consumer Surplus and Producer Surplus of a *subsidy*. If a tax as a hindrance to trade is associated with an efficiency loss (apart from any mere transfers that may also be involved), does it follow that a subsidy as an encouragement to trade will generate actual efficiency gains?

8 MONOPOLY

CORE CHAPTER

A monopoly is said to exist when the industry contains only a single firm. If that firm is able to drive out competitors because its costs of production are lower, the situation is termed "natural monopoly." Not all monopolies are "natural," however. One other important source of monopoly is exclusive privilege granted by government, as in the case of a franchised public utility or a legal patent. At the other extreme from monopoly is the large-numbers or "competitive" case. Actually, the number of firms is economically significant only as a clue to behavior. In the large-numbers situation, what is essential is *price-taking behavior:* each firm has so negligible an effect upon price that it acts as if price were independent of its own output decision. (But, as we shall see when cartels are examined in Section 8.F, large numbers of firms can sometimes behave like a collective monopolist.) In the case of a single firm, or a small number of firms in an industry, price-taking is not plausible behavior. The impact of each firm's output decision upon the price of the product is too large to be disregarded.

Where more than one but still only a very few firms survive in an industry, the market structure is called "oligopoly"—competition among the few. Under oligopoly each single firm's output decision noticeably affects the demand conditions faced by *other* firms. As a result there is *conscious interaction* among firms, a condition that leads to "strategic" rather than price-taking behavior, as will be explored in Chapter 10. Another important market structure is "monopolistic competition," which arises when different firms produce distinct products that nevertheless compete closely with one another—like brands of toothpaste. Monopolistic competition will be covered in Chapter 9. The present chapter takes up only the cases of: (1) a single-firm monopolist and (2) a cartel of firms acting collectively as a monopoly.

8.A
MONOPOLY AND NON-PROFIT GOALS

Do monopolists seek profit more than or less actively than competitive firms? Demagogic orators often suggest that monopolists are exceptionally ruthless in their search for profit. On the other hand there is some reason to believe that a monopoly firm, sheltered from competition, would be inclined to give more weight to *non-profit* goals (as discussed in Chapter 6). For a competitive firm there is always a problem of survival. As we saw in the preceding chapter, competitive downward pressure on product prices and upward pressure on input prices are continually forcing profits toward zero. So in pure competition no firm can have much leeway for indulging non-profit goals. Monopolistic firms, in contrast, may have some freedom of choice.

Among the possible non-profit goals of a monopolistic firm might be empire-building for ambitious managers (or, alternatively, an easy life for un-ambitious ones), support of charitable institutions, favors to friends and relatives, and exercise of discrimination against unpopular demographic groups. Some of these activities could be intended to generate favorable public notice, others would better be left unpublicized.

However, the argument that monopolies are especially able to pursue non-profit goals is by no means clear-cut. Owners of a monopolistic firm are likely to put just as much pressure upon managers to maximize profit as would owners of a competitive firm. Consider a monopoly organized as a corporation with trad-able shares. The value of those shares depends upon the firm's present and future profits. If a monopoly earns less than it otherwise could, the loss will be borne by shareholders—who can be expected to complain, in extreme cases to sue in the courts, or to support an alternative management group that is threat-ening to take over the firm.[1] It seems likely that non-profit goals, creditable or discreditable, will be significant mainly for those firms—whether monopolists or not—whose managements are protected against threats to their managerial pos-itions. One such instance has already been described: "non-profit" savings and loan associations (in Chapter 6). In this chapter, however, we will assume that profit-maximization remains the operative goal, even for monopolistic firms.

8.B
MONOPOLY PROFIT-MAXIMIZING OPTIMUM

8.B.1   □ Price–Quantity Solution

Figure 8.1 displays the basic price–quantity optimum for the monopolistic firm. As usual the upper panel here shows the solution in terms of the Total Cost function C and Total Revenue function R. And the lower panel shows the solution in terms of AC, AR, MC, and MR (the corresponding average and marginal functions of output Q).[2] The bold line-segment labelled Π^* in the

---

[1]If *owners* are unwilling to accept a reduction of profits to achieve non-profit goals, does that mean that empire-building, nepotism, group prejudice, and the like will in fact not occur? Such a conclusion is unwarranted. It may be that suppliers of resource services will accept a lower hire-price in order to achieve such goals. A manager might serve at lower pay if able to hire relatives, for example. Or men might work for less if women employees are (or, perhaps, are not) also employed, or vice versa.

[2]The capital letter Q has previously been used to signify *industry* output. Since the monopolist is a single-firm industry, Q can be used to denote the output of a monopolist firm.

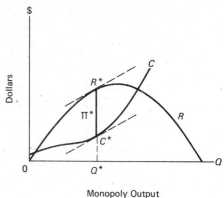

Monopoly Output

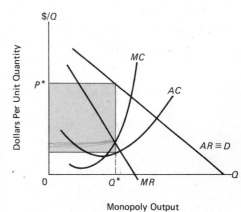

Monopoly Output

FIGURE 8.1 Monopoly Profit-maximizing Solution. Maximum profit Π* occurs at output Q*, where the vertical difference between the Total Revenue curve R and the Total Cost curve C in the upper panel is greatest. At this output the R and C curves are parallel (note dashed tangent lines). In the lower panel, it follows that the curves of Marginal Revenue MR and Marginal Cost MC intersect at output Q*. Profit in the lower panel is represented by the shaded area, equal to Q* times the difference between price P* and Average Cost AC* at that output: Q*(P* − AC).

upper panel is the maximized profit—the excess of Revenue over Cost at the optimal output Q*. At this optimal output the R and C curves are farthest apart, so their slopes must be parallel as suggested by the dashed tangent lines drawn at the points R* and C*. Consequently, in the lower panel the Marginal Revenue MR (representing the slope of the Total Revenue function) and the Marginal Cost MC (representing the slope of the Total Cost function) intersect at this same output Q*. The maximized profit Π* is represented in the lower panel by the shaded rectangle, whose base is the optimum quantity Q* and whose height is P* − AC ≡ AR − AC.

The difference between the competitive and monopoly solutions lies on the revenue side. For the competitive firm of Figure 6.1, the constancy of price P led to a Total Revenue curve R taking the form of a ray out of the origin. But for the monopolistic firm, price P is a falling function of output. The consequence is that the Total Revenue curve R in the upper panel of Figure 8.1 is concave downward, like the cross-section of a mountain.

Geometrically, we know that Marginal Revenue MR is the slope along the Total Revenue curve R. Along the concave-downward R function, slope decreases algebraically throughout (from a high positive magnitude at small Q, to zero slope at the point where R reaches a maximum, and then to increasingly negative slope as the R curve turns downward). The MR curve in the lower panel is correspondingly first positive, then zero, then negative; it decreases along its entire length. The demand curve, we know, is the Average Revenue curve AR, since Price P is Average Revenue R/Q. Since the monopolist by definition faces a downward-sloping demand curve, AR also declines throughout.

In the lower panel MR always lies below AR, i.e., Marginal Revenue is less than Average Revenue. This follows from the logical relations between average and marginal magnitudes discussed in Section 2.B. Proposition 2.2a there states: *When the average magnitude is falling, the marginal magnitude must lie below it.*

> *WARNING:* It is important not to confuse the *price* charged for the last unit sold with the *Marginal Revenue MR*. Note the two shaded areas in Figure 8.2. As sales increase from Q to $Q + 1$ units, the demand curve D shows that price must fall slightly from P' to P''. We can think of P'' as the price received for the last unit, represented by the thin tall rectangle of width unity and height P''. But to see the full effect on Revenue of a unit increase in quantity, it is necessary to remember that price has fallen from P' to P'' *on all the other units* sold. The effect of this price reduction is represented by the flat thin rectangle of width Q and height $P' - P''$.

There are, therefore, two elements entering into Marginal Revenue. First is the positive price P received for the last unit. Second is the price reduction on all the other units. Marginal Revenue can be expressed as the algebraic sum of these two elements:[3]

(8.1)
$$MR \equiv P + Q\frac{\Delta P}{\Delta Q}$$

[3]This equation is strictly valid only if Marginal Revenue is defined as the *limit* of the ratio $\Delta R/\Delta Q$ for small changes in quantity. But if the "better approximation" MR_2 for Marginal Revenue (see Chapter 2) is used, equation (8.1) will be found to hold almost exactly.

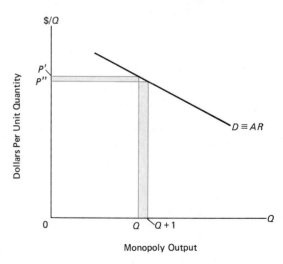

FIGURE 8.2 **Marginal Price versus Marginal Revenue.** Marginal *price,* the price of the last unit sold, corresponds in revenue terms to the area of the tall shaded rectangle of unit base and height P''. To calculate *Marginal Revenue* we must deduct from this amount the thin wide rectangle of height $P' - P'' \equiv \Delta P$ and width Q. This rectangle corresponds to the loss of receipts due to lowering the price on units that could have been sold at P'.

240

Since $\Delta P/\Delta Q$, the slope along the demand curve, is negative for a monopolist, it follows that the second term has negative sign. Then Marginal Revenue MR must be less than Average Revenue $AR \equiv P$.

The cost function for the monopolistic firm, as shown in terms of total magnitudes in the upper panel of Figure 8.1 and in terms of average and marginal magnitudes in the lower panel, has essentially the same appearance as for the competitive firm. Of course, the monopolistic firm may be of relatively large size, so that the horizontal scale would then be correspondingly large. In connection with this, there is one difference of substance. The competitive firm was assumed to be a price-taker not only with respect to the product market but also with respect to *factor prices*. In consequence, the competitive firm's cost function does not allow for any effects on factor prices; only after turning to the supply function of the competitive industry in Chapter 7 was the factor-price effect encountered (as an "external" diseconomy). But the single monopolistic supplier is itself an entire industry. Hence, any factor-price effect would be displayed *within* the cost function of the monopolist firm. Since an increase in industry output will tend to push factor prices upward, the factor-price effect makes the monopolist firm's cost functions—total, average, and marginal—all tend to rise more sharply as output increases.

Formally, the monopolist's optimizing problem can be expressed as:

(8.2) $$\text{Max } \Pi \equiv R(Q) - C(Q) \equiv P(Q)Q - C(Q)$$

Here the parenthesis notation (Q) is to call attention to the fact that the R, C, and P variables are all functions of output Q. (In the solution for the competitive firm, price P was *not* a function of firm output.) As usual, the condition of optimality (maximum of profit or minimum of loss) is the equality of Marginal Cost and Marginal Revenue:[4]

(8.3) $$MC = MR \equiv P + Q\frac{\Delta P}{\Delta Q} \qquad \text{Maximum-Profit Condition, Monopolist Firm}$$

As in Chapter 6 for the competitive firm, there is again the technical qualification that the MC curve must cut the MR curve *from below* to have a profit maximum. If MC cuts MR *from above*, profit is a *minimum* (or loss a maximum) at that output.[5] Furthermore, the "no shut-down" conditions of Chapter 6 also remain applicable: The firm will produce a positive output in the short run only if Total Revenue covers at least Total Variable Cost, and in the long run only if Total Revenue covers Total Cost.

[4]*Mathematical Footnote:* Taking derivatives of profit Π as defined in (8.2) and setting equal to zero:

$$\frac{d\Pi}{dQ} = \frac{dR}{dQ} - \frac{dC}{dQ} = P + Q\frac{dP}{dQ} - \frac{dC}{dQ} = 0$$

Marginal Revenue dR/dQ is $P + Q(dP/dQ)$, and Marginal Cost is of course dC/dQ.

[5]*Mathematical Footnote:* The second-order condition for a maximum of Π is $d^2R/dQ^2 < d^2C/dQ^2$. That is, MR must be falling relative to MC, i.e., MC must cut MR from below.

The maximum-profit equation (8.3) is evidently a generalization of the similar condition (6.3) that applied to a competitive firm. For the competitive firm as a price-taker, the ratio $\Delta P/\Delta Q$ is zero and (8.3) reduces simply to $MC = MR \equiv P$.

The (price) elasticity of demand was defined in Chapter 5. In terms of the notation of this chapter, the elasticity of demand is:

(8.4)
$$\eta \equiv \frac{\Delta Q/Q}{\Delta P/P} \equiv \frac{\Delta Q}{\Delta P} \cdot \frac{P}{Q}$$

(Recall that η ordinarily has a negative sign.) We can use (8.3) and (8.4) to obtain an important expression connecting Marginal Revenue MR and price elasticity η. First, equation (8.4) can be rewritten:

$$\frac{\Delta Q}{\Delta P} \equiv \eta \frac{Q}{P} \quad \text{or} \quad \frac{\Delta P}{\Delta Q} \equiv \frac{1}{\eta} \frac{P}{Q}$$

Substituting for $\Delta P/\Delta Q$ on the right-hand side of (8.3), we have:

$$MR \equiv P + Q\left(\frac{1}{\eta} \frac{P}{Q}\right) \equiv P + \frac{P}{\eta}$$

This is usually written in the form:

(8.5)
$$MR \equiv P\left(1 + \frac{1}{\eta}\right) \quad \text{or} \quad MR \equiv P\left(1 - \frac{1}{|\eta|}\right)$$

Since elasticity η is ordinarily negative, we see again that MR is less than $P \equiv AR$.

We saw also in Section 5.B that elastic demand (η greater than unity in absolute value) corresponded to increasing consumer expenditure on a good as its price P falls (and quantity purchased Q rises). *Consumer expenditure* is, of course, the opposite side of the same coin as *Revenue* to the firm. So elastic demand corresponds to the region where Total Revenue R is an increasing function of output Q in the upper panel of Figure 8.1, or equivalently to the region of positive Marginal Revenue MR in the lower panel. Inelastic demand corresponds to the region of falling Total Revenue in the upper panel or negative Marginal Revenue in the lower panel. Since Marginal Cost MC is surely positive, the condition $MC = MR$ dictates that the monopolist optimum must be in the region where the Total Revenue curve is rising so that $MR > 0$, i.e., in the range of *elastic* demand.

PROPOSITION: A profit-maximizing monopoly firm will always operate (that is, will always choose a price–quantity solution) in the region of elastic demand along the market demand curve.

8.B.2 ☐ Monopolist versus Competitive Solution

Table 8.1 illustrates a hypothetical set of revenue and cost data for a monopolist firm. The cost data are exactly the same as those employed for a hypothetical competitive firm in Table 6.1. But on the revenue side, the monopolist's demand function is assumed here to be $P = 132 - 8Q$; price is a declining function of output. The equation has been so chosen that if the monopolist *were* following the competitive optimality rule $MC = P$ he would be led to the same output ($Q = 9$) as in Table 6.1. For although the demand curve here is a declining function of Q, the numbers have been so contrived that, at $Q = 9$, Marginal Cost MC and price P are both equal to 60.

TABLE 8.1

Revenue and Cost Functions: Monopolist Firm

$P = 132 - 8Q$, or $R = 132Q - 8Q^2$
$C = Q^3 - 14Q^2 + 69Q + 128$

Q	P	R	MR₁	MR₂	MR	C	MC	η
0	132	0	—		132	128	69	− ∞
				124				
1	124	124	124	**116**	116	184	44	−15.5
				108				
2	116	232	108	**100**	100	218	25	− 7.25
				92				
3	108	324	92	**84**	84	236	12	− 4.5
				76				
4	100	400	76	**68**	68	244	5	− 3.125
				60				
5	92	460	60	**52**	52	248	4	− 2.3
				44				
6	84	504	44	**36**	36	254	9	− 1.75
				28				
7	76	532	28	**20**	20	268	20	− 1.36
				12				
8	68	544	12	**4**	4	296	37	− 1.06
				−4				
9	60	540	−4	**−12**	−12	344	60	− 0.83
				−20				
10	52	520	−20	—	−28	418	89	− 0.65

The monopolist, therefore, has it in his power to behave like a competitive firm. But, in the interests of profit-maximization he will set $MC = MR < P$ [equation (8.3)]. In the Table here, once again we have three approximations for Marginal Revenue. MR_1 is the "poorer approximation." Here the revenue difference $R_{Q+1} - R_Q$ is considered the Marginal Revenue at $Q + 1$. MR_2 is the "better approximation" of Chapter 2, where this same difference is taken as the Marginal Revenue at $Q + \frac{1}{2}$. In this column, the boldface numbers have been interpolated to show MR_2 at integer values of Q. The *true* Marginal Revenue MR (the perfect approximation) is given in the third column. This can be found by calculus techniques, which show that if the demand function is $P = 132 - 8Q$ then Marginal Revenue is $MR = 132 - 16Q$.[6] As can be seen from the Table, the "better approximation" MR_2 is in this case precisely correct. (This will always be true for a quadratic revenue function.)

It is easy to prove the following, without using calculus.

PROPOSITION: Given any *linear* demand curve $P = A - BQ$, the true corresponding Marginal Revenue function is $MR = A - 2BQ$. Geometrically, starting at the same vertical intercept on the P-axis, the MR curve falls twice as fast as the AR curve. *Proof:* From equation (8.3), $MR = P + Q(\Delta P/\Delta Q)$. Now $\Delta P/\Delta Q$ is by definition the slope of the demand curve, a constant for a linear demand curve. Given the demand equation $P = A - BQ$, this slope is equal to $-B$. Substituting on the righthand side of (8.3): $MR = (A - BQ) + Q(-B)$ or $MR = A - 2BQ$.

COROLLARY: The MR curve bisects the horizontal distance between the vertical axis and the demand curve, if the latter is a straight line.

As for the Marginal Cost MC, only the "true" figures are taken over from Table 6.1. The condition $MC = MR$ is met at $Q = 7$, which is the monopolist's profit-maximizing output. The corresponding profit-maximizing price (or Average Revenue) is $P = 76$. Total Revenue is $R = 532$ and Total Cost $C = 268$, so that the maximized profit is $\Pi^* = 264$.

It was argued above that the monopolist's solution must lie in the elastic range of demand, i.e., where $|\eta| > 1$. The last column of Table 8.1 shows the elasticity at the various levels of output. The computation was based on the relation $\eta \equiv P/(MR - P)$, derived by solving equation (8.5) above for η. Note that had the monopolist been following the competitive rule so as to choose $Q = 9$, the solution would have been in the inelastic range from the viewpoint of industry demand. We thus see that it is quite possible for a *competitive* price–quantity equilibrium, but not for a monopolist's price–quantity optimum, to be in the inelastic range of demand.

PROPOSITION: The monopoly output solution occurs where $MC = MR < P$. Since competitive firms produce to where $MC = P$, a monopolized industry achieves higher price and produces smaller output than would a competitive industry.

What might be called "monopoly power" is indicated by the divergence

[6]*Mathematical Footnote:* If $P = 132 - 8Q$, then $R \equiv PQ = 132Q - 8Q^2$. Differentiating: $MR \equiv dR/dQ = 132 - 16Q$.

between Marginal Revenue MR (equal to Marginal Cost MC) and price P. From equation (8.5) we see that the difference between MR and P is greater the *smaller* (in absolute value) is the price elasticity η. It is more convenient to measure monopoly power by the *ratio $P/MC = P/MR$*. The more the ratio exceeds unity, the greater the monopoly power. From equation (8.5), and since $MC = MR$, it is algebraically easy to see that:

(8.5a)
$$\frac{P}{MC} = \frac{|\eta|}{|\eta| - 1}$$

As the elasticity gets larger and larger in absolute value, the ability of the monopolist to achieve a divergence between price P and Marginal Revenue diminishes. In the limit, for a price-taking firm the elasticity of demand is infinite and the ratio approaches unity—there is no monopoly power.

Exercise 8.1: Suppose that the demand equation is $P = 10 - Q$. (a) What is the equation for Marginal Revenue? (b) If Marginal Cost is given by $MC = 1 + Q$, what is the profit-maximizing price–quantity solution? (c) What is the elasticity of demand at this solution?

Answer: (a) The "better approximation" MR_2 for Marginal Revenue would give the exact answer here. But noticing that the demand curve is linear in the form $P = A - BQ$, we can use the Proposition that $MR = A - 2BQ$—specifically here, $MR = 10 - 2Q$. (b) Setting $MC = 1 + Q$ equal to $MR = 10 - 2Q$, the solution is $Q = 3$, $P = 7$. (c) Since the demand-curve slope is $\Delta P/\Delta Q = -1$, the elasticity of demand η is

$$\frac{P}{Q} \frac{\Delta Q}{\Delta P} = \frac{7}{3}(-1) = -\frac{7}{3}$$

which as expected is in the elastic range.

EXAMPLE 8.1

Specialists on the New York Stock Exchange

Each security listed for trading on the New York Stock Exchange (NYSE) is assigned to a member of the Exchange who becomes the "specialist" for that stock. The specialist's function is to "make the market" in the stock, by always standing ready to buy or sell. At each moment the specialist is required to quote the lowest price he will accept to sell and the highest price at which he will buy. On average, of course, if the specialist is to make money his selling price must exceed his buying price. The difference between the two, or "bid–ask spread," reimburses the specialist for taking on the market-making function.

Only one specialist is assigned to a security listed on the New York Stock Exchange and so each such specialist has a monopoly position for dealings on the Exchange. But the Exchange may not have a monopoly of the trading process for a given security; some stocks are listed on other organized exchanges as well as on the NYSE. A study by S. M. Tinic showed that competition worked in the expected direction: The bid–ask spread on the New York Stock Exchange was lower, other things equal, *for those securities that were traded on other exchanges as well as on the NYSE*.[a] The Stock Exchange's specialist has a monopoly on that exchange, but competitors (firms offering similar services) on other organized exchanges reduce the specialist's monopoly power.

[a]S. M. Tinic, "The Economics of Liquidity Services," *Quarterly Journal of Economics*, v. 86 (Feb. 1972).

Apart from the number of firms in an industry, the underlying elasticity of consumers' demand for the product (the elasticity of the *industry* demand curve) will also be highly relevant. If in a particular industry the demand happens to be highly elastic to begin with, even a single-firm monopolist will have little *monopoly power* (will be unable to profitably raise price P much above Marginal Cost MC).

What determines the elasticity of consumers' demand for a product? We saw in Chapter 5 that luxuries tend to have more elastic demands than necessities (since the income effect of the price change—making the consumer richer if price falls, or poorer if price rises—reinforces the pure substitution effect). It then follows that a monopolist tends to have greater monopoly power—ability to raise price—if the commodity is a necessity. The second major determinant emphasized in Chapter 5, and probably much the more important, is *closeness of substitutes*. If a good substitute for a commodity is available, a price increase will lead to a large loss of sales; demand tends to be elastic, and monopoly power is necessarily small.

EXAMPLE 8.2
Gas and Electric Utilities

Public utility corporations are generally granted exclusive (monopoly) rights to serve a particular locality. Among such public utilities are companies providing gas and electricity. But in some areas these two commodities are provided by the *same* company, while in other communities the services are separately supplied. Since gas and electricity as alternative sources of energy are close *substitutes* over a considerable range of uses, a company providing only one of those commodities faces an effectively more elastic demand (has less monopoly power). Such a company would always be seriously concerned about shift of business to the other energy source if it were to raise its price.

Bruce M. Owen made a comparative study of prices and outputs of combined versus separated gas and electricity services.[a] He found that private

[a]Bruce M. Owen, "Monopoly Pricing in Combined Gas and Electric Utilities," *The Antitrust Bulletin*, v. 15 (Winter 1970).

companies supplying combined gas and electric services charged, other things equal, on average about 6% more for electricity while providing about 15% less output in comparison with companies supplying only electricity. (On the other hand, there seemed to be no significant effect of combined versus separated service upon gas prices. Perhaps gas may have relatively elastic demand for reasons apart from availability of electricity as a substitute.)

> COMMENT: Privately owned public utility corporations are almost always *regulated* (as will be discussed in Section 8.D); the prices they charge must be approved by a government agency. The evidence above of seeming ability to exploit monopoly power suggests that regulation may have been ineffective, at least to some degree.

8.B.3 □ An Application: Author versus Publisher

In the publishing industry, it is common practice for authors' royalties to take the form of a simple percentage of sales receipts. The question arises: Is there any difference between the incentives of author and publisher as to how high a price should be set on a book?

Since there is only one seller of any single text, monopoly theory is applicable. Suppose that the author receives as royalty just 10% of Total Revenue R. Denote his royalty as $R_a = 0.1R$. Writing the net revenue to the publisher as R_p, it must be that $R_p = 0.9R$. This problem is most simply analyzed in "total" units, by an extension of the geometry in the upper panel of Figure 8.1. In Figure 8.3

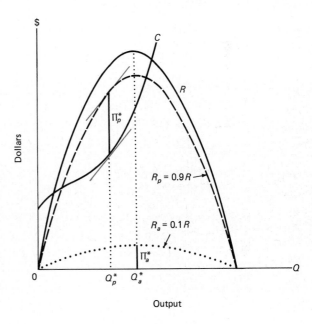

FIGURE 8.3 Author versus Publisher. Of the receipts from sales indicated by the Total Revenue curve R, 10% go to the author (R_a curve) and 90% to the publisher (R_p curve). Since the author bears no costs of production, from his point of view the optimal output is Q_a^* at the maximum of the R_a curve (where his income is Π_a^*). The publisher's maximum profit Π_p^* occurs at output Q_p^*, where the R_p curve has the greatest vertical divergence over the Total Cost curve C. The publisher will prefer a smaller output (will want to set a higher price) than the author.

the Total Revenue R received from customers is divided between the dashed R_p (nine-tenths the height of R) and the dotted R_a (one-tenth the height of R). The publisher would prefer the output Q_p^* such that the *slopes* along R_p and along the Total Cost curve C are equal; his profit Π_p^* at that output is indicated by the height of the upper bold line-segment. The lower solid line-segment drawn along the same vertical, between R_a and the horizontal axis, indicates the corresponding royalty to the author.

This is *not* the preferred output from the point of view of the author. *Since the author incurs no cost of production,* for him the optimum output Q_a^* is simply that which maximizes R_a. But $R_a = 0.1R$, and so the author wants to set a price that will simply maximize sales (Revenue R) without regard to cost. The author's "ideal" royalty in the diagram is shown by the bold line-segment Π_a^*, but then the corresponding profit to the publisher will be less than ideal from the latter's point of view. The upshot of the analysis is that *it is in the interest of the publisher to set a higher price (implying a smaller number of books sold) than the author would rationally prefer.*

In the publishing industry authors do not normally have the power to fix price, which is the sole domain of the publisher. However, it might be advantageous for an author to make a deal accepting a smaller royalty percentage in return for the publisher setting a lower price for his book.

Exercise 8.2: The demand function for a certain text is given by $P = 20 - 0.0002Q$, while the publisher's Marginal Cost is $MC = 6 + 0.00168Q$. The author's royalty is 20% of Total Revenue R. What is the publisher's preferred price–quantity solution? The author's?

Answer: The publisher wants to set his Marginal Revenue $MR_p = 0.8MR$ equal to Marginal Cost. Since the combined Marginal Revenue from sales is $MR = 20 - 0.0004Q$, eight-tenths of this is $MR_p = 16 - 0.00032Q$. Equating MR_p to MC, the publisher's optimum is $Q = 5000$, $P = 19$. The author simply wants to choose Q to maximize Revenue, i.e., to set Marginal Revenue equal to zero. $MR = 20 - 0.0004Q = 0$ implies $Q = 50,000$, $P = 10$. Note the enormous difference between the two solutions.

EXAMPLE 8.3
Economists as Authors

P. M. Horvitz[a] surveyed 98 authors of textbooks in economics, receiving 71 usable replies to questionnaires. He was interested in determining the degree of participation of authors in the pricing process, and in particular their awareness of the conflict of interest between author and publisher.

The results seemed rather disappointing as clues to the acumen of economist-authors. Only 7 reported participating in the pricing process, and nearly all were satisfied with the publisher's pricing decision. However, the direction of dissatisfaction is of some interest. Of the 5 who reported dissatis-

[a]P. M. Horvitz, "The Pricing of Textbooks and the Remuneration of Authors," *American Economic Review,* v. 56 (May 1966).

faction, all would have preferred a lower price. And 3 others among the satisfied group also indicated that a lower price would have been preferred. No author would rather have had a higher price set on his book.

8.C
MONOPOLY AND ECONOMIC EFFICIENCY

Monopoly leads to higher price and lower output as compared with competitive supply. Is this a good or a bad thing? Obviously, while high price is bad for the customers it is good for the monopolist. The possibility of making valid statements concerning the impartial or *social* desirability of alternative economic states of affairs will be discussed under the heading of "Welfare Economics" in Chapter 15. However, recall the Fundamental Theorem of Exchange—*trade is mutually beneficial*. We can use the concepts of Consumer Surplus and Producer Surplus to show that monopoly can be regarded as a *hindrance to trade*. As such, it leads to an "efficiency loss," apart from the mere transfers associated with high monopoly price.[7]

Figure 8.4 illustrates the interpretation of monopoly as a hindrance to trade. Assume that there are no economies or diseconomies of scale tending to shift the cost function downward or upward for a single producer in comparison with an aggregate of small competitive suppliers. Then the Marginal Cost curve MC of the monopolist is essentially the same as the competitive supply function S of Figure 7.2. (The factor-price effect, if any, due to expanding industry supply is already incorporated in the shape of the monopolist's MC curve.) The monopoly solution is at quantity Q_m (the quantity level at which $MC = MR$) and price P_m (the height of the demand curve at quantity Q_m). The hypothetical competitive solution would be at quantity Q_c and price P_c (the intersection of the demand curve D and supply curve S).

The hindrance to trade can be analyzed on the analog of Figure 7.9 that showed the effect of a tax on transactions. The rectangular shaded area $(P_m - P_c)Q_m$ is the buyers' loss of Consumer Surplus due to the higher monopoly price on the quantity Q_m. As the monopolist seller derives an exactly equal benefit, this is a "transfer" that does not enter into efficiency calculations. The upper roughly triangular (dotted) area is the deadweight loss in Consumer Surplus for units that *would have been* produced and purchased at the price P_c but are not purchased at the higher price P_m. The lower dotted area is the corresponding deadweight loss in Producer Surplus. The monopolist could have produced these additional units at marginal costs less than the price P_c that could have been received for each unit had the quantity Q_c been supplied. Of course,

[7]However, we cannot therefore conclude that monopoly "should" be abolished. (Any more than we could conclude in Chapter 7 that taxes, as the cause of losses in Consumer Surplus and Producer surplus, "should" therefore be abolished.) There may be other considerations to be balanced against the efficiency loss.

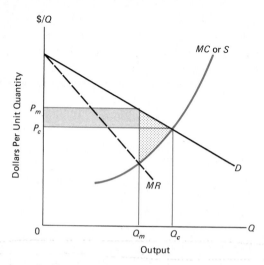

$/Q

Dollars Per Unit Quantity

P_m

P_c

MC or S

MR

D

0   Q_m Q_c Q

Output

FIGURE 8.4 Monopoly and Efficiency Loss. If there are no *productive* losses or gains from organization of the industry into a single large firm versus competing small firms, the supply curve S of the competitive industry is identical with the Marginal Cost curve MC of the monopolist. The competitive equilibrium would occur at price P_c and quantity Q_c; the monopoly optimum at the higher price P_m and smaller quantity Q_m. In comparison with the competitive outcome, the shaded area is a transfer from consumers to the monopolist supplier (equal to the price difference times the quantity still produced). The upper dotted area is the loss of Consumer Surplus due to the reduction in quantity traded (inability of consumers to buy the amount $Q_c - Q_m$ at the old price P_c). The lower dotted area is the analogous loss in Producer Surplus on the amount $Q_c - Q_m$, since Marginal Cost would have been less than price P_c in that range.

the monopolist chose not to provide so large a quantity because at smaller output a higher profit was obtained.

Thus, for the monopolist the net advantage of the monopoly over the competitive solution is the shaded area (a transfer) less the lower dotted area (a dead-weight loss). As for the consumers, the upper dotted area represents their dead-weight loss, and, in addition, they are on the losing side of the transfer. The transfer cancels out; the *efficiency loss* is measured by the two dotted areas alone.

CONCLUSION: In comparison with the competitive outcome, monopoly involves a transfer from consumers to suppliers. There is also an efficiency loss, the reductions in Consumer Surplus and Producer Surplus that are due to the lessened volume of trade.

EXAMPLE 8.4
Monopoly Efficiency Loss

A. C. Harberger[a] estimated the aggregate magnitude of the efficiency loss due to monopoly in the United States, for the period 1924–28. He was able to

[a] A. C. Harberger, "Monopoly and Resource Allocation," *American Economic Review,* v. 54 (May 1954).

do so only by making a number of heroic assumptions, in particular, that Marginal Cost MC was constant for all industries, and that the price elasticity of demand was *unity* everywhere. Identifying monopolized industries on the basis of high average profit rate on assets, he obtained a surprisingly low estimate of the loss: only around 0.1% of national income.

Harberger's results were criticized by G. J. Stigler[b] on several grounds, among them: (1) a rational monopolist will always produce in the range where elasticity is *greater* than unity (as we have just seen in Section 8.B); (2) reported profit rates for monopolists may omit monopoly returns in the form of disguised "cost" items such as patent royalties and executive salaries; and (3) for monopoly firms, "intangible" items may become counted among assets, so as to reduce the reported profit as a percentage of assets.

A number of later studies examined different sets of data, allowing in various ways for Stigler's objections. D. R. Kamerschen[c] studied the period 1956–61, making rather strong assumptions toward the opposite extreme from Harberger. For example, he included royalties, intangibles, and advertising expenditures with the monopoly returns. He obtained demand-elasticity estimates by industry, averaging around (minus) 2 or 3. On this basis Kamerschen concluded that the annual welfare loss due to monopoly is around 6% of national income. Still later, D. A. Worcester, Jr.,[d] studied the period 1965–69, using *firm* rather than *industry* data for added precision. Taking account of the Stigler objections in a variety of ways, and using an overall elasticity figure of (minus) 2, he still obtained low "maximum defensible" estimates of the welfare loss due to monopoly, in the range of 0.5% of national income.

COMMENT: As this very condensed report suggests, we have here an as-yet-unresolved economic controversy, involving issues both of theory and of statistical data. Even if the low estimates prove correct, it would be wrong to infer automatically that anti-monopoly activities of government should be suspended. Perhaps the low monopoly losses are to be attributed to the success of those very activities.

[b]G. J. Stigler, "The Statistics of Monopoly and Merger," *Journal of Political Economy,* v. 64 (Feb. 1956).

[c]D. R. Kamerschen, "An Estimation of the 'Welfare Losses' from Monopoly in the American Economy," *Western Economic Journal,* v. 4 (Summer 1966).

[d]D. A. Worcester, Jr., "New Estimates of the Welfare Loss to Monopoly, United States: 1956–1969," *Southern Economic Journal,* v. 40 (Oct. 1973).

There is, however, a possible *additional* source of efficiency loss not considered in the preceding analysis: whatever sacrifice of resources is involved in acquiring or defending the monopoly position itself. How much would a potential monopolist be willing to pay to win and retain such a privilege? Evidently, any amount short of the net monopoly gain. In Figure 8.4, the amount would be the excess of the shaded rectangular area (representing the transfer gain to the monopolist of an industry) over the lower dotted triangle (representing loss of Producer Surplus when the industry reduces output). If instead of a single claimant there were competing contenders all struggling for the monopoly position, each would have to discount this possible net gain in accordance with his estimate of his chances of success in the contest—but in the aggregate, the costs that *all* the contenders together would be willing to incur probably remain comparable to the monopoly gain.[8]

The degree to which costs incurred to gain a monopoly position are *efficiency losses* depends, however, on the way in which the contest takes place. Suppose a government authority simply auctioned off a monopoly privilege. (Something like this now occurs for the right to supply cable television service; communities generally grant an exclusive franchise to whichever cable company makes the most attractive bid.) In an ideal auction, where the expenses incurred by losing bidders are negligible and the cost to the winning bidder is simply the amount bid, the payment would represent a mere transfer—in this case from the monopolist (ultimately, from consumers of the monopolized product) to the government. There is no *additional* efficiency loss due to the contest for monopoly position. But to the extent that an auction involves real costs (for example, if contestants hire economists to advise on how high to bid), resources will be diverted from alternative employments and the striving for monopoly privilege will itself cause an efficiency loss.

Since economists are not too expensive (alternative employments are not that valuable), this efficiency loss might not seem large. But consider other forms of struggle for monopoly position. One that comes immediately to mind is violence. Chicago-style gang wars were attempts to gain monopoly over crime—evidently, a highly costly process to all concerned. Less picturesque, entirely lawful, but still often quite costly are contests in which prizes are awarded at the discretion of a government authority. The Federal Communications Commission awards broadcasting channels, the Patent Office grants patents, local city councils bestow cable franchises, and so on. Here the proceedings typically involve extremely expensive documentary submissions, often leading to burdensome litigation, and perhaps very large costs incurred to bring political or other pressures to bear upon the awarding agency.[9]

Note that these *costs of achieving monopoly rights* are not essentially different from the costs involved in acquiring or defending any form of rights in our society. Rights to property, rights to sue in court, and even "civil" rights like freedom of speech can often only be gained or exercised at considerable cost.

---

[8]Estimates of the expenses incurred to achieve monopoly positions in a number of industries are provided in R. A. Posner, "The Social Costs of Monopoly and Regulation," *Journal of Political Economy,* v. 83 (Aug. 1975).

[9]What if the prize were given instead simply to the contestant offering the highest bribe? This is like an auction, so that (to a first approximation, at least) there would be no efficiency loss. Only a transfer is involved, in this case going to the private purse of the corrupt official rather than to the government treasury. Note that illegal or immoral methods may involve an efficiency loss (gang war) or may not (bribery), just as legal and moral methods may or may not. (This may perhaps suggest that efficiency ought not be the *sole* criterion for social judgments.)

REGULATION OF MONOPOLY

Between the two extremes of *laissez-faire* toleration of monopoly, on the one hand, and "trust-busting" on the other, lies a third possibility—regulation of monopoly. Regulation is almost universal for privately owned public utilities providing power, water, gas, and telephone service, all generally considered to be "natural monopolies." But not all regulation is of monopolized industries, and not all monopolized industries are regulated.

It is sometimes thought that "natural monopoly" requires that potential supplier's Average Cost functions all be downward-sloping, the seeming implication being that one firm can always produce any given output more cheaply than if that output were divided among a number of firms. But this is mistaken. Natural monopoly exists when, in the relevant region for satisfying the entire market demand, a single supplier's Marginal Cost is lower than the Average Cost of any of its potential competitors. Clearly, a single large firm's Average Cost function might be rising in the relevant range, but its Marginal Cost might still be lower than the lowest Average Cost achievable by any smaller firm. Consequently, regulated natural monopolies may have either rising or falling Average Cost curves in the relevant demand region.

The usual regulatory goal is that monopoly revenue should be allowed to cover only costs plus a *normal profit*, i.e., an amount necessary to attract and retain the resources employed in the industry. But the "normal" profit to the owners of a firm is (as explained in Chapter 6) the economic or opportunity cost of the resources provided by them. Hence regulatory policy can be interpreted as aiming at zero *economic profit* for the firm.

Figure 8.5 repeats the comparison of the monopoly solution (Q_m and P_m) and the competitive solution (Q_c and P_c) of the preceding diagram, and adds the regulatory solution (Q_r and P_r) as interpreted above. The regulatory zero-

FIGURE 8.5 Regulation of Monopoly: Increasing Cost. The regulatory solution, fixing price so that the firm achieves zero economic profit, is the price–output combination P_r, Q_r where the AC and AR curves intersect. If this occurs in the range where Average Cost AC is rising, regulated output Q_r will be even greater than the competitive equilibrium output Q_c. In comparison with the competitive solution, the shaded rectangle is a transfer from suppliers to consumers. The dotted area is an efficiency loss due to *excessive* output.

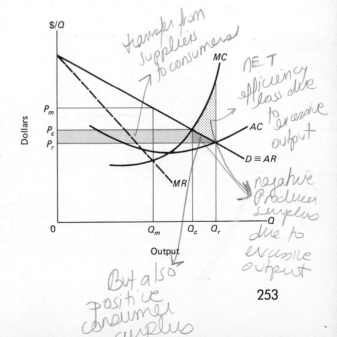

economic-profit condition is equivalent to setting a price and output such that $AC = AR$. Note that whereas the laissez-faire monopoly solution had "too small" output and "too high" price in comparison with the competitive outcome ($Q_m < Q_c$ and $P_m > P_c$), in this diagram the regulatory correction "overshoots" the competitive outcome ($Q_r > Q_c$ and $P_r < P_c$).

A striking feature of Figure 8.5 is that, in the range of output greater than Q_c, Marginal Cost MC exceeds demand price (marginal "willingness to pay"). Thus there is an efficiency loss from "too great" a regulated output, as represented by the dotted area in Figure 8.5. This, plus the small shaded triangle, represents *negative* Producer Surplus due to the excessive output. On the other hand, this triangle is also a region of positive Consumer Surplus. So the triangle cancels out, leaving the dotted area as the *net* efficiency loss. (Consumers receive also a transfer gain represented by the shaded rectangle.)

Regulation is, as has been indicated, the policy often chosen by government for declining with "natural" monopolies. One type of natural monopoly is characterized by an Average Cost curve AC that is falling throughout the relevant range. If all potential firms in an industry had the same cost function, with AC *declining* throughout, any single firm able to achieve an output lead over the others would be able to produce more cheaply. Since the cost advantage grows as the output lead increases, the ultimate outcome is likely to be a single surviving firm.

This type of natural monopoly is pictured in Figure 8.6. Since AC is falling in the diagram, Marginal cost MC lies always below it (Proposition 2.2a). Note that in Figure 8.6 the regulatory solution (Q_r and P_r) lies *between* the monopoly solution (Q_m and P_m) and the competitive solution (Q_c and P_c). It follows that in this type of regulated natural monopoly, there is still "too small" output and "too high" a price. The dotted region shows the efficiency loss due to "too small" a regulated output.[10]

An implication of this analysis is that regulated firms should be rather less interested than unregulated firms in making technological adances so as to reduce Average Cost, or in heading off cost increases from any source. Indeed, if regulation were perfectly effective in maintaining the condition $AC = P_r$, the firm would have no incentive at all to hold costs down. Any cost increase would be immediately reflected in allowable higher prices, maintaining the "normal" profit of the firm. However, there is always a regulatory lag. If costs rise or fall, some time will pass before the regulatory commission gets around to adjusting prices. Consequently, the cost-reducing incentive, while somewhat attenuated, is not completely eliminated for regulated monopolies.

---

[10]Falling AC leads to a paradox. At the competitive solution, since $MC = P$ and $MC < AC$, then $AC > P$. So at the competitive outcome Average Cost exceeds price; the firm suffers a financial loss. It might therefore seem that the competitive solution could hardly serve as standard of efficiency. Nevertheless, the competitive solution remains the efficient one in the situation of Figure 8.6, as may be seen from the following argument. At the regulatory solution, $AC = P$, and there would be no financial loss. Now, given that output is at the regulatory level Q_r, is it or is it not efficient to expand production further to Q_c? Clearly it is, since in the region between Q_r and Q_c the demand price is always greater than the Marginal Cost. The resulting price drop, leading to the result $AC > P$, is a pure "transfer" not relevant for calculations of efficiency.

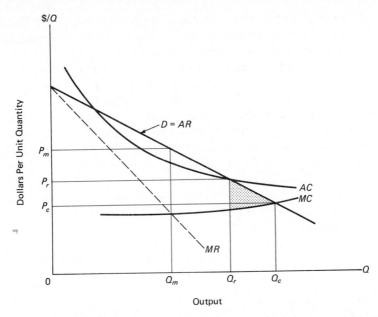

FIGURE 8.6 Regulation of Monopoly: Decreasing Cost. Here the regulatory solution P_r, Q_r at the intersection of the AC and AR curves (zero economic profit) occurs in the range where Average Cost is falling. In this "natural monopoly" situation the regulated output Q_r, though greater than the profit-maximizing monopoly output Q_m, is still less than the ideally efficient output Q_c where $MC = P$. In comparison with the efficient outcome, the dotted areas represent losses of Consumer Surplus and Producer Surplus due to insufficient output.

8.E
MONOPOLISTIC PRICE DISCRIMINATION

A monopoly firm is a "price-maker" rather than "price-taker." But up to now it has been assumed that the monopolist offers all customers a single price—at which they are free to choose desired quantities. In certain circumstances, however, a monopolist may be able to engage in more complex *price discrimination*. By offering different terms to different purchasers, it would be possible to divide the market (*market segmentation*). Or, for any given purchaser, the monopolist might be able to impose a price schedule of greater or lesser complexity (*multi-part pricing*). In the limiting case a different price can be charged to each consumer for each successive infinitesimal unit purchased; this is called *perfect discrimination*.

8.E.1 ☐ Market Segmentation

In the most elementary segmentation scheme, the monopolist divides the market into two and quotes a different price to customers in each portion. Apart from questions of legality, this can only be achieved by the monopolist when the two segments are effectively *insulated* one from another. If they are not insulated, customers in the low-price sector of the market would be able to reap an imme-diate windfall gain by resale to the high-price sector—and the whole scheme would necessarily break down.[11]

The underlying logic of the market-segmentation solution is perhaps easier to grasp than the geometrical representation. Denote the separate demand or Average Revenue functions of the two segments as $ar_1(q_1)$ and $ar_2(q_2)$. (The parentheses indicate that ar_1 is a function of q_1 and ar_2 of q_2.) There are, of course, corresponding Marginal Revenue functions $mr_1(q_1)$ and $mr_2(q_2)$. The monopolist's Marginal Cost function can be expressed as $MC(Q)$, where $Q \equiv q_1 + q_2$.

Now, at any level of output Q, whenever $mr_1 \neq mr_2$ the monopolist would want to reallocate units from the sector with lower to the sector with higher Marginal Revenue. Consequently, one optimality condition is $mr_1 = mr_2$. Also, he would want to produce more units of output so long as, and only so long as, $MC < mr_1 = mr_2$. Putting these conditions together, we have:

(8.6)
$$MC(Q) = mr_1(q_1) = mr_2(q_2) \qquad \text{where } Q \equiv q_1 + q_2$$

Market-Segmentation Optimality Condition[12]

The geometrical construction appears in Figure 8.7. The key device is the curve labeled Σmr, the *horizontal* sum of mr_1 and mr_2. The intersection of the firm's Marginal Cost curve MC with Σmr at the point W establishes optimal output $Q \equiv q_1 + q_2$. The separation into q_1 and q_2 is determined by picking off the lengths $ST(= q_1)$ and $TW(= SU = q_2)$ along the horizontal $STUW$. The final step is the determination of the segment prices P_1 and P_2; these are simply the prices associated with the respective quantities q_1 and q_2 along the segment demand curves ar_1 and ar_2.

From equation (8.5), and knowing that $mr_1 = mr_2$, we see that:

(8.7)
$$P_1\left(1 + \frac{1}{\eta_1}\right) = P_2\left(1 + \frac{1}{\eta_2}\right)$$

It follows that if, for example, $|\eta_1| > |\eta_2|$ (demand in segment 1 is the more elastic), then $[1 + (1/\eta_1)] > [1 + (1/\eta_2)]$, so that $P_1 < P_2$. Thus, *the segment with more elastic demand receives the lower price.*

This feature explains the phenomenon called "dumping abroad," i.e., sell-ing to foreigners at a price lower than the price a monopolist charges in the domestic market. In the international market the suppliers of all nations com-pete, and so demand tends to be much more elastic. (More precisely, the elasticity of demand facing any *single* seller tends to be relatively great.) A monopolist able to insulate its domestic market (for example, by inducing the government to impose a tariff or ban upon imports) generally finds it profitable to charge a lower price abroad than at home.

---

[11]However, the insulation of the two segments need not be *total*. The monopolist could accept some "leakage" and still remain ahead.

[12]The technical qualification earlier, that MC must cut MR from *below*, here takes the form: MC must cut the horizontal sum of the mr curves (see Figure 8.7) from below.

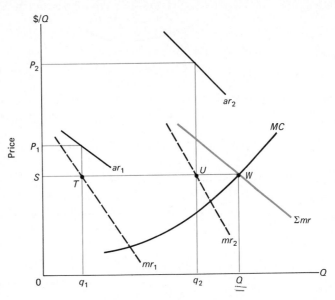

FIGURE 8.7 Market Segmentation. The market is divided into segments 1 and 2, whose independent demand curves are ar_1 and ar_2. The profit-maximizing solution for the firm is to produce where $MC = mr_1 = mr_2$. Geometrically, the optimal output Q is at the intersection of Marginal Cost MC with the Σmr curve representing the horizontal sum of the separate Marginal Revenue curves mr_1 and mr_2. Of this total output the amount q_1 (which equals ST) is sold to the first sector at price P_1, while q_2 (SU, which equals TW) is sold to the second sector at price P_2.

Firm Output and Segment Sales Quantities

Exercise 8.3: A monopolist in a certain country has its domestic market protected by law from import competition. The domestic demand curve for its product is given by $P_d = 120 - q_d/10$. The firm can also export to the world market, where the price is $P_e = 80$ independently of the quantity q_e exported. (That is, this firm is a price-taker so far as the world market is concerned.) The monopolist's Marginal Cost is given by $MC = 50 + Q/10$, where $Q \equiv q_d + q_e$. (a) Find the best overall output Q and its division between the two markets. (b) Compare the prices and demand elasticities in the domestic market versus the world market.

Answer: (a) We know that the Marginal Revenues in the two markets, mr_d and mr_e, and also Marginal Cost MC, must all be equalized. Since the domestic demand curve is linear, we have: $mr_d = 120 - q_d/5$. And since the export demand curve is horizontal: $mr_e = P_e = 80$. Equating the Marginal Revenues: $120 - q_d/5 = 80$, which implies $q_d = 200$. Equating MC to mr_e leads to: $50 + Q/10 = 80$, which implies $Q = 300$. It follows that $q_e = 100$. (b) The export price remains $P_e = 80$, and demand elasticity in that market is minus infinity. In the domestic market, $q_d = 200$ implies $P_d = 100$. The demand elasticity is:

$$\eta_d = \frac{P_d}{q_d}\frac{\Delta q_d}{\Delta P_d} = \frac{100}{200}(-10) = -5$$

The price is higher in the less elastic domestic market.

8.E.2 ☐ Multi-Part Pricing

A second type of monopolistic price discrimination, a multi-part pricing scheme, is illustrated in Figure 8.8. It involves the monopolist's presenting a single price *schedule* to each separate consumer, such that a relatively high price

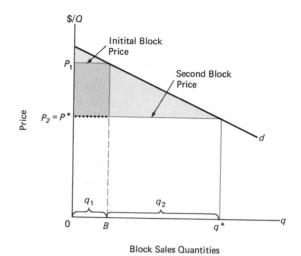

$/Q

Inititial Block Price

P_1

Second Block Price

Price

$P_2 = P^*$

d

q_1 q_2

0   B q^* q

Block Sales Quantities

FIGURE 8.8 Two-Part Pricing. Here P^* is assumed to be the profit-maximizing simple price for a monopolist. If d is the demand curve of a typical consumer, the illustration shows that the monopolist can do even better by charging a higher price P_1 on an initial block quantity B, and $P_2 = P^*$ thereafter. This two-part pricing scheme allows the monopolist to capture the portion of Consumer Surplus represented by the rectangle lying within the shaded area. (The diagram is strictly correct only if the consumer's purchases in the second block are not affected by higher outlays for the first block. Ordinarily, the income effect would bring about a reduction of second-block sales, so the monopolist engaging in two-part pricing could not do quite so well as shown.)

P_1 is charged for initial units up to some given limit B, and a lower price P_2 for additional units taken thereafter. The basic intent of such a scheme is to capture for the seller a portion of the Consumer Surplus that would otherwise have gone to buyers.

In Figure 8.8, the monopolist is facing the individual demand curve d of one typical consumer. The cost function cannot be shown in this diagram, but we may assume that the intersection of MC and MR as pictured in the lower panel of Figure 8.1 leads to the determination of an optimal *simple* monopoly price P^*. At this price the consumer would have chosen the quantity q^*. Simple pricing would leave the shaded area under the demand curve as Consumer Surplus.[13] A two-part pricing scheme might specify an initial higher P_1 up to the limit B, and the lower $P_2 = P^*$ thereafter as indicated in the diagram. Suppose we can assume that the same total quantity $q_1 + q_2 = q^*$ will still be purchased by the individual as under simple monopoly. The consumer would buy $q_1 = B$ units at the price P_1, and $q_2 = q^* - B$ units at the price P_2. Then the revenue received by the seller would obviously be greater than under simple pricing, by the area $(P_1 - P^*) \, q_1$ of the rectangle shown as cutting into the Consumer Surplus.

This is, however, somewhat of an idealized situation. The monopolist would ordinarily not be able to do quite so well as pictured. First of all, the adverse "income effect" (Section 4.D) of paying the higher price P_1 for the first B units

[13] It follows from the normally positive income effect, however (see below), that the conventional shaded area in Figure 8.8 somewhat exaggerates the true Consumer Surplus.

would *tend to reduce the consumer's demand for additional units.* The ordinary demand curve d is constructed on the hypothesis of simple uniform pricing; only in the case of goods for which the income effect is zero (the income elasticity of demand is zero) will the curve remain the same when multi-part pricing is employed to extract more revenue from the consumer. Consequently, the monopolist must consider, as a partial offset to the advantage gained from selling the first B units at the high price P_1, that there will be a reduction in the overall number of units that can be sold.

Another, generally more important, qualification stems from *differences among consumers.* The monopolist would ideally like to offer differing price schedules to different customers. But legal restrictions, or perhaps the cost of making such distinctions among customers, may dictate a common price schedule in which P_1, P_2, and B are the same for all purchasers. Then there are likely to be a number of buyers in the situation of Figure 8.9. For these customers B is so large that the initial price P_1 becomes a simple price for them: they will not purchase any additional units at all at the lower price P_2 quoted for units beyond B. Since by assumption above $P_2 = P^*$ was supposed to be the profit-maximizing simple price, for a typical consumer any further increase in price would mean *less* profit for the firm. So if it is not feasible to offer different price schedules to different customers, the profitability of multi-part pricing will be much less.

The two qualifications reduce the advantage of multi-part pricing to the monopolist. In addition, of course, the transaction cost of more complex pricing schemes will be greater. Not only will more detailed metering and recording of sales be required, but it will be necessary to control "leakage" of units from low-price to high-price buyers. Thus, it is not always evident that the monopolist will find such discrimination advantageous.

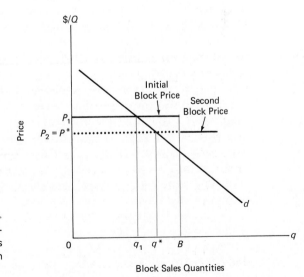

FIGURE 8.9 Unsuccessful Two-Part Pricing. Here we see a two-part pricing scheme inappropriate for this particular consumer. No sales are actually made at the second block price, so in effect a simple price P_1 is being charged.

At first sight, it may appear that discrimination via multi-part pricing is very common. Electric and water utilities, for example, normally charge on a "declining-block" basis. There is an initial high price for the first block consumed in any period, and a lower price thereafter. Utility price schedules may often have four or five parts (blocks), and also, possibly, some segmentation of different classes of customers. Printers and furniture-movers also commonly have declining-block pricing arrangements. Indeed, wherever "quantity discounts" are encountered multi-price discrimination may be suspected.

However, the suspicion is not conclusive; the pricing scheme may be due not to discrimination but to the costs incurred in serving different classes of customers. In the case of electric utilities, for example, there may be a recurrent "fixed" cost of providing the consumer's connection to the main cable, a cost that is essentially independent of the number of kilowatt-hours consumed. Similarly, for printing jobs there is normally a "fixed" cost per transaction (e.g., the cost of setting up the type for a printing order) and a variable cost representing the actual run of the press. Ideally, then, bills should have a fixed and a variable component. For a variety of reasons, it may be more convenient to express the recurring fixed component as a premium price on the first few units taken. Thus, the question of the actual prevalence of discriminatory multi-part pricing versus "cost-justified" quantity discounts remains subject to some controversy.

8.E.3 ☐ Perfect Discrimination

Finally, we can now go to the logical extreme of *perfect* discrimination. This of course is not a practical possibility, but is illuminating to analyze. It combines the *interpersonal* discrimination of market segmentation and the *intrapersonal* discrimination of multi-part pricing. In addition, these processes are imagined as carried to their limits. Each separate consumer is charged according to an individually tailored price schedule, which specifies a different amount to be paid for each successive infinitesimal unit he purchases.

In Figure 8.10 we see a four-part pricing schedule, an extension of the two-part schedule pictured in Figure 8.8. As in the previous analysis, we make the simplifying assumption of zero income effect (zero income elasticity of demand) for the commodity. Then the quantities taken at the lower prices are unaffected by the higher amounts paid out for earlier units. As can be seen, such a multi-part schedule can transfer great portions of the Consumer Surplus to the seller; in Figure 8.10, only the small shaded areas remain as Consumer Surplus.

When this process is carried to the limit, with different prices for each successive infinitesimal unit, *all* the Consumer Surplus will have been transferred from the buyer to the seller. By repeating this process with every separate consumer, the perfectly discriminating monopolist absorbs essentially all the achievable mutual advantage of trade.

Despite the seeming "inequity" of this totally unbalanced distribution of the benefits from trade, the remarkable thing about the perfect-discrimination solution is that it is *efficient*—there are no efficiency losses, only transfers! For the last infinitesimal unit purchased by each consumer, the monopolist will charge an

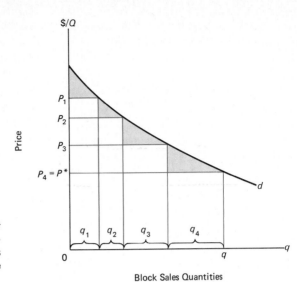

FIGURE 8.10 Four-Part Pricing. In contrast with the two block prices in the preceding diagrams, here there are four blocks. The block sizes and prices, in the case illustrated, leave only the shaded areas as Consumer Surplus.

amount equal to Marginal Cost. Since each buyer's marginal willingness to pay (demand price) is thus equal to the seller's Marginal Cost of production, there is no social gain available from increasing or decreasing output. So the perfectly discriminating monopolist cannot be said to produce "too little" or "too much" from the point of view of economic efficiency.

8.F
CARTELS

A cartel may be defined as a group of independent firms attempting, via collusive agreement, to behave as a collective monopoly. Each firm in a cartel agrees to produce less than it would under unrestrained competition, the overall effect being to drive the price up so that all in the group will benefit.

Cartels have an Achilles heel. However desirable the arrangement is to the firms as a group, for any single one of them it pays to "chisel" on the agreement. Consider a firm in a cartelized industry that would otherwise have been perfectly competitive. Figure 8.11 illustrates such a situation. At the price P° that would rule in perfect competition, d° is the familiar horizontal demand curve *as viewed by* the competitive firm. Assuming that Average Variable Cost is covered, the firm would produce output q° where Marginal Cost $MC = P^\circ$. If a cartel is organized with the objective of raising prices, industry output Q must somehow be cut back—for example, by fixing production quotas for each firm. Suppose that this firm is assigned an output quota q', and furthermore that the cartel is successful in pushing prices up to P'. The incentive to chisel is evident. The new demand curve *as viewed by* the firm (a tiny slice of the industry demand curve) is d'—effectively horizontal, just like the d° curve before cartelization. This means that by charging an infinitesimally lower price, any single firm can get as much business as desired, taking away sales from others. Even at the old competitive

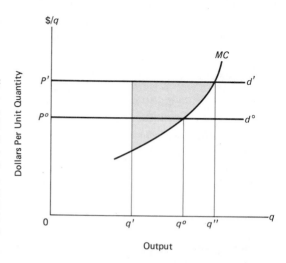

$/q

FIGURE 8.11 **Incentive to Chisel under a Cartel.** If the competitive equilibrium price is $P°$, this price-taking firm would produce output $q°$ (at the intersection of its MC curve with its perceived horizontal demand curve $d°$). If a cartel is organized, it can drive up price only by forcing its members to cut back production. If this firm's assigned production quota were q', and the cartel succeeded in driving price up to P', the firm's potential gain from chiselling (increase in profit due to exceeding its quota) would be the shaded area. Note that, at the high price P', the firm would find it profitable to produce output q'', *greater* than its competitive output $q°$.

price $P°$, the firm was motivated to produce $q°$, more than the quota q'. (Cartel production quotas must of course be smaller than competitive firm outputs, or the price could not rise from $P°$ to P'.) But once the cartel has raised price, the incentive to chisel is that much greater. At the price P' the firm would want to sell output q'' in the diagram. The potential profit increment available to a chiseler, assuming all the other firms are faithfully abiding by the cartel agreement so that price does not fall, is indicated by the shaded area in the diagram.

CONCLUSION: Cartels can only raise prices by cutting firm outputs. But at the higher prices, member firms are motivated to produce even more than at competitive equilibrium. So the more successful the cartel, the greater the incentive to chisel.

Exercise 8.4: Suppose that there are 100 identical firms in an initially competitive market. Market demand is given by $P = 10 - Q/200$ and supply by $P = 1 + Q/200$. (a) Find the competitive equilibrium price P, industry output Q, and firm output q. (b) If the 100 firms formed an effective cartel, what would be the price–quantity solution for maximum aggregate profit? [Assume that the industry supply curve is simply the horizontal sum of the firm Marginal Cost curves.] (c) At this price, to what output would the typical firm have to be limited? How much would it like to produce?

Answer: (a) Equating supply and demand, we have: $10 - Q/200 = 1 + Q/200$. The solution is $Q = 900$, $q = 9$, and $P = 5\frac{1}{2}$. (b) Since the demand curve is linear, Marginal Revenue is $MR = 10 - Q/100$. Marginal Cost for industry output as a whole is, by assumption, $MC = 1 + Q/200$. The profit-maximizing solution for the industry is $Q = 600$, $P = 7$. (c) At this price the typical firm would have to be limited to output $q = 6$. But it would like to set its $MC = 1 + q/2$ equal to $P = 7$, implying a desired output $q = 12$.

Cartels, therefore, require enforcement devices. The power of the state may do the trick; the law may treat the cartel agreement as a legally enforceable contract. This had indeed been the situation in a number of European countries. Some jurisdictions take a neutral position: the cartel agreement is not unlawful, but the power of the state will not enforce it. Finally, as typically has been the case in the United States, the law may be actively hostile to cartels as "conspiracies in restraint of trade." In such a situation, a cartel would require enforcement devices that are *both effective and secret*—an unlikely combination when any detected chiseler can threaten to complain to the authorities.

Collusive agreements alleged to be in restraint of trade are prosecuted in the United States mainly by the Anti-Trust Division of the Department of Justice and by the Federal Trade Commission. (In addition, it is possible for individuals or firms to sue for damages suffered as victims of such agreements.) But it is a curious paradox that other branches of the United States government are themselves active in the organization and enforcement of cartel agreements. A number of agricultural products, for example, are sold subject to governmentally sponsored "marketing orders" designed to limit production and sales.

EXAMPLE 8.5
Agricultural Marketing Orders

On the basis of legislation of the federal government, and of some states as well, the growers of certain agricultural products may draw up an agreement to limit supply and assign marketing quotas. If two-thirds of the growers (by number or by volume) vote for such an agreement the Secretary of Agriculture is authorized to make it binding upon *all* growers.

Quantities produced beyond the marketing quotas are "dumped" abroad, used in special government programs outside normal trade channels (e.g., school lunches), or simply destroyed. In effect, the cartel (representing the growers as an aggregate) buys up excess production in order to limit supplies and drive up price in the "primary" market. However, this means that each individual producer has an incentive to produce more and more. In addition, the higher the price, the more growers of *other* commodities tend to shift over to the cartelized product. Consequently, we would expect over time to see an increasing percentage of the cartelized crops having to be diverted away from "primary" markets. This trend is illustrated in the Table.

Percentage of Annual Supply Diverted from Primary Markets under Federal Marketing Orders

CROP	1960–64 AVG.	1965–68 AVG.
California raisins	28.2	39.6
California–Arizona lemons	55.2	62.5
California almonds	15.0	21.2
California–Oregon–Washington walnuts	0.8	7.5
Oregon–Washington filberts	21.8	27.5
California dates (Deglet Noor)	21.4	28.2

Source: John A. Jamison, "Marketing Orders and Public Policy for the Fruit and Vegetable Industries," *Food Research Studies in Agricultural Economics, Trade, and Development.* v. 10, no. 3 (1971), p. 347.

Of course, there can hardly be anyone in the world unfamiliar with the most successful cartel in history—the Organization of Petroleum Exporting Countries (OPEC).

EXAMPLE 8.6
The OPEC

In pre-OPEC days, before 1960, the international oil companies (especially the seven or eight "majors" such as Royal Dutch Shell and Standard Oil of New Jersey) were often accused of acting as a cartel. If their aim was to keep prices high they failed, as became evident later when the OPEC came into existence and *really* raised prices. In fact, it was the attempt of the majors to cut oil prices that led the exporting nations to establish the OPEC in 1960. (The U.S. State Department, in what must have been an all-time low point for intelligent foreign economic policy, actively encouraged formation of the OPEC!) The subsequent history of the world petroleum market may be divided into four phases.

Phase 1 (1960–1973): The OPEC nations, by requiring the private oil companies to reduce production levels, prevented prices from falling. Over most of this period the price was around $1.80/barrel for Arabian light crude, rising to $2.59 by 1973.[a] Also during this period the exporting nations solidified their control over pricing and production, in effect expropriating the private oil concessions. (Thenceforth, the private oil companies in OPEC countries received only what amounted to fees for providing extraction and marketing services. For example, Saudi Arabia captured as government take all but about $.60 of the price in effect on January 1, 1973.)

Phase 2 (1973–1978): In solidarity with the attack of Egypt and Syria upon Israel in late 1973, the Arab countries dominating OPEC decided to use oil as an economic weapon. While the attempt to embargo shipments to Europe and America was unsuccessful, the associated cutback of production drove the price dramatically upward. By January 1, 1974 the official OPEC price had more than quadrupled, to $11.65/barrel. It says something about economic gullibility that the Shah of Iran, the King of Saudi Arabia, and other oil potentates succeeded in convincing a large part of the Western public that the "shortage" and high prices were due not to OPEC's dictated production pinch but to the machinations of the wicked private oil companies. (These companies were in fact typically receiving from their OPEC concessions little more than the same $.60/barrel they had been earning before.)

The problem for the OPEC was and is to hold production down despite member countries' incentives to "chisel." Each separate exporting nation can gain by expanding output so long as the others are holding back. In fact, in

---

[a] Data on prices have been collected from several sources including *International Economic Report of the President*, Washington, D.C.: U.S. Government Printing Office, Feb. 1974, pp. 110–11, and *Los Angeles Times* (March 15, 1983), p. 1.

the period from 1974 to late 1978 most of the member countries were probably not holding back but were instead producing all-out. The cartel was viable in that period because a few major producers, notably Saudi Arabia and Kuwait, were willing to diminish their production (or maintain it at a relatively low level). Nevertheless, OPEC's power was gradually weakening. While the official price rose from $11.65 per barrel at the beginning of 1974 to $13.00 five years later (an increase of about 12%), the U.S. dollar depreciated by around 38% over the same period. Thus, by January 1, 1979 the real price of OPEC crude oil was down substantially from its peak.

Phase 3 (1979–1982): The turmoil in Iran that paralyzed production there and eventually displaced the Shah permitted OPEC to start another round of price increases. Even after the new government took over, Iranian exports remained drastically less than before. The official price rose, in several steps, ultimately to $34/barrel in late 1981. (And at the peak some OPEC suppliers were demanding and receiving a premium of as much as $5 above the official price.) However, especially toward the end of the period, maintaining these high prices necessitated increasingly severe production cutbacks by the major OPEC producers—in particular, by Saudi Arabia.

Among the adverse features from the OPEC point of view were: (1) *Elasticity of demand:* As economic theory suggests, demand elasticity proved greater in the long run than in the short run. The continuing high price impelled consuming nations to use oil more economically, and to shift toward substitute fuels. (The international recession starting in 1981 led to a cyclical reduction of demand as well.) (2) *Inducement of new entry:* High prices encouraged non-OPEC nations like Britain and Mexico to develop and expand their capacity to extract crude oil. The combined effect of lesser demand and increased non-OPEC supply was drastic indeed, leading to:

Phase 4 (beginning early 1982): In this phase, OPEC has attempted to defend its high quoted price while coping with the "oil glut" inevitably created by that high price. The only possible way of doing so has been for OPEC to cut back production. OPEC output fell from a 1979 peak of 32 million barrels per day (bgd) to less than half that amount by early 1983.[b] And within OPEC, the brunt of the decline has fallen upon the largest producer, Saudi Arabia, which has been forced to curtail its output from a peak of 10.2 bgd to less than 4 bgd. (Even so, the nominally fixed $34/barrel price was slipping in real terms; the dollar depreciated about 5% between October 1981 and March 1983.) Bowing to economic reality, in March 1983 OPEC was finally forced to cut the dollar price to $29/barrel. Whether even this price can be maintained will depend, of course, upon the ability of the cartel to hold down production. At this writing, the OPEC members have been unable to agree upon the production quotas each nation must accept.

[b]Production figures from S. Fred Singer, "What Do the Saudis Do Now?" *Wall Street Journal* (March 18, 1983), p. 20.

With a small number of firms in an industry, *price-taking* behavior is unlikely. Each firm will be aware of the effects of its own output decision upon market price. The extreme case, where only a single firm is viable in an industry ("natural monopoly"), occurs where one firm can always produce more cheaply than and so drive out any larger number. But monopolies may also be the result of exclusive government privileges or franchises.

Monopolists, like ordinary firms, are assumed to be profit-maximizers. Profit is maximized by setting output (or price) such that:

$$MC = MR$$

For the monopoly firm, in contrast with the price-taking firm, Marginal Revenue MR is less than price P. The relation between these two variables involves the demand elasticity η:

$$MR \equiv P(1 + 1/\eta).$$

"Monopoly power" may be measured by the divergence between $MC = MR$ and price P; it tends to decrease with the number of firms in the industry, and with the consumers' elasticity of demand for the product. Thus, monopoly power tends to be greater for necessity goods and for goods without close substitutes.

Monopoly output is smaller than output would be if the industry had a competitive structure. There is an efficiency loss (reduction in Consumer Surplus and Producer Surplus) due to the smaller volume of production and exchange, and also a pure transfer from consumers to the monopolist seller. There may also be an additional efficiency loss, of a different type, if resources are expended in the struggle to gain and maintain a monopoly position.

Monopolies, and in particular franchised public utilities, are often subjected to regulation. The goal of regulation is commonly to ensure that the monopolist receives only enough revenue to attract and retain the resources employed in the industry, i.e., receives only a "normal" profit and no *economic* profit. Then Average Revenue and Average Cost must be equal. If the monopolist's Average Cost curve is rising, the intersection of AC and AR "overshoots" the competitive equilibrium; there will be an efficiency loss due to *excessive* production in this industry. On the other hand, if AC is in its falling range, the regulated solution lies between the monopolist's profit-maximizing output and the competitive outcome.

By engaging in price discrimination, a monopolist can acquire still more revenue from given consumer demands (can capture more of what would have been Consumer Surplus). Under *market segmentation,* the monopolist would set overall Marginal Cost of production equal to the Marginal Revenue in each segment. It follows from the equation relating P, MR, and elasticity η that higher prices will be charged in segments with less elastic demands. *Multi-part pricing*—an alternative form of price discrimination—captures some of Consumer Surplus via a declining-block price schedule. This type of discrimination is most effective if an individualized schedule can be offered to each consumer. *Perfect discrimination* is a limiting case in which each consumer is charged the maximum he or she would be willing to pay for each unit—so that no Consumer Surplus at all remains. Surprisingly, there is no efficiency loss under perfect discrimination.

Cartels are associations of smaller firms able to act collectively like a monopolist. Since a higher price can only be achieved if production is cut back, output quotas typically have to be imposed on members of a cartel. Each member is therefore motivated to "chisel" (produce beyond quota). As a result, cartels have historically been fragile except where supported by government power.

☐ QUESTIONS FOR CHAPTER 8

MAINLY FOR REVIEW

*R1. Why will a monopolist's profit-maximizing rate of output always be in the region of elastic demand?

R2. Why is monopoly power over price smaller as elasticity of demand increases?

*R3. "Monopoly is a bad thing for consumers, but a good thing for producers. So, on balance, we can't be sure that monopoly is responsible for any loss in economic efficiency." Analyze.

R4. A competitive industry may have its equilibrium in the range of inelastic demand. Then the industry would receive more revenue if its output were smaller. Does it follow that such a competitive industry is producing "too much" of the good in terms of efficient use of resources?

*R5 Monopoly firms are accused of pursuing "non-profit goals" to a greater degree than competitive firms. Why might a monopolist be any less interested in profit than a competitor?

R6. Compare the profit-maximizing conditions for simply monopoly, for market-segmentation monopoly, and for perfect-discrimination monopoly. Why is only the last of these said to be *efficient*?

*R7. In making efficiency comparisons between a monopolized and a competitive industry, the Marginal Cost function of the monopolist was said to correspond to the supply function of the competitive industry. Explain why.

R8. When will zero-profit regulation of a monopoly lead to too high a price from an efficiency point of view? Too low a price?

R9. Show how behavior of its own members may threaten the survival of a cartel. Show how behavior of outsiders may threaten it.

FOR FURTHER THOUGHT AND DISCUSSION

*T1. Is there a contradiction between the assertions that: (1) the oil industry is an effective monopoly (cartel), and (2) higher prices for petroleum products will do little to discourage demand?

T2. Is it better (more efficient) to have a monopolized industry, or no industry at all?

*The answers to asterisked questions appear at the end of the book.

*T3. In comparison with a simple monopolist, does a perfectly discriminating monopolist *possibly* or *necessarily* produce more output? Does a market-segmentation monopolist? A multi-part pricing monopolist?

*T4. Price discrimination tends to be more common in the sale of services (e.g., discrimination by income for medical services, by age for transportation services) than in the sale of manufactured goods. Explain.

*T5. Movie theaters often offer price discounts to the young. Is there likely to be a "leakage" problem in this form of market segmentation?

*T6. Observers have noted that pornographic movie theaters seem to discriminate against single patrons (a discount price is offered to couples). Can you explain this?

T7. Doctors often charge poorer customers lower fees for medical services. They usually explain this as a charitable gesture. Might another explanation be offered?

T8. It has been alleged that sellers' cartels are more effective in dealing with *government* as a buyer because of the existence of public records of all transactions in which government engages. Explain. How might the contention be tested?

T9. Historically, governments have sometimes auctioned off the right to monopolize a commodity (the *gabelle,* or salt monopoly of pre-Revolutionary France, was an example). Show diagrammatically the maximum amount the government might expect to acquire by auctioning off a monopoly. Is this likely to generate more or less income for the government than the most lucrative excise tax the government might impose?

*T10. If an organization like the Mafia effectively monopolized illegal activity, would you expect to observe less crime than under competitive free entry into this "industry"?

PRODUCT AS A VARIABLE: VARIETY AND QUALITY

SUPPLEMENTARY
CHAPTER

☐ We have studied the decisions of the competitive firm in choosing the amount of output offered on the market, and of the monopolistic firm in determining the most profitable price–quantity combination to offer consumers. But we have not yet allowed for the fact that a firm producing wheat or haircuts or electricity can also select, to some extent at least, the *characteristics of the product* being offered. Different strains of wheat can be grown, haircuts come in different styles, and even electricity can be generated with different voltages, frequency, reliability, etc. The "new theory of consumption" (Chapter 5) indicated that consumers are not really interested in the physical commodities as such. Rather, consumer preferences should be thought of as attaching to the attributes or characteristics represented by or contained in the commodities. Market goods are desired only because and insofar as they constitute convenient packages of attributes.

In this chapter two main types of situations will be investigated. First, suppose that consumers' tastes and desires for a particular product are distributed over a range of some quantifiable characteristic such as size, color, or weight. Some customers like red roses, some pink, some white. Some people like small cars, others prefer big ones.[1] The market response to this situation will typically be to offer an assortment of products to consumers. This will be called the problem of *variety*. Section A of this chapter will cover the variety or product assortment decision of a monopolistic supplier. Section B takes up the market structure known as "monopolistic competition"—where each firm offers consumers its own unique product, but there may be many closely competing firms.[2] The remainder of the chapter considers a second type of situation, called the problem of *quality*. Here consumers do not have diverging preferences. Instead, all consumers agree on the desirability of some objective quality attribute (e.g., strength or durability) contained, to greater or lesser degree, in the products

[1]For some commodities, one or more of the preference-determining characteristics may not be objectively quantifiable. Toothpaste may have a sweet or spicy taste, clothing may be in mod or conservative style, an automobile may or may not have a sporty design. We deal here only with attributes that can be objectively scaled.

[2]Under monopolistic competition, we will assume that each firm specializes by producing only a single type of product. Variety is offered to consumers by the market as a whole, rather than by any single firm. This of course will not always or even usually be the case, but it provides a simple starting point for analysis.

offered for sale. But higher quality will, in general, involve higher cost of production. The problem is the determination of the equilibrium level of quality offered in the market.

9.A
OPTIMAL PRODUCT ASSORTMENT: MONOPOLY

Before bringing in the element of competition, let us consider how a monopolist would solve the problem of variety—the profit-maximizing assortment of products to be offered on the market. Products may of course vary in an indefinitely large number of ways, but for simplicity consider a single dimension of variation. In the case of clothing, think in terms of the assortment of *sizes* to be offered. Alternatively, the assortment of *colors* might be a relevant consideration.

A locational metaphor or analogy will help to visualize the problem. With clothing *size* as the attribute, imagine that consumption preferences are distributed over a line-segment as in Figure 9.1 (linear attribute preference). For example, a consumer looking for a small-sized product can be regarded as located toward the left, one desiring a large size toward the right. We would normally expect to find greater density toward the middle. As indicated in Figure 9.1, desires for extreme sizes are less common than demand for intermediate sizes. However, it will be sufficient for our purposes to imagine that preferences are *uniformly* distributed over the range. One other analytically convenient change will be made from the picture given by Figure 9.1: we will assume that the varying product characteristic or attribute does not have a lower limit and upper limit but instead can be described by a ring, as in Figure 9.2. *Color* might be such a characteristic. If as many prefer red as yellow as green, and so on, consumers can be thought of as distributed uniformly around the color circle of Figure 9.2.

In this locational metaphor the variety (color) preferred by a particular consumer can be regarded as a *consumption locale*, i.e., as the geographical location of the consumer's residence on the ring. Similarly, any given variety actually produced and offered in the market can be regarded as a *production locale*. Since only a few consumers would be located exactly at production locales, the typical consumer would have to pay some transport cost to cover the shipment of the good from the nearest production point. Geographical distance in this picture illustrates the imperfect matching of consumer preferences with the available

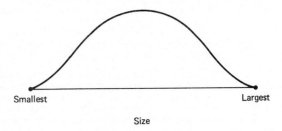

FIGURE 9.1 Distribution of Linear Attribute Preferences. Differing consumer preferences for an attribute like size of goods can be pictured as a distribution over a line-segment. Ordinarily, more consumers will be found toward the middle than toward the ends (intermediate sizes will be more popular than extreme sizes).

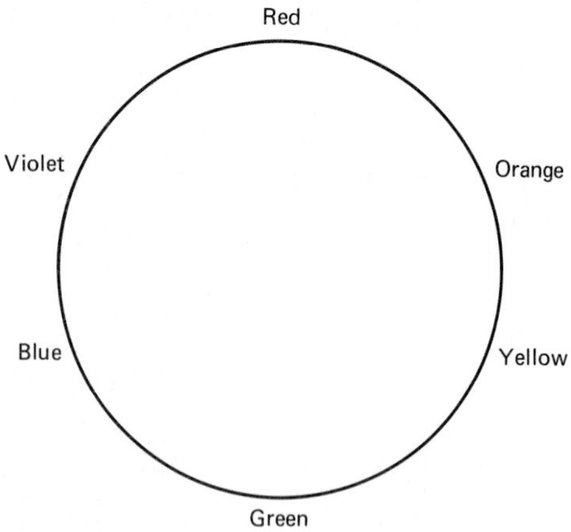

FIGURE 9.2 **Ring of Circular Attribute Preferences.** An attribute like color may be described as a circle, rather than as a line-segment with end-points. (It is assumed that consumer preferences are uniformly distributed around the ring.)

products. For example, a consumer wearing size 9 dresses might find that only sizes 8 and 10 were available on the market. After making a purchase she might employ someone for alterations, or do them herself at home, or simply tolerate the imperfect fit. Whichever she chooses, the loss she suffers corresponds to the transport cost in a locational situation.

Returning to the ring of Figure 9.2, the first problem for the monopolist is to determine *how many* varieties to produce, i.e., the number of distinct production locales to establish around the ring. Having done so, it will then be necessary to decide *how much* to produce at each production point, and what *prices* to charge for the outputs. There is an advantage to be gained by increasing the number of production locales (of "plants"), since this will reduce transport costs and therefore increase the amount of consumers' expenditures that the monopolist is able to capture as revenue. What prevents carrying this process to the limit (a separate plant for each consumer) is *economies of scale*. Over some range, at least, Average Cost per plant will ordinarily be a decreasing function of plant output. So the monopolist must balance savings in production costs against savings in transport costs. Put another way, the monopolist must choose between returns to large-scale production versus the advantage of offering consumers a better assortment of products.

For simplicity again, assume that the monopolist's cost of production is *identical* at all possible locations around the ring. Then, given a uniform distribution of consumers, the producing plants (whatever their number) should be spaced evenly around the ring to minimize the transport costs of delivery to consumption locales. And, it also follows from the symmetry of the situation that the price at the factory (the "f.o.b. price") will be identical at each producing plant. Each consumer, of course, must pay this f.o.b. price *plus* the unit transport cost from the nearest plant.

Looking first at the demand side, note in Figure 9.3 the limiting (highest) aggregate consumer demand function D_∞. This represents the ideal case in which there are an infinite number of production locales around the ring. As consumers then incur no transport costs, their desires for product become wholly reflected in the effective demand curve faced by the monopolist. At the opposite

272

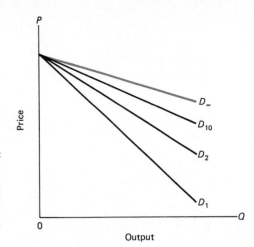

FIGURE 9.3   Aggregate Demand as Related to Number of Producing Plants. $D_1, D_2, \ldots, D_\infty$ show the aggregate effective demand, as viewed by a monopolist seller, for increasing numbers of plants (production locales) spaced evenly around the ring of Figure 9.2. Effective demand increases with the number of plants (since there is less wastage in transport costs), but at a decreasing rate.

extreme is the curve labeled D_1, which shows effective demand with just a single productive plant (placed at any arbitrary point on the ring). Here the worst-off consumer must pay for shipment halfway around the ring; the *average* transport cost corresponds to a quarter-circle of circumference about the ring. Any amounts expended to cover transport costs leave that much less of the consumers' outlays as receipts to the seller, hence whenever Q is positive D_1 must lie below D_∞. The curve D_2 represents the effective demand faced by a monopolist with two plants, so that the average consumer is separated by an eighth-circle from the nearest production locale. The D_{10} curve in the diagram shows the effective demand with 10 plants.[3] Note that the curve of effective demand shifts upward, *but at a decreasing rate*, as the number of plants is increased, i.e., as the assortment offered more closely approximates the distribution of consumer preferences.

To arrive at the monopolist's solution we also need the cost function for output. This is conveniently illustrated under the special assumption that plant production costs are linear. Thus for the nth plant, $C_n = A + Bq_n$. Here A is the Fixed Cost of each plant, and B the Marginal Cost. Then if there are N identical plants, the overall Total Cost will be symbolized here as $TC_N = \Sigma_{n=1}^{N} C_n$. Thus $TC_N = \Sigma_{n=1}^{N} (A + Bq_n) = NA + BQ$, where $Q \equiv \Sigma_{n=1}^{N} q_n$ is the monopolist's overall output of product. For a range of possible numbers of plants N, the overall Total Cost functions TC_N are shown by the dashed lines $TC_1, TC_2, \ldots$ in Figure 9.4. Because of the existence of the Fixed Cost A *per plant*, the Total Cost of producing any aggregate output Q rises with *number* of plants N.

[3]The picture in Fig. 9.3 is somewhat oversimplified, however. The picture is correct in that all the demand curves from D_1 to D_∞ must intersect at the same point along the vertical axis. However it can be shown that, for sufficiently large Q, the different demand curves eventually become *parallel* to one another. The explanation for the convergence of the curves near the vertical axis is that, for any finite number of plants, when price becomes high enough the sum of price plus transport cost chokes off some people's demand entirely. And the "choke price" at which aggregate demand Q becomes zero is the same regardless of the number of plants. But for sufficiently low price, where everyone is consuming some positive quantity of the product, the unit transport cost is like a unit tax and the demand curves are parallel.

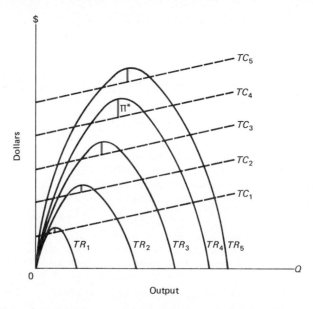

FIGURE 9.4   Monopoly Total Revenue and Total Costs, as Related to Number of Plants. The aggregate Total Revenue curves TR_1, TR_2, . . . represent the same data as shown by the aggregate demand curves (curves of Average Revenue) D_1, D_2, . . . of the previous diagram. As number of plants N rises, Total Revenue TR_N also rises *but at a decreasing rate.* The Total Cost curves TC_1, TC_2, . . . show the aggregate cost of producing any output Q with 1, 2, . . . plants. Under the assumption of an identical linear cost function for each plant, TC_N shifts upward by a constant amount as N rises (since an additional Fixed Cost is incurred each time a new plant is brought into production). The bold vertical segments show the highest achievable profit for each N; the greatest of these is the profit maximum Π^*, which occurs here at $N = 4$.

The Total Revenue functions corresponding to different numbers of plants are also shown in Figure 9.4. TR_1 is the Total Revenue curve corresponding to the effective demand curve D_1 of the previous diagram, TR_2 similarly corresponds to D_2, etc.

For any given number of plants N, the monopolist chooses the f.o.b. price P_m and the associated quantity Q by using the familiar condition $MC = MR$ so as to maximize profit—the vertical distance between the appropriate pair of TR_N and TC_N curves (compare the upper panel of Figure 8.1). For different numbers of plants N, the various possible profits are indicated by the vertical bold line segments in Figure 9.4. As may be seen, there will normally be a range in which profit increases as N rises. In this range the gain from better matching of products to consumer desires (i.e., from the fact that consumers are willing to pay more when they avoid the metaphorical "transport costs"), evidencing itself by upward shifts of the TR curve, is greater than the increased cost due to the larger number of production locales. But the gains from increasing N tend to taper off. Meanwhile costs tend to rise steadily as N grows, because of the necessity of incurring another fixed-cost element A each time a new plant is added. There will, consequently, be an optimum number of plants. In Figure 9.4, the largest profit Π^* (greatest of the bold vertical line-segments) is achieved at $N = 4$; having exactly four production locales represents the best compromise between production costs and transport costs.

9.B
MONOPOLISTIC COMPETITION

The monopoly solution of the preceding section provides the needed background for analyzing the market structure known as *monopolistic competition*. This market structure combines the following characteristics: (1) competition among plants, now treated as independent *firms*; (2) free entry; and (3) differentiated products among firms. The first two characteristics represent the competitive aspects of monopolistic competition. The monopolistic aspect is represented by the third element, the uniqueness of the firm's product offered to the market. This uniqueness would correspond to a degree of *geographical* monopoly. Each firm will have a "clientele" consisting of those consumers located closer to it than to any other firm around the ring of preference.

It will be convenient first to provide a reinterpretation of the monopoly solution in terms of an average-marginal diagram as in Figure 9.5. In a monopoly with N identical plants, the effective aggregate demand (Average Revenue) is D_N, a curve some distance below the "ideal" D_∞. Marginal Revenue is MR_N. Now consider the *pro-rata shares* of D_N and MR_N attributable to any single plant, $D_n \equiv D_N/N$ and $MR_n \equiv MR_N/N$. Geometrically, these are found simply by dividing the respective aggregate curves horizontally by N. If $N = 4$, the pro-rata plant curves D_n and MR_n, will simply represent one-fourth the quantities along the aggregate curves D_N and MR_N, respectively. The profit-maximizing solutions for aggregate *firm* output Q_N^* and for *plant* output $q_n^* \equiv Q_N^*/N$ can be seen by inspection of Figure 9.5. The *plant* output q_n^* is determined by the intersection of

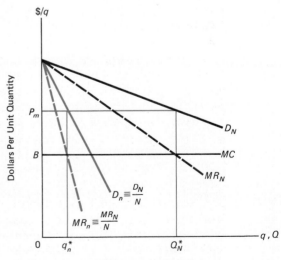

FIGURE 9.5 Monopoly Solutions, Aggregate and Plant. For a given number of plants N, the monopolist's effective *aggregate* demand curve is D_N. And $D_n \equiv D_N/N$ is the pro-rata *plant* demand curve. MR_N and $MR_n \equiv MR_N/N$ are the associated Marginal Revenue curves. Under the linear cost assumption, the constant Marginal Cost is shown by a horizontal MC curve at the level B. The profit-maximizing *aggregate* output is Q_N^* (where $MC = MR_N$), and *plant* output is q_n^* (where $MC = MR_n$). Of course, $Q_N^* \equiv Nq_n^*$. For either the plant or the firm solution, the same profit-maximizing price P_m is found along the associated demand curve.

Plant Output and Aggregate Output

MC with MR_n. (Under the linear cost assumption $C_n = A + Bq_n$, the Marginal Cost curve MC is horizontal at the level B.) The aggregate *firm* output Q_N^* is found at the intersection of MC with MR_N. The monopoly price, P_m, may be found equally well along the aggregate demand curve D_N (at quantity Q_N^*), or along the plant pro-rata demand curve D_n (at quantity q_n^*). Of course, $Q_N^* = Nq_n^*$.

We now shift gears, in order to introduce the element of *competition*. Imagine that each *plant* of the monopolist becomes a separate small *firm*. For the moment, we will assume there is some definite number N of such firms, that all of them have identical cost functions, and that they have distributed themselves evenly around the preference ring of Figure 9.2. Then the monopolist's *aggregate* demand curve of Figure 9.5 can be regarded as the *industry* demand curve, since from the consumers' point of view the transport costs incurred are the same regardless of whether shipment is from a monopoly plant or an independent firm. The pro-rata demand curve $D_n (\equiv D_N/N)$ in Figure 9.6 is therefore also the same as the correspondingly labeled curve in the previous diagram; it now indicates, at every price, the share of the industry output that can be sold by each of the *firms*. At the intersection of MC and MR_n, we see once again what the profit-maximizing monopoly plant output q_n^* would be.

But the key point is that, once the plant has become an independent firm, the monopoly plant output will *not* be the solution arrived at. The reason is that, for a plant that is an autonomous firm, *the perceived demand function* d_n *becomes more*

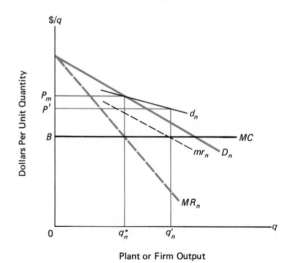

FIGURE 9.6 **Monopoly Plant versus Monopolistic-Competition Firm, at Monopoly Solution.** The solution for the monopoly plant, where $MC = MR_n$ at output q_n^* and associated monopoly price P_m, is the same as in the preceding diagram. But once the monopoly plant becomes an independent firm, at the price P_m the *perceived* demand curve would be d_n. This is more elastic than the pro-rata demand curve D_n, since the firm can win customers from its neighbors if it lowers its price relative to theirs. Under monopolistic competition the firm will therefore attempt to achieve the solution where Marginal Cost MC cuts the curve mr_n, the latter being the Marginal Revenue curve associated with the perceived d_n demand curve. At this attempted solution, firm output would be q_n' and price P'.

elastic (flatter) than the D_n curve that represents the monopoly plant's pro-rata share of the overall demand curve. The curve d_n is more elastic than D_n because, by lowering price relative to its neighbors, each firm figures that it can win customers away from them—whereas the monopoly plant's demand curve D_n was based on the premise that the *same* (f.o.b.) price P_m will be charged by all N plants. (It is not in the interest of the monopolist, of course, to have his plants cutting price at one another's expense.) Corresponding to the *more elastic* firm demand curve d_n in Figure 9.6 is a *higher* perceived Marginal Revenue curve mr_n.[4] The firm in Figure 9.6 will therefore be competitively motivated to attain the larger output q_n' where $mr_n = MC$. Doing so implies setting a lower price $P' < P_m$ for its particular variety of product.

Figure 9.6 suggests that the output of a monopolistic-competition firm will surely be larger than the per-plant output of an ordinary monopolist. But we are not yet entitled to draw that conclusion. The reason is that the seeming firm solution in Figure 9.6, with output q_n' sold at the price P' along demand curve d_n, is not possible as an *overall equilibrium* of the industry. With a fixed number N of producing locations (whether plants of a monopolist, or competing firms), the sales achievable per location at any given price can be no greater than those represented by the pro-rata demand curve $D_n \equiv D_N/N$. Each firm's flatter demand curve d_n is an illusion (akin to the illusion of the seemingly horizontal demand curve faced by the firm in pure competition). Any single firm can hope to cut price so as to expand output along d_n. But the symmetry of the situation, with N identical firms, dictates that in equilibrium *they must all end up choosing the same price*. They each cut price, hoping to sell output q_n' at price P'. But the result of their collective action is that output expands less than expected, along the steeper pro-rata demand curve D_n in the diagram.

The overall equilibrium must therefore represent a point on the pro-rata demand curve D_n, like S in Figure 9.7. Each firm produces quantity q_n'', and the associated price is P''. Once again the firm *perceives* a flatter demand curve d_n, but the d_n pictured in Figure 9.7 is such that the firm's desired price–output combination P'', q_n'' (determined by the intersection of MC with mr_n) lies along the pro-rata demand curve. Thus, the solution on the firm level is now in balance with the overall consumer demand for the industry's production. At this solution each firm's output is clearly greater (and price to consumers lower) in comparison with the monopoly pro-rata solution P_m, q_n^*.

We are not yet at the full or *long-run* equilibrium for monopolistic competition, however. Possible changes in the *number* of firms in the market (associated with the condition of free entry) must also be taken into account. Depending upon the level of the fixed cost per firm, the short-run equilibrium shown in Figure 9.7 might either be a profitable one for firms in the industry (inducing

---

[4]This will be evident from the geometry, recalling (from the "Corollary" of Section 8.B.2) that the Marginal Revenue curve bisects the horizontal distance from the axis to a linear demand curve. Or, consider the definition $MR \equiv P + Q(\Delta P/\Delta Q)$, where the ratio $\Delta P/\Delta Q$ represents the slope of the demand curve. For a given (P, Q) combination, the smaller the slope in absolute value (the flatter the demand curve), the smaller in absolute magnitude is the second term in the definition of MR. But this second term is of negative sign. So the flatter the slope of the demand curve, the greater is Marginal Revenue.

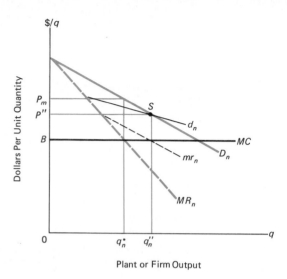

FIGURE 9.7 Monopoly Plant versus Monopolistic-Competition Firm, at Monopolistic-Competition Equilibrium. With N firms, price P'' and per-firm output q_n'' represent a monopolistic-competition equilibrium (point S in the diagram). Each firm is maximizing profit since $MC = mr_n$, where mr_n is the Marginal Revenue associated with the *perceived* (flatter) firm demand curve d_n. And this outcome is consistent with overall equilibrium of the industry as a whole, since the combination of output q_n'' and price P'' constitutes a point on the pro-rata demand curve D_n. Price is lower and output greater than in the monopoly case.

entry) or an unprofitable one (dictating exit). Let us assume that the short-run equilibrium is profitable, with price P'' greater than the representative firm's level of Average Cost AC_n at the production rate q_n. As entry of new firms occurs, both the true pro-rata demand curve $D_n \equiv D_N/N$ and the illustory d_n as viewed by an existing firm will *shift inward* toward the vertical axis.[5] The long-run solution is as shown in Figure 9.8 for the representative firm. Here, in addition to the conditions satisfied in the preceding diagram, that $MC = mr_n$ and that the firm's price–output combination be consistent with the pro-rata demand curve D_n, we have a *zero-profit solution*. This is represented in the diagram by the tangency at point L of the firm's demand curve d_n with its Average Cost curve AC_n, the output being q_n''' and price P'''.

> CONCLUSION: In comparison with multi-plant monopoly, under monopolistic competition aggregate output will be greater and hence product price lower. And in long-run equilibrium zero economic profit will be earned. But there may or may not be a larger number of producing locales. Thus, while consumers benefit from a lower price, they may or may not find a better assortment of varieties available under monopolistic competition as compared with monopoly.

[5]This shift is due to dividing the aggregate demand curve D_N horizontally by a larger N. There is a countervailing factor, however, since a larger N is associated with a more perfect matching of consumer desires, so that the aggregate curve D_N itself shifts upward as N rises (as shown in Figure 9.3). So both the numerator and the denominator of the ratio D_N/N (which defines the pro-rata demand curve D_n) rise as N increases. However, the numerator tends not to rise as fast as the denominator. If we go from two to three firms there is a 50% increase in N, but not in general such an enormous improvement in the matching of production locales to consumer preferences as to warrant a 50% increase in quantity demanded at any given price. So, despite this countervailing factor, the D_n curve (and therefore also the d_n curve) must, at least eventually, shift inward as N rises.

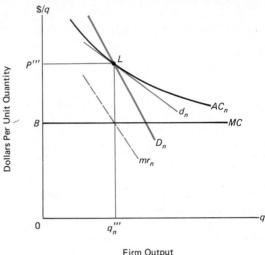

FIGURE 9.8 Long-Run Equilibrium, Representative Firm in Monopolistic Competition. For long-run equilibrium in monopolistic competition, the short-run equilibrium conditions of the preceding diagram continue to hold: $MC = mr_n$, and the representative firm's price–output combination constitutes an achievable point on the true pro-rata demand curve D_n. The additional long-run condition is that entry or exit takes place until the representative firm is earning zero profit (price equals Average Cost). All these conditions are met at point L in the diagram, where the representative firm's output is q_n''' and price is P'''.

9.C
EQUILIBRIUM QUALITY LEVEL: COMPETITIVE INDUSTRY

We now turn to quite a different type of product variation. Suppose there is some single attribute or characteristic that all consumers want from the product. From light bulbs, buyers might simply be seeking light output in lumens. From gasoline, mileage might be the desired feature. It is no longer a matter of some customers preferring white shirts and others blue, or big men wanting big sizes and small men small sizes. Instead, an objectively agreed measure of *quality* exists. (Of course, quality may be multi-dimensional. Gasoline may be valued for rapid acceleration and easy starting as well as miles per gallon. The color or shape or size of light bulbs might be important to customers, aside from light output in lumens. In the interests of simplicity, however, we will think of quality as measurable by some single characteristic.)

Many different questions might be asked about quality equilibrium. One is: Will a monopolist tend to produce a higher-quality or lower-quality product than a competitive industry? This topic will be considered in Sections 9.D and E below. The issue to be considered here is: Will a competitive industry tend to settle on a single grade of quality of product, or will a quality assortment be produced? And if the latter, will it be the case (as might seem plausible) that poorer people would tend to buy a lower-quality product?

There is one key idea to be kept in mind. Only superficially are consumers and producers dealing in quantities of *product Q* (e.g., gasoline); more fundamentally, consumers are demanding and firms are supplying quantities of *attribute K* (e.g., mileage). Thus we are concerned here with conditions of equilibrium in the *market for the quality attribute* (mileage).

Assume to begin with a fixed number N of competitive firms. Each separate firm will, it is assumed, choose a quality grade z_n as well as an output rate q_n for its physical product. Then, the firm's *output of the attribute k_n* will simply be:

$$(9.1) \qquad\qquad k_n \equiv z_n q_n$$

For example, a firm producing $q_n = 1,000,000$ gallons of gasoline per day, with quality grade $z_n = 20$ miles per gallon, is effectively producing $k_n = 20,000,000$ units per day of "mileage" for sale to consumers.

Since it is the attribute that they are really concerned with, the underlying demand function of the consumers shows the aggregate quantity of *attribute* they demand, K_d, as a function of the *"price of attribute" P_k* that is implicit in the prices charged by the various firms for their physical products. On the assumption that consumers are always fully informed as to quality, the price P_n of the nth firm's physical product will depend strictly upon its attribute content:

$$(9.2) \qquad\qquad P_n \equiv z_n P_k$$

If one gasoline is known to yield 10% greater mileage per gallon than another, its price must be 10% higher.

The equilibrium *price of attribute P_k* is determined by the overall supply and demand of attribute. The supply quantity K_s, to be balanced against the demand quantity of K_d as a function of price P_k, is simply the sum of the separate firms' outputs of attribute:

$$(9.3) \qquad\qquad K_s \equiv \sum_{n=1}^{N} k_n$$

The firm's decision problem, as a competitive price-taker in the market for attribute, is to choose the profit-maximizing combination of z_n and q_n. A possible situation is illustrated in Figure 9.9. Suppose an initial quality grade $z_n = z^{\circ}$ were chosen by the firm. The associated Average Cost and Marginal Cost functions, indicated by the solid curves $AC(z^{\circ})$ and $MC(z^{\circ})$, lead to the optimal attribute output k_n°. Knowing k_n and z_n, the required physical output of commodity is then given, from equation (9.1), as $q_n = k_n/z_n$.

But attribute output of k_n° is optimal only given the initial choice of quality grade $z_n = z^{\circ}$. What would happen if other quality grades were considered? It might be that a 20% increase in quality z_n (miles per gallon) would only raise cost by 10% per unit of physical commodity (gallons of gasoline). This would imply that the cost *per unit of attribute* (mileage) is lower at higher quality. Geometrically, this would be reflected in Figure 9.9 by a downward displacement of MC and AC, as suggested by the dashed curves $AC(z')$ and $MC(z')$ in the diagram. With $z_n = z'$, the optimal output of attribute is k_n'.

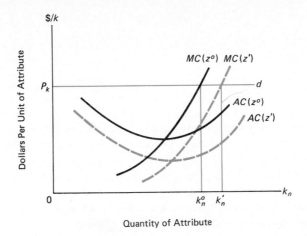

FIGURE 9.9 **Uniform Optimal Quality.** The horizontal scale represents amounts of attribute $k_n \equiv z_n q_n$ produced by the nth firm, where q_n is the firm's output of the commodity and z_n the quality grade (attribute content per unit of commodity produced). The ruling market price for attribute, P_k, is shown by the firm's horizontal demand curve d. In the situation pictured, quality z' is always more profitable than $z°$, because $AC(z')$ lies always below $AC(z°)$. Any desired output of attribute can be produced more cheaply at quality grade z' than at $z°$ (where z' might represent either higher or lower quality than $z°$).

What is the *best* z_n to choose? If for some choice of z_n such as z' in Figure 9.9, $AC(z')$ were *uniformly lower* than the Average Cost curve associated with any other z_n, then clearly z' is the profit-maximizing quality grade.

In general, however, things may not be quite so simple. It might be the case that, as illustrated in Figure 9.10, some quality grades are less costly at low production levels ($z_n = z°$ in the diagram), some at middling output levels ($z_n = z'$), and still others at high production levels ($z_n = z'$). Then the optimal

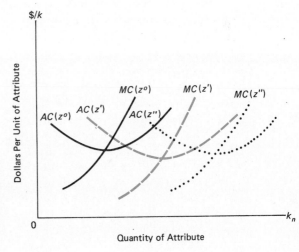

FIGURE 9.10 **Optimal Quality Varying with Output.** Here the optimal quality grade associated with the firm's lowest-cost way of generating attribute varies with the scale of output. Since the firm will always want to choose the lowest Average Cost of producing attribute, the optimal quality changes as P_k varies.

choice of quality will vary with optimal firm output, which will itself be a function of the market price P_k. At a very high price, for example, the firm will want to produce large amounts of attribute for the market, which can best be done by choosing quality grade $z_n = z''$ in the diagram. But at lower prices, a different level of production and consequently a different choice of z_n may be dictated.

When we take into account the possible variation of cost functions as among non-identical firms, we see that there is no presumption that competitive firms will all choose the same quality level. In mining, for example, some firms will be exploiting richer and others leaner deposits. Each firm will market an ore whose richness (mineral content per ton) represents its quality level z_n. But, assuming informed purchasers, the prices offered for ores of different mineral content will be such as to reflect (after due allowance for any special chemical or physical features) a single underlying price P_k for the mineral contained.

We have already in effect answered the question posed above, as to willingness of consumers to pay for differences in quality grades. If all buyers are interested only in the attribute content (mileage) of the commodity produced (gasoline), and all are fully informed, then in equilibrium all will be paying the same going market price P_k *for the attribute*. Neglecting special features like costs of extraction or storage, each firm's product must sell at a price representing simply its attribute content. At these equilibrium prices, every consumer will be *indifferent* as to buying higher-quality or lower-quality goods (obtaining the same mileage with fewer gallons of high-quality but expensive gasoline or with more gallons of low-quality but cheap gasoline). And in particular, there is no reason to expect poorer consumers to buy goods of lower quality than richer consumers.

CONCLUSION: Each firm will, at its optimal level of output, choose the quality grade minimizing its Average Cost of producing attribute. The chosen quality may vary with output, and between different firms, so an assortment of qualities will normally be offered by firms. But, with fully informed consumers, the equilibrium price of any firm's output will be proportional to its attribute content; at these prices, all consumers will be indifferent as among the outputs of any of the firms.

EXAMPLE 9.1
Price and Quality: Movie Theaters

R. D. Lamson studied the relation between quality attributes and the prices charged for movie admissions in a large metropolitan area over the period 1961–64.[a] As suggested by the preceding analysis, there was considerable variation in quality attributes of different theaters.

For 1961 the adult evening admission price P (in cents) was estimated from

[a] R. D. Lamson, "Measured Productivity and Price Change: Some Empirical Evidence on Service Industry Bias, Motion Picture Theaters," *Journal of Political Economy*, v. 78 (March/April 1970).

the data by the equation:

$$P = 4.13 + 31.46 \log_{10} U + 5.77L + 8.21T - 7.68D$$
$$- 1.13F + 27.09S + 0.81R$$

The symbols used on the right-hand side represent the explanatory (quality) variables:

U: average percentage of unused seating capacity per showing

L: theater location (1 if suburban, 0 if city center)

T: theater age (1 if less than 10 years since construction or major renovation, 0 otherwise)

D: type of theater (1 if outdoor, 0 if indoor)

F: parking (1 if provided, 0 otherwise)

S: screening policy (1 if first-run, 0 otherwise)

R: average film rental (cents per ticket charged by distributor)

The results were generally in the directions anticipated. For example, other things equal, newer (or renovated) theaters charged on the average 8.21 cents more per admission; first-run houses charged 27.09 cents more; each penny per ticket paid for film rental (a measure of *film* quality or, at least, film popularity) was associated with a 0.81 cents increment to admission price; etc. The one paradoxical component of the equation is parking provision, associated with a 1.13 cent *reduction* in price. This might possibly be due to an inter-correlation of parking availability (a positive quality element) with remote or low rental location (an unfavorable element) not captured in the crude index L.

One rather important element is the role of U, unused capacity. This can be regarded as a quality measure of movie seating–*uncrowdedness*. The equation shows that a 10% increase in unused seating capacity (e.g., from 20 to 22%) is associated with a 1.3 cent increase in admission price. It is of interest to note that since *quality* in the form of uncrowdedness U automatically rises when *quantity* of sales falls off in response to a rise in admission price, the true (quality-constant) elasticity of demand for movie admissions must be greater than that implicit in these data.

9.D
EQUILIBRIUM QUALITY LEVEL: MONOPOLY VERSUS COMPETITION

The question to be considered here is: Will a monopolist producer tend to offer a lower quality level to consumers than would a competitive industry? Since a monopolist produces a lesser *quantity* of product than a competitive industry (see Section 8.B), by analogy one might anticipate a lower *quality* of product as well. But, as it turns out, this superficial analogy is mistaken.

The essential feature at work can be seen in terms of the simplest case of a uniformly best quality level, as illustrated for a competitive firm in Figure 9.9 above. Clearly, if Average Cost is lowest with quality $z = z'$ for *all* outputs of attribute k, then *that same quality grade would be selected by a monopolist as well as by a competitive firm.*

A somewhat more complicated situation is shown by the cost picture of Figure 9.10, where the quality grade representing lowest Average Cost of producing attribute k varies at different outputs. Since we would expect the attribute output of a monopolist to be large (in comparison with the output of a *single* firm if the industry in question had a competitive market structure), the monopolist would tend to choose a quality permitting low-cost production at large firm output. But there seems to be no general reason to presume that this quality grade is necessarily higher or lower than the most profitable quality level for small outputs.[6]

---

[6]Conceivably, at small outputs it might be most economical to use hand labor, and at large outputs machinery. Hand labor may often produce work of higher quality than machinery, but this is by no means a universal phenomenon.

EXAMPLE 9.2
Monopoly and Quality: Baseball

H. G. Demmert, in a study of the economics of professional team sports,[a] examined the determinants of the "quality" choices made by owners of the various major league baseball clubs. An owner can most obviously upgrade quality by hiring more skilled players, coaches, and so forth. A natural quality measure is how well a particular team fares in its games.

Using a sample of 282 observations on 16 major league baseball teams over the period of 1951–69, two determinants were found to be important. First, teams in more populous areas were, on the average, of higher quality. This seems reasonable, since fans generally prefer winning teams and a greater population base can better afford to "buy" this objective. Specifically, a population difference of 5,000,000 was found to be associated with a difference of 0.018 in the team's win ratio.

More closely relevant to the discussion of this section, it was found that teams with major league baseball competitors (where more than one team was franchised in a given population area) were of poorer quality than teams with monopoly positions in their area. Specifically, it was found (other things held equal) that the existence of a competitor was associated with a *decrease* of 0.034 in the win ratio.

[a]H. G. Demmert, *The Economics of Professional Team Sports* (Lexington, Mass.: D. C. Heath, 1973), esp. p. 71.

At least for this peculiar good, then, a monopolist tended to produce a product of higher quality than did a firm facing a competitor or competitors in its market area.

9.E
AN APPLICATION: SUPPRESSION OF INVENTIONS

Monopolists are sometimes accused of suppressing inventions. Let us interpret "invention" to mean a discovery permitting production of a higher-quality product at given cost, or a given-quality product at lower cost.[7] Then it can be shown, under the key assumption that buyers are fully informed as to the quality improvement, that suppression is *never* rational.

Take the instance of a monopolist of gasoline, where consumers are interested only in the quality attribute yield (mileage). The monopolist discovers a way, let us say, of doubling the mileage per gallon of gasoline, without any additional cost of production. We can see immediately, that in terms of a cost function like that in Figure 9.9, the Average Cost of producing mileage will be halved at all output levels if the new invention is adopted. Then, regardless of whether the monopolist decides to produce more output or less, it would surely be absurd to suppress such an invention.

The assumption of *full knowledge* on the part of consumers is, however, a strong one. If the invention really improves product quality but the consumers do not believe it, they would not (at least not initially) be willing to pay any more for the higher-mileage gasoline. Under the reasonable assumption that it costs somewhat more per gallon to produce gasoline of doubled mileage yield, the monopolist's incentive to introduce the innovation would be impaired. In this case, however, we should really consider the *cost of informing consumers* as a part of the economic cost of the invention. It is not really "suppression" when an invention, even though a genuine improvement of quality, cannot be put on the market except at a cost that is too great (including the cost of spreading the information) in comparison with the benefit received.

Another possible motivation for suppression emerges in a case where the invention *would destroy the monopoly*. Consider a monopolist of the only currently exploitable aluminum ore—bauxite. Conceivably, this monopolist might come into possession of a cheap process for extracting aluminum from alumina. The latter, one of the most plentiful components of the earth's crust, could not effectively be monopolized. But even here, the monopolist can in principle do better by using than suppressing the invention. The monopoly *of the information* as to how to reduce alumina is more valuable than the previous monopoly of

[7]Obviously, there is no problem in explaining the "suppression" of discoveries that lead to production of a *lower*-quality product at the same cost, or a constant-quality product at *higher* cost!

bauxite. The monopolist could patent and license the new process, or alternatively use it while keeping the key steps a secret.[8]

It is of some interest to work through the monopolist's solution for a cost-reducing invention, to see the implications for *output of attribute K* (mileage) versus *output of product Q* (gasoline).

Let us return to the simple assumption that the invention doubles the quality (mileage per gallon) of the product without any added cost of production. Then the situation may be pictured as in Figure 9.11, a diagram in "Total" units with attribute quantity k (mileage) on the horizontal axis. The original Total Cost curve is $C°$. At any given cost of producing the commodity (gasoline), the invention doubles the mileage output k. This shifts the Total Cost curve in mileage units to the position C'—a horizontal doubling (stretching) to the right. The key assumption, that consumers are fully informed, means that the *Total Revenue curve in terms of attribute* k *remains unchanged.* Consumers have no interest in gasoline as such; whether quality is high or low, they only pay for what concerns them—the mileage content.

In Figure 9.11 the profit-maximizing levels of attribute output are $k°$ for the pre-invention situation and k' for the post-invention situation. The pre-invention profit $\Pi°$ is the bold line-segment indicating the greatest vertical differ-

---

[8]In practice, however, there might be difficulties either with patenting or with maintaining secrecy. Thus, a rational motivation for suppression might persist in the case of an invention tending to destroy one's own monopoly.

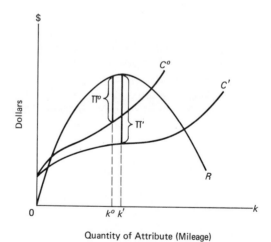

FIGURE 9.11 A Quality-improving (Cost-reducing) Invention, Attribute Units. In the case pictured, a monopolist is considering adoption of an innovation that costlessly doubles the quality (attribute content) of the product. Since the horizontal axis represents amount of attribute k, the original Total Cost curve $C°$ shifts to C'—attribute quantity is doubled at each level of cost. Fully-informed consumers are interested only in amount of attribute, and so in terms of attribute the Total Revenue function R is unchanged. The monopolist will necessarily achieve a higher profit by adopting rather than suppressing such an invention. In the situation pictured, the increased profit is Π'; consumers also benefit, since greater attribute output is produced to be sold at a lower price.

ence between the Total Revenue curve R and the original Total Cost curve C°. The necessarily larger post-invention profit Π' similarly represents the greatest vertical difference $R - C'$. The diagram illustrates a "normal" case in which output of attribute increases ($k' > k^\circ$) but by less than a doubling ($k' < 2k^\circ$). This means that consumers benefit from having more attribute k (mileage), while the firm saves some cost by having to produce less physical output q (gallons of gasoline).

If the Total Revenue curve were rising almost linearly, however (i.e., if Marginal Revenue MR were almost constant), it might conceivably happen that output of attribute k *more* than doubles. The stretching of the Total Cost curve from C° to C' may have the effect of lowering Marginal Cost MC in the relevant range. If throughout the doubling interval MC remains lower while MR is nearly unchanged, the profit-maximizing output of attribute k will be *more than* twice the pre-invention amount.

Paradoxically, it is logically possible for the output of attribute at the post-invention solution to fall ($k' < k^\circ$). In this case, while the invention will not have been suppressed, the consumers are nevertheless worse off! How this might happen is more clearly visible in Figure 9.12, which is an Average-Marginal diagram. On the horizontal axis we see attribute quantity k as before, while the verti-

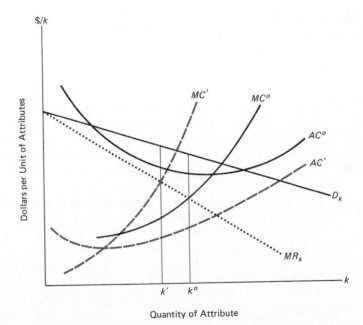

FIGURE 9.12 **A Quality-improving (Cost-reducing) Invention Adverse to Consumers.** Here the diagram is in Average-Marginal units. A quality-improving invention is equivalent to a reduction in the Average Cost of producing the quality attribute k, and so the new AC' curve lies everywhere below the original AC° curve. Nevertheless, as shown here, there may be a range in which the new Marginal Cost MC' is *higher* than the original MC°. As a result, the new $MC' = MR$ intersection may determine a profit-maximizing attribute output k' that is *smaller* than the original output k°. If so, consumers will be worse off for the invention.

cal axis is in units of dollars/k. Corresponding to the Total Revenue curve of the preceding diagram is the monopoly firm's negatively sloped demand curve D_k for the attribute. The quality-improving invention is equivalent to a reduction in Average Cost of producing any amount of attribute—the new AC' curve (dashed) is therefore everywhere lower than the original $AC°$ curve (solid). But, as the diagram illustrates, there may be a range in which the Marginal Cost MC' associated with the new technology is *higher* than the original $MC°$. If, as shown here, the intersection of Marginal Cost with Marginal Revenue occurs in this range, the firm's profit-maximizing output of attribute will be smaller ($k' < k°$). This implies that monopoly price must be higher, and consumers must be worse off!

> CONCLUSION: Monopoly cannot validly be accused of *suppressing* inventions (given the assumption of fully informed buyers). But it remains open to the accusation of possibly using inventions in such a way that consumers may derive no benefit therefrom, or may even be made worse off.

☐ SUMMARY OF CHAPTER 9

In previous chapters a firm could vary only the *amount* of output produced and possibly (if it has monopoly power) also the *price*. In this chapter it is assumed that a firm may also be in a position to change the characteristics that define its own product. Under this general heading, two main topics are considered: the problem of *variety*, and the problem of *quality*.

The problem of *variety* arises when consumer preferences are distributed over a range of some characteristic (size, color, weight) of the commodity. Then the greater the number of different varieties produced, the less the average consumer's dissatisfaction from having to choose a good with characteristics less close to what he or she desires. A locational metaphor permits us to think of "closeness" in geographical terms.

The solutions for the profit-maximizing number of varieties offered consumers (and for the associated price and quantity decisions) were compared for two market structures: *monopoly* and *monopolistic competition*. Under monopoly, while there are separate producing locations (plants), a combined profit-maximizing policy is pursued in the interest of the firm as a whole. Under monopolistic competition, each producing location becomes an independent firm. The monopolistic element in monopolistic competition is the monopoly power of each separate firm over those consumers closest to its production locale; the competitive element is the presence of neighboring firms to whom customers can transfer their business. In comparison with ordinary monopoly, the industry under monopolistic competition produces greater aggregate output at lower price, but may or may not provide consumers with more variety to choose from.

The problem of *quality*, in its simplest form, assumes unanimity of consumer preference for larger amounts of some underlying attribute contained in the physical goods produced. Demand and supply ultimately determine an equilibrium price and quantity of *attribute*. Each firm will produce that quality grade (amount of attribute per unit of commodity) which minimizes its Average Cost of producing attribute. In general, because of differing production conditions, firms' outputs will be of differing quality grades. But there is no reason to expect a monopolist's output to be of higher or lower quality than a competitive industry's average quality grade. If consumers are fully informed, they will be paying only for attribute content of the goods purchased, at the going equilibrium price for attribute. It follows that the price of each firm's product must be simply proportional to its attribute content, so that in equilibrium consumers are indifferent as to buying higher-quality or lower-quality products.

When consumers are fully informed, a rational monopolist would never suppress an invention that *increases quality*, since such an invention is equivalent to one that *reduces cost* (of producing the underlying attribute desired by consumers). By adopting the invention, the monopolist necessarily increases profit. The consumers usually gain as well, from increased output of attribute. It is, however, logically possible for the monopolist's profit-maximizing output of attribute to fall, in which case the consumers would be worse off after adoption of the invention.

☐ QUESTIONS FOR CHAPTER 9

MAINLY FOR REVIEW

*R1. If consumers are distributed among different locations, is it true that the greater the number of distinct producing plants the larger will be aggregate demand for the product? How is this argument analogous to one concerning the number of distinct *varieties* offered consumers?

*R2. What stops the monopolist from offering an infinite number of varieties? Under what circumstances will only a single variety be produced?

R3. How does monopolistic competition differ from pure competition? From pure monopoly?

R4. In monopolistic competition, why is the firm's "perceived" demand curve flatter than the "true" demand curve (as in Figure 9.6)?

R5. Why is the firm's "perceived" demand curve in monopolistic competition analogous to the horizontal demand curve faced by the firm in pure competition?

*R6. If a monopolist normally produces less *quantity* of a product than a competitive industry would, why is it not correct to presume that the monopolist would normally also offer a product of lower *quality*?

*R7. Would a monopolist ever suppress an invention reducing the cost of producing its given product? Would it ever suppress an invention raising the quality of product at its given cost? Will consumers in either case be necessarily better off if the invention is adopted?

*The answers to asterisked questions appear at the end of the book.

FOR FURTHER THOUGHT AND DISCUSSION

*T1. Is there a reason to expect monopolistic competition (rather than pure competition) to emerge when the desired commodity is really a single "quality" attribute contained in the marketed good? Explain.

T2. Would the price-quantity equilibrium under monopolistic competition tend to lie between that achieved under pure monopoly on the one hand, and pure competition on the other hand? Explain.

*T3. Could a quality-improving invention in a *competitive* industry ever be adverse to the consumers' interests?

*T4. It is sometimes argued that only relatively high-quality products can "bear the cost" of shipment to distant locations. Thus, California oranges shipped to New York are (on the average) better quality than those consumed by Californians at home. Does this follow from the analysis in this chapter? [*Hint:* Does it cost much more to ship high-quality oranges than low-quality ones?]

*T5. In seeming contradiction to the statement in the preceding question about California versus New York oranges, for lobsters it is said that one can never get top quality except by going oneself to the New England shore. Can this be explained?

*T6. Would imposition of a fixed per-unit tax (e.g., 10 cents per gallon of gasoline) tend to increase or decrease the equilibrium *quality* of gasoline (miles per gallon) offered on the market?

T7. A says: "A monopolist will produce a product of higher quality, since cut-throat competition must lead to a decline in quality." B says: "A monopolist produces a smaller *quantity* of product than would a competitive industry, and by the same logic will also produce a product of lesser quality." Is either correct, or are they both wrong?

*T8. Poor people seem to purchase articles of lower quality than do rich people. Can this be explained in terms of the analysis in the text?

*T9. In an attempt to reduce tobacco production and thereby raise prices received by tobacco farmers, a government program introduced in 1933 allotted quotas to farmers that fixed the number of *acres that could be planted.* Over the years production expanded anyway, since the farmers responded by applying more fertilizer, irrigating more intensively, etc. In 1965 the program was reformed, replacing acreage limitations with quotas that fixed the number of *pounds that each farmer could sell.* Would you expect the original and the reformed programs to have different effects upon the *quality* of tobacco produced by American farmers? Explain.

OLIGOPOLY

SUPPLEMENTARY CHAPTER

□ *Oligopoly is competition among the few*. But, as explained in Chapter 8, looking only at the number of firms in an industry does not conclusively tell us how the market functions. While large numbers normally lead to competitive (price-taking) behavior, under certain circumstances the firms may act collectively as a monopolist (cartel). Conversely, a single firm in an industry normally behaves as a monopolist price-maker, but sometimes may be unable to achieve monopoly profit. In the case of oligopoly a variety of outcomes are possible, *depending upon the degree to which the firms act either as rivals or as cooperators*.

10.A
OLIGOPOLY AND STRATEGIC BEHAVIOR

A "strategic" situation arises when a number of economic agents, with at least partially conflicting interests, are aware that their decisions interact. The concept of *optimizing*, choosing a "best" outcome, can become somewhat hazy in a strategic situation. What is best for A to do may depend upon B's choice, and B in turn must take into account the options open to A. Thus, there is room for conscious *cooperation* or *conflict*. Behavior in strategic situations may involve promises, threats, or other types of communications among the parties. These topics are studied in the "theory of games," a relatively new field of mathematics stimulated in large part by the economic problem of oligopoly.

In all market interactions there are elements of conflict and elements of parallelism of interests—among sellers as a group, among buyers as a group, and between buyers and sellers. The sellers have a common group interest in keeping prices high, but within the group a conflict of interest as to which suppliers are to obtain larger fractions of profitable sales. The buyers have a common interest in keeping prices low, but a conflict of interest as to which ones will be able to make purchases at an attractively low price. Between sellers as a group and buyers as a group there is of course conflict of interest over the price to be set, but the two still have a strong shared interest in having exchange take place (the mutual advantage of trade).

The theory of games provides a systematic way of exploring the mixture of conflicting versus parallel interests in social interactions. As an extreme limiting case, Table 10.1 illustrates a situation of completely conflicting interests—a so-

TABLE 10.1
Zero-Sum Game: Land or Sea?

		DEFENDER'S CHOICE OF STRATEGY	
		Land	Sea
ATTACKER'S CHOICE OF STRATEGY	Land	+10 / −10	−5 / +5
	Sea	−25 / +25	+20 / −20

called "zero-sum" game. Imagine that an Attacker can invade by land or by sea. The Defender, let us suppose, will win the battle *if* he guesses the attack route correctly and so can dispose his forces accordingly, but if he guesses wrong Attacker will win. Along the left margin of the Table are Attacker's strategy choices—attack by Land or by Sea—and across the top are the corresponding Defender's choices. Within each of the four cells of the Table the payoff to Attacker appears at lower left, and the payoff to Defender at upper right. The numbers shown for the payoffs might or might not be realistic (it is assumed that a sea attack involves greater potential gain or loss to both players than a land attack), but the crucial point is that in each cell the payoffs add up to zero—the Attacker's gain is always the Defender's loss, and vice versa. This is therefore a situation of *pure conflict of interests*.

But situations of pure conflict are uninteresting to the economist. Economics is concerned with social patterns where, potentially at least, there is some prospect for mutual gain (recall the Fundamental Theorem of Exchange). Let us therefore pass on to the opposite case—*pure parallelism of interests*. Table 10.2 pictures a situation where two players will both win if they coordinate their strategies, but otherwise will both lose. Imagine that two drivers are traveling in opposite directions along a dark road, where the options are "Drive on the right" versus "Drive on the left." Here again the numbers inside the cells are somewhat arbitrary—it is assumed that both players do a little better driving on the right (earning +10 instead of +8), perhaps because they are used to doing so. But the

TABLE 10.2
Mutuality of Interests: Drive on Right or Left?

		B'S CHOICE OF STRATEGY	
		Right	Left
A'S CHOICE OF STRATEGY	Right	+10 / +10	−100 / −100
	Left	−100 / −100	+8 / +8

main point, of course, is that failure to coordinate would be disastrous for both: if one drives on the right and the other on the left, the outcome for each is -100.

It might seem that the players in Table 10.2 should have no difficulty agreeing to drive on the right. (And notice that neither has any incentive to diverge from the agreement once made.) Even if separated and therefore unable to come to an understanding in advance, two intelligent players equipped with the information in the Table should be able to figure out that driving on the right is the better strategy for both. But pure-coordination games like that of Table 10.2 are also rather uninteresting to economists. In economics, we are almost always concerned with mixed cases containing elements of conflict as well as elements of mutuality.

How conflict and mutuality of interests can be mixed together is exemplified by an important type of social interaction situation studied in the theory of games: the Prisoners' Dilemma. Suppose that the police have apprehended two men, accomplices in a crime, but have rather poor evidence against them. Lacking a confession from one or both, the authorities will be able to convict the prisoners only of a minor infraction carrying a mild penalty. With a confession, on the other hand, conviction on a major count is guaranteed. Keeping the prisoners out of communication with one another, the district attorney offers to let either of them off for turning state's evidence—provided that he confesses, but the other does not! (Should both confess, each will receive a reduced yet still substantial penalty.)

The choice situation is summarized in Table 10.3. Along the left margin we see the possible strategies of prisoner A: *Confess* versus *Don't confess*. Across the top are the same choices for prisoner B. Within each cell of the Table, at the lower left is the penalty (months of imprisonment) to be imposed on prisoner A. Similarly, at the upper right in each cell we see the corresponding outcome for B. (Since imprisonment outcomes are bad, they have minus signs attached.)

The prisoners evidently have a *mutual* interest, in that both gain from both choosing "Don't confess" so as to incur only a mild penalty (1 month's imprisonment) each. But looking at the Table from A's point of view, note that *he is better off choosing "Confess" regardless of what B has chosen!* Suppose that B has chosen "Confess." Then, comparing the two cells in the left-hand column, A will notice that should he select "Confess" he gets -24; should he select "Don't

TABLE 10.3

The Prisoners' Dilemma: Months of Imprisonment

		B'S CHOICE OF STRATEGY	
		Confess	Don't confess
A'S CHOICE OF STRATEGY	Confess	−24 / −24	−36 / 0
	Don't confess	0 / −36	−1 / −1

confess" he gets −36. So, A will say to himself: If my partner is a fink, why should I be a hero? But what if B were bravely to choose "Don't confess"? Looking at the right-hand column of the Table, A sees that selecting "Confess" yields him 0 (the best possibility of all), while if he selects "Don't confess" he gets −1. Even when his partner is a hero, therefore, it still pays A to be a fink. And B will reason in exactly the same way.

So, in the Prisoners' Dilemma situation, it appears that both will confess and both suffer 24 months' imprisonment. In the language of game theory, the strategy-pair "Confess, Confess" is called the *Nash*[1] *solution* for this game. It is an equilibrium since, once the strategy-pair is arrived at, neither party has any motive to change his choice. Each is doing the best he can for himself, given the decision of the other.

While the Prisoners' Dilemma is a picturesque story, is there any reason to believe that it corresponds to any broadly applicable economic situation? We can show that there is by re-writing the situation in the more general form of Table 10.4. The two strategies here are called "Be loyal" versus "Be disloyal" (to one's partner or partners), corresponding to hero versus fink behavior in the original tale. The numbers indicate, for each player, the *rank* ordering of the outcomes: 4 is best, 3 second best, 2 next, and 1 is worst. Any situation describable in the form of Table 10.4 corresponds logically to a Prisoners' Dilemma. The "Nash solution" is at the upper left where each party receives 2 (his or her next-to-worst outcome)—although by suitable cooperation each could have achieved 3 (the next-to-best outcome).

As an instance, recall the problem of "chiseling" in cartels (Chapter 8, Section F). Despite the mutual gain to all firms together if they can all resist temptation, each firm separately is motivated to be disloyal and chisel—to make profitable sales by expanding output. Whether or not everyone else is resisting temptation or succumbing, each firm separately does best for itself by increasing production so long as its Marginal Cost *MC* is less than price *P*. [*Query:* Can you think of other forms of social interaction that are Prisoners' Dilemmas? What of the problem of international armaments? Of the hunting of whales to near-extinction?]

[1]J. F. Nash, contemporary American mathematician.

TABLE 10.4

The Prisoners' Dilemma: Rank-ordered Outcomes

		B'S CHOICE OF STRATEGY	
		Be disloyal	Be loyal
A'S CHOICE OF STRATEGY	Be disloyal	2　　2	1　　4
	Be loyal	4　　1	3　　3

But cartels do sometimes persist (see the OPEC example of Chapter 8). There may be ways of escaping the Prisoners' Dilemma, particularly when the parties know one another's identity and are likely to have a continuing relationship. Under oligopoly—competition among the few—these conditions are often met. As a result, a number of different outcomes become possible under oligopoly.

To avoid needless complications, let us assume (except where otherwise specified) that: (1) there are exactly *two* selling firms, so that oligopoly becomes the special case called "duopoly"; (2) the firms are identical, except possibly in strategic skill or aggressiveness; (3) production is carried on at zero cost (i.e., the Total Cost, Average Cost, and Marginal Cost functions are all zero throughout). A traditional example, more or less fitting these conditions, has been of two firms each of which owns a mineral spring gushing forth costlessly and in unlimited volume forever.

We will take up separately the two cases of *homogeneous* versus *heterogeneous* oligopoly. In the homogeneous case the products are identical. At least so far as the consumers are concerned, the two springs produce identical waters. Then even a slightly lower price quoted by one seller will deprive the other of all sales, and so no price differential between the two firms can persist in homogeneous oligopoly equilibrium. But if the consumers can distinguish the two outputs, some preferring the first spring and others the second, each firm will have a "clientele"; up to a point, it can raise price without losing all of its customers. Hence, in heterogeneous oligopoly equilibrium a price differential may persist.

10.B
HOMOGENEOUS PRODUCTS

A pure competitor is always a price-taker; his choice variable is *quantity* of output. A monopolist is usually regarded as deciding upon *price*, letting quantity be determined in the market. Sometimes, however, it is convenient to think of the monopolist as choosing *quantity* and letting the market process determine the price at which that quantity can be sold. Since the result is the same point on the industry demand curve in either case, it makes no difference whether we think of a monopolist as choosing the most profitable price or the most profitable quantity. But in the oligopoly case, whether price or quantity is the decision variable may turn out to be important for the *interaction* of the parties. Consequently, the final result may be affected.

Let us first take *quantity* as the decision variable. Table 10.5 categorizes a number of different oligopoly (duopoly) "solutions."[2] The Table was constructed on the hypothesis that the overall *industry* demand curve is expressed by the equation $P = 100 - Q$, where the industry output Q is the sum of the two firm outputs: $Q \equiv q_1 + q_2$. (Recall that zero production cost is assumed.)

The first solution shown in the Table is the Collusive outcome. Here the two firms act together as a collective monopolist or cartel, sharing the gain equally.

[2]A somewhat similar Table appears in M. Shubik, "Information, Duopoly and Competitive Markets: A Sensitivity Analysis," *Kyklos*, v. 26 (1973), p. 748.

TABLE 10.5

Duopoly Solutions, with Industry Demand Curve $P = 100 - (q_1 + q_2)$

	q_1	q_2	Q	P	Π_1	Π_2
Symmetrical						
Collusive	25	25	50	50	1250	1250
Cournot	$33\frac{1}{3}$	$33\frac{1}{3}$	$66\frac{2}{3}$	$33\frac{1}{3}$	$1111\frac{1}{9}$	$1111\frac{1}{9}$
Competitive	50	50	100	0	0	0
Asymmetrical						
Pre-emptive	50	25	75	25	1250	625
Threat	50	0	50	50	2500	0

A collective monopolist would want to set Marginal Revenue MR equal to Marginal Cost MC, both defined for the industry as a whole. Since production costs are assumed zero throughout, $MC = 0$ for each firm and therefore $MC = 0$ for the industry as well. Marginal Revenue for the industry is readily obtained from the demand curve for the industry, using the Proposition (Section 8.B.2) describing Marginal Revenue when the demand curve is *linear*: If $P = A - BQ$, then $MR = A - 2BQ$. In this case the industry demand equation has the linear form $P = 100 - Q$, so industry Marginal Revenue is $MR = 100 - 2Q$. Since Marginal Cost MC is zero, the monopoly-optimum condition $MR = MC$ becomes $100 - 2Q = 0$, so that $Q = 50$ is the profit-maximizing industry output. Then $P = 50$ is the associated price along the demand curve for the industry. Total Revenue $R \equiv PQ$ is 2500 which, in the absence of any costs, is also the total profit Π. With equal division, each firm's profit under the Collusive solution will be $\Pi_1 = \Pi_2 = 1250$.

The Collusive solution assumes that the problem of the Prisoners' Dilemma has somehow been solved by the two parties, who have achieved the mutually most profitable outcome. But what if the problem cannot be solved? Skipping to the third line of the Table, note that this is called the Competitive solution. It is based upon two assumptions: (1) That cooperation is not achieved, so that each firm operates in its own short-run selfish interest. (2) And, in addition, that each firm is so ignorant of the effect of its own output upon price P as to behave like a price-taker. That is, the firms are each assumed to be adopting the decision rule $MC = P$, an erroneous policy in this case since the correct rule is always $MC = MR$, and here $MR < P$. (The Competitive solution is therefore a highly implausible outcome if there really are only two firms; it becomes a more realistic possibility, the larger the number of firms.) Since $MC = 0$, acting as price-takers the firms would each be willing to produce indefinitely large amounts for *any* price P greater than zero. The consequence, of course, is that the competitive equilibrium price ends up at $P = 0$. Combined output is then 100, as dictated by the demand equation, but revenue and profits are zero.

On the second line of the Table, lying between the Collusive and the Competitive outcomes, is the "Cournot solution."[3] Here the assumptions are:

[3] Antoine Augustin Cournot (1801–1877), French mathematician and economist.

(1) As in the Competitive case, cooperation is not achieved. (2) Unlike the Competitive case, however, here each firm correctly evaluates the effect of its own output in lowering price along the industry demand curve. (3) But, on the other hand, the firm fails to allow for any interdependence between its own output decision and *the other firm's output decision.* The assumptions underlying the Cournot solution correspond therefore to the Nash equilibrium in game theory: each decision maker is doing the best he can *given* the decision of the other. (This outcome is accordingly sometimes known as Nash–Cournot solution.) Then for any output level q_1 that might be chosen by the first firm, there will be some unique optimal output choice q_2 for the second firm. In effect, firm 2 becomes a monopolist over the demand not satisfied by the first firm's output q_1 already on the market. Specifically, the demand equation for firm 2 becomes $P = (100 - q_1) - q_2$, with q_1 regarded as constant. This is still a linear demand equation, so for firm 2 the Marginal Revenue is $MR_2 = (100 - q_1) - 2q_2$. For example, if $q_1 = 10$ the condition $MR = MC$ for firm 2 leads to the equation $90 - 2q_2 = 0$, so that firm 2's output would be $q_2 = 45$. Plotting the q_2 chosen by firm 2 as a function of the given output of firm 1 leads to a "Reaction Curve" RC_2 like that shown in Figure 10.1. Since the firms are symmetrically situated, by a corresponding process a Reaction Curve RC_1 can be developed for firm 1. The curves are *mutually consistent only at the point of intersection,* which is therefore declared to be the equilibrium. At the solution point the outputs are $q_1 = q_2 = 33\frac{1}{3}$, intermediate between the Collusive and the Competitive solutions.[4] Thus the Cournot solution may be regarded as representing a kind of imperfect collusion technique.

[4]To verify that $33\frac{1}{3}$ is indeed the equilibrium, we can proceed as follows: If firm 1 sets $q_1 = 33\frac{1}{3}$, the demand equation for firm 2 is $P = 66\frac{2}{3} - q_2$. The associated Marginal Revenue is $MR_2 = 66\frac{2}{3} - 2q_2$. Setting $MR = MC = 0$, we obtain $q_2 = 33\frac{1}{3}$. Reversing the process, we see that under the assumed reaction conditions both firms are satisfied to set output at $33\frac{1}{3}$.

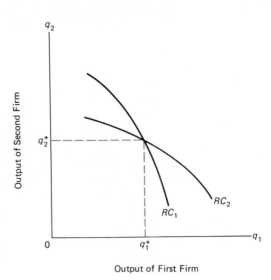

FIGURE 10.1 Duopoly Reaction Curves. Given any output q_2 of the second firm, the first firm can determine its profit-maximizing output q_1—in which it makes use of its monopoly power over the *remainder* of the market. Considering all possible levels of q_2, a Reaction Curve RC_1 for the first firm is thereby defined. Similar reasoning (based on taking q_1 as given) leads to the construction of RC_2, the Reaction Curve of the second firm. The intersection of the two Reaction Curves is a Nash equilibrium, since each firm is then at its optimum *given* the decision of the other.

Output of First Firm

Exercise 10.1: Find the equations for the Reaction Curves RC_1 and RC_2 in the numerical example above, and verify whether their intersection is indeed the Cournot solution of Table 10.5.

Answer: For firm 2, since it takes the output q_1 of firm 1 as given, Marginal Revenue is: $MR_2 = (100 - q_1) - 2q_2$. Marginal Cost MC_2 is zero, and so the firm sets $MR_2 = 0$, implying $q_2 = 50 - q_1/2$. This is the equation of RC_2. Similar reasoning yields the equation $q_1 = 50 - q_2/2$ for RC_1. Note that the curves are generally similar to those pictured in Figure 10.1—in particular, RC_1 will be steeper than RC_2—except that here the two Reaction Curves are actually straight lines. Solving RC_1 and RC_2 simultaneously, the solution is indeed $q_1 = q_2 = 33\frac{1}{3}$.

The Cournot solution represents rather shortsighted behavior on the part of the two firms. While each of them modifies its output in response to the output decision of the other—this is what the Reaction Curves show—each makes its own decision *without* allowing for the fact that the other will so react! This is unreasonable. Unfortunately, when analysts turn to more plausible assumptions for each party to make about the behavior of the other, matters rapidly become much more complicated and it is difficult to arrive at any definite solution.

EXAMPLE 10.1
Oligopoly Experiment

A pioneering series of economic experiments was conducted by the economist Lawrence E. Fouraker and the psychologist Sidney Siegel.[a] In these trials each experimental subject acting as a "seller" chose a quantity of output on the basis of a tabulated profit schedule, which depended upon the quantities offered by the two sellers together. Two separate cases were considered: (1) complete information was provided to each subject about all previous quantity choices and profits of the other; (2) the quantity decision but not the profits of the other seller were reported to each subject.

The results of 28 trials (14 for each of the two informational conditions) were as follows: (1) In the complete-information case, 5 trials most closely approximated the Collusive solution, $7\frac{1}{2}$ the Cournot solution, and $1\frac{1}{2}$ the Competitive solution. (The fraction was due to a tie.) (2) In the incomplete-information case, all 14 trials most closely approximated the Cournot solution.

The sensitivity of the experimental observations to the informational conditions is an extremely interesting result. Later studies have shown that the actual details of the market process—for example, whether prices are secretly negotiated or openly posted—will also have a very significant effect upon the extent to which the final outcome approaches the collusive or the competitive end of the spectrum of possibilities.[b]

[a]L. E. Fouraker and S. Siegel, *Bargaining Behavior* (New York: McGraw-Hill, 1963).
[b]See the extensive discussion in Charles R. Plott, "Industrial Organization Theory and Experimental Economics," *Journal of Economic Literature*, v. 20 (Dec. 1982).

Another aspect of oligopoly is revealed once we allow for *asymmetrical* behavior. In the lower portion of Table 10.5, firm 1 is assumed to be aggressive while firm 2 is passive. In effect, firm 1 *acts* while firm 2 only *reacts*. Such an aggressive firm, if sufficiently knowledgeable, can make use of the other's Reaction Curve RC_2 to improve its situation.

The *Pre-emptive* solution in the lower part of Table 10.5 (also known as the Stackelberg[5] solution) occurs when, knowing firm 2's Reaction Curve, firm 1 picks an output level and proclaims that it will not modify that decision regardless of the other firm's behavior. If the proclamation is believed, the best that firm 2 can do is indeed to behave as a Cournot reactor along its Reaction Curve RC_2. Of course, firm 1 will choose that output q_1 which, when combined with the other firm's correctly predicted output q_2, leads to the most profitable outcome for itself. Specifically in the text example, firm 1 optimizes by setting $q_1 = 50$, in which case it achieves as much profit for itself as under the symmetrical Collusive solution. Firm 2 then monopolizes the remainder of the market, setting $q_2 = 25$, and reaping half the profit of the other firm.[6]

The *Threat* solution is a still stronger asymmetrical outcome. Suppose firm 1 proclaims that if the other firm enters the market at all, it (the first firm) will produce enough to drive price P down to zero. If this proclamation is believed, the second firm will see no way to make a profit in the market. Hence it might as well stay out entirely. (A very small side-payment from the first firm would provide a positive inducement for the second to remain on the sidelines.) In the Threat solution, the first firm does as well as if it had the *sole* monopoly of the industry.

What would happen if *both* firms attempted to act as aggressors? Each would make his threat, only to be defied by the other. Actual execution of the threats would then force the situation into the symmetrical Competitive outcome of the upper part of the Table.

Table 10.5 was constructed upon the premise that the decision variable for both firms was *quantity* of output. What if *price* rather than quantity were the decision variable? Here the key point to appreciate is that, since the products are identical, the firm quoting the lower price will (however small the price differential) attract *all* the customers. Then the Cournot solution of the Table disap-

---

[5]Heinrich von Stackelberg, twentieth-century German economist.

[6]This solution may be verified as follows. Firm 1, the aggressor, knows that firm 2 will behave as a Cournot reactor, i.e., that firm 2 will choose output q_2 to satisfy the equation $MR_2 = (100 - q_1) - 2q_2 = 0$. So $q_2 = (100 - q_1)/2$, and this is known to firm 1. Substituting in the industry demand curve:

$$P = 100 - Q = 100 - q_2 - q_1 = 100 - \frac{100 - q_1}{2} - q_1 = 50 - \frac{q_1}{2}$$

This becomes the overall demand curve facing firm 1, and is again linear. Then $MR_1 = 50 - q_1$, and $MR_1 = MC_1 = 0$ leads to $q_1 = 50$. For firm 2, the condition $MR_2 = MC_2 = 0$ becomes $MR_2 = 50 - 2q_2 = 0$, so that $q_2 = 25$. The total industry output is $Q = 50 + 25 = 75$, and market price is $P = 25$.

pears, or rather it coalesces with the Competitive solution shown there.[7] Given any price P_2 quoted by firm 2, firm 1 will quote a P_1 just barely undercutting it. But then firm 2 will proceed to barely undercut P_1, and there is no stable outcome short of $P_1 = P_2 = 0$—the Competitive solution.

The asymmetrical Pre-emptive solution also must disappear if price is the decision variable. It does no good for firm 1 to announce that it will quote some fixed price regardless of what firm 2 does, because again firm 2 will then just barely undercut and reap all the profit. On the other hand, the asymmetrical Threat solution is still valid. Here firm 1 announces that, if firm 2 attempts to do any business at all while charging a positive price, firm 1 will quote a price of zero and so drive its competitor out. If this threat is believed, firm 2 might as well stay out of business completely. Firm 1 gains all the profit—as on the bottom line of Table 10.5.[8]

[7]This was the point of a famous attack upon the Cournot model by the French nineteenth-century mathematician Joseph Bertrand.

[8]The student will find it interesting to plot these solutions in terms of the firms' Reaction Curves, but with the *prices* charged by the two firms on the two axes.

EXAMPLE 10.2
Predatory Price-Cutting

The Threat solution of Table 10.5, but with price rather than output as the decision variable, corresponds to what is known as "predatory" price-cutting. A single firm sufficiently well equipped with resources and ruthlessness might always stand ready to undertake a price war to drive out any competitors. Having achieved this reputation, the predator firm would not need to execute its threat often. Occasional punishment meted out to foolish interlopers would suffice to deter all others from entering.

The leading instance cited of a predatory price-cutter firm is John D. Rockefeller's old Standard Oil Company—dissolved in 1911 as a result of a landmark anti-trust decision. Standard Oil had achieved, before that date, a substantial degree of monopoly in oil refining through merger and acquisitions. Common opinion, as illustrated in historical writing about the period, is that these mergers and acquisitions were mainly secured under threat of predatory price-cutting.

A study by John S. McGee demonstrated, surprisingly, that the tale is a myth.[a] Standard Oil rarely if ever started costly price wars to achieve its monopoly. Rather, its practice was to buy out competitors on relatively handsome terms, made possible by the prospect of higher monopoly profits achievable by the withdrawal of competition.

[a]J. S. McGee, "Predatory Price Cutting: The Standard Oil (N.J.) Case," *Journal of Law and Economics*, v. 1 (Oct. 1958).

10.C
HETEROGENEOUS PRODUCTS

In the preceding section we saw that, depending upon the degree of rivalry among the sellers, there are a number of solution concepts for oligopoly with a single or *homogeneous* product. All the different solutions had one condition in common: the firms' identical products must sell in the market at a single common price. But when oligopolists produce differing or *heterogeneous* products, the situation to be considered here, the prices will in general *not* be identical. Nevertheless, the same underlying forces remain operative. There is on the one hand an incentive for the sellers to cooperate so as to achieve a collusive monopoly outcome, but on the other hand a temptation for each to benefit at the expense of the others (as in the Prisoners' Dilemma) by aggressive or rivalrous behavior.

10.C.1 □ The "Kinked" Demand Curve: A Partial Solution?

One idea relating to equilibrium under heterogeneous oligopoly has been the subject of considerable controversy. After an equilibrium pattern of prices and outputs for the different firms is once achieved, it has been alleged, the demand curve for any single oligopolist has a "kink" at the point of equilibrium. Figure 10.2 pictures the situation of a single oligopolist firm in a position to

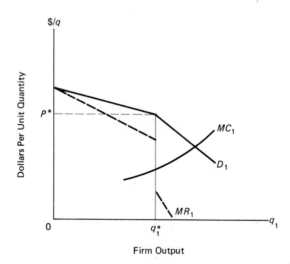

FIGURE 10.2 Kinked Demand Curve: Heterogeneous Oligopoly. For oligopolists producing heterogeneous (non-identical) products, it is supposed that an initial equilibrium exists where the pictured firm produces output q_1^* at price $P_1 = P^*$. If the firm were to cut its price, the other oligopolists meet the price reduction so that the price-cutter's sales gain is small; if the firm raises price, the others do not follow the increase and the sales loss is large. These assumptions define a *kink* in the firm's demand curve D_1 which is associated with a *vertical gap* in the curve of Marginal Revenue MR_1. The profit-maximizing condition $MC_1 = MR_1$ is therefore met at the initial equilibrium. The equilibrium price P^* will be relatively stable, since demand and cost conditions can shift somewhat without affecting the fact that the MC_1 curve cuts through the vertical gap of the MR_1 curve.

choose output q_1 (or price P_1) after an initial price for its product has been established at P^*. The argument goes as follows. Suppose that one oligopolist, firm 1, attempts to sell more by cutting its price P_1. Then all other firms will respond by *meeting* the price cut, so that firm 1 will reap only a relatively small increase in sales. In other words, in the region below the initial equilibrium price P^* the demand curve D_1 as seen by firm 1 will be steep. What if firm 1 attempted to raise price? Then, assertedly, competing oligopolists would *not* meet the price increase, so that firm 1 suffers a relatively large decline in sales. In other words, in the region above the initial equilibrium price P^* the demand curve as seen by firm 1 is relatively flat. Note that the argument makes sense only in the heterogeneous case, since only then can any price difference persist.[9]

This hypothesis is not a complete theory. It says nothing about how the original ruling price P^* was determined. But there is nevertheless an interesting implication: *Equilibrium prices arrived at by oligopolistic sellers should be relatively stable over time*.

Consider the *marginal* curves in Figure 10.2. Note that the kink in the demand or Average Revenue curve D_1 for firm 1 becomes a *vertical displacement* in the Marginal Revenue curve MR_1. It is simple to verify this geometrically in the special case where the two branches of the demand curve are linear. We know (from the "Corollary" in Section 8.B.2) that for any linear demand curve the Marginal Revenue curve must bisect the horizontal distance to the vertical axis. With two separate linear branches of the demand curve, there must then be a vertical break or jump in the MR_1 curve as shown.

For the price–quantity situation (P^*, q^*) to be an equilibrium, it must be the case that Marginal Cost equals Marginal Revenue for firm 1 at q_i^*. Of course, a similar condition must hold for the other oligopolists. Then, as illustrated for firm 1 in the diagram, the MC_1 curve must *cut through* the vertical jump of MR_1. The tendency toward price stability stems from this feature. Suppose some disturbance brought about a moderate change in the cost function of oligopolist 1. Its MC_1 curve would accordingly move up or down. But this could occur, to some extent, *without* affecting the fact that the intersection of MC_1 with MR_1 occurs in the vertical break of the latter, in which case optimal price and output remain unchanged for this firm. Even if the disturbance affected other firms as well, their behavior also might not be affected, leaving the equilibrium unchanged. Alternatively, suppose that a force operated to increase or decrease *demand* for firm 1's output. Again, it will be evident geometrically that moderate shifts of MR_1 to the right or left are likely to preserve the property that the Marginal Cost curve MC_1 cuts through the vertical jump of MR_1. Where this holds, price $P_1 = P^*$ quoted by firm 1 will remain unchanged, but output q_i^* will increase or decrease in accordance with the direction of shift of the Marginal Revenue function.

The competing oligopolists' behavior, on this hypothesis, is *strongly rivalrous*. One might therefore wonder how the initial equilibrium, which suggests a degree

---

[9]*Query:* Assume, under *homogeneous* oligopoly, that a single firm finds that competitors meet its price cuts but do not meet its price increases. Would the firm's demand curve here also be "kinked"? What would the shape of the demand curve be above the initial equilibrium price P^*? Below P^*?

of cooperation, could have come about. One possible explanation: the firms might have agreed on a collusive initial solution which is to be *enforced by* punitive behavior against any single firm that departs from the agreement. In short, cooperation and conflict are not entirely mutually exclusive but are often, as asserted above, intertwined in observed patterns of behavior.

EXAMPLE 10.3
Oligopoly and Price Rigidity

Under the hypothesis of the kinked oligopolist-firm demand curve, demand and cost conditions can vary (to some extent) without affecting the equilibrium prices charged by firms. For a simple monopolist, on the other hand, any shift of the Marginal Cost or the Marginal Revenue curves should lead to a new optimizing price. Consequently, an implication of the kinked-demand hypothesis is that oligopoly prices should be relatively rigid.

This implication was tested by G. J. Stigler. The data in the Table are typical of his findings. As can be seen, there is a strong indication that oligopoly prices are *less* rigid than monopoly prices. This is certainly true in terms of the *number* of monthly price changes, and tends to be confirmed by the *quantitative* measure of price change represented by the "coefficient of variation" (the standard deviation of monthly prices divided by their mean).

Price Flexibility (June 1929–May 1937)

	NUMBER OF FIRMS IN INDUSTRY	NUMBER OF MONTHLY PRICE CHANGES	COEFFICIENT OF VARIATION OF PRICES
Oligopolies			
Bananas	2	46	16
Grain-binder	2	5	3
Plows	6	25	6
Tires	8	36	9
Monopolies			
Aluminum	1	2	6
Nickel	1	0	0

Source: G. J. Stigler, "The Kinky Oligopoly Demand Curve and Rigid Prices," *Journal of Political Economy*, v. 55 (1947), p. 443.

One possible objection to Stigler's test is that *inter-industry comparisons* of price changes cannot be made with very much confidence. Customs and conditions of conducting business vary from one industry to another, and it may have just so happened that the "monopolized" sectors in the Table would have had relatively rigid prices regardless of number of firms. Another objection is that what is statistically reported as a *single* industry is often mere convention. Had aluminum and nickel been placed together in a single "non-ferrous metals" category, they would have been classed as an oligopoly rather than as two separate monopolies.

A study by Julian L. Simon[a] employed data that were less vulnerable to these objections. He studied prices quoted for business-magazine advertising, where the magazines had been classified into groups by the Standard Rate and Data Service (SRDS). Since all the groups fell into the business-magazine category, there was relative uniformity in conditions and methods of price quotation. And since the group classification by SRDS was undertaken for the convenience of customers (advertisers), it presumably represented an economically meaningful rather than a merely conventional categorization.

The numbers of magazines in the 148 groupings on which data were provided varied from 1 to 29. A magazine without competitors in its grouping could then be considered a monopolist. The data for two different periods, 1955–61 and 1961–64, both suggested that the monopoly groups had *more* rigid prices than the oligopoly groups. Simon's test thus confirmed Stigler's previous negative conclusion as to the kinked-demand hypothesis. (However, the *quantitative* differences found by Simon were by no means as great as those reported by Stigler.)

> COMMENT: One possible explanation of the observations, consistent with assigning at least some degree of validity to the kinked-demand hypothesis for oligopoly, runs in terms of *non-profit goals* of the firm. We saw in Section 8.A that monopoly firms, sheltered from competition, may be in a relatively better position to pursue goals other than economic profit. It might well be that an important non-profit goal for monopoly firms is the easy life, avoidance of difficult decisions. Changing price, rather than just leaving things as they are, can be a difficult decision. Not only is sheer mental effort required, but "rocking the boat" is more liable to elicit complaint or political scrutiny than simple inaction. We might then expect monopoly and oligopoly prices *both* to be rigid, for different reasons: for oligopolists the kinked-demand hypothesis might be valid, while for monopolists the "easy life" goal might lead to even greater rigidity of prices.

[a]J. L. Simon, "A Further Test of the Kinky Oligopoly Demand Curve," *American Economic Review*, v. 59 (Dec. 1969).

10.C.2 □ Variation of Product

In heterogeneous oligopoly there is another dimension of behavior for the firm to consider: the specification of the product itself. One oligopolist can compete with others not only by raising or lowering price, but also by varying the nature of the commodity placed on the market.

Product variation was studied in the preceding chapter under a number of market structures: monopoly, pure competition, and monopolistic competition. Two main types of product variation were considered: (1) product *variety* (the degree to which the range of products offered in the market coincides with the range of subjective consumer preferences), and (2) product *quality* (the degree to which an objective quality attribute, desired by all consumers, is contained in the market commodity).

The topic of product *quality* under oligopoly will not be considered here. But we will deal with one model of oligopolistic product *variety* that has received considerable attention. This model employs a *linear* locational metaphor like that of Figure 9.1 to represent the range of consumer preferences. Specifically, in Figure 10.3 the consumers are supposed to be *uniformly* distributed along a line-segment scaled from 0 to 1, with mid-point $M = \frac{1}{2}$. There is a constant unit transport cost t from any producing location to the consumer. If P is the f.o.b. price at the producing location R, the solid lines show what the delivered price $P + ts$ would be at any distance s from point R; the dashed lines show the delivered prices if the production locale is at the mid-point M.

A curious solution to this problem has been proposed by H. Hotelling.[10] Assume that there are just two firms (duopoly), with identical costs of producing and delivering the commodity. Now suppose that consumers everywhere along the line-segment want exactly one unit of the commodity, and are willing to pay any price for it. (Each person's demand is absolutely inelastic, but only for a single unit of the good.) Suppose that one firm is located at the mid-point M in Figure 10.3 and the second firm at some other point R. Then the firm at M will have a larger share of the market. Comparing the dashed and solid lines, we see that location at M leads to lower delivered price for all consumers located to the left of M and also for some of the consumers located to the right—those nearer to M than to R. So the firm at R would have an incentive to move toward the mid-point M. (The firm at M might seem also to have an incentive to move farther toward R, but it would thereby leave itself vulnerable to the other firm

[10]H. Hotelling, "Stability in Competition," *Economic Journal*, v. 39 (March 1929).

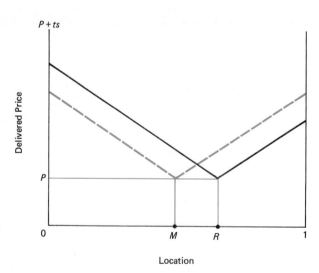

FIGURE 10.3 Delivered Price. If P is the f.o.b. price, t is the unit transportation cost, and s the distance from a production point, the delivered price from that point to any consumer location is $P + ts$. The solid lines in the diagram show the delivered prices from a production locale at R; the dashed lines show the delivered prices from a production locale at the mid-point M.

skipping over it and relocating to *its* left.) The conclusion is that in equilibrium the duopolists would locate back-to-back, an infinitesimal distance apart at either side of the mid-point M. In that way each is closer to half of the market which serves as its "clientele."

Interpreting the locational metaphor in terms of product *variety*, the equilibrium here has both firms supplying nearly identical products of middling character. Essentially no variety is offered to consumers at all. As an interesting extension, Hotelling and others have commented that similar forces not only make different companies' toothpastes and refrigerators very much alike but tend to make the Republican and Democratic political platforms converge toward a centrist position, to induce the Catholics and Protestants to minimize their theological differences, and so forth.

In the Hotelling equilibrium, *not enough* variety is offered consumers. Putting it in locational terms, avoidable waste of resources is incurred in transporting the good to consumers from distant production points. When both firms are located at M, the average distance between consumers and the nearest production locale is $1/4$. If the two firms were to spread apart and ideally locate at the quartile points, the average distance would be reduced to $1/8$ instead. Thus, by offering more differentiated products the two firms could better satisfy the range of consumer preferences without incurring additional cost. In terms of Table 10.5 the Hotelling result is analogous to a Cournot solution; each firm reacts (with respect to location as a decision variable) on the presumption that the other firm's decision will remain fixed.

The assumption of absolutely inelastic demand is of course highly unreasonable. Indeed, if this were the case the duopolists' Collusive solution (raise price indefinitely high) would yield *infinite* revenue and profit, regardless of location. Once we allow for elasticity of consumer demand, the duopolists would be pulled away from the mid-point locations. In Figure 10.3, suppose there are initially two firms located back-to-back at M—the firm just to the right having as "clientele" all those to the right of M, while the one just to the left takes the remainder. Suppose that the right-hand firm were to shift location toward position R. Since it could then reduce price to most of its old clientele, and in particular to everyone remaining to the right of R, it could sell more product to them—while losing to the other firm only a small fraction of its old clientele (those located in the neighborhood of M). As the other firm would behave similarly, under this more reasonable demand assumption some variety would after all be offered to consumers. However, the degree of variety remains less than efficient; the firms are not motivated to move away from one another as far as the ideal quartile locations.

Another oddity of the Hotelling model is that the whole argument collapses when numbers increase beyond two. A third oligopolist would want to locate an infinitesimal distance on one or the other side of the initial duo. But then one of the firms would be boxed in between two others, leaving it without clientele. This firm would then surely "jump" to the outside, to be followed by the one now left in the middle, and so on in an unending musical-chairs situation. So with more than two firms there cannot be a Cournot–Hotelling equilibrium.

More acceptable results may be obtained using the locational metaphor of consumers distributed uniformly *around a ring* (see Figure 9.2) rather than along a line-segment. Assuming a degree of demand elasticity, as is certainly appropriate, Cournot behavior in the ring model would lead to an efficient result: for any arbitrary location of one firm, the other would place itself 180° away around the circle. This would of course minimize transport cost. The ring model also generalizes easily to any number of firms, which are motivated to spread themselves evenly around the circle. Of course, whether the ring metaphor or the line-segment metaphor is more appropriate depends upon the actual situation.[11]

10.D

OLIGOPOLY AND COLLUSION

The intricacies of strategic models of oligopoly are intellectually challenging, but the results seem unsatisfyingly inconclusive. Another approach[12] has been to treat oligopoly situations as *imperfect collusive arrangements* (i.e., imperfect cartels as described in Section 8.F). Since there is a joint advantage of collusion, all firms under this approach agree upon that aim. However, they all also recognize that each cannot be restrained from "chiseling" (see Figure 8.11) except through a policing mechanism. That is, the assumption is that anyone who can cheat, will. Given that there are costs of trickery on the one hand, and of detection on the other hand, there will be some equilibrium amount of slippage from the Collusive solution that represents the achievable ideal for the sellers (although not, of course, for consumers). Thus, the parties involved will agree upon forming a cartel with some kind of policing scheme, in the anticipation that it will be tolerably (though imperfectly) effective.

What forces promote oligopolistic collusion? First and most obviously, the fewer the firms involved, the easier it is for them to police one another. And, hence, the more effective the cartel. Second and almost equally obvious, secret price cuts are more likely to be offered to large than to small buyers. To increase business 10% by a chiseling deal with a single customer is one thing; to try secretly to get the same increase of business from ten small customers is stretching secrecy too far. Third, enforcement of collusion should be much easier where the product is homogeneous. Otherwise, price cuts can take the hard-to-penetrate guise of better quality. (Even where the physical commodity is homogeneous, there may be an element of heterogeneity in aspects of the transaction such as credit terms or delivery date.) Fourth, the more unstable the conditions of the industry, the harder it will be to negotiate and maintain agreements. And fifth, certain "institutional practices" of the industry, such as the offer of price guarantees to purchasers, may facilitate collusion—as the discussion following suggests.

[11]In terms of politics, for example, it is sometimes argued that a ring is a better picture than a line-segment. It has been noted that supporters of extreme-left parties are often psychologically very similar to those on the extreme right—the extremes may have more in common with one another than either has with moderate positions.

[12]Proposed in G. Stigler, "A Theory of Oligopoly," *Journal of Political Economy*, v. 72 (Feb. 1964).

10.D.1 □ An Application: "Most-Favored Customer" Clauses[13]

Imagine two duopolists producing distinct products, and therefore able to set different prices P_1 and P_2. For simplicity, however, assume that firm 1 considers only two possible price quotations, high and low: P_1^H and P_1^L. Similarly, firm 2 will be choosing between high and low prices P_2^H and P_2^L. Suppose that the profit payoffs to each firm are summarized by the game matrix of Table 10.6. Comparison with our earlier payoff matrices reveals that the duopolists here once again are caught in a Prisoners' Dilemma. By both choosing the high-price strategy each could attain its second-best outcome (numerically, a profit of 100). Yet, once this is achieved each firm is tempted to cut its price so as to gain at least a temporary profit of 140. Indeed, for either firm the low-price strategy is superior regardless of what the other does. So the two are likely to end up at their next-to-worst outcome—numerically, a profit of 70 each.

Each firm here would be willing to bind itself to quote its high price—provided that the other did the same. However, in the United States such an agreement would be a clear violation of the anti-trust laws; even if not detected by the law-enforcement authorities, the contract could not be enforced against a price-cutter. But the same effect might be achieved by subtler means. In particular, imagine that each duopolist "generously" offers to guarantee to each of its buyers that no other customer will be offered the product at a lower price. That is, should a later reduced price be offered to anyone else, the earlier customers will also get the benefit. (This is called a "Most-Favored Customer" clause.)

On the surface there appears to be no reason why a purchaser should decline a Most-Favored Customer clause, as it seems to offer the possibility of a later rebate at no additional cost. But notice in Table 10.7 how this has changed the firms' payoff matrix. Now, if the P_1^H, P_2^H strategy-pair is achieved, neither firm has any motivation to diverge from it. If firm 1, for example, were to cut price its profit will be 90 instead of 100—while it may gain new profitable sales at the

---

[13]This analysis is based largely upon Steven C. Salop, "Practices That (Credibly) Facilitate Oligopoly Coordination," in J. E. Stiglitz, ed., *New Developments in Market Structure* (forthcoming).

TABLE 10.6

The Prisoners' Dilemma: Oligopoly Prices

		FIRM 2	
		P_2^H	P_2^L
FIRM 1	P_1^H	100 / 100	140 / −10
	P_1^L	−10 / 140	70 / 70

expense of the other firm, it will have to provide substantial rebates to its old customers.

Notice that Table 10.7 is somewhat similar to Table 10.2, if we consider only the *rankings* of outcomes rather than the absolute payoffs within the cells. It is not quite the same, however. Table 10.2 represented pure parallelism of interest, whereas here some conflict of interest does remain (in the off-diagonal cells). But the logic leading to the likely mutual achievement of the best outcome (at the upper left, in each case) remains equally compelling. We can imagine that one of the firms, let us say firm 1, has the first move. Then it will reason: "If I choose the high price P_1^H then the other firm's superior strategy is to follow me and also choose P_2^H, whereas if I choose P_1^L he will choose P_2^L. Either way, he will match my choice, hence I do better to start off with the high price P_1^H." Even if the firms were each to choose its price strategy in ignorance of the other's move, they both should be able to realize the mutual logic of choosing the high price.

A seeming paradox here is frequently encountered in the theory of games: sacrificing an opportunity may actually lead to a gain, *once the effect upon other players' decisions is taken into account.* In this case, by arranging matters so that it will lose rather than benefit by cutting price, each firm assures the other that it will not be a price-cutter, hence the mutually profitable high-price solution becomes achievable.

Other contractual provisions that might be offered buyers could have much the same effect. One example is the Meet-or-Release clause: here the seller guarantees a customer (who has not yet taken delivery) that any lower price on the market will be matched by the seller, or else the customer will be released from his obligation to purchase. (The Most-Favored Customer clause guarantees that buyers will get the advantage of the seller's *own* later price cuts, if any; Meet-or-Release guarantees that buyers will get the advantage of *other firms'* lower prices.) The Meet-or-Release clause has the side-effect of inducing the customer to report when competitors are cutting prices, thus reducing the likelihood that an oligopolistic high-price equilibrium will be subverted by secret discounts and chiseling.

We should not, however, jump to the conclusion that the Most-Favored Customer clause or the Meet-or-Release clause or similar arrangements are employed only or mainly as devices to facilitate oligopolistic price coordination.

TABLE 10.7

Escape from the Prisoners' Dilemma

		FIRM 2	
		P_2^H	P_2^L
FIRM 1	P_1^H	100 100	90 −10
	P_1^L	−10 90	70 70

They have other functions as well, for example, providing buyers with insurance against being the targets of price discrimination. Therefore, such clauses are not conclusive evidence of anti-competitive collusion among sellers.

□ SUMMARY OF CHAPTER 10

Oligopoly is *competition among a small number* of firms in an industry. With small numbers, all the decision-makers are likely to be conscious of the interdependence of their choices: what is best for each to do depends upon what the others are doing. Behavior in such contexts is called *strategic*. Strategic behavior is a topic studied in the mathematical theory of games. Depending upon the degree of rivalry versus cooperation, there are a number of different equilibrium or solution concepts possible for games in general, and for oligopoly in particular.

"The Prisoners' Dilemma" typifies social interactions in which there are potential gains from cooperation, and yet it is in the private interest of each party to behave selfishly—so that, in what is called the *Nash solution*, all lose. But where the parties know one another's identity and may be engaging in repeated interactions or plays of the game, as is often the case under oligopoly, they may be able to achieve a cooperative outcome.

Oligopoly may be *homogeneous* (all the firms produce exactly the same product) or *heterogeneous* (the firms produce distinct, though similar commodities). In the former case, no price difference between the firms can persist in equilibrium.

Under homogeneous oligopoly, and assuming for simplicity just two firms (duopoly), first consider that *quantity* of output is the decision variable. If the two firms behave symmetrically, at one extreme they may *collude* to attain the monopoly outcome—while at the other extreme they may act as *competitive* price-takers. But if each firm simply reacts optimally to what is perceived as a fixed output decision of the other, the "Cournot" equilibrium (a special case of the Nash solution) is attained, intermediate between the Collusive and Competitive outcomes. The key idea is that each firm chooses the best monopoly output for the *remainder* of the market, after subtracting the other firm's given production. If *asymmetrical* behavior is allowed, the more aggressive firm may be able to gain more profit by forcing the other to an inferior position—in the limit, driving the other out entirely.

Considering instead that *price* is the decision variable, and that the firms behave symmetrically, then given each firm's choice of price the optimal reaction for the other firm is to just barely undercut it. Then the Cournot outcome reduces to the Competitive one. Possibilities remain, however, for profitable symmetrical *collusion* on price, or for asymmetrical gain to a more aggressive firm.

In *heterogeneous* oligopoly, in contrast, a price difference between the firms may persist. Apart from this, the analysis of the symmetrical and asymmetrical outcomes is much the same. In particular, the Cournot solution remains intermediate between the Collusive and Competitive outcomes.

For oligopolists producing heterogeneous products, one particular type of assumed strategic interaction leads to a "kinked" demand curve for any single firm. If the other producers will meet any price cut, the firm's demand curve below the current price will be steep (inelastic); if the others will not meet any price increase, above the current price the firm's demand curve will be flat (elastic). The effect is to discourage price changes. This theory does not explain how the equilibrium price was originally arrived at, but suggests that once equilibrium is attained price will be rather stable.

A new element arising in heterogeneous oligopoly is the problem of product variety. The much-discussed Hotelling model concludes that an oligopolistic industry would provide *too little* variety to consumers. This result depends, however, upon doubtful features of the model, among them that preferences can be linearly ordered. And in any case, the Hotelling model breaks down if there are more than two firms.

Oligopolists, even if disposed to be cooperative, find it difficult to enforce collusion—given the temptation of each to chisel (as in the Prisoners' Dilemma). Collusion is easier if the number of oligopolists is small, if there are no large buyers, if the product is homogeneous, and if market conditions are stable. Certain contractual arrangements between buyers and sellers, such as Most-Favored Customer clauses, may also facilitate collusion.

☐ QUESTIONS FOR CHAPTER 10

MAINLY FOR REVIEW

R1. What is strategic behavior? Why are suppliers more likely to engage in strategic behavior when there are only a few of them in the market? What if there is only one supplier (monopoly)?

*R2. What is the "Prisoners' Dilemma"? Do the participants in this game have an unexploited mutual gain from trade, and if so, why?

*R3. Distinguish oligopoly from monopolistic competition.

*R4. Justify the statement in the text that the Cournot oligopoly outcome is a special case of the Nash solution in the theory of games.

R5. Explain the Cournot solution to the duopoly problem.

R6. Diagram the Reaction Curves for the asymmetrical "Pre-emptive" and "Threat" cases of Table 10.3 (letting output be the decision variable).

*R7. Why does a "kinked" demand curve tend to lead to rigid prices? How might a kinked demand curve for a single oligopolist result from the behavior of others designed to enforce a collusive agreement?

FOR FURTHER THOUGHT AND DISCUSSION

T1. It seems somewhat strange that different duopoly solutions are obtained depending upon whether price or quantity is the decision variable. Which outcomes are different, and why?

*The answers to asterisked questions appear at the end of the book.

*T2. Under the assumptions of the Cournot model, each duopolist *incorrectly* imagines that the other's output is a fixed constant. Over time, however, each would surely learn that this assumption about the other's behavior is incorrect. What would then be likely to happen?

*T3. Can a kinked demand curve arise under *homogeneous* duopoly? If so, what would be its shape?

T4. In recent anti-trust cases, the courts appear to believe that small numbers almost inevitably imply cartel-like collusion. Is this inference justified?

*T5. Some economists have argued that "predatory price cutting" to enforce the Threat solution will almost never be observed. The reason given is that the symmetrical Collusive solution is typically better for both parties. Is this necessarily correct? Is it ever correct? Under what circumstances will predatory price cutting be likely to emerge, if ever?

11
THE DEMAND FOR FACTORS OF PRODUCTION

CORE CHAPTER

In previous chapters we have studied the *product market,* in which individuals demand and firms supply consumer goods. Now we turn to the *factor market,* to the supply of and demand for productive services. (In terms of the circular flow diagram of Figure 1.1, attention is shifting from the upper portion to the lower portion of the picture.) This chapter surveys the demand side of the factor market—the decisions of firms as to how much land, labor, or other productive services to hire. The following chapter takes up the supply side, the offer decisions made by owners of resources.

In the equilibrium of the factor market, *market structure* (degree of competition) continues to play an important role. Indeed, we have to take account of market structures not only in the factor market itself but also in the associated product market or markets. The two structures are quite separate. A company may be a monopolist in its product market and still be only one among many employers (and therefore be a competitive or "price-taking" buyer) of a productive service like secretarial help in a large city. Conversely, a textile firm may face a highly competitive world market for its product and still be a "price-making" or *monopsonist*[1] employer of labor in a small town.

This is a rather complicated chapter, which proceeds in the following sequence. In Sections 11.A through 11.C the factor markets are assumed to be perfectly competitive *on both sides;* demanders of factor services (firms) and suppliers of factor services (resource-owners) all behave as price-takers. (This assumption still allows for the possibility that an employing firm might have monopoly power in its *product* market.)[2] Section A covers the simplest case, analyzing the firm's demand for a single variable factor—the amounts employed of all other factors being fixed. (I.e., this is the firm's demand for a variable factor in the "short run.") Section B takes up the "long run" case, the firm's demand for several variable factors. (Although marked with an asterisk on account of difficulty, this section covers a number of topics important for students on the intermediate level.) Section C moves on from the firm to the industry, asking how the factor demands of the separate firms within an industry are aggregated into

---

[1]A monopolist is a sole *seller* in a market; a monopsonist is a sole *buyer.*

[2]Firms might also be *oligopolists* or *monopolistic competitors* in their respective product markets, as discussed in Chapters 9 and 10, but only the polar cases of pure competition and pure monopoly will be covered here.

an overall industry demand curve for the factor. Section D diverges from the previous assumption of price-taking behavior to consider *monopsony,* where a single firm is the sole demander of a factor. Section 11.E will apply the concepts of the chapter to the analysis of minimum-wage laws.

11.A
FIRM'S DEMAND FOR A SINGLE VARIABLE FACTOR

11.A.1 ☐ The Production Function

Suppose that a firm is producing a single output good Q by using resource inputs $A, B, C, \ldots$. Its production function can be written abstractly as:

(11.1) $$q = \Gamma(a, b, c, \ldots)$$

This expression means simply that there is some relation determining output q given the inputs $a, b, c,$ etc. We will be assuming in this section that the quantities of all but a single input A are *fixed*. (Accordingly, we are dealing here with "the short run.") Then the production function can be written more simply as:

(11.2) $$q = \gamma(a)$$

The quantities of the fixed factors $B, C, \ldots$ no longer appear in the equation. But of course they still have an effect; the amounts of the fixed factors help determine the *shape* of the $\gamma(a)$ function, showing how much Q can be obtained from a given input of A.

> NUMERICAL ILLUSTRATION: Suppose that the underlying production function for output Q has two inputs A and B, specifically, $q = 6a^{1/2}b^{1/4}$. This corresponds to equation (11.1). If the quantity of factor B is held fixed at $b = 1$, the equation corresponding to (11.2) would take the simpler form $q = 6a^{1/2}$. With $b = 16$, however, (11.2) would become $q = 12a^{1/2}$.

There is a famous technological relation between the amount of factor input on the one hand, and output quantity on the other. This relation is known as the *Law of Diminishing Returns*—already described in Chapter 6 as the fundamental reason why firms' Marginal Cost and Average Cost curves eventually take on rising form. (That is, diminishing returns correspond to increasing costs.)

> THE LAW OF DIMINISHING RETURNS: If one factor (or group of factors) is increased while another factor (or group of factors) is held fixed, output or Total Product q will at first tend to rise. But, eventually at least, a point will be reached where the rate of increase, the Marginal

Product[3] $mp_a \equiv \Delta q/\Delta a$ associated with increments of the variable factor, begins to fall; this is the point of diminishing *marginal* returns. With further increases of the variable factor, the Average Product $ap_a \equiv q/a$ will also eventually begin to fall; this is the point of diminishing *average* returns. As the amount of factor A employed rises still more, A may actually become counterproductive, reducing the Total Product q. This is the point of diminishing *total* returns to factor A.

The Law of Diminishing Returns is illustrated in Figure 11.1. The upper panel shows the Total Product curve tp_a relating output quantity q and factor

[3]*Mathematical Footnote:* Formally, the Marginal Product is (like all marginal concepts) defined as a limit:

$$mp_a \equiv \lim_{\Delta a \to 0} \frac{\Delta q}{\Delta a} \equiv \frac{dq}{da}$$

(Henceforth in the text, note of the translation of marginal concepts into derivative notation will not be taken except where there may be a danger of misunderstanding.)

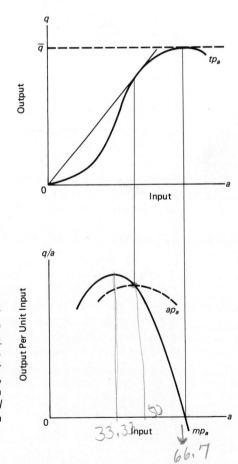

FIGURE 11.1 The Law of Diminishing Returns. The upper panel shows the Total Product function tp_a or $q = \gamma(a)$; the lower panel shows the corresponding Average Product function ap_a or q/a, and Marginal Product function mp_a or $\Delta q/\Delta a$. For the production function pictured here, diminishing *marginal* returns to employment of factor A set in first (the mp_a curve reaches its peak), then diminishing *average* returns set in (the ap_a curve reaches its peak), and finally diminishing *total* returns set in (the tp_a curve reaches its peak, at the maximum producible output $\bar{q}$).

input a. The lower diagram shows the corresponding average function (the Average Product curve ap_a representing q/a as the factor input a varies) and marginal function (the Marginal Product curve mp_a showing $\Delta q/\Delta a$ as a function of factor input a). The relations among the total, average, and marginal magnitudes here are of course consistent with the general laws developed in Section 2.B. As Total Product tp_a is rising or horizontal or falling, Marginal Product mp_a is correspondingly positive or zero or negative (Propositions 2.1a, 2.1b, 2.1c). And the Marginal Product curve mp_a lies above the Average Product curve ap_a when the latter is rising, intersects it when ap_a is horizontal, and lies below it when ap_a is falling (Propositions 2.2a, 2.2b, 2.2c).

Exercise 11.1: A firm's Total Product function for factor A is given by the equation $tp_a \equiv q = 100a^2 - a^3$. The Average Product function is then, evidently, $ap_a \equiv q/a = 100a - a^2$. It can be shown by calculus that the exact Marginal Product function is given by $mp_a \equiv \Delta q/\Delta a = 200a - 3a^2$. (The "better approximation" for marginal magnitudes, as explained in Section 2.B, would come very close to this exact relation.) (a) When do diminishing marginal returns set in? (b) Diminishing average returns? (c) Diminishing total returns? (d) Verify that when Total Product reaches a maximum, Marginal Product is zero. (e) Verify that when Average Product reaches a maximum, Marginal Product equals Average Product.

Answer: (a) It can be determined by calculus (or else by tabulating the function) that Marginal Product reaches its maximum at $a = 33\frac{1}{3}$. This is where diminishing marginal returns set in. (b) Similarly, Average Product reaches a maximum and diminishing average returns set in at $a = 50$. (c) Total Product reaches a maximum and diminishing total returns set in at $a = 66\frac{2}{3}$. (d) At $a = 66\frac{2}{3}$, the formula for Marginal Product shows that $mp_a = 0$. (e) At $a = 50$, the formulas show that Average Product and Marginal Product are equal: $ap_a = 2500 = mp_a$.

The Law of Diminishing Returns is a physical law, taken as an "outside" fact or premise by economists; it is not a proposition of economic science. But the commonsense of the Law is understandable in economic terms. There will, in general, tend to be (at any level of output) some most effective *proportion* among the several factors. When we increase the quantity of factor A from a very low level (say, from zero) with other factor quantities held fixed, we are likely to be getting closer to the most effective proportion of factors. Hence, Total Product is likely to be increasing rapidly. Then the Marginal Product of factor A will be high (and may even be increasing over a certain range). When we reach this most effective proportion and push beyond to further augment the quantity of the variable factor A, Total Product will still tend to increase, but at a decreasing rate (*declining* Marginal Product of factor A). For, while the additional units of factor A are useful, input proportions are increasingly diverging from optimal. Eventually indeed, we may so swamp our productive process with factor A that additional quantities of it actually interfere with production (*negative* Marginal Product of factor A).

EXAMPLE 11.1
Cotton Irrigation Experiment

In 1960 A. Marani and Y. Fuchs conducted a cotton irrigation experiment in Israel. On April 3 "Pima 32" variety cotton was planted. All plots received 50 mm of water immediately after planting, but none thereafter until July 4. On that date plots were irrigated with varying quantities of water. The Table shows the results at harvest.

Irrigation Treatment and Yield

WATER APPLIED JULY 4 (MM)	GROWTH IN HEIGHT AFTER JULY 4 (CM)	COTTONSEED YIELD (G/M²)	LINT YIELD (G/M²)
0	1	58	19
100	8	99	31
150	22	136	42
200	33	131	40

Source: A Marani and Y. Fuchs, "Effect of Amount of Water Applied as a Single Irrigation on Cotton Growth under Dryland Conditions," *Agronomy Journal*, v. 56 (May/June 1964), p. 282.

In this case there are two outputs of interest: cottonseed and lint. However, the Total Product curves are quite similar for each. The lack of observations at the intermediate 50 mm level unfortunately leaves some doubt as to the shapes of the Total Product curves in the early ranges. But for both products it is evident that over the range from 150 to 200 mm of irrigation water there are diminishing *total* returns, i.e., Marginal Product is negative. (The plants do actually grow higher at 200 mm than at 150 mm, but the seed and lint yields are both less.)

11.A.2 □ From Production Function to Cost Function

This section is a slight digression. It is intended to show how the production function introduced in this chapter serves as underpinning for the shapes of the various cost functions (Total Cost, Average Cost, Marginal Cost) employed in Chapter 6 and afterward.

The firm is best thought of as *hiring* the factors of production, that is, the firm buys the *services* of the factors rather than the factors themselves.[4] The "hire-prices" of factors A, B, . . . will be symbolized as h_a, h_b, ... We assume in

[4]In some cases a firm may be able either to *hire* or to *buy* a factor. Thus, a business may be able to rent office space or to buy a building for that purpose. Later we will find it useful to distinguish the hire-price h_a of factor A from the price P_A of the factor itself—of the *source* of the productive services used by the firm. But in this chapter we will deal only with the hire-price h_a, the price of the factor's *services*.

this chapter that the firm is a "price-taker" with regard to these factor-market prices of inputs. Therefore, all the hire-prices are taken as known constants.

In general, the firm's cost for any given combination of inputs is:

$$(11.3) \qquad C \equiv h_a a + h_b b + h_c c + \cdots$$

In our special case where all factors except A are held "fixed," cost can be divided into a fixed component F and a variable component V, and can be expressed as:

$$(11.3') \qquad C \equiv F + V \equiv F + h_a a$$

Here $h_a a$, the expenditure on factor A, corresponds to the "variable cost" V.

The only additional step required is to transform (11.3) into a function of output q rather than of input a. To do this, we need to "invert" the production-function equation (11.2) so as to express a in terms of q. For example, if (11.2) had the specific algebraic form $q = \sqrt{a}$, the "inverted" relation is $a = q^2$, so that (11.3') could be written as $C = F + h_a q^2$. More generally, the "inverted" production function can be expressed algebraically as:

$$(11.4) \qquad a = \phi(q)$$

Then the cost function, for a single variable factor A, is:

$$(11.5) \qquad C \equiv F + h_a \phi(q)$$

This relation between cost and output is completely determined upon insertion of the fixed cost F and the hire-price h_a.

The geometrical interpretation is illustrated in Figure 11.2. The shape of the Total Variable Cost curve V in the first panel suggests the shape of the tp_a curve in the upper panel of Figure 11.1, rotated 180° and flipped over. And in particular, the dashed *vertical* bound on the right represents the same maximum producible output $\bar{q}$ that was indicated by the dashed *horizontal* bound in the upper panel of the earlier diagram. (The dotted upper branch of the Total Variable Cost curve in Figure 11.2, above the point of contact with the vertical bound, is economically irrelevant—the firm would not produce a given output at greater cost if it can produce the same output at lower cost.) As for the Total Cost C, this curve must evidently lie above V by the amount of the fixed cost F.

Comparing the lower panels of the diagrams, a kind of inverse relation is apparent to the eye. Analytically, the logical connection between the Marginal Cost MC and the Marginal Product mp is:

$$(11.6) \qquad MC \equiv \frac{\Delta C}{\Delta q} \equiv \frac{h_a \Delta a}{\Delta q} \equiv \frac{h_a}{\Delta q / \Delta a} \equiv \frac{h_a}{mp_a}$$

Since the hire-price h_a is assumed constant, Marginal Cost moves inversely to Marginal Product. In particular, *rising* Marginal Cost corresponds to *diminishing* Marginal Product (diminishing marginal returns to employing factor A).

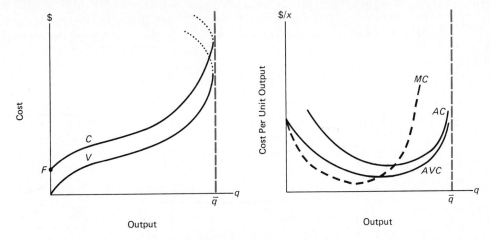

FIGURE 11.2 From Production Function to Cost Function: Geometry. If we multiply the horizontal axis of the previous diagram by the constant hire-price h_a, the dimensionality shifts from units of input (a) to units of Variable Cost ($h_a a$). Rotated 180° and flipped over, the tp_a curve of Figure 11.1 thus in effect becomes the Total Variable Cost V curve above. By similar reasoning the mp_a curve of the previous diagram can be converted into the Marginal Cost MC curve above, and the ap_a curve into the Average Variable Cost AVC curve above.

A corresponding inverse relationship holds between Average Product ap_a and Average *Variable* Cost $AVC \equiv V/q$:

$$(11.7) \qquad AVC \equiv \frac{V}{q} \equiv \frac{h_a a}{q} \equiv \frac{h_a}{q/a} \equiv \frac{h_a}{ap_a}$$

Because of the presence of the fixed cost term F, a slightly more complicated relation connects Average Cost AC and Average Product ap_a:

$$(11.8) \qquad AC \equiv \frac{C}{a} \equiv \frac{F + h_a a}{q} \equiv \frac{F}{q} + \frac{h_a}{ap_a}$$

Exercise 11.2:   Suppose that the firm's short-run production function [equation (11.2)] is $q = 2\sqrt{a}$. This of course is also the Total Product function tp_a. (a) For hire-price $h_a = 4$ and fixed cost $F = 50$, find the Total Variable Cost function V and the Total Cost function C. (b) Relate Average Variable Cost AVC to Average Product ap_a. (c) Relate Marginal Cost MC to Marginal Product mp_a.

Answer: (a) The "inverted" function [equation (11.4)] is: $a = q^2/4$. Then $V \equiv h_a a = 4a = q^2$. And $C \equiv F + V = 50 + q^2$. (b) $AVC \equiv V/q = q^2/q = q$. And $ap_a \equiv tp_a/a = 2\sqrt{a}/a = 2/\sqrt{a}$. Equation (11.7) tells us that $AVC \equiv h_a/ap_a$, which can be verified as follows: $h_a/ap_a = 4/(2/\sqrt{a}) = 2\sqrt{a} = q = AVC$. (c) By calculus or tabulation (using the "better approximation"), Marginal Cost can be found to be $MC = 2q$. Similarly, Marginal Product is $mp_a = 1/\sqrt{a}$. Equation (11.6) tells us that $MC \equiv h_a/mp_a$, which we can verify: $h_a/mp_a = 4\sqrt{a} = 2q = MC$.

Having seen how the shape assumed in Chapter 6 for the firm's cost function depends upon the underlying production function, we now return to the main business of this chapter—demand for the services of factors of production.

11.A.3 ☐ The Firm's Demand for Factor Services

In Figure 11.3, the horizontal line drawn at the level of the hire-price h_a can be regarded as the *factor supply curve* s_a for a price-taking firm in the factor market. Denoting the total expenditure on (the total cost of hiring) factor A as $C_a \equiv h_a a$, where a is the quantity of factor A employed by the firm, this supply curve can be interpreted as a curve of *Average Factor Cost* ($afc_a \equiv C_a/a$). And, since the price per unit is constant, it is also a curve of *Marginal Factor Cost* ($mfc_a \equiv \Delta C_a/\Delta a$).

To determine its optimal (profit-maximizing) employment of factor A, the firm must balance the *returns* from hiring A against the hire-price h_a. Two elements are involved in calculating these returns: (1) the *physical productivity* of A as an input to production, and (2) the *revenue* gained from the units of commodity produced.

In successively choosing whether or not to hire one more unit of factor it is evident that, so far as physical productivity is concerned, only *Marginal* Product will be relevant to the firm's decision. However great the contribution to *Total* Product may have been for earlier units of factor, only the incremental yield from an additional unit will be considered in hiring that last unit. Thus, the Marginal Product mp_a curve, as in the lower panel of Figure 11.1, pictures the physical productivity element.

In dealing with the revenue element, by similar reasoning it is only the *Marginal* Revenue that matters. But where the firm is a price-taker in the product market, the increment to revenue from sale of one more unit of product is simply the given product price P. Valuing the factor's physical productivity at this price P leads to the concept called *Value of the Marginal Product* of factor A.

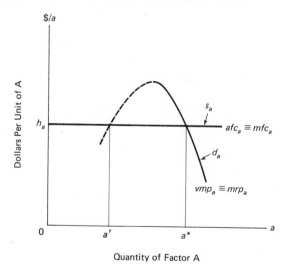

FIGURE 11.3 Optimal Factor Employment, Price-taking Firm in Both Factor Market and Product Market. The horizontal line at the level of the going hire-price h_a for factor A is the curve of Average Factor Cost (afc_a) and of Marginal Factor Cost (mfc_a) to the price-taking firm, and is also its factor supply curve s_a. If the firm is a price-taker in the product market as well, the Value of the Marginal Product (vmp_a) curve and the Marginal Revenue Product (mrp_a) curve coincide. The firm's demand curve d_a for factor A is then the downward-sloping branch of the $vmp_a \equiv mrp_a$ curve.

DEFINITION: Value of the Marginal Product vmp_a equals product price P times physical Marginal Product mp_a.

(11.9)
$$vmp_a \equiv P(mp_a)$$

Since P is assumed constant, the curve showing vmp_a in Figure 11.3 will have the same graphical shape as the mp_a curve in the lower panel of Figure 11.1. The only difference, due to the multiplication by a constant P, is the change of the vertical scale—from output per unit of input (q/a) to dollars of revenue per unit of input ($\$/a$).

Turning to the employment decision, if the Value of the Marginal Product vmp_a exceeds the price h_a of factor A, it will surely pay the firm to employ an additional unit of A. Thus, the optimum condition for employment of factor A by a price-taking firm can be expressed as:

(11.10)
$$vmp_a = h_a$$

It so happens that this equality is satisfied at the two different employment levels a' and a^* in Figure 11.3. However, a subsidiary condition for an optimum is that the vmp_a curve be *falling* relative to the horizontal $afc_a \equiv mfc_a$ curve,[5] and this holds only at a^* in the diagram.[6] In terms of economic logic, to employ only a' units of A would be to forego the profitable range where the return from hiring an additional unit of the factor (vmp_a) exceeds the cost (h_a).

The conclusion, therefore, is that for a price-taking firm the demand curve for factor A is represented by a portion of the vmp_a curve, specifically the downward-sloping range along that curve.

Exercise 11.3: Suppose that the firm's Total Product function is $q = 2\sqrt{a}$ as in Exercise 11.2. Let the price of the product be $P = 60$, and the factor hire-price be $h_a = 4$. (a) Find the vmp_a curve, and the optimal factor employment a^*. (b) What is the associated output q^*? (c) What is the firm's demand curve for factor A?

---

[5]This condition corresponds to the technical qualification (see Chapter 6) that the output optimum for the firm occurs at $MC = MR$ *provided that the* MC *curve cuts* MR *from below.* Here the optimum occurs when vmp_a cuts mfc_a *from above.*

[6]*Mathematical Footnote:* The firm chooses the amount of A to maximize profit $\Pi \equiv R - C \equiv Pq - h_a a - F$ (where F stands for fixed costs representing expenditures on factors other than A). Differentiating Π and setting the derivative equal to zero, we have as *first-order* condition:

$$P\frac{dq}{da} = h_a \quad \text{or} \quad P(mp_a) \equiv vmp_a = h_a$$

verifying (11.10). Taking the second derivative of Π, the *second-order* condition for a maximum is:

$$P\frac{d^2q}{da^2} < 0 \quad \text{or simply} \quad \frac{d^2q}{da^2} < 0$$

This means that Marginal Product mp_a (and so the curve vmp_a) must be *falling* to have a profit maximum.

Answer: (a) We saw above that, for this tp_a function, Marginal Product is $mp_a = 1/\sqrt{a}$. Thus, $vmp_a \equiv P(mp_a) = 60/\sqrt{a}$. To find the optimal factor employment set $vmp_a = h_a$, or $60/\sqrt{a} = 4$, which implies $a^* = 225$. (b) The associated output is $q^* = 2\sqrt{a^*} = 30$. (c) Since the vmp_a curve here is downward-sloping throughout, the demand curve is identical with the vmp_a curve. The demand-curve equation is $h_a = 60/\sqrt{a}$.

Now suppose that the firm employing factor A, while still a price-taker in the *factor market*, is no longer a price-taker (now has monopoly power) in the *product market*. Figure 11.4 indicates how the firm's returns from increased factor employment will be adversely affected by the falling tendency of price P as more output is produced. For a monopolist firm, the return on the margin from the employment of an additional unit of factor A is not the *value* of the physical Marginal Product but the *revenue increment* achievable by sale of that Marginal Product. This leads to the concept known as *Marginal Revenue Product* of factor A, denoted mrp_a:

(11.11)
$$mrp_a \equiv MR(mp_a)$$

DEFINITION: Marginal Revenue Product mrp_a equals Marginal Revenue MR times physical Marginal Product mp_a.

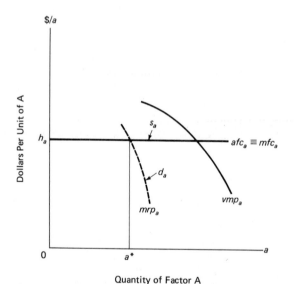

FIGURE 11.4   **Optimal Factor Employment: Monopolist in Product Market.**   The firm pictured here (like the firm in Figure 11.3) is a price-taker or competitive purchaser in the factor market, as indicated by the horizontal supply curve s_a at the level of the going hire-price h_a for factor A. But here the firm has monopoly power in the product market. The consequent divergence between price P and Marginal Revenue MR is reflected in the divergence between the vmp_a (Value of the Marginal Product) and mrp_a (Marginal Revenue Product) curves. The firm's optimum is at the intersection of s_a and mrp_a, leading to employment a^* of factor A. The downward-sloping branch of the mrp_a curve is also the firm's demand curve for factor A.

Returning to the competitive (price-taker) firm in the product market (Figure 11.3), product price P is perceived as constant—in which case Marginal Revenue MR identically equals price P. It follows immediately that, *for a competitive firm in the product market the* vmp$_a$ *and the* mrp$_a$ *curves are identical*. This was indicated by the labeling $vmp_a \equiv mrp_a$ in Figure 11.3. For a firm with monopoly power in the product market, on the other hand, Marginal Revenue MR and product price P are both decreasing functions of output. And the MR curve falls faster than the demand or Average Revenue curve—as shown, for example, in the lower panel of Figure 8.1. So, *for a monopoly firm, the* mrp$_a$ *curve must lie below the* vmp$_a$ *curve*, as in Figure 11.4. The optimal factor employment $a*$ for the firm with monopoly power in the product market is determined in this diagram as the intersection of the mrp_a curve with the horizontal factor-supply curve $afc_a \equiv mfc_a$.[7] It follows that, in the situation of Figure 11.4, the firm's demand curve d_a for factor A is given by the mrp_a curve rather than by the vmp_a curve.

Exercise 11.4: Using the same Total Product function as before, $q = 2\sqrt{a}$, and recalling that Marginal Product is $mp_a = 1/\sqrt{a}$, assume now that the firm has monopoly power—and specifically, that it faces the downward-sloping demand curve $P = 90 - q$. Let the hire-price be $h_a = 4$ as before. (a) Find the vmp_a and mrp_a functions, and verify that mrp_a lies below vmp_a. (b) What is the optimal factor employment $a*$ and associated output $q*$? (c) What is the monopoly firm's demand curve for factor A? (d) Compare the solutions with those of Exercise 11.3.

Answer: (a) As before, $vmp_a \equiv P(mp_a)$, but now P is itself a function of output q and therefore of input a. Thus, $vmp_a = (90 - q)(1/\sqrt{a}) = (90 - 2\sqrt{a})(1/\sqrt{a}) = 90/\sqrt{a} - 2$. Since for the linear product demand curve $P = 90 - q$ we know that Marginal Revenue falls twice as fast as price, we have $MR = 90 - 2q$. Then $mrp_a = 90/\sqrt{a} - 4$, so that mrp_a is always less than vmp_a. (b) Setting $mrp_a = h_a$ we have $90/\sqrt{a} - 4 = 4$, which implies $\sqrt{a} = 90/8 = 11.25$ or $a* = 126.56$. The associated output is $q* = 22.5$. (c) Since the mrp_a curve is everywhere downward-sloping, the demand curve coincides with it. The demand-curve equation is $90/\sqrt{a} - 4 = h_a$. (d) The firm here could produce 30 units of output and sell them at the market price $P = 60$, as did the price-taking firm of Exercise 11.3. But, because of its monopoly power, it produces only 22.5 units of output (and sells them at the higher price $P* = 90 - q* = 67.5$). Correspondingly, it employs fewer units of factor A (126.56 instead of 225).

Since for the competitive firm in the factor market vmp_a and mrp_a are identical, equation (11.10) can be superseded by the following more general Factor Employment Condition that holds for *both* monopolist and pure competitor in the product market:

[7]*Mathematical Footnote:* The firm is maximizing $\Pi = R - C = Pq - h_a a - F$ as before, but now recognizes that P is a decreasing function of output q—and so, indirectly, of input a. Differentiating and setting equal to zero, the first-order condition is:

$$P\frac{dq}{da} + q\frac{dP}{dq}\frac{dq}{da} = h_a \quad \text{or} \quad \left(P + q\frac{dP}{dq}\right)\frac{dq}{da} = h_a$$

The element in parentheses is Marginal Revenue. So the condition can be expressed as:

$$MR(mp_a) \equiv mrp_a = h_a$$

$$(11.12) \qquad mrp_a = h_a \qquad \begin{array}{l}\text{Factor Employment Condition,} \\ \text{Price-Taking Firm} \\ \text{in Factor Market}\end{array}$$

Again, we have as a technical qualification that the mrp_a curve must cut the horizontal factor-supply curve from *above*.

> CONCLUSION: For a factor-price-taking firm facing a given hire-price h_a, the optimal employment of factor A occurs when $mrp_a = h_a$ (in the downward-sloping range of the mrp_a curve). The curve of Marginal Revenue Product mrp_a is (in its downward-sloping range) the firm's demand curve for A.[8] In Figure 11.3, picturing a competitor firm in the product market, the factor demand curve d_a coincides with the curve of $vmp_a \equiv mrp_a$. In Figure 11.4, for a monopolist in the product market, the factor demand curve d_a coincides with mrp_a (and *not* with vmp_a).

The separate treatments of the firm's *output* decision in Chapters 6 and 8 (for the competitive and monopolist firm, respectively) and of the *factor-employment* decision in this chapter might suggest that these are two distinct choices. But the two decisions are inextricably connected. Having made the factor-employment decision, output is determined; there is no further degree of freedom for the firm to choose a level of output. And, so long as we are dealing with a *single* variable factor, the converse is also true. Choosing output necessarily determines factor employment.[9]

The equivalence of the output decision and the factor-employment decision follows almost immediately from the logically necessary connection between Marginal Cost MC and the Marginal Product mp_a for a single variable factor A, which will be repeated here:

$$(11.13) \qquad MC \equiv \frac{h_a}{mp_a}$$

Dividing both sides by Marginal Revenue MR, we have:

$$(11.14) \qquad \frac{MC}{MR} \equiv \frac{h_a}{MR\,(mp_a)} \equiv \frac{h_a}{mrp_a}$$

So satisfaction of the Factor Employment Condition (11.12), $h_a = mrp_a$, directly implies $MC = MR$, which is the general Maximum-Profit condition of equation (8.3). The converse also holds, of course.

---

[8]A technical qualification: Strictly speaking, this holds only for that portion of the downward-sloping range where the total expenditure $C_a \equiv h_a a$ on the variable factor A is less than Total Revenue R.

[9]With several variable factors, however, the determination of output still leaves a range of freedom for selection of the best resource combination to produce that output. This topic will be taken up shortly.

Exercise 11.5: For Exercises 11.3 and 11.4, verify that the solution for optimal input $(mrp_a = h_a)$ also implies that for optimal output $(MR = MC)$.

Answer: We saw in Exercise 11.2 that the Marginal Product relation $mp_a = 1/\sqrt{a}$ implied that Marginal Cost is $MC = 2q$. For the price-taking firm of Exercise 11.2, with $P = 60$, the Maximum-Profit Condition $MC = MR \equiv P$ says that $2q = 60$, or $q^* = 30$—which confirms the result obtained earlier using the Factor Employment Condition $vmp_a = mrp_a = h_a$. For the monopolist firm of Exercise 11.4, using the demand curve $P = 90 - q$ the Maximum-Profit Condition $MC = MR$ becomes $2q = 90 - 2q$, or $q^* = 22.5$, once again confirming the earlier result.

*11.B
FIRM'S DEMAND FOR SEVERAL VARIABLE FACTORS

When only a single factor is considered to be variable, the firm is acting in the "short run"—whereas, when the firm makes "long-run" decisions, all factors become variable. Having more than one variable factor makes the analysis of factor demand considerably more intricate. To minimize complications the exposition here will assume there are just two variable factors, A and B.

11.B.1 ☐ The Production Function

In some ways, the firm deciding upon employment of factors is like the individual choosing consumption goods and services. Just as consumption goods can be regarded as generating *utility,* so factors as inputs generate *product.* The relation between inputs and output is the production function of the firm. If there are just two variable factors, the production function (11.1) can be written:

(11.15)
$$q = \Psi(a, b)$$

Diagrammatically, the production function is the "output hill" of Figure 11.5, which shows output quantity q as a function of input quantities a and b. Chapter 3 contained a discussion of the difficulty or impossibility of quantifying "cardinal" utility for scaling the vertical axis of the utility hill. Here, however, there is no such problem. The quantity of the output commodity Q provides a natural "cardinal" scale for the vertical axis of a three-dimensional production function (output hill). Still, the convenience of working in just two dimensions is such that we will often make use of the "contour map" instead, as illustrated here in Figure 11.6. But we can always attach some definite numerical output quantity index q to each contour or *isoquant* of the contour map; we are not restricted, as we were in the case of utility, to merely "ordinal" comparisons of higher and lower.

There are two essential aspects of the multi-factor production function: (1) the effect of changes in *relative factor proportions,* and (2) the effect of changes in

*The section between the asterisk and the symbol ■ may contain somewhat more difficult or advanced material.

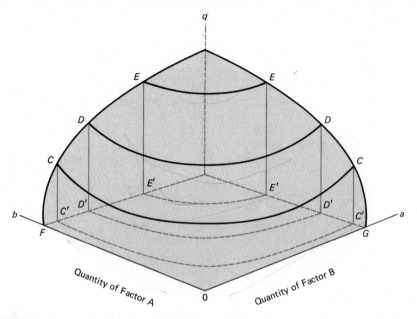

FIGURE 11.5 Output as a Function of Two Inputs. Output q, measured vertically, is shown as a function of the input quantities a and b. *CC, DD,* and *EE* are contours of equal height (output) along the three-dimensional surface. The curves $C'C'$, $D'D'$, and $E'E'$ are the projections of these contours in the base plane.

scale (i.e., of proportionate increases or decreases in all factors simultaneously).

With regard to *relative* factor proportions, the Law of Diminishing Returns continues to hold (as a postulated technological fact) in the two-factor case. Consider Figure 11.7. Here, along the surface of the output hill are sketched several curves showing the change in output quantity q as one input varies with

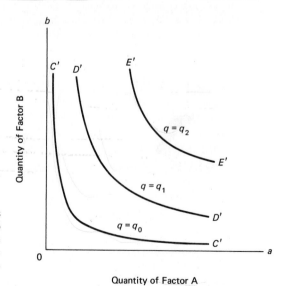

FIGURE 11.6 Isoquants of Output. The projections $C'C'$, $D'D'$, and $E'E'$ in the base plane of Figure 11.5 are shown here as isoquants (curves of equal output) in a contour map, without the overlying vertical dimension. Each isoquant is associated with a definite quantity of output (q_0, q_1, or q_2).

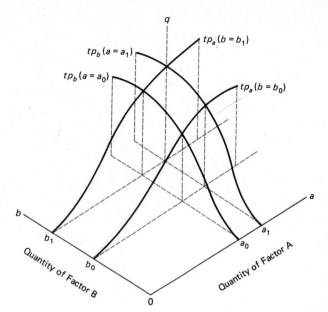

FIGURE 11.7 Total Product Functions.
Here Total Product curves are drawn along an output hill like that of Figure 11.5. The Total Product curves for factor A, designated tp_a, hold constant the amount of the other factor B. However, the heights of the tp_a curves depend upon the specific constant values assumed for b in each case, and similarly the tp_b curves depend on the values assumed for a.

the other input held constant. These can be regarded as *Total Product curves*, analogous to the tp_a curve defined for a single variable factor A in the previous section. But there are now Total Product curves for each of the two factors—tp_a and tp_b. Indeed, for each factor there is an infinite family of such curves, since in general both tp_a and tp_b will depend also upon the specific magnitude at which the *other* factor is held constant. The Total Product curves for factor A are given labels like $tp_a(b = b_0)$ and $tp_a(b = b_1)$. Each such curve shows the variation of Total Product q with changes in the input quantity of factor A, factor B held constant—in the one case at $b = b_0$ and in the other at $b = b_1$. And a set of tp_b curves can correspondingly be defined. It is possible, of course, to associate with any of the Total Product curves of Figure 11.7 an Average Product curve and Marginal Product[10] curve as in the lower panel of Figure 11.1.

In Figure 11.8 the two families of Total Product curves are shown suggestively on (q, a) and on (q, b) axes, respectively. Each single curve has a form similar to the tp_a curve of Figure 11.1, as dictated by the Law of Diminishing Returns. In Panel (a) the entire tp_a curve is shown as shifting upward as quantities of the other factor B rise from b_0 to b_1 to b_2, and similarly for the other factor in Panel (b). Such an upward shift must occur, if the "other" factor is productive.

With regard to changes in *scale*, the shape of the output hill in Figure 11.5 shows that a kind of diminishing returns *may* prevail even where both factors increase proportionately. We will assume here that, eventually at least, *diminishing returns to scale* also apply. (That is, when all inputs are increased in the same

[10]*Mathematical Footnote:* With two or more variable factors, the Marginal Product of any single factor such as A becomes a *partial* derivative:

$$mp_a \equiv \lim_{\Delta a \to 0} \frac{\Psi(a + \Delta a, b) - \Psi(a, b)}{\Delta a} \equiv \frac{\partial q}{\partial a}$$

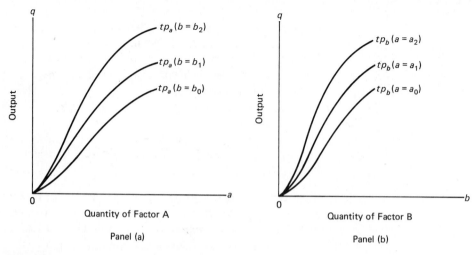

FIGURE 11.8   Families of Total Product Curves.   Here tp_a curves like those drawn along the output hill of Figure 11.7 are shown on q,a axes in Panel (a); the tp_b curves are similarly shown on q,b axes in Panel (b).

proportion, output rises in a lesser proportion.) However, constant or even increasing returns to scale would not be a contradiction of the Law of Diminishing Returns as defined for *varying factor proportions*. Total Product curves can have the normal diminishing-returns shape even on an output hill with constant or increasing returns to scale.

EXAMPLE 11.2
Missouri Corn

An agricultural experiment in Missouri reported by J. Ambrosius examined the response of corn yield (bushels per acre) to variation in two inputs *A* and *B* (*number of plants* per acre and *pounds of nitrogen* per acre). Reading horizontally across any single row, the Table shows selected points on the Total

Bushels of Corn per Acre (q)

POUNDS OF NITROGEN PER ACRE (B)	NUMBER OF PLANTS PER ACRE (A)				
	9000	12,000	15,000	18,000	21,000
0	50.6	54.2	53.5	48.5	39.2
50	78.7	85.9	88.8	87.5	81.9
100	94.4	105.3	111.9	114.2	112.2
150	97.8	112.4	122.6	128.6	130.3
200	88.9	107.1	121.0	130.6	135.9

Source: John Ambrosius, "The Effects of Experimental Size upon Optimum Rates of Nitrogen and Stand for Corn in Missouri" (1964), quoted in J. P. Doll, V. J. Rhodes, and J. G. West, *Economics of Agricultural Production, Markets, and Policy* (Homewood, Ill.: Richard D. Irwin, 1968), p. 89.

Product curve tp_a for plants per acre—with b, nitrogen input per acre, held constant along the row. Reading vertically down any column, points are shown on the tp_b curve for nitrogen input b—holding fixed the number of plants per acre, a. The entire tp_a curve tends to shift upward as b increases, and the tp_b curve tends to shift upward as a increases.

It is also possible to see that diminishing returns apply here even to *proportionate variation* in both factors together. For example, a doubling of both inputs from the combination $a_0 = 9000$, $b_0 = 50$ to the combination $a_1 = 18{,}000$, $b_1 = 100$ raises corn output from 78.7 only to 114.2.

The "Missouri Corn" example suggests a possible rationale for diminishing returns to scale (i.e., to proportionate variation of factors). Nitrogen and number of plants as inputs were varied in the experiment, but there was at least one other factor—the number of acres—still held constant. Since (as argued earlier) in the real world it will not generally be possible to vary literally *all* inputs, we are always in practice dealing still with changes in *relative* factor proportions. So even though all *marketable* inputs are varied in proportion, the condition wherein some inputs are physically "fixed" is, in some degree, ultimately inescapable.

EXAMPLE 11.3
Pigs

The agricultural economist E. O. Heady[a] reported an experiment which involved varying the amounts of corn (high in carbohydrate content) and soybean oilmeal (high in protein content) fed to young pigs. The experiment was conducted on 302 pigs, carried from a weaning weight of 34 pounds to a market weight of around 250 pounds. Observations on weight gain were used to estimate output as a function of these two inputs.

It was found that rather different production functions were appropriate for different weight ranges, as the effects of inputs of carbohydrate versus protein upon weight gained tended to be different for younger (smaller) versus older (larger) pigs. The results obtained (rounded off) were as follows, where G indicates weight gain, P is input of soybean oilmeal (protein), and C is input of corn (carbohydrate)—all measured in pounds per pig.

$$G = 1.60P^{.30}C^{.53}, \quad \text{for the weight interval 34–75 pounds}$$

$$G = 0.71P^{.14}C^{.77}, \quad \text{for the weight interval 75–150 pounds}$$

$$G = 0.46P^{.09}C^{.86}, \quad \text{for the weight interval 150–250 pounds}$$

The exponents of P and C in the different functions indicate, as is reasonable,

[a] E. O. Heady, "An Econometric Investigation of the Technology of Agricultural Production Functions," *Econometrica*, v. 25 (April 1957).

that weight gain in young pigs responds relatively more to protein input while weight gain in older pigs responds more to carbohydrates.

> COMMENT: It can be shown mathematically that, in functions of this form, there would be increasing returns to scale (more than proportionate effect upon output for proportionate variation of both inputs) if the *sum* of the exponents exceeds unity. Constant returns to scale hold if the sum of exponents exactly equals unity, and decreasing returns to scale if the sum falls short of unity. Evidently, all three production functions here show decreasing returns to scale.

11.B.2 ☐ The Factor-Employment Decision: Geometry

The factor-employment decision of a firm using two variable factors has, like the production function itself, two aspects: (1) the determination of optimal relative factor *proportions,* and (2) the determination of most profitable *scale.* Following the procedure applied to the consumption decision (in Section 4.A), we shall first adopt a geometrical and then an analytical point of view.

To isolate the aspect of factor proportions, hold scale constant by assuming a fixed level of cost $C' = h_a a + h_b b$. We want to determine the a, b input combination, at this given level of cost, that is most advantageous for the firm. Clearly, the best combination is that which maximizes the quantity of output. Geometrically, it will be evident in the contour map or isoquant diagram of Figure 11.9 that the tangency point Q' is optimal. The factor employments at point Q' are a' and b', leading to output level q'.

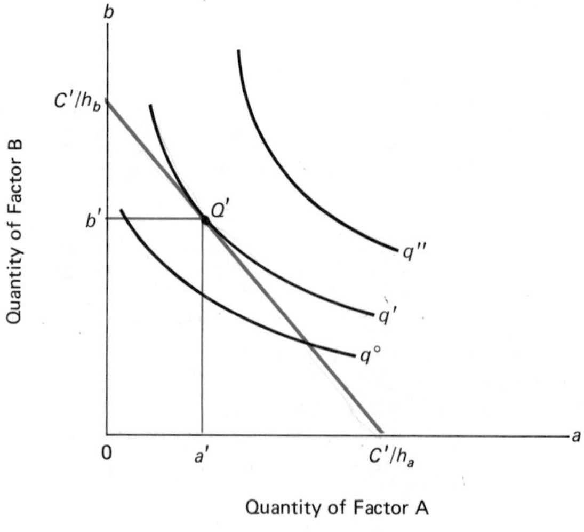

FIGURE 11.9 Optimal Factor Balance. At a given cost level $C' = h_a a + h_b b$, the best factor employments are a' and b' at point Q'—the tangency of the iso-cost line C' with the highest attainable output contour q'.

Note the analogy with the optimum of the consumer that was pictured in Figure 4.1. There the consumer was maximizing utility by choice of consumption quantities x and y, at a specified level of income $I = P_x x + P_y y$. Here the firm maximizes output by choice of factor employments a and b, at a specified level of cost $C' = h_a a + h_b b$.

But of course we want to consider different levels of cost, i.e., of *scale* of output. As cost expands in any proportion, the cost line in the diagram will move out from the origin along both axes in the same proportion. Figure 11.10 pictures a family of cost lines (isoquants of *cost*) $C°, C', C'', \ldots$, as well as a family of production contours (isoquants of *output*) $q°, q', q'', \ldots$. All the cost lines will have the same fixed slope (see below). Since at any level of cost the tangency point represents the optimal proportion or balance of factors, a curve drawn through all such tangency points must contain the overall best position for the firm. This curve may be called the Scale Expansion Path (SEP), in analogy with the consumer's Income Expansion Path (IEP) of Section 4.B.

There are a number of different ways of locating the overall best position of the firm. Perhaps the simplest is to convert the data of the Scale Expansion Path SEP into Total Cost and Total Revenue curves. For any tangency point such as Q' along the SEP in Figure 11.10, there are associated quantities q' of output and C' of cost. With this q,C information for all levels of cost $C°, C', C'', \ldots$, the Total Cost curve $C(q)$ can be plotted as in Figure 11.11. To obtain the Total Revenue curve, the only additional information needed is the *demand function* relating price P to the firm's output q. Thus, for each level of q there is a unique P. Multiplying the output indexes $q°, q', q'', \ldots$ by the appropriate P in each case, we see that isoquants of output q in Figure 11.10 can equally well be regarded as isoquants of Total Revenue $R \equiv Pq$. (If the firm is a price-taker in the product market, P is a constant so that R increases proportionately with output. Then all

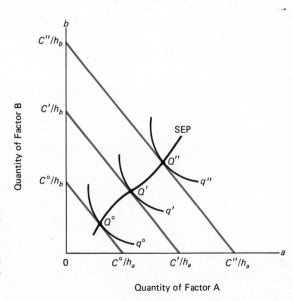

FIGURE 11.10 Scale Expansion Path. Along any iso-cost line, the tangency with an output isoquant represents the largest output attainable at that cost. Each such tangency shows the best factor proportions for that level of cost and output. The Scale Expansion Path SEP connects all these tangency positions.

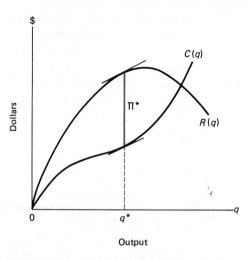

FIGURE 11.11 Total Revenue and Total Cost Functions.
Each point on the Scale Expansion Path of the previous diagram is associated with a particular level of cost C and output q. This information permits plotting the Total Cost curve $C(q)$ above. Also, each level of output q is associated with a certain revenue $R = Pq$, given the firm's demand function. This information permits plotting the Total Revenue curve $R(q)$ above. The profit-maximizing output q^* determined in this diagram also determines the optimal factor employments a^* and b^* in the preceding diagram.

the different q-contours are multiplied by the *same P* to become R-contours.) The q,R information can be plotted as the Total Revenue curve $R(q)$ in Figure 11.11, which corresponds to the monopoly-power case—note that the diagram is identical with the upper panel of Figure 8.1.

The best output q^* is that for which profit $\Pi \equiv R - C$, i.e., the vertical distance between the $R(q)$ and $C(q)$ curves in the diagram, is greatest. The optimal q^* tells us which particular q-contour is best in Figure 11.10. The intersection of this contour with the Scale Expansion Path SEP determines, finally, the optimal factor employments a^* and b^*.

11.B.3 ☐ The Factor-Employment Decision: Analysis

Let us now consider this factor-proportion decision analytically. Assuming diminishing marginal productivity for each of the two factors, at any level of cost the firm will be at an (interior) optimum when the Factor Balance Equation holds.[11]

(11.16) $$\frac{mp_a}{h_a} = \frac{mp_b}{h_b} \qquad \text{Factor Balance Equation}$$

[11]*Mathematical Footnote:* We can use again "the method of Lagrangian multipliers" to maximize output $q = \Psi(a, b)$ subject to a given level of cost $C = h_a a + h_b b$.

$$\underset{(a,b,\lambda)}{\text{Max}}\, L = q + \lambda(h_a a + h_b b - C)$$

The first-order conditions are:

$$\frac{\partial q}{\partial a} + \lambda h_a = 0 \qquad \frac{\partial q}{\partial b} + \lambda h_b = 0 \qquad h_a a + h_b b - C = 0$$

The first two conditions can be written as:

$$-\lambda = \frac{\partial q/\partial a}{h_a} = \frac{\partial q/\partial b}{h_b}$$

That is, at any given scale the relative factor employments are optimal when the Marginal Products *per dollar* spent are equal for each variable factor employed.[12]

MRS_Q, the Marginal Rate of Substitution in Production between factors A and B with regard to product Q, is defined as the amount of factor B which can be substituted for a small reduction of factor A in such a way as to hold output q constant. Geometrically, this can be interpreted as the absolute slope at any particular point along an output isoquant. Thus:

$$MRS_Q \equiv -\frac{\Delta b}{\Delta a}\bigg|_q$$

(For the analogous concept of the Marginal Rate of Substitution in Consumption MRS_C, representing the absolute slope of the consumer's indifference curve, see Section 4.A.2.) And the *Marginal Rate of Substitution in Exchange* between the two factors, MRS_E, is the absolute slope of the iso-cost line. So the tangency condition of Figure 11.10 representing optimal factor balance also can be written as:

(11.16′)
$$MRS_Q = MRS_E$$

That (11.16′) corresponds to the Factor Balance Equation (11.16) follows from the identities:

$$MRS_E \equiv \frac{h_a}{h_b} \quad \text{and} \quad MRS_Q \equiv \frac{mp_a}{mp_b}$$

The equivalence of MRS_E with a price ratio is familiar by now. The equivalence of MRS_Q, the absolute slope along the output isoquant, with the ratio of marginal products[13] may be illustrated by a simple example. MRS_Q is, for small changes,

---

So these first-order conditions correspond to the Factor Balance Equation. With more than one variable factor, however, diminishing Marginal Product ($\partial^2 q/\partial a^2 < 0$, $\partial^2 q/\partial b^2 < 0$) does not guarantee that the *second-order* conditions for a maximum are met. (Compare the analogous statement about diminishing Marginal *Utility* in Chapter 4.) An additional required condition is:

$$\frac{\partial^2 q}{\partial a^2}\frac{\partial^2 q}{\partial b^2} > \left(\frac{\partial^2 q}{\partial a\,\partial b}\right)^2$$

[12]If D is some third factor *not* actually being employed ($d = 0$) at current factor prices, its Marginal Product per dollar is related by an *inequality* condition to the others:

$$\frac{mp_a(a > 0)}{h_a} = \frac{mp_b(b > 0)}{h_b} > \frac{mp_d(d = 0)}{h_d}$$

For the optimal employment of D to be zero, its Marginal Product per dollar must be less than that of other factors, even for the very first unit of D.

[13]*Mathematical Footnote:* Along any output isoquant, q is constant. Thus:

$$dq = \frac{\partial q}{\partial a}da + \frac{\partial q}{\partial b}db = 0$$

Then

$$-\frac{db}{da} = \frac{\partial q/\partial a}{\partial q/\partial b} \quad \text{or} \quad MRS_Q = \frac{mp_a}{mp_b}$$

the additional number of units Δb of factor B required to maintain output intact (i.e., to get back to the same output isoquant) after a unit reduction $\Delta a = -1$ in employment of factor A. If $mp_a = 10$ and $mp_b = 5$ and if we are dealing with small changes (so that the marginal products are approximately constant), it follows that 2 units of B will be required to make up for 1 of A. That is, $2 = 10/5$ is the MRS_Q, equal to the ratio mp_a/mp_b.

The analytical condition for the firm's optimum *scale of output* took the form $MC = MR$ in equation (8.3). We now want to express this same result in terms of employment of factors A and B. First, note the following interpretation of the Factor Balance Equation:

$$(11.17) \qquad \frac{h_a}{mp_a} = \frac{h_b}{mp_b} = MC$$

That is, Marginal Cost $MC \equiv \Delta C/\Delta q$ equals, for factor A, its hire-price $h_a \equiv \Delta C/\Delta a$ divided by its Marginal Product $mp_a \equiv \Delta q/\Delta a$. Similarly, of course, for factor B. At the correct factor proportions dictated by the Factor Balance Equation, it is equally costly to expand output by hiring a small increment of A, or of B, or any mixture of the two.[14]

Dividing through by Marginal Revenue MR, we have:

$$(11.18) \qquad \frac{MC}{MR} = \frac{h_a}{mrp_a} = \frac{h_b}{mrp_b}$$

Then satisfaction of the Maximum-Profit Condition $MC = MR$ implies the joint Factor Employment Conditions:

$$(11.19) \qquad \begin{cases} mrp_a = h_a \\ mrp_b = h_b \end{cases} \qquad \begin{array}{l} \text{Factor Employment Conditions,} \\ \text{Price-taking Firm} \\ \text{in Factor Markets} \end{array}$$

Thus, the scale of factor employments is correct if (for each factor actually employed) Marginal Revenue Product equals factor hire-price. For a firm with no monopoly power in the product market, $MR \equiv P$. For such a firm, therefore, equations (11.18) and (11.19) could be written in terms of Value of the Marginal

---

[14]*Mathematical Footnote:* First, $dq = (\partial q/\partial a)da + (\partial q/\partial b)db$. Since $C = h_a a + h_b b$, $dC = h_a\,da + h_b\,db$. So:

$$MC \equiv \frac{dC}{dq} = \frac{h_a\,da + h_b\,db}{(\partial q/\partial a)\,da + (\partial q/\partial b)\,db}$$

Since $h_a/(\partial q/\partial a) = h_b/(\partial q/\partial b)$ from the Factor Balance Equation, it follows algebraically that:

$$MC = \frac{h_a}{\partial q/\partial a} = \frac{h_b}{\partial q/\partial b}$$

Product *vmp* (price times Marginal Product) instead of *mrp* (Marginal Revenue times Marginal Product). The equations in their present general form, however, hold whether the firm is a monopolist or a competitor in the product market.

Equations (11.19) are of course a direct generalization of the single-factor employment condition of equation (11.12). But there is one important complication in the multi-factor case: the Marginal Product mp_a and therefore the Marginal Revenue Product mrp_a may depend not only upon the amount of factor *A* but also upon the associated employment of the other factor *B*—and similarly, of course, mp_b and mrp_b may depend upon the amount of factor *A*.[15]

Two factors are said to be *complementary* if increased employment of one raises the Marginal Product of the other. Complementarity represents a kind of harmonious or mutually helpful interaction of factors: executives and secretaries, ships and sailors, land and fertilizer are examples of complementary pairs. In the absence of such an interaction, where increased employment of one factor has no effect upon the marginal productivity of the other, the two are said to be *independent*. Handcraftsmen and mass-production machines might be such a pair. If a firm simultaneously produces high-quality hand products and low-quality machine products, it may be that the handcraftsmen work entirely apart from the machines so that there is no interaction one way or the other between them.

If increased employment of one factor actually *reduces* the Marginal Product of the other, the negative interaction is called *anti-complementarity*.[16] Classes of inputs that are close substitutes for one another tend to be anti-complementary. An increase in employment of *A* necessarily reduces its *own* Marginal Product mp_a (in the economically relevant range where the Law of Diminishing Marginal Returns applies). But if resource *A* is a close substitute for *B*, increased employment of *A* might also reduce mp_b. Examples might be male versus female labor, large machines versus small machines, or one brand of fertilizer versus another.[17]

A complementary interaction between two factors *A* and *B* is illustrated in Figure 11.12. The family of Marginal Product curves mp_a shown in Panel (a), and the family of mp_b curves shown in Panel (b), may be regarded as derived in the usual way from the corresponding families of *Total* Product curves tp_a and tp_b in the two panels of Figure 11.8. The crucial point is that the mp_a curves shift *upward*

---

[15]*Mathematical Footnote:* If $q = \Psi(a, b)$, the Marginal Products or partial derivatives $\partial q/\partial a$ and $\partial q/\partial b$ will in general both be functions of *a* and *b*. Geometrically, in Figure 11.7 we see that the slope along the Total Product curves tp_a in the *a*-direction $(\partial q/\partial a)$ varies not only as *a* increases, but also from one curve to the next as *b* increases. And similarly of course for the slope along the tp_b curves $(\partial q/\partial b)$.

[16]*Mathematical Footnote:* The presence or absence of complementarity corresponds to the sign of the second cross-derivative of the production function. In the normal *complementary* case, $\partial(\partial q/\partial a)/\partial b \equiv \partial^2 q/\partial a\,\partial b$ is positive. *Independence* corresponds to a zero cross-derivative, and *anti-complementarity* to a negative cross-derivative.

[17]Anti-complementarity should be distinguished from what might be called *interference,* where the two factors actually hamper one another. In a situation such that sex differences are distracting, hiring more females might actually reduce output and therefore reduce the *Total* Product of the male employees—and vice versa if more male workers are employed. In the anti-complementary cases to be considered here, however, employing more of one factor *A* leads to a fall in the *Marginal* Product of *B* $(\Delta q/\Delta b)$ but not to a reduction in the *Total* Product *q*. To employ interfering factors may be irrational, but employment of anti-complementary factors is not at all absurd.

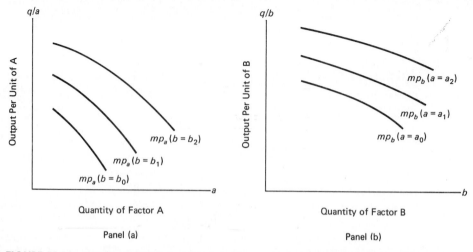

FIGURE 11.12 Families of Marginal Product Curves: Complementary Factors. The family of Marginal Product curves mp_a in Panel (a) is derived from the corresponding family of Total Product curves tp_a in Panel (a) of Figure 11.8. The mp_b curves in Panel (b) correspond similarly to the tp_b curves in Panel (b) of Figure 11.8. In the illustrated range here, the curves have negative slope (the Marginal Product of each factor is a decreasing function of its own quantity). But the curves shift upward as the quantity of the *other* factor increases (the Marginal Product of each factor is an increasing function of the quantity of the other input). This illustrates the normal case of complementarity.

as the associated amount of factor B increases from b_0 to b_1 to b_2; similarly, the mp_b curves move higher as A rises from a_0 to a_1 to a_2.

11.B.4 ☐ Shifts in Factor Prices: Substitution and Scale Effects

We saw in Chapter 4 that a change in the price of consumer good had a *substitution effect* and an *income effect* upon purchases. Analogously here, a change in the price of a factor has a *substitution effect* and a *scale effect* upon factor employment. The substitution effect follows from the change in factor proportions due to the shift in *relative* factor prices h_a/h_b; the scale effect follows from the effect on optimal output due to the implied change in Marginal Cost MC.

The substitution effect is illustrated in Figure 11.13. Here the initial position Q° represents a typical point on the Scale Expansion Path SEP° (see Figure 11.10), at a tangency of a cost isoquant C° and an output isoquant q°. A fall in h_a, the price of factor A, necessarily lowers (flattens) the absolute slope h_a/h_b of the cost isoquants. The dashed C' is that member of the family of flatter cost isoquants tangent to the initial output isoquant (at position Q'). The new Scale Expansion Path SEP' will therefore be displaced to the right, as indicated in the diagram. *There will be a shift of optimal factor proportions toward the relatively cheapened factor A.*

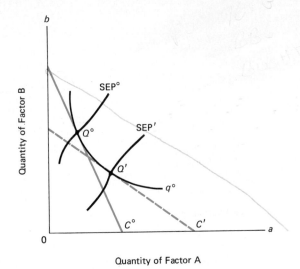

Quantity of Factor B

Quantity of Factor A

FIGURE 11.13 Factor Substitution Effect. At initial hire-prices h_a^0 and h_b^0, a Scale Expansion Path (SEP°) connects all points of tangency between isoquants of cost C and isoquants of output q. That is, all points where the slope $\Delta b/\Delta a$ along isoquants like $q°$ equals the slope $-h_a^0/h_b^0$ along cost lines like $C°$. If h_a falls to h_a', the new isoquants of cost have flatter slope, like C'. The changed price ratio h_a'/h_b^0 determines a new Scale Expansion Path SEP'. From an initial position $Q°$, the *factor substitution effect* is the increased employment of A due to moving to a new tangency at Q'—where the original output isoquant q is just attained along a cost line C' whose slope represents the new hire-price ratio.

EXAMPLE 11.4
Factor Prices and Ocean Shipping

Newly constructed ships used by Japanese, continental European, and British shippers during the years 1952–55 were examined by W. Y. Oi in order to compare the relative factor proportions employed. In ocean shipping the important factors of production may be divided into: (1) "capital" (amortization of construction expenses, plus ship maintenance), (2) fuel, and (3) labor (wages plus subsistence at sea). In the period studied, fuel prices were very similar for all shippers. So the essential element was the capital cost versus labor cost comparison..Labor costs were relatively cheapest for the Japanese shippers and most expensive for the continental Europeans, with the British in between.

One consequence of relatively high labor cost (or, equivalently, relatively low capital cost) is the employment of ships with a high designed speed. Faster ships are costlier to construct and maintain, but permit a saving of labor time per voyage. The Table indicates that, as anticipated, the Japanese chose ships with lowest and the continental Europeans with highest designed speed.

Median Design Speed (knots)

	SMALL SHIPS (3000–9000 DWT.)	LARGE SHIPS (OVER 9000 DWT.)
Japanese shippers	11.46	13.81
British shippers	14.00	14.04
European shippers	14.86	14.93

Source: W. Y. Oi, "The Cost of Ocean Shipping," in A. R. Ferguson *et al.,* eds., *The Economic Value of the United States Merchant Marine* (Evanston, Ill.: The Transportation Center at Northwestern University, 1961), p. 160.

The scale effect is somewhat trickier. Figure 11.14 shows the effect of a fall in h_a alone (from h_a° to h_a') upon a typical initial cost isoquant. Evidently there is an outward rotation of the cost isoquant, from the position C° to C''. The new tangency will necessarily be on a higher output isoquant q''. Thus, *at any given cost* it will be optimal for the firm to produce more output after a cheapening of a factor. Or, put another way, any given output can be produced at a lower Total Cost than before.

Figures 11.13 and 11.14 together show that if *output* is held constant after hire-price h_a falls, cost will be less—while if *cost* is held constant, output will be greater. But no general conclusion is warranted as to whether cost will in fact be lower or output greater at the new optimum position. It might have seemed plausible to expect that a fall in factor price would surely lead to an expansion of the optimum scale of output, but this does *not* necessarily follow. It is true that the Total Cost curve falls with a cheapening of any factor. But the optimal output is determined by the relation between *Marginal* Cost and *Marginal* Revenue ($MC = MR$) i.e., between the *slopes* of the Total Cost and Total Revenue curves.

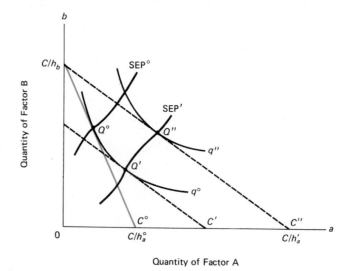

FIGURE 11.14 Cheapening of Factor A. As in the preceding diagram, Q' is the factor combination attained upon shifting from an initial combination Q° in response to a fall in hire-price h_a. As between Q° and Q', output q is held constant. This diagram shows also the new position Q'' reached if Cost C is held constant instead of output q. The points Q' and Q'' are both on the new Scale Expansion Path SEP'.

PART 4 FACTOR MARKETS AND INCOME DISTRIBUTION

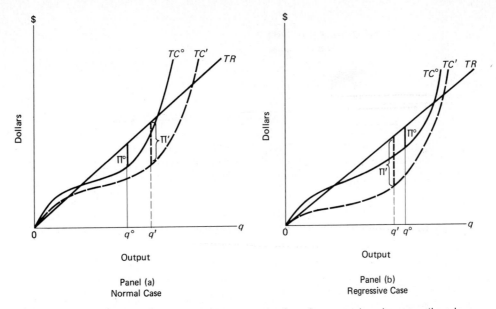

FIGURE 11.15   Scale Effect.   A fall in the hire-price h_a of any factor employed necessarily reduces the Total Cost of producing any level of output q, so in both panels here the new TC' curve lies everywhere below the original $TC°$ curve. But profit $\Pi = TR - TC$ is greatest where Marginal Revenue (slope along the TR curve) equals Marginal Cost (slope along the TC curve). In the "normal case" shown in Panel (a), the TC' curve is not only lower than the $TC°$ curve at each output but also flatter—so Marginal Cost has also fallen everywhere. Then the new optimal output q' is greater than the previous $q°$. But in the "regressive case" of Panel (b), the TC' curve is lower but (over a portion of its range) *steeper* rather than flatter than $TC°$. In this range *Marginal* Cost is greater than before, and so the new optimal output q' is less than $q°$. In both cases, the new profit Π' is necessarily greater than the original profit $\Pi°$.

Panel (a) in Figure 11.15 shows a normal situation in which the lowering of the Total Cost curve from $TC°$ to TC' does lead to an expansion of optimal output from $q°$ to q' (note the location of the profit magnitudes $\Pi°$ and Π'). Panel (b) shows the more surprising case in which the lowering from $TC°$ to TC' is combined with a *steepening* of the slope (thus increasing the MC) in the relevant region, so that the new optimal output q' is less than $q°$.

   In this latter case, A is called a "regressive factor." It is not difficult to give an economic interpretation of the seemingly paradoxical result, however. Think of A as a factor particularly specialized to and useful for small-scale production, for example, skilled craftsmen. If the price of skilled craftsmen falls, it may pay a firm to shift away from a large-scale mass production technique so as to earn more profit with smaller output—by making better use of the now cheaply available craft skills.

> CONCLUSION: A change in factor price leads to a substitution effect and a scale effect upon factor employment and firm output. The substitution effect is *always* in the normal direction: more of the now relatively cheaper factor will be used. The scale effect of a fall in factor

price is normally to increase output, and of a rise in factor price to decrease output. But in the case of a "regressive" factor, the scale effect is reversed; cheapening of a factor *may* lead to smaller output.

11.B.5 □Firm's Demand for Factors

In the single-factor situation, the firm's demand curve for the variable factor was given by its Marginal Revenue Product curve *mrp*.[18] In the multi-factor analysis, the firm's demand curve for any of the variable factors still depends upon the Marginal Revenue Product of that factor. However, it is necessary now to take account of the interaction among the factor Marginal Products associated with the concept of complementarity.

In deriving the demand curve for either of two variable factors, for example factor A, we will suppose that the firm is at an initial position where the Factor Employment Conditions in equations (11.19) are all met. In Figure 11.16, point G is supposed to represent such a position. At the initial hire-price h_a°, employment of factor A is the amount a° such that $mrp_a(b = b^\circ) = h_a^\circ$. (The expression on the left-hand side represents the Marginal Revenue Product for A as measured along the particular mrp_a curve associated with the amount b° of factor B.) It is understood that, correspondingly, employment $b = b^\circ$ of the other factor B is also such that $mrp_b(a = a^\circ) = h_b^\circ$.

Now let the hire-price h_a fall from h_a° to the level h_a'. If the quantity of the other factor B remained unchanged, the firm would find it advantageous to employ $a = \hat{a}$ units of factor A since, at that level of employment, $mrp_a(b = b^\circ) = h_a'$. But now we must allow for the complementarity effects. Suppose that factors A and B are actually complementary. Analysis of the interaction proceeds as follows. Let price h_a° fall to h_a', leading to an initial employment expansion from a° to $\hat{a}$ as just indicated. But this is not the full adjustment. The condition $mrp_b = h_b$ for the *other* factor B is now violated—since the increased employment of A will, assuming complementarity, have shifted the entire mrp_b curve upward. A corresponding diagram for factor B would show that such an upward shift dictates more employment of factor B as well. When the secondary adjustment of factor B's employment is made, mrp_a will now in turn shift upward, and so on. This reciprocal interaction must have a limit, however. That is, there must be some increased employment of *both* factors such as to restore the equalities (11.19). The restored equalities can be expressed more explicitly as:

$$\begin{cases} mrp_a(b = b') = h_a' \\ mrp_b(a = a') = h_b^\circ \end{cases}$$

Note that the hire-price of B is still at its original level; only the price of factor A has changed.

The upshot is that the firm's demand curve for factor A is related in a somewhat more complex way to the mrp_a curves than in the case where A was the

[18]More precisely, by a portion of the downward-sloping branch of the *mrp* curve, as explained above.

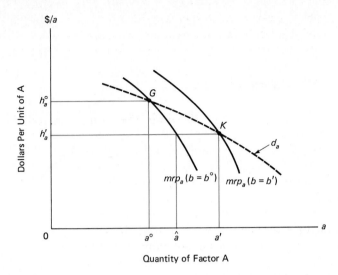

$/a

Dollars Per Unit of A

h_a°

h_a'

G

K

d_a

$mrp_a(b = b^\circ)$ $mrp_a(b = b')$

0   a° $\hat{a}$ a' a

Quantity of Factor A

FIGURE 11.16   Firm's Demand Curve for Factor A.   At the initial hire-price h_a it is supposed that the Factor Employment Conditions (11.19) are met by employments $a = a^\circ$ and $b = b^\circ$. Thus $mrp_a(b = b^\circ)$ equals h_a° at G—providing one point along the firm's demand curve for factor A. If the hire-price of A falls to h_a', increased employment of A in the amount $\hat{a}$ would be indicated by a movement along $mrp_a(b = b^\circ)$. But this movement throws the employment condition for factor B out of equality, if there is any complementarity (or anti-complementarity) between A and B. Restoring the equality for factor B will then (regardless of whether the interaction is complementary or anti-complementary) raise the Marginal Product of factor A. The conditions in equations (11.19) can only be re-established at a point like K, where h_a' is set equal to $mrp_a(b = b')$—with b' representing the adjusted amount of the *other* factor. The firm's demand curve d_a for factor A is therefore flatter than the general slope of the mrp_a curves, wherever there is a complementary (or anti-complementary) interaction between the factors.

only variable factor. In Figure 11.16 the demand curve goes through points like G (showing employment of a° at price h_a°) and K (showing employment of a' at price h_a').

If the factors are *independent* rather than *complementary* in production, however, the interaction effect disappears. Given an initial adjustment from a° to $\hat{a}$ along the mrp_a curve in response to a fall in price from h_a° to h_a', the condition $mrp_b = h_b$ for the *other* factor B is in no way disturbed. The initial adjustment is then the full adjustment. The initial mrp_a curve remains the firm's demand curve for factor A, as in the case of a single variable factor. Putting it more generally: In the case of productive *independence* between factors, each factor's family of mrp curves coalesces into a single mrp curve that is not affected by the employment of the other factor.

What about "anti-complementary" factors? Intuition might suggest that if the firm's demand curve for factor A is *flatter* than the mrp_a curves in the complementary case and is *the same* as the (unique) mrp_a curve in the intermediate independent case, then it should be *steeper* than the mrp_a curves in the anti-complementary case. *This is incorrect!* In the anti-complementary as in the normal complementary case, the firm's demand curve for factor is *flatter* than the mrp curves, as illustrated in Figure 11.16. [The student can verify this, making use of equations (11.19) in parallel with the argument used for the case of complementarity. *Hint:* After the initial adjustment from $a°$ to $\hat{a}$, do the mrp_b curves shift up or down? What is the direction of the secondary effect upon the employment of B? How does that secondary effect further react upon the mrp_a curves?][19]

> CONCLUSION: Given complementarity or anti-complementarity between factors, the demand curve for any factor is flatter (more elastic) than the Marginal Revenue Product curves. One implication is that employment of a variable factor tends to be more sensitive to price changes in the *long run,* when the amounts of the "fixed" factors can be varied. ∎

11.C
INDUSTRY DEMAND FOR FACTORS

In proceeding from the *firm's* demand to the *industry's* demand for a factor of production, we can begin with the simple case of a single variable factor as in Section A.

First, consider the demand of a *monopolized* industry (i.e., an industry composed of a single seller in the product market) for a factor A. Evidently, the industry demand will be identical with the demand of the monopolist firm itself. The demand curve d_a of Figure 11.4 then becomes without further change the factor demand curve of the monopolized industry. (Where more than one factor is considered to be variable, it is the demand curve d_a of Figure 11.16 that is relevant.)

If the industry consists of a large number of *competitive* producers in the product market, however, there is a complication. The two panels of Figure 11.17 show a typical firm and then the competitive industry as a whole. Suppose an initial equilibrium exists at factor price $h_a = h_a°$ and product price $P = P°$. The firm's demand curve, derived from its curve of Marginal Revenue Product mrp_a (in this competitive case, identical with the firm's Value of Marginal Product vmp_a), is shown in Panel (a) as the curve labeled $d_a(P = P°)$. Along the $d_a(P = P°)$ curve, $a°$ is the indicated employment of factor A. For the industry as a whole, we can sum these firm demand curves horizontally so as to obtain the curve labeled $\Sigma d_a(P = P°)$. At the initial factor price $h_a°$, this horizontal summation curve shows industry employment $A° = \Sigma a°$ of the factor (at point K).

Now let factor price fall to h_a'. In Panel (a) the firm will first move along the initial demand curve, $d_a(P = P°)$, to employment level $\hat{a}$ of factor A. The corresponding industry-wide movement in Panel (b) would be to the aggregate employment level $\hat{A}$ (point N). But this is not the full solution. The increased

---

[19]A direct implication is that there cannot be a "Giffen factor"—that is, a factor whose demand curve has positive rather than negative slope. (Compare the discussion of possible "Giffen consumption goods" in Chapters 4 and 5.) We know that, in the range of relevant economic interest, Marginal Product must be declining (the Law of Diminishing Marginal Returns), which implies that the curve of Marginal Revenue Product must have negative slope. But the demand curve d_a is, if anything, even flatter than the mrp_a curves; there is no possibility of its becoming so steep as to eventually "curl back."

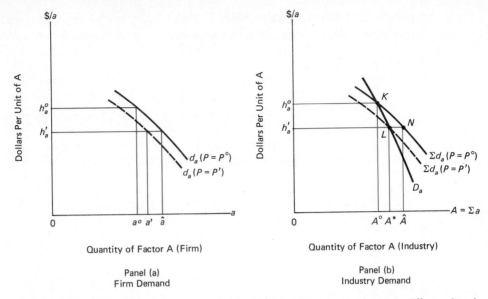

FIGURE 11.17   Demand for Factor: Competitive Firm and Industry, Product-Price Effect.   Panel (a) pictures a firm's demand for factor A; Panel (b) pictures industry demand. At an initial factor hire-price h_a^o, position K in Panel (b) represents a point on the industry demand curve for A associated with a product price P^o. This product price is regarded by the firm as fixed, as indicated by the associated (solid) firm demand curve $d_a(P = P^o)$ in Panel (a). In Panel (b) the solid curve $\Sigma d_a(P = P^o)$ is the horizontal summation of these firm demand curves. When factor price falls to h_a', the firm aims to expand production from a^o to $\hat{a}$—the corresponding industry-wide summations in Panel (b) being A^o and $\hat{A}$. But as employment of A expands, industry-wide output Q also tends to rise, driving down product price to some level P'. Thus the firm's demand curve will fall to a position like the (dashed) curve $d_a(P = P')$ in Panel (a); the dashed summation curve in Panel (b) will move similarly. The consequence is that the new point on the industry factor demand curve in Panel (b) will be L. Thus, the product-price effect tends to make the industry demand curve for a factor relatively inelastic.

employment of factor A will normally entail increased firm output q. Correspondingly, the industry as a whole will expand its aggregate output Q. Given a normally downward-sloping consumers' demand curve for good Q, the rise in output will necessitate a fall in product price P. And since $vmp_a \equiv P(mp_a)$, each firm will observe a downward shift of the overall position of its d_a curve taking place.

After taking the product-price effect into account, the factor demands of the firm and industry at the new factor price h_a' are illustrated by the dashed curves in the two panels of Figure 11.17. Here *product* price P has fallen to the level P'. The firm operates along the lower (dashed) factor demand curve labeled $d_a(P = P')$ to employ a' units of factor A. The industry correspondingly employs A' units in the aggregate, at point L on the horizontal summation curve $\Sigma d_a(P = P')$. The precise amount that product price must fall is determined, of course, by the elasticity of the consumers' demand for the increased output of Q. The true industry demand curve for factor A is illustrated in Panel (b) by the bold curve D_a that cuts through points K and L on the two different horizontal-summation curves.

Exercise 11.6: With production function $q = 2\sqrt{a}$ and product price $P = 60$, the price-taking firm's demand equation for factor A was found in a previous Exercise to be $h_a = 60/\sqrt{a}$. Suppose that the industry consists of 1000 identical such firms, and that the industry demand curve for product Q is given by the equation $P = 90 - Q/1000$. (a) What is the equation corresponding to the curve labeled $\Sigma d_a(P = P°)$ in Figure 11.17? (b) What is the industry demand equation D_a for factor A?

Answer: (a) The individual firm's factor-demand equation, when $P = P° = 60$, can be rewritten as $a = 3600/h_a^2$. Then industry employment for 1000 identical firms, when $P = 60$, must be $A \equiv 1000a = 3,600,000/h_a^2$. (b) Now allowing for the variation of product price with industry output, since $Q \equiv 1000q$ the industry's demand curve for product can be written $P = 90 - q$. And we know from an earlier Exercise that $mp_a = 1/\sqrt{a}$. Since each price-taking firm sets $vmp_a \equiv P(mp_a) = h_a$, we have $(90 - q)(1/\sqrt{a}) = h_a$. But $q = 2\sqrt{a}$, and so $(90 - 2\sqrt{a})(1/\sqrt{a}) = 90/\sqrt{a} - 2 = h_a$. Then, since $A \equiv 1000a$, the industry's demand equation for factor A can be written $A = 8,100,000/(h_a + 2)^2$.

What if there are other variable factors? As employment of A expands in response to a fall in its hire-price h_a, in the normal complementarity case the industry will be attempting also to increase use of other factors $B, C, \ldots$. But the consequence on the industry level will be that the hire-prices $h_b, h_c, \ldots$ will tend to *rise;* therefore, employment of these cooperating factors will not increase as much as would otherwise have been the case. And so the demand for factor A will not benefit as much from complementarity as the picture in Figure 11.16 might suggest. The complementary-factor-price effect therefore reinforces the product-price effect in tending to make industry demand D_a for factor A steeper (less elastic).

One other consideration has not yet been taken into account. Given a reduction in the hire-price of factor A, production becomes more profitable so that *new firms will tend to enter* the industry. Therefore, in Panel (b) of Figure 11.17 the *number* of firms over which the summation is taken in the lower (dashed) summation curve $\Sigma d_a(P = P')$ will tend to exceed the number of firms relevant for the (solid) summation curve $\Sigma d_a(P = P°)$. The effect of entry (or of exit, if a rise rather than a fall in h_a were to take place) considered alone would tend to make the dashed summation curve in Panel (b) of the diagram lie *above* rather than below the solid summation curve.

Weighing the counterbalancing considerations, in general we cannot say which way the final result will go. If the product-price effect is very big (if consumer demand for the industry's product is quite inelastic, so that P falls sharply when industry output rises) then the entry–exit effect tends to be small— few new firms will be induced to enter. Then the D_a curve will tend to be steeper than the summation curves, Σd_a, as pictured in Figure 11.17. But if the product-price effect is small (if consumer demand for Q is quite elastic so that P falls very little), the fall in h_a will bring about a sharp rise in profits. This will tend to induce considerable new entry, and thus to reverse the situation pictured in the diagram—the D_a curve would be flatter than the summation curves. With several variable factors, the analog of a big product-price effect would be a big complementary-factor-price effect—if the supply curves of the cooperating factors are highly inelastic, h_b, h_c, . . . will tend to rise sharply. As in the case of the product-price effect, a big factor-price effect tends to reduce the entry incentive for new firms.

> CONCLUSION: The industry's demand curve for a factor A tends to be steeper (less elastic) than the horizontal-summation curves that represent the aggregate of firms' factor demand curves for A: (1) when the consumers' demand curve for the industry's product is highly inelastic (strong product-price effect), and (2) when the supply curves of other factors B, C, . . . complementary to A are highly inelastic (strong factor-price effect). If consumer demands and cooperating-factor supplies are highly elastic, on the other hand, the product-price effect and factor-price effect will be weak, inducing a strong entry–exit effect tending to make the industry's demand curve for factor A more highly elastic.

11.D
MONOPSONY IN THE FACTOR MARKET

The analysis so far has allowed for the possibility of monopoly power in the *product* market, while assuming competitive conditions (price-taking behavior) on both sides of the *factor* market. The possibility of monopoly *on the supply side* of the factor market will be considered in the next chapter. Here we turn to the analysis of a single buyer or "monopsonist" *on the demand side* of the factor market.

The situation of such a monopsonist is illustrated in Figure 11.18. The worth of incremental units of factor A to the firm is indicated, as before, by the

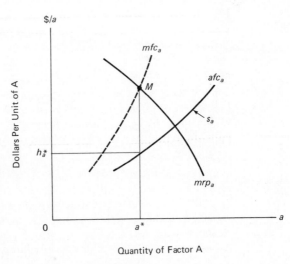

FIGURE 11.18 Monopsony in the Factor Market. The rising supply curve of A to the firm, s_a, is also a curve of Average Factor Cost afc_a. The curve of Marginal Factor Cost mfc_a will then lie above afc_a, as shown here. The optimum factor employment for the firm is a^*, where the mfc_a and mrp_a curves intersect (point M). The associated hire-price h_a^* is the price along the s_a curve at this level of employment.

curve of Marginal Revenue Product mrp_a. But the monopsonist firm recognizes that the supply curve of factor that it faces is upward-sloping (rather than effectively horizontal as in Figures 11.3 and 11.4). The firm is so large an employer of factor A that its own decisions to hire more or fewer units drive the price h_a up or down.

Recall that $C_a \equiv h_a a$ is the total expenditure of the firm in hiring factor A. The supply curve s_a is a curve of Average Factor Cost afc_a, since $h_a \equiv C_a/a$ is the average amount that must be paid to hire any specified number of units of factor A. The *additional* expense incurred by the firm in hiring an incremental unit of factor A is its *Marginal* Factor Cost $mfc_a \equiv \Delta C_a/\Delta a$.

When the supply curve s_a, or equivalently the Average Factor Cost afc_a, is horizontal, the curve of Marginal Factor Cost mfc_a coincides with it at the level of the given market hire-price h_a. But here the afc_a curve is a rising function of factor quantity. Therefore the mfc_a curve must lie above it (Proposition 2.2b).

More explicitly, the increment of expense due to hiring an additional unit of factor is the sum of two elements: h_a is the payment to the additional unit of factor itself, and $a \Delta h_a$ is the expense due to the increased price paid to all units previously employed.

(11.20)
$$mfc_a \equiv \frac{\Delta C_a}{\Delta a} \equiv h_a + a\frac{\Delta h_a}{\Delta a}$$

Here the rising supply curve means that $\Delta h_a/\Delta a$ is positive in sign, thus verifying that $mfc_a > h_a \equiv afc_a$.

For any factor A, the monopsonist firm maximizes profit by equalizing the marginal benefit and the marginal expense of hiring A.

(11.21) $mrp_a = mfc_a$ Factor Employment Condition, Monopsony Firm

In Figure 11.18 this equality is found at employment level $a*$. The firm will then pay the factor price h_a^* required to elicit this quantity of factor, as indicated by the height of the supply curve s_a at $a = a*$. Note that h_a^* lies *below* the intersection of mrp_a and mfc_a at point M in the diagram.

Exercise 11.7:   Suppose that the firm described in Exercise 11.4, with production function $q = 2\sqrt{a}$, not only has monopoly power in its product market (faces demand curve $P = 90 - q$) but also has monopsony power in the factor market. Specifically, let the supply curve of factor A to the firm be $h_a = 1 + a/75$. What is the profit-maximizing solution for employment of input and production of output?

Answer: The firm will set $mrp_a \equiv MR\,(mp_a) = mfc_a$. Marginal Revenue is $MR = 90 - 2q$, and Marginal Product here is $mp_a = 1/\sqrt{a}$. With a linear factor supply curve, it can be verified that the curve of Marginal Factor cost is also linear and rises twice as fast. Thus, $mfc_a = 1 + 2a/75$. The condition $mrp_a = mfc_a$ can then be expressed either in terms of the variable q or the variable a. Either way, a cubic equation is obtained. Working for convenience in terms of q, the equation becomes $(90 - 2q)(2/q) = 1 + (q^2/2)/75$, which reduces to $q^3 + 750q = 27,000$. The solution is $q* = 21.9$, which implies $a* = 120.2$.

EXAMPLE 11.5
Monopsony in Professional Baseball

The leading (and perhaps the only important) example of labor-market monopsony exists in the realm of professional sports. Here a legal quirk, perhaps based upon the idea that sports are play (a "pastime") rather than a business, has permitted the organization of buyers' cartels with respect to employment of players. The most important cartel instrument is the "reserve clause," which (with certain exceptions) makes the player the exclusive property of the team that first signs him up, or to which he is "traded" thereafter. Should a player refuse to accept the wage offer of the team whose property he is, he cannot play for any other team in the cartel.

Gerald W. Scully investigated the effect of the reserve clause in major league baseball. He anticipated that the buyers' cartel would cause a divergence between Marginal Revenue Product *mrp* and wage (see Figure 11.18).

But first, differences in player *quality* (i.e., in *mrp*) had to be allowed for. Using 1968 and 1969 data, Scully estimated the "gross" *mrp* in terms of the player's effect on gate receipts and broadcast revenues. Deducting related expenses, and in particular player development costs, led to estimates of "net" *mrp* for players of different qualities. Since substantial player development costs, on the order of $300,000, are incurred before it is known how successful the athlete will be, it sometimes happens that net *mrp* turns out to be negative. On the average, however, in a competitive situation wages should be equal to net *mrp*. If the actual structure is one of monopsony, on the other hand, wages on the average would fall short of net *mrp*.

The Table shows some of Scully's results. For batters and pitchers falling into different quality groups, net *mrp* and average salary are compared. While for "mediocre" players salary is above net *mrp*—and indeed, the latter is actually negative—for "average" and "star" players, net *mrp* far exceeds salary. Thus, on balance there is considerable evidence of monopsony power.

Quality versus Pay of Baseball Players

	QUALITY GROUP	NET mrp	SALARY
Hitters	Mediocre	$-30,000	$17,200
	Average	128,300	29,100
	Star	319,000	52,100
Pitchers	Mediocre	-10,600	15,700
	Average	159,600	33,000
	Star	405,300	66,800

Source: G. W. Scully, "Pay and Performance in Major League Baseball," *American Economic Review*, v. 64 (Dec. 1974), p. 928.

COMMENT: Contrary to common opinion among fans and sports writers, star players are not "overpaid." In fact, they receive far less than their economic worth. Since the time of Scully's study, the "reserve clause" in professional sports has been substantially weakened. And in consequence, as would be expected, stars' salaries have tended to rise.

Having to allow for the effects upon factor demand of both product-market structure and factor-market structure has made for a relatively intricate analysis. Table 11.1 provides a compact summary of the main results. (But recall that these market-structure combinations refer only to *the demand side* of the factor market; monopoly in the *supply* of resources will be taken up in the chapter following.)

The Table shows, for each market-structure combination, the associated forms of the Factor Employment Condition (best amount of input to hire) and the Optimal Output Condition (best amount of product to sell). Of course, as has been shown above, these two conditions are equivalent: the best amount of factors to employ must generate the most profitable level of output to produce. The *general* result, which allows for the possibility of both monopoly power in the product market and monopsony power in the factor market, is the pair of conditions in the upper-left corner of the Table: $MC = MR$ and $mfc = mrp$. There are two limiting cases: (1) absent monopoly power in the *product* market, $MR \equiv AR \equiv P$ so that the two conditions can be rewritten in a more special form as $MC = MR \equiv P$ and $mfc = mrp \equiv vmp$ (right-hand column of the Table); (2) absent monopsony power in the *factor* market, $mfc \equiv afc \equiv h$ so that the Factor Employment Condition can be rewritten as $h \equiv mfc = mrp$ (lower row of the Table).

TABLE 11.1

Factor Employment and Optimal Output Conditions

FACTOR MARKET STRUCTURE	PRODUCT MARKET STRUCTURE	
	Monopolist	Price-taker
Monopsonist	$\begin{cases} mfc = mrp \\ MC = MR \end{cases}$	$\begin{cases} mfc = mrp \equiv vmp \\ MC = MR \equiv P \end{cases}$
Price-taker	$\begin{cases} h = mfc = mrp \\ MC = MR \end{cases}$	$\begin{cases} h = mfc = mrp \equiv vmp \\ MC = MR \equiv P \end{cases}$

11.E
AN APPLICATION: MINIMUM-WAGE LAWS

Two economic models are in contention for explaining or predicting the consequences of minimum-wage legislation: the *competitive-market model* versus the *monopsony-market model*.

The competitive model is illustrated in Figure 11.19. The commodity is a certain grade or class of labor L, whose hire-price is the wage rate w. A competitive equilibrium exists at wage w_c and employment L_c. Now a legal minimum

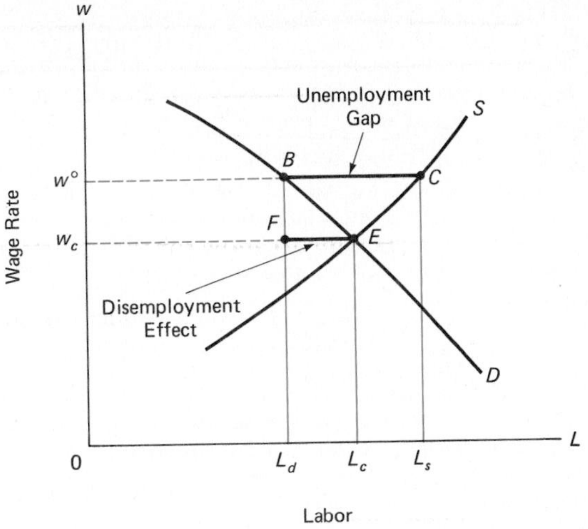

FIGURE 11.19 Minimum Wage: Competitive Model.
The competitive equilibrium at point E is associated with wage w_c and employment L_c. If a wage floor or minimum wage were imposed at the level $w°$, employment would fall to L_d. The quantity FE is the "disemployment effect." At the higher wage there would be L_s units of labor seeking employment, so the perceived "unemployment gap" would be the larger quantity BC.

wage $w°$ is imposed, at a level higher than w_c.[20] At wage $w°$ the labor offered on the market is the quantity L_s but the labor demanded is only L_d. The perceived *unemployment gap* at the legal wage is the quantity BC or $L_s - L_d$. However, the *disemployment effect* actually due to the wage floor is the somewhat lesser quantity FE or $L_c - L_d$. Analysts using the competitive-market model would clearly predict some degree of *disemployment* and a larger degree of *unemployment,* as a result of imposition of a minimum wage higher than the pre-existing market equilibrium wage.

The monopsony model leads to rather different implications, illustrated in Figure 11.20. The pre-existing situation has employment L_m (at the intersection of the *mrp* and *mfc* curves); the wage $w_m < mrp$ is determined along the labor supply curve S. With the introduction of an effective minimum-wage law, *the market supply curve is replaced by a horizontal line at the level of the imposed minimum wage* (in the range where the market supply curve S lies below the level of the minimum wage). That is, the monopsonist employer is *forced to be a price-taker* at the minimum wage, wherever the market supply conditions would otherwise have permitted establishing a monopsony hire-price lower than the legally imposed floor.

Three classes of possibilities are illustrated in Figure 11.20. First, suppose that the minimum wage is only a little higher than w_m, for example w' in the diagram. Then the *effective* supply curve to the firm is horizontal at the level w' until the S curve is reached at point N. In this range the Marginal Factor Cost *mfc* also equals w'. If the firm could actually hire as many units as desired at wage w', it would employ the quantity associated with point G, where $w' = mrp$. But this is not possible. Beyond point N, the effective supply curve of labor to the firm rejoins the original S curve; the laborers are not willing to supply more than L' units at wage w'. It follows also that, beyond employment L', the effective Marginal Factor Cost leaps upward discontinuously to rejoin the original *mfc* curve

[20]A legal minimum wage *lower* than w_c would clearly be without effect.

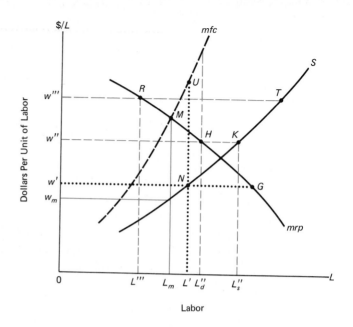

FIGURE 11.20 Minimum Wage: Monopsony Model. Under monopsony, the optimality condition $mfc = mrp$ determines the wage w_m at employment L_m. At a relatively low imposed minimum wage w', the optimality condition is satisfied at employment L'—both wage and employment rise slightly. At an intermediate imposed wage w'', the optimal employment is L''_d. Here there is a considerable increase in both wage and employment; nevertheless, a perceived "unemployment gap" HK arises, since at wage w'' the offered employment has increased to L''_s. At the high imposed minimum wage w''' the wage has risen even further, but now employment falls (to L''')—as in the competitive model of the preceding diagram.

(at point U). Since the *mrp* curve in the diagram passes through this vertical discontinuity of the *mfc* curve, the firm will find it optimal to employ L' workers at wage w'. Note that, relative to L_m, the minimum-wage law here has *increased* employment! Nor is there any perceived unemployment at the legally imposed wage.

Now consider a somewhat higher minimum wage, w''. At this wage the firm would again be forced to be a price-taker, and would not want to employ more than L''_d units (at point H), using the condition $w'' = mrp$. This employment is also greater than the L_m of the unregulated monopsony solution; no *disemployment* takes place. However, at wage w'' some *unemployment* will be perceived. At the w'' wage the offered labor supply would be L''_s, which is more than the firm wants to hire. The resulting unemployment gap is indicated by the distance HK in the diagram.

Finally, w''' represents a still higher minimum wage, higher than the level at which the *mrp* and *mfc* curves intersect. Here the effective employment would be reduced to L'''. Thus, a minimum wage as high as w''' would lead to the same qualitative implications as in the competitive-market model. With this high wage there would be some *disemployment* as compared with L_m, and a large *unemployment* gap represented by the distance RT in the diagram.

CONCLUSION: The competitive-market model unambiguously implies both disemployment (less L employed) and unemployment (a supply-demand gap) as a result of any imposed minimum wage higher than the unregulated equilibrium. The monopsony-market model has three possible outcomes: (1) At a relatively low minimum wage w', employment *increases* and there is no perceived unemployment. (2) At an intermediate minimum wage w'', employment increases but there is also some unemployment. (3) At a relatively high minimum wage w''', there is both disemployment and considerable unemployment.

Which of these models is the more relevant? That is an empirical question which has been investigated by a number of economists.

In determining the effects of minimum-wage legislation upon wages and employment, it is essential to appreciate that there is a spectrum of labor skill and quality. Some workers will already be earning more than the imposed minimum and others less. Under any market model, minimum-wage laws will have quite different impacts upon high-wage and low-wage workers.

Using the *competitive* model, low-skilled (low-wage) workers would be affected as in Figure 11.19. Their wage rates would rise, but some workers would find themselves disemployed. For higher-skilled workers, in contrast, the equilibrium wage level is likely to be already above the imposed minimum wage—so no direct impact is to be expected. If the *monopsony* model of Figure 11.20 were valid, on the other hand, a more complex set of observations would be anticipated: (1) For very low-skilled workers the imposed minimum wage would be effectively at a high level, like w''' in Figure 11.20—so higher wages but lesser employment would be expected. (2) For medium-skilled workers, the w'' picture might be appropriate—*both* wage rate and employment might increase. (3) For quite high-skilled workers, the imposed minimum wage would be relatively low, even lower than w' in Figure 11.20—little or no direct effect on wages or employment would be anticipated.

EXAMPLE 11.6
Minimum-Wage Legislation

An early study by A. F. Hinrichs[a] classified plants in the seamless hosiery industry by wage group. It was found that, after imposition of the 25-cent minimum wage in October 1938, low-wage plants had a relatively greater loss in employment (and a relatively greater rise in average hourly earnings) than high-wage plants. Indeed, despite generally improving business conditions, the lowest-wage plants suffered an *absolute* loss in employment. A more extensive study by J. M. Peterson[b] confirmed Hinrichs' results as to the seamless hosiery industry, and showed a similar picture for Southern sawmills and for men's cotton garments, over several steps of minimum-wage increases between 1938 and 1950. The pattern was consistent, in that in each case low-wage plants lost relatively more in employment while paying a relatively greater wage increment. In addition, Peterson showed a relative loss in employment position for low-wage versus high-wage *cities,* and a *regional* tendency of industry to shift away from the low-wage South. The regional effect

[a] A. F. Hinrichs, "Effects of the 25-Cent Minimum Wage on Employment in the Seamless Hosiery Industry," *Journal of the American Statistical Association,* v. 35 (March 1940).
[b] J. M. Peterson, "Employment Effects of Minimum Wages, 1938–50," *Journal of Political Economy,* v. 65 (Oct. 1957).

was emphasized in a study by M. R. Colberg,[c] who examined the impact of the 1957 $1.00 minimum-wage law upon high-wage and low-wage *counties* in Florida. The law was found to have caused a relative decrease in employment in low-wage counties.

A number of recent studies have directed attention specifically to low-wage *workers*, and particularly to the effects of minimum-wage laws on *teenagers*. In general, teenagers are relatively lacking in the skills and experience necessary to earn high wages. Hence a large fraction of them are likely to be in the position where a uniform legal minimum wage is higher than their equilibrium market wage. Under the competitive model, in consequence, a relatively large disemployment effect upon teenagers would be anticipated. A study by Y. Brozen[d] found that successive increases in the legal minimum wage were indeed reflected by rises in the teenage unemployment rate. But as productivity and inflation progressed over time, the equilibrium wage for teenagers tended to "catch up" with the legally fixed minimum so as to erode the disemployment effect, until the next round of minimum-wage legislation began the cycle over again.

A sophisticated statistical regression analysis over the period 1954–68 by T. G. Moore allowed not only for the *level* of the minimum wage but also for *coverage* of the labor force (since, over time, not only level but coverage has tended to increase). Some of Moore's results are shown in the following Table.

Effect of Minimum Wage upon Younger Age-Group Unemployment

	DETERMINING VARIABLES	
UNEMPLOYMENT RATE OF:	Employed Workers Covered by Minimum Wage (%)	Minimum Wage as Proportion of Hourly Earnings
Nonwhites, 16–19	0.2549	1.75927
Whites, 16–19	0.077	0.58461
Males, 16–19	0.080	0.61649
Females, 16–19	0.171	0.73988
Males, 20–24	0.063	0.05346

Source: T. G. Moore, "The Effect of Minimum Wages on Teenage Unemployment Rates," *Journal of Political Economy*, v. 79 (July/Aug. 1971), p. 901

The data in the Table may be interpreted as follows, using the first row as an example. The unemployment rate of nonwhites aged 16–19: (1) increased 0.2549% for each percent rise in the *coverage* of the minimum-wage law, and (2) increased 1.75927% for each percent increase in the *ratio* of the legal minimum wage to the average hourly earnings of production workers in

[c] M. R. Colberg, "Minimum Wage Effects on Florida's Economic Development," *Journal of Law and Economics*, v. 3 (Oct. 1960).

[d] Y. Brozen, "The Effect of Statutory Minimum Wage Increases on Teen-Age Unemployment," *Journal of Law and Economics*, v. 12 (April 1969).

private nonagricultural employment. Note that males aged 20–24, above the teenage category, were *not* substantially affected by the minimum-wage legislation (bottom row).

> COMMENT: All these studies provide solid confirmation for the predictions of the competitive model of Figure 11.19. The monopsony model of Figure 11.20, being consistent with a variety of outcomes, is not conclusively refuted by these results. However, none of the studies shows any hint of the *favorable* effect of a minimum-wage law on employment of some middle-quality workers that would be anticipated on the basis of the monopsony model.

Regardless of economic impact, minimum-wage legislation must have satisfied some criteria of *political* effectiveness to have become so important a feature of the economic situation. The supposed "beneficiaries"—low-wage workers previously receiving less than the minimum wage (largely teenagers and "minorities")—incur mixed consequences from such legislation. While many of them will indeed receive a wage increase, a good proportion are likely to end up disemployed. The most significant political pressure for higher minimum wages seems to come not from the "beneficiaries" but from organized labor, in particular the AFL–CIO. Few of the relatively high-paid workers represented by the AFL–CIO are in the directly impacted group that would otherwise be receiving less than the minimum wage. For such skilled high-wage workers an increased minimum wage may, however, represent an indirect kind of benefit. A higher minimum wage raises the cost to employers of hiring unskilled relative to skilled workers. The consequence is to induce firms to employ fewer of the unskilled workers, raising relative demand for the skilled workers represented by the AFL–CIO. [*Query:* An imposed minimum wage making low-skilled labor more expensive would clearly raise *relative* demand for high-skilled workers, but can we be sure that actual overall demand for high-skilled labor would rise? Does the answer depend upon the presence or absence of complementarity between high-skilled and low-skilled workers?]

☐ SUMMARY OF CHAPTER 11

This chapter deals with the demand for factors of production. A key theme is that the optimal *output* decision on the one hand (studied in Chapter 6 for the competitive firm and in Chapter 8 for the monopoly firm), and on the other hand the optimal *input* decision examined here, are logically interconnected rather than independent choices.

The profit-maximizing Factor Employment Conditions for the firm depend upon *market structure*—both in the product market (whether the firm is a price-taker or else has monopoly power with regard to the output commodity) and in the factor market (whether the firm is a price-taker or else has "monopsony" power with regard to the input commodity).

The Factor Employment Condition for a single variable factor A, in most general form, is:

$$mfc_a = mrp_a$$

That is, the firm sets the Marginal Factor cost mfc_a of hiring another unit of A equal to the Marginal Revenue Product mrp_a. In the special case where the firm is a *product-market* price-taker, vmp_a (Value of the Marginal Product) can be substituted for mrp_a on the right-hand side of the Factor Employment Condition. [Since Marginal Revenue MR equals price P for a product-market price-taker, $mrp_a \equiv MR(mp_a)$ equals $vmp_a \equiv P(mp_a)$.] In the special case where the firm is a *factor-market* price-taker, the hire-price h_a can be substituted for mfc_a on the left-hand side of the Factor Employment Condition. (Since $mfc_a \equiv h_a + a$ $\Delta h_a / \Delta a$, it follows that if h_a is constant then $mfc_a = h_a$.)

If the firm is a price-taker in the factor market, its demand curve for factor A is simply the downward-sloping branch of the mrp_a curve. From the definition of Marginal Revenue Product, it is evident that factor demand depends upon the marginal physical productivity of the factor (mp_a) and upon the value to the firm of the additional output produced (MR).

If there are several variable factors, productive interdependencies among them must also be taken into account. With just two factors A and B, the Factor Employment Conditions (for a factor-price-taking firm) are:

$$\begin{cases} h_a = mrp_a \\ h_b = mrp_b \end{cases}$$

The productive interdependence between A and B is called *complementary* if an increase in employment of either raises the Marginal Product of the other, and *anti-complementary* if the reverse holds. Complementarity is the normal case. (If there is no interdependence, the factors are called *independent* in production.) Any productive interdependence, whether complementary or anti-complementary, tends to make the firm's demand curve for either factor more elastic.

As factor prices shift, there will be both a *substitution effect* and a *scale effect* upon factor employment. The substitution effect, considered alone, dictates increased employment of the relatively cheapened factor and decreased employment of the other. For a fall in a hire-price h_a, the scale effect (due to increased firm output) will normally increase employment of the cheapened factor A further. (But a "regressive" case is possible, in which cheapening of a factor leads to a reduction in the optimal output.)

The competitive *industry's* demand for a factor is, to a first approximation, the summation of the member firms' demands. But there are several complications. As the hire-price h_a falls, the industry tends to expand employment of A and thus (apart from the regressive case) also its output Q. The effect will be to lower product price P, and therefore to reduce the degree of industry response to changes in h_a (i.e., to make the industry demand for A more inelastic). Similarly, induced changes in prices of related factors h_b, h_c, . . . also tend to reduce industry response to changes in h_a. But there is one important consideration cutting the other way. A reduction in h_a will make the industry more profitable and thus induce entry. The entry–exit effect tends to make the industry demand for a factor *more* elastic.

Summing up: Demand for a factor *A* tends to be *greater*: (1) where the employers are product-market competitors rather than monopolists, and are factor-market price-takers rather than monopsonists; (2) where the physical Marginal Product mp_a is high; and (3) where the additional output produced by employing *A* is highly valued by consumers. Demand for *A* tends to be *more elastic*: (1) the more elastic is the consumers' demand for the output; (2) the less powerfully the Law of Diminishing Returns operates as employment of *A* increases; (3) the greater the normal productive interdependence (complementarity) between *A* and other factors; (4) the more elastic is the supply of these complementary factors; and (5) the greater the exit–entry effect as the hire-price h_a changes.

□ QUESTIONS FOR CHAPTER 11

MAINLY FOR REVIEW

R1. Distinguish the *productivity* and the *revenue* considerations entering into a firm's demand for a factor.

*R2. Does the curve of Marginal Revenue Product for factor *A*, mrp_a, necessarily lie below (to the left of) the curve of Value of the Marginal Product, vmp_a? Explain. Which is the firm's demand curve for factor *A*?

R3. Why is $mrp_a = h_a$ the Factor Employment Condition for a price-taking firm in the *factor* market? What if the firm is not a price-taker in the *product* market? Is this condition sufficient, or are there other subsidiary conditions that must be met?

*R4. Is it ever rational to employ so much of a factor as to be in the region of diminishing marginal returns? In the region of diminishing average returns? In the region of diminishing total returns?

*R5. With two factors *A* and *B*, explain why the conditions $mrp_a = h_a$ and $mrp_b = h_b$ lead not only to the choice of optimal factor proportions but also to the optimal *scale* of output.

*R6. With two factors of production, is the slope of the output isoquant equal (in absolute value) to the ratio of the Marginal Products? Explain. Interpret the absolute slope of the *cost* isoquant as a ratio.

R7. Explain why, if two factors are complementary, the demand curve for either is flatter than its *mrp* curves. What if the factors are anti-complementary?

*R8. Is the factor demand curve of a competitive industry necessarily less elastic than the summation of the demand curves of the separate firms present in the industry at a particular moment?

*R9. True or false? (Explain in each case.) The economy-wide demand curve for factor *A* will be more elastic:

*The answers to asterisked questions appear at the end of the book.

a. The more elastic the consumer demand for goods in the production of which *A* is employed.

b. The weaker the operation of the Law of Diminishing Returns as employment of *A* is varied.

c. The more elastic is the *supply* of factors complementary to *A*.

R10. In the competitive minimum-wage model of Figure 11.20, why is the "unemployment gap" bigger than the "disemployment effect"?

R11. Show how, upon imposition of a minimum-wage law, the monopsony model might predict *increased* employment. Given an initial dispersion of wage rates (high-skilled, mid-skilled, and low-skilled workers) under this model, which groups would tend to find employment decreasing and which increasing? Compare the predictions with the competitive model.

FOR FURTHER THOUGHT AND DISCUSSION

*T1. Are there examples in this text providing empirical support for the Laws of Diminishing Marginal and Average Returns? Would you expect to find any exceptions?

*T2. Can a demand curve for factor *A* be derived if the employer of *A* is a *monopsonist*? That is, is there a relation that shows the quantity employed as a function of price? Why or why not?

T3. With regard to Table 11.1, the monopolist–monopsonist Factor Employment Condition $mfc_a = mrp_a$ is said to be the "most general." Show that this condition also covers the case of a firm that is a price-taker in both product and factor markets.

*T4. Why might a firm at a given moment hire positive amounts of two factors that are anti-complementary? Would it ever simultaneously hire "interfering" factors?

T5. Would you expect, typically, that combinations of different classes of labor (like skilled versus unskilled) are more or less likely to be complementary—in comparison with combinations of labor and machines?

T6. Assuming that labor organizations were interested only in the selfish gains of their members, would you expect them to oppose immigration?

*T7. Historically, wages in the United States have been high relative to wages elsewhere. Does the chapter shed light on this phenomenon? Explain.

*T8. Would you expect technological progress to raise wage rates, on the average?

T9. A minimum wage law raises firms' *relative* demand for skilled labor versus unskilled. Would it tend to raise the *absolute* demand for skilled labor, if skilled and unskilled are complementary? If they are anti-complementary? How does your answer bear upon the attitudes of trade unions toward minimum wage laws?

12 FACTOR
SUPPLY
AND
FACTOR-MARKET
EQUILIBRIUM

CORE CHAPTER

This chapter takes up the *supply side of the factor market*. Upon completing the chapter we will have rounded the entire circuit of economic activity pictured in Figure 1.1—having previously surveyed the demand side of the product market in Chapters 3 through 5, the supply side of the product market in Chapters 6 through 10, and gone on to cover the demand side of the factor market in the preceding chapter.

The supply of factors of production reflects how resource-owners choose between market employment and self-employment—between offering factor services for hire versus retaining them for non-market or *reservation uses*. These choices are discussed in the first two sections of the chapter. Sections 12.C and 12.D then bring supply and demand together to study *equilibrium* in the market for factors. The next subject covered is the distribution of income, the division of the national product among various categories of resource-owners. This leads finally into the analysis of "capital," a topic that has been the source of great confusion and controversy in economics.

12.A
THE OPTIMUM OF THE RESOURCE-OWNER

In the analysis of consumption and demand in Chapter 4, the individual was supposed to be already in possession of a given income I out of which he or she could purchase desired consumption goods. But, of course, this income does not come out of thin air. *Income consists of earnings received from the employment of resources (factors) owned.* The consumers and the resource-owners thus are the same persons, although viewed from different aspects.

As resource-owner, everyone has a decision problem. It is necessary to decide how much to supply on the market, as against the alternative of reserving some or all of one's owned resources for non-market use. For concreteness, think of labor capacity as the owned resource. Then the decision problem is to choose *between labor income and "leisure."*[1]

---

[1]"Leisure" perhaps suggests a mere lazing away of time. But the term as used here may include productive activities—so long as these are outside the market context. An enormously important example is homemaking, an activity which involves productive services that would be extremely costly to procure on the market.

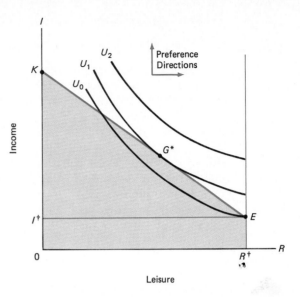

FIGURE 12.1 Optimum of the Resource-Owner. The resource-owner's preferences, as indicated by indifference curves U_0, U_1, U_2, . . . , show that Income I and reservation uses (or "leisure") R are both goods. At endowment position E the person has $R^\dagger$ of leisure and possibly some initial income $I^\dagger$ as well. The slope of the budget line EK indicates the terms (the hire-price or wage) at which the individual can obtain income by sacrificing leisure uses of the resource. The tangency point G^* is the resource-owner's optimum position.

Figure 12.1 shows an individual's preference map in terms of indifference curves between *income I* (which stands here as a proxy for the consumption goods purchasable out of income) and *leisure R* (i.e., reservation uses of one's time). The arrows showing preference directions indicate that income and leisure are both "goods" rather than "bads." Before any exchange takes place, the individual at endowment position E has $R^\dagger$ units of leisure (24 hours per day, let us say) and $I^\dagger$ units (dollars) of non-labor income (from property earnings, perhaps). The diagram is bounded both on the right and on the left. The bound on the right at $R^\dagger$ says that, no matter what, the individual cannot "buy" more than 24 hours of leisure per day; the bound on the left at zero says that the individual cannot sell more than 24 hours of the labor per day.

The opportunity set is the shaded area lying below the budget line EK. Starting from E, as an hour of labor is sold (as an hour of leisure is sacrificed) the person receives in exchange the hourly wage rate h_L, where h_L is the "hire-price" of labor. If the individual is a price-taker with respect to the wage rate, the budget line has constant slope $\Delta I/\Delta R = -h_L$.[2] The wage rate h_L can be regarded either as the price of an hour of *labor* or of an hour of *leisure*.

The individual's *resource-employment optimum* (balance between market and reservation uses of labor-time resource) is at the tangency position G^* in Figure 12.1. The logic is entirely parallel to that used in finding the *consumer's optimum* in Chapter 4 (compare Figure 4.1).

Let us now look more formally at the determination of the resource-employment optimum. First, the equation of the budget line is:

(12.1) $$h_L R + I = h_L R^\dagger + I^\dagger$$

[2]More explicitly, the slope of the budget line might be expressed as $-h_L/P_I$, where P_I is the "price" of a unit of income. But P_I is by definition unity, since income is measured in units of *numéraire* (in this case, dollars).

This equation tells us that the value of the individual's endowment, shown on the right hand side as non-labor income $I^\dagger$ plus the market value $h_L R^\dagger$ of endowed time, must equal achieved income I plus the market value $h_L R$ of the leisure that the person "purchases" (by not working). Alternatively, this same relation can be formulated in terms of *labor or working hours* L rather than leisure hours R, where by definition $L \equiv R^\dagger - R$. Then (12.1) can be rewritten:

$$(12.1') \qquad\qquad\qquad I^\dagger + h_L L = I$$

In this form, the budget equation says that the person's achieved income I is composed of endowed or property income $I^\dagger$ plus labor earnings $h_L L$.

At the optimum point $G^\dagger$, the tangency condition can be expressed as a Substitution Equivalence Equation (like that in Section 4.A) between two Marginal Rates of Substitution:

$$(12.2) \qquad\qquad\qquad MRS_R = MRS_E \equiv \dot{h}_L$$

This equation, in exactly the same form as equation (4.4), says: At a tangency optimum the *Marginal Rate of Substitution in Resource Supply* (i.e., the ratio $-\dfrac{\Delta I}{\Delta R}\Big|_U$ representing the amount of additional income ΔI for which the individual is just willing to sacrifice another unit of leisure ΔR) must be equal to the *Marginal Rate of Substitution in Exchange* between income and leisure (i.e., the ratio $-\dfrac{\Delta I}{\Delta R}\Big|_E$ representing the income increment h_L that the market *permits* him to acquire in exchange for another hour of leisure). MRS_R is the absolute value of the indifference-curve slope in Figure 12.1; following the argument of Section 4.A, MRS_R can also be interpreted as the ratio of the *Marginal Utilities* of leisure and income—$MRS_R \equiv MU_R/MU_I$. And MRS_E is the absolute slope of the budget line, or in this case simply the wage rate h_L. So (12.2) can equivalently be written:[3]

[3]*Mathematical Footnote:* Using the method of Lagrangian multipliers, the optimization problem of the resource-owner can be expressed as:

$$\underset{(I,R,\lambda)}{\text{Max }} L = U(I, R) + \lambda(h_L R + I - h_L R^\dagger - I^\dagger)$$

Then:

$$\frac{\partial L}{\partial I} = \frac{\partial U}{\partial I} + \lambda = 0$$

$$\frac{\partial L}{\partial R} = \frac{\partial U}{\partial R} + \lambda h_L = 0$$

$$\frac{\partial L}{\partial \lambda} = h_L R + I - h_L R^\dagger - I^\dagger = 0$$

Eliminating λ in the first two equations:

$$\frac{\partial U/\partial R}{\partial U/\partial I} = h_L$$

This is the form of (12.2').

$$(12.2')$$ $$\frac{MU_R}{MU_I} = h_L$$

As in Chapter 4, *convexity* of the indifference curves here is justified by the observation of "diversification" between income and leisure. (People normally work somewhere between zero and 24 hours per day.) Of course, an individual very well endowed with property income (very large $I^\dagger$) might choose not to work at all. In terms of the geometry, such a "corner solution" would be preferred if the indifference curve U_0 in Figure 12.1 were steeper than the budget line EK at the endowment position E.[4]

Exercise 12.1: An individual is endowed with $R^\dagger = 24$ hours of leisure per day and $I^\dagger = 120$ units of income (dollars) per day. His Marginal Rate of Substitution in Resource Supply is $MRS_R = I/R$. The wage facing him is $h_L = 10$. How many hours of labor will he supply, and what will be his income from labor?

Answer: His budget constraint in the form of equation (12.1) is $10R + I = 10(24) + 120 = 360$. Using (12.2), he will set $MRS_R = I/R = h_L = 10$. Putting the equations together, the solution is $R^* = 18$, $I^* = 180$. Thus, he works 6 hours per day and earns 60 dollars per day from labor.

Continuing to pursue the analogy with the consumption optimum of Chapter 4, consider what happens: (1) when endowed (non-labor) income $I^\dagger$ varies, and (2) when the hire-price (wage) h_L changes.

Variation of income is illustrated in Figure 12.2, where the budget line takes successively higher positions from $E^\circ K^\circ$ to $E'K'$ to $E''K''$. Both income I and leisure R are, it is reasonable to assume, "normal" (or "superior") goods. That is, an upward shift of the budget line due to a rise in endowed non-labor income $I^\dagger$ would be expected to lead to choice of increased consumption income I *and* increased leisure R. The consequence is a positively sloped *Income Expansion Path* (IEP). The individual takes only part of the benefit of any increment of endowed income in the form of consumption goods; the remainder of the gain is taken in the form of increased leisure.

Figure 12.3 shows the consequence of variation in h_L, the wage rate or "price of leisure." As the wage rate rises, the budget line rotates around the endowment position E so as to become increasingly steep. The *Price Expansion Path* (PEP) goes through all the tangency-optimum positions along these steepening budget lines EK°, EK', EK'', ... For relatively low wage rates the negative slope of PEP indicates that more labor L will be offered (i.e., less leisure R "purchased") as the wage rises. But for sufficiently high wage rates, it is quite possible for PEP to

---

The form (12.2) follows directly from the equivalences:

$$-\frac{dI}{dR}\bigg|_U \equiv \frac{\partial U/\partial R}{\partial U/\partial I} \equiv MRS_R \quad \text{and} \quad -\frac{dI}{dR}\bigg|_E \equiv h_L \equiv MRS_E$$

[4]The analytical condition for this corner solution is that at $R = R^\dagger$, $MRS_R > MRS_E$.

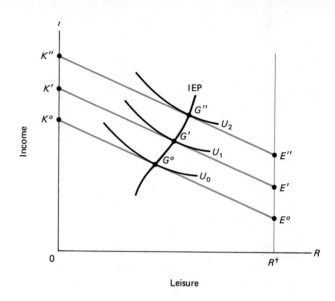

FIGURE 12.2 Income Expansion Path.
As endowed income $I^\dagger$ rises, with the hire-price (wage) held constant, the budget line shifts upward parallel to itself. If I and R are both normal (superior) goods, the successive resource-employment optimum positions G°, G', G'', . . . show that more income and more leisure will be chosen. Thus, the Income Expansion Path (IEP) has positive slope.

enter a range of positive slope (in the diagram, the range above point G') where a higher wage will lead to a *lesser* quantity of labor offered.

This seemingly puzzling situation is due to the interaction of the *income effect* and the *substitution effect* of the change in h_L. As explained in Chapter 4, when the substitution effect alone of a price change is considered (i.e., when real income is held constant), a *rise* in price must lead to a *fall* in quantity purchased. In this case, an increase in the wage rate h_L means a rise in the price of leisure and so less leisure will be "purchased." And since choice of a smaller amount of leisure

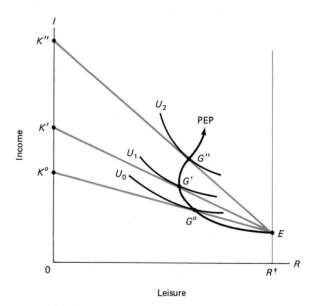

FIGURE 12.3 Price Expansion Path. As the wage or hire-price h_L increases, the slope of the budget line rotates clockwise around E. In an initial range where the wage rate is still low, increases in h_L will lead to choice of more income but less leisure (that is, more labor will be offered). Thus, the Price Expansion Path (PEP) has negative slope. A range *may* be reached where further increases in h_L lead to less labor being offered—the PEP curve may "bend backward," taking on a positive slope for sufficiently high h_L.

means that labor supplied must be larger, the pure *substitution effect* dictates that the higher the wage h_L the greater the hours worked L.

But an increase in wage is not a pure substitution story. Since the individual is a *seller of labor,* he is effectively enriched by any increase in the wage rate. And since leisure is a normal good, the income or enrichment effect would lead to *greater* "purchases" of leisure as the wage rises. Thus, the income and substitution effects of a wage change normally act in opposite directions. (This contrasts with the situation in the theory of consumption where, for a "normal" superior good, the substitution effect and the income effect of a price change are *reinforcing.*)

Not only does the income effect act in opposition to the substitution effect in the labor-supply decision, but the *magnitude* of the income effect is relatively large. The reason is the contrast between "diversification in consumption" and "specialization in production." Since the consumer generally buys a wide variety of products, a rise in the price of any single commodity is not likely to impoverish him or her substantially. But in terms of factor-supply, there is one single price that will be *very* important for the resource-owner, namely, the wage of the particular type of labor service in which the individual specializes. Changes in this wage will typically represent a very considerable shift in real income.

Despite the potential importance of the income effect, *the substitution effect must nevertheless dominate the labor-supply decision at very low wage rates.* This may be seen as follows. Since the indifference-curve slope is negative at the endowment position E, there is some wage rate so low (corresponding to this slope) that it would elicit from the person a zero offer of labor.[5] If we consider wage rates only slightly above this, any income or enrichment effect must be very small. The enrichment due to a wage increase is on the order of $L(\Delta h_L)$, where Δh_L is the wage increment and L is the hours worked. If L is close to zero hours, the person cannot be *substantially* enriched by a wage-rate change. It is only in the upper regions of the PEP curve that enough hours are worked to make the enrichment $L(\Delta h_L)$ substantial, in which case it might overcome the substitution effect so as to cause the PEP curve to enter a range of reversed slope as shown in Figure 12.3.

> CONCLUSION: In the resource-employment decision the income and substitution effects of changes in hire-price h_L normally work in opposite directions. The substitution effect must dominate (more employment will be chosen as h_L rises) at low hire-prices; the income effect may dominate, however, for sufficiently high h_L.

[5] As would, of course, any still lower wage.

EXAMPLE 12.1 _____
Retirement Decisions

In recent years the labor force participation of the elderly has declined markedly. Of white males aged 65 and over, 46.5% participated in the labor force in 1948 but only 22.5% in 1974. For non-white males the decline was from 50.3% to 21.7%.[a] A study by Michael J. Boskin[b] sought to explain this development by evaluating the retirement decisions of white married males who were aged 61–65 in 1968.

The statistical evidence for the period 1968–72 indicated that, other things equal, an increase of $1000 in annual income from assets (equivalent to an upward shift of the endowment point E in Figure 12.2) *increased* the probability of retirement by 15%. An increase of $1000 in net earnings (equivalent to a clockwise rotation of the budget line in Figure 15.3) *reduced* the probability of retirement by about 60%.

Boskin was particularly concerned to investigate the effect of Social Security benefits upon retirement decisions. He found that a $1000 increase in these benefits more than doubled the probability of retirement. Since increased Social Security benefits act like increased income from assets and shift the endowment point E upward as in Figure 12.2, it seemed puzzling that the Social Security effect was so large. There are a number of possible explanations, some of the more important of which are connected with the fact that *receiving Social Security payments limits the income that an individual is legally permitted to receive from working*. During the period in question, any income from employment earned by Social Security recipients fell into four ranges: (1) there was a certain exempt level that the recipient could retain without penalty; (2) above the exemption, a certain range where earned income was in effect taxed 50% (by a corresponding reduction in Social Security benefits); (3) above the 50% bracket, another bracket where earned income was taxed 100%; (4) and above the 100% bracket, a final range where income earned could again be fully retained (since no Social Security benefits remain to be reduced as earnings increase). The key point is that an increase in Social Security benefits, if not linked to an increase in the exemption level, would for many people be largely taxed away *unless* they chose to retire (or, at any rate, chose to work considerably less than before). Since eligibility for increased Social Security benefits depended heavily upon the individual's not working, increases in benefits had a powerful tendency to promote retirement.

[a] From *Manpower Report of the President, 1975* (Washington, D.C.: U.S. Government Printing Office).

[b] Michael J. Boskin, "Social Security and Retirement Decisions," *Economic Inquiry*, v. 15 (Jan. 1977).

12.B
AN APPLICATION: THE "NEGATIVE INCOME TAX" PROPOSAL

Existing relief or "welfare" arrangements for support of the unemployed have a strongly adverse effect upon the incentive to work. The Negative Income Tax proposal is an attempt to overcome this adverse effect.

With some oversimplification, welfare-relief may be pictured as in Figure 12.4. The individual here is assumed to have no property income, and so the

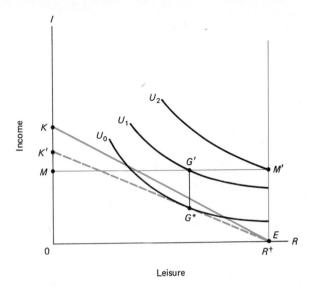

FIGURE 12.4 Employment versus Welfare, I.
For a person with endowment E, initial non-labor income $I^\dagger$ is zero. In the absence of taxes, EK would be the budget line. Assuming a simple proportional income tax, the effective after-tax (dashed) budget line EK' leads to a resource-employment optimum at G^*. Welfare arrangements guaranteeing income M would provide a cash supplement so as to bring the individual up from G^* to G'. But if leisure is always a good, the person will prefer the point M' where income M is received without any work at all.

endowment position E lies along the horizontal axis at $R = R^\dagger$ (24 hours of leisure per day). The pre-tax wage rate at which the person could work is reflected in the slope of the solid budget line EK; in the absence of taxes or a welfare system, the tangency optimum would lie along EK. But in actuality income and Social Security taxes would have to be paid on labor earnings, so that the effective or post-tax budget line is the dashed EK'.[6] Along EK', the employment optimum is indicated by the tangency with indifference curve U_0 at G^*.

Now suppose that the welfare system provides a level of *minimal income maintenance* represented by the horizontal line MM'. This means that, should earnings from employment be less than the amount $OM = EM'$, they will be supplemented to bring income I up to that level. Persons who attain G^* by working would therefore receive a cash payment bringing them up to position G' on MM'. But if leisure is always a good, the position M' on indifference curve U_2, attainable without working at all, is clearly preferred to G' on indifference curve U_1. Subject to the proviso that income and leisure are both *goods* (preference directions are north and east), no one will work at all if his or her employment optimum G^* along EK' lies below MM'.[7]

Furthermore, even for some individuals whose employment optimum G^* would otherwise lie *well above* MM', the no-work position M' available under welfare may still be preferable. In Figure 12.5 indifference curve U_1 through M' represents a higher level of satisfaction than can be achieved at the employment optimum G^*. Even though G^* would generate more spendable income I than the amount received under the dole, the increased leisure at point M' may be valued more highly by the individual.

---

[6]The diagram assumes that taxes on income are a simple proportion of earnings. Ideally, we should allow for exemptions, progressivity, and other complex features of the tax structure. But doing so is not essential for our purposes.

[7]Welfare administrators sometimes attempt to force those capable of working to do so. But, *de facto*, effective control is very limited. An unwilling worker can easily convince his employer to fire him.

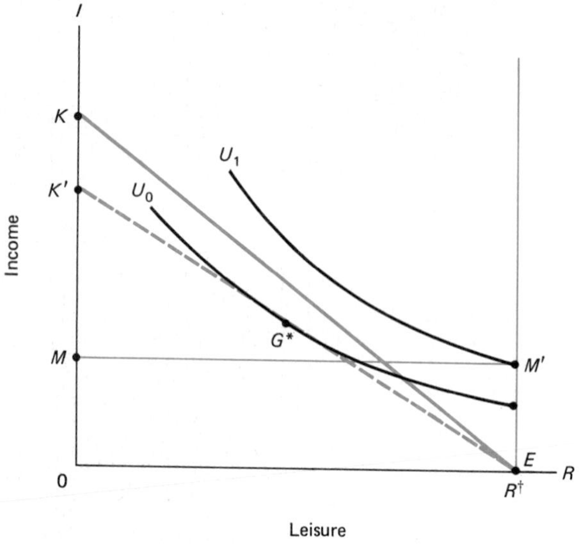

FIGURE 12.5 **Employment versus Welfare, II.** Here, in the absence of welfare-relief the individual would attain position G^* along his after-tax budget line EK', earning more than the guaranteed welfare level M. Nevertheless, the person's tastes are such that position M' (yielding income M without working) would be chosen under a welfare system in preference to G^*.

EXAMPLE 12.2
Interwar Unemployment in Britain

British economists in the period after World War I were puzzled by the high levels of unemployment in that country (never below 9.5% in the period 1921–38), levels that were much higher than those observed before the first Great War. (The seeming failure of labor markets to come to an equilibrium may have promoted the development of Keynesian macroeconomic theories in Britain during this period.) However, a later re-evaluation by the economists D. K. Benjamin and L. A. Kochin[a] indicated that the difficulty may not have been any flaw in the market for labor, but rather the liberalization of Britain's unemployment insurance program—the "dole"—in comparison with the pre-war years.

This liberalization included extending unemployment compensation to cover many more workers, increasing the payments in comparison with wages from ordinary employment, and shortening the waiting period before benefits could be received. Using data on the ratio of unemployment benefits to wages, and adjusting for fluctuations in general business conditions, Benjamin and Kochin estimated that the unemployment insurance program raised the unemployment rate by five to eight percentage points. Had unemployment benefits been no more generous than in the prewar years, they claimed, unemployment in Britain would have been at normal levels throughout most of the inter-war period.

[a]D. K. Benjamin and L. A. Kochin, "Searching for an Explanation of Unemployment in Interwar Britain," *Journal of Political Economy*, v. 87 (June 1979).

The Negative Income Tax (NIT), as an alternative to the existing welfare system, is pictured in Figure 12.6. We see once again the pre-tax (solid) budget line EK and the after-tax (dashed) budget line EK' of the preceding diagram, with an employment optimum G^* that is inferior (in the eyes of the individual) to the unemployment position at M' attainable under the welfare system. The NIT alternative is based upon the following considerations: (1) The income maintenance level MM' is still guaranteed, whether or not the individual works. (2) A "breakeven level" of income is established, represented by the horizontal line BB' in the diagram, that is *higher* than MM'. (3) Above the breakeven level the individual is a payer of (positive) taxes; below, a recipient of (negative) taxes.

The effect is to make a different NIT budget line, represented in Figure 12.6 by the dotted line $M'K''$, relevant for the individual's employment decision. $M'K''$ incorporates the effect of positive or negative taxes. It intersects the horizontal breakeven line BB' at the point B'' which also lies on the pre-tax (solid) budget line EK. A person who supplied so much labor as to exactly attain the position B'' would neither pay taxes nor receive any supplementary income. Beyond B'', the person would be a net payer of taxes,[8] but short of B'' would be a net recipient of income supplement.[9] In the case illustrated in the diagram, the individual chooses the position G^{**}, offering $L \equiv R^\dagger - R'$ hours of labor. Pre-tax earnings are $R'H$ in the diagram, and the income supplement is HG^{**}. The person is working (at least some hours) under the NIT, and there is to that extent a social gain over the welfare system that led him or her to prefer total unemployment.

[8]That is, the pre-tax budget line EK is *higher* than the NIT budget line $M'K''$ in this range.
[9]That is, in this range EK is lower than $M'K''$.

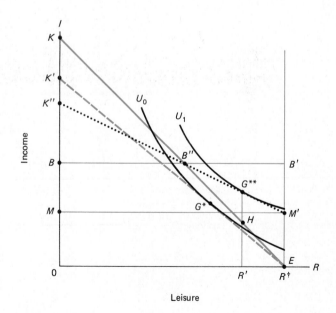

FIGURE 12.6 NIT versus Welfare, I.
The Negative Income Tax (NIT), as an alternative to welfare, again guarantees an income level M. There is a breakeven level of income, however, such that earned incomes below the line BB' receive supplementation (negative taxation) while those above BB' pay positive taxes. If EK (solid) is the pre-tax budget line, and EK' (dashed) the usual after-tax budget line, under NIT the effective after-tax budget line becomes $M'K''$ (dotted). Here NIT has a "favorable" effect: an individual who would have chosen G^* in the absence of either welfare or NIT, and who would have shifted to M' (choosing complete unemployment) under welfare, is now motivated to choose G^{**}—he or she is induced not to totally abandon employment.

Defenders of NIT point to the psychologically corrosive effect of welfare-induced unemployment upon the worker's sense of independence and self-esteem. Opponents, on the other hand, argue that the NIT may itself constitute a source of psychological corrosion for a *much larger* number of workers who will now be receiving "unearned" income supplements from government, even though remaining (to some extent, at any rate) employed. Furthermore, the higher *marginal* tax rate under NIT (flatter slope of $M'K''$ as compared with EK' in Figure 12.6) is likely to induce working individuals to choose a lesser *degree* of employment.

Both of these adverse effects are illustrated in Figure 12.7. This diagram again compares the welfare after-tax budget line EK' (dashed) with the NIT after-tax budget line $M'K''$ (dotted). (The *pre-tax* budget line EK of the previous diagram is not needed here, and so has been omitted.) But the individual's preferences and opportunities are now such that under the welfare system the preferred position along EK' is at $G*$ on indifference curve U_0; he or she does not accept relief, but on the contrary shows relatively great willingness to work. Along $M'K''$, however, the preferred position is $G**$ on indifference curve U_1. As is evident, under NIT the individual will work far fewer hours, and furthermore has been induced to abandon a position of sturdy tax-paying independence at $G*$ in favor of a socially dependent role below the breakeven income level BB'.

It is even possible that an individual who would have chosen employment under the welfare-relief system could turn to unemployment under the NIT. Such a situation is illustrated in Figure 12.8. The analysis (showing that $G*$ along EK' would have been preferred to the welfare-unemployment position M', but that unemployment at M' is superior to any other attainable position along the NIT budget line $M'K''$) is left to the student as an exercise.

Whether the NIT proposal is on balance a desirable one depends, at least

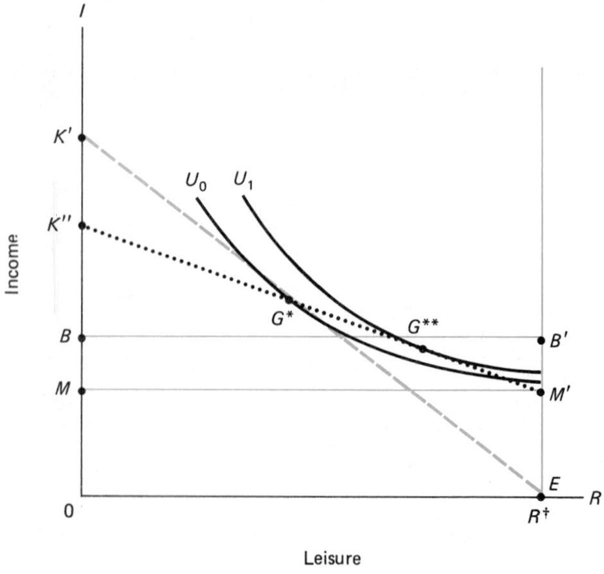

FIGURE 12.7 NIT versus Welfare, II. In contrast with the preceding diagram, this illustrates that an individual under the welfare system who would have chosen $G*$ along EK', in preference to unemployment at M', may be induced under NIT to work considerably less (at position $G**$). Further, the individual shifts from being a positive taxpayer at $G*$ to becoming a social dependent (recipient of negative taxes) at $G**$.

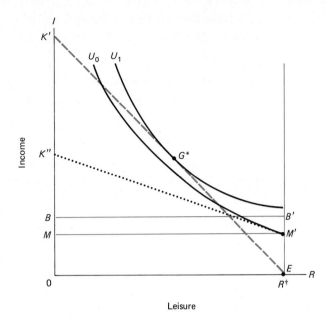

FIGURE 12.8 NIT versus Welfare, III. This illustrates an even more extreme possible adverse result of NIT. An individual who would have worked rather than remain unemployed under welfare (choosing G^* along budget line EK' over M') now finds unemployment at M' preferable along the NIT budget line $M'K''$.

in part, upon the frequency with which the various types of situations described in these diagrams will be encountered. A number of experiments have been conducted to cast light upon this question.

EXAMPLE 12.3
Negative Income Tax Experiments

The Federal Office of Economic Opportunity initiated an extensive experiment in 1967 aimed at estimating the effect of the Negative Income Tax (NIT) upon work incentives. Subject families in four cities in New Jersey and Pennsylvania were assigned to one of eight experimental NIT programs or to a control group.

One of the important considerations in evaluating the statistical results was that acceptance of assignment to an NIT program was voluntary; a family could not be compelled to participate. A family that refused participation remained subject to ordinary taxation and also eligible for welfare-relief. (Note that the family in Figure 12.8 would have chosen *not* to participate.) Had the program been introduced nationally, however, it would presumably have entirely replaced ordinary taxation and relief. As would be expected, participation in the program tended to increase the *higher* the guaranteed income offered under NIT and the *lower* the tax rate (in our diagrams, the higher the point M' and the steeper the slope of the $M'K''$).

A study by John F. Cogan[a] found, among those families choosing to par-

---

[a] John F. Cogan, *Negative Income Taxation and Labor Supply: New Evidence from the New Jersey–Pennsylvania Experiment*, The Rand Corporation, R–2155–HEW (Feb. 1978).

ticipate, a rather substantial work disincentive effect: an average reduction of 5 to 7 labor-hours per week. The reduced level of employment would also be associated with a heavy increase in required transfer payments under NIT. Thus, this experiment suggests that the possible favorable effects of NIT upon employment incentives and taxpayer burdens (as in Figure 12.6) may be outweighed by the negative possibilities (pictured in Figures 12.7 and 12.8).

Another series of experiments, in Seattle and Denver, was analyzed by N. B. Tuma and P. K. Robbins.[b] Once again the results indicated significant adverse consequences: individuals enrolled in the NIT program were more likely to leave employment, and incurred lengthier spells of unemployment, in comparison with experimental control families not enrolled in the program.

[b] N. B. Tuma and P. K. Robbins, "A Dynamic Model of Employment Behavior: An Application to the Seattle and Denver Income Maintenance Experiments," *Econometrica*, v. 48 (May 1980).

12.C
RESOURCE SUPPLY TO THE MARKET, AND FACTOR-MARKET EQUILIBRIUM

The data represented by a person's Price Expansion Path PEP of Figure 12.3 could be plotted in a separate diagram on R, h_L axes as his or her "demand curve for leisure." It is more usual, however, to present the data on L, h_L axes as the individual's *supply curve for labor* (where by definition $L \equiv R^+ - R$, as before).

Figure 12.9 shows such an individual supply curve s_L. The hire-prices h_L°, h_L', and h_L'' in Figure 12.9 correspond respectively to the slopes of the budget lines EK°, EK', and EK'' in Figure 12.3. The lower range in which the PEP curve of the earlier diagram is moving westward corresponds to the range of prices below h_L in which the supply curve s_L has normal positive slope—where an increased

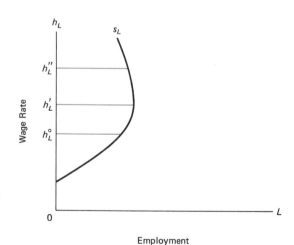

FIGURE 12.9 **Backward-bending Supply Curve of Labor.** The supply curve of labor shown here, s_L, has normal positive slope for wage rates up to h_L' but "bends backward" above that wage.

wage elicits increased labor-hours. Above this range, however, the PEP curve *may* (as shown in Figure 12.3) be moving eastward. This means that, once wage rates are sufficiently high, a further wage augmentation could lead to a decreased labor offer; should that occur, the labor-supply curve is said to be "backward-bending." (A backward-bending supply curve as in Figure 12.9 is a strong possibility, but is not a logical necessity.)

EXAMPLE 12.4
Animal Labor Supply

A study by R. C. Battalio and J. H. Kagel[a] examined the labor-supply behavior of rats under simulated working conditions. The rats had to press a lever in order to obtain a food reward (sucrose solution). The "wage" was varied by changing the number of presses required to obtain a fixed quantity of reward.

The rats' responses typically generated a backward-bending supply curve (as in Figure 12.9). In one experiment with 16% sucrose solution as reward, the increasing-supply range applied as the wage rose from a low of one reward per 320 presses up to a high of one reward per 20 presses. A further wage increase, requiring only 10 presses per reward, brought about reduced supply.

[a] R. C. Battalio and John H. Kagel, "Labor Supply Behavior of Animal Workers: Towards an Experimental Analysis," in V. L. Smith, ed., *Research in Experimental Economics*, v. 1 (Greenwich, Conn.: JAI Press, 1979).

When individual supply curves are aggregated (summed horizontally), the overall factor-market supply curve S_L is obtained as in Figure 12.10. The aggregate S_L is likely to have a normal positive slope even if some of the component individual supply curves have backward-bending ranges, since the various

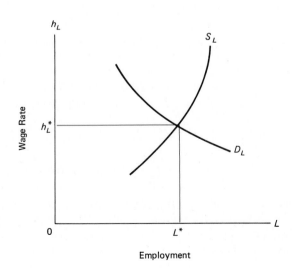

FIGURE 12.10 Equilibrium in the Factor Market.
The intersection of the aggregate demand curve for labor D_L and the aggregate supply curve of labor S_L determines the equilibrium wage rate h_L^* and the level of market employment L^*.

individuals' h'_L points as in Figure 12.9 will differ. But it is possible that even the aggregate supply curve may be found to be backward-bending at sufficiently high wage rates.

In considering the possibility of backward-bending supply, one important qualification must be kept in mind. While supply of labor *to the market as a whole* (as against the alternative of unemployment or leisure) may quite easily be backward-bending above a certain wage level, supply of labor *to a limited sector or to a particular type of employment* is unlikely to be backward-bending. The reason is that there are many more alternatives. As the wage rises in a particular sector, individuals are attracted not only from leisure but from other areas or activities. Thus, the supply of labor to a limited sector is always *much more elastic* than the supply of labor to the economy as a whole.

EXAMPLE 12.5
Braceros and the Supply of "Stoop Labor"

From 1953 to 1964 the supply of agricultural workers in the United States was supplemented by foreign contract workers primarily from Mexico, who were known as "braceros." When domestic political pressures arose to ban bracero labor, employers contended that it would not be possible to find American workers willing to do the "stoop labor" in the fields. Presumably, the contention was that higher wages would make Americans no more and perhaps even less willing to provide the required amounts of this form of labor (the supply curve of American "stoop labor" was supposedly vertical or even backward-bending).

Despite these arguments the bracero program was in fact terminated in 1965. Growers did, as it turned out, find it possible to attract American labor—though at a much higher wage. A study by Donald E. Wise[a] indicated that, for two California crops (winter melons and strawberries), the labor-supply elasticity was quite high: in the range from 2.7 to 3.4. For California winter melons, the results of abolition of the bracero program included: a 67% increase in wage rate, a 262% increase in employment of American workers (but a 22% reduction in *total* employment, since braceros were no longer used), and a 23% reduction of output.

[a] Donald E. Wise, "The Effect of the Bracero on Agricultural Production in California," *Economic Inquiry*, v. 12 (Dec. 1974).

Market equilibrium under conditions of competition is of course determined by the intersection (as shown in Figure 12.10) of the aggregate supply curve just discussed and the aggregate demand curve derived in the preceding chapter. Changes in equilibrium price and quantity, as always, come about as a result of shifts in supply or demand functions, or both.

In terms of the discussion of determinants of factor demand in Section 11.C, we know that the forces that may shift *demand* function for factors include:

1. *Technological change:* Technical progress tends to shift Marginal Product (*mp*) upward, and hence to raise the curve of $mrp \equiv MR\,(mp)$ that determines firms' demand for factors.[10]

2. *Demand for final products:* Similarly, an increase in the demand for some product, leading to a rise in its price and associated Marginal Revenue, raises the demand for any factor used in its production.

3. *Supply of cooperating or competing factors:* The demand for any one factor will be affected by changes in the availability of other factors that can complement it or substitute for it in production. In particular, an increase in the *supply* of one of a pair of complementary factors will raise the *demand* for the other.

Some of the important influences operating to shift *factor supply* functions are:

1. *Wealth:* Higher endowed wealth increases resource-owners' ability to "purchase" *reservation uses* of owned factors, and hence tends to diminish the supply offered on the market.

2. *Social trends and legal context:* Social and legal forces may at times encourage, at other times discourage, market availability of factors. In some societies women have been excluded from all but domestic activity. In other communities there have been severe restrictions upon the permitted market uses of land or other resources.

3. *Investment and accumulation:* In recent centuries in the Western world, stocks of produced resources ("capital goods") have accumulated enormously over time. Each generation has so arranged its affairs as to leave its successor generation better endowed with these man-made resources. (The process of intertemporal choice leading to this result will be considered in the next chapter.)

4. *Demography:* The growth of population has paralleled the accumulation of goods over time. (Of course, human beings are also a kind of "produced resource," though generated in response to somewhat different motivations.) The aggregate size of the human population and its detailed age-sex composition obviously affect the supply of labor available to the market.

---

[10]This is the normal situation. But consider "labor-saving" inventions. These surely raise the average productivity of labor. Nevertheless, since employers end up hiring fewer workers, such inventions must reduce the demand for labor. The explanation is that demand for a factor depends upon *Marginal* Product; an invention can raise a factor's Average Product *ap* while reducing its Marginal Product *mp* (at least over a certain range).

EXAMPLE 12.6
The Black Death[a]

The Black Death (1348–50) is generally believed to have wiped out between a quarter and a third of the population of Western Europe. Later recurrences of plague in 1360–61, 1369, and 1374 may each have killed perhaps 5% of the populations remaining. There was a drastic reduction in labor supply, with an immediate effect on wages: "The increase due to the plague is 32% for the threshing of wheat, 38% for barley, 111% for oats in the eastern counties. In the middle counties the percentages of rise are 40, 69, 111; in the south, 33, 38, 75; in the west, 26, 41, 44; in the north, 32, 43, and 100."[b]

The English government responded to this shock with what we would now call a "wage freeze," eventually formalized as the Statute of Laborers (1351). This decree not only froze wages but forbade idleness and required reasonable prices for necessities. Another ordinance in the same year prohibited emigration. But all these regulations failed. The economic logic of the situation (the increased scarcity of labor relative to other resources and, in particular, relative to land) dictated a rise in wages and in per-capita incomes of the laboring classes. This is evidenced by innumerable reports of individuals stepping up to fill vacant higher places in the manorial economy, by records of remissions and recontracts of feudal dues owed the lords, as well as by loud complaints against unwontedly lavish living by the lower orders. (For example, a Statute of Dress of 1363 forbade the lower classes to imitate upper-class attire.)

COMMENT: The feudal system was about as far removed from the economists' competitive model as can be imagined. Feudal economic relationships are in principle dictated solely by custom and status. Nevertheless, competitive forces could not be denied. The system could not withstand the pressure of such a drastic and sudden change in factor availabilities as represented by the Black Death; hence the complaints about flight of labor, vagrancy, "wasting," etc., and calls upon the government to cancel the market concessions granted to the upstart workers. An attempt in the reign of Richard II to reverse the clock and enforce feudal status relationships led to the Peasants' Revolt of 1381, which came within a hair of overturning the monarchy. Among the peasants' demands were the abolition of serfdom, of feudal dues and services, of governmental monopolies, and of restrictions on buying and selling. In short, the peasants anticipated Adam Smith; they wanted *laissez faire* so that marketplace revisions of economic status could proceed in their favor.

[a] Discussion based upon J. Hirshleifer, *Disaster and Recovery: The Black Death in Western Europe*, The Rand Corporation, Memorandum RM–4700–TAB (Feb. 1966).

[b] H. Robbins, "A Comparison of the Effects of the Black Death on the Economic Organization of France and England," *Journal of Political Economy*, v. 36 (Aug. 1928), p. 463.

MONOPOLIES AND CARTELS
IN FACTOR SUPPLY

"Monopsony" on the *demand* side of factor markets was studied in the preceding chapter. Monopoly on the *supply* side of the factor market is the subject here.

As every firm's product is in some respects unique, every firm has *some* degree of monopoly power in the product market. Similarly for resources: every resource has some degree of uniqueness and therefore every resource-owner has *some* monopoly power in the factor market. But if a sufficient range of close substitutes is available the competitive model, which postulates price-taking behavior of market participants, will nevertheless be a satisfactory approximation of reality. Ownership of resources is typically very widely diffused. So individual *monopoly* power over resource supply is likely to be significant only in very unusual cases. (Motion picture stars and athletic champions are possible examples.) On the other hand, *cartels* of resource-suppliers (e.g., trade unions) are very common.

*12.D.1 □Optimum of the Monopolist Resource-Owner

The optimal solution for the resource-monopolist is very simple in the special case where he or she has no reservation uses for the factor. Then the monopolist will merely seek to maximize "Total Revenue" or, we shall say, *Total Factor Income (TFI)*. *TFI* is equal to the factor earnings $h_L L$ from the owner's given endowment $R^\dagger$ of resources. This maximization *may* dictate holding some units of the resource off the market, not for reservation uses (as, by assumption, there are none) but simply in the interests of obtaining a higher price through monopoly power. Figure 12.11 illustrates such a situation, in terms of a "total" function in the upper panel, and "average-marginal" functions in the lower. The monopolist's income-maximizing employment L^* occurs at the maximum of the *TFI* curve in the upper panel; the lower panel shows, equivalently, how L^* is determined at the point where *Marginal Factor Income MFI* $\equiv \Delta I / \Delta L$ falls to zero. The wage set by the monopolist will be h_L^*, the height of the factor demand curve D_L at $L = L^*$; this equals the slope of the dotted line in the upper panel. Since $h_L \equiv TFI/L$, the factor demand curve can be identified with the factor-monopolist's *Average Factor Income* function (*AFI*).

What if the curve of Total Factor Income *TFI* is rising throughout the relevant range where $L \leq R^\dagger$ (meaning that the factor demand curve is *elastic* throughout)? Then, even absent reservation uses, the resource-monopolist will *not* find it advantageous to hold any units off the market. In that case *MFI* remains greater than zero at $L = R^\dagger$, where all of the resource available is employed.

---

*The section between the asterisk and the symbol ■ may contain somewhat more difficult or advanced material.

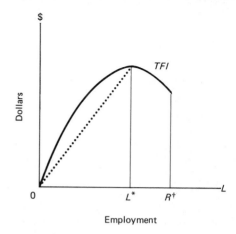

FIGURE 12.11 Factor Monopoly: No Reservation Uses. In the upper panel, the curve of Total Factor Income *TFI* represents total earnings of a monopolist seller of a resource service. In the lower panel, the corresponding curve of Average Factor Income *AFI* is also the market demand curve D_L for the factor. The dashed line is the associated Marginal Factor Income *MFI*. At employment L^*, *TFI* is at its peak while *MFI* is zero. L^* will be the preferred employment offer of a factor monopolist with no alternative uses of the resource.

Exercise 12.2: An individual is a monopolist of a resource A, for which he has no reservation uses. (a) If the demand equation is $h_A = 120 - A$, how many units will he hold off the market if his endowment is $R_A = 100$? (b) If the endowment is $R_A = 50$?

Answer: (a) The hire-price h_A is also the Average Factor Income *AFI*. Since $AFI = 120 - A$ is a straight-line equation, Marginal Factor Income is $MFI = 120 - 2A$. Setting $MFI = 0$, we have $A^* = 60$. He will therefore hold $100 - 60 = 40$ units off the market. (b) If he is endowed only with 50 units of A, then *MFI* remains positive even when he sells all 50 units, so he will not hold any off the market.

If there are *reservation uses* of the factor, the monopolist would have to balance these uses against increased factor earnings in the market. The decision may be illustrated in terms of the preference diagram of Figure 12.12. This differs from Figure 12.1 in that the shaded opportunity set is now bounded by a concave curve rather than a straight line. The concave "budget curve" represents the fact that the wage h_L is *not* constant, but rather is a decreasing function of employment $L \equiv R^\dagger - R$. The monopolist's optimum position is of course at the indifference-curve tangency G^*; the reservation quantity is R^*, and the corresponding employment quantity is L^*.

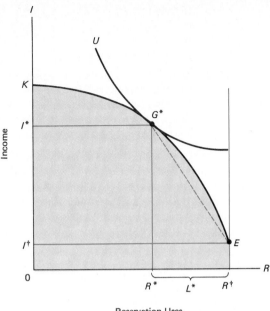

FIGURE 12.12 Factor Monopolist with Reservation Uses, I. On R,I axes a factor monopolist will have a "budget curve" EK bounding the shaded market opportunity set. If there are alternative uses for the resource, the monopolist's preferences can be expressed by indifference curves of standard shape. In the diagram, the monopoly optimum is at G^*, the tangency of EK with the highest attainable indifference curve U. Retained reservation uses are R^*; offered employment is $L^* \equiv R^\dagger - R^*$. The slope of the dashed line EG^* represents the market wage for the offered level of employment. EK can also be regarded as a Total Factor Income curve as L increases to the left, the factor income being the *excess* of the income I attained along EK over the endowed income $I^\dagger$.

This solution is translated to a price–quantity diagram on L,h_L axes in Figure 12.13. The Marginal Factor Income $MFI \equiv \Delta I/\Delta L$ for any employment level L is the absolute slope $-\Delta I/\Delta R$ (since $\Delta L \equiv -\Delta R$) of the concave budget curve in Figure 12.12. This is the "Marginal Revenue" in income units of sacrificing an hour of leisure. What corresponds to "Marginal Cost" for the factor-monopolist is the *marginal value of reservation uses*, which is nothing but his Marginal Rate of Substitution MRS_R as analyzed in Section 12.A. The rising curve MRS_R in Figure 12.13 shows increasing "Marginal Cost" of accepting income in place of leisure. So the tangency at G^* in Figure 12.12 (equality of the budget-curve slope and indifference-curve slope) corresponds to the intersection

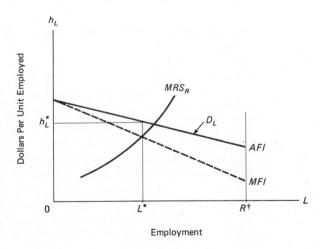

FIGURE 12.13 Factor Monopolist with Reservation Uses, II. The curves of Average Factor Income AFI (the demand curve D_L for the factor) and of Marginal Factor Income MFI are derived from the budget curve EK of the previous diagram. The curve MRS_R, representing the Marginal Rate of Substitution in Resource Supply, plays the role of Marginal Cost. The intersection of MFI and MRS_R determines the factor monopolist's optimum level of employment, with h_L^* the associated price along the demand curve.

of MFI and MRS_R in Figure 12.13. The monopoly optimum wage h_L^* in Figure 12.13 similarly corresponds to the absolute slope of the dashed line EG^* in Figure 12.12.

Exercise 12.3: An individual is endowed with $R^\dagger = 24$ hours of leisure and $I^\dagger = 40$ units of income (dollars). His Marginal Rate of Substitution in Resource Supply between income I and reservation uses R is $MRS_R = I/R$. He is the monopolist of a special type of labor for which the demand is $w = 50 - 4L$, where w is the wage rate and $L \equiv 24 - R$. How much labor should he offer? At what wage? What is the attained income I?

Answer: He will want to set MRS_R equal to Marginal Factor Income MFI. Since Average Factor Income $AFI = w = 50 - 4L$, $MFI = 50 - 8L$. So the equation to solve is $50 - 8L = I/(24 - L)$. The achieved income is $I = 40 + wL = 40 + (50 - 4L)L$. After substituting, a quadratic equation is obtained whose solutions are $L = 5$ and $L = 19.33$. The latter implies $MFI < 0$, so $L = 5$ is the correct result. When 5 hours of labor are put on the market, the wage is $w = 30$. His attained income is $I = 40 + 5(30) = 190$.

> CONCLUSION: The monopolist supplier of a resource, like the monopolist supplier of a product, will set Marginal Revenue equal to Marginal Cost. In the factor market, Marginal Revenue corresponds to Marginal Factor Income MFI. Marginal Cost corresponds to MRS_R, the owner's Marginal Rate of Substitution between income and reservation uses of the resource. If there are no reservation uses, MRS_R will be everywhere zero. Even so, the monopolist factor-supplier may still hold some units of the factor off the market, if MFI falls to zero before the marketed quantity exhausts the owned supply. ∎

12.D.2 ☐ Resource Cartels

Trade unions are often accused of being labor monopolies. Technically, they are *cartels*, associations or coalitions of resource-suppliers. Their members have little or no monopoly power individually, but as a collective group they may be able to influence the price–quantity outcome of the market process.

As was explained in Chapter 8, cartels have an Achilles heel. Given that the other members are loyally abiding by the agreement, it pays any single member to "chisel" by undercutting the standard terms. All cartels therefore require enforcement devices, most commonly achieved through use of government power. In the case of trade unions in the United States, an election is normally held under the terms of the National Labor Relations Act to determine "collective-bargaining representation." Whichever union wins a majority of the votes cast becomes the exclusive bargaining agent for *all* workers in the collective-bargaining unit.[11] ("No union" is also one of the options.) When a collective-bargaining agent has been officially certified, individual bargaining is prohibited—thus ruling out, or at any rate minimizing, the possibility of the

---

[11]The administrative-legal process that determines just what is the appropriate "bargaining unit" may be quite crucial for the final outcome of the election.

worker "chiseling" by accepting less than the standard pay for the given work or offering more work at the standard pay.

EXAMPLE 12.7
Unionization and Hotel Workers[a]

Before 1929 there was very little unionization of hotel workers. In the two decades after 1929 the Hotel and Restaurant Employees and Bartenders International Union was able to organize in a number of cities. As may be seen in the Table, wage rates rose somewhat faster in the unionized cities.

Average Hourly Earnings of Hotel Employees (1929 = 100)

	1929	1935	1939	1948
Weighted mean index, 19 union cities*	100	81	88.4	188
Weighted mean index, 12 non-union cities[†]	100	76	80	168
Ratio (union/non-union)	1.0	1.06	1.10	1.12

Source: Joseph Scherer, "Collective Bargaining in Service Industries: A Study of the Year-Round Hotels," Ph.D. dissertation, University of Chicago, 1951.

*More than 35% of hotel workers organized in 1948.

[†]Less than 10% of hotel workers organized in 1948.

After adjustment of the data to eliminate regional wage effects (since unionized cities tended to be northern and non-unionized cities southern), the ratio of union to non-union wage indexes was found to be 1.06. That is, wages in the union cities grew about 6% more, in the course of twenty years, as compared with non-union cities.

Note, however, that the union versus non-union differential is small in comparison with the overall wage swings over the twenty years covered by the Table.

[a] Discussion based on H. Gregg Lewis, *Unionism and Relative Wages in the United States* (Chicago: University of Chicago Press, 1963), p. 58.

Since different interests must be reconciled in collective decisions, the determination of the market policy of any cartel creates internal political conflict. In the case of trade unions, elaborate internal machinery often exists to solve this "problem of collective action."[12]

But trade unions are by no means the only cartels effective in resource supply. Professional associations, such as the American Medical Association (see the Example "Returns to Medical Education" below) are frequently charged with cartel-like behavior. In general, loosely organized resource-supply cartels find it easier to achieve their ends by *restricting entry to the trade* than by trying to gain agreement on prices. Entry is relatively visible, while price-chiseling may be

---

[12]The topic of "collective action" will be considered more fully in Part Seven.

hidden. A sufficiently tight lid on supply, through control of entry, will inevitably force up the market price even though market behavior remains competitive for those actually in the trade. In a supply–demand equilibrium like that of Figure 12.10, entry control may have shifted the supply curve S_L so far to the left as (essentially) to achieve a monopoly-like price-quantity outcome.

EXAMPLE 12.8
Barbers

In 1962 a study by Simon Rottenberg[a] showed that 47 of the old 48 states had laws licensing barbers. The main impetus for the legislation was lobbying by barbering associations. Educational requirements for securing a barber's license are an important barrier to entry. The Illinois law, for example, requires (among other things) 1872 study hours in a recognized barber school as well as passing an examination covering topics related to the theory and practice of barber science and art. These include anatomy and physiology, hygiene and sanitation, barber history and law, pharmacology, electricity and light, and even haircutting, shaving, etc. Apprenticeship rules may be an even more important restriction on entry: a minimum apprenticeship of $2\frac{1}{4}$ years must be served, and no shop may employ more than one apprentice for each registered barber. The barber associations also oppose licensing reciprocity among states (for then students would acquire licenses in the less restrictive jurisdictions).

While the barbering associations have also pressed for minimum price-fixing, only fourteen states had such laws.

COMMENT: Non-legal methods were at one time a significant deterrent to price "chiselers." A disproportionately large number of unexplained fires used to occur, from time to time, on the premises of price-cutting barbers.

[a] Simon Rottenberg, "The Economics of Occupational Licensing," in H. Gregg Lewis et al., Aspects of Labor Economics (Princeton, N.J.: Princeton University Press, 1962).

One notable exception to tight control over occupational entry is the legal profession. A very large increase in the capacity of law schools and in their throughput of students into the profession has occurred in the United States recently, without apparent objection on the part of those in the trade. This exception is, however, understandable and in a sense "proves the rule." Each additional barber or doctor or accountant competes with his fellows and takes business away from them. But the legal process is such that each additional practitioner, by adding to the number of lawsuits, presentments, hearings, trials, pleadings, appeals, writs, demurrers, briefs, rebuttals, rejoinders, etc., makes *more* business for his colleagues.[13]

[13] Old folk saying: "When will a lawyer be poor? When he's the only lawyer in town."

Of course, cartels may be effective over non-labor resources as well.

EXAMPLE 12.9
Tobacco Allotments

Under the market order[a] regulating the supply of tobacco, certain specific acres of farmland carry "allotments" permitting tobacco to be grown thereon. Anyone may grow tobacco, but must compete with all other growers to buy or rent some "allotted" acres on which to do so. Thus, the government-sponsored cartel works in behalf of owners of the resource of "allotted" land, not in behalf of growers as such. One study has estimated the *premium* paid by growers for land with an allotment (over equivalent land without allotment) as between $962 and $2500 per acre (for land suitable for growing flue-cured tobacco in North Carolina and Virginia counties in the period 1954–57).[b] A later study[c] estimated that the premium had risen to $3281 per acre in 1962 for allotted land in eastern North Carolina.

[a] See also Example 8.5, "Agricultural Marketing Orders."
[b] F. H. Maier, J. L. Hedrick, and W. L. Givson, Jr., "The Sale Value of Flue-Cured Tobacco Allotments," Agricultural Experiment Station, Virginia Polytechnic Institute, Technical Bulletin No. 148 (April 1960), p. 40.
[c] James A. Seagraves, "Capitalized Values of Tobacco Allotments and the Rate of Return to Allotment Owners," *American Journal of Agricultural Economics*, v. 51 (May 1969).

12.E
THE "FUNCTIONAL" DISTRIBUTION OF INCOME

12.E.1 ☐ The Problem of Classification

Factors of production have traditionally been classified under the headings of *labor, land,* and *capital.* These were thought to correspond to three categories of "functional" factor returns, namely: *wages* to labor, *rent* to land, and *interest* to capital. In the emerging period of economic thought, most particularly in England in the late eighteenth and early nineteenth centuries, this categorization had political and sociological relevance. The three factor groupings corresponded to major social classes of the time. Land was mainly owned by the aristocracy, capital (material assets other than land) by the rising bourgeoisie, while the working classes could be regarded as owning their labor power. Even sociologically speaking, this classification was never very useful for societies (like America) lacking a feudally-based aristocracy; with changes in economic circumstances it hardly remains interesting today.[14] And in any case, the claim that these

[14] Ditch-diggers and corporate presidents both appear within the category of "labor," while the category of "landowners" includes impoverished southern blacks together with the descendants of John Jacob Astor.

three factors are "functionally" distinct in economic terms is analytically indefensible.

LAND VERSUS CAPITAL: *Land* is traditionally defined as the "natural and inexhaustible productive powers of the soil," i.e., its native fertility, topographical features, and geographical location. *Capital* in contrast with land is thought of as "produced means of production." But the distinction collapses once it is realized that the actual powers of the soil are as much a human creation as any building or machine. Human effort went into the discovery of the vast new lands of America, and, for that matter, into the draining of marshes and clearing of wasteland in the Old World. Nor can the fertility of land be maintained except by continuing human effort and sacrifice. Most important of all, the original *source* of any productive power is only of historical, not of economic or functional, significance.

It is sometimes claimed that a useful distinction between land and capital can be made in terms of supply curves. Supposedly, the supply of land is absolutely fixed by Nature (a vertical supply curve) while the supply of man-made resources is responsive to price (a positively sloping curve). But more land *will* be provided at a price (if necessary, reclaimed from the ocean), while existing land will be permitted to erode away if the reward for maintaining it is insufficient. Furthermore, as long as there are any reservation uses of land, its supply *to the market* will not in general be fixed (independent of price).[15]

LABOR VERSUS CAPITAL: Nor is it possible in the last analysis to distinguish between *labor power* (the source of human services) and capital. In modern society a worker does not sell raw labor power, but rather his or her trained and educated capacity to apply effort. Training is part of the worker's capital ("human capital"), just as a tool a worker owns is a part of capital. There is no functional difference between the worker's sacrificing time and effort to acquire training (to improve labor skills) on the one hand, or to purchase a set of tools on the other.[16]

[15]The supply curve of land to *all* uses (including reservation uses) will indeed be a vertical line independent of price. But this is true for any resource, including labor. (If "leisure" is counted as a use of labor, the supply of labor is necessarily the entire amount in existence.) Meaningful supply curves always refer to quantities offered for *market* use, excluding reservation uses.

[16]There remain, of course, important differences between human capital and material capital. For one thing, training is less subject than material property to confiscation. (It is said that the emphasis of the Jews upon education is based upon the "portability" of this form of capital.) On the other hand, human capital perishes instantly with the death of its possessor, and can only with difficulty be transferred to others.

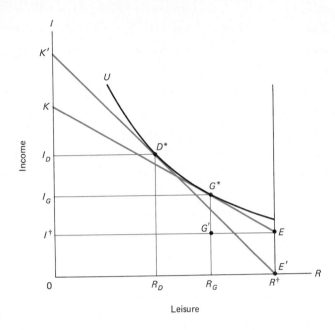

FIGURE 12.14 Returns to Education.
The individual here is just indifferent between making or not making an investment in education. With endowment at E, the initial budget line EK permits attainment of position G^* on indifference curve U. Incurring a cost of education, represented by the vertical distance EE', raises the market wage, allowing the person to move instead along the steeper budget line $E'K'$. But the tangency optimum D^* along $E'K'$ is located on the same indifference curve U. Comparison of D^* with G^* indicates that the individual making the educational investment will thereafter choose less leisure.

12.E.2 ☐ An Application: Investment in Human Capital

There is an interesting interaction between the returns from investment in human capital and the income-versus-leisure choice (the resource-employment decision) discussed in Section 12.A.

Figure 12.14 shows a situation in which an individual is *indifferent* between two situations G^* and D^* on indifference curve U. The endowment E, consisting of $R^\dagger$ of labor capacity and $I^\dagger$ of property income, lies on budget line EK. At the resource-employment optimum G^* the person has labor earnings equal to G^*G', making his total income I_G. But now suppose there is another alternative—adding to "human capital" by investing in education. Let us assume it is necessary to give up all of endowed property income $I^\dagger$ (sacrifice all his non-human capital) to acquire this training; the effective position after this sacrifice therefore becomes E' on the horizontal axis. But as a result of the education this worker now earns a higher wage, so that the new budget line $E'K'$ is steeper than EK.

Although position D^* is by hypothesis indifferent to G^*, the income I_D achieved at D^* is much greater than while the leisure R_D is less than at G^*. Those who become educated should rationally work harder ever after!

EXAMPLE 12.10
Returns to Medical Education

The professional medical associations, in particular the AMA, have been accused of functioning as an entry-restricting cartel. Evidence has been brought forward showing that, *in terms of income achieved,* there seems to be an "excess" return to investment in medical education. That is, medical education seems to be more profitable than is normal for investment in material capital, suggesting that there may be a cartel at work effectively limiting entry into this profitable form of training.

C. M. Lindsay has contended, however, that this comparison in terms of additional income achieved fails to allow properly for the *lesser leisure* typically associated with the resource-employment decisions made after human-capital investments, and after medical training in particular. A true comparison should adjust for this lesser leisure.

In the Table the "unadjusted" MD returns represent the seeming excess value of medical education ($24,376) in comparison with college graduates generally. This measures the net balance of additional income achieved, deducting the cost of medical training, but *without* any offset for additional working hours of MDs. There are two ways of allowing for the difference in working hours: adjusting college-graduate hours worked *up,* or adjusting MD hours worked *down.* (The true comparison must lie between the results of these two alternative adjustments.)

Reportedly, MDs worked 62 hours per week on the average. For the sake of comparison, alternative assumptions of a 40- and a 45-hour average workweek were used for college graduates. If college graduates are working 45 hours per week, the Table shows that a differential or excess net return to medical education persists, the true number lying somewhere between the alternative adjusted excess-return figures of $10,830 and $1950. On the 40-hour assumption, however, the two adjustments average out very close to zero. So if college graduates generally are working close to 40 hours per week, there is no evidence of an excess return to medical education *once the MDs' loss of leisure is properly taken into account.*

Excess Returns to Medical Education

	40-HOUR WEEK	45-HOUR WEEK
Unadjusted MD excess returns	$24,376	$24,376
Adjusted by raising college graduate hours (to 62)	4,660	10,830
Adjusted by lowering MD hours	−4,580	1,950

Source: C. M. Lindsay, "Real Returns to Medical Education," *Journal of Human Resources,* v. 8 (Summer 1973), p. 338. An interest rate of 10% was used to represent the "normal" return from which the "excess" was calculated. (The original source shows the computation in terms of interest rates of both 5% and 10%).

COMMENT: The 62-hour figure for MDs may be suspect, however. Doctors (like others) are apt to report themselves working harder than they really are. If doctors do not in fact work as many as 62 hours per week, the evidence here would tend to support the hypothesis of an excess (cartel-like) return to medical education.

12.E.3 ☐ Capital versus Income: The Rate of Interest

The key to understanding the nature of "capital" lies not in the distinction between capital and land or labor, but in the *contrast between capital and income.* This contrast rests upon the difference between a source of productive services and the productive services themselves. The human being is the source of labor services, but the labor service proper is the "man-hour" (or other such unit representing the employment of a worker over some defined period of time). Similarly, land is a source of productive services, but the service itself is measured in units like acre-years. And again, it is necessary to distinguish buildings and machines (both sources) from the services of building and machines.

Sources and their services may both be traded in markets. There is a price for an acre of land, and a price for a year's use of an acre of land (the latter being the hire-price or rental). There is a price for a building, and a rental for use of the building over some period of time. In a non-slave economy, in contrast, the *sources* of labor services (the human beings themselves) may not be sold, though labor still can be hired for a periodic wage (the hire-price per man-hour). The "factor prices" discussed in this and previous chapters have been the *hire or rental prices of the productive services,* the "wage rates" per unit of time for the use of the resources—not the prices of the resources themselves.

The sources of factor services constitute an individual's or a nation's "capital." Land is capital, machines and buildings are capital, and the human being's training, strength, and skill, as sources of labor power, are capital.

EXAMPLE 12.11
Capital in the Slave-Owning South

The following Table, based on a study by Louis Rose, summarizes the value of various categories of property (capital) in the 15 states where slaves were emancipated by President Lincoln's proclamation. Slave values varied of course with age and other characteristics; the mean was $933. Emancipation constituted an enormous loss to the slave-owners but this was balanced by a corresponding gain to the slaves in the form of the transferred ownership of their own persons. (Indeed, since free labor is certainly more productive, the economic value of the gain to the former slaves must have exceeded the loss to the slave-owners.)

Wealth Data, 15 Southern States, 1860 (millions of dollars)

Value of real estate and personal property	$8644
Value of land in farms	2550
Value of implements and machinery in use	104
Value of livestock	515
Value of slaves emancipated	3685

Source: L. Rose, "Capital Losses of Southern Slaveholders Due to Emancipation," *Western Economic Journal,* v. 3 (Fall 1964), pp. 43, 49.

Two important senses of the word "capital" must be carefully distinguished: *real-capital* versus *capital-value*. Real-capital refers to the sources themselves— buildings, land, labor power, etc. Capital-value is the market valuation of these sources. (To avoid the ambiguity of the word "capital" standing alone, it is good practice always to specify whether it is real-capital or capital-value that is meant.) There are two corresponding senses of the word "income." The services of land generate a flow of *real-income* (e.g., bushels of wheat per year). But if the prefix "real" is omitted, the word "income" standing alone is commonly understood to be in value terms. Thus, an acre of land yields a rental income (dollars per year) to the owner, corresponding to the dollar value of the real-income in bushels per year actually produced.

Consider the Factor Employment Condition of the previous chapter: $h_a = mrp_a \equiv MR(mp_a)$. Here the physical Marginal Product mp_a is the real-income produced in units of the good Q, so the dimensionality of mp_a might be bushels per acre per year. The dimensionality of Marginal Revenue MR is dollars/Q (dollars per bushel) so Marginal Revenue Product mrp_a is in units of dollars per acre per year. On the left-hand side of the equation, the hire-price or "wage" of land is of course also in units of dollars per acre per year.

If a resource as source of productive services is itself tradable, there will be a market-determined ratio between the *annual value of the service* and the *value of the source*, i.e., the ratio of income to capital-value. This ratio, the proportionate *yield* on the capital-value of the source, corresponds to the *rate of interest* earned from ownership of the resource. Suppose that an acre of land is valued at $1000 and generates real-income (has a Marginal Product) of 50 bushels of wheat per year. If the price of wheat is $2 per bushel, the income is $100 per year. Then the rate of interest r earned upon the investment in land is $100/$1000 or 10% per annum. More generally, for any asset:

$$(12.3) \qquad \text{Rate of interest earned } r \equiv \frac{\text{Annual income}}{\text{Value of asset}}$$

In performing this calculation, however, it is important to account for all aspects, both positive and negative, of annual "income." For example, suppose the asset *depreciates* in value during the year because of wear-and-tear or obsolescence. Then the loss due to the depreciation during the year must be taken into account as an offset in calculating the true income from the source. If we symbolize as P the value of any source of income, as ΔP the positive or negative change in this value (appreciation or depreciation) during the year, and as z the "cash-flow" generated during the year, equation (12.3) defining the annual rate of interest r can be written more explicitly as:

(12.3')
$$r \equiv \frac{z + \Delta P}{P}$$

With income properly accounted for, there is a fundamental proposition that governs the relation between income and capital-value:

PROPOSITION: The proportionate yield (the rate of interest earned) on all assets tends to come into equality.

If the yield on asset T were lower than on another asset S, holders of T would be trying to sell out in order to buy S instead. This would drive down the price P_T (capital-value) of T and drive up the price P_S (capital-value) of S. As may be seen from equation (12.3), as the dollar value of source T falls its percent yield must rise, while as the dollar value of source S rises its percent yield must fall. In this way the incentives of individuals to achieve the maximum returns on their asset-holdings tend to bring the rate of interest earned on all assets into equality.

Taking this point into account together with equation (12.3') leads to an important implication: assets whose values are expected to *depreciate* during a given time-period should yield relatively large cash-flows z; assets whose values are expected to *appreciate* may be attractive despite small cash-flows. As an example, a land speculator may pay a steep price for a city lot, even though intending to hold it vacant for a year or more. Here there would be no positive cash-flow at all, and indeed very likely a substantial negative cash-flow when taxes are taken into account. But the decision may prove to be correct, *if* the value of the site appreciates enough to surpass the earnings that could have been achieved via alternative investments.

Exercise 12.4: In an economy where the interest rate is $r = 5\%$, there are three assets: acres of land (A), for which the annual cash flow is $z_A = 50$ and neither appreciation or depreciation is anticipated; barrels of maturing wine (B), for which the cash flow is $z_B = -30$ (there are no receipts, only storage expenses) but which are expected to appreciate 8% in value over the year; and machines (M), yielding a cash flow $z_M = 100$ but expected to depreciate 5% in value over the year. Find the asset prices P_A, P_B, and P_M.

Answer: In each case we will use the equation $r = (z + \Delta P)/P$. For asset A, $\Delta P = 0$ and so the equation has the simple form $0.05 = 50/P$, the solution being $P_A = 1000$. For asset B, the expected appreciation is $\Delta P = 0.08P$. Thus the equation becomes $0.05 = (-30 + 0.08P)/P$, so that $P_B = 1000$ also. For asset M, $\Delta P = -5\%$ and so the equation is $0.05 = (50 - 0.05P)/P$. Once again the solution is $P_C = 1000$. All three assets have the same value; the numbers are such that for asset B a negative cash flow exactly offsets anticipated appreciation, while for asset M a positive cash flow exactly offsets depreciation.

We can now see more clearly into the relation between interest and the traditional "functional" categories—such as rent as return to land and wages as return to labor. Since rent is the hire-price of land, *annual rent* on land will (in equilibrium) be equal to *the interest yield on the price or capital-value* of the land. In a slave economy, annual wages as the hire-price of labor would tend to equal the interest yield on the capital-value of the slave. And even in a free economy, the additional income due to investment in training would, allowing for loss of leisure, tend to equal the interest yield on the cost of acquiring that training (see the Example, "Returns to Medical Education").

In equation (12.3), dollars/year of net income from the services of any factor A must equal the hire-price h_a. Dollar value of the source, the price of factor A itself, can be denoted as P_A. For any factor A, then, in equilibrium:

(12.4) $$h_a = rP_A$$

CONCLUSION: Interest is not the return to a particular factor called "capital." Rather, any factor income represents the interest yield on the price or *capital-value* of the corresponding resource. Or put another way: The interest rate is, for any factor, the ratio between the hire-price of the factor and the market value of the *source* of the factor services.

12.F
ECONOMIC RENT AND PRODUCER SURPLUS

A portion of the income earned by any factor may constitute what is sometimes called "economic rent," to wit, that part of the return to the factor in excess of the minimum amount required to induce it into employment.

Consider Figure 12.15. Here, for some factor service A, the supply curve S_a is vertical; i.e., there are no reservation uses. It follows that the entire income payment for the hire of that resource, the shaded rectangle in the diagram, is an "excess" payment and therefore constitutes economic rent. For, the vertical supply curve shows that the quantity A^* would be forthcoming even at an infinitesimal wage. With an upward-sloping factor supply curve as in Figure 12.16, the region of "excess" payment is the shaded area lying above S_a but below the market price h_a^*. Here not all of factor income is economic rent, because of the existence of reservation uses (compare the upward-sloping MRS_R curve of Figure 12.13).

Economic rent as pictured in Figure 12.16 looks very similar to the representation of *Producer Surplus* in Figure 7.7. And indeed, economic rent is the analog of Producer Surplus. Producer Surplus measures a selling individual's net gain from trade *in the product market*. Economic rent measures the net gain from

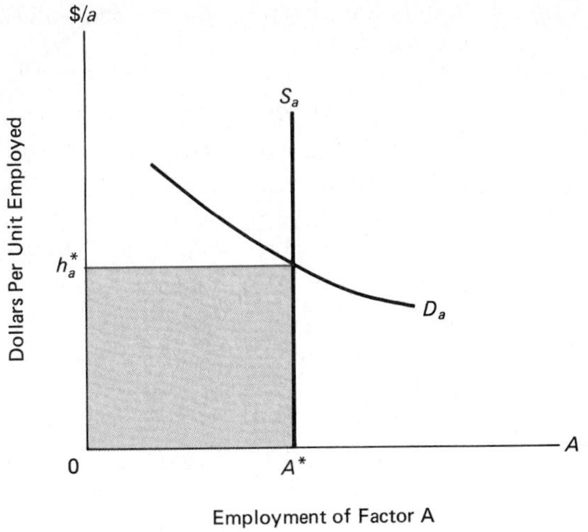

$/a

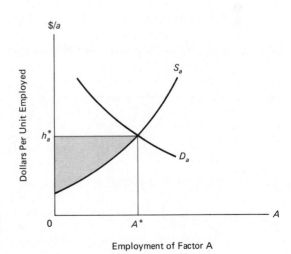

S_a

h_a^*

D_a

0   A^* A

Employment of Factor A

FIGURE 12.15 Economic Rent, I. If the supply curve S_a of factor A is vertical, the entire market receipts to suppliers (the rectangle whose height is the hire-price h_a^* and whose base is employment A^*) is "economic rent"—an excess over the minimum payment required to call the units of the factor into market employment.

trade *in the factor market,* that is, from market employment (as opposed to non-market or reservation uses) of the resources the person owns.

Economic rent is a rather slippery category, one that must be handled with care. Its magnitude depends upon the range of alternatives being considered. If we are thinking of supply of a resource to *all* market employments (as against the alternative of non-market or reservation uses) the economic rent is likely to be large. But if we speak of supply to some narrower range of activity, the economic rent received by the resource-owner is only the excess over the *next-best* employment—which is likely to be much smaller. Diagramatically, in Figure 12.16 the supply curve S_a to a narrow range of activity is likely to be much more elastic than the supply curve to a wider category of activities, and so the shaded area is likely to be smaller.

$/a

S_a

h_a^*

D_a

0   A^* A

Employment of Factor A

FIGURE 12.16 Economic Rent, II. If S_a is upward-sloping, economic rent is the area lying above the supply curve but below the market equilibrium hire-price h_a^*.

EXAMPLE 12.12

Economic Rent and the Military Draft

Until recently a sizable fraction of U. S. military personnel were conscripted. Wages to enlistees were low, and military requirements were met by supplementing volunteers with draftees.

In 1967 Walter Oi[a] analyzed the losses in economic rents that would be suffered, given a continuation of conscription, by suppliers of labor services to the armed forces. For a desired intake of 472,000 recruits annually, it was estimated that the yearly recruitment at the then-current starting wage of $2500 per year would be composed of 263,000 "true" volunteers, 153,700 "reluctant" volunteers (individuals induced to volunteer only to gain some advantages over being drafted), and 55,300 draftees.

The draft as a "tax" on economic rent affects all three of these groups. The true volunteers are those already willing to serve at the $2500 rate. But if military salaries were raised enough to eliminate any need for reluctant volunteers or draftees, the true volunteers would also receive more pay. Under the most favorable assumption as to the elasticity of voluntary supply to the armed forces, Oi estimated that to attract the required numbers the annual wage would have to be $5900. (Under what he regarded as a more realistic supply-elasticity assumption, the wage would have to be $7450.) The loss of this benefit (the economic rent that a true volunteer would otherwise have received) is therefore $3400 per true volunteer per year.

The reluctant volunteers, it is reasonable to assume, had better market opportunities than the true volunteers. As a result of enlistment at the $2500 rather than $5900 wage, they were estimated to lose on average $918 per year from foregoing these market opportunities, leaving $2482 as their average loss in economic rent (where $918 + $2482 = $3400). For the draftees, individuals who had to be compelled to serve, market opportunities were presumably better still. Oi estimated the loss to them as $3165 per year in foregone market opportunities and only $235 per year in economic rent. (These estimates for reluctant volunteers and draftees are minimal figures, which would be appropriate only if individuals drafted or induced to volunteer were those with the poorest alternative non-military employments.)

[a] W. Y. Oi, "The Economic Cost of the Draft," *American Economic Review,* v. 57 (May 1967), pp. 39–62.

12.G

CAPITAL, INTERTEMPORAL CHOICE, AND THE CIRCULAR FLOW

We have now taken account of the individual in two decision-making aspects, as *consumer* and as *resource-owner*. But there remains at any moment of time a third dimension of choice: *between consumption and increased resource-ownership.*

Each person not only has to make decisions as to how to employ currently owned resources and how to consume income, but also whether and to what extent to refrain from consuming now (to save) so as to provide for the future. Having chosen to save, the individual has funds available for increasing his or her resource-ownership. This might be done by purchasing already-existing sources of factor services (land, machines, buildings, etc.) from someone else. Over the economy as a whole, of course, such transactions cancel out as there must be a seller for each buyer. But a firm or an individual might also physically *produce* a social increment of real-capital by manufacturing new resources not previously in existence, or, for that matter, by "manufacturing" new human capital through undergoing training. *Saving* is the process of refraining from consumption; the process of actually building new real-capital is called *investment*.

From the individual's point of view, today's consumption-versus-saving decision can be reinterpreted as an intertemporal choice between *present* consumption and *future* consumption. By not consuming today and saving instead, the person builds up a stock of owned resources so as to augment future income—convertible into consumption at later dates. Eventually, in retirement perhaps, the person is likely to "dis-save" by gradually disposing of owned re-

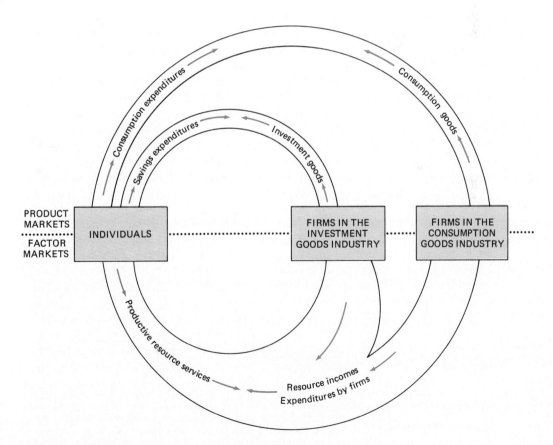

FIGURE 12.17   The Circular Flow: Consumption and Investment.

sources (real-capital) to provide for consumption in old age. (He or she may, however, plan to leave a legacy to descendants, thereby participating by proxy in consumption activities beyond death.) We are thus led to the topic of *intertemporal choice*, the subject of Chapter 14.

The familiar picture in Figure 1.1 of the circular flow of economic activity can now be made more realistic by separating consumption and saving (see Figure 12.17). We now imagine that there are two types of firms: those producing *consumption goods* and those producing real-capital or *investment goods* (buildings, land, machines, etc.). In the upper portion of the diagram (the product market) the two types of goods are purchased by consumption expenditures and savings expenditures, respectively. In the lower part of the diagram (the factor market), resource-owning individuals supply factor services to the employing firms. A decision to save rather than to consume will increase the individual's stock of owned resources. Then, at some later date, he will be able to supply a larger quantity of productive services and thereby earn more future income.[17]

☐ SUMMARY OF CHAPTER 12

Just as individuals face the product markets as demanders of consumer goods, they face the factor markets as suppliers of resource services. Their receipts from provision of factor services become their incomes available for spending on consumer goods.

The services of owned resources can be sold on the market, or else retained for reservation (leisure) uses. The individual can be regarded as having preferences for alternative combinations of income I and reservation uses R_a of any factor A. At the resource-owner's optimum, the Marginal Rate of Substitution in Resource Supply MRS_R (the marginal value of reservation uses) will be equal to the factor hire-price h_a. As endowed income (income from other sources) rises, an Income Expansion Path IEP will be traced out. Assuming that R_a and I are both normal goods, the IEP will have positive slope—showing that as income rises more reservation uses will be chosen (less of the factor will be supplied). As hire-price h_a varies, a Price Expansion Path PEP will be traced out. In decisions as to factor supply, the income and substitution effects normally work in opposite directions. At very low hire-prices (in the neighborhood of the all-leisure corner solution) the substitution effect must dominate, so that the PEP has normal negative slope. But for sufficiently high h_a the income effect may dominate, so that the PEP may "bend backward."

Corresponding to the possible backward-bending range of PEP would be a hire-price h_a' above which the supply curve of resource A to the market also bends backward (less is offered as the hire-price rises). However, even if there should be a range where the overall supply curve *to the entire market* (as against the

---

[17]The implicit assumption underlying the diagram is that all resources are *owned* by individuals and *rented* to firms for productive employment. In actuality firms themselves may legally own as well as hire resources. But resource-ownership on the part of firms can be regarded merely as a convenient fiction, since ultimately all firms are themselves owned by individuals.

alternative of leisure) bends backward, the supply of resource *to any limited sector or particular activity* is almost certain to have the standard positive slope—since there are so many other alternatives to draw supply from as h_a rises.

Market equilibrium for any factor A under conditions of competition is determined by the intersection of an overall demand curve and an overall supply curve. Factor demand tends to rise with technological progress (raising Marginal Product), with higher consumer demand for final products, and with increased supply of cooperating factors. On the supply side, greater wealth in the form of stocks of human and non-human resources increases overall factor availability, but at the same time tends to decrease the fraction provided to the market—since suppliers can afford to "purchase" more reservation uses of their resources.

A monopolist owner of a factor would in effect have a "budget curve" rather than a budget line in the indifference-curve diagram. This can be translated into a curve showing Total Factor Income *TFI* as a function of the amount of resource supplied. The corresponding curves of Average Factor Income *AFI* (an Average Revenue or demand curve) and Marginal Factor Income *MFI* (a Marginal Revenue curve) are declining functions of the amount supplied. The relevant Marginal Cost for such a monopolist would be the Marginal Rate of Substitution in Resource Supply, MRS_R, representing the marginal value of reservation uses. The factor-monopolist would offer the market an amount such that $MRS_R = MFI$ (akin to a product-monopolist setting $MC = MR$). In the absence of reservation uses, the factor-monopolist would have MRS_R of zero and so would simply maximize Total Factor Income *TFI* (would set $MFI = 0$).

Trade unions and other forms of resource cartels represent attempts on the part of smaller suppliers to act together as a collective monopolist. As in the case of product-market cartels, there are strong incentives to "chisel"—which, for the most part, can be effectively countered only by government support of the cartel.

A traditional classification divides factors of production into the categories of *land* (resources provided by Nature), *capital* (resources provided by human sacrifice and forethought), and *labor* (the human resource itself). This classification is not logically defensible: elements provided by Nature and elements provided by human effort enter into all three of the usual categories.

A more valid distinction is that between the *sources* of productive services (which can be regarded as "real-capital," whether in the form of land or machines or human beings) and the *services* themselves. The services are sold in the factor markets and earn *hire-prices*. If the sources themselves can be sold, a logical relation must hold between the price of the source and the hire-price of its services. The *interest rate r* is defined as the ratio between the annual net income of any asset (adjusted for depreciation or appreciation) and the value of the asset itself, or in particular between the hire-price and the purchase price of any factor.

The excess return paid to any factor, over and above the amount necessary to call it into the service considered, is *economic rent*. Economic rent is the analog, in factor-market units, of what was called Producer Surplus in Chapter 7. Economic rent is smaller the narrower the range of uses considered: even if economic rent in all market uses taken together (as against the alternative of non-market uses) is large, the economic rent in the best market use (as against the second-best use) may be quite small.

At any moment of time the individual must make choices as to purchases of consumption goods (the decision problem of the consumer) and as to the employment of resources (the decision problem of the resource-owner). A third decision problem is between consumption and increased resource-ownership, the latter taking place via saving and investment. This is in effect a choice between present consumption and future consumption.

☐ QUESTIONS FOR CHAPTER 12

MAINLY FOR REVIEW

R1. Explain, in terms of income and substitution effects, how a "backward-bending" supply curve of a resource service can come about.

*R2. If leisure were an inferior good, would a backward-bending supply curve of labor be possible?

*R3. Why *must* the substitution effect dominate the income effect at very low wage rates?

*R4. Is the supply curve of a resource to a particular employment likely to be more or less elastic than the supply to all market uses? Why?

R5. In what way does the market opportunity set of a factor-monopolist differ from that of a competitive supplier of factor services? How will the optimum of the resource-owner be affected?

*R6. An individual who invests heavily in developing labor skills will afterward earn a higher wage. But he or she is then likely to work more hours than otherwise would have been the case. Explain why.

R7. Explain the traditional "functional" classification of factors of production.

*R8. How can land and labor power be thought of as capital?

*R9. What is the relationship between the hire-price of a factor and the purchase price of that factor?

R10. What causes the rate of return on all assets to tend toward equality?

*R11. What is economic rent? What is its relation to Producer Surplus?

R12. Show that an individual who would have chosen employment under a welfare-relief system *might* prefer to remain unemployed if there is a Negative Income Tax.

FOR FURTHER THOUGHT AND DISCUSSION

T1. What would be the effect upon the budget line and the resource-employment optimum of a *progressive* income tax on labor earnings? Of a time-and-a-half rule for overtime work?

*T2. Apart from leisure as a reservation use of labor, what other resources are likely to have nonmarket reservation uses yielding utility to their owners?

The answers to asterisked questions appear at the end of the book.

T3. Diagram a situation in which a resource-owner chooses a "corner solution" so as to devote all of his resource to reservation uses. Does this necessarily imply that income *I* must be a "bad" or a "neuter" commodity at the solution point? Diagram a situation in which the resource-owner's optimum is such that no reservation uses *R* are retained. Does this imply that *R* must be a "bad" or a "neuter" commodity at the solution point? Explain.

*T4. With the advent of the women's liberation movement, there is reason to believe that women's preferences may be changing so as to make reservation uses of their time less attractive than before, in comparison with market employment. What effect would such a taste change have upon the supply curve of female labor? Upon the relative market wages of male and female workers?

*T5. In modern times, real wealth and real wage rates have steadily increased throughout the Western world. But average working hours in market employment have steadily fallen. Would the pure "income effect" (due to rising per-capita wealth) tend to lead to reduced market employment? Would the pure "substitution effect" (due to the relative price shift represented by the rising wage rate) tend to have this effect? Comment upon the relative importance of the two in light of the evidence.

*T6. Consider the situation of a slave who has no market opportunity set for disposition of his labor power. Suppose the master simply provided a fixed "income" *I* (in the form of consumption rations) to the slave. What would be the optimum *I, R* position from the point of view of the slave? What position would the master prefer? How is the divergence likely to be resolved? Might it be in the interests of the master to free his slave and pay him wages? Might it not?

T7. Suppose that entry into a particular field of employment for a resource like labor or land is restricted by the requirement to obtain a special license, where the license is traded in the market. Assuming a fixed number of licenses, use supply–demand analysis to determine the equilibrium price of a license. How is the market demand curve for licenses derived from the demand curve and supply curve for the resource service?

T8. In some nations, higher income taxes are imposed upon "unearned" as opposed to "earned" income (i.e., higher taxes upon income from property as opposed to income from labor services). What are the likely effects upon investment in human capital in comparison to investment in physical capital? On the other hand, it has been maintained that most income taxes are biased against labor income by failing to allow any deductions for *depreciation* of the worker's labor power over time. What would be the consequence of allowing such deductions?

*T9. According to the "single tax" movement, a tax on land is likely to be particularly effective. (Allegedly, the supply curve of land is vertical, and so its availability to society will not be affected no matter how heavy is the tax on land.) If a land tax is levied upon *market uses* of the resource (income tax), would the market availability of land be affected? If the tax were levied instead upon *ownership* of the resource (wealth tax), would the market availability of land be affected? Then make an analogous comparison, in terms of the market availability of labor, of an *income* tax upon labor earnings versus a *wealth* tax upon labor capacity. (The latter is a so-called "facultative" tax, a fixed sum proportioned to a person's *ability* to earn rather than to his actual market earnings.)

*T10. Following up Question T7 in the preceding chapter, what *supply-side* considerations may help explain the relatively high wages received by U.S. workers?

T11. Over a century ago Karl Marx, in what is known as the "immiserization hypothesis," predicted that workers' wages and incomes in the advanced industrial countries would tend to fall—thus bringing on a socialist revolution. This prediction has failed. Some defenders of Marx have argued that the reason why "immiserization" did not occur is that in the meantime capitalism has adopted "socialistic" reforms. Among these might perhaps be classed minimum-wage laws, the forty-hour week, welfare relief for the unemployed, and laws encouraging trade unions and collective bargaining. What effects would you expect each of these reforms to have upon wage rates? Upon workers' incomes?

*T12. Wage rates are high in New York City, compared to the rest of the United States. But so is the cost of living. Explain why this pattern exists.

CORE CHAPTER

THE BENEFITS OF EXCHANGE, TRANSACTION COSTS, AND THE ROLE OF MONEY

The Fundamental Theorem of Exchange—that voluntary trade is mutually beneficial—was introduced in Chapter 7. We also saw there how Consumer Surplus and Producer Surplus measure the benefits of exchange to buyers and sellers, respectively. Errors of economic reasoning (for example, the most commonly encountered arguments for protective tariffs) often rest upon failure to appreciate the obvious truth that voluntary trade is mutually beneficial.

There are, it must be conceded, certain debatable aspects of this proposition. (1) Suppose that trickery has taken place: a purchaser pays good money for a beachfront lot that turns out to be a mile out to sea. Here there was no actual *agreement*, no meeting of minds, so the transaction was not really a mutually voluntary exchange. (2) The momentary desires on which an exchange is based may not represent an individual's true considered preferences. Esau sold his birthright to Jacob for a mess of pottage, and regretted the transaction afterward. (3) Still more seriously, the question remains as to whether individuals truly benefit from having even their fully considered preferences satisfied. That a person's desires do not necessarily lead to where true benefit lies has been a theme of moralists through the ages.

While these philosophical questions cannot be studied here, we see that there are possible qualifications to the Fundamental Theorem. Nevertheless, accepting the postulate of rationality, it remains the case that each participant in exchange benefits *as he sees it at the time of decision*, although possibly not in the opinion of an outside observer (or even in his own opinion at some later date).

There are two distinct elements in the mutual gain from trade. The first element is an *improved allocation of consumption goods* over individuals. Suppose there are two persons, let us call them John and Karl, both endowed with equal quantities of tea and coffee (perhaps as a result of a wartime rationing system). If John prefers tea and Karl prefers coffee, the potential gain from trade will be obvious. Nor are differences of taste necessary. Suppose that John and Karl, having the same preferences, find themselves in possession of quantities of bread and butter, except that John has all the bread and Karl all the butter. Again, trade can lead to improved consumption patterns for both.

The second source of improvement, an indirect consequence of the first, is *rearrangement of production* rather than of consumption. In the illustration just given, if John were better at baking bread and Karl at churning butter, the possibility of later trading would permit each to specialize in the activity for which he is better suited. Specialized production would make greater *totals* of goods available to all, apart from the improved consumption distributions that trade brings about after the goods are produced.

> CONCLUSION: Voluntary exchange is mutually beneficial because traders can: (1) reallocate existing stocks of consumption goods so that each achieves a preferred bundle, and (2) specialize in production so as to increase the social totals of goods available.

In this chapter we will be probing more deeply than before into the familiar supply–demand equilibrium of markets. We will also face the fact that exchange is not a costless process, and that *transaction costs* place a limit upon the achievable benefits from trade. The role of *money* in minimizing such costs of transacting will be the last topic of the chapter.

13.A
PURE-EXCHANGE EQUILIBRIUM: THE EDGEWORTH BOX

How exchange improves the allocation of consumption goods is pictured by the "Edgeworth box" in Figure 13.1. For John the origin O_j is at the lower-left corner as usual; his preference map (consisting of indifference curves U'_j, U''_j, ...) is drawn upon axes representing his consumption quantities x_j and y_j of commodities X and Y, respectively. For Karl the directions are reversed. Karl's origin O_k is at the upper-right corner of the box; his indifference curves are drawn with respect to his consumption quantities x_k and y_k. The arrows attached to the axes indicate that, for commodity X, John's quantity x_j is measured by distance to the *right* of O_j and Karl's quantity x_k by distance to the *left* of O_k; similarly, John's y_j is measured *upward* from O_j and Karl's y_k *downward* from O_k.

The width and height of the Edgeworth box are determined by the social totals $\overline{X}$ and $\overline{Y}$ of the two commodities, where $\overline{X} \equiv x_j + x_k$ and $\overline{Y} \equiv y_j + y_k$. The fixed social totals, the dimensions of the Edgeworth box, mean that no production takes place (since production, by its very nature, changes the total availabilities of commodities). It follows that if John's consumption x_j of commodity X increases then Karl's x_k must correspondingly decrease, unit for unit, and similarly for commodity Y.

The initial allocation of the two goods between John and Karl is shown by the *endowment* position E. John's endowment consists of the quantities $x_j^\dagger$ and $y_j^\dagger$ measured to the east and to the north, respectively, from his origin O_j. Karl's endowment consists of the quantities $x_k^\dagger$ and $y_k^\dagger$ measured to the west and to the south from his origin O_k. Trading entails a shift to some other allocation of the social totals, i.e., to some position other than E in the box. If X and Y are *goods* for both parties, then each will insist upon receiving more of one commodity in exchange for giving up some of the other. The allocations permitted by this condition (i.e., achievable by voluntary exchange) are those lying either toward the southeast *or* toward the northwest of the initial endowment position E.

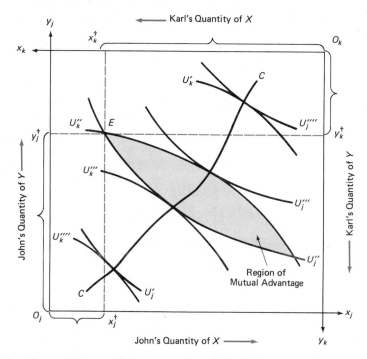

FIGURE 13.1 Edgeworth Box. John's consumption of X and Y is measured in the usual way by distances east and north of the origin O_j. For Karl the axes are inverted: his consumption of X is measured by distance west of the origin O_k, and his consumption of Y by distance south of O_k. John's preferences are represented by the indifference curves U'_j, U''_j, ... with utility increasing moving northeast, Karl's by the curves U'_k, U''_k, ... with utility rising moving southwest. The overall width of the box corresponds to the fixed social total $\overline{X}$, and the overall height to the fixed social total $\overline{Y}$. Any point in the diagram represents an allocation of these social totals between John and Karl. Starting at the endowment position E, the allocations preferred to E by both parties (on higher U_j and U_k indifference curves) are shown by the shaded Region of Mutual Advantage.

But a still stronger condition can be placed on the mutually advantageous exchanges that are possible. Consider the traders' respective indifference curves U''_j and U''_k that pass through the endowment position E. If trade is voluntary and the individuals are rational, neither will ever move to a point at a lower preference level than he has already attained at E. Each will only move "uphill" from E on his utility surface. Consequently, the possible final allocations are only those lying within the shaded lens-shaped region in the diagram between U''_j and U''_k. This area is called the *region of mutual advantage*.

EXAMPLE 13.1 _____
Economic Exchange and the American Civil War

Before the Civil War the northern and southern states had engaged in a mutually advantageous economic exchange. The South produced a vast surplus of cotton which was sold in the North (and also abroad), the proceeds being used to purchase manufactured products. Less than 10% of the total pre-war (1860) national value of manufactures had been produced in the seceded states.[a]

• With the onset of the war, direct North–South trade was interrupted. The interruption hit the Confederacy much harder than the Union. While cotton prices in the North jumped, this was an inconvenience rather than a catastrophe. But the Union blockade largely prevented the South from exporting cotton or importing manufactured products. (The small blockade-running traffic was largely used for the import of luxury goods. "When Captain Hobart Pasha of the *Venus* asked a southern woman in England what was most needed in the Confederacy, she unhesitatingly replied, 'Corsets'.")[b] Despite valiant effort to redirect production, the South was brought to economic and military collapse by inability to acquire essential manufactured civilian products and implements of war, while huge stocks of unsalable cotton piled up uselessly in her storehouses.

Confederate trade policy was seriously misguided. Export of the huge cotton crops of 1861 and 1862 to earn credits abroad would have been possible, since the Union blockade did not really become effective until later years. The Confederate government discouraged this export. They reasoned that, since "Cotton was King," withholding the crop would force northern and foreign industrial interests to support the secession. Relying on their opponents' loss of the advantage of trade, the South's leaders failed to realize how much more vulnerable a largely one-crop economy was to the interruption of mutually advantageous exchange.

An even more striking error was the policy of the Confederate government that banned trade through the lines with the North, partly on moralistic grounds, partly again to withhold "King Cotton." This was illogical for several reasons, one of which was that most of the cotton run through the blockade to Cuba or Bermuda was transshipped to the North anyway. But more important, a strict ban on trade through the lines was, for the Union, a logical complement to the sea blockade, a component of the "anaconda" policy of strangling the southern economy. In contrast, it was in the interest of the South to break this overland ban almost as much as it was to evade the sea blockade. It is true that the cotton and tobacco that could have been sent North would, to some degree, have helped the northern war economy. But the Confederacy, its economy collapsing because of inability to dispose of its surpluses for needed imports of all kinds, was in a position where it had to grasp every opportunity. Actually, a substantial amount of illegal trade did pass through the lines; despite the attempts of officials on both sides to stop the practice, the temptations of corruption and the real needs of the southern economy at times proved to be an overwhelming combination. Curiously, even

[a]Albert D. Kirwan, ed., *The Confederacy* (New York: Meridian Books, 1959), p. 63.
[b]Clement Eaton, *A History of the Southern Confederacy* (New York: Macmillan, 1954), p. 144.

today historians commonly take a moralistic attitude on this question. They fail to appreciate the fundamental asymmetry that made maintenance of the land blockade a wise policy for the Union, but an unwise one for the Confederacy.[c]

[c] This discussion is based on J. Hirshleifer, *Disaster and Recovery: A Historical Survey*, The Rand Corporation, Memorandum RM–3079–PR (April 1963), Section IV.

Figure 13.2 illustrates the determination of market prices, where John and Karl are *competitive* traders or "price-takers." The price ratio P_x/P_y is the absolute value of the slope of the budget line in this double indifference-curve diagram. Suppose hypothetically that prices are such that the dashed line KL is the budget line. For John, KL passes through his endowment position $E = (x_j^\dagger, y_j^\dagger)$ and represents an upper (northeast) boundary of his market opportunities (just as in

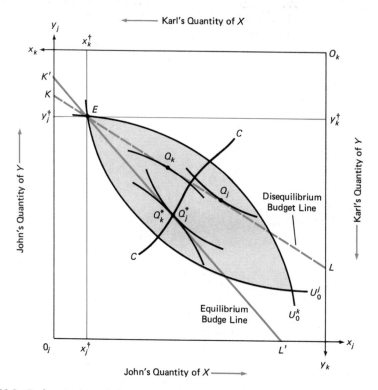

FIGURE 13.2 Budget Lines and Competitive Equilibrium. Any price ratio P_x/P_y determines the slope of a corresponding budget line through the endowment position E. Each such budget line is a northeast boundary of the opportunity set for John, a southwest boundary for Karl. The dashed budget line KL does not correspond to a competitive market equilibrium for these two traders, since along KL John's optimum Q_j and Karl's optimum Q_k do not coincide. K'L' does correspond to an equilibrium price ratio, since the optimum positions Q_j^* and Q_k^* do coincide. A *mutual tangency* of indifference curves therefore exists at that point. If the endowment position were to vary, any equilibrium solution would still have to be at a point of mutual tangency of indifference curves; the contract curve CC shows all such possible equilibrium solutions.

Figure 4.1). But in the Edgeworth box KL must also serve as budget line for Karl, passing through his endowment position $E = (x_k^\dagger, y_k^\dagger)$. Since Karl's axes are inverted, KL as upper limit for him bounds the market opportunity set toward the *southwest* rather than the northeast.

With KL as budget line in Figure 13.2, John would want to proceed to a consumptive optimum indicated by the position Q_j. Similarly, Karl would want to move to his optimum along KL at Q_k. But the two points Q_j and Q_k do not coincide! This means that the quantity of X that John wishes to purchase, offering Y in exchange in accordance with the price ratio represented by the slope of KL, is *not* equal to the quantity that Karl is prepared to supply at that price ratio. The situation is not one of competitive equilibrium. The difficulty is that KL represents a price ratio P_x/P_y such that X is too cheap relative to Y, the buyer (John) seeking to take more of X than the seller (Karl) is willing to offer.

An *equilibrium price ratio* for competitive trading is represented by the steeper line $K'L'$ in Figure 13.2, corresponding to a higher price ratio P_x'/P_y'. At this price ratio both parties are led to *coinciding* preferred positions $Q^* = Q_k^*$, meaning that the amount of commodity X offered by Karl equals the amount willingly purchased by John. (Correspondingly, of course, the quantity of Y offered by John in payment must also exactly balance the amount required by Karl.)

> PROPOSITION: In the Edgeworth box, the competitive equilibrium allocation of the two commodities (1) lies in the region of mutual advantage, and (2) represents a mutual tangency of both traders' indifference curves with one another and with a common budget line.

Now imagine a number of possible variations of the endowment position E. For each such E, there will be a different region of mutual advantage and a different equilibrium budget line. But the only potential competitive equilibria are the points representing mutual tangencies of indifference curves of John and Karl, since only there do the consumptive optimum positions coincide. The curve connecting these mutual tangencies is known as the *contract curve*, shown as CC in Figures 13.1 and 13.2.

In equilibrium each market participant must be at his tangency optimum, that is, each must be (1) on his budget line, and (2) at a point where his Marginal Rate of Substitution in Consumption, MRS_C, equals the price ratio. Thus, for John and Karl the following equations must hold:

(13.1)
$$P_x x_j + P_y y_j = P_x x_j^\dagger + P_y y_j^\dagger \quad \text{and} \quad P_x x_k + P_y y_k = P_x x_k^\dagger + P_y y_k^\dagger$$
$$MRS_C^j = P_x/P_y = MRS_C^k$$

And the second condition of equilibrium is that the sum of the individuals' desired consumption quantities must equal the social total available, for each commodity. This condition corresponds to the equations:

(13.2)
$$x_j + x_k = \overline{X}$$
$$x_j + y_k = \overline{Y}$$

Exercise 13.1: Suppose that John's Marginal Rate of Substitution in Consumption is $MRS^j_C = y_j/x_j$, and for Karl similarly $MRS^k_C = y_k/x_k$. Let the endowments be $(x^†_j, y^†_j) = (10, 100)$ and $(x^†_k, y^†_k) = (50, 20)$. Verify that if Y is the *numéraire* (so that $P_y \equiv 1$), the equilibrium price is $P^*_x = 2$.

Answer: First finding John's consumptive optimum at $P_x = 2$, the equations that must be satisfied are:

$$2x_j + y_j = 2(10) + 100 \qquad \text{and} \qquad y_j/x_j = 2$$

The solution is $(x^*_j, y^*_j) = (30, 60)$. For Karl the corresponding equations are $2x_k + y_k = 2(50) + 20$ and $y_k/x_k = 2$, leading to the same numerical solution for him: $(x^*_k, y^*_k) = (30, 60)$. Verifying that the social totals are met:

$$x_j + x_k \equiv \overline{X} \equiv x^†_j + x^†_k = 60$$

$$y_j + y_k \equiv \overline{Y} \equiv y^†_j + y^†_k = 120.$$

13.B
SUPPLY AND DEMAND IN PURE EXCHANGE

Let us reinterpret this pure-exchange equilibrium in terms of supply and demand, examining more specifically the *transacting* that takes place.

The Price Expansion Path PEP in Panel (a) of Figure 13.3 looks very much like the PEP of Figure 4.3 except for one novel feature. In the diagram of Chapter 4, as the budget lines tilted in response to changes in P_x they all remained anchored to a fixed point K on the vertical axis. This anchoring point corresponded to the quantity I/P_y—or simply I, if Y is the *numéraire* commodity so that $P_y \equiv 1$. But here the situation is slightly different. John comes to market not with a fixed *income I*, but rather with fixed *endowment quantities* of X and Y. Therefore, the anchoring position through which the budget lines all pass is not necessarily a point on the vertical axis; the endowment point E_j may lie anywhere in the diagram. (The previous analysis therefore corresponded to a special case in which the individual had an endowment consisting only of units of Y, none of X.)

This modification has an important consequence. In Figure 4.3 the individual could only be a demander of X, never a supplier. But here John's endowment position E_j lies toward but not quite at the vertical axis; he has a large endowment of Y, but also some positive endowment of X. We would therefore expect him *usually* to be a demander of X from the market, but not necessarily *always*. There is some price ratio P_x/P_y so high (some budget line $K°L°$ so steep) that he will prefer to stand pat with his endowment combination and not make any additional purchases of X. This is called the "sustaining" price ratio. And for even higher price ratios (even steeper budget lines through E_j), John would actually be a net supplier of X to the market—that is, his consumptive optimum position would then be at a point northwest of E_j. (Of course, every time that John is a demander of X from the market he is necessarily a supplier of Y, and *vice versa*.) Similarly for Karl; Panel (b) reveals that while he will usually be a supplier of X (demander of Y), at a sufficiently low price ratio P_x/P_y his market behavior would reverse.

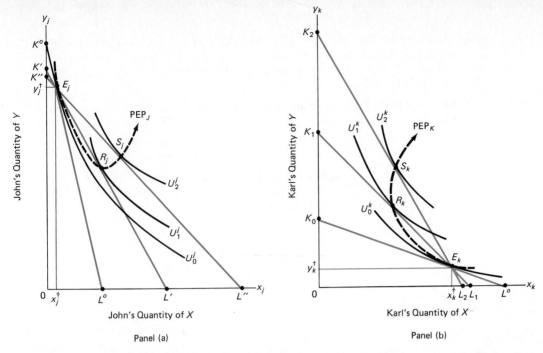

FIGURE 13.3 Price Expansion Paths. Changes in the price ratio are reflected by tilting of the budget lines which, however, must all pass through the endowment positions E_j for John in Panel (a) and E_k for Karl in Panel (b). Since John's endowment is toward the northwest in Panel (a), he will ordinarily be a demander of X from the market (supplier of Y). More specifically, for price ratios leading to points on PEP_j east of E_j, John will be a net demander of X; at the "sustaining" price ratio (budget line $K°L°$) leading to a tangency at E_j itself he will stand pat and not trade; for still higher price ratios he will be a supplier of X (indicated by the range of PEP_j to the west of E_j). A corresponding analysis holds for Karl in Panel (b).

The next step is the transfer of the data represented by the Price Expansion Paths of Figure 13.3 to generate demand and supply curves on x, P_x axes. This can be done in two different ways, which we must be careful not to confuse. The first runs in terms of the whole or "full" quantities demanded or supplied, the second in terms of the net or "transaction" quantities. On the demand side, the "full" quantity demanded of good X *includes* the quantity of X endowed—this is the demand concept relevant for purposes of consumption. The "transaction" demand quantity *excludes* the quantity endowed (the quantity self-supplied) and thus represents demand relevant for purposes of market trading. On the supply side the "full" quantity is simply the fixed endowment amount, while the "transaction" quantity is that portion of the endowment offered to the market. We can think of the "full" quantities as those demanded from or supplied to the *economy*, while the "transaction" quantities are those smaller amounts demanded from or supplied to the *market*.

The relation between transaction demands and full demands, for any individual i, is given by:

(13.3)
$$x_i^t \equiv x_i - x_i^\dagger$$
$$y_i^t \equiv y_i - y_i^\dagger$$
Transaction Demands and Full Demands

The first equation says that the transaction quantity of commodity X demanded by individual i from the market, x_i^t, is equal to the full quantity desired for purposes of consumption, x_i, minus the quantity already in the individual's possession before trading, $x_i^\dagger$. The second equation expresses a corresponding relation for commodity Y. In Panel (a) of Figure 13.3, the *full* quantity of X associated with any consumptive optimum position like E_j, R_j, or S_j along the PEP_j curve is simply the x-coordinate of that position—the horizontal distance from that point on the PEP_j curve to the vertical axis. The transaction quantity is this horizontal distance *less* the endowed amount $x_j^\dagger$, the x-coordinate of E_j. It follows that at his sustaining price ratio John's *full* demand for X equals $x_j^\dagger$ and his *transaction* demand for X is zero.

The transaction demands x_i^t and y_i^t in equation (13.3) can be positive or negative. Negative transaction demand is, of course, positive transaction supply. But the full demand magnitudes x_i and y_i and the endowed or full supply quantities $x_i^\dagger$ and $y_i^\dagger$ are necessarily non-negative; neither consumption nor endowment can ever be less than zero.

The distinction between full and transaction magnitudes is important in a number of areas, among them taxation. A tax on *consumption* of good X is levied upon the full demands; a tax on *purchases* of X burdens only the transaction demands. Put another way, endowed quantities that are self-consumed escape a "transaction tax" on purchases, but do not escape a tax on consumption. A special case of a transaction tax is a tariff, which burdens international trading but not domestic trading (the latter representing quantities that are "self-supplied" from the viewpoint of the nation as a whole). One important practical implication is that as transaction taxes become higher, individuals will find it increasingly attractive to self-supply their wants rather than deal in the market. It seems very likely that the growth of the "do-it-yourself" movement is in large part a response to the growing weight of taxes on market transactions.

As the price ratio P_x/P_y (or simply P_x, if Y is the *numéraire* so that $P_y \equiv 1$) varies, Figure 13.4 shows how the individual's supply and demand curves for

FIGURE 13.4 Full and Transaction Supply and Demand Curves in Pure Exchange. For an individual i in pure exchange, the *full demand curve* d_i shows, at any price P_x, the desired consumption quantity. The *full supply curve* $s_i^\dagger$ represents i's fixed endowment quantity. The *transaction demand curve* d_i^t shows, at any price P_x, the amount demanded from the market (horizontal difference between d_i and $s_i^\dagger$). In the range where transaction demand d_i^t is negative, it is usually more convenient to speak of a positive *transaction supply curve* s_i^t. Transaction demand and supply are exactly zero at the sustaining price $P_x^\dagger$.

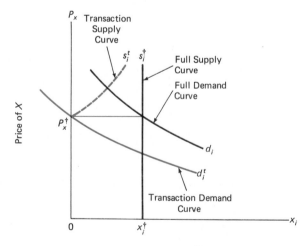

Full or Transaction Quantity of X

commodity X are traced out. The "full demand curve" corresponds to the desired consumption quantity x_i, the "full supply curve" to the endowed quantity $x_i^\dagger$, and the "transaction demand curve" to the difference between the two—x_i^t. Note that above the "sustaining price" $P_x^\dagger$ it is more convenient to diagram a positive "transaction supply" rather than a negative "transaction demand." [Justifying the relations among the shapes of these curves is left as an exercise for the reader.]

Figure 13.5 brings supply and demand together in two different ways—in terms of the transaction magnitudes in Panel (a), and the full magnitudes in Panel (b). Recall that John was relatively poorly endowed with X and Karl relatively well endowed with X. Accordingly in Panel (a), in the neighborhood of the equilibrium price P_x^* the social total D^t of the transaction demand is due to John's net demand d_j^t, and the social total S^t of the transaction supply to Karl's net supply s_k^t. (More generally, of course, S^t and D^t would sum up the transaction choices of many traders on each side of the market.) Panel (b) shows the other instructive way of looking at the two-person supply–demand equilibrium. Instead of net quantities supplied to or demanded from *the market*, the diagram pictures the full magnitudes demanded (for consumption) from or supplied (via endowment) to *the economy*. [Verification of the correspondence between the two panels is left also as an exercise for the reader.] One final point to appreciate is that at the supply–demand equilibrium of commodity X, the equilibrium for commodity Y is also being implicitly determined. [*Query:* Why?]

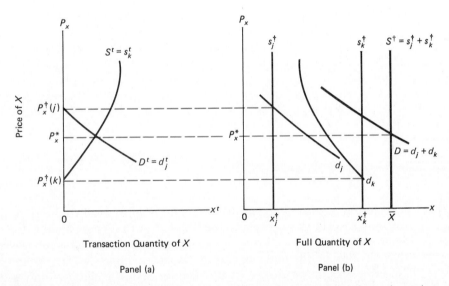

Panel (a) — Transaction Quantity of X

Panel (b) — Full Quantity of X

FIGURE 13.5 Supply–Demand Equilibrium. Panel (a) shows a competitive demand–supply equilibrium for commodity X in terms of the *transaction* quantities; Panel (b) pictures the same equilibrium in terms of the *full* quantities. Since John is relatively poorly endowed and Karl well endowed with commodity X, the equilibrium in Panel (a) is at the intersection of John's *transaction demand curve* d_j^t and Karl's *transaction supply curve* s_k^t. In Panel (b) the aggregate *full supply curve* $S^\dagger$ to the economy as a whole is the sum of John's $s_j^\dagger$ and Karl's $s_k^\dagger$. The aggregate *full demand curve* D is similarly the sum of d_j and d_k. The $S^\dagger$ and D curves in Panel (b) must intersect at the same equilibrium price P_x^* as at the intersection of S^t and D^t.

CONCLUSION: Competitive supply–demand equilibrium can be expressed in two ways. The intersection of the aggregate *transaction* supply curve and the aggregate *transaction* demand curve determines the equilibrium price and the quantity actually traded in markets. The intersection of the aggregate *full* supply curve and the aggregate *full* demand curve determines the same equilibrium price, but the quantity shown is the entire economy-wide consumption, which must equal the aggregate full amount supplied. (In pure exchange, this quantity would be the sum of the individual endowments.)

We should, of course, be thinking of the equilibrating process as involving not just two commodities X and Y but rather all goods simultaneously. The result is a *general* equilibrium of prices and quantities. However, the underlying principles—that individuals optimize, and that demand and supply balance in the market—are in no way different from the principles illustrated in the simplified two-good world.

Exercise 13.2: Using the data of Exercise 13.1, find: (a) the "full" supply and demand curves for each individual and for the society, and (b) the corresponding "transaction" supply and demand curves. Verify the solution $P_x^* = 2$ in each case.

Answer: (a) John's budget equation is $P_x x_j + y_j = 10P_x + 100$ and his Substitution Equivalence Equation is $y_j/x_j = P_x$. Eliminating y_j, his "full" demand equation is $x_j = 5 + 50/P_x$. Karl's optimality conditions are $P_x x_k + y_k = 50P_x + 20$ and $y_k/x_k = P_x$, leading to his "full" demand equation $x_k = 25 + 10/P_x$. The aggregate full demand equation is then $X_d = x_j + x_k = 30 + 60/P_x$. The "full" supplies are simply $x_j^\dagger = 10$ and $x_k^\dagger = 50$, so that in aggregate $X_s = 60$. Letting $X_s = X_d$, the solution is indeed $P_x^* = 2$. (b) John's "transaction" demand is $x_j - x_j^\dagger \equiv x_j^t = -5 + 50/P_x$. Karl's is $x_k - x_k^\dagger \equiv x_k^t = -25 + 10/P_x$. In the neighborhood of equilibrium John is a net demander of X and Karl a net supplier. So the aggregate transaction demand is $X_d^t = x_j^t = -5 + 50/P_x$. For the aggregate transaction supply we can take the negative of Karl's transaction demand: $X_s^t = -x_k^t = 25 - 10/P_x$. Letting $X_d^t = X_s^t$, the solution once again is $P_x^* = 2$.

13.C
EXCHANGE AND PRODUCTION

So far in this chapter we have considered trade in a world without production, a world of "pure exchange." Under pure exchange individuals can alter their endowments *only* through market trading. But in the actual world individuals can also modify endowments by *production*, by transacting (so to speak) with Nature. As the opposite extreme, Robinson Crusoe could deal only with Nature; he could produce and consume, but could not trade. What we really want to analyze is a world where transactions both with Nature (production) and with other persons (exchange) are taking place.

In each panel of Figure 13.6 the shaded region shows the *productive opportunity set*—all the possible baskets of commodities X and Y that an individual might have the capacity to produce. The northeast boundary QQ of the pro-

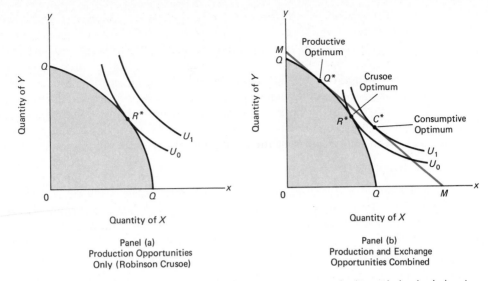

FIGURE 13.6 Productive and Consumptive Optimum Positions.   In both panels the shaded region shows a *productive opportunity set* subject to diminishing returns as the individual specializes in production of either *X* or *Y*. Panel (a) is the situation of a Robinson Crusoe, whose best attainable point *R** is a joint productive–consumptive optimum. In Panel (b) the individual has *both* productive and exchange opportunities. The productive optimum is at *Q**, allowing trade to a consumptive optimum at *C**. The final *C** outcome made possible by exchange is superior to the Robinson Crusoe outcome at *R**.

ductive opportunity set is called the *transformation locus* or *Production-Possibility Curve* (PPC). Its "concave" shape reflects diminishing returns. Suppose that an individual or a nation tried to specialize by concentrating upon the production of commodity *X*, i.e., tried to produce a combination well toward the *X*-axis along *QQ*. As specialization is pushed further and further, each increment of *X* requires a greater and greater sacrifice of *Y*—*increasing opportunity costs* are encountered.

For a Robinson Crusoe possessing *only* productive transformation opportunities, the optimum consumption basket in Panel (a) of Figure 13.6 is *R**, the tangency of his transformation locus *QQ* with his highest attainable indifference curve U_0. Since Crusoe cannot engage in trade, *R** represents for him a *joint productive–consumptive optimum*. The tangency condition can be expressed as the equation:

(13.4) $$MRS_C = MRS_T \qquad \text{Robinson Crusoe Optimum}$$

Here MRS_C, the Marginal Rate of Substitution in Consumption, corresponds as we know to the absolute indifference-curve slope. The new symbol MRS_T stands for the *Marginal Rate of Substitution in Productive Transformation;* more briefly, *Marginal Rate of Transformation*. MRS_T is the absolute slope of the Production-Possibility Curve, the additional amount of *Y* that can be produced per unit small sacrifice of *X*. Note how the opposing curvatures (of the transformation locus QQ versus the indifference curves) guarantee that there will be a unique tangency R^*.[1]

> CONCLUSION: A Robinson Crusoe, possessing productive transformation opportunities but isolated from opportunities for exchange with other individuals, would find his joint productive–consumptive optimum at the point where his Marginal Rate of Substitution in Consumption MRS_C equals his Marginal Rate of Transformation MRS_T along the boundary of his productive opportunity set.

Robinson Crusoe situations may seem fanciful, but this is not necessarily so. We might, for example, sometimes want to consider a nation as a whole as an acting entity; history has shown a number of instances in which a nation has isolated itself from external trade.

[1]*Mathematical Footnote:* In terms of derivatives, the condition can be expressed as:

$$\frac{dy}{dx}\bigg|_U = \frac{dy}{dx}\bigg|_Q$$

In addition, the individual must be on his Production-Possibility Curve, so that the equation $Q(x, y) = 0$ is satisfied.

EXAMPLE 13.2
Animal Robinson Crusoes

Trade is a human invention. Since they do not engage in exchange with one another, non-human animals make all their economic decisions under Robinson Crusoe conditions. An example of such a decision is the problem of "optimal diet breadth," which biologists have analyzed in a way that corresponds exactly to Panel (a) of Figure 13.6.[a]

Think of X and Y as two sources of food—for example, two prey species for a predator. Because of diminishing returns the predator's productive opportunity set typically has a shape like the shaded region in the diagram. The more the predator concentrates upon consuming prey species X, the scarcer and harder to capture X becomes relative to the availability of Y (increasing Marginal Rate of Transformation). The predator also has "preferences" as represented by the indifference curves in the diagram. Each such curve represents a set of equally acceptable diets. The convexity of the indifference curves presumably reflects the fact that variety helps provide the many metabolic inputs required by living organisms. The greater the consumption of food

[a]The discussion here is based on D. J. Rapport, "An Optimization Model of Food Selection," *The American Naturalist*, v. 105 (Nov.–Dec. 1971) and M. L. Cody, "Optimization in Ecology," *Science*, v. 183 (March 22, 1974).

source X, the harder it becomes to achieve nutritional needs by additional consumption of X as compared to the nutritional benefit of a unit of Y (decreasing Marginal Rate of Substitution in Consumption).

The optimal position for the animal is of course at the "Robinson Crusoe" tangency point R^*, which will ordinarily represent an interior (mixed-diet) solution.

Now let us drop the Robinson Crusoe case and consider an individual having both productive and trading opportunities. We can imagine that Crusoe is discovered by the world market in which he becomes a competitive trader or "price-taker." Market opportunities are shown in Panel (b) of Figure 13.6 by the line MM just tangent to the transformation locus QQ. The absolute slope of the market line represents the ruling price ratio P_x/P_y. The existence of market opportunities permits a trader to *separate the productive and consumptive decisions*. Specifically, the formerly isolated individual can now attain his consumptive optimum (most preferred combination of x and y) at C^* on indifference curve U_1 by a two-step procedure. First, he moves along QQ to his *productive optimum Q^**, the tangency of the Production-Possibility Curve with the market line MM. From Q^*, by exchanging X for Y he can move southeast along MM so as to finally achieve the *consumptive optimum* at C^*. A comparison of the Crusoe solution R^* with the improved optimum C^* now attainable reveals the advantage gained from the separation of productive and consumptive decisions made possible by trade.

The productive optimum position Q^* is associated with the equation:

(13.5) $$MRS_T = MRS_E \equiv \frac{P_x}{P_y} \qquad \text{Productive Optimum Condition}$$

The individual sets the Marginal Rate of Transformation along QQ equal to the Marginal Rate of Substitution *in Exchange*, the absolute price ratio P_x/P_y ruling in the market. This condition in effect moves the individual *onto* the market line MM at point Q^*. The familiar consumptive optimum condition, achieved by movement *along MM* to C^*, is:

(13.6) $$\frac{P_x}{P_y} \equiv MRS_E = MRS_C \qquad \text{Consumptive Optimum Condition}$$

Since (13.5) and (13.6) together imply $MRS_T = MRS_C$, equation (13.4) holds in a world of exchange as well as for an isolated Robinson Crusoe. But for Crusoe MRS_C and MRS_T are equated *at the same point R^* along QQ*, whereas someone engaged in trade can generally do even better by being able to set $MRS_T = P_x/P_y$ at the productive optimum Q^* and $P_x/P_y = MRS_C$ at the consumptive optimum C^*.

Exercise 13.3:   Robinson Crusoe's Production-Possibility Curve is expressed by the equation $f^2/2 + g = 150$, where f is the amount of fish and g the amount of grain he can obtain depending upon the way he divides his time and effort. (Think of g as plotted on the vertical axis, f as on the horizontal axis.) Robinson's Marginal Rate of Substitution in Consumption is $MRS_C = g/f$. (a) Find Robinson's production–consumption optimum R^*. (b) If Robinson is discovered by a world market in which $P_f = 5$, where grain is the *numéraire* so that $P_g \equiv 1$, determine his productive optimum Q^* and consumptive optimum C^*. (c) Verify that he prefers C^* to R^*.

Answer: (a) Robinson's Marginal Rate of Transformation MRS_T is the absolute slope along his Production-Possibility Curve. By calculus it can be found that $MRS_T = f$. (This can be approximately verified by tabulating $\Delta g/\Delta f$ for small increments along the PPC.) Setting $MRS_T = MRS_C$, the condition becomes $f = g/f$, or $g = f^2$. Substituting in the PPC equation, the R^* solution is obtained as $f = 10$, $g = 100$. (b) Robinson finds Q^* by setting $MRS_T = P_f = 5$ in his PPC equation. Thus, $f = 5$, $g = 137.5$ is his productive optimum. To find his consumptive optimum, we use the budget condition and Substitution Equivalence Equation. That is: $5f + g = 5(5) + 137.5$ and $g/f = 5$. The C^* solution is therefore $f = 16.25$, $g = 81.25$. (c) He has it in his power to buy the R^* combination and even have something left over—e.g., he can give up 6.25 units of f and obtain 31.25 units of g, leaving him with the R^* combination plus 12.5 units of g in addition—yet chooses not to do so.

The forces determining the market equilibrium price in a world of production and exchange can be summarized as usual in terms of supply and demand. Once again it will be useful to distinguish "full" versus "transaction" supply and demand concepts.

Figure 13.7 is analogous to Figure 13.4, with one important difference. In pure exchange the individual's full supply of X to the economy was simply a given endowed quantity $x_i^\dagger$ independent of price (the vertical line $s_i^\dagger$ in Figure 13.4). But in a world of production and exchange, an individual's full supply of X is the result of a productive decision in response to the ruling market price. In Figure 13.7 the full supply curve s_i^q represents, for any price P_x, the x-coordinate of the *productive optimum* Q^* in Panel (b) of Figure 13.6. As P_x rises (with P_y held constant), the market line MM in Figure 13.6 grows increasingly steep. The tangency of MM with the transformation locus QQ at Q^* therefore shifts around to the southeast. This shift represents an increased quantity of X produced, thus demonstrating that the individual's full supply curve s_i^q for commodity X is a rising function of price P_x. The full demand curve d_i of Figure 13.7 similarly represents, for any price P_x, the x-coordinate of the individual's *consumptive optimum* C^* in Panel (b) of Figure 13.6. The s_i^q curve and the d_i curve in Figure 13.7 reflect the movement of the C^* position and the Q^* position of the preceding diagram as price changes.

What about the individual's transaction demand from or transaction supply to *the market*? In parallel with the discussion of the preceding section, the s_i^t curve of Figure 13.7 represents the positive net amounts supplied (for prices higher than the "autarky price"[2] P_x°) and the d_i^t curve the positive net amounts demanded

---

[2]The autarky price is analogous to the "sustaining price" $P_x^\dagger$ of pure exchange; each represents the price at which the individual does not participate in trade.

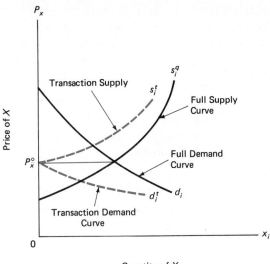

FIGURE 13.7 Individual Demand and Supply, with Production. For an individual i, at any price P_x (or price ratio P_x/P_y, with P_y fixed) the full supply provided to the economy as a whole is the x-coordinate of the productive optimum Q^* in Panel (b) of the preceding diagram. As P_x rises, an increased quantity of X is produced, so the full supply curve s_i^q is rising. The individual's full demand is the x-coordinate of C^* in Panel (b) of Figure 13.6, which generally decreases as P_x rises. The transaction supply and demand of X are exactly zero at the "autarky price" P_x^o, the price at which the full demand curve and the full supply curve intersect. Above this price full supply exceeds full demand, so there will be positive *transaction supply*—increasing as P_x rises. Below this price full demand exceeds full supply, so there will be positive *transaction demand*—increasing as P_x falls.

(at prices lower than P_x^o). Of course, at the autarky price itself the net amount demanded and supplied is zero.

Figure 13.7 describes the supply and demand curves for a single person. Equilibrium in the market as a whole is based of course upon balancing aggregate supply and aggregate demand. This is pictured in Figure 13.8, which simultaneously shows the solutions for: (1) X^*, the full social total of X produced and consumed, and (2) X^{t*}, the transaction amount of X exchanged in the market.

At the equilibrium price P_x^* the aggregate quantity *produced* (along the aggregate full supply curve S^q) must equal the aggregate amount *desired for consumption* (along the aggregate full demand curve D). Of course, S^q is the horizontal sum of the individuals' s_i^q curves, and D the horizontal sum of their d_i curves. The same price P_x^* obtains at the intersection of the aggregate transaction supply curve S^t and the aggregate transaction demand curve D^t. Note that, for any single individual, s_i^t and d_i^t intersect only along the vertical axis; no person is ever simultaneously a positive net supplier to and a positive net demander from the market. But at the market equilibrium *some* persons will be supplying and others demanding, so that X^{t*}, the volume of transactions, is positive. The difference between X^* and X^{t*} represents, as we have seen, the aggregate amount of X produced by individuals for personal consumption rather than for trade in markets.

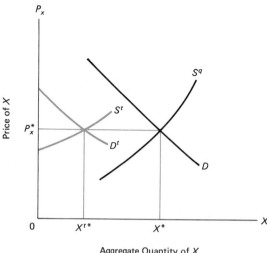

FIGURE 13.8 **Equilibrium of Supply and Demand, with Production.** The aggregate full supply curve S^q and full demand curve D represent horizontal summations of the corresponding individual curves of the preceding diagram and similarly for the aggregate transaction supply and transaction demand curves S^t and D^t. The equilibrium price P_x^* is determined by the intersection of either pair of curves. At the equilibrium, the aggregate full quantity produced and consumed is X^* while the aggregate transaction quantity traded among individuals is X^{t*}. (The difference is the aggregate quantity self-supplied by individuals for their own consumption.)

The pure-exchange model was appropriate for highlighting one of the two advantages of exchange: the reallocation of existing stocks of goods among individuals so as to achieve a mutually preferred combination. The model of production and exchange now permits us to appreciate the second advantage of exchange: the fact that greater social totals of goods are generated by *productive specialization.*

In Figure 13.9 the two panels show Production-Possibility Curves QQ for John and Karl. John can more easily or efficiently produce commodity Y, while Karl can advantageously specialize in producing X. Yet, in the absence of trade, their diversified preferences would dictate "Robinson Crusoe solutions" R_j^* and R_k^* that both lie toward the middle of their respective Production-Possibility curves QQ. To meet his desires for both commodities, each person would have to devote a large portion of his efforts to manufacturing a good that is unsuited to his productive talents.

The opening of trade makes available market lines MM (of slope $-P_x/P_y$) to both John and Karl. The former takes advantage of the market by shifting his productive solution northwest along QQ to Q_j^*, i.e., he now *specializes in producing* Y. And this does not in any way require of him a corresponding loss of "diversity in consumption," for he will trade the excess Y to Karl. Correspondingly, of course, Karl is enabled to become a specialist in the production of X, the excess to be traded to John. It is the adjustment of relative prices P_x/P_y, reflecting the relative scarcities of goods in society as a whole, that induces each person (as if led by an "Invisible Hand") to serve the interests of the other.

That both individuals benefit is evident from the superiority of their C_j^* and C_k^* consumptive optimum positions in a world of exchange, in comparison with their "Crusoe" solutions R_j^* and R_k^*. And inspection reveals that the social totals available of *both* X and Y have increased. As a natural application of this conclusion, economists have usually argued that free trade between two nations will benefit both.

416

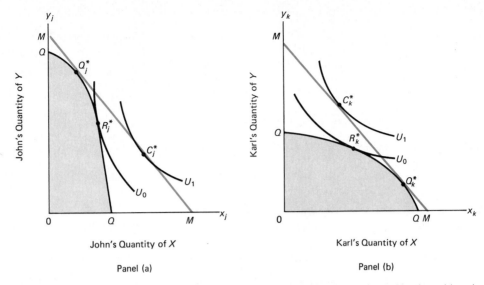

FIGURE 13.9 **Productive Specialization.** In the absence of exchange, John and Karl would each find an optimum productive–consumptive combination at his "Robinson Crusoe" solution R*. The opening of trade permits each to specialize in producing the commodity favored by his transformation opportunities. John's productive solution Q* involves heavier production of Y, Karl's involves heavier production of X. By trading with one another thereafter, each can move along a market line MM to achieve a superior consumption basket C*.

EXAMPLE 13.3
International Specialization

Individuals tend to specialize in production but diversify in consumption. We work at just one job, or a very few, but consume hundreds of different products. Should we expect the same thing of countries? To some extent, surely yes. But we would probably anticipate that the degree of productive specialization will be less for *larger* countries, which tend to have more highly varied resources and productive opportunities, and thus are less dependent upon international trade to secure diversity in consumption.

A study by M. Michaely compared the extent of specialization in the exports and imports of 44 countries, in terms of 1954 (or, in some cases, 1953 or 1952) data. The Table shows, for a number of countries, indexes of specialization in exports and in imports. The measure of specialization employed was the "Gini coefficient," which in this case has a possible range of from 8.2 to 100.0.[a] The countries in the Table are ranked in decreasing order of export (productive)

[a]The Gini coefficient for exports is defined as $100 \sqrt{\sum_{i=1}^{N}(x_i/X)^2}$; x_i is a nation's annual value of exports of a particular good i, and X is its total annual value of exports. The goods were classified into $N = 150$ categories. If only a single good were exported by a country, the formula would show a specialization index of 100.0. If it exported all 150 goods in equal amounts, the result would be an index of 8.2. The measure of import specialization is similarly defined and has the same range.

specialization. As can be seen, the highly specialized group at the top tend to be small countries while the group at the bottom tend to be large countries. No particular pattern is evident in the specialization index for imports, a result consistent with the principle of diversity in consumption.

Indexes of Specialization of International Trade

COUNTRY	EXPORTS	IMPORTS
Egypt	84.2	18.6
Colombia	84.0	23.9
Gold Coast	83.5	21.4
Iceland	80.3	19.1
Finland	38.1	19.2
Mexico	35.0	26.8
Libya	34.1	18.9
Spain	33.9	24.5
Italy	20.5	20.7
U.K.	19.2	16.1
U.S.	18.8	20.5
France	18.0	20.4

Source: Michael Michaely, "Concentration of Exports and Imports: An International Comparison," *Economic Journal*, v. 68 (Dec. 1958), p. 725.

13.D
IMPERFECT MARKETS: COSTS OF EXCHANGE

In previous chapters we have sometimes diverged from the assumption of *perfect competition* (price-taking behavior on both sides of the market)—for example, in the chapters on monopoly and oligopoly. But one assumption has been maintained up to now: *perfect markets*. A market is said to be perfect (even if not competitive) if at any moment of time there is a single price, known to all participants, and at which transactions may be executed without further fee or penalty. Elaborating a bit, there are three main characteristics of perfect markets:

1. *Perfect communication:* The market must be an integrated whole, not segmented by limitations of information. Real-world markets have informational imperfections, as we can see by the efforts made to overcome them: the use of classified newspaper advertising to communicate supply–demand offers, specialized "middlemen" (such as real-estate brokers) through whom buyers and sellers can reach one another, and organized exchanges (such as the New York Stock Exchange) which aim to bring all relevant offers into a single combined marketplace.

2. *Instantaneous equilibrium:* A market can be viewed as a mechanism, taking as input all potential traders' supply and demand functions, and yielding as

output the equilibrium or "market-clearing" price at which purchases and sales are all to be executed. A perfect market would instantaneously digest the inputs and proclaim the correct market-clearing price. But no such magic machine exists in the real world. So a farmer bringing vegetables to a city produce market may by cleverness or chance realize a sale at a price higher than the (unknown) true equilibrium. Or, unluckily, the farmer may accept a price lower than might have been obtained. Thus, in real-world markets there is some "trading at false prices." (One of the functions of *speculation* is to minimize such accidental fluctuations of price that lead to false trading, since speculators enter the market so as to buy when they perceive that the price is accidentally too low and to sell when price is accidentally too high.)

3. *Costless transactions:* Markets that are perfect would also be costless. In the real world, market "middlemen" such as wholesalers and retailers, brokers, dealers, and jobbers exist, and obviously must be paid for their services. While these middlemen improve the perfection of the market in other respects, the fees and payments they receive constitute a burden on the process of exchange. Transaction taxes, in which *government* collects "middleman" payments (possibly reflecting actual services to taxpayers, but possibly not), are another important factor.

CONCLUSION: Absence of costs of exchange is one element of the concept of *perfect markets*, the other elements being perfect communication and instantaneous equilibrium. While transaction costs considered alone are an element of imperfection, such costs are ordinarily incurred in order to reduce other imperfections—for example, when someone selling a house is willing to pay a commission to a real-estate broker for establishing communication with potential homebuyers.

EXAMPLE 13.4
Experiments in Perfect and Imperfect Markets

An interesting series of economic experiments on the functioning of markets has been conducted by Vernon L. Smith.[a] One question studied was the following: given that real-world market situations, whether arising naturally or in artificially constructed experiments, can never fully meet the theoretical conditions of "perfect markets," how far can the conditions diverge from "perfection" and still achieve the same essential *results*? For example, if traders are not in perfect communication, or if "trading at false prices" may occur, to what extent is it the case that equilibrium is nevertheless attained quite quickly and at a price–quantity outcome close to the theoretical ideal?

[a]V. L. Smith, "An Experimental Study of Competitive Market Behavior," *Journal of Political Economy*, v. 70 (April 1962); "Effects of Market Organization on Competitive Equilibrium," *Quarterly Journal of Economics*, v. 78 (May 1964); "Experimental Auction Markets and the Walrasian Hypothesis," *Journal of Political Economy*, v. 73 (Aug. 1965).

In one experiment Smith provided each participant with information only as to his or her demand price (the maximum he or she should be willing to bid if buying) or supply price (the minimum he or she should be willing to accept if selling). Thus only the experimenters and not the subjects knew the *aggregate* supply and demand functions and the "true" equilibrium price. Under the experimental conditions any buyer (or seller) could make an offer at any time, which, if accepted by another trader, became a binding contract. The process was public, so that the terms of any deals consummated became known to as-yet-uncommitted traders.

A trading "week" consisted of five trading "days" (periods) within which supply and demand conditions remained unchanged. A typical experimental series went as follows. In the first week the supply and demand conditions implied a theoretical equilibrium price of 465; while the experiment revealed some trading at false prices in the first couple of days, after the end of the third day practically all transactions took place exactly at the correct price of 465. At the beginning of the second week demand and supply conditions were shifted to make the equilibrium price 285; the participants were now more experienced, and practically all trading settled down to the correct price by the end of the second day. For the third week a new set of supply–demand conditions made the equilibrium price 735; convergence to the new equilibrium was so rapid that virtually all trades were made at the equilibrium price, almost from the very beginning.

The model of perfect markets therefore provided an excellent prediction of actual transaction prices in this experiment. Furthermore, the *quantities* exchanged were also very close to the theoretical ideal. In short, substantially all the potential advantages of trade (in the form of Consumer Surplus and Producer Surplus) were in fact achieved despite the experimental departure from ideal conditions.

Results such as these suggest that the economist's perfect-market model is "robust," in the sense of having a high degree of predictive reliability even though the exact conditions for its validity are not fully met. A very similar situation in physics is the model of a "perfect gas" that leads to the prediction known as Boyle's Law. No actual gas can meet the requirements of a "perfect gas," and yet Boyle's Law is a very reliable predictive equation in physics.

In the discussion that follows, markets will generally be assumed perfect *except* for transaction or exchange costs. This amounts to assuming that middlemen function so effectively as to totally eliminate the other two types of market imperfection—informational segmentation, and false trading at non-equilibrium prices. But of course these efficient middleman services must be compensated by fees or charges upon transactions. Costs of exchange have, we shall see, important consequences for the scope of trading and for the degree of specialization in production and consumption.

EXAMPLE 13.5
Costs of Trading on the New York Stock Exchange

An organized exchange like the New York Stock Exchange goes a considerable way toward the ideal of a perfect market. The key feature of an organized exchange is the guarantee of the transaction, i.e., of the quality of merchandise delivered, of payment arrangements, etc., by the exchange authorities themselves. As a result the buyer can forego personal inspection of the merchandise, and the seller need not be concerned with the credit standing or the character of the buyer. In dealing on the New York Stock Exchange, the buyer does not have to worry about whether the stock certificates acquired are counterfeit, nor need the seller fear that the buyer may be making payment with a bad check.

However, there are costs of trading on the New York Stock Exchange. These fall into two main categories: (1) commission charges, and (2) bid–ask price spread. The *commission charges* are the explicit fees paid to brokers by buyers and sellers. These charges are quoted separately from the amounts paid or received for the securities themselves. The *bid–ask spread* is a less obvious portion of the cost of transacting. At any instant of time the market price of a stock like General Motors to a seller, the "bid price," is less than the "ask price" that a buyer of GM stock would have to pay. The difference goes mainly to the Exchange's "specialist" in General Motors stock (see Example 8.1) who plays the role of making a continuous market in that security. Specialists, like retail or wholesale merchants, must on the average buy for less (the bid price) than they sell for (the ask price) if they are to remain in business. (The customer's *broker*, in contrast with the specialist, is normally a pure intermediary who does not buy or sell for his own account.)

A study by Harold Demsetz[a] indicated that in 1965 the bid–ask spread on the New York Stock Exchange comprised about 40% and explicit commission charges about 60% of total transaction cost, on the average. The two together amounted to about 1.3% of the value of the securities exchanged. The study also found that the bid–ask spread is normally much lower for frequently traded than for infrequently traded securities. This is reasonable if we regard the Exchange's specialist as a merchant who must hold an "inventory" of securities in order always to stand ready to sell. On average the specialist's funds must be tied up longer, and therefore also at greater risk of price fluctuation, in the case of a "slow-moving" commodity like an infrequently traded stock. Commission charges also proved to be relatively lower for bigger transactions, which is easily understandable in terms of a saving in communications and recording costs.

[a]H. Demsetz, "The Cost of Transacting," *Quarterly Journal of Economics*, v. 82 (Feb. 1968).

Large proportions of national resources appear to be devoted to the process of exchange. In 1982 around 22% of U.S. non-agricultural employment was reported as engaged in the occupational category Wholesale and Retail Trade. And many workers classified under other headings—e.g., Transportation and Communication; Finance, Insurance, and Real Estate; and Services—might also be regarded as associated with the exchange process. This suggests that "middleman" (transaction-facilitating) activities are a truly enormous drain upon the nation's resources. It might seem astonishing that such heavy burdens remain even after the invention of money, banking, and other sophisticated devices designed to economize upon the costs of market exchange.

This initial impression is misleading. A crucial distinction must be made between two logically distinct classes of interpersonal "transactions." The *trading* of goods and services between self-interested individuals, i.e., the social process of market exchange, is one thing. The sheer physical *transfer* of possession or control of commodities is quite another. Any economy that integrates the activities of a great number of individuals so as to take advantage of productive specialization and the division of labor, whether it be an economy of saints, of monks, of slaves, of ants, or of utility-maximizers under free markets, would still involve physical transfer of commodities. *Activities and costs that are intrinsically due to the mere physical fact of transfer must not be attributed to the particular process that achieves interpersonal integration via market trading.*

Consider an extreme "command economy" in which all economic decisions are made by a central authority. The economy might be a slave society in which everyone works for the benefit of a single master. Or it might be a socialist dictatorship, centrally planned (let us say) to achieve popular well-being. Specialization in production would be achieved by command rather than by an "Invisible Hand." Farmers would be ordered to grow crops and turn them over to railroads; railroads ordered to ship them to cities, and turn them over to warehouses; warehouses ordered to store them, and turn them over to the next recipients in the chain, and so forth. Every transfer of control of goods would involve costs: handling, shipping, storing, record-keeping, and so forth.

The costs associated with the physical transfers that would persist even in a totally dictated economy fall logically under the economic category of *production* costs rather than exchange costs. This accounts for essentially all transportation services, for one thing. "Adding" transportation to a good so as to physically bring it to a consumer is in principle the same as "adding" baking services to dough so as to make bread that the consumer can eat. The consequence is that *the costs of market exchange as a process are not nearly so great as might have first been thought.* Even wholesaling and retailing expenses, as usually classified, are in large part due to the physical warehousing of goods that would still have to take place in a total command economy with no market process at all.

What then are the *costs of exchange* proper? These are the costs, in a non-command or "free" economy, that stem specifically from the contending wills and property interests of the parties. In such an economy physical transfers of commodities take place only if consistent with the perceived mutual advantages of the traders involved. To arrange transactions, offers must be communicated and alternatives compared. Contracts must be negotiated, and their execution verified. Fraud or other non-performance must be guarded against. All these activities involve costs.[3] All of the expenses of an institution like the New York Stock Exchange, for example, fall under one or more of these headings. (Without private ownership there would be no need for a Stock Exchange, since there would be no corporate shares.)

EXAMPLE 13.6
Farmer, Consumer, Middleman

"Consumerists" contend that food prices are too high, while farmers can be counted on to complain that the prices they receive are too low. It is natural for both groups to fasten upon the "middleman" as the culprit. And, in fact, payments to middlemen have over the years been accounting for an increasing share of consumer expenditure on food.

But of course middlemen are providing services for the income they receive: processing, transporting, packaging, distributing, and so forth. Over time the middleman services incorporated into food products have been increasing. We have been choosing to consume food that has traveled further, been processed more elaborately, and distributed in more complex ways than in earlier times.

One explanation of this phenomenon is that middleman services are a relatively superior or "luxury" commodity compared to raw farm products themselves. That is, the *income elasticity of demand* for off-farm food services is greater than for farm products alone. Confirming this, one study has indicated an overall income elasticity of demand of 0.705 for food products—but when this figure is divided between the farm and off-farm components, the income elasticity of demand is only 0.279 for the farm but 1.322 for the off-farm element.[a] So the rising share of the middleman in food sales in the United States is largely a result of rising consumer income, which has permitted an increase in the purchases of middleman services that constitute a relatively superior good as a component of food at the point of consumption.

[a] E. W. Bunkers and W. W. Cochrane, "On the Income Elasticity of Food Services," *Review of Economics and Statistics*, v. 30 (May 1957), p. 217.

Costs of exchange are generally a function of: (1) the volume of goods traded; (2) the number of distinct transactions per unit of time; (3) the number of parties involved in a transaction; and (4) the number of distinct commodities per transaction. In the next sections we will be dealing only with two-party, two-commodity trades, ruling out the third and fourth elements above. (Some comments upon costs of multi-party and multi-commodity trading will be made in later sections.) For simplicity, we will analyze special cases that isolate each of

---

[3] Of course there would also be great communication and enforcement problems in any actual attempt to construct a functioning *command* economy. "Costs of command"—the resource wastage in attempting to enforce an economic dictatorship—would almost surely far exceed the costs of market exchange.

the two sources of exchange cost to be considered here. Specifically, the implications of *transaction costs strictly proportional to volume* will be studied first; afterward, *costs dependent solely on the number of separate transactions* will be taken up.

13.D.1 □ Proportional Transaction Costs

We have already noted in Chapter 2 (see Figure 2.6) certain consequences of a particular type of proportional transaction cost—a uniform tax on sales. If an excise tax of $1 per unit were levied upon purchases of a commodity X, then the *gross price* P_x^+ paid by buyers would necessarily be $1 per unit greater than the *net price* P_x^- received by sellers. Figure 13.10 here is equivalent to the earlier diagram. It indicates that, as compared with a no-tax situation with price P_x^* and quantity X^*, after imposition of the tax the quantity exchanged would be only X'. As for price, the gross price P_x^+ paid by buyers will always be higher than, but the net price P_x^- received by sellers will be lower than, the no-tax equilibrium price P_x^*. The shaded area in the diagram, equal to $X'(P_x^+ - P_x^-)$, represents the tax collections.

But a more generalized interpretation of the diagram is possible. We can think of it as representing the effects of *any* proportional transaction cost, not just a tax. The *price gap* $G \equiv P_x^+ - P_x^-$ is the rate charged by middlemen (e.g., the "bid–ask spread" of Example 13.5 above) to effectuate the exchange of a unit of X. The shaded area is then the aggregate amount received by middlemen for their services in this market.

Let us now consider the situation from the viewpoint of an individual trader. In Figure 13.11 a price-taking trader in a world of *costless* exchange could, starting from an endowment combination E, attain any position along the solid market line KL. The market opportunity set would be the entire triangle OKL,

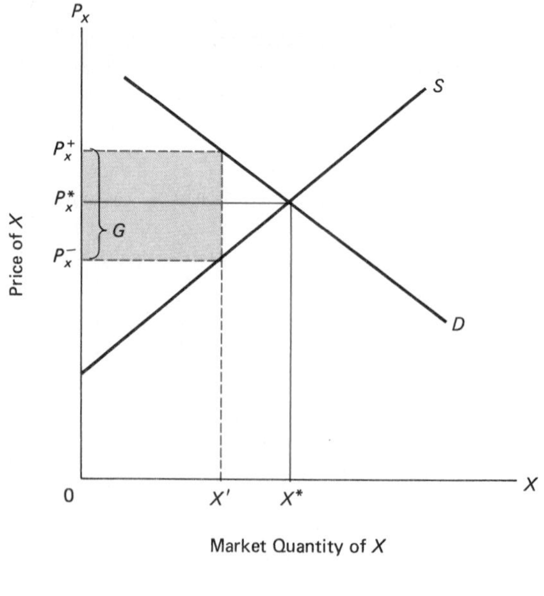

FIGURE 13.10 Proportional Transaction Costs.
A proportional transaction charge in the amount of G per unit of commodity X exchanged means that, in equilibrium, there must be a price gap of this amount between the price paid by demanders (P_x^+) and the price received by suppliers (P_x^-). The quantity exchanged is X', and the shaded area represents the aggregate transaction costs paid by traders.

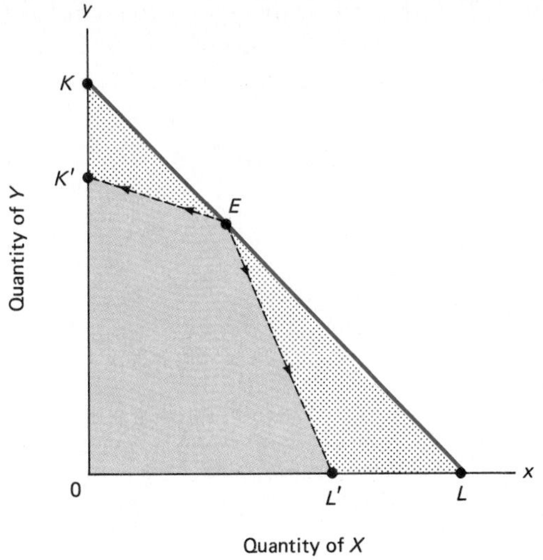

FIGURE 13.11 **Individual Trading Opportunity: Cost-less versus Costly Exchange.** An individual with trading opportunities and initial endowment E would have, under costless exchange, a market opportunity set consisting of the entire triangle OKL. But if there is a proportional transaction charge, the person would face a steeper budget line as buyer of X (line-segment EL') or a flatter budget line as seller of X (line-segment EK'). The market opportunity set is therefore reduced to the shaded area.

the shaded area plus the dotted areas. The slope of the market line is $-P_x/P_y$, or simply $-P_x$ since as usual we interpret Y as a *numéraire* (representing "all other goods") with price $P_y \equiv 1$. In contrast, the dashed line-segments show the impact of a proportional trading charge. Trying to buy X by moving *southeast* from E (note direction of the arrows) along the line-segment EL', there is a steeper slope because P_x^+ is greater than P_x. And if the person tries to sell X by moving *northwest* along EK', he or she receives only the lower price P_x^- reflected in the flat slope of EK'. The existence of transaction costs narrows the individual's opportunity set, from the triangle OKL that would be relevant under costless exchange to the quadrilateral $OK'EL'$ bounded by the dashed line-segments (shaded area in the diagram).

Transaction costs reduce the gains from trade and therefore tend to prevent people from arriving at mutually preferred redistributions of consumption goods. Furthermore, transaction costs also tend to curtail specialization in production. In the limiting case, transaction costs may lead individuals to choose *autarky*.

Whether or not autarky solutions will be preferred under costly exchange depends upon the buying and selling prices P_x^+ and P_x^- and of course also upon the shapes of the individual's productive opportunities and preferences. In Figure 13.12 the two dotted areas show the increments to the individual's overall opportunity set still provided by the possibility of trading (even though a transaction charge is being levied). Consider the dotted area at the upper left. A is the point where the Production-Possibility Curve QQ has the same slope as (is tangent to) the dashed market line-segment whose flatter slope represents the lower selling price P_x^-. Hence, in attempting to move northwest (acquire Y by giving up X) beyond A the individual does better along AK' (selling X for Y in the market) than along QQ (converting X into Y via productive transformation). A corresponding argument applies, of course, for the dotted area at the lower right

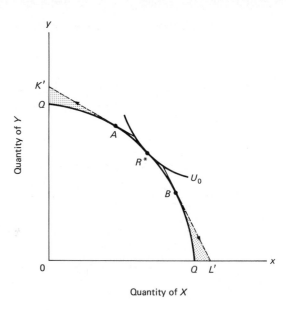

FIGURE 13.12 **Opportunity Set with Transaction Costs: Autarky Solution.** The gross price P_x^+ determines the slope of the line-segment BL' tangent to the Production-Possibility Curve QQ at point B, thus adding the lower-right dotted area as a portion of the individual's overall opportunity set. Similarly, the net price P_x^- determines the slope of the line-segment AK' tangent to QQ at point A, which adds the upper-left dotted area to the overall opportunities. Nevertheless, here the autarky solution R^* remains preferred, since R^* lies between A and B.

bounded by the steeper line-segment BL' whose slope represents the higher buying price P_x^+.

Now if the preference map is, as shown in Figure 13.12, such that the Crusoe tangency R^* *falls between* A *and* B, autarky is preferred. The high buying price P_x^+ and the low selling price P_x^- *straddle* the common value of $MRS_C = MRS_T$ at the autarky point. On the other hand, if the shape of the preference map and/or transformation locus QQ are such that R^* falls outside the range AB along QQ, the individual will engage in market trade as a net buyer or seller. Specifically, suppose that the R^* tangency falls northwest of A along QQ as in Figure 13.13. But in this range the individual can do better (can attain a higher

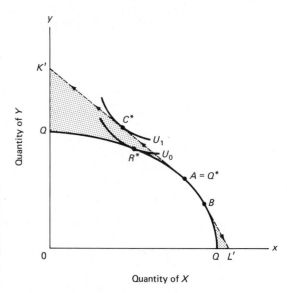

FIGURE 13.13 **Opportunity Set with Transaction Costs: Non-Autarky Solution.** Here R^* does not lie between the tangency points A and B on QQ. The productive optimum Q^* is at point A (the individual specializes in production of good X). The consumptive optimum C^* lies to the northwest along AK', indicating that the individual sells some of the produced X (at the low selling price P_x^-) to obtain the desired consumption quantity of Y.

426

indifference curve) along the market line-segment AK' than along AQ. The *productive* optimum Q^* would then be at the point A and the person would sell X for Y to attain a *consumptive* optimum C^* along AK'.

Thus, the condition for the individual to become a net seller of X (specializing in production of X), despite the existence of a price gap G due to proportional transaction costs, is that *the low net price* P_x^- *must exceed* the common value of $MRS_C = MRS_T$ at the autarky point. Again, a corresponding argument will apply to the opposite case of specialization in production of Y: this will occur only if the *high gross price* P_x^+ *is less than* the common value of $MRS_C = MRS_T$ at R^*.

With proportional costs of transacting, the individual and overall market situations are represented in Figure 13.14. In Panel (a) the autarky price P_x^o for any individual is the common value of $MRS_C = MRS_T$ at his Crusoe solution R^*. If the low *net* price P_x^- exceeds P_x^o, the individual will be a supplier to the market as shown by the dashed curve labeled $s(P_x^-)$. Similarly, this person will be a net demander only if the high *gross* price P_x^+ is lower than P_x^o, as shown by the solid curve labeled $d(P_x^+)$. Thus, it is the *inner pair* of curves that picture the individual's market behavior. It is convenient, however, also to show the (solid) supply curve in terms of the gross price, $s(P_x^+)$, and the (dashed) demand curve in terms of the net price, $d(P_x^-)$. Each of these differs from its partner by the constant vertical distance G—the price gap.

Summing over all the individuals, we have the corresponding pairs of aggregate market supply and demand curves shown in Panel (b). Now we can see

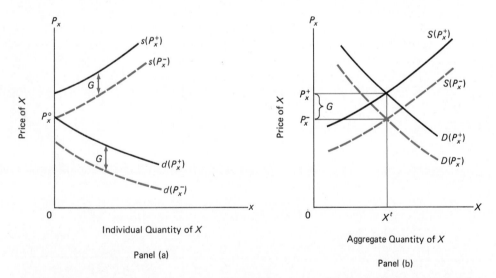

Panel (a)

Individual Quantity of X

Panel (b)

Aggregate Quantity of X

FIGURE 13.14 Supply and Demand: Proportional Exchange Cost. In Panel (a), for a given individual the inner pair of curves represent the transaction supply as a function of the *net* selling price P_x^- (where this exceeds the autarky price P_x^o) and the transaction demand as a function of the *gross* buying price P_x^+ (where this is less than the autarky price). The upper solid curve shows supply as related to the gross price, and the lower dashed curve shows demand as related to the net price. Panel (b) pictures the market-wide aggregates of these four curves. The equilibrium quantity X' is found at the intersection of either the two (solid) curves defined in terms of the gross prices or the two (dashed) curves defined in terms of the net prices; the equilibrium gross and net prices are determined accordingly.

why it was convenient to draw the curves in terms of both gross and net prices. For, the solution that determines the gross or buying price P_x^+ will be at the intersection of $S(P_x^+)$ and $D(P_x^+)$, the two solid curves. This intersection will be at the same market quantity X^t as the intersection of the two dashed curves $S(P_x^-)$ and $D(P_x^-)$ that determines the net or selling price P_x^-. The two prices differ by the fixed gap G that represents the fee charged by middlemen.

What would happen if the bid–ask spread, the size of the gap G, were to increase? In Panel (a) of Figure 13.14 the *inner pair* of curves would remain unchanged, since they directly represent individual behavior in terms of the relevant (gross or net) prices. But the outer pair of curves would be pushed further outward as G rises. Since the equilibrium solution determined in Panel (b) necessarily involves an intersection with one or the other of the outer curves, the *consequence of higher transaction costs is a fall in the volume of transactions.*

CONCLUSION: Proportional transaction costs create a gap between buying price and selling price. The higher the transaction charges, the more likely that individuals will choose autarky solutions, and the smaller the aggregate volume of market trading.

EXAMPLE 13.7
Urban–Farm Food Cost Differentials

In the absence of transaction costs there would be no reason for a specialist in the *production* of commodity X to be a particularly heavy consumer of X. The tailor would not have an unusually ample wardrobe, the candlestick maker would not substitute his product for electric lights in his home, and the Detroit assembly-line worker would have no special inducement to drive a car rather than use public transit. It follows that where we *do* observe a producer heavily consuming his or her own product, transaction costs are likely to be an important factor.

Urban and farm consumption expenditures for 1960–61 were studied by F. Y. Lee and K. E. Phillips. As can be seen in the Table below, farmers spend relatively more on "Food prepared at home," urban-dwellers relatively more on "Food prepared away from home." There seems little reason to doubt that transaction costs impose a greater degree of autarky upon farmers, making it more advantageous for them to consume home-prepared food.

On the other hand, costs of *exchange* are not the sole explanation of the divergence visible in the Table. Costs of *transfer* also play a role: for example, the cost of transporting food from farm to factory and then back to farm might dictate that farmers consume more home-prepared food even under a command economy. It is also possible that farmers simply have a greater comparative preference for home-prepared food (if not, they might not have chosen farming as an occupation). Perhaps more important, in the period studied farm families on the average were poorer than urban families. Since "Food prepared away from home" is a relatively superior good (income elasticity greater than unity), the income difference may also provide a partial explanation.

Total Consumption Expenditures (Percent of)

	NORTHEAST		WEST	
EXPENDITURE	Urban	Farm	Urban	Farm
Food prepared at home	21.0	31.0	18.9	27.5
Food prepared away from home	4.8	3.0	4.9	2.9

Source: F. Y. Lee and K. E. Phillips, "Differences in Consumption Patterns of Farm and Non-farm Households in the United States," American Journal of Agricultural Economics, v. 53 (Nov. 1971), p. 575.

It has been observed that certain types of markets, visible in poorer countries, seem to disappear as a country gets wealthier: for example, the market for used containers or for cigarettes by the unit (rather than by the pack). The market for used clothes is one that has substantially disappeared in recent years in the United States; it has become cheaper to throw used clothes away. It appears that in advanced economies the enormous range and variety of commodities available for purchase and sale put heavy pressure upon the resources involved in facilitating exchange. Accordingly, marketing services become quite expensive even as transportation and communication become quite cheap, and as overall availability of commodities increases. Eventually, the gap G between the gross price P_x^+ and the net price P_x^- for some commodity X may grow so large, relatively speaking, that the market for X becomes non-viable. This tends especially to happen, of course, if commodity X is of concern only to the declining fraction of poorer people in the economy.

*13.D.2 □ Lump-Sum Transaction Costs

The model of proportional exchange costs discussed above is a simplification. But it does explain a number of important aspects of the process of exchange observed in the world: among them, the normal gap between buying and selling prices, and the viability or non-viability of markets as transaction costs rise or fall. But one crucial aspect of exchange has not been explained: the holding of *inventories* (stocks of goods) for purposes of trading. All the models so far studied in this book have taken the form of continuous *flows*—of production, consumption, and exchange—over time. In such models, at least in the simple versions dealt with to this point, there was no need for *stocks* of commodities to be held by anyone. But in real life people do not transact continuously; we go to market at discrete separated moments of time. Over the intervals between trans-

---

*The section between the asterisk and the symbol ■ may contain somewhat more difficult or advanced material.

actions, everyone has to accumulate and decumulate inventories of goods purchased or to be sold.

Let us make the extreme assumption here that costs of exchange take the form only of a fixed lump-sum *charge per transaction*. This obviously provides a strong incentive to minimize the number of transactions engaged in per unit of time. On the other hand, the less frequent the transactions the larger the inventories needed to bridge over the intervals between successive trips to market. The cost of holding inventories must be balanced against the cost of frequent trading.

Suppose the lump-sum charge is a fixed amount F, incurred for each transaction. Think of it as an "entry fee." The individual trader's decision problem may be interpreted as the choice of an *optimal trading interval* θ. Figure 13.15 shows a possible inventory history for an individual with constant production and consumption flows of a commodity X, making discrete trades at a time-interval of θ. There is a self-supplied productive flow at the rate x^q. At discrete intervals θ, 2θ, 3θ, etc., the individual purchases a quantity χ (not a flow, but a stock magnitude) of commodity X. This makes it possible to maintain a level consumption flow of $x^c = x^q + (\chi/\theta)$ continuously. For example, if $x^q = 10$ units per day, χ is 140 units, and $\theta = 7$ days, a consumption rate of $10 + (140/7) = 30$ units per day can be maintained.

As a net purchaser of X, this person would have to be a net seller of the "other" commodity Y; a similar diagram, showing regular accumulation rather than decumulation of inventory between trades, could be constructed to portray his inventory history for commodity Y.

Now let us consider the individual's decision as to *autarky*, i.e., as to the desirability of engaging in trade at all. Figure 13.16 shows a situation where autarky is preferred; the "Robinson Crusoe solution" R^*, at the tangency of the Production-Possibility Curve QQ and the indifference curve U_1, is the best position attainable. In the lump-sum transaction cost model, it is important to appreciate that there are two distinguishable disadvantages of trading. The first is

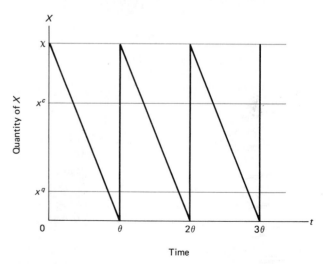

FIGURE 13.15 Inventory History for an Individual. The individual has a self-supplied continuous production flow x^q while maintaining a continuous consumption flow x^c, the difference being made up by discrete market purchases at time-intervals θ. At each multiple of θ, inventory falls to zero and a new stock quantity χ is purchased to recommence the cycle.

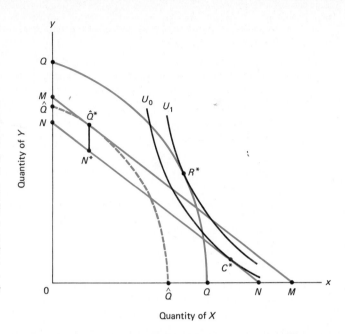

FIGURE 13.16 Autarky and Lump-Sum Transaction Costs. An autarky solution can be attained at R^* on the (solid) Production-Possibility Curve QQ. But if trading is engaged in, inventories must be held, reducing the effective production possibilities to the (dashed) $\hat{Q}\hat{Q}$. Also, lump-sum transaction charges F must be paid, representing a cost of F/θ per unit of time—represented by the vertical distance $\hat{Q}^*N^*$. The best the individual can do via trading is to move along the market line NN. In this diagram the autarky solution R^* (on indifference curve U_1) is preferred to the best position C^* (on U_0) that can be attained through trading.

inventory holding costs. In the diagram these have the effect of contracting the production possibilities of X and Y from the solid QQ curve to the dashed $\hat{Q}\hat{Q}$ curve; resources devoted to maintaining inventories cannot be applied to production. The second disadvantage is, of course, the *lump-sum trading charges* themselves—the explicit fees F paid at each transaction. In the diagram, the average fee incurred per unit of time is represented by the vertical distance $\hat{Q}^* - N^*$. This distance is equal to F/θ, paid out in units of Y. The key point to appreciate is that the individual in this model must, if not choosing the autarky solution, trade along the market line NN parallel to but below the market line MM that is tangent to $\hat{Q}\hat{Q}$. The line NN represents the *effective* trading opportunities, the combinations of X and Y achievable in the market after payout of the average lump-sum charges F/θ per unit of time.

Autarky is of course not inevitable. Lowered costs of holding inventories would decrease the gap between QQ and $\hat{Q}\hat{Q}$; lowered transaction charges would decrease the gap between MM and NN. Either of these forces would tend to make the trading solution (the tangency C^* with the highest indifference curve attained along the market line NN) relatively more attractive in comparison with the autarky solution R^*. For the trading solution to be superior, C^* would of course have to lie on a higher indifference curve than R^*.

Even with trading costs held constant, the outcome as to autarky or trading will depend upon the market price P_x. Returning to Figure 13.16, as P_x falls the absolute slope of MM and NN will decrease. The tangency of MM with $\hat{Q}\hat{Q}$ (the point $\hat{Q}^*$) will rotate along $\hat{Q}\hat{Q}$ to the northwest, enlarging the trading opportunity set toward the southeast of the diagram. Eventually, a price may be reached at which the trading optimum C^* along NN will be preferred to R^*—the individual will enter the market as a net demander of X. Similarly, at a sufficiently high price P_x the person may enter the market as a net supplier of X.

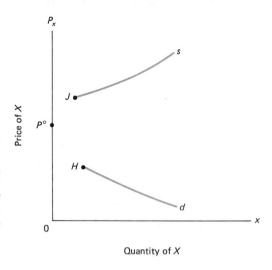

FIGURE 13.17 **Individual Net Supply and Demand: Lump-Sum Transaction Cost.** Market price must diverge from the autarky price P_x° by a certain discrete amount before the individual will enter the market as a supplier or a demander. If the price divergence is just great enough, the individual will offer or demand a minimal discrete quantity—represented by the point J where the supply curve begins and the point H where the demand curve begins.

Translating this information into a supply–demand representation leads to Figure 13.17. Here there is no divergence between the buying price and selling price; in this case, middlemen are reimbursed by lump-sum transaction payments F, not by a price gap G. As before, for each individual there is an autarky price P_x° represented by the common slope $MRS_C = MRS_T$ at his Crusoe solution R^*. There will now be a *range* of prices around the autarky price for which it will not pay the individual to undergo both the inventory holding costs and the lump-sum transaction charges of entering the market. But as the market price P_x increasingly diverges from P_x°, consumptive combinations that are attainable only by trading become increasingly attractive. For a sufficiently wide divergence, it will pay to incur the average trading fee F/θ and the inventory costs associated with market exchanges.

Another interesting feature of Figure 13.17 is that the supply and demand curves do not go all the way to the vertical axis, but are shown as beginning at the respective points J and H in the interior of the diagram. There must be a certain minimal discrete divergence of P_x upward or downward of the autarky price P_x° before it pays to trade at all—and when trade does begin to pay, there will also be a discrete minimal quantity offered or demanded. [Verification of this point is left as a challenge to the reader.]

The individual transaction supply and demand curves can as usual be aggregated into market-wide supply and demand curves. Again, for lump-sum transaction costs as for proportional transaction costs there is a serious possibility that the market-wide curves do not intersect. If so, the market disappears; there is no price at which any buyer–seller pair of traders are willing to incur the transaction charges and associated inventory costs of market dealings in preference to autarky solutions.

CONCLUSION: Lump-sum transaction costs do not create a price gap. But they dictate that exchanges take place at discrete intervals, so that inventories must be held. Transaction charges plus inventory costs due to trading make individual autarky solutions more likely, reduce the aggregate volume of market trade, and may even totally destroy the market. ■

13.E
THE ROLE OF MONEY

Money is a device that reduces the cost of market trading. But it does not, and in the nature of the case cannot, *reduce the cost of physical transfers*—which are, as described above, essentially an aspect of production. As to transportation, for example, geographical dispersion of producers and consumers will dictate shipping costs that would have to be incurred even in a perfectly functioning command economy. Money can do nothing to reduce these shipping costs. And similarly, imperfect synchronization of production and consumption will require commodity inventories at various places along the manufacturer–wholesaler–retailer–consumer chain. Again, money cannot eliminate this category of expense.

What money does is to reduce trading costs proper, the cost of integrating individual activities through the process of voluntary exchange. Money thus tends to counter the tendency toward autarky so as to promote a more efficient division of labor. It does so by serving the two key functions of *medium of exchange* and *temporary store of value*. These functions can be best visualized if we consider three social regimes in logical succession: (1) pure command economy, with no trading whatsoever but only dictated physical commodity transfers; (2) barter economy, with trading but without any monetary commodity; and (3) money economy.

Money as medium of exchange:

To fix ideas suppose that there are N commodities, each produced by a single individual. In the absence of any transfer or trading costs, imagine that all N persons would be willing to consume positive quantities of all N goods. Thus, there is specialization in production but desired diversity in consumption—the normal situation.

Under a pure command regime, let us suppose that the dictator is perfectly efficient and benevolent. In this economy there is no resource "wastage" due to costs of *trading*, i.e., no bidding, negotiating, contracting, etc. Even so, pure costs of *transfer* such as transportation expense may rule out some of the $N(N-1)$ possible commodity movements as uneconomic. Suppose that oranges are produced in California, and lobsters in Maine. Lobsters might be so expensive to ship that, from the viewpoint of overall economic efficiency, the dictator correctly decides that Californians would have to do without them. But if oranges are not very costly to ship, the dictator might still find it feasible and efficient to command that California oranges be sent to Maine.

Now suppose that a revolution displaces the dictator, substituting a regime of barter trade. In this regime, we will suppose, *only two-party trade is feasible.*

(Multi-party barter transactions can and do take place, but they seem to be exceedingly costly to negotiate and enforce and are therefore relatively rare.) Then, and this is the crucial point, instead of the $N(N-1)$ possible *one-directional commodity movements* that were available to the dictator in a command economy, under bilateral barter only $N(N-1)/2$ possible *two-way channels of exchange* are possible. If shipment of Maine lobsters to California is barred by the high costs of physical transfer (transportation cost), then the two-way channel is blocked. The California oranges cannot go to Maine either, since the lobstermen cannot provide appropriate compensation. As compared with an ideal command economy (perfectly efficient and benevolent dictator), not only is there wastage of resources due to the necessity of negotiating trades but also an inferior allocation of production and consumption due to a higher degree of autarky.

We can now see how the invention of a universal *medium of exchange* improves matters. The medium of exchange can be one of the original N goods or it can be an artificial $(N+1)$th commodity like paper money. In either case, the effect is *to make multilateral trading indirectly possible through a bilateral accounting device*.

Suppose, to begin with, that one of the N initial commodities is chosen as medium of exchange. In the prisoner-of-war situation of Example 4.1, *cigarettes* served this function. But in keeping with modern economic history, we will speak of *gold* as medium of exchange. Then all the other commodities are no longer traded for one another, but only for gold. This involves a saving, in that there is a drastic reduction in the number of markets that must be provided.

In the barter economy the number of two-way trading channels required is $N(N-1)/2$. Then if there are five goods (four ordinary consumption goods A, B, C, D, plus gold G), Figure 13.18 pictures the 5(4)/2 or *ten* trading channels. But if all other commodities are traded only for gold, *four* channels or markets will

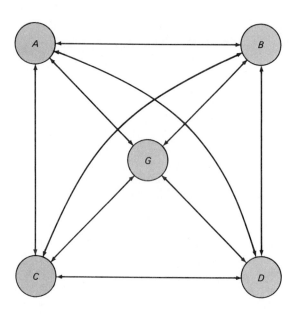

FIGURE 13.18 Trading Channels: Five Goods.
With five commodities, under two-way barter exchange there would have to be *ten* channels of trade or markets. If commodity G is instead the sole "medium of exchange," only *four* markets would be needed.

suffice. In general, the market system of a money (gold) economy would be required to generate prices and to execute exchanges for only $N - 1$ types of transactions. As compared with barter, there will be a considerable reduction of the costs of finding partners and negotiating, recording, and enforcing trades.

But this direct saving has less overall importance than the *indirect* gain due to the greater degree of productive specialization made possible. Consider the lobster-orange example once again. With gold as medium of exchange, the Maine lobsters will still not go to California; the physical transfer costs remain excessive. But the California oranges can now go to Maine! The Maine lobstermen can pay for oranges in gold, which they obtain by selling lobsters to other, non-Californian customers. Thus, gold makes possible triangular or still more complex turnovers, without requiring anything beyond bilateralism in trading.

One element of cost is likely to be greater in a gold economy than in a barter economy: there will be increased handling and shipping of *gold*, the monetary commodity itself. Clearing arrangements, one aspect of banking, will arise to reduce these costs. Also, gold as medium of exchange can be replaced by an artificial commodity (e.g., paper money) for which the shipping and handling costs are less. Ultimately the money economy tends to move toward a nonphysical, purely abstract medium of exchange, *banking deposits*, to minimize these handling and shipping costs.

Money as temporary store of value:

The other important role of money is as *temporary store of value* ("abode of purchasing power"). Inventories of money bridge time gaps between receipts and payments. By carrying an inventory of money a baker can obtain meat today, even though out of bread for sale until tomorrow.

To grasp the significance of this, let us return first to our imagined pure command economy. Even there, where no voluntary exchange occurs, imperfect synchronization of the processes of production, transportation, and consumption will require the holding of inventories as goods are passed along the interpersonal transfer chain. Now, if a revolution takes place overthrowing the dictator in favor of a regime of bilateral voluntary barter exchange, additional costs in the form of *trading inventories* have to come into existence. Let three individuals a, b, and c be sole specialized producers of commodities A, B, and C, respectively. Imagine that to meet consumption preferences the desired pattern of trade is triangular: commodity A is to flow from a to b, commodity B from b to c, and commodity C from c to a. If multilateral trading is ruled out, we have here the famous "double coincidence" problem of barter. Consider individual b, who wants commodity A from individual a but produces nothing that the latter wants from him. Although b can provide commodity B to individual c, the latter produces nothing that b desires.

This dilemma is resolved by having some or all individuals hold a trading inventory of the third commodity, i.e., of the one they neither produce nor consume. People accept "trade goods" in exchange for commodities they do produce, in order to have something available to exchange (when opportunity permits) for commodities they wish to consume.

Rather than hold a multiplicity of different trading inventories, it is obviously efficient for all traders to agree to accept in exchange some single "store of value" commodity. It should be a commodity both cheap to produce and cheap to store, and preferably one that is not eroded (as were cigarettes in the P.O.W. example) by consumption. These criteria will enter into the selection of gold (or some alternative commodity) as the monetary medium. Again, there will be a natural tendency to move toward a purely abstract money commodity like banking deposits, almost costless to produce and to store, and not needed for consumption.

CONCLUSION: The invention of money reduces the costs of market trading, not the costs of physical transfers which would be required in any economic system employing a division of labor. With money serving as *medium of exchange*, all other goods may be traded for amounts of the single monetary commodity. This reduces the number of two-way market channels required, and makes triangular or even more circuitous trade patterns viable that would be excessively costly or impossible under barter. Where inventories of goods must be carried for trading purposes, this is done most economically by holding the single monetary commodity—which then serves also as *temporary store of value*.

EXAMPLE 13.8
Barter in the East Indies

An interesting network of exchanges among primitive peoples in the East Indies was analyzed by the anthropologist M. Sahlins.[a] A puzzling problem was described by Sahlins. The Busama, who serve as middlemen between the Tami Islanders and certain southern villages, allegedly acquire bowls worth 10 to 12 shillings from Tami Island which they then carry to the south and exchange one-for-one against pots worth only 8 shillings!

The supposed explanation is that, while pots and bowls are desired throughout the region, the Busama are producers of taro which is wanted only by the southern villagers. The latter can only pay in pots. As these are in excess of the Busama's own requirements, the Busama carry the excess pots to Tami and exchange them against bowls as the only product there available. The quantity of bowls thus acquired being again in excess of the Busama's own needs, some are carried back down to the southern villages to be traded along with taro once again for pots.

[a]Marshall Sahlins, *Stone Age Economics* (Chicago: Aldine, 1972), Chap. 6.

COMMENT: It is clearly not rational for the Busama to carry bowls from Tami—where they are, according to the report, *more* highly valued than pots (10 to 12 shillings against 8)—to southern villages where bowls are relatively *less* highly valued (one against one). Indeed, the logic of the situation strongly suggests that the relative values have been misreported. Surely the pots are relatively less highly valued where they are plentiful, at their origin in the south, and the bowls relatively less highly valued at their origin on Tami Island. Only if this is the case does the two-way shipping traffic of the Busama become understandable. The Busama must accept pots from the southern villagers, their only customers for taro, but nothing forces the Busama to carry bowls from north to south at a loss.

Another point to note is that since this is a situation of barter exchange, the cited shilling values may lack any real meaning. Since shillings are not actually employed everywhere in the region as a medium of exchange, price quotations may be reported that do not reflect the actual terms at which trades are taking place. Thus, a pot may be "worth" 8 shillings somewhere, but not necessarily on Tami Island if shillings are not actually exchanged for pots there.

☐ SUMMARY OF CHAPTER 13

This chapter examines the process of exchange and the benefits of trade. Transaction costs are analyzed, and the role of money in overcoming such costs is explained.

Benefits of exchange fall into two main categories: *reallocation of the existing stocks* of goods to the mutual advantage of all consumers, and *increased quantities* of goods made possible by specialization in production.

The first benefit stands out most clearly in a world of "pure exchange," where society has fixed stocks of all commodities. In such a world the Edgeworth box shows how two parties can both achieve greater satisfaction by trading into the "region of mutual advantage." At competitive equilibrium in pure exchange, each trader will have set his Marginal Rate of Substitution in Consumption MRS_C equal to the price ratio P_x/P_y. This corresponds to achieving a point on the "Contract Curve" in the Edgeworth box.

In a world of production and exchange, the individual's *productive optimum* Q^* will in general be distinct from his *consumptive optimum* C^*. At Q^* the condition met is $MRS_T = P_x/P_y$, where MRS_T is his Marginal Rate of Substitution in Productive Transformation (or Marginal Rate of Transformation); at C^* the condition is $MRS_C = P_x/P_y$ as before. The availability of trade widens the opportunities available in comparison with autarky; it leads to specialization in which each trader concentrates on the activity at which he is most productive. The increased output thus achieved is the second benefit of trade.

Full demand (the desired consumption quantity at any given price) and *full supply* (the total amount endowed or produced at that price) should be distinguished from *transaction* demand and supply. The latter represent amounts desired from or offered to the market at a given price. Summing over all individuals, the intersection of the aggregate *full* demand and supply curves shows the total quantity consumed and produced in the economy; the intersection of the aggregate *transaction* demand and supply curves shows the amount exchanged in the market.

Perfect markets involve perfect communication between buyers and sellers, instantaneous equilibrium with a single price at which all trading takes place, and absence of transaction charges. Actual markets can only approximate these ideal conditions. "Middlemen" tend to overcome market imperfections but do so at a cost—since the middlemen must be compensated. The costs of *trading*, properly speaking, are the costs of operating a market system in which self-interested individuals negotiate with one another while protecting themselves against fraud and coercion. Not all "middleman" services represent costs of trading. Some of them, like transportation, warehousing of goods, and retail distribution, would persist even in a total command economy.

Costs of trading are, among other things, a function of the physical volume of goods exchanged and of the number of distinct transactions per unit of time. The former source of cost was analyzed by assuming that transaction costs are proportional to the quantity of goods changing hands, and then the latter by assuming that the costs are incurred as a fixed lump-sum each time a transaction takes place.

Proportional transaction costs are similar, from the traders' point of view, to excise taxes. In equilibrium the gross price P_x^+ paid by buyers will exceed the net price P_x^- received by sellers, by the amount of the unit transaction expense. And of course the volume of goods exchanged will be less than in a hypothetical world free of transaction costs. *Lump-sum* transaction costs provide an incentive to minimize the number of distinct transactions. In consequence, inventories of goods purchased and sold must be held between trading dates. Both types of transaction costs diminish the extent of specialization in production, and make autarky solutions more likely.

Money is a device that reduces the cost of trading. As *medium of exchange* the existence of money lessens the number of different two-way channels of exchange that must be provided (in comparison with barter). This lowers the costs of collecting information, keeping records, and shipping goods to settle transactions. Even more important, it opens up triangular or even more complex patterns of trade that would be blocked under two-way barter. As *store of value*, money economizes on inventories that would have to be carried for trading purposes under barter. As a result of these cost savings, the institution of money makes possible more generally preferred distributions of consumption goods, together with larger output due to a higher degree of specialization in production.

MAINLY FOR REVIEW

R1. Explain how the possibility of trade can lead both to *consumptive* benefits (preferred allocations of given social totals of goods over the different individuals) and *productive* benefits (larger social totals of desired goods). How is the consumptive improvement illustrated in the Edgeworth box? Which diagram illustrates the productive improvement?

*R2. If two persons have identical preferences (indifference-curve maps), does it follow that they cannot trade to mutual advantage? What if they have identical preferences *and* identical endowments in a world of pure exchange? In a world of production, what if they have identical preferences and identical productive opportunities?

*R3. We normally observe a strong tendency toward specialization in production but diversification (non-specialization) in consumption. What shapes of the individuals' Production-Possibility Curves and preference maps lead to this pattern of behavior? Is trade necessary to bring it about?

R4. What is meant by an individual's "sustaining price" for a particular good? What happens at higher prices? At lower prices? How does the "sustaining price" differ from the "autarky price"?

R5. What condition must hold for each individual at competitive equilibrium in a world of *pure exchange*? What additional condition characterizes the market as a whole?

*R6. What are the productive and consumptive conditions that must hold for each individual in a world of *production and exchange*? What additional conditions characterize the market as a whole?

R7. Justify the assertion that the *productive* improvement due to trade necessarily implies greater social totals of desired goods. [*Hint:* Consider the two individuals' Marginal Rates of Transformation with and without trade.]

*R8. If market equilibrium takes place at the intersection of the aggregate *transaction* demand and *transaction* supply curves, how can the intersection of the full demand and full supply curves also determine the equilibrium?

R9. "For every individual, the s_i' and d_i' curves must intersect along the vertical axis, as in Figure 13.7. It is therefore quite impossible for the aggregate S' and D' curves to intersect in the interior, as in Figure 13.8." True or false? Explain.

R10. What are perfect markets? What is perfect competition?

*R11. Can autarky occur in costless exchange? Why is autarky more likely, the higher the transaction costs? Do you think the increasing burdens of payroll taxes (income tax, Social Security tax) and sales taxes in recent decades have anything to do with the "do-it-yourself" trend observed in such areas of activity as furniture construction and repair, car maintenance, dressmaking, etc.?

R12. Some markets are illegal (markets for babies, for narcotic drugs, for government favors, and so on). Law enforcement that is short of being *totally* effective can be regarded as imposing a transaction cost upon participants. In terms of this

*The answers to asterisked questions appear at the end of the book.

chapter's analysis, what effects would you anticipate from increased law-enforcement effort against the narcotics traffic? Would the volume of transactions be affected? What about the gross price paid by buyers in comparison with the net price received by sellers?

R13. Illustrate how sufficiently heavy *proportional* transaction costs might make a market non-viable. Do the same for *lump-sum* transaction costs.

*R14. Since the existence of markets necessarily involves some burden of transaction costs, wouldn't a command economy dispensing with markets always be more efficient? Explain.

R15. Distinguish between transfer costs and exchange costs. How would you class transportation of goods between producer and consumer? What about the costs of negotiating a contract? Enforcing a contract?

FOR FURTHER THOUGHT AND DISCUSSION

T1. From Omar Khayyam:

> I often wonder what the Vintners buy
> One half so precious as the Goods they sell.

Omar seems to be suggesting that vintners ought not to engage in exchange, since wine is more precious than anything else. Does this make sense in economic terms? Interpret.

*T2. Compare the likely effects of a tax upon *consumption*, upon *production*, and upon *exchange* of a commodity.

*T3. Why do we assume diminishing marginal returns in production but not in exchange?

T4. It was shown in the text that the opening of trade between two formerly autarkic producers tends to lead to greater specialization in production. The demonstration was based on the premise that preferences are relatively diversified (unspecialized) in comparison with productive opportunities. Show that if, on the contrary, two traders have relatively specialized tastes (one strongly preferring X, the other Y) and unspecialized productive opportunities, then the opening of trade would lead to a *lesser* degree of productive specialization. Does this mean that there is no productive benefit from trade? Explain.

*T5. Imagine an initial Edgeworth-box competitive equilibrium, starting from an endowment position where individual i has all of commodity C (corn) and individual j has all of commodity Y (*numéraire*). Suppose that i's endowment of corn doubles, everything else remaining unchanged. Can we be sure that i is better off at the new competitive equilibrium? That j is better off? That at least one of them is better off? [*Hint:* Are corn farmers necessarily better off if the crop is large? What about consumers of corn?]

*T6. Give examples of markets that have existed historically, but do not now exist. Can you explain their disappearance?

T7. According to economist K. E. Boulding, a tariff can be regarded as a "negative railroad." Whereas a railroad *connects* trading communities, a tariff *separates* them. Is the analogy valid?

*T8. How can integration of individuals' productive and consumptive choices be achieved *without* the use of markets? Can it be achieved with markets, but without the use of money?

*T9. Flowers provide bees with nectar, while bees facilitate the pollination of flowers. Is this exchange?

T10. Fresh fruits are cheaper at farm roadstands than in city markets. Does the price difference reflect transfer costs or exchange costs, or are there elements of each?

T11. Give examples of exchange costs that are reduced by the existence of money as a *medium of exchange*. Of money as a *store of value*.

*T12. If *rationing* is introduced, money is no longer fully effective as a medium of exchange. What types of additional exchange costs emerge in a world where ration coupons and cash are *both* required in order to effectuate a transaction?

*T13. According to elementary textbooks, a commodity selected to serve as money should be portable, divisible, storable, generally recognizable, and homogeneous. In terms of the discussion in this chapter, why are these desirable qualities? Can you think of other desirable qualities? [*Hint:* Think of cigarettes serving as money in a prisoner-of-war camp.]

T14. Suppose a gasoline tax is imposed, taking the form of a fixed number of cents per gallon (the same for regular and for premium gas), and assume that the supply curves for regular and premium gas are both horizontal. Consider the following arguments. (1) While we'd expect the quantity demanded of both premium and regular gasoline to fall after the tax is imposed, there should be a *relatively smaller* effect for the premium quality—since a fixed number of cents is a smaller *proportionate* tax for the premium gas. (2) On the contrary, we'd expect a *relatively bigger* effect for the premium quality—because premium gasoline is more of a "luxury" good, and the regular gasoline more of a "necessity" good. Is one or the other of these arguments totally wrong, or is it a matter of which of two valid arguments is the stronger? Analyze each argument separately, and explain.

14 INTERTEMPORAL CHOICE: SAVING, INVESTMENT, AND INTEREST

SUPPLEMENTARY
CHAPTER

Up to now we have studied two main types of individual decisions: (1) how to spend current income (that is, what consumption goods to purchase) and (2) how to earn current income (that is, what amounts of resource services to offer on the market). In this chapter a third type of decision is examined: how to strike a balance between consuming today versus arranging, via saving or investment, to have more income in the future.

What is meant by "saving" and "investment"? *Saving* is simply refraining from current consumption. *Investment,* in contrast, refers to the actual creation of new sources of productive services like buildings or machines. For an isolated Robinson Crusoe, saving must match investment. When Robinson refrains from eating some of his current corn, he is automatically investing—he is creating new resources in the form of a stock of seed that will yield future corn. In an exchange economy, however, those who save and those who invest do not have to be the same people. The person who saves by not consuming all his income, putting money in the bank instead, is not generally the one who creates a new resource by constructing a house. But the builder of the house, who makes the actual investment, will probably have borrowed. As we shall see, through the process of borrowing and lending the market works to make the economy-wide totals of saving and investment equal to one another.

Why would you save or invest, rather than consume today? Only so you, or your heirs, can consume more in the future. Someone who builds a house is arranging for future shelter; an orchardist who plants a tree is intending to reap future fruit; a business that incurs costs to maintain its machinery is assuring that its owners will have future earnings.

Section 14.A analyzes these choices between present and future. We will see how the *interest rate* serves as a kind of price in the market process that determines aggregate saving and investment. Section 14.B takes up an important practical topic: the criteria used by business firms and by government agencies in making their investment decisions. The role of risk is examined in Section 14.C, and the distinction between real interest and monetary interest is introduced in Section 14.D. The concluding section reviews the underlying forces that explain why interest rates are high in some countries, low in others—or have been high in some eras, while low in other historical periods.

14.A

CONSUMPTION AND PRODUCTION OVER TIME

For simplicity here we can sweep away the complications of multiple commodities and assume that there is only a single desired consumption object C (corn). The "goods" entering into the analysis are *dated* quantities of C symbolized as C_0 (this year's corn), C_1 (corn one year from now), C_2 (corn two years from now), etc. To begin with, let us consider elementary two-period choices: between consumption this year versus consumption next year.

14.A.1 ☐ Borrowing–Lending Equilibrium

The key to understanding the intertemporal decision process (the choice between C_0 and C_1) is to notice that the underlying logic is exactly the same as in choosing between ordinary commodities X and Y within a single period of time. Figure 14.1 looks almost exactly like the "optimum of the consumer" diagram first encountered in Figure 4.1. Once again there is a *preference map* (indifference curves U', U'' U''', . . .) and a *budget line* (KL). The optimum of the consumer will again be at a tangency point C^*—here representing a best "consumption basket" in the form of c_0^* of current corn and c_1^* of future corn.

The intertemporal endowment position E shows the individual's starting-point in the form of initial entitlements of current consumption ($c_0^{\dagger}$) and anticipated future consumption ($c_1^{\dagger}$).[1] When the individual trades northwest along the budget line KL from endowment position E, he or she is said to be "lending"—

[1]*Uncertainty* is ruled out here, so that anticipations as to the future are sure to be realized.

FIGURE 14.1 Intertemporal Consumptive Optimum. The decision between consumption this year C_0 and consumption next year C_1 has the same elements as the simple problem of consumer choice: preference map (indifference curves U', U'', U'''), endowment position (E), budget line (KL), and optimum position (C^*). The individual here chooses to lend the amount $c_0^{\dagger} - c_0^*$ of current claims, receiving in repayment the amount $c_1^* - c_1^{\dagger}$ of future claims. $W_0^{\dagger}$ is the endowed wealth measured in units of current claims C_0.

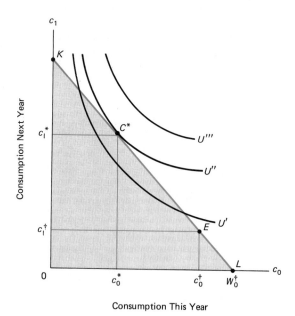

Consumption This Year

giving up current corn C_0 in exchange for future corn C_1. Should the person move southeast, obtaining more C_0 at the expense of C_1, he or she is said to be "borrowing." The individual pictured in Figure 14.1 chooses to be a lender in the amount of $c_0^\dagger - c_0^*$, the anticipated repayment next year being $c_1^* - c_1^\dagger$. Had the endowment position E been to the northwest of the intertemporal optimum C^* along the budget line, the individual would have been a borrower. Such a person, with an endowment mainly in the form of future income, is like the "heir with great expectations" in Charles Dickens' novel. He is poor today but has rich prospects for the future.

What is the rate of exchange at which the market will permit borrowing or lending, that is, the trading of current consumption entitlements C_0 against future entitlements C_1? This rate corresponds geometrically to the slope of the budget line. Let the price of C_0-claims be symbolized as P_0 and the price of C_1-claims be P_1. Then the ratio at which the two claims can be exchanged, $\Delta c_1/\Delta c_0$, equals $-P_0/P_1$. (The minus sign is needed since, as usual, Δc_1 and Δc_0 have opposite signs—one must be given up to obtain more of the other.) We will be assuming that current claims C_0 serve as the *numéraire* or basis of pricing, so that $P_0 \equiv 1$.

In the analysis of intertemporal exchange, the *interest rate r* is a special kind of price. Specifically, the annual rate of interest r is the *premium* on the relative value of current consumption claims over one-year-in-the-future consumption claims—the extra worth of corn today over corn next year. Looking at it the other way, the price P_1 of a future consumption claim is such that $1 + r$ units of future claims have the same value today as a single unit claim to current income:

$$(14.1) \qquad P_1(1 + r) \equiv P_0 \equiv 1$$

It is also useful to keep in mind the logically equivalent expressions:

$$(14.1') \qquad \frac{P_1}{P_0} \equiv \frac{1}{1 + r}$$

$$(14.1'') \qquad r \equiv \frac{P_0}{P_1} - 1$$

Consequently, the slope $-P_0/P_1$ of the budget line in Figure 14.1 can also be written as $-(1 + r)$.

Exercise 14.1: (a) If the interest is $r = 10\%$, what is the implied price P_1 of a one-year future claim? (b) What if $r = 100\%$? (c) If future claims become almost valueless (P_1 approaches zero), what would happen to r? (d) Are negative interest rates ($r < 0$) meaningful?

Answer: (a) Using (14.1'), if $r = 0.1$ then $P_1/P_0 = P_1 \equiv 1/1.1 = 0.9091$. (b) If $r = 1.0$ then $P_1 = 1/2 = 0.5$. (c) As P_1 approaches zero, r goes to infinity. (d) Yes, $r < 0$ means only that $P_1 > P_0$—that a future claim is worth *more* than a present claim. This is not at all impossible. For example, it might come about if people anticipated great scarcities in the future.

In the analysis of consumption in a single period (Section 4.A), it was the individual's *income I* that constrained choices according to the budget equation, $P_x x + P_y y = I$. This equation failed to allow for the fact that people often spend less than their current income (they may save) or more than their income (they may borrow). We are now in a position to correct this flaw in the preceding analysis. It is not *income I* that limits the individual's consumption choices over time but rather endowed *wealth* $W_0^\dagger$.

DEFINITION: Endowed wealth $W_0^\dagger$ is the value of an individual's intertemporal endowment of present and future claims.

In terms of the prices of present and future claims, endowed wealth would be expressed as follows:

$$(14.2) \qquad\qquad W_0^\dagger \equiv P_0 c_0^\dagger + P_1 c_1^\dagger$$

And in terms of the alternative "interest" notation, since $P_0 \equiv 1$ and $P_1 \equiv 1/(1 + r)$, endowed wealth is:

$$(14.2') \qquad\qquad W_0^\dagger \equiv c_0^\dagger + \frac{c_1^\dagger}{1 + r}$$

Geometrically, if $P_0 \equiv 1$ then the endowed wealth is the horizontal intercept of the budget line *KL*. Note the subscript 0 attached to the symbol for wealth. The reason is that wealth signifies a *present* market value, the worth *today* (in *numéraire* or C_0-units) of the dated income combination or time-stream.

The constraint itself, the budget line *KL* of Figure 14.1, can similarly be expressed in two ways:

$$(14.3) \qquad\qquad P_0 c_0 + P_1 c_1 = W_0^\dagger$$

$$(14.3') \qquad\qquad c_0 + \frac{c_1}{1 + r} = W_0^\dagger$$

These expressions describe all the c_0, c_1 combinations purchasable out of a given endowed wealth.

The intertemporal borrowing–lending equilibrium is derived in exactly the same way as the familiar market equilibrium involving commodities X and Y. By imagining different prices P_1 (or interest rates r) determining different budget lines through the endowment position, a Price Expansion Path is obtained for each individual. And these can then be translated into "full" or "transaction" supply and demand curves—first for the separate individuals, and then for the market as a whole. The final result is pictured in Figure 14.2, which corresponds to Panel (a) of Figure 13.5. The L^t curve is the market supply of lending, the summation over individuals of the "transaction quantities" of C_0 offered on the loan market at each interest rate r. B^t represents the market demand for borrowing, the aggregate transaction quantity of C_0 demanded at any r by those whose

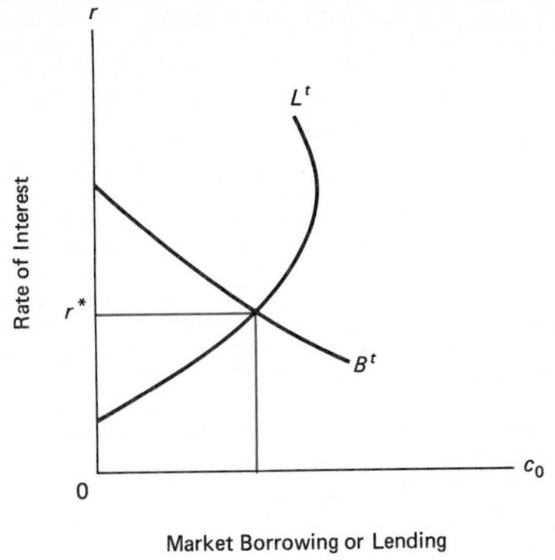

FIGURE 14.2 Borrowing–Lending Equilibrium. The L^t curve shows the aggregate supply of current claims offered for lending at each interest rate r; the B^t curve shows the aggregate demand for borrowing at each r. The intersection determines the equilibrium amount borrowed and lent, and the equilibrium interest rate r^*.

current endowments fall short of desired consumption at that interest rate. On the vertical axis of the borrowing–lending diagram it is usual to put the interest rate r, so that the supply–demand intersection determines the equilibrium rate of interest r^*—the premium paid for current corn relative to future corn.

Exercise 14.2: Suppose that John's Marginal Rate of Substitution for intertemporal consumption is given by $MRS^j_C = c^j_1/c^j_0$ and Karl's by $MRS^k_C = c^k_1/c^k_0$. Let the corresponding intertemporal endowments be $(c^{tj}_0, c^{tj}_1) = (10, 100)$ and $(c^{tk}_0, c^{tk}_1) = (50, 20)$. (a) Find John's demand for borrowing b_0 and Karl's supply of lending l_0. (b) Express the market equilibrium in terms of both the price ratio and the interest rate.

Answer: (a) To find John's consumption optimum, the usual equations are $c^j_1/c^j_0 = 1/P_1(\equiv P_0/P_1)$ and $c^j_0 + P_1 c^j_1 = 10 + 100P_1$. Eliminating c_1 we have: $c^j_0 = 5 + 50P_1$, or $c^j_0 = 5 + 50/(1 + r)$. This equation represents John's "full" demand curve for current corn (inclusive of his own consumption). His demand for borrowing is a "transaction" demand curve, specifically, $b^j_0 = c^j_0 - c^{tj}_0 = -5 + 50/(1 + r)$. A similar analysis for Karl leads to $c^k_0 = 25 + 10/(1 + r)$, implying $l^k_0 = c^{tk}_0 - c^k_0 = 25 - 10/(1 + r)$. (b) The equilibrium is at $r = 100\%$, or $P_1/P_0 = 1/2$. Here John borrows 20 units of C_0, equal to the amount that Karl is willing to lend.

14.A.2 ☐ Saving–Investment Equilibrium

In the pure borrowing–lending equilibrium just discussed, the lenders were saving (refraining from consumption). But their saving was exactly counterbalanced by *dis-saving* on the part of the borrowers; by assumption, no *investment* was taking place. Investment, the construction of new real-capital in the form of durable assets like machines or buildings, is a kind of production. Consequently, the analysis of the saving–investment equilibrium here will closely parallel the discussion of "Exchange and Production" in Chapter 13. (In fact, the correspondence is so close that only a few high points need be covered.) The upshot is that, in equilibrium, the net total of saving will be a positive amount that exactly balances (or "finances") the actual investment taking place in the economy.

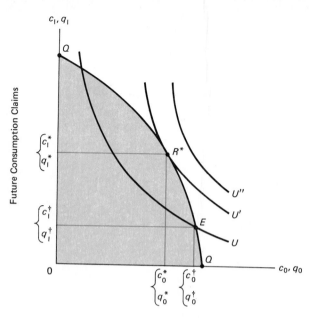

FIGURE 14.3 Intertemporal Productive–Consumptive Optimum: Robinson Crusoe.
A Robinson Crusoe has no intertemporal *exchange* (borrowing–lending) opportunities, but can engage in *productive* transformations between consumption this year and consumption next year. QQ is the Production-Possibility Curve through the endowment position E. The Crusoe optimum is at R^*, where QQ is tangent to the highest attainable indifference curve. This is an "autarky" solution: the amounts produced (q_0^*, q_1^*) equal, respectively, the amounts consumed (c_0^*, c_1^*).

Figure 14.3 shows the intertemporal productive–consumptive situation of a Robinson Crusoe isolated from all trade. Starting from an intertemporal endowment combination $E = (c_0^\dagger, c_1^\dagger)$, Robinson's productive transformation opportunities are indicated by his Production-Possibility Curve QQ. Evidently, the optimum position for Robinson is the tangency point R^* in the diagram. This is a joint productive–consumptive optimum: $R^* = (c_0^*, c_1^*) = (q_0^*, q_1^*)$.

We can now interpret the Crusoe or "autarky" solution in terms of the special terminology of intertemporal choice. Robinson's *saving* (refraining from consumption) is, as before, the horizontal distance $c_0^\dagger - c_0^*$. But here no lending occurs, as there is no other person with whom an exchange of current for future consumption claims can take place. Rather, Robinson's saving is used solely for physical *investment* (planting seed): $c_0^\dagger - c_0^* = q_0^\dagger - q_0^*$. The yield in terms of future corn is shown in the diagram by the vertical distance $q_1^* - q_1^\dagger = c_1^* - c_1^\dagger$. For an isolated Robinson Crusoe, therefore, plantings of seed (investing) exactly equal non-consumption of current corn (saving).

Once there is a possibility of exchange with other persons, the saving–investment equality need no longer apply for any single person separately. Figure 14.4 pictures an individual possessing *both* productive opportunities and market opportunities. The productive opportunities are represented, as before, by the Production-Possibility Curve QQ. The market opportunities can be represented by straight market lines of slope $-P_0/P_1 \equiv -(1 + r)$ through attainable points on QQ. Each market line is associated with a particular magnitude of attained wealth according to the equation:

(14.4)
$$W_0 = q_0 + \frac{q_1}{1 + r}$$

448

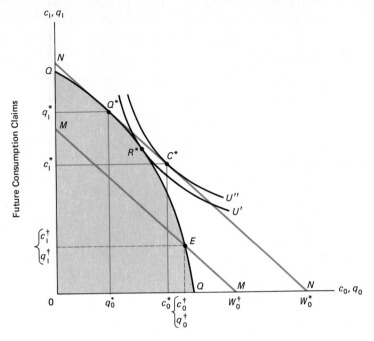

FIGURE 14.4 Intertemporal Productive–Consumptive Optimum with Exchange. The individual here has intertemporal productive opportunities (shown by the Production-Possibility Curve QQ) as well as exchange opportunities indicated by the market lines like MM and NN of slope $-P_0/P_1 \equiv -(1 + r)$. The productive optimum Q^* involves physical investment in the amount $q_0^\dagger - q_0^*$. The consumptive optimum C^* indicates that only the amount $c_0^\dagger - c_0^*$ is provided by this individual's own saving: the remainder of his investment is financed by borrowing in the market.

One such line, MM, shows the possibilities for market exchange from the endowment position E—the associated wealth being $W_0^\dagger$ as before. But it is obviously superior for the individual here first to attain a productive optimum at Q^*, where QQ is tangent to the *highest* attainable market line NN. This line NN is associated with the maximum attainable level of wealth, W_0^*:

(14.5)
$$W_0^* = q_0^* + \frac{q_1^*}{1 + r}$$

Having made the productive decision that maximizes wealth, the person can *then* engage in market exchange along NN, attaining a consumptive optimum at C^* far superior to what could have been achieved by isolated production. The attained wealth W_0^* becomes the effective *constraint* or budget line for his consumptive optimization decision:

(14.6)
$$c_0 + \frac{c_1}{1 + r} = W_0^*$$

In terms of the special intertemporal terminology, the individual pictured in Figure 14.4 is engaging in physical *investment* (planting of seed corn) to the extent of the horizontal distance $q_0^\dagger - q_0^*$. But his *saving* is a lesser amount, indicated by the horizontal distance $c_0^\dagger - c_0^*$. The individual is saving a portion of his endowed current income, but not enough to fully "finance" the investment. It follows that some other members of the society must be saving enough to make up the deficiency, i.e., to provide the remainder of the needed seed corn.

Market equilibrium is shown in Figure 14.5 in two ways: (1) as a balance between the overall "supply of saving" S_S and "demand for investment" D_I, and (2) as a balance between the overall "supply of lending" L^t and "demand for borrowing" B^t. The analogy with Figure 13.8 of the preceding chapter, showing solutions in terms of "full" supply and demand versus "transaction" supply and demand, is evident. [The derivation of the curves in Figure 14.5, proceeding as usual from the individual optimization diagram to individual supply and demand curves and then to market-wide supply and demand, is left for the reader.] Note that the difference between the magnitude of saving–investment versus the amount of borrowing–lending is accounted for by the economy-wide real investment that is *self-financed*—through investors' own savings rather than by recourse to the market for borrowing and lending.

> CONCLUSION: In the absence of productive investment opportunities, at any given interest rate r each individual will engage in borrowing or lending so as to achieve a preferred intertemporal pattern of consumption. At the equilibrium interest rate r^* the supply of lending balances the demand for borrowing. If there are investment opportunities, however, each individual will choose the scale of investment maximizing wealth—while also borrowing or lending as required to achieved a preferred time-pattern of consumption. Then the equi-

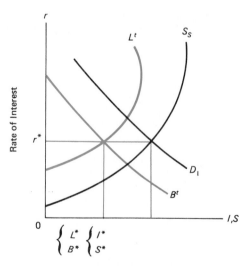

FIGURE 14.5 Intertemporal Equilibrium with Productive Investment. When productive investment can take place, the determination of the equilibrium interest rate r^* can be interpreted in two equivalent ways: (1) r^* is the interest rate that balances the aggregate *supply of saving* S_S with the aggregate *demand for investment* D_I, or (2) r^* is the interest rate that balances the aggregate *supply of lending* L^t with the aggregate *demand for borrowing* B^t. The difference between the two magnitudes is accounted for by the amount of investment self-financed out of investors' own savings.

450

librium interest $r*$ will balance the aggregate supply of saving with the aggregate demand for investment, and *also* balance the aggregate supply of lending with the aggregate demand for borrowing.

EXAMPLE 14.1 _____
Social Security, Saving, and National Income

Before the Social Security program came into effect, individuals generally provided for their retirement years by saving out of income earned in their productive working years. Whether in the form of bank deposits, annuities, stocks and bonds, or productive assets like real estate, such saving served to finance economy-wide real investments that increased the real-capital of the nation.

Upon the introduction of Social Security, however, retirement income was guaranteed to beneficiaries—reducing their need to save during their working years. Also, Social Security taxes on earnings reduced income available for saving. Thus, aggregate *private* saving would be expected to decline as a result of the Social Security program. On the other hand, the federal government was receiving huge inflows of Social Security contributions. Had the government adopted a policy of "funding" these contributions, the cash inflows would have been used to purchase stocks and bonds, real estate, etc. (Indeed, this is precisely what insurance companies do with premiums paid in under their private "social security" programs for individuals who purchase retirement annuities.) Then the collective saving of the Social Security Administration would have balanced the reduction in private savings of contributors.

However, the decision was made *not* to fund Social Security. Instead, Social Security tax revenues were used to support the current expenses of government. Some economists have contended that, in consequence, there has been a severe adverse effect upon aggregate saving in the economy (and therefore also upon aggregate real investment). Martin Feldstein[a] estimated that the Social Security program has reduced overall private saving by 38%—without, as just explained, providing any compensating increase in collective or government saving. The lower scale of saving and investment over the years has substantially reduced the nation's stock of real-capital. And since real-capital contributes to production (raises the Average Product of labor and other resources), total and per-capita national income have also been affected. Feldstein estimated that, by 1972, the Social Security program had led to a startling reduction in GNP—between 11 and 15%.

These calculations and estimates have since been subjected to searching criticism by other economists. One objection raised was that Feldstein had assumed all private saving was for retirement purposes, whereas in actuality many people save in order to pass on bequests to heirs. Taking account of this

[a]Martin Feldstein, "Social Security, Induced Retirement, and Aggregate Capital Accumulation," *Journal of Political Economy*, v. 82 (Sept./Oct. 1974).

and other criticisms, Michael R. Darby[b] has produced revised estimates. He concluded that Social Security was responsible for a decrease of between 5 and 20% in the capital stock, and between 2 and 7% in national income. These results tend to confirm Feldstein's point about the way in which the Social Security program affects saving and national income, but the calculated effects are numerically smaller than Feldstein's original estimates.

[b]Michael R. Darby, *The Effects of Social Security on Income and Capital Stock* (Washington, D.C.: American Enterprise Institute for Public Policy Research, 1979), esp. p. 79.

14.B
INVESTMENT DECISIONS
AND THE PRESENT-VALUE RULE

The analysis of consumption and production patterns over time is a branch of economics that is of intense and immediate concern for practical men of affairs. Decision-makers in government and business continually face such choices as: What investment projects to adopt? How to finance the set of chosen projects? Over what time frame to pay out the benefits? We can now begin to analyze certain of these investment decision problems.

14.B.1 ☐ The Separation Theorem

An essential feature of Figure 14.4 is that *the productive optimum position is entirely independent of the individual's preferences.* No matter how the indifference curves may shift around, the productive optimum Q^* is unchanged; the location of Q^* depends only on the Production-Possibility curve QQ and the slope of the market lines. This independence, called the *Separation Theorem,* applies only if there are perfect and costless markets (see Chapter 13) for borrowing and lending. Suppose instead that such transactions were costly, that (for example) an individual could only borrow at a higher rate of interest than the rate at which he could lend. Then the amount to be invested, the choice of Q^* on the Production-Possibility Curve, would depend in part upon preferences, upon the person's willingness to self-finance (to save). If so, the productive and consumptive decisions would not be entirely separated. Take the extreme case of an isolated Robinson Crusoe, where costs of transacting are infinite (there are no market opportunities at all). For Robinson Crusoe the productive and consumptive decisions must be identical; *all* his physical investment must be self-financed, and so his preferred time-pattern of consumption will surely affect his scale of investment.

If the conditions underlying the Separation Theorem can be regarded as approximately applicable, there are very important practical implications. Suppose that one individual (the "principal") were to delegate productive decisions to another (the "agent"). *The agent would not have to know anything about the subjective time-preferences of the principal.* If the agent maximizes attained wealth W_0^*, an objective market magnitude, this suffices to assure that the principal is made as well off as possible.

Even more important, an agent could work simultaneously for a number of *different* principals with diverging time-preferences. These principals are thus more able to combine their productive opportunities by forming a *firm* or corporation (see Chapter 6). An agent maximizing the wealth of the corporation also maximizes the wealth increments going to each and every one of the owners, regardless of divergences in their intertemporal consumption desires. So the types of investments a firm could advantageously undertake will be the same whether the owners are "heirs with great expectations," or forethoughted savers, or any mixture thereof.[2]

14.B.2 □The Present-Value Rule

Suppose that a "project," i.e., an investment (or disinvestment) opportunity, is under consideration for adoption. What is the appropriate *investment decision rule?*

A project can be regarded as characterized by a sequence of dated cash flows or payments. In a simple two-period model these would correspond to increments (or decrements) z_0 and z_1 to investors' income. If z_0 is negative and z_1 is positive, present income is being sacrificed for future income and we have an *investment* project. If z_0 is positive and z_1 negative, it would be a *disinvestment* project.

No matter what the pattern of positive or negative elements, the *Present Value* V_0 of a project is defined as:

$$(14.7) \qquad V_0 \equiv z_0 + \frac{z_1}{1 + r}$$

Comparison with the definition of wealth in equation (14.4) shows that Present Value can be regarded as a *wealth increment* associated with adoption of the project in question. *If* the Separation Theorem is applicable, wealth-maximization is the object of all productive decisions: positive wealth increments are unambiguously desirable and negative wealth increments undesirable. These considerations lead to:

PRESENT-VALUE RULE 1: Adopt any project for which Present Value V_0 is positive; reject any project for which Present Value V_0 is negative. (Note that this rule has the same form for investment and disinvestment projects.)

There are possibilities of complications where projects are *interdependent*. Conceivably, adoption of any one project might change the z_0, z_1 payoff sequence

---

[2]When the Separation Theorem is *inapplicable,* there is said to be a "clientele effect" in the decisions of the firm. We would expect principals of different tastes to sort themselves out, becoming owners of different types of firms, each of which would cater to the particular time-preferences of its owners.

associated with another. The obvious implication is to adopt that *set* of projects whose combined payment stream has maximum Present Value. We shall not go through all the interdependence possibilities here, but rather state the rule that applies when projects or combinations of projects are *mutually exclusive:*[3]

> PRESENT-VALUE RULE 2: If two projects (or combinations of projects) are mutually exclusive, adopt that which has the higher Present Value V_0.

Exercise 14.3: (a) For a certain project the anticipated cash-flows are $z_0 = -100$, $z_1 = 125$. Is this an investment or a disinvestment? What is its Present Value V_0 when the interest rate r is 10%? At $r = 20\%$? At $r = 30\%$? What is the highest rate of interest at which the project should be adopted? (b) The Table shows alternative payments sequences for two interdependent projects M and N. The columns headed "alone" show the payments associated with each if it were adopted separately. The other columns show the payments associated with each if the other were also be to adopted. If the interest rate r were 20% and you were required to adopt no more than one project, which (if any) should be adopted? If you could adopt both together, would you want to do so?

| | ALONE | | WITH THE OTHER PROJECT | |
PROJECT	z_0	z_1	z_0	z_1
M	−100	125	−95	110
N	−50	90	−60	95

Answer: (a) This is an investment project. When $r = 10\%$, $V_0 = -100 + 125/(1 + 0.1) = 13.64$. When $r = 20\%$, $V_0 = 4.167$. When $r = 30\%$, $V_0 = -3.85$. To find the highest rate of interest at which the project should be adopted, solve for r in $V_0 = 0 = -100 + 125/(1 + r)$. The answer is $r = 25\%$. The project should be adopted for any r *below* 25%. (b) The easiest way to do this is to compare Present Values of the three mutually exclusive investment alternatives M, N, and MN—in comparison with the do-nothing alternative 0. At 20%, $V_0(M) = -100 + 125/1.2 = 4.17$ and $V_0(N) = -50 + 90/1.2 = 25$. For the combination MN the combined payments are $z_0 = -155$ and $z_1 = 205$, so that $V_0(MN) = -155 + 205/1.2 = 15.83$. The best option is to adopt N alone, even if you could adopt both.

14.B.3 ☐ Multi-period Analysis

The discussion to this point has been limited to consumption and investment choices over two dates: "now" (time-0) and "one year from now" (time-1). But the same general principles apply to more complex time-patterns of decisions. We can think of individuals as attempting to attain preferred consumption combinations over any number of dates from "now" to an economic horizon at some future date T. However, we must generalize the concept of

---

[3] Any list of alternative projects, interdependent or not, can be grouped into mutually exclusive combinations. Thus, three projects A, B, C can be sorted into the eight mutually exclusive combinations 0, A, B, C, AB, AC, BC, and ABC (where 0 represents adopting *no* project at all).

Present Values to a multi-period form. We can write the prices of consumption claims at different dates as $P_0, P_1, \ldots, P_T$.[4] As usual we can set $P_0 \equiv 1$, letting current income claims continue to serve as *numéraire*.

In translating from *prices* to *interest rates*, there are two different formulations in common use.

Consider the successive one-year price ratios $P_1/P_0, P_2/P_1, \ldots, P_T/P_{T-1}$. These can be used to define the successive one-year "short-term" interest rates $r_1, r_2, \ldots, r_T$ on the left side of the Table of Interest-Rate Equivalents below. Here r_1 is the rate appropriate in exchanging or "discounting" time-1 claims into their present or time-0 equivalents, r_2 the rate for discounting time-2 claims into time-1 equivalents, etc.

Alternatively, we can consider the ratios $P_1/P_0, P_2/P_0, \ldots, P_T/P_0$—defined so that P_0 appears in all the denominators. These can be used, as on the right side of the Table, to define the "long-term" interest rates $R_1, R_2, \ldots, R_T$. These rates are appropriate for discounting the claims of any date *directly* into current (time-0) equivalents.

Table of Interest-Rate Equivalents

SHORT-TERM INTEREST RATES	LONG-TERM INTEREST RATES
$\dfrac{P_1}{P_0} = \dfrac{1}{1 + r_1}$	$\dfrac{P_1}{P_0} = \dfrac{1}{1 + R_1}$
$\dfrac{P_2}{P_1} = \dfrac{1}{1 + r_2}$	$\dfrac{P_2}{P_0} = \dfrac{1}{(1 + R_2)^2}$
$\cdots$	$\cdots$
$\dfrac{P_T}{P_{T-1}} = \dfrac{1}{1 + r_T}$	$\dfrac{P_T}{P_0} = \dfrac{1}{(1 + R_T)^T}$

The Present Value of a multi-period sequence of income increments (or decrements) can be correspondingly expressed in two different forms:

$$(14.8) \qquad V_0 \equiv z_0 + \frac{z_1}{1 + R_1} + \frac{z_2}{(1 + R_2)^2} + \cdots + \frac{z_T}{(1 + R_T)^T}$$

$$(14.9) \qquad V_0 \equiv z_0 + \frac{z_1}{1 + r_1} + \frac{z_2}{(1 + r_2)(1 + r_1)}$$

$$+ \cdots + \frac{z_T}{(1 + r_T) \cdots (1 + r_2)(1 + r_1)}$$

For some purposes the first formulation is the more convenient, for other purposes the second. There is no ultimate difference between them. The "long-

---

[4]It is important to note that while the claims represent rights to income at different dates, the prices are those quoted in the trading that takes place now. P_1 is the price *today* of a claim to income payable one year in the future, P_2 is the price *today* of a claim payable two years in the future, etc.

term" rate R_t applicable for discounting claims dated t years from now is obviously a kind of average of the "forward" short-term rates $r_1, r_2, \ldots, r_t$ between now and that date.

While there are important economic forces leading to systematic patterns in the "term structure" of the r_t or R_t interest rates, in most practical investment-decision applications it is customary to assume that the currently applicable rate will maintain itself into the future. Of course, if the r_t are all equal to some common value r then all the R_t will also be equal to r, so that the two formulations (14.8) and (14.9) become identical in the form:

$$(14.10) \qquad V_0 \equiv z_0 + \frac{z_1}{1 + r} + \frac{z_2}{(1 + r)^2} + \cdots + \frac{z_T}{(1 + r)^T}$$

Let us modify equation (14.10), which defines the Present Value V_0 of a project at some constant intertemporal interest rate r, in the following ways. First, assume that the "economic horizon" T is infinite. Second, suppose that returns on the project begin at time-1. And third, assume that the future receipts $z_1, z_2, \ldots$ extending out to infinity remain at some constant level z. Then (14.10) reduces to the simple form:[5]

$$(14.10') \qquad V_0 \equiv \frac{z}{r} \qquad \text{or} \qquad r \equiv \frac{z}{V_0}$$

This formulation can be interpreted as the relation between the annual interest payments (z) and the principal sum (V_0) of a loan. Or, in accordance with equation (12.3) of Chapter 12, as the relation between the annual income derivable from a source of productive services (z) and the current market value of the source itself (V_0). Note the two different aspects of the interest rate r: it expresses both the time-premium, the extra market value of earlier over later consumption income, and also the ratio between income flow and the value of the source of income.

[5]*Mathematical Footnote:* The derivation proceeds from (14.10), under the special assumptions above, as follows:

$$V_0 = z \left[\frac{1}{1 + r} + \frac{1}{(1 + r)^2} + \cdots \right]$$

Let $1/(1 + r)$ be denoted k. Then

$$V_0 = z(1 + k + k^2 + \cdots) - z = \frac{z}{1 - k} - z$$

But

$$1 - k = 1 - \frac{1}{1 + r} = \frac{r}{1 + r}$$

So

$$V_0 = z \left(\frac{1 + r}{r} \right) - z = \frac{z}{r}$$

Exercise 14.4: (a) If the one-period (short-term) interest rate is $r_1 = 10\%$ and the two-period (long-term) interest rate is $R_2 = 20\%$, what is the implied "forward" short-term rate r_2? Assuming $P_0 \equiv 1$ as usual, what are the implied prices P_1 and P_2 for one-year-future and two-year-future claims, respectively? (b) Suppose that a three-period project has the cash-flow sequence $-1, 2, 1$. Assuming the interest rate r is constant over time, what is the range of r for which this is a good project? What if the cash-flow sequence is $-1, 5, -6$?

Answer: (a) Since $P_2/P_0 = (P_2/P_1)(P_1/P_0)$, from the Table of Interest-Rate Equivalents we can see that $(1 + R_2)^2 = (1 + r_2)(1 + r_1)$, or numerically here $(1.2)^2 = 1.1(1 + r_2)$. The solution for the forward short-term rate is $r_2 = 30.9\%$. The implied prices for the future claims are $P_1 = 1/(1 + r_1) = 0.91$ and $P_2 = 1/(1 + R_2)^2 = 0.69$. (b) We want to find the range of r for which $V_0 > 0$. With the first cash-flow sequence the inequality becomes: $-1 + 2/(1 + r) + 1/(1 + r)^2 > 0$. Solving the quadratic, the root is $r = 141.4\%$. Thus the Present Value is positive for any interest rate $r < 141.4\%$. (The quadratic has another root, $r = -141.4\%$, but interest rates less than -100% are impossible.) For the second cash-flow sequence it turns out that V_0 is negative for all allowable interest rates below 100%, becomes positive in the range between $r = 100\%$ and $r = 200\%$, but then turns negative again for still higher r.

EXAMPLE 14.2
Education and Earnings

A study by A. Razin and J. D. Campbell[a] calculated Present Values of lifetime earnings for holders of bachelor's degrees in various fields. National Science Foundation 1968 data on yearly incomes of scientific manpower were used. The authors assumed that earnings begin in the 5th year after admission to college, and terminate in the 44th year, so that equation (14.10) was applied in the special form:

$$V_0 = \frac{z_5}{(1 + r)^5} + \frac{z_6}{(1 + r)^6} + \cdots + \frac{z_{44}}{(1 + r)^{44}}$$

Calculating in terms of an interest rate $r = 3\%$, the Table indicates some of the results obtained. (The relatively favorable position of the economics de-

Present Values of Earnings for Bachelor's Degrees

Mathematics	$342,068
Economics	339,482
Computer sciences	306,733
Political science	300,000
Physics	282,758
Psychology	262,127
Agricultural science	225,118
Biological science	215,691
Sociology	213,590

[a] Assaf Razin and James D. Campbell, "Internal Allocation of University Resources," *Western Economic Journal*, v. 10 (Sept. 1972), esp. p. 315.

gree is consistent with the salary standing of economics instructors reported in Example 1.2.)

These numbers do not represent the *net* or overall Present Value of going to college and receiving the degree. Only the benefits, the earnings received by holders of the degree, have been shown. The cost side of the picture, which would allow for college-related outlays (tuition, living expenses, books, etc.) and also for earnings foregone by students during the four college years, has not been taken into account.

There is still another difficulty: we cannot assume that the higher earnings of educated individuals are due to their education alone. People who go to college may earn more because they are smart to begin with, or come from more affluent families, etc. To eliminate such sources of bias J. R. Behrman, R. A. Pollak, and P. Taubman[b] compared the earnings of pairs of *identical twins* who had received different amounts of schooling. They found that the following formula best fitted the observations:

$$\log \left(\frac{E_1}{E_2} \right) = 0.28 \log \left(\frac{S_1}{S_2} \right) + 0.014$$

where E_1 and E_2 represent the annual earnings of the two members of the twin pair, and S_1 and S_2 their years of schooling.

With this equation we can estimate that if an individual has a twelfth-grade education and earns \$18,400 per year (these were typical figures in 1980) then his twin with four years of college will earn \$20,225 per year—an improvement of \$1825 or only 9.9%! Assuming a forty-year working life and an interest rate of 3%, the Present Value of additional earnings due to four years of college is \$42,176. Note how much smaller this figure is than those in the Razin–Campbell study, and recall that neither study makes any allowance for the *costs* of attending college.

Does this mean that college is a bad investment? Not necessarily. Presumably, individuals are deriving some benefits from college apart from improvement in future earnings. Among the possibilities are intellectual enrichment, new friends, potential marriage partners, and even fun and games.

[b]Jere R. Behrman, Robert A. Pollak, and Paul Taubman, "Parental Preferences and Provision for Progeny," *Journal of Political Economy*, v. 90 (Feb. 1982).

14.C
THE EFFECTS OF TIME AND RISK ON INTEREST RATES

The numerical interest rate r employed usually has a very substantial effect upon Present Value. This is especially the case when the annual payments z_t, whether negative (representing costs) or positive (representing benefits or receipts), extend to a relatively distant time-horizon T.

EXAMPLE 14.3
Present Values of the Feather River Project

The Feather River Project is an enormous undertaking of the State of California conveying water from a dam and reservoir in the northern part of the state to numerous delivery points in the central and southern portions. The Table that follows shows the results of an independent assessment (made prior to construction) of the prospective costs and receipts of the project and of the net balance of the two, all calculated in terms of Present Values. Three alternative routes then under consideration were evaluated. The present-value calculation considered two alternative interest rates, 2.7% and 5%.

While all the Present Values were negative, the higher 5% interest rate was associated with relatively lower figures for both costs and receipts. Since the cost sequence is a series of positive payments at each date, and the receipts sequence also a series of positive elements, the larger the r the smaller the discounted sum for each, as may be seen from equation (14.10). But the Table shows that the impact of a higher r upon receipts is greater than upon costs. The reason is that costs are typically incurred *earlier* in time than receipts are received, so that a rise in the discount factor $(1 + r)$ operates more powerfully to reduce the latter. *The higher the* r, *the less attractive the project* is a reliable general rule.

Present Values of the Feather River Project (millions of dollars)

INTEREST RATE	COSTS	RECEIPTS	NET PRESENT VALUE	NET PRESENT VALUE, ADJUSTED*
2.7%				
Route 1	$1241	$1079	$−162	$− 97
Route 8A	1123	1012	−111	− 46
Route 10A	1029	919	−110	− 46
5%				
Route 1	1035	515	−520	−502
Route 8A	860	445	−415	−397
Route 10A	799	409	−391	−372

Source: J. C. DeHaven and J. Hirshleifer, "Feather River Water for Southern California," *Land Economics*, v. 33 (Aug. 1957), p. 201. (Some technical footnotes omitted.)

*Adjustment credits an allowance for flood-control benefit and salvage value.

COMMENT: The Feather River Project was adopted, despite the showing of negative net Present Value. Thus, the investment decision rule of this chapter was violated. Indeed, the route adopted was that which had the *most unfavorable* receipts-cost balance. (Reasons why this might have occurred are suggested in the analysis of the political process in Chapter 16.)

The next example also illustrates the powerful effect of interest rates upon Present Values.

EXAMPLE 14.4
Professors and Publications

Professors in general, and economics professors in particular, devote a considerable portion of their time to research. The output of successful research usually takes the form of articles published in scholarly journals. Publications lead to professional recognition and so tend to raise the lifetime earnings of their authors.

H. P. Tuckman and J. Leahey[a] conducted a study estimating the worth to authors of a published article. Their results indicate that a *first* article by an Assistant Professor is associated with an increase of $12,340 in Present Value of lifetime earnings, calculated at an interest rate of 5%. At a higher 10% interest rate, the future earnings gains are discounted more heavily, however, leading to a lower estimate of $7074.

The Present Values of lifetime income increments due to articles published by Associate and Full Professors were generally lower than for Assistant Professors, the main explanation being the fact that the higher-rank professors are nearer retirement age. Another interesting point observed was the operation of the Law of Diminishing Returns. At the lower $r = 5\%$, the Present Value of a marginal article published by an Assistant Professor steadily declined from $12,340 for the first article, to $4310 for the fifth article, down to only $1544 for the thirtieth published article!

[a]Howard P. Tuckman and Jack Leahey, "How Much Is an Article Worth?" *Journal of Political Economy*, v. 83 (Oct. 1975).

An interest rate of $r = 3\%$ was used in one of the studies reported above; a second employed two alternative rates, 2.7% and 5%; and the third used 5% and 10%. Can all these be correct? How do we determine the correct rate to use?

Interest rates may vary for a number of reasons. First, they change historically, so that decisions involving Present Values calculated in 1950 or 1960 were subject to a different r than were 1970 or 1980 decisions. And even at a specific moment of time, as we saw above there is a "term structure" of interest rates—differing rates for discounting near-future cash flows versus far-future cash flows. On December 3, 1982, for example, U.S. Treasury issues (bonds and notes) of different maturities were selling at prices representing different net interest yields to purchasers. Issues maturing in the nearer future (1982 and 1983) were typically yielding from 9.0% to 9.25%; issues maturing in the medium future (1986) were yielding about 10.75%; while distant future maturities (beyond 2000) were yielding around 11% per annum.

The major reason for a variety of interest rates existing at a moment of time, however, is the element of *risk*. Even if maturity and all other elements of the transaction are the same, bonds of foreign governments or of municipalities or of private corporations are generally considered riskier than U.S. Treasury issues—and so can only be sold at prices generating a higher risk-compensating interest yield to their holders. Similarly, a potential borrower will find that a bank or other lending institution may offer a variety of interest rates—a higher rate for an unsecured loan than for a loan secured by a mortgage or other collateral or guarantees.

Two rather different aspects of risk should be distinguished:

1. *Default risk:* Some transactions, like a bank loan or a bond issue, represent an explicit promise of performance by the borrower (promise to pay interest and to repay principal). If these promises are not fully carried out, the borrower has to some degree defaulted. Suppose that a bank makes a one-year $1000 loan to an individual at a contractual (promised) interest rate of 10%, and imagine that the bank has 99% confidence in the borrower's performance but believes there is a 1% chance of a complete default on both principal and interest. Then the "expected" or average interest yield for the bank is not 10% but only 8.9%.[6] It is the 8.9% that approximates the "true" interest rate; 10% is the "nominal" interest rate, the difference being an adjustment or premium for default risk.

2. *Variability Risk:* Some financial instruments, like equity shares of corporate stock, do not have any explicit promise of performance. The returns to the lender or investor in the form of dividends or other cash payments may vary considerably up or down from the average; this is variability risk. In general, there is an aversion to variability risk. As between two securities with the same average yield, the typical investor will prefer the one more nearly approaching a fully certain yield. It follows that securities whose returns are highly uncertain will sell at prices yielding their holders *greater* average earnings—the difference being the adjustment or premium for the greater variability risk.

[6]The bank anticipates receiving $1100 at the end of the year if all goes well (99% probability), but otherwise receiving nothing. Its "expected" or average net interest return is 0.99($1100) + 0.01($0) − $1000, or $89, which is a rate of yield of 8.9% on the $1000 principal amount.

EXAMPLE 14.5
Term and Risk Premiums

R. G. Ibbotson and R. A. Sinquefield examined the actual yields obtained over the period 1926–81 by investors holding a number of different classes of financial instruments. In the Table, a difference between the average yield on long-term government bonds versus short-term U.S. Treasury bills would represent a *term premium* offered investors. Over the period studied this difference, as can be seen, was nil. On the other hand, the excess of experienced yield on common stocks over government bonds indicates that during this period those investors willing to incur *variability risk* received a substantial premium for doing so.

Experienced Average Yields, 1926–1981 (%)

	ARITHMETIC MEAN	GEOMETRIC MEAN
U.S. Treasury bills	3.1	3.0
Long-term government bonds	3.1	3.0
Common stocks	11.4	9.1

Source: Roger G. Ibbotson and Rex A. Sinquefield, *Stocks, Bonds, Bills and Inflation: The Past and the Future* (Charlottesville, Va.: Financial Analysts Research Foundation, 1982), esp. p. 71.

The difference between the results calculated in terms of the arithmetic mean versus the geometric mean of the annual experienced yields is also of significance. The arithmetic mean answers the question, "On the basis of the annual data, what yield can be expected *in any given year* on this type of investment?" The geometric mean answers the question, "On the basis of the cumulative record, what *average annual compounded yield* can be expected on this type of investment?"

The problem of choosing an interest rate, for calculating Present Value via equation (14.10), may arise in either *normative* or *positive* analysis (see Section 1.A.3). From the *positive* point of view we may ask: "What interest rates are decision-makers actually employing in their investment decisions?" From a *normative* point of view we could be asking: "What interest rate ought a decision-maker employ in accepting or rejecting an investment project?"

In Example 14.2 on the Present Value of a bachelor's degree, the economists were engaging in positive analysis; their choice of *r* was an estimate of how heavily college students were discounting anticipated future earnings in deciding whether or not to earn a college degree. Example 14.4 on the worth of a published article, and Example 14.5 on the realized rates of return observed in the financial markets, also represent positive analyses. In these terms it seems that the 3% discount rate employed in Example 14.2 was on the low side. The decision to invest time and resources in obtaining a bachelor's degree is obviously a highly risky one; a rational investor would demand a very substantial variability-risk premium before doing so. In contrast, Example 14.4 studies a considerably less risky decision (whether or not to invest in producing a single publishable article), and uses a considerably higher range of interest rates (5% and 10%).

Example 14.3 is on a rather different footing. It represents *normative* analysis. The economists there were concerned with the question: "Should the Feather River Project have been built by the State of California?" What is the appropriate rate to use for such a normative analysis? In general, the correct rate (the one that would lead to the correct decision in terms of maximizing California citizens' wealth) would be the rate used by the market in evaluating investments of comparable risk.

EXAMPLE 14.6
On Appreciating Art

The return received from holding a durable asset may take a number of forms, including: (1) productive yield, as from agricultural land, (2) consumptive utility, as from clothing, or (3) anticipated appreciation of market value. The prospect of value appreciation is often important for individuals deciding whether to invest in works of art.

By examining auction prices from 1946 to 1968, J. P. Stein[a] estimated the appreciation gain from ownership of paintings. He found that over this period the return averaged 10.5% per annum, as compared to 14.3% for dividends plus appreciation on corporate stocks. In part the discrepancy might be explained by the fact that paintings offer somewhat less variability risk than stock market investments. But even after adjusting for risk and certain other special circumstances, Stein found the financial return on paintings to be about 1.6 percentage points less than comparable stock returns. The explanation, presumably, is that investors were willing to sacrifice some financial gain for the consumptive utility derived from ownership of fine works of art.

[a]John P. Stein, "The Monetary Appreciation of Paintings," *Journal of Political Economy*, v. 85 (Oct. 1977).

14.D
REAL INTEREST AND MONEY INTEREST: ALLOWING FOR INFLATION

So far in this chapter we have been analyzing the *real* rate of interest. Following the usual practice in microeconomics we have looked behind the "veil of money." Recall that the exchange ratio between present and future real claims can be expressed as:

(14.11)
$$-\frac{\Delta c_1}{\Delta c_0} \equiv 1 + r$$

Here the rate of interest r is the market premium on C_0 relative to C_1—on current versus future claims to real consumption income.

But in common parlance "the rate of interest" is ordinarily understood to be associated with the lending and borrowing of *money*. The *money rate of interest,* which can be symbolized as r', will not in general equal the *real* rate of interest r. The money rate of interest is the premium on *current money* m_0 relative to *future money* m_1. That is, when current money is exchanged in the loan market against future money, in the amounts Δm_0 and Δm_1, the exchange ratio defines the *money rate of interest* in the expression:

(14.12)
$$-\frac{\Delta m_1}{\Delta m_0} \equiv 1 + r'$$

What is the relation between the real rate of interest r and the money rate of interest r'? This is connected with movements of the "price level," that is, with changes in the prices (in contemporaneous *money* units) of *real* goods. At time-0, money is traded for real goods in the exchange ratio $\Delta m_0/\Delta c_0$. At time-1, the ratio is $\Delta m_1/\Delta c_1$. These exchange ratios (in absolute values) define the current and future money *price levels* P_0^m and P_1^m:

(14.13)
$$P_0^m \equiv -\frac{\Delta m_0}{\Delta c_0} \quad \text{and} \quad P_1^m \equiv -\frac{\Delta m_1}{\Delta c_1}$$

These imply:

$$\frac{\Delta m_1}{\Delta m_0} = \frac{P_1^m(\Delta c_1)}{P_0^m(\Delta c_0)}$$

Finally, this can be rewritten, using the preceding equations:

(14.14)
$$1 + r' = (1 + r)\frac{P_1^m}{P_0^m}$$

In terms of economic logic, equation (14.14) is readily understandable. The left hand side, $1 + r'$, is what a lender receives in future money in return for giving up one unit of current money. The amount so received must depend, in part, upon the *real* future return $1 + r$ per unit of current *real* claims sacrificed. But money may rise or fall in value relative to the underlying real claims. Hence, the rate of money interest r' must be sufficiently high to make up for any increase in the price level that makes future *real* claims more expensive relative to future *money*.

The ratio of the money price levels, P_1^m/P_0^m, is a measure of the rate of inflation. More specifically, let a be the *anticipated rate of price-level inflation*:

(14.15)
$$\frac{P_1^m}{P_0^m} \equiv 1 + a$$

It follows then that:

$$1 + r' = (1 + r)(1 + a)$$

Simplifying, we have:

(14.16)
$$r' = r + a + ra$$

Accordingly, the money rate of interest equals the real rate of interest plus the anticipated rate of price inflation, plus the cross-product of the latter two. When r and a remain in their usual range of percentage points, the cross-product term can to a fair approximation be ignored. With *compound* interest, the shorter the period of compounding the more correct it is to drop the cross-product. For continuously compounded interest, the cross-product drops out entirely and we have exactly:

(14.17)
$$r' = r + a$$

It is in this simple form that the relation between real and money interest is usually expressed.[7]

> PROPOSITION: The money rate of interest equals the real rate of interest plus the anticipated rate of price inflation.

[7]*Mathematical Footnote:* If i is any annual interest rate, a dollar will grow in value to $1 + i$ dollars at the end of one year. With quarterly compounding of interest, the terminal value will be $(1 + i/4)^4$; with any compounding frequency of f per year, it will be $(1 + i/f)^f$. For continuous compounding, we let f approach infinity. Then $\lim_{f \to \infty} (1 + i/f)^f \equiv \lim_{h \to \infty} [(1 + 1/h)^h]^i$ where $h \equiv f/i$. But the limit within the brackets is e, the base of the natural logarithms. The terminal value of a dollar continuously compounded at interest rate i, at the end of a year, is then e^i. The terminal value of Z dollars at the end of T years is Ze^{iT}.

Expressed in terms of continuously compounded rates, equation (14.14) becomes:

$$e^{r'} = e^r e^a$$

Taking logarithms, (14.17) follows directly.

EXAMPLE 14.7
Real and Money Rates of Interest

William E. Gibson[a] examined the effects of inflationary expectations upon the "nominal" (money) rates of interest paid on U.S. Treasury securities in the period 1962 to 1970. In all such studies the practical problem is to find a measure of "inflationary anticipations," which are not a directly visible magnitude. The measure used by Gibson was derived from a semi-annual survey of economists conducted by Joseph Livingston, a nationally syndicated financial columnist.

Using this information as an estimate of anticipations a, and the recorded interest rates as the measure of the money rate r', Gibson estimated statistically an equation in the form:

$$r' = H + Ka$$

Here H and K were the parameters of the line of best fit to the observed data.

[a]William E. Gibson, "Interest Rates and Inflationary Expectations: New Evidence," *American Economic Review*, v. 62 (Dec. 1972).

On the assumption that the *real* rate of interest r was constant over this period, comparison with equation (14.17) above shows that the fitted parameter H is an estimate of the real rate r. Also, the fitted parameter K should be simply equal to unity.

The statistical evidence varied somewhat according to the type of security considered. But the H figures obtained suggested a *real* rate of interest between 2% and 3% (much lower than the nominal interest rates in this period, of course). And the K estimates were not far from unity (for example, 0.9300 for three-month Treasury bills, 0.8959 for three-year to five-year Treasury notes).

One interesting point is that the K estimates were closer to unity in the latter than in the earlier portion of the period. The suggestion is that the general public was gradually learning to adjust to the prospect of continuing inflation.

Equation (14.17) is connected with important issues of *macro*economic policy. Suppose the government desires, for reasons that do not concern us here, to reduce the money interest rate r'. One thing the government can do is to increase the aggregate money balances in the economy (for example, by paying its bills with newly printed money). In the short run, as the aggregate amount of current money m_0 rises, this does tend to lower the money rate of interest. For, if people have more m_0 in their hands they are more inclined to make market exchanges Δm_0 of current money against future money, i.e., they are more inclined to *lend* money for future return. As we can see in equation (14.12), when the denominator Δm_0 on the left-hand side rises then r' on the right-hand side falls. However, there is an important after-effect to consider. When government increases the aggregate of current money m_0, equation (14.13) tells us that the current price-level P_0^m also tends to rise ("more money chasing the same amount of goods"). It *may* happen that this process tends to generate public anticipations of further price inflation. People may think that if the government has found it convenient to print more money forcing up the current price-level P_0^m, they will find it convenient to do so again in the future. Should these anticipations become general, a rises in equation (14.17), so that the money rate of interest r' must rise. Hence a successful attempt to lower r' *in the short run* may only serve to raise it higher *in the long run*.

The main lesson to be learned from this discussion is that high monetary or "nominal" rates of interest do not necessarily imply high real yields to investors. In fact, taking inflation into account the experience of investors over the past half-century has been unimpressive.

EXAMPLE 14.8
Nominal and Real Yields, 1926–1981

In the Table below the first column, repeated from Example 14.5, shows the arithmetic mean of the *nominal* annual returns from holding various types of securities over the 55-year period 1926–81. The second column shows the inflation-adjusted or *real* average annual returns. As can be seen, the real return has been practically zero on both short-term and long-term government issues. Only common stocks show a positive real return. Thus, while there has been some reward for bearing variability risk over this period, savers and investors have on average received little or no premium in future real income for current sacrifices of consumption.

Nominal and Real Yields, 1926–1981 (%)
(arithmetic means)

	NOMINAL YIELD	REAL YIELD
U.S. Treasury bills	3.1	0.1
Long-term government bonds	3.1	0.3
Common stocks	11.4	8.3

Source: See Example 14.5.

Furthermore, the returns from holding Treasury or corporate securities are taxable to investors. The real *tax-adjusted* returns, while varying across individuals depending upon tax brackets, will all be smaller than those shown in the Example above. As a final twist of the screw, in the United States (and many other nations as well) the income tax is levied not on the real but on the nominal return. This has a most damaging effect. Consider an individual who purchases a common stock for $100, gets a better-than-average 12% nominal yield in terms of dividends, and finds his stock still priced at $100 at the end of the year. Suppose that the rate of inflation is 10%, and his marginal tax rate is $33\frac{1}{3}$%. He will pay in $4 in tax, which knocks down his 12% pre-tax yield to 8% after-tax yield. But, with 10% inflation, the real end-of-the-year value of his common stock is not $100 but $100/1.1 = $91 (approximately). So the depreciation of the real value of his security has exceeded his real after-tax dividend return; his true real yield has been negative. U.S. investors have generally incurred negative real after-tax yields over the past half-century— even for securities like common stocks which offer a premium return due to variability risk. We should not be surprised, therefore, to learn that the amount of saving in relation to income in the United States has become disturbingly low, in the opinion of many observers.

14.E
DETERMINANTS OF INTEREST RATES

What are the underlying forces tending to cause interest rates to be high in some countries and low in others, high in some historical periods and low in others? In line with the analysis here, the determinants of *real* interest rates may be classified under the headings of: (1) time-preference, (2) time-endowment, and (3) time-productivity. Given these determinants of *real* interest, the *money* interest rate is accounted for by incorporating the anticipations of price-level inflation as shown by equation (14.17).

1. Time-preference: The more intense the preference in a community for *current* as against *future* consumption, the steeper the indifference curves on c_0, c_1 axes (as in Figure 14.1) tend to be. The market price ratio $P_0/P_1 \equiv 1 + r$ (the absolute slope of the market lines) must to a greater or lesser extent reflect this, so that *high time-preference causes high interest.* Low time-preference is associated with personal characteristics such as fore-thoughtedness, strong family ties, willingness to defer enjoyment, etc. The latter years of the Roman Empire were characterized by a decline in such "Puritanical" attitudes, and interest rates were accordingly high. A similar shift in values appears to be taking place in the Western world today, which might help explain the recent tendency of Western interest rates to rise.

2. Time-endowment: As we have seen, an "heir with great expectations," whose personal income-endowment lies mainly in the future, tends to be a borrower. In Figure 14.1 the endowment position E for such an heir would lie toward the northwest, in the region where the indifference curves are steep. If an entire society were in the situation of expecting future income to be much greater than current income, the interest rate (reflecting the absolute slope of the market lines) would correspondingly tend to be high. A notable example is a community struck by a disaster. It is usually the case that a catastrophe damages goods relatively close to consumption more drastically than the basic productive powers of the economy. A drought or a hurricane, for example, may destroy growing crops while leaving long-term productive fundamentals such as fertility of the land unimpaired. Since present or near-future income-endowments are affected more seriously than far-future endowments, interest rates tend to rise when disaster strikes.

3. Time-productivity: Higher time-productivity of investment is represented by greater ratios $-\Delta q_1/\Delta q_0$, i.e., steeper absolute slopes of individuals' intertemporal Production-Possibility Curves QQ in Figure 14.4. If this pattern is typical of a community, the market interest rate must to a greater or lesser extent reflect it. Thus interest rates have tended to be high in newer and more productive communities, e.g., higher in America than in England, and higher in California than in Massachusetts. Also, technological change works somewhat like new settlement of territory in making available improved opportunities for investment. Thus, interest rates tend to be higher in technologically progressive than in more static countries and eras.

Finally, a very important consideration is the *degree of isolation* of a community. There may be a very special or idiosyncratic situation as to time-preference, time-endowment, or time-productivity in a small local area. Nevertheless, unless that region is isolated from commerce the interest rates there cannot diverge too far from the more normal rates representing the typical picture in the outside world. The process of exchange will lead to a flow of investments and loans (in the form of money and real claims) from the low-interest area to the high-interest area of any integrated market. The differences historically observed between interest rates in England and America, or between Massachusetts and California, have therefore been much smaller than would have been the case had the communities in question been isolated from one another.

EXAMPLE 14.9
Interest and the Gold Rush[a]

Gold was struck in California in 1848, and the gold rush was on. The gold miners (and most other Californians as well) typically thought of themselves as having little current endowed income, but as prospectively very rich. Thus, they were in a situation comparable to that of "heirs with great expectations," and would be expected to be borrowers.

However, until the completion of the first transcontinental railroad in 1869, California was largely isolated from the rest of the world. Hence, Californians for the most part could only borrow from one another. Consequently, the interest rate during the period of the gold rush was generally very high, 24% per annum being a typical figure. This was far higher than the rate then ruling in the East. In the decade following the completion of the transcontinental railroad, it became much more feasible to transfer real resources from the East, and the interest rate in California dropped to around 6%.

[a]See Irving Fisher, *The Theory of Interest* (New York: Macmilian, 1930; reprinted [Fairfield, N.J.: Augustus M. Kelley] 1955), Chap. 18.

☐ SUMMARY OF CHAPTER 14

Individuals' decisions as to saving or investment are based upon their preferences and their opportunities regarding intertemporal consumption. *Saving* is consuming less than income; *investing* is a productive operation that actually transforms potential current consumption into future income. These decisions interact in the market to determine the price ratio between current and future claims, P_0/P_1. This ratio is also defined as $1 + r$, where r is the rate of interest representing the market premium of current real consumption claims over one-year future real claims.

In a world of pure exchange, without intertemporal productive opportunities, each individual would choose a preferred intertemporal pattern of consumption subject to a fixed wealth constraint. Saving by some (lending) would necessarily be balanced by the dis-saving of others (borrowing). The intersection of the aggregate supply curve of lending and the aggregate demand curve for borrowing would determine the equilibrium interest rate and the amount of borrowing and lending. Where there are productive opportunities, however, individuals would choose a wealth-maximizing *productive optimum* solution, determining their level of investment, together with a utility-maximizing *consumptive optimum* solution determining their level of saving. In the market as a whole, the intersection of the aggregate supply curve of saving and the aggregate demand curve for investment would determine the equilibrium rate of interest and the amount of saving and investment. At this interest rate, aggregate borrowing would also equal aggregate lending.

If markets for intertemporal claims are perfect, the Separation Theorem holds. As the productive decision then involves maximizing an objective market quantity, wealth, the task can more easily be delegated to an agent. This feature facilitates the formation of firms. If managers exploit productive opportunities so as to maximize wealth of the firm, they will also be maximizing wealth for all the owners individually.

A project or set of projects that is wealth-increasing has a positive Present Value V_0. In the simple two-period case, in terms of cash-flow payments z_0 and z_1, Present Value is defined as:

$$V_0 \equiv z_0 + \frac{z_1}{1 + r}$$

Any project with positive Present Value should be adopted; any project with negative Present Value should be rejected. The equation defining Present Value can be generalized to the multi-period case, making use of the anticipated stream of payments $z_0, z_1, \ldots, z_T$ and the sequence of forward interest rates $r_1, \ldots, r_T$. If the interest rate is expected to be constant at the level r over time, the generalization takes the simple form:

$$V_0 \equiv z_0 + \frac{z_1}{1 + r} + \cdots + \frac{z_T}{(1 + r)^T}$$

An important issue in many empirical studies or practical choice situations is the selection of an appropriate interest rate r for the Present-Value calculation. The major problem is to allow properly for risk. Securities promising fixed payments (e.g., bonds) are subject to *default risk;* securities with uncertain returns varying around some expected average level (e.g., stocks) are subject to *variability risk.* For any type of investment, market opinions as to risk attach an appropriate risk-premium to the promised or expected return that the decision-maker should take account of in calculating Present Value.

The *real* interest rate r is the premium commanded in the market by current real claims over future real claims. The *money* interest rate r' is the premium on current monetary claims over future monetary claims. The latter premium is affected by the anticipated rate of price-level inflation, a, so that:

$$r' = r + a$$

Someone who borrows money, in order to repay in money, must offer the lender an additional monetary return to cover the increase in the money price of real claims anticipated by the time of repayment.

The determinants of the real interest rate r in a community include: the individuals' patterns of *time-preference* (more urgent desires for current goods raise interest rates), *time-endowment* (anticipations of higher future income raise interest rates), and *time-productivity* (remunerative investment opportunities raise interest rates). And since the observed interest rate in a community is normally the monetary rate r', *anticipations of inflation* will also raise quoted interest rates.

☐ QUESTIONS FOR CHAPTER 14

MAINLY FOR REVIEW

R1. Explain the analogy between the intertemporal optimum of the consumer (choice between current consumption C_0 and future consumption C_1) and the optimum of the consumer at a moment of time (choice between consumption of commodity X and commodity Y). What determines the shape of the intertemporal market opportunity set?

*R2. Which is correct?
   a. The annual rate of interest is the ratio P_0/P_1, the price of a current consumption claim divided by the price of a consumption claim dated one year in the future.
   b. The annual rate of interest is the *premium* on the value of current relative to one-year future claims, as given by the expression $(P_0/P_1) - 1$.
   Explain.

R3. What is *wealth*? How is it related to current and future *incomes*?

*R4. In a pure-exchange situation, at market equilibrium the total of borrowing equals the total of lending. What can be said about saving and investment?

*R5. In a productive situation, at market equilibrium the total of saving equals the total of investment. What can be said about borrowing and lending?

R6. What is the Separation Theorem? What is its importance? What would tend to happen if it were not applicable?

*R7. What is the Present Value Rule? Will this rule always lead decision-makers to correct choices of projects when the Separation Theorem holds? What if the Separation Theorem does not hold?

R8. Explain the relation between the rate of interest r as defined in the equation $r = (P_0/P_1) - 1$ and as defined in the equation $r = z/V_0$.

R9. What is the *money* rate of interest, and how is it related to the *real* rate of interest?

FOR FURTHER THOUGHT AND DISCUSSION

T1. In a two-period preference diagram, illustrate plausible endowment positions in the following cases. Indicate whether each person is likely to be a borrower or a lender.
   a. A young man with an elderly, wealthy, loving uncle in Australia.
   b. A farm-owner whose crop has been destroyed by hurricane.

*The answers to asterisked questions appear at the end of the book.

c. A sugar-*beet* farmer who has just learned that this year's sugar-*cane* crop has been destroyed by hurricane.

d. A 35-year-old star baseball player.

*T2. "Saving need not equal investment for any single individual, but the two must be equal for the market as a whole." Is this necessarily true in equilibrium? Would it be true in a disequilibrium situation, as might result from a floor or ceiling upon interest rates?

*T3. In a newly settled country, resources are likely to have great potential but are as yet undeveloped. Would you expect the real interest rate to be high or low? Comparing situations in which the new country is or is not in close contact with the rest of the world, in which situation will the interest rate be higher? In which will more investment take place? Explain.

*T4. One country is "stagnant" (i.e., little investment and little economic growth are taking place) because productive opportunities yielding a good return on investment are lacking. Another "stagnant" country has excellent investment opportunities, but little investment because time-preferences are very high. Which country would tend to have a high, and which a low, real interest rate? Explain.

T5. Money interest rates have been on a sharply rising trend over the past thirty years throughout the world. Indicate which of the following might provide part of the explanation, and analyze:

a. Higher rates of time-preference (changes in tastes).

b. Higher rates of time-productivity (changes in investment opportunities).

c. Lower ratios of current to anticipated future incomes (increased relative scarcity of current endowments).

d. Higher rates of inflation (changes in anticipations as to monetary policies of governments).

*T6. Are negative rates of interest impossible? Is there a limit upon how negative the interest rate can be?

T7. "Annual income twenty pounds, annual expenditure nineteen nineteen six, result happiness. Annual income twenty pounds, annual expenditure twenty pounds ought and six, result misery"—Mr. Micawber in Dickens' *David Copperfield.* Is this sound economics? Analyze.

*T8. In the April 1972 issue of *Consumer Reports,* a publication of the well-known consumer advice organization Consumers Union, the question was raised whether a homebuyer might advantageously finance purchase of appliances by an addition to his or her home mortgage. The alternatives considered were: (1) purchase of appliances through a retail store for $675, financed by a two-year contract at 15% interest; and (2) purchase of the same appliances for $450 through the homebuilder, financed by a mortgage add-on 27-year contract at $7\frac{3}{4}$% interest. The *CR* article contended that the first option was superior. The justification offered was that, for the two-year 15% contract, the total of interest-plus-principal payments would add up to only $785—whereas, for the 27-year mortgage add-on contract at $7\frac{3}{4}$%, the total payments would eventually sum to $1075. Analyze.

15

WELFARE ECONOMICS: THE THEORY OF ECONOMIC POLICY

SUPPLEMENTARY CHAPTER

In this book the main emphasis has been upon economics as a *positive* science. The intent has been to analyze how the market economy works—either when left alone by government, or when subjected to state interventions such as import tariffs or quotas, price ceilings, etc. But the discipline of economics was originally called "political economy," a title reflecting the concern of early economic thinkers with *normative* questions of public policy. This raises the question: How are we to decide whether a possible intervention or reform is a good idea or not? In other words, what are the theoretical justifications for economic policies that a government might adopt? This area of study, known as "welfare economics," is the subject of the present chapter.

The first section of the chapter considers the *goals* of policy. Section 15.B reviews Adam Smith's "Theorem of the Invisible Hand," which attributes certain very desirable qualities to the unregulated *laissez-faire* economy. A discussion of the real or alleged failures of the Invisible Hand then follows. Finally, Section 15.D considers the ever-challenging issue of economic equality.

15.A
GOALS OF ECONOMIC POLICY

Economic theorists have concentrated attention almost entirely upon only two of the many possible goals of policy: (1) efficiency, and (2) distributive equity. Roughly speaking, these two criteria represent the *size* of the economic pie and the *distribution* of slices among the possible claimants.

15.A.1   ☐ Efficiency versus Equity

To begin with, suppose that an individual's well-being can be summarized simply by the amount of income I available for consumption. For two persons John and Karl the alternative social allocations of income might be represented on I^j, I^k axes as in Figure 15.1. The shaded area shows the set of I^j, I^k combinations potentially available to this two-person community. The shape of this "social opportunity set" will depend upon the processes and rules governing the production of goods and the assignment of income claims to individuals.

The curve II' that bounds the social opportunity set on the northeast, the Social Opportunity Frontier, might have any of a variety of shapes. As drawn it

474

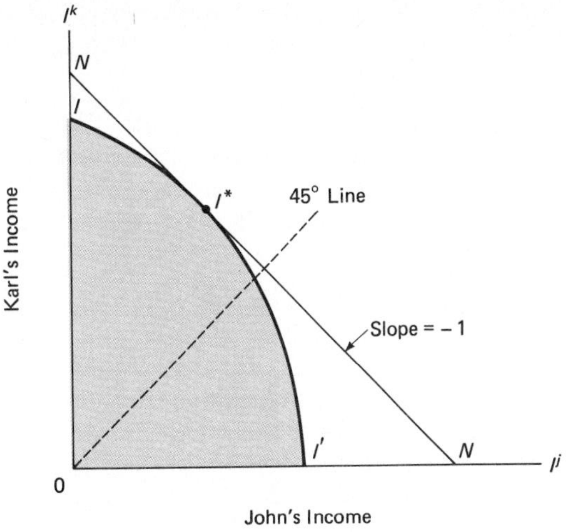

FIGURE 15.1 Social Allocations of Income. The shaded region is the social opportunity set, showing the attainable combinations of income for John (I^j) and income for Karl (I^k); its boundary is the Social Opportunity Frontier II'. The aggregate income is maximized at I^*, where II' is just tangent to a line of slope -1 (line NN).

is concave to the origin, suggesting that a greater *aggregate* social income $I^T \equiv I^j + I^k$ could be attained toward the middle of II' rather than at the corners. This might be plausibly justified as follows. At the lower right corner Karl receives literally nothing—$I^k = 0$. But then Karl will surely exit from the community (by death or emigration), in which case his productive powers will no longer be available to augment the aggregate social product I^T. If production is a cooperative process, providing Karl with some incentive in the way of income I^k will, up to a point at least, make the aggregate I^T larger than it would otherwise be. In a different terminology, the social mechanism that generates and distributes income is not a "constant-sum game." If Karl is induced to produce more as a result of receiving more, John will not lose the entire amount that Karl gains.

Let us now consider *efficiency* as a goal of social policy. It might seem natural to define efficiency as achieving the largest *sum* of income I^T. Geometrically, this maximum is reached at I^* in Figure 15.1. I^* is the point of contact of II' with the dashed line NN, the highest attainable line of slope -1 in the diagram (aggregate income I^T being constant along any such line). But this is not the way the economist defines efficiency. For, treating I^* as some kind of social maximum involves a hidden assumption—that it would be acceptable to deprive John of one dollar if Karl thereby gets two dollars, or to deprive Karl of a smaller amount if John can thereby get a larger amount. Instead, the economist uses a somewhat weaker concept of efficiency. Any particular income distribution I^j, I^k is called efficient if it corresponds to a point on the Social Opportunity Frontier II' rather than in the interior of the shaded region.[1]

---

[1]It might be asked, why not have the parties go initially to I^* and then *redistribute* the maximized aggregate income I^T along NN on any basis agreed between them? Moving along NN, a point could always be found that is superior for both parties (yields higher income for each) as compared with any point along II' away from I^*. But such redistribution is not possible, by the definition of II' as the Social Opportunity Frontier. (If it were possible, the line NN would *be* the frontier.) Presumably, the costs of redistribution, or the inability of the parties to agree on how to go about it, dictates a "concave" curvature of the Social Opportunity Frontier.

We know, however, that money income, or even "real" income, is not an adequate index of an individual's well-being. First of all, a person may derive satisfaction from *reservation uses* of resources (e.g., leisure) as an alternative to maximizing market income. Second, how the individual *spends* income over the many different consumption goods will clearly affect his or her achieved level of satisfaction. Perhaps most important, markets might be imperfect or even non-existent, as in a feudal or a communist society. In such an environment, "income" defined as the market earnings from owned resources would be a defective or even entirely meaningless measure of well-being.

We can get around this problem by using the familiar concept of *utility U* as index of the degee of satisfaction. Figure 15.2 shows the social opportunity set in terms of achievable utilities U^j and U^k of the two individuals. Utility, we saw in Chapter 3, is regarded as only an *ordinal* magnitude. An individual is assumed to be able to distinguish a more preferred from a less preferred outcome, but not be able to quantify the utility difference between them. Also, utility is *incommensurable* between individuals. For both these reasons we cannot meaningfully speak of aggregate utility $U^j + U^k$, or of maximizing any such aggregate. Consequently the Social Opportunity Frontier in terms of utilities (*LL'* in Figure 15.2) has no meaningful shape apart from the *ordinal* property represented by its negative slope. This negative slope tells us only that one party cannot be made somewhat better off without making the other somewhat worse off.

DEFINITION: One allocation of goods in an economy is said to be "Pareto-preferred,"[2] in comparison with another, if in the first arrangement all parties concerned are *at least* as well off and one or more of the parties is actually better off than in the second.

Consider the allocation D in the interior of the social opportunity set of Figure 15.2. Comparing D' with D, Karl is better off and John is no worse off, so D' is Pareto-preferred to D. At D" John is better off and Karl is no worse off, so the allocation D" is also Pareto-preferred to D. And for any point *between D'* and *D"* along the boundary LL', *both* parties are better off so that any such point is Pareto-preferred to D.

Generalizing this reasoning, for any point like D in the interior of the social opportunity set there will be points on the frontier LL' that are Pareto-preferred to it. But comparing any two allocations along the boundary LL' itself, the utility gain to one party will necessarily be associated with a utility loss to the other. Hence, for no point on the frontier will there be any other allocation Pareto-preferred to it.

The set of boundary points, the Social Opportunity Frontier, is called the set of *Pareto-optimal* allocations. Any of these points can be said to "maximize the size of the economic pie," in the weak sense represented by the absence of any allocation Pareto-preferred to it. *In utility terms, the efficient set of income allocations is the Pareto-optimal set.*

---

[2]Vilfredo Pareto (1848–1923), Italian economist and sociologist (mentioned also in Chapter 3).

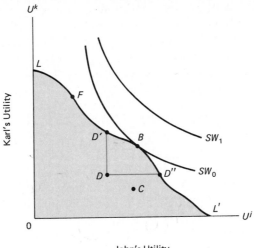

John's Utility

FIGURE 15.2 Social Allocations of Utility. Since utility has no unique cardinal scaling, in utility units only the *ordinal* properties of the Social Opportunity Frontier *LL'* are relevant—in particular, the negative slope along *LL'*. This slope indicates that John cannot be made better off without making Karl worse off, and vice versa. SW_0 and SW_1 are hypothetical indifference contours of social well-being or "welfare," which would be maximized at point *B*. But if comparisons can be made only in terms of the Pareto criterion, no such contours exist. All that can be said is that distributions to the northeast of any point like *D* (those in the shaded region *DD'BD''*) are preferred to *D*. The Social Opportunity Frontier *LL'* is the set of Pareto-efficient distributions; Pareto comparisons cannot be made between points on *LL'*.

What about the goal of distributive equity? Here we lack any principle with as compelling appeal as Pareto-optimality.[3] *Equality* as a goal receives a great deal of support, but because of non-cardinality and incommensurability the "equality of utilities" is meaningless. In practice, something like *equality of incomes* is often taken as an important goal. (This question is considered further in Section 15.D.) Another issue is whether the initial distribution, the *status quo*, has any presumptive standing as an equitable ranking. It is said that "possession is nine points of the law." That is, under our legal system the *status quo* is generally enforced unless there is some special reason to the contrary. But from a sufficiently abstract point of view, there is perhaps no sound justification for attaching even such tentative validity to the *status quo*.

One tradition in welfare economics "solves" the social optimality problem by imagining a special kind of interpersonal utility measure summarized in a so-called *social welfare function*. In Figure 15.2 we might lay down indifference contours of interpersonal utility or "welfare" (SW_0 and SW_1 in the diagram) and declare that the social optimum of perfect bliss occurs at point *B* where the boundary *LL'* touches the highest attainable welfare-indifference contour. The "only" difficulty is the absence of any agreement as to what the content of such a social welfare function might be!

---

[3]Not everyone would agree that Pareto-optimality is a very compelling principle. (See below.)

15.A.2 ☐ Utilitarianism

Turning to somewhat deeper issues, not everyone will agree with the *utilitarian* philosophy underlying welfare economics.[4] The main theses of utilitarianism may be summarized in the two-fold assertion: (1) Social policies, rules, and institutions are to be judged solely in terms of their *consequences;* and (2) the only relevant consequences are *individuals' gratifications* ("pleasures and pains").

The first assertion represents a kind of social pragmatism. For utilitarians all social practices or arrangements (e.g., monarchy or voting or the market or capital punishment or the family or the nation) are merely means or instruments. They should not be adopted or rejected because they agree or disagree with the word of the Bible, or with natural law, or with the dictates of ethical principles, or with historical tradition or timeless custom. Instead, the only criterion is: Do they give rise to desirable social outcomes? Where others might say "The ends do not justify the means," the utilitarian replies: "What can justify means except the ends attained?"

The second assertion represents a radical individualism. Policies may or may not serve the purposes of God, may or may not advance science and learning, may or may not promote the survival of the race or nation or the gene pool; none of this is relevant for the utilitarian. What counts is whether the results comport with the desires of individuals. President John F. Kennedy once declared, "Ask not what your country can do for you, ask what you can do for your country!" To which a utilitarian might reply, "Why have a country except for what it can do for you?"

A somewhat separate question turns on the issue of *hedonism.* In calculating social well-being, do only individuals' sensate satisfactions count, as the hedonists would have it? What about "higher wants," for example benevolent desires to help others? The economic utilitarians generally answer this question by saying that it is the satisfaction of factually observable wants, whether sensate or "higher," that should govern policy. On this approach, benevolent desires are counted as well as hedonistic ones, but of course only to the extent that they are actually present—as measured, for example, by individuals' willingness to sacrifice sensate gratifications for higher goals. Unfortunately, in the world as we know it there are also "lower wants," for example malevolent urges to punish or dominate others. What legitimate weight to attach to such wants remains a problem for utilitarians.

Upon departing from utilitarian premises, *both* efficiency and equity as goals lose much of their force. Non-utilitarians might make any of the following arguments:

1. Social policy should be directed not at giving individuals what they *want,* but what they *ought to have.* As the great moralists and our sacred texts have told us, as observation of others and candid self-examination reveal, and as history demonstrates, most of what people want most of the time they would be better off not

---

[4]The similarity between the words "utility" and "utilitarianism" is not accidental. Both are due to Jeremy Bentham.

getting. Efficiency is a goal for raising pigs, not for the social life of a community of people. Even the "equity" goal means little more than fair division among pigs at the trough.

2. Even admitting that an efficient and equitable distribution of satisfactions of individual wants might to some extent be a legitimate aim, it is absurd to assert that this is the only relevant social goal. Liberty, justice, order, community—all express goals of policy that transcend the satisfaction of individual wants.

3. Apart from the social allocation of *outcomes* (the attainment of goals) is the question of the *means* by which these social outcomes are achieved. Far better to have an allocation of goods and services that is both inefficient and inequitable, but arrived at in a spirit of voluntary cooperation under law, than a perfectly ideal allocation established by dictatorial decree or political trickery.

4. What individuals desire is very largely a result of their social conditioning. Much more important than the *want-satisfaction* process is the *want-creation* process. The main goal of policy should be to get people to desire the proper things.

No resolution of these difficult philosophical questions can be provided here. It is clear that utilitarianism can be criticized from many different points of view: dictatorial or democratic, radical or conservative, ethical or cynical. In any case economics is the science of the *instrumental*, of the choice of proper means for given ends. However defective utilitarian aims may be, they do carry a great deal of consensus in modern societies and therefore must be reckoned with in the analysis of economic policy.

15.B
THE THEOREM OF THE INVISIBLE HAND

Adam Smith asserted that the invisible hand of self-interest "frequently" leads men to effectually promote the interests of society. Economists in modern times have refined this idea into a more precise theorem that can be worded as follows: *Given a number of ideal conditions, optimizing behavior on the part of individuals and firms under pure competition leads to an efficient (Pareto-optimal) social outcome.* In this section we shall go through the meaning of this "Theorem of the Invisible Hand." The ideal conditions, and what happens when they are violated, are discussed further in Section 15.C. But note that the theorem relates solely to the social goal of *efficiency*. The question of distributive *equity* will be considered further in Section 15.D.

A formal demonstration of the Theorem of the Invisible Hand requires rather high-level mathematics, and will not be attempted here. Intuitively, however, we can see that efficiency for the economy as a whole requires: (1) *efficiency as among consumers* (in the allocation of consumption goods), (2) *efficiency as among resource-owners* (in the provision of resources for productive uses), and (3) *efficiency as among firms* (in the conversion of resources into consumable goods). What will be shown here (as a reminder of previous results, rather than as anything really new) is that *all three of these conditions are met in competitive equilibrium*.

To isolate the question of *efficiency among consumers*, we can return to the analysis of Chapter 13. Equation (13.1) can be repeated, in slightly changed notation, here:

$$(15.1) \qquad MRSC^j_{XY} = \frac{P_x}{P_y} = MRSC^k_{XY}$$

This says that, for any pair of individuals John and Karl, as a condition of competitive equilibrium each person's *Marginal Rate of Substitution in Consumption*, here denoted $MRSC_{XY}$, must equal the price ratio P_x/P_y. Let us pierce the veil of money and think in terms of real commodities only. One of the consumption goods, in particular Y, can be chosen as the *numéraire* or basis of pricing. Then P_y is necessarily unity (the price of Y, in units of Y, must be 1) so that P_x/P_y reduces to P_x. With this understood, the condition of efficiency among consumers can be expressed more simply as:

$$(15.1') \qquad MRSC^j_{XY} = P_x = MRSC^k_{XY} \qquad \text{Efficiency among Consumers}$$

It is the equality $MRSC^j_{XY} = MRSC^k_{XY}$ that represents the condition of efficiency. Its meaning is that, on the margin, John is just as willing as Karl to sacrifice a unit of Y (in order to obtain more X). Inequality between these Marginal Rates of Substitution would imply inefficiency, since then the two parties could mutually benefit from trade. (The one more willing to give up Y in exchange for X would do so, receiving in payment some X from the one more anxious to acquire Y). A benevolent and omniscient dictator might directly impose such an equality between $MRSC^j_{XY}$ and $MRSC^k_{XY}$ without the aid of any market system. In a regime of competitive markets, however, the equality emerges from the self-regarding actions of each trader in setting his own $MRSC_{XY}$ equal to the market exchange rate between X and Y, i.e., to the price P_x. Thus, the market price P_x *mediates* the efficient equality of the individuals' Marginal Rates of Substitution in Consumption.

For *efficiency among resource-owners*, an exactly corresponding argument leads to the condition that can be expressed as:

$$(15.2) \qquad MRSR^j_{al} = h_a = MRSR^k_{al} \qquad \text{Efficiency among Resource-Owners}$$

This equation follows, again with slightly changed notation, from equation (12.2). As described in Chapter 12, each owner of a resource A sets his or her *Marginal Rate of Substitution in Resource Supply*, the MRS between reservation uses of A and market income I, equal to the hire-price h_a of factor A. Since Y is the *numéraire* commodity in which real income is measured, $MRSR_{al}$ is equivalent to $MRSR_{aY}$, that is, to the Marginal Rate of Substitution between reservation uses of A and consumption of the *numéraire* commodity Y. Again, the individuals' separate Marginal Rates of Substitution are not equated directly, as might be done by a dictator. Rather, in a regime of competitive markets the separate optimizations are mediated and brought into efficient equality by the hire-price h_a of factor A.

With regard to *efficiency among firms,* think of production as the process of converting resource A into good X. We know from Chapter 11 that the competitive (price-taking) firm sets vmp_a, the Value of the Marginal Product of factor A, equal to the hire-price h_a. Specifically, equation (11.7) implies that for any two price-taking firms f and g:

(15.3) $$vmp_a^f = h_a = vmp_a^g \qquad \text{Efficiency among Firms}$$

That this is an efficient condition is immediately evident. Recall that price P_x will be the same for all firms in the market. Then, if (15.3) did not hold, the physical Marginal Products mp_a^f and mp_a^g would differ. It would then be socially more efficient to shift some units of resource A away from the firm with lower mp_a and to the firm with higher mp_a. Once again, the efficient equality condition is not imposed by dictation but rather emerges from the mediating role of the competitive price system.

An alternative version of the efficiency condition as among firms takes the familiar form:

(15.3') $$MC_x^f = P_x = MC_x^g$$

This condition differs from (15.3) only in being expressed in units of output X rather than units of input A.[5]

To prove the efficiency of competitive equilibrium, these results should be generalized to deal with any numbers of individuals, of firms, of products, and of resources. But doing so would be a mere complication; the essence of the efficiency conditions is contained in what has already been set down.

15.C
WHAT CAN GO WRONG? ALMOST EVERYTHING!

The trouble is, the Theorem of the Invisible Hand is too good to be true. There are many ways in which things can go wrong.

15.C.1 ☐ Monopoly

First of all, consider *monopoly.* Monopoly can and does exist, to some degree at least, on both sides of the various product and factor markets in the economy. Firms might be monopolist sellers of product or monopsonist employers of resources; individuals might be monopolist sellers of resources or monopsonist

---

[5]The equivalence of the two formulations follows immediately from the identity:

$$MC_x \equiv \frac{h_a}{mp_a}$$

Since $vmp_x \equiv P_x(mp_a)$, simple algebra converts (15.3') into the form (15.3).

buyers of products. And it is not necessarily monopoly or monopsony in the strict sense that lead to failure of the theorem. Any non-price-taking behavior, whether due to cartels, oligopoly, or to any of the market-structure situations analyzed in Chapters 8 through 10, implies violation of the efficiency conditions of the preceding section.

An important policy distinction has been made between *natural* and *contrived* monopoly. In "natural" monopoly, productive economies such as the advantage of large scale make it possible for one firm to produce more cheaply than can a larger number. Public utilities (electricity, telephone, gas, etc.) are commonly believed to fit into this category. Traditional policy with regard to natural monopoly has been to retain the single large firm but to prevent monopolistic exploitation through a regulatory process (see Section 8.D). "Contrived" monopoly is said to arise when the economies of scale are not a dominant feature; certain other circumstances have somehow blunted competitive forces. Here government "trust-busting" has attempted to break up monopolistic concentration. Despite this supposed dedication to competition, however, government policy has in many ways tended to support the monopolization, or at any rate the cartelization, of sectors of the economy.[6]

Given either natural or contrived monopoly, the Invisible Hand does not induce behavior that serves the interests of others, at least not to the optimal degree. The profit-maximizing monopoly firm is motivated to set $MC_x = MR_x$ rather than $MC_x = P_x$ (see Chapter 9), thus violating equation (15.3'). Since $MR_x < P_x$, the monopolist ordinarily produces "too little" output of X. In terms of factor units, it is equation (15.3) that is violated. As shown in Chapter 11 the profit-maximizing factor-employment condition for the firm is $mrp_a \equiv MR_x(mp_a) = h_a$ whereas the efficiency condition (15.3) is $vmp_a \equiv P_x(mp_a) = h_a$. Then $MR_x < P_x$ implies $mrp_a < vmp_a$. So "too little" of factor A will be hired by the monopolist firm.

By corresponding arguments it can be shown that a monopsonist employer of a factor, or a monopolist supplier of a factor, or even a monopsonist consumer of a product (should that case ever arise) will all violate one or more of the efficiency conditions of the preceding section.

CONCLUSION: Under both monopoly and monopsony there is "too little" market exchange. And in consequence, there will also be "too little" productive specialization and "too little" market employment of factors.

In effect, monopoly deprives society of some of the mutual benefits of trade. Although the economic agent possessing monopoly power derives advantages therefrom, in principle it would be possible to improve matters by achieving a Pareto-preferred solution. If price-taking behavior were substituted for monopolistic exploitation, the gain would be great enough to permit compensating the monopolist while still leaving something over for the rest of society.

[6]See, for instance, Example 8.5, "Agricultural Marketing Orders" and Example 12.8, "Barbers."

15.C.2 ☐ Disequilibrium

Another extremely important source of difficulty is *market disequilibrium.* Section 15.B demonstrated the mediating role of prices in bringing the separate optimizing decisions of individuals and firms into accord. But what if the currently quoted price is not the right one for clearing a market? It is true that there will then surely be corrective forces at work tending to restore equilibrium, as explained in Chapter 2. But given a world in which the determining conditions are ever-changing, the chances are that prices will always be some distance from and scarcely ever at their equilibrium values. Disequilibrium is therefore the prevalent state of affairs.

Since prices will sometimes be too high and at other times too low, it might be thought that the effects of disequilibrium would tend more or less to cancel out. That, however, is not the case. Prices that diverge from equilibrium levels, whether too high or too low, tend to *reduce* quantities exchanged in markets and therefore limit the economy's ability to derive the advantages of specialization in production. Like monopoly, disequilibrium wipes out some of the potential gains from trade.

This is easy to see in Figure 15.3, which pictures a market with normally sloping supply and demand curves. The price P' is too high to equate supply and demand. At that price the effective quantity exchanged Q' is the *lesser* of the supply and demand quantities, in this case, the demand quantity. It is true that at the high price P' there are unsatisfied sellers, but they cannot find customers. ("It takes two to tango."). The price P'' on the other hand is too low to clear the market, but again here it is the *lesser* (offered) quantity Q'' that governs; there are now unsatisfied buyers, but they cannot find willing suppliers. While price is in the one case above and in the other case below the equilibrium $P*$, in both situations the quantity exchanged is *less* than the equilibrium $Q*$.

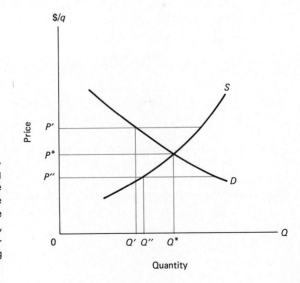

FIGURE 15.3 Disequilibrium. At the equilibrium, price is $P*$ and quantity exchanged $Q*$. If the ruling price were at the high disequilibrium level P', the associated quantity exchanged would be Q'; at the low disequilibrium price P'' the quantity would be Q''. Whether price is above or below equilibrium, the quantity exchanged is always *less* than the equilibrium amount—since trade requires both willing buyers and willing sellers.

CONCLUSION: Disequilibrium, like monopoly, leads to non-Pareto-optimal outcomes because of reduced volumes of trade.

Disequilibrium in one or more particular markets may have significant *macroeconomic* consequences. The incomes that consumers have available for spending on goods do not come out of the air; they derive from earnings received as resource-owners. A market disequilibrium, reducing the scale of production in one or more markets, must adversely affect individuals' real incomes. Factor suppliers will have to select less remunerative alternative employments or less desired reservation uses of the resources they own. The reduction in real incomes will in turn affect consumers' demand functions for goods, in accordance with the "Engel curve" analysis of Chapter 5. Thus, disequilibrium in *one* market will tend to reduce demand (to shift demand curves to the left) *in all other* markets. A second-order adjustment in these other markets will then carry the process further. A self-reinforcing process may thus ensue in which an initial disequilibrium has a multiplied negative effect upon resource employment and real incomes. According to some macroeconomic theories, this "multiplier" process plays a central role in causing fluctuations in overall business activity.

15.C.3 □ Externalities and Coase's Theorem

"Externalities" are said to arise when the decisions of some economic agents—whether in production, in consumption, or in exchange—affect other economic agents in ways that do not set up legally recognized rights of compensation or redress. But this definition is too broad for present purposes. Each individual person is affected by the infinitely varied actions of people all over the globe that may tend to raise or lower the prices of commodities he or she either consumes or produces. We here rule out merely "pecuniary" externalities that affect others only through movements in market prices. Rather, we will be concerned with *direct* externalities—which come about when one decision-maker's actions have an immediate effect upon the consumption or production possibilities available to others.

Consider *pollution.* An upstream use of water may degrade water quality, for example, chemical pollution may reduce potability for downstream consumers, or heat pollution may make the river less effective for downstream industrial cooling. A related problem is called *congestion.* Congestion is a special case of pollution, in which the operations of one economic agent (firm or individual) adversely affect other economic agents engaged in the same industry or activity. Thus, each additional driver crowds the highways for other drivers; each additional broadcasting station impairs reception of other stations' signals; each additional well reduces water levels in neighbors' wells.

But a direct externality may also be beneficial. An upstream user's activities may actually improve the quality of river water. What might be called a "beneficial congestion" externality can also occur, for example, in drainage of marshy soils. Each farmer's attempt to drain his own land lowers water levels and therefore improves the productivity of neighboring land.

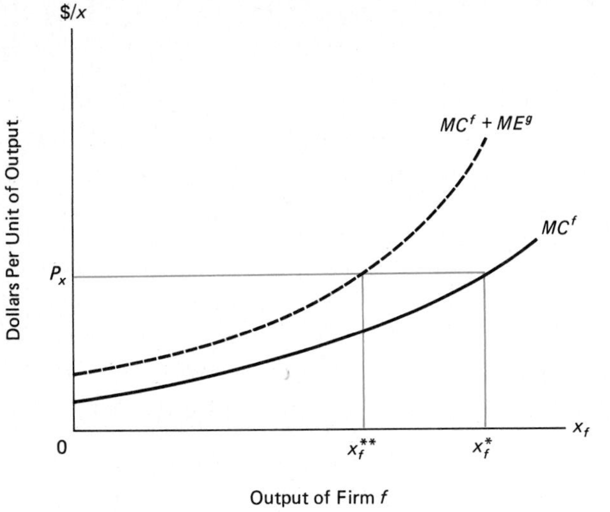

FIGURE 15.4 Harmful Externality. The competitive firm *f* is motivated to produce output x_f^*, where its perceived Marginal Cost MC^f equals price P_x. But, counting also the Marginal Externality ME^g imposed on another firm *g*, the true social Marginal Cost is the vertical summation $MC^f + ME^g$ (dashed curve); the efficient output would be x_f^{**}.

Output of Firm *f*

A harmful externality, which might or might not be of congestion type, is pictured in Figure 15.4. We can suppose that a competitive (price-taking) firm *f* produces commodity *X*, aiming to maximize profit by setting perceived Marginal Cost MC^f equal to price P_x at output x_f^*. But as the firm's production x_f increases, an externality is imposed on some other firm *g*. The true social Marginal Cost *MC* at any output x_f is then the vertical sum $MC^f + ME^g$, where ME^g may be called the Marginal Externality. The output x_f^{**} at which true *MC* equals price P_x, the efficient output, is evidently less than x_f^*. [*Query:* Analyze the case of a beneficial externality.]

EXAMPLE 15.1
Health Costs of Nuclear Power Versus Coal Power

A great deal of concern has been expressed about the health consequences of nuclear power. In judging these, a comparison with the health consequences of electricity generation from alternative sources (predominantly from coal) is highly relevant.

L. B. Lave and L. C. Freeberg[a] analyzed coal versus nuclear power, taking into account the entire fuel cycle from exploration through extraction, transportation, refining, generation, and recovery. So far as the occupational health effects were concerned (effects upon workers in the industry), the mining phase was the main consideration in each case. For nuclear the costs of mine accidents and chronic diseases were estimated at around 2.4 cents per 1000 kilowatt-hours of energy produced—but at around 32 cents per 1000 kWh, over 13 times as great, for coal. (*Note:* If these *occupational* health hazards are

[a]Lester B. Lave and Linnea C. Freeburg, "Health Effects of Electricity Generation from Coal, Oil and Nuclear Fuels," *Nuclear Safety*, v. 14 (Sept./Oct. 1973).

reflected in higher wages, the associated costs would not be *externalities*—they would be paid for and thus taken into account by producers. On the other hand, to the extent that occupational health costs are borne by others, as in the case of the government program to help coal-miners suffering from "black-lung disease," an externality is being imposed on the rest of the community.)

A much more uncertain part of the analysis examined health effects upon the outside public, which are undoubted externalities. Several elements had to be left out of the comparison for lack of generally agreed data, among them the risk of nuclear accidents, the chance of terrorist hijacking of nuclear materials, and the long-term environmental effects of coal and nuclear waste disposal. Setting these aside, the public health costs were mainly the result of chronic low-intensity radiation exposure in the case of nuclear, and pollution of air and water by combustion waste products in the case of coal. For nuclear the estimated public health costs were within the range of 0.0003 to 0.03 cents per 1000 kWh; note that even the upper limit is small relative to the already small occupational health costs. For coal, on the other hand, the estimated range for public health costs was 10 cents to $5.00 per 1000 kWh—over 3000 times as great as nuclear at the upper limit, and 16,000 times as great as nuclear at the lower limit! These results suggest, therefore, that some of the concern about the health hazards of nuclear power might better be redirected toward the very large health externalities associated with coal power.

> COMMENT: Unfortunately, as often occurs in analysis of practical decision problems, the unknown or "unquantifiable" elements might be very large here. The accident record at nuclear plants has on the whole been excellent, and accidental nuclear detonation is considered close to impossible. But, as the 1979 Three Mile Island incident in Pennsylvania indicated, the *potential* consequences should a major accident occur are truly enormous. (Though no identifiable health injury ensued from that accident.) It is more difficult still to estimate the likelihood or the consequences of a terrorist group's acquiring enough fissionable material to fabricate atomic weapons. While nuclear power has an enormous advantage with regard to calculable health costs and externalities, it would be foolhardy not to attach high weights to these less quantifiable hazards.

> CONCLUSION: Direct externalities, beneficial or harmful, lead the Invisible Hand astray. In the interests of efficiency the agent generating the externality ought, if the externality is beneficial, to be induced to engage in the process even more than private self-interest would dictate. If the externality is harmful, the generating agent ought to be induced to diminish the scale of polluting activity in comparison with what self-interest would dictate.

Externalities, therefore, represent sources of social gain or loss that do not get translated into the market signals that constitute the Invisible Hand. Traditional policy analysis has recognized a number of alternative remedies for this problem.

1. *Tax-subsidy adjustments:* A tax placed on the generation of a harmful externality will tend to reduce the amount of externality imposed on others. An ideal corrective tax would add to the private Marginal Cost, the cost that is recognized by the polluting producer in terms of self-interest, a penalty just equal to the Marginal Externality suffered by others. Then the sum of the tax penalty and the private Marginal Cost would bring home to the generating agent the total true social Marginal Cost of carrying on the polluting activity. For a beneficial externality, a corrective *subsidy* would be called for to induce an ideal (greater) level of the externality-generating activity.

2. *Unitization:* If the upstream and the downstream productive processes using the river water were merged or "unitized" under the control of a single economic agent, what was previously an externality would be *internalized.* The single integrated water-using enterprise would now carry on the polluting activity at a socially efficient level, i.e., it would pollute only so long as the marginal upstream gain exceeded the marginal downstream loss. A particularly important instance of unitization occurs in oilfield operations. The externality here is a congestion effect: pumping at any well adversely affects the output of other wells in the same field (by drawing away the fugitive oil, and by reducing gas pressure). Under diversified ownership the consequence is inefficient over-drilling and over-pumping. The owner of each well is motivated to pump faster than he otherwise would, to capture oil under others' land and to prevent others from capturing the oil under his land. And the owner of land is similarly induced to drill more wells, and to locate them inefficiently all along the boundaries of his tract so as to minimize oil loss to others. With unitization, the sole ownerships of individual wells would be exchanged for *pro rata* shares in the overall operation of the oilfield. This eliminates the motivation to over-pump or to over-drill.

3. *Property Reassignment:* The fundamental source of the externality problem is inappropriate assignment of legal property rights. If the span of actual effect always coincided with the span of legally recognized control, externalities would not occur. In the river-water example, the downstream user should ideally be assigned a property right to receive water of some specified quality. A first user who degrades the quality below this level should be liable for the damages suffered by later users. Conversely, the upstream user who leaves the water in better condition than legally required should in principle be entitled to compensation from later users. An assignment of property entitlements to water quality would not, as might first be thought, simply freeze the pattern of uses in accordance with the legally defined titles. Should some other arrangement be mutually preferred, the parties concerned could negotiate an exchange of property rights. If the downstream user was initially entitled to absolutely pure water,

for example, the upstream producer could nevertheless buy from him the right to pollute the river to some specified degree.[7]

This last concept has been generalized into what is known as *Coase's Theorem*,[8] which can be stated as follows:

COASE'S THEOREM: Regardless of the specific initial assignment of property rights, in market equilibrium the final outcome will be efficient—provided that the initial legal assignment is well-defined and that transactions involving exchange of rights are costless.

The thrust of Coase's Theorem is that the Invisible Hand is much more effective than the above argument about externalities at first suggests. For, there are natural market forces at work tending to bring the "external" effects into the calculations of the responsible parties. If a producer initially owns the right to generate a harmful externality, those adversely affected can offer him a financial reward for *not* exercising that right. Or if the other parties are initially entitled to be safe from the externality, it is up to the producer to offer terms of compensation at which they will accept a degree of harm. (In the case of a beneficial externality, of course, the argument applies in reverse.) So long as the legal rights are well-defined and marketable, the Invisible Hand will tend to lead the parties to an efficient outcome, i.e., to a result that exhausts all possibilities for further mutual gain.

---

[7] Where the valuable resource takes the form of a "common pool," as in the case of fish in the ocean or underground water or petroleum, it has recently been proposed to establish a new kind of property right—marketable entitlements to uncaught fish, or to unpumped water or oil. Over-exploitation would be discouraged by the fact that anyone extracting a unit of the resource must also purchase an entitlement to do so. The market price of these titles would reflect investors' estimates of the market value of the resource in *future* uses. See Vernon L. Smith, "Water Deeds: A Proposed Solution to the Water Valuation Problem," *Arizona Review*, v. 26 (Jan. 1977).

[8] R. H. Coase, "The Problem of Social Cost," *The Journal of Law and Economics*, v. 3 (Oct. 1960).

EXAMPLE 15.2
The Apples and the Bees

One of the classical illustrations used in economists' discussions of externalities has been a tale of the apples and the bees. The apple-grower's orchard provides the beneficial externality of nectar for his neightbor's bees, a contribution to the production of honey for which the orchardist receives no reward. And the bees return the compliment by pollinating the apple blossoms *gratis*, thus contributing to the output of the orchard. These interacting externalities were assumed to represent a clear case of inadequate guidance by the Invisible Hand. Government action was supposed to be necessary to induce the orchardist to optimally cooperate with the beekeeper, i.e., to grow *more* nectar-yielding apple blossoms than the orchardist's self-interested calculation would dictate. And similarly, it was supposed, something had to be done to induce the beekeeper to provide *more* pollination benefits to his apple-growing neighbor than would ensue as a merely incidental side-effect of profitable honey production.

Upon looking into beekeeping in the state of Washington, however, Steven N. S. Cheung found the Invisible Hand alive and well! In actual fact, beekeepers and orchardists are quite aware of the beneficial externalities. In consequence, active market dealings govern the placement of hives. The market terms depend upon the relative values of the two interacting "external" benefits: the honey yield to the beekeeper as against the pollination services gained by the grower. The Table here illustrates that, where honey yield is great, the beekeeper ordinarily pays an "apiary rent" for the right to place his hive on the grower's land. Where the honey yield is small, the grower pays pollination fees for the privilege of having hives placed on his land. Washington bees are even exported to California to help pollinate the early-season almond crop. Evidently, market processes are at work to bring "externalities" into private economic calculations.

Honey Yields and Pricing Arrangements, Washington 1970–1971

SEASON	CROP	SURPLUS HONEY (POUNDS PER HIVE)	POLLI-NATION FEES	APIARY RENT PER HIVE
Early spring	Almond (Calif.)	0	$5–$8	—
	Cherry	0	$6–$8	—
Late spring (major pollination season)	Apples and soft fruits	0	$9–$10	—
	Blueberry (with maple)	40	$5	—
	Cabbage	15	$8	—
	Cherry	0	$9–$10	—
	Cranberry	5	$9	—
Summer and early fall (major honey season)	Alfalfa	60	—	13–60¢
	Alfalfa (with pollina-tion)	25–35	$3–$5	—
	Fireweed	60	—	25–63¢
	Mint	70–75	—	15–65¢
	Pasture	60	—	15–65¢
	Red clover	60	—	65¢
	Red clover (with pollination)	0–35	$3–$6	—
	Sweet clover	60	—	20–25¢

Source: Steven N. S. Cheung, "The Fable of the Bees: An Economic Investigation," *The Journal of Law and Economics,* v. 16 (April 1973), p. 23.

Alas for the economists' fable, apple growing yields little or no honey. (The "apple honey" sold in markets seems to be an instance of imaginative labeling.)

So far so good. But Coase's Theorem seems to prove too much. Consider the case of simple monopoly, which (by the standard analysis) leads to an inefficient outcome—underproduction of the monopolized good. But wherever there is inefficiency there must be a mutual advantage of trade. Then, according to Coase's Theorem, the Invisible Hand should lead the monopolist and his customers to get together in some efficient arrangement; the monopolist can be made at least as well off as before, while the customers will do better. So monopoly should disappear, along with externalities!

The problem with the application of Coase's Theorem to "solve" the problem of monopoly, as in its application to "solve" the problem of externalities, is that the negotiations required may be impracticable. Where large numbers are involved, it may be impossible to secure a sufficient degree of unanimity. *Unitization*, for example, as an efficient solution of the externality problem in oilfields should, according to Coase's Theorem, tend to come about simply in response to the Invisible Hand. But in practice it has been necessary to pass special legislation whereby hold-out minority tract-owners in an oilfield are compelled to comply with a unitization agreement favored by a sufficiently large majority. It is the "free rider" problem that makes unanimity almost impossible. If the majority agree to cease overpumping their wells, it pays to be a member of the non-complying minority. The latter secure the advantage of others' pumping reductions, while still pumping as hard as they wish themselves.[9]

If the numbers involved are small, on the other hand, the problem becomes one of *strategic behavior* (as discussed in Chapter 10). When a small number of bargainers face each other, the mere possibility of a mutually advantageous agreement does not guarantee that such an agreement will be reached.

[9]The motivation is essentially the same as that of the "chiselers" in a cartel situation (see Section 8.F). But, it should be noted, absolutely unanimous cooperation is not strictly necessary for a workable degree of agreement in either the unitization or cartel contexts.

EXAMPLE 15.3
An Experimental Test of the Coase Theorem

E. Hoffman and M. L. Spitzer conducted a series of two-person and three-person experiments to examine the conditions under which student subjects could arrive at mutually beneficial outcomes.

In each two-person group one subject was chosen at random to be the "controller"—a role corresponding to the property-owner, the individual who has the legally assigned power to impose an externality upon the other party. In these experiments the controller had a choice of two options: option A might (say) yield him $10 and the other subject $2; option B might yield him $4 and the other party $10. Thus option B is socially more efficient, but it is (initially) in the controller's private interest to choose option A. However, the rules allowed negotiations in which the second party might offer the controller a sufficient inducement to shift the choice from A to B.

The experiment studied achievement of cooperation with and without a continuing relationship between the parties. A continuing relationship meant that the pair faced two successive opportunities, without knowing during the first session which person would become controller in the second session. A continuing relationship was expected to improve achievement of efficiency, since noncooperative behavior in the first session might lead to reprisal in the second. It was also expected that the efficient outcome would more frequently be arrived at under full information about each other's payoffs than where such information is absent.

The Table indicates very striking ability to achieve efficiency. While continuing relationship and full information did lead to some improvement, efficiency was almost always achieved even lacking their aid.

In the three-person interactions, the experimenters introduced the complication of "joint controllers," who had to agree whether or not to accept any offer made by the third party. This factor, it was expected, would tend to reduce the likelihood of efficient outcomes. Overall, however, in the three-person experiments efficiency was again achieved the great majority of the time. Even for the worst case considered, joint controllership with limited information, efficiency was achieved in 9 of 15 cases.

Achievement of Efficient Outcomes in Two-Party and Three-Party Interactions

	CASES IN WHICH EFFICIENCY ACHIEVED	CASES IN WHICH EFFICIENCY NOT ACHIEVED
TWO-PARTY INTERACTIONS		
Full information		
Continuing relationship	12	0
No continuing relationship	11	1
Limited information		
Continuing relationship	8	0
No continuing relationship	11	1
THREE-PARTY INTERACTIONS		
(with continuing relationship)		
Full information		
Single controller	12	1
Joint controller	15	1
Limited information		
Single controller	19	2
Joint controller	9	6

Source: Extracted from Elizabeth Hoffman and Matthew L. Spitzer, "The Coase Theorem: Some Experimental Tests," *Journal of Law and Economics,* v. 25 (April 1982), esp. p. 92.

From a policy point of view, Coase's Theorem strongly suggests that *the unambiguous assignment of exchangeable property rights,* whatever the specific nature of the assignment may be, might be an important step in promoting the achievement of efficiency.

EXAMPLE 15.4
Water Law[a]

In the eastern states the law governing the use of flowing streams is based mainly upon the "riparian" doctrine; in the West, the "appropriation" doctrine dominates.

While the legislation of each state has unique features, the basic idea of the riparian principle is that every owner of land bordering a stream has an equal right to reasonable use of the flow. The riparian doctrine of property rights in water is defective *both* in terms of ambiguity and exchangeability. What is a "reasonable" use for one party relative to others is a subject of continual contention before administrative agencies and law courts. Water-users are deterred from making costly investments, however efficient, for fear that a judicial or administrative redetermination of "reasonable" uses may later deprive them of supply. Nor can any user buy another's water right, since all are equally entitled to the flow. In particular, it is generally impossible to buy the right to transfer water away from the stream onto "non-riparian" land, however productive such a transfer may be.

In the relatively arid western states, scarcity of water made the riparian doctrine intolerable. The appropriation doctrine adopted instead is based upon the concept that "first in time is first in right." Subject to qualifications and conditions that vary from state to state, first users were given the right to appropriate specified quantities of flow, sometimes limited also as to time, place, or manner of diversion. In particular, appropriated water was no longer tied to "riparian" uses but could be transferred away from the stream. The appropriation doctrine represented a considerable improvement from the point of view of *certainty* of rights. However, the *exchangeability* of rights has remained subject to erratic legal intervention.

In recent years there has been a tendency, even in the western states, for administrative agencies or courts to redetermine what constitutes "reasonable" use for the award or deprivation of water rights. In consequence, the ambiguity of rights to water use has been increasing rather than decreasing. The California Supreme Court, for example, ruled in 1983 that under the "doctrine of public trust" environmentalist groups could challenge diversions of water by the City of Los Angeles from the Mono Basin—despite the fact that the city had long ago purchased the appropriative rights to those waters, and had made extensive investments to develop them and to build aqueduct connections to the metropolis. Recent legislation has also tended to be increasingly hostile to market exchanges of water rights. Under the statutes of Colorado, for example, it is illegal to sell water found in the state outside its boundaries. Colorado legislators seem to lack confidence in the ability of naive Coloradans to exact an appropriate price from wily out-of-staters.

---

[a]Discussion based upon J. Hirshleifer, J. C. DeHaven, and J. W. Milliman, *Water Supply: Economics, Technology, and Policy* (Chicago: University of Chicago Press, 1960), Chap. 9.

15.C.4 ☐ Public Goods

A commodity is called a "public good" if its consumption by any one person does not reduce the amount available for others. Or putting it another way, a good is "public" if providing the good for *anyone* makes it possible to provide it for *everyone*, without additional cost. Public goods thus represent a particular type of beneficial externality. A private good (e.g., a banana) is used or consumed *exclusively*; a public good is (or may be) used *concurrently* by many economic agents.

The traditional example is the lighthouse. If one ship receives the benefit of the warning signal, that in no way deprives others from doing so. Or in radio or television, a broadcast program is available non-exclusively to any and all persons equipped with suitable receivers.[10]

If Z is a public good, with the *numéraire* commodity Y remaining a private good, the efficiency condition as between a producing firm f and two consumers John (j) and Karl (k) can be expressed as:

$$(15.4) \qquad MC_z^f = MRSC_{ZY}^j + MRSC_{ZY}^k$$

That is, the Marginal Cost of the producing firm must be set equal to the *sum* of the consumers' marginal valuations of the public good. Geometrically, the picture is as in Figure 15.5. The two individuals' separate demand curves are shown as d^j and d^k. Recall that the demand curve d^j can be regarded as a schedule of John's $MRSC_{ZY}^j$, and d^k as a corresponding schedule for Karl. The aggregate value of any additional unit of Z, produced for concurrent consumption by the two consumers together, is then shown in the diagram by the social valuation function Σ—the *vertical* summation[11] of d^j and d^k. The intersection of the MC_z and Σ curves represents the satisfaction of condition (15.4) above, so that z^* is the efficient level of output.[12]

The problem for the theorem of the Invisible Hand is: Can achievement of

[10]Since there are *some* costs to users (stationing a lookout to watch for the lighthouse, buying a receiving set for the broadcasts), the goods mentioned are not absolutely "pure" public goods. This qualification is minor in the cases given. But many goods lie in the intermediate range of the spectrum between wholly private and wholly public. A stage performance, for example, is "public" as among the members of a given audience. But the capacity of the theater sets a limit on the number who can be concurrently served, all others being excluded. In this discussion only "pure" public goods will be considered.

[11]The familiar market demand curve applicable to private goods is the *horizontal* summation of the individual demand curves (see Chapter 4). The curve Σ is *not* a market demand curve in this usual sense.

[12]If one individual's d schedule were such as to make his $MRSC_{ZY}$ actually negative for sufficiently great public-good output, on the margin Z would be a *bad* rather than a good for him. Given a "free disposal" possibility (as in the case of broadcasting, where one can simply turn off the receiver), any negative $MRSC_{ZY}$ need not be suffered, so that the social valuation function Σ would be a summation only of the *positive* ranges of the individual d curves. But if it were not possible for an individual to evade consumption of a public good, even after it becomes a bad, the Σ curve would be the *algebraic* sum of both positive and negative values along the individual d curves. (A possible example is national defense. This may be a public good for the majority, but a public bad for a minority of traitors who favor the enemy!) In what follows, it will be assumed that public goods do not ever become bads.

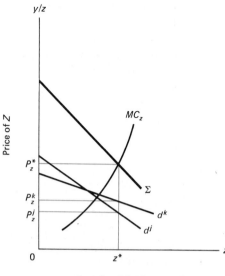

FIGURE 15.5 Public Good. MC_z represents the Marginal Cost of producing a public good Z, cost being measured in terms of amounts of the real *numéraire* good Y sacrificed. If John has demand curve d^i and Karl has demand curve d^k, the relevant total demand for the two consumers is the *vertical* summation curve Σ—since John and Karl consume the public good concurrently rather than exclusively. If the price P_z^i were charged to John, and P_z^k to Karl, and if the supplying firm behaved as a price-taker with regard to the summation price P_z, correct signals would be given to both supplier and demanders. The efficient output z^* would be produced, and that same quantity would be concurrently purchased and consumed by each demander.

the efficiency condition (15.4) be mediated by market prices? First of all, let us assume that, in principle at least, it is possible to charge for the use of the public good and to *exclude* those who do not pay. In television, for example, a coded or "scrambled" message could be broadcast that is only interpretable with the aid of a paid descrambling device.[13] Then private firms can contemplate producing public goods for market sale.[14] The market prices that would serve the needs of mediation are P_z^i and P_z^k in Figure 15.5, each price being equal to the respective consumer's separate $MRSC_{ZY}$ at the efficient output level z^*. The price-mediating conditions are:

(15.5)
$$\begin{cases} MRSC_{ZY}^i = P_z^i \\ MRSC_{ZY}^k = P_z^k \end{cases} \quad \text{and} \quad MC_z = P_z^* \equiv P_z^i + P_z^k$$

It is evident that these equations imply satisfaction of the efficiency condition (15.4).

So there is a set of prices that would fill the bill. But could these prices be arrived at by a market-equilibrium process?

Note, first, that *price discrimination* is required since, in general, $P_z^i \neq P_z^k$. It was shown in Chapter 8 that a monopolist seller could—where resale of the good between consumers is impossible—segment the market so as to be able to charge different prices to different consumers. In the case of public goods, it may again be possible to segment the market (to prevent resale). Then a monopolist *could*

---

[13]Sometimes, however, this may be impracticable. Consider mosquito abatement. This is clearly a public good. But to exclude non-payers from the benefit, it would be necessary to somehow train or signal the mosquitoes that some targets were permissible.

[14]Radio and television broadcasts are provided privately even *without* explicit charge to the consumer. But of course the listeners are really paying something, in being willing to have their time and attention captured by commercial messages.

satisfy conditions (15.5) corresponding to the intersection of MC_z and Σ in Figure 15.5. But there would be no motivation to do so. The monopolist would want to choose an output such that Marginal Cost MC_z equals the sum of the *Marginal Revenues* mr_z^j and mr_z^k in the segmented markets represented by the two individuals, rather than the sum of the prices P_z^j and P_z^k. Each person's Marginal Revenue curve mr would of course lie below his associated demand (Average Revenue) curve d, so that the vertical sum $mr_z^j + mr_z^k$ would lie below the vertical sum of the prices represented by the Σ curve. It follows that the monopolist, as one would expect, chooses an output *smaller* than that required by the efficiency condition (15.5).

Suppose, on the other hand, that the monopolist were somehow induced to act as a price-taker, calculating in terms of $P_z^j + P_z^k$ rather than $mr_z^j + mr_z^k$. But if price discrimination is ruled out, the monopolist would have to set $P_z^j = P_z^k$ at whatever level of output is chosen. (Even if discrimination were technically and legally feasible, the monopolist might not be able to secure the information about individual demand functions necessary for doing so.) Then the effective vertical summation curve Σ' from a revenue point of view (not shown in the diagram) would lie somewhat *below* the true Σ. The consequence, as before, would be a less than efficient output of the public good.

Exercise 15.1: John's demand curve for the public good Z is given by $P_z^j = 10 - 2z^j$, Karl's is $P_z^k = 20 - 4z^k$. The Marginal Cost of producing Z is $MC_z = 6$. (a) What is the efficient output of Z, and what prices should be charged? (b) If the producer of Z were a discriminating monopolist, what would be the profit-maximizing output and price?

Answer: (a) Adding the demand curves *vertically*, the equation becomes $\Sigma \equiv P_z^j + P_z^k = 30 - 6z$, where $z = z^j = z^k$. Setting $MC = \Sigma$, the result is $6 = 30 - 6z$ or $z = 4$. To dispose of this output, the respective prices to John and to Karl must be $P_z^j = 2$ and $P_z^k = 4$. (b) The monopolist would set $MC_z = mr_z^j + mr_z^k$ or $6 = (10 - 4z^j) + (20 - 8z^k) = 30 - 12z$. The solution is $z = 2 = z^j = z^k$. The prices charged would be $P_z^j = 6$ and $P_z^k = 12$. [*Query:* What would happen if the monopolist had to charge the same price to each consumer?]

A public good might, conceivably at least, be provided *competitively* rather than monopolistically. Television broadcasting is a case where we see hot competition among firms (channels). However, product differentiation among competing broadcasters makes the instance closer to "monopolistic competition" (see Chapter 9) than to pure competition. So even a hypothetical competitively supplied public good is likely to be "under-produced."

CONCLUSION: The efficiency conditions for public goods require price discrimination in accordance with consumers' Marginal Rates of Substitution in Consumption. Because of the difficulty and costs of excluding non-payers, and of charging correct discriminatory prices, public goods are likely to be under-supplied by private firms.

One other consideration reinforcing this conclusion is the existence of *transaction costs* associated with the conversion of a public good into excludable private property. If a television broadcast is "scrambled" to permit charging a fee for receiving the program, society is bearing a cost in terms of the resources used for scrambling and unscrambling, as well as for the efforts involved in negotiating over price, billing, and all other costs of the market exchange process. Again, these costs lead to under-production.

According to some welfare theorists, the various difficulties in private supply of public goods dictate that they be "publicly" (i.e., governmentally) provided instead. Indeed, some have thought that the concept of public goods serves to define the proper scope of government: "Private goods" ought to be privately supplied, and "public goods" ought to be publicly supplied. But in fact we do observe private firms supplying public goods. Television broadcasting is the obvious example, but even lighthouse services have at times been privately provided. And on the other hand government agencies, while supplying public goods like national defense, are also in the business of producing a vast range of private goods. Among the many examples are electric power (TVA), irrigation water (the U.S. Bureau of Reclamation), insurance (Social Security), education (public schools), and of course postal services (the U.S. Postal Service).

Government provision is inevitable only for those public goods for which *exclusion* of non-payers is unfeasible. Here the same "free rider" problem arises as already discussed under the heading of "Externalities" above. If a non-payer can derive benefits on essentially the same terms as someone who does pay, each and every person will be motivated to let the others foot the bill. In such circumstances provision of the public good by private firms may be impossible. But the difficulty is due to the *non-exclusionary* aspect rather than to the *public-good* aspect. Even a perfectly ordinary private good, not collectively consumed (e.g., food in a restaurant), could not be profitably provided on a private basis if non-payers could invade the premises and obtain service on the same basis as the paying customers!

15.C.5 ☐ Appropriative Activity or "Rent-Seeking"

Coase's Theorem asserts that market trading will always lead to an efficient outcome—provided, among other things, that property rights are "well-defined." What does this condition mean, and what happens when property rights are not "well-defined"?

Property rights can be said to be well-defined if: (1) all resources are *appropriated* (belong legally to someone), and (2) legal rights to property are perfectly and costlessly *enforced*.

Consider the latter condition. If legal rights are *not* perfectly and costlessly enforced then, evidently, some individuals may find it possible and advantageous to steal. Even without violating the law, some people can unilaterally attempt to gain control over resources owned by others—by instituting more or less groundless lawsuits, by inducing legislators to change the law (or inducing bureaucrats to re-interpret the law) in their favor, or even by appealing to the charitable impulses of the present owners. The present owners are likely to respond with defensive measures: patrolling their property to prevent theft or invasion, hiring expensive lawyers to fight lawsuits, lobbying in Washington against new legislation, and so forth. All such proceedings, both offensive or defensive, come under the heading of *appropriative activity*—efforts to impose or to prevent involuntary changes in the ownership of property. Such efforts, known also as "rent-seeking," are not costless. They absorb resources that could have been devoted to production and exchange activities instead.

Turning back now to the first condition, suppose that some resources are not presently appropriated at all. If those resources are valuable, the consequence again will be appropriative activity. A dramatic historical instance was the Oklahoma land rush of 1889. When the settlers raced to stake out former Indian territories, the resources devoted to "rushing" so as to gain possession ahead of others constituted a social efficiency loss.[15] Some of the externality problems of Section 15.C.3 are also associated with attempts to gain control of unappropriated resources: over-pumping of oil is due to the fact that the petroleum is no-one's property until brought to the surface. Settling new territories or pumping oil are productive actions in and of themselves; what is inefficient is the waste in "rushing" to act before others do.

The efficiency loss due to appropriative activity, it is important to emphasize, is not a consequence of the *existence* of property rights under law. It is a consequence of *imperfections* in their assignment or enforcement. A totally lawless society would not avoid appropriative activity; on the contrary, such activity would become everyone's main occupation.

15.D
THE PROBLEM OF EQUALITY

Equality of income has historically been an important political objective, especially in democratically governed societies. Attempts have been made to defend equality on utilitarian grounds. Suppose that individuals had cardinal and interpersonally comparable utility functions, characterized by diminishing Marginal Utility, and furthermore that *all these utility funcitons were essentially identical.* Then the total social aggregate of utility would be maximized by dividing income equally. This argument involves strong assumptions, of course, over and above acceptance of the philosophical premises of utilitarianism.

Alternatively, equality of income might be proclaimed as an "ethical" postulate in its own right, independent of utilitarian philosophizing. At first glance an ethic of equality seems appealing. But note that achieving equality would require imposing a tax of 100% upon *any* above-average income an individual might receive. Such a tax would obviously have a drastically adverse effect upon incentives to engage in burdensome toil, to invest long years of effort in training, and so forth. But apart from such practical considerations, even from an ethical point of view most of us would not want to deprive the individual of *all* reward to his or her extra effort.

[15]The famous Oklahoma "Sooners" were those who cheated by beating the starting gun.

15.D.1 □ An Application: Rawls' Concept of "Justice"

The philosopher John Rawls has recently proposed a strongly egalitarian criterion of "social justice."[16] The criterion deals primarily with distribution of the measurable goods of society, and so can best be regarded as mappable on the objective income axes I^j, I^k of Figure 15.1 rather than on the subjective utility axes U^j, U^k of Figure 15.2.

Rawls' key concept is what he calls the "difference principle." Inequality in a society, he asserts, is justified *only* to the extent that it benefits the *least* advantaged. In Figure 15.6, the 45° line shows all the conceivable income allocations I^j, I^k for which equality holds, i.e., for which $I^j = I^k$. Now consider the shaded social opportunity set bounded by the curve II'. The best attainable point on the 45° line is evidently the point F; this it the equality optimum. In moving from F toward the point S along the Social Opportunity Frontier II', a degree of inequality is being created (since, northwest of the 45° line, John's income I^j exceeds Karl's income I^k). But this is *justified*, according to Rawls, in that even the poorer individual (Karl) is thereby made better off.

It will be evident that the application of Rawls' difference principle leads to selection of the point S as the social optimum in Figure 15.6. More generally, his rule is equivalent to asserting a particular shape for the interpersonal or social "welfare" function (compare Figure 15.2). The isoquants of social welfare in the form of Rawlsian "justice"[17] are rectangular with corners on the 45° line, as exemplified by SW_0 and SW_1 in the diagram.

[16]John Rawls, *A Theory of Justice* (Cambridge, Mass.: Harvard University Press, 1971).

[17]Rawls' identification of the word "justice" with "equality" is questionable terminology. Our ordinary understanding of "justice" is as a proper *relationship between a man's actions and his rewards.* The Biblical "eye for an eye" may be a primitive concept of justice, but it is the sort of thing that we mean by justice. In contrast, Rawls' concept would deprive some individuals and reward others *independent of any actions on their part.* This is confiscation, not justice.

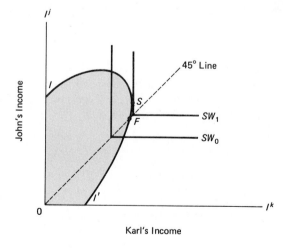

FIGURE 15.6 Rawls' Social Optimum. The philosopher John Rawls regards as "just" only those departures from equality of income that benefit the least advantaged. If II' is the Social Opportunity Frontier, F is the highest attainable point of equal incomes (along the 45° line). At S, in contrast, incomes are unequal. But, since even the less well-off party (Karl) has gained in moving from F to S, that move is supposedly "justified." In effect, Rawls' conception has indifference curves of "social welfare" like SW_0 and SW_1; right-angled, with the corners on the 45° equality line.

Now consider instead a social opportunity set like that portrayed in Figure 15.1, where the frontier *II'* has negative slope throughout (i.e., John cannot gain unless Karl loses, and vice versa). Under these circumstances the Rawlsian optimum always requires *absolute equality of income.*

15.D.2 ☐ Equality and Pareto-Optimality

A different approach to the problem of equality emphasizes that purely private motivation, in a world of individuals who are not completely selfish, will suffice to bring about a certain degree of equality. And indeed, the equality thus voluntarily achieved will represent an efficient (Pareto-optimal) allocation of incomes.

In Chapter 3, "preference for charity" was studied. Apart from minor changes in notation, Figure 15.7 here is essentially equivalent to the lower panel of Figure 3.11 in the earlier chapter. I have preferences as between "My income" I^m and "His income" I^h, such that *both* I^h and I^m are "goods" for me when $I^h < I^m$ (i.e., I am benevolent to someone poorer than myself). Given an initial endowment allocation E of incomes such that $I^h < I^m$, the opportunity locus or "budget line" EK shows the allocations I can attain by unilaterally transferring my income to him.

In the situation of Figure 15.7, my transfer optimum is the tangency T^*. Furthermore, if his preference function is like mine, the circumstances that impel me to donate to him (I am richer than he) also motivate him to accept the gift (he is poorer than I). Being mutually desired, the transfer is Pareto-optimal.

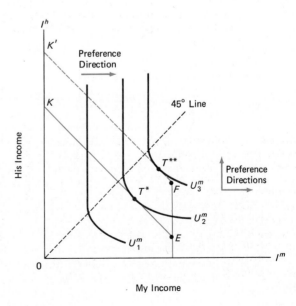

FIGURE 15.7 The Economics of Charity. My preferences shown here represent benevolence to others when they are poorer than myself. Given an initial endowment allocation of incomes *E*, and if I can transfer income to the other party along the line *EK*, my private optimum is at *T**. If he has similar preferences, since he is poorer than I he will also surely gain in utility terms. Thus, the move from *E* to *T** is Pareto-preferred. If a third party were to give him a contribution *EF*, the revised endowment allocation from my point of view becomes point *F*. I will then move along *FK'* to point *T***, making a somewhat smaller contribution.

15.D.3 ☐ Equality as a Public Good

Still another approach emphasizes that equality can be regarded as a "public good." An increased degree of equality that satisfies the benevolent desires of any one individual will, without additional cost, also increase utility for any other person who is similarly situated and has similar benevolent preferences.

Returning to Figure 15.7, suppose that, before I make my voluntary transfer changing the income allocation from the endowment position E to the optimum T^*, some third party A were to make a gift to my prospective beneficiary H. Specifically, if A's gift to H is in the amount EF, the initial endowment allocation of income between H and myself shifts upward to point F. My opportunity locus then becomes the dashed line FK'. Clearly, I can attain a higher level of satisfaction (tangency T^{**} with a higher indifference curve on I^m, I^h axes) than before. A's gift has, to some degree, enabled me to satisfy my taste for benevolence without cost to myself.

Furthermore, this is an example of a *non-excludable* public good. Having made the gift to H, the third party A is in no way able to prevent me from enjoying the effects of that act. The consequence is, once again, a "free rider" problem. I transfer to H only the amount of income needed to move from F to T^{**}, whereas without A's intervention I would have been willing to make the larger transfers required to move from E to T^*. To some extent, therefore, as a potential donor I am free-riding on others' contributions. Similarly, the third party A (and other potential donors as well) may contribute less than they otherwise would, expecting to free-ride on my contribution. Following the familiar free-rider theme, it follows that a less-than-efficient amount of income transfers would be underaken by private individuals. This analysis therefore provides a rationale for government intervention via *fiscal redistribution,* whereby taxes levied on the wealthier classes are collected for transfer to poorer groups.

To fit ideally into the model of benevolence as a public good, however, the redistributive taxes would have to be voluntarily levied upon themselves by the wealthier groups! A more cynical explanation of the phenomenon of fiscal redistribution would not make any use of benevolence as a motive, but would run simply in terms of political realities. This topic is considered further in the next chapter.

But in any case, *private* charity is an important phenomenon. Hence, benevolent preferences surely do exist, and so cannot be entirely dismissed as motivation for fiscal redistribution.

15.E

WELFARE ECONOMICS: CONCLUSION

Welfare economics has been primarily preoccupied with the problem of *efficiency*, i.e., with the determination of the conditions leading to allocations on the Social Opportunity Frontier (as shown, for example, by the curve LL' in

Figure 15.2). Any such allocation is characterized by the condition that there exists no other that is Pareto-preferred to it.

Achievement of efficiency is, however, neither necessary nor sufficient as a criterion of ideal social policy. The *distribution* of income as among individuals and social classes is another important criterion. Even granting the appropriateness of a certain tilt toward distributive *equality*, the question remains how far to go in sacrificing efficiency. And there are, of course, many other criteria with some claim to be considered in social policy: liberty to retain and use lawfully acquired talents or property, communitarian versus individualistic values, and other non-utilitarian considerations.

Nevertheless, economists' emphasis upon the efficiency criterion has probably played a useful social role. The political processes that determine social policy tend to overlook considerations of efficiency almost entirely. Whether the issue be the progressive income tax, the protection of some industries by tariffs and quotas, penalization of others for "excessive" profits, combating monopoly, or choosing the proper scale of government, it has become a function of the economist to point out that there are efficiency implications to be considered. To wit, which policy will bring about the largest aggregate "pie" of income, apart from the question of how the pie is to be sliced up?

An older generation of welfare economists tended to think in terms of a policy shotgun with two barrels: (1) a presumption in favor of *laissez faire*, based on the Theorem of the Invisible Hand as discussed in Section 15.B above, but modified by (2) a presumption in favor of government intervention to remedy the specific failures and distortions of the Invisible Hand reviewed in Section 15.C. Neither barrel of the shotgun quite hits the target. The efficiency ideally attainable by the Invisible Hand is, as we have seen, not a fully satisfactory guide to policy. On the other hand, a failure of the Invisible Hand to achieve efficiency does not of itself provide any warrant for belief that government intervention will improve matters.

This last question suggests the need for a study of political or governmental decision-making. Economists have indeed, though only very recently, turned to serious *positive* analysis of government, i.e., to examining the economic consequences of what government *actually* does as opposed to what in some ideal sense it "ought" to do. Recent developments in this field of inquiry will be examined in the following chapter.

☐ SUMMARY OF CHAPTER 15

The study of the principles underlying correct public policy is called "welfare economics."

While there are many possible goals of policy, economists' attention has traditionally been concentrated on only two: efficiency, and distributive equity. Efficiency is increased by making any change that is Pareto-preferred, i.e., that increases the utility of any person or persons without decreasing the utility of any other. An outcome is said to be efficient or Pareto-optimal when there are no other outcomes Pareto-preferred to it. (However, it is not true that an efficient outcome is Pareto-preferred to *every* outcome that is not efficient.) The goal of distributive equity is ordinarily interpreted as *equality*. But while equality may be definable in terms of objective incomes, there is no way to say when two individuals' utilities are equal. Both efficiency and equality as goals are based on utilitarian philosophy. Non-utilitarians have criticized such goals as, among other things, excessively individualistic and excessively materialistic.

The Theorem of the Invisible Hand states that, under ideal conditions, a *laissez-faire* economy will achieve an efficient utilization of resources. As economic agents respond to the ruling equilibrium prices, efficiency will be attained among consumers in the allocation of finished products, among factor-owners in the choice between market employment and reservation uses of their resources, and among firms in using resources and producing final products.

However, there are several grounds on which the Invisible Hand might fail in the actual world. (1) Monopolies of many types exist, all leading to inefficient outcomes if operated for private gain. (2) Disequilibrium prices do not give the correct signals to buyers and sellers. (3) If the existing structure of property rights allows some agents to impose direct externalities on others, incentives are distorted. Coase's Theorem asserts that property rights will be exchanged to eliminate inefficient externalities, but this holds only under ideal conditions: property rights must be well-defined, and transactions costless. (4) Public goods represent a special type of externality, where a commodity is concurrently rather than exclusively consumed—so that if a public good is provided for one person, there is no additional cost in providing it to others. If a public good is or can be made excludable in the market, it can be privately provided. There is a pattern of discriminatory prices that can achieve efficiency in the private production and use of excludable public goods, but in practice such goods are likely to be under-supplied in the market. If a public good is non-excludable, on the other hand, it can scarcely be provided by the market at all. (But neither could a non-excludable *private* good.) (5) Where property rights are not well defined, individuals will be motivated to undertake activities aimed at changing the effective structure of rights (or at preventing such changes). Resources devoted to such "appropriative" activities represent a loss of efficiency.

The ethical position associated with the philosopher Rawls demands absolute equality of income, except where a move in the direction of inequality would help the worst-off. If potential donors have benevolent motivations, private incentives tend to bring about some Pareto-preferred moves toward equality of income. But such equality becomes a kind of non-excludable public good, and so underprovided by private incentives.

In view of the uncertainties of distributive equity (or its usual practical counterpart, income equality) as goals, economists have tended to concentrate upon achievement of efficiency. This has probably served a socially useful function. While one must treat with reserve the proposition that an actual *laissez-faire* economy would approximate an efficient outcome, it remains to be seen whether actual government interventions normally tend to correct any failure to do so.

☐ QUESTIONS FOR CHAPTER 15

MAINLY FOR REVIEW

R1. Explain and justify the normally "concave" shape of the Social Opportunity Frontier in income terms (Figure 15.1). What can be said about the shape of the Social Opportunity Frontier in utility terms (Figure 15.2)?

*R2. Show how a Social Opportunity Frontier in utility terms for two individuals may be derived from the *contract curve* of the Edgeworth box diagram of Chapter 13.

*R3. What meaning, if any, can be given to the concept of a "social optimum"? How valid is "efficiency" or Pareto-optimality as a criterion of social optimality?

R4. What is the Theorem of the Invisible Hand?

*R5. What are the conditions of "efficiency" reached under ideal conditions by the unregulated market process? Can the conditions be achieved, in principle, without use of the market?

R6. Why does disequilibrium of markets lead to inefficiency?

*R7. Explain why a firm that is a monopolist in the product market is said to hire "too little" of the factors it uses for production. Explain why a firm that is a monopsonist in the factor market is also said to hire "too little." Given these effects, does it follow that too large a proportion of the community's resources are employed by competitive firms, or are retained for reservation uses by resource-owners, or both?

R8. What are public goods? What are externalities? Is a public good a special case of an externality?

R9. How would inability to exclude non-payers affect the private supply of public goods? The private supply of private goods?

*R10. What is the efficiency condition for optimal provision of a public good? In what sense is it appropriate in the case of public goods to sum individual demand curves *vertically*, whereas for private goods the summation takes place *horizontally*?

*R11. What limits the possibility of private supply of public goods? Will public provision mean that a more nearly optimal amount will be supplied?

R12. What is the Coase Theorem? Explain the relevance of each of the following conditions for the actual empirical applicability of the theorem: (a) well-defined property rights, and (b) low costs of negotiating and enforcing agreements.

R13. What is "appropriative" activity? What are the implications of such activities for economic efficiency?

FOR FURTHER THOUGHT AND DISCUSSION

*T1. Fragment of a conversation based upon Robert Browning's poem, "My Last Duchess":

But my dear Dr. H., your own textbook proves that in terms of economic efficiency I was amply justified in taking the life of my last duchess. For, being of not inconsiderable means,

*The answers to asterisked questions appear at the end of the book.

I was willing to pay more for her death than she could have afforded to pay to prevent it.

The Duke of Ferrara

Is the Duke's analysis correct?

*T2. "An efficient allocation of resources maximizes the dollar value of national income." True or false? Explain.

T3. In the apples–bees example in the text, the externality is mutually beneficial. Provide an example of a reciprocal relation in which the mutually imposed externalities are harmful. Can there be a case in which in one direction the effect is beneficial but in the other direction harmful?

*T4. What sorts of real-world considerations may forestall the working of Coase's Theorem by making property rights ambiguous or uncertain? By raising the costs of negotiating and enforcing contracts?

T5. What are the major considerations bearing upon the likelihood or effectiveness of achieving efficiency through market versus nonmarket means?

*T6. "An ideal market would achieve a Pareto-efficient outcome, but only one that is Pareto-preferred to the endowment situation; an ideal dictatorship would not be so limited." True or false? Explain.

*T7. Recently, steps have been taken in the United States to ban the commercial market in human blood. (One of the arguments given was that commercially provided blood is more likely to be infected with hepatitis than volunteered blood.) Can this ban be justified on efficiency grounds, or any other grounds?

*T8. One "market intervention" is the law against polygamy. Through much of human history polygyny (multiple wives) has been very common and even polyandry (multiple husbands), although rare, has occasionally occurred. It has been contended that the laws banning polygyny work to the *disadvantage* of women as suppliers of wife-services—just as a law forbidding more than one car per customer would be disadvantageous to suppliers of automobiles. Is this sound? Who are the main losers and main gainers from the monogamy laws? Can the monogamy laws be defended in terms of efficiency? In terms of equality?

16

POLITICAL ECONOMY: COOPERATION AND CONFLICT

SUPPLEMENTARY
CHAPTER

Market transactions are voluntary. One person contracts to sell, the other to buy, under terms to which both of them consent. But the political sphere is characterized by *involuntary* transactions. To pay for a service like a public road, a government will typically tax many people in the community who will be deriving no benefit whatever from the road, who may even be injured by it. What is far more drastic, governments define certain behaviors as crimes for which citizens may be punished by fines, imprisonment, or death. Or, a government may make war against its enemies, possibly drafting unwilling citizens as soldiers. Involuntary transactions like these are dictated ones. The essence of politics is who dictates to whom, who governs and who is governed.

Some philosophers contend that people always behave selfishly in the marketplace, but when it comes to politics they are more inclined to act in the public interest. This naive view is rejected here. Market decisions and political choices are made by the same people, with the same motives. To explain observed differences between market behavior and political behavior we must look not to differences in motives but to differences in the rules of the game.

The first portion of the chapter takes up a hypothetical "service state"— a government characterized by a minimum of dictation. Such a state acts solely to satisfy its citizen-consumers' desires for goods and services. But, in contrast with the market mechanism where preferences are expressed by willingness to buy and sell, in the service state preferences are registered by some system of "public choice"—e.g., by voting. While the economist naturally thinks of government in this way, as a system in which individuals band together to acquire goods and services, the concept of the service state fails to illuminate some of the most central issues of politics. *Political conflict* must be given at least as much weight as public choice, and this topic will be addressed later in the chapter.

16.A
THE SERVICE STATE: IMPERFECTIONS OF PUBLIC CHOICE

The service state can best be grasped by thinking of *political parties* as akin to *business firms*. Business firms offer goods and services, at specified prices, to the consumers. Political parties offer packages of government policies, at certain costs in the form of taxes and other burdens, to the citizens. Firms are groupings of individuals trying to make a profit by providing *consumers* with what they want. Political parties are groupings of individuals trying to make a "profit" (which might, in some degree, represent satisfactions like power or glory apart from pecuniary remuneration) by providing *citizens* with what they want.

Ideal free enterprise in the economy corresponds to ideal democracy in the polity.[1] What forces businessmen to satisfy the desires of consumers is the same as what pushes politicians to satisfy the desires of citizens—the pressure of *competition*. In the ideal market economy, perfect competition among firms drives profits to zero in long-run equilibrium (see Chapter 7). Then firms have no power to do anything other than what consumers want, since any firm that fails to satisfy consumers will be driven out of business by other firms. In the ideal polity, perfect competition among parties similarly drives political "profit" to zero. Parties would have no power to do anything other than what citizens want, since any party that fails to satisfy citizens will be voted out. Thus, Adam Smith's Invisible Hand—the force that induces individuals, in their own self-interest, to satisfy the needs of others—operates to some degree in the political arena as well as in the market economy.

It was emphasized in the preceding chapter that imperfections of real-world market systems (monopoly, disequilibrium, externalities, etc.) do not imply that government necessarily "ought" to intervene. Before drawing any such conclusion, we should look into the *flaws of the political process*. Let us now take up this topic, the shortcomings of political mechanisms viewed as ways whereby citizen-consumers attempt to achieve their desires.

16.A.1 ☐ Political Competition

Just as ideal democracy in the polity corresponds to perfect competition in the market, political dictatorship corresponds to monopoly in the market. But political dictatorship has far more drastic consequences. We can usually avoid doing business with a market monopolist who overcharges, but escaping an oppressive government may be impossible. Furthermore, the market monopolist wants only our money—while the political dictator may want our very lives. Yet even the most absolute dictator still faces competition. Possible conquest from outside or revolution from within set a limit on how much a dictator can prudently exploit the citizenry.

Democratic political systems are characterized by relatively free entry into the contest for political power. But, there appear to be strong economies of scale in the political process. As a result, most commonly there are only two or at any rate only a very few effective political parties. So democratic political competition is closer to oligopoly (Chapter 10). Furthermore, rare exceptions apart, citizens do not vote directly on policies. They vote only for delegates in the legislative, judicial, and executive branches of government; these delegates make the actual policy decisions. But elections of delegates are relatively infrequent. Whereas

[1]See Gary S. Becker, "Competition and Democracy," *Journal of Law and Economics*, v. 1 (Oct. 1958).

consumers make and reconsider market choices every single day, citizens can choose or recall their political representatives only at election intervals measured in years. And some of the most important political decision-makers, such as U.S. Supreme Court Justices, are only indirectly "elected" and once chosen are beyond effective recall.

The *limited options* available further erode the control that citizens have over their delegates. There is considerable "bundling" of issues in the election process. A voter may prefer the position of one candidate on one question, of a competing candidate on a second issue, and so forth. But the delegate elected will be representing (or misrepresenting) the voter in *all* decisions to be made during his or her term of office.

So even in a highly democratic system delegates may have a considerable degree of "power" (i.e., of leeway to violate the preferences of their constituents). The clearest evidence of this is the willingness of candidates and parties to expend enormous sums to win political office. U.S. Senate and House candidates were reported by the Federal Elections Commission to have spent around $314 million seeking congressional seats in the 1982 election.[2] And this figure is surely much too low: it takes no account of volunteer efforts of sympathizers and party workers, free publicity from supporting newspapers and other media, propaganda put out by unions and businesses hoping to win favors, etc.

A number of political institutions have been devised to widen the role of individual citizens in public decisions. (1) In some states of the U.S., voters may bypass the elected legislature to pass laws via the *initiative,* and may *recall* elected officers between scheduled elections. (2) Within parties, the "primary" and other techniques of participation provide ways for citizens to influence the final slate of candidates offered the voters in the actual election. (3) Under a federal system, the citizen may support one party for national office and a different one for local office. (4) Similarly, where there is separation of powers the voters may choose one party to represent him in the legislative branch and another party in the executive branch of government.

But these are all highly imperfect arrangements. Indeed, while improvements from the single point of view of *representation* of citizen preferences, some or all of the devices may be objectionable on other grounds. They may be inconsistent, for example, with effectiveness of government—with simply getting things done. In any case, the scope of individual choice remains drastically less in the political arena than in the marketplace.

16.A.2 ☐ Majority and Minority

Modern democratic political systems operate mainly on the principle of *majority rule.* The necessity of making decisions through delegates poses a problem, as we have seen, since the delegate may not faithfully serve constituents' interests. But what if the constituents differ among themselves? Then, to be elected, delegates need only serve the majority interest; they must please only 50%-plus-one of those who turn out to vote.

[2]*Los Angeles Times,* Jan. 7, 1983, p. 1.

This obviously puts the minority at a grave disadvantage. Conceivably, even their most vital interests may be at the mercy of the majority. If on some policy issue 75% of the constituency prefer alternative 1 and 25% prefer alternative 2, the delegate's support will be unlikely to be divided in this proportion. Rather, the delegate will be motivated to give full support to the majority, those favoring alternative 1. In contrast, majority and minority preferences are normally *both* provided for, in due proportion, in a market economy. If 75% of consumers prefer chocolate and 25% prefer vanilla, chocolate and vanilla flavors will tend, other things equal, to be provided in just about these proportions.

Devices have emerged tending to provide partial remedies for the majority-minority problem. *Constitutional protection* limits the types of laws a majority can pass, thus affording some minimal security for minority rights. A very interesting phenomenon, which arises most visibly on the higher or legislative level, is called "log-rolling." Suppose that the minority legislators feel very strongly on a particular issue *A*. Then to swing over votes on issue *A*, they may promise other legislators to support *their* positions on separate issues *B, C, D,* etc. In this way the *intensity* of minority preferences is registered, to some degree, as a counter-weight to the mere numbers of the majority.

The process of log-rolling can be regarded as a partial injection of market considerations into the political process. Through "political exchange," delegates' votes on some issues are "bought," to be "paid for" later by votes on other issues. Log-rolling, though generally considered an evil, reminds us of the *mutual advantage of trade*. Indeed, efficiency in the sense of a *Pareto-optimal* outcome—a result in which it is no longer possible to achieve any further gains to anyone without hurting others (see Chapter 15)—would be achieved if legislators' votes on issues could be openly purchased for money!

The underlying logic is this. An ideal system of "political exchange" would be one requiring *unanimous* consent for every action. To achieve agreement, every dissenter's vote would have to be bought by the winning side. This would guarantee that all political actions undertaken are actually Pareto-preferred over the initial situation (i.e., would constitute an improvement for some, and an injury for none). Those who suffer from the chosen action are compensated by the purchase of their votes. With majority rule and log-rolling, it is true that compensation is not paid to all those affected—only to a number sufficient to comprise a voting majority. Nevertheless, since *both* sides will be trying to buy votes, the winning side will be the one able to bid higher. Hence under a bought-vote system the more highly-valued alternative would always be chosen. The result is Pareto-*optimal*, though not in general unanimously preferred (Pareto-*preferred*) over the status quo.

That the purchase of votes seems repugnant is a consequence of the problem of *delegation* discussed above. In a *direct* democracy, offering compensation, to win the approval of those adversely affected by a proposed policy alternative, would surely be quite reasonable. But our knowledge of the world leads us to suspect that any compensation privately paid to the delegate in a *representative* democracy may be pocketed rather than translated into benefits for the constituents. That is true enough, but we should realize where the real objection lies: in the delegation of decision-making power, not in the process of offering compensation to win the approval (buy the votes) of those injured by proposed public decisions.

There is still another curious problem of majority decision. Suppose a majority prefer option 1 over 2, and a majority also prefer 2 over 3. Still, it does not follow that a majority will prefer 1 over 3! Imagine that three individuals must make a collective decision as to color, say of their joint living quarters. Two of them may favor red over green, two favor green over yellow, and yet two favor yellow over red. This problem of "cycling" means that majority preferences are not necessarily *transitive*. (Recall that transitivity of *individual* preferences was treated as an Axiom in Chapter 3.) It follows that it is not in general possible to construct a consistent rank ordering of majority preferences. In such circumstances, the way in which the issues are presented for voting (the "agenda") can easily determine the outcome. (It has been said that whoever controls the agenda, controls the meeting.)

16.A.3 □ The Problem of Voting

It is the *vote* that represents the ultimate discipline that individual citizens can exercise upon their delegates. But the effectiveness of a single vote is so minuscule that the ordinary citizen is scarcely motivated to go to the polls at all. Even if the election of the preferred candidate were worth an enormous sum to the voter, one person's voting will actually have an effect upon the outcome only in a fantastically improbable situation, i.e., the case where that ballot gives the candidate a majority of one. Or if the citizen is not so interested in electing a particular candidate as in swelling the poll for an ideological position, again one vote more or less would scarcely ever be noticeable. And even if the voter has no selfish aims at all but intends to cast a purely public-spirited ballot, that single vote will no more measurably serve the *public* interest than it would the voter's own *selfish* interest.

If it were possible and legal for a candidate to *buy* votes, there would be no problem of motivating the voter. Parallel to the argument for log-rolling, a surprisingly good case can be made for buying citizens' votes at election time. What this means is that the politicians will be paying the constituents in advance for the rewards of office. Competition for votes before election would compensate for the scarcely controllable power granted the delegates after their election.

If votes are not paid for, and if the chance of affecting the outcome is negligible, why are so many votes actually cast in elections? If citizens are rational, it can only be that the *costs of casting a ballot are low*. And indeed, at least for city-dwellers and when the weather is good, the cost is small. Voting may actually be fun; it provides sociability and a feeling of civic accomplishment to offset the small travel and time cost involved.

The imperfections of the political representation process have certain less obvious consequences. In the marketplace you "get what you pay for." In the political arena, it is all too easy to vote in a candidate and not get desired results out. (The main cost to the individual of such an outcome is not the trivial effort of wasted voting, of course, but the taxes and other burdens of undesired policies.) In view of the problems of electing a candidate supporting the whole bundle of one's preferred policies, and of ensuring that he abides by the platform upon which he was elected, it simply is not worthwhile for the rational citizen to invest large resources in determining what *are* the best policies. Voting is cheap, but voting *intelligently* may be quite costly. And so, citizens typically find themselves ill-informed on the issues about which they are casting ballots.

EXAMPLE 16.1 _____
Determinants of Voter Turnout

If a citizen rationally considers whether to turn out and vote, his decision to incur the costs thereof should depend in part upon (1) the importance of the election, and (2) the probability of affecting the outcome. Y. Barzel and E. Silberberg[a] investigated the impact of these determinants upon the proportion of citizens actually casting ballots in U.S. gubernatorial elections in the years 1962, 1964, 1966, and 1968 (122 elections).

They found, among other results, that:

1. *The larger the population, the smaller the percent of turnout.* This represents rational behavior, since the larger the population the smaller is the probability of a single vote determining the election. An *increase* of 1,000,000 in voting-age population of the state was associated with a 6% *decline* in the percent voting.

2. *The more one-sided the election, the smaller the turnout.* Again rational, since if voters had some inkling in advance of the one-sidedness they would place lower credence upon their own single ballot affecting the outcome. Statistically a 10% *increase* in the majority fraction was associated with a 7.7% *decline* in percentage voting.

3. *Coincidence of non-gubernatorial with gubernatorial elections increased turnout.* Statistically, a presidential candidacy raised the fraction voting by 11.1%; a senatorial candidacy by 5.5%. Obviously, it is more rational to vote if the election is more important.

COMMENT: It would have been of interest to see if the difficulty and cost of voting significantly affected turnout. One would anticipate a larger fraction voting the better the weather, the less the average distance to the polls, the more convenient the voting hours, etc. As another point, it is also reasonable to expect a larger turnout on the part of those who expect to be able to cast *intelligent* ballots. (College graduates? Economics students?)

[a] Y. Barzel and E. Silberberg, "Is the Act of Voting Rational?" *Public Choice*, v. 16 (Fall 1973)

PUBLIC GOODS, FREE RIDERS, AND PRESSURE GROUPS

According to the traditional "welfare-economics" view, any imperfection of the market process was a presumptive justification for remedial government action. But the drastic imperfections of government, viewed as a mechanism for achieving individual ends, might tempt us to swing to the other extreme. So the question arises: Can an affirmative case be made for decision-making through the institution of government, to explain why at least a *portion* of economic activity is channeled through the state rather than through the market?

One explanation concerns "public" or "collective" goods—commodities which if supplied to one member of the community can without additional cost be supplied to all. Lighthouses and radio broadcasting are the traditional examples, but the most important collective good is undoubtedly *defense* of the community against external and internal enemies. We saw in the preceding chapter that the market tends to under-provide public goods. So, even though government may be an inefficient tool for satisfying citizen-consumer desires, when it comes to public goods there may as a practical matter be no alternative. This point can be brought out more clearly if we re-examine the provision of public goods, with emphasis upon the *free-rider* problem.

The free-rider problem characterizes externalities of all kinds (and public goods represent a special type of externality). No-one is eager to incur private costs in producing a public good; everyone is motivated to free-ride, to let others pick up the tab. While a community of self-interested individuals will typically generate some positive amount of a collective good, three propositions can be asserted: (1) As we already know, the amount provided will be less than Pareto-optimal; (2) furthermore, wealthy individuals will produce *disproportionately* more, and those with small stakes in the economy disproportionately less of the public good; and (3) as numbers in the community increase, the public good will be increasingly underprovided.

In Figure 16.1 a typical individual is choosing how much to produce and consume of an ordinary private good X and of a public good G. In his initial endowment position at $E°$, a Robinson Crusoe alone on his island starts with $x^†$ of the ordinary good and zero of the collective good. However, he can produce G at the expense of X, as indicated by the Production-Possibility Curve $E°g°$. The optimum productive-consumptive solution for Robinson when he is isolated is at the tangency R_0^* along indifference curve $U°$. Now suppose that other settlers arrive, also capable of producing quantities of G. Any such quantity would be available "free" to Robinson. Let F be the free amount provided by other inhabitants. If $F = E' - E°$, Robinson's endowment position would be shifted upward by that distance along the dashed vertical in the diagram. His PPC would shift upward correspondingly to $E'g'$, and his new optimum would be at R_1^*. What might be called the Free-Rider's Expansion Path (FEP curve) illustrates how Robinson's optimum combination would shift as F increases. [*Query:* FEP appears to change direction at point E'''—explain why.]

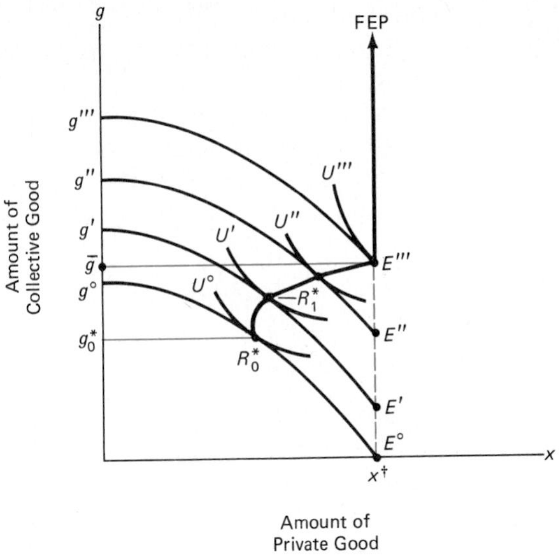

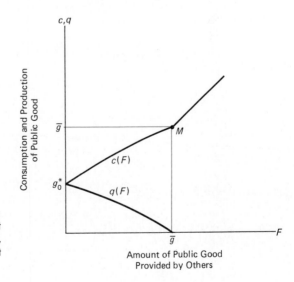

FIGURE 16.1 **Choice between Private Good and Collective Good.** The isolated individual's endowment position is $E°$. His productive-consumptive optimum is R_0^*, where the Production-Possibility Curve $E°g°$ is tangent to indifference curve $U°$. If other individuals provide an amount F of the public good, the endowment position and the associated PPC shift upward by that amount. The FEP curve traces out the individual's optimum consumption combinations as F increases.

Figure 16.2 contrasts the individual's *consumption* c of the collective good with his *production* g—in response to changes in F, the amount provided by others. When Robinson is alone, his production and consumption are equal in the amount $g°$. As F increases, $c(F)$ rises steadily but $g(F)$ falls. Eventually, when others are providing as much as $\bar{g}$, Robinson's own production of G falls to zero. [*Query:* Starting at point M in the diagram, the $c(F)$ curve becomes a 45° line—explain why.]

Why the wealthy (those with larger X-endowments) are likely to produce *disproportionately* more of G will be evident from the diagrams. In Figure 16.2, $\bar{g}$ for a poor individual may be so low that even a small amount F provided by

FIGURE 16.2 **Individual's Production versus Consumption of a Collective Good.** As F, the amount of the public good provided by others, increases, the amount c *consumed* by the individual rises but the amount q *produced* falls.

others may lead him to suspend his own production of G entirely. Think of Robinson Crusoe and Friday as sharing living quarters, where warmth (achieved by cutting wood for the fireplace) is the public good G, while berries for eating are the private good that each forages for himself. Suppose Robinson owns most of the better land and can collect berries easily, while Friday must hunt long and hard for his berries. Then they both know that Friday can't afford to spend a lot of time and effort cutting wood. So, if any warmth is to be supplied, it is pretty much up to Robinson to do so.

EXAMPLE 16.2
The Economics of Alliance

An *alliance* between independent nations is generally undertaken in the interests of mutual defense. But defense is, to an important degree at least, a public good for the allied powers. Destruction of an enemy's bombers, for example, reduces the threat against each and all of the possible target nations. Since each participating nation receives only a portion of the benefit of any marginal increment of expenditure, all are tempted to free-ride on the efforts of the others. But the larger nations are not in a position to free-ride to nearly the same degree as the smaller allies.

A study of the North Atlantic Treaty Organization (NATO) defense expenditures in 1964 verified the differential expenditures of larger and smaller participants. The Table compares the rankings of NATO nations as to size (measured by GNP) and as to proportion of budget devoted to defense expenditures. The association is evident to the eye, and statistical testing indi-

NATO Statistics

	GNP, 1964		DEFENSE BUDGET AS PERCENT OF GNP	
	$ Billion	Rank	Percent	Rank
United States	569.03	1	9.0	1
Germany	88.87	2	5.5	6
United Kingdom	79.46	3	7.0	3
France	73.40	4	6.7	4
Italy	43.63	5	4.1	10
Canada	38.14	6	4.4	8
Netherlands	15.00	7	4.9	7
Belgium	13.43	8	3.7	12
Denmark	7.73	9	3.3	13
Turkey	6.69	10	5.8	5
Norway	5.64	11	3.9	11
Greece	4.31	12	4.2	9
Portugal	2.88	13	7.7	2
Luxembourg	0.53	14	1.7	14

Source: M. Olson, Jr., and R. Zeckhauser, "An Economic Theory of Alliances," *Review of Economics and Statistics*, v. 48 (Aug. 1966), p. 267.

cates a high degree of significance. (The most conspicuous exception, Portugal, is explainable on other grounds. That nation, tiny in GNP, supported a large defense budget because of its colonial commitments in Africa rather than its participation in NATO.)

It is conceivable, then, that collective wants can be provided for, given small numbers, even without a government. NATO may be performing adequately, for example, without being in any way a super-government capable of coercing its members. But the NATO community in this period had only 14 constituents. As population size N increases, each individual member becomes more and more like Friday in the fable above—only a small element in the picture relative to everyone else taken together. So the larger N is, the more inadequate is voluntary provision of the public good,[3] and the stronger is the case for coercive governmental action. Such action can overcome the free-rider problem because, in voting (if only indirectly, through elected delegates) for the supply of certain public goods, citizens are also voting to impose the burden of the costs thereof *upon others as well as upon themselves.*

The difference between the effectiveness of large and small groups in achieving collective ends has an important implication for observed political behavior. Members of a compact "special interest" (for example, businessmen and workers in a particular industry) are few in number compared to the population at large. Nevertheless, they are often successful in achieving political favors like tariffs or subsidies at the expense of the general consuming public. The reason is that the effective influence of the individual citizen-voter upon government is, for the reasons outlined in the preceding section, extremely weak. Filling the vacuum are "pressure groups," which are sub-collectives of individuals interested in pushing particular policies or points of view upon the delegated representatives of the voters. Special interests have two factors on their side in forming pressure groups. First, their motivation is stronger. Since their financial interest is concentrated (as in the case of a tariff affecting a single industry), they gain far more from appropriate political action than any comparably sized group of the general public stand to lose, even though the *entire* public may suffer in the aggregate a much greater loss. Second, being small in number they are more able to overcome the free-rider problem in organizing their pressure group.

[3] While the *under*-provision or shortfall increases with N, nevertheless the *absolute* production of the public good G rises as population grows—if G is a normal superior good. [Verification of this point is left as a challenge for the reader.]

EXAMPLE 16.3
Regulated Electricity Rates

Electricity, as a "natural monopoly," is now governmentally regulated in almost all states. The problem of collective action suggests that *large* consumers of electricity will have an advantage over the multitude of *small* consumers of electricity in forming a pressure group that can influence the political agencies responsible for regulating rates.

This hypothesis was tested by George Stigler and Claire Friedland, making use of data from earlier years when there were still a considerable number of unregulated states. Since it can be presumed that *industrial* users of electricity are relatively large in scale (and small in number) in comparison with *residential* users, the ratio of the residential price to the industrial price is a relevant measure of the hypothesis that large users are favored over small. This ratio alone is not a satisfactory criterion, however, since there may well be differences in the cost of service that would warrant some degree of rate inequality between industrial and residential users. But there is no obvious reason *for the ratio to differ as between regulated and unregulated states.*

Average Ratio $\dfrac{\textit{Residential Price}}{\textit{Industrial Price}}$ for Electricity

	1917	1937
Regulated states	1.616	2.459
Unregulated states	1.445	2.047

Source: G. J. Stigler and C. Friedland, "What Can Regulators Regulate? The Case of Electricity," *Journal of Law and Economics,* v. 5 (Oct. 1962), p. 9.

The data showed that the ratio was indeed substantially higher for the regulated states, consistent with the hypothesis that regulation works to the comparative advantage of large consumers over small consumers.

Of course, the political strength of "special interest" groups is only one side of the picture. It is easier for a small specialized group to organize and bring its weight to bear, but it remains a group small in number. Landlords can organize *against* rent controls more effectively than tenants *for* them, but a politician cannot ignore the fact that there are many more tenant votes than landlord votes. The "pressure group" phenomenon counterbalances somewhat the tendency of the democratic polity to override the interest of minorities. But it does so in a rather capricious way, protecting only those minorities strategically positioned (by reason of concentration) to influence the political process. One important point is that since production is generally a *specialized* activity and consumption an *unspecialized* one, government interventions have historically tended to favor producers over consumers.[4] As we are all *both* producers and consumers, it might

[4]The political success of one important "pro-consumer" intervention, residential rent control, is connected with the fact that consumers *are* somewhat "specialized" when it comes to housing. The single rental transaction typically accounts for a large fraction of consumption budgets. So it may pay renters to form a pressure group, aimed at securing a political determination of the terms of the housing transaction.

be thought that the effects cancel out. But the political measures that favor producers (for example, permitting formation of a cartel) tend to be anti-competitive. This leads to a loss of economic efficiency, apart from possibly objectionable effects upon wealth distribution.

16.C
BUREAUCRACY

So far we have thought of the governing group simply as *elected delegates* of the citizens. But of course the situation is more complicated than that. Because their incentives are different, elected executives will behave differently from elected legislators and both of these differently from elected or appointed judges. We might similarly expect different kinds of decisions from officials on the national, state, and local levels of government, from representatives of majority versus minority parties, and so forth. All of these pose very interesting issues that cannot be taken up here. Instead, let us consider the motivation and behavior of another important group of participants in the political game—the governmental bureaucracy.

The bureaucracy consists of that class of government personnel not responsible for *making* policy decisions but for *implementing* them. Supposedly impartial and neutral, bureaucrats are not subject to election or recall at the hands of the voters. It follows that if bureaucrats really do determine the actual outcomes of decisions, then the ability of citizens to achieve their desires through the political mechanism (i.e., through their control over elected delegates) is even weaker than has previously been indicated.

Now it is an obvious fact of common knowledge that implementation is as important as decision. For all practical purposes, implementation *is* the actual decision. So the bureaucracy surely does have substantial power.

What are the interests of the bureaucracy? Apart from high wages for easy work, a critical aim is *security of tenure*. This not only keeps jobs safe, but provides valued clout: a bureaucrat who could be easily dismissed would have to tread warily in dealing with elected delegates or with outside pressure groups. In modern times, the governmental bureaucracy has achieved extraordinary job security through civil-service regulations that forbid demotion or dismissal except "for cause." While civil-service reform is in many respects preferable to the spoils system, it has nevertheless changed the balance of power within government in favor of the bureaucrats.

In any government agency, a natural aim of the officeholders is *agency growth*. All those involved generally benefit by building empires, by increasing the resources under their control. According to "Parkinson's Law,"[5] no matter how much the business of a governmental unit may fall off, the number of officials will still increase. Let the Royal Navy diminish in size, the Admiralty bureaucracy will grow. Let the colonies declare their independence, Her Majesty's Colonial Office in London will continue to expand. And in the United States the De-

---

[5]C. Northcote Parkinson, *Parkinson's Law* (Boston: Houghton Mifflin, 1957).

partment of Agriculture will go on swelling in budget and employment even while the number of farmers shrinks.

EXAMPLE 16.4
Taxicab Regulation

Taxicab service tends to be regulated under one of two alternative systems: (1) municipal agency, or (2) independent commission. In a study of 33 cities, Ross D. Eckert argued that these modes of regulation are associated with different incentive structures for the regulators.

The decision-making officeholders in a municipal agency have, one would expect, the typical motivations of bureaucrats. As the degree of detailed supervision of the taxicab industry increases, a larger budget and staff will be "needed," with correspondingly higher salaries for the directors of such a massive and important regulatory activity. Independent commissioners, however, are in quite a different position. They generally engage in other public or private activity; their commission service is only a part-time occupation. Complex and detailed taxicab regulation, with consequent need to supervise large staffs, hear complaints, grant exceptions, etc., would require costly sacrifice of their time and effort. And since commissioners normally hold office only for a limited term of years, any long-run return (e.g., an upward trend in salaries for commissioners) that may result from more energetic regulatory activity may go only to benefit their successors in office.

One way of *reducing* the level of regulatory effort is to have a single "responsible" operator of all the taxicabs in a city. Outright monopoly situations are indeed more common in commission-regulated than in agency-regulated cities. But, for a variety of reasons, literal monopoly is rare. Many cities, however, have partial degrees of regulation-imposed monopoly effected through division of the market by quotas, territory assignments, or exclusive taxistands. The hypothesis is that commissioners would prefer this situation, whereas agency bureaucrats would welcome the necessity for elaborate and detailed regulatory dealings with a multiplicity of small operators. The data below show that the hypothesis was verified.

Taxicab Regulatory Status in 1967, for 22 U.S. Cities

	MONOPOLY OR MARKET DIVISION (NUMBER OF CITIES)	NEITHER MONOPOLY NOR MARKET DIVISION (NUMBER OF CITIES)
Commissions	5	1
Agencies	5	22

Source: Ross D. Eckert, "On the Incentives of Regulators: The Case of Taxicabs," *Public Choice*, v. 14 (Spring 1973), p. 90.

POLITICAL CONFLICT

So far we have looked only at the *service state*. Government has been regarded as an instrument whereby citizens engage in "public choice." Certain imperfections were considered: elected delegates may not be entirely motivated to represent the desires of constituents, there is a problem of balancing majority versus minority rights, etc. But what is a much more drastic real-world "imperfection," rulers may not be serving the population at all. The goal of a government might be to fleece and rob its subjects, or perhaps to use them as slaves or cannon fodder. What might be called the *exploitation state* is at least as important historically as the service state.

Actual historical regimes fall somewhere between the two extremes of the service state and the exploitation state. The democratic government of classical Athens made public choices on behalf of an upper class of citizens, while exploiting a lower class of slaves. According to radical critics today, the supposedly democratic governments of the Western world are instruments whereby (depending upon who is talking) the capitalists or the WASPs or the intellectuals are oppressing everyone else. Toward the other end of the spectrum are those governments that scarcely pretend to be democratic—one-party Marxist regimes, for example, or traditional military tyrannies. Even obviously exploitative political systems like these will generally *claim* to be actually serving the population, and to at least a small degree may be doing so.

Let us now go to the opposite extreme and develop the idea that *conflict* rather than "public choice" is the essence of politics. Conflict arises in many contexts: among nations, between rulers and subjects within nations, between criminals and victims, etc. It is also useful sometimes to think of activities like lawsuits or industrial strikes and lockouts as instances of conflict, even though bodily violence may not be involved. Conflict may be said to occur when each party to an interaction is incurring costs in order to impose his will upon the opponent—rather than come to a compromise settlement. From one point of view, conflict is "an agreement to disagree." It is also in a way an educational process: each contender tries to convince the other that he is the one better able to take and to deliver punishment.

Among the important sources of conflict are:

1. *Antipathy:* One party may be willing, from sheer causeless hatred or envy, to incur costs in seeking to injure the other. An example was Hitler's war against the Jews.
2. *Rivalry:* If resources are too scarce to meet the requirements of both parties, one or the other may try to improve his position through aggression. While antipathy leads to hot emotion-laden conflict, rivalry may be deadly yet quite cool. ("I got nothin' against you, Wyatt Earp, but this town ain't big enough for the two of us.")
3. *Over-confidence:* The stronger the belief in one's own chances of winning the battle, the less the willingness to come to a compromise settlement.
4. *Non-enforceability of agreements:* Sometimes both parties might be happy to come to a compromise settlement. But, if there is no way to prevent violation, there is no point in compromise.

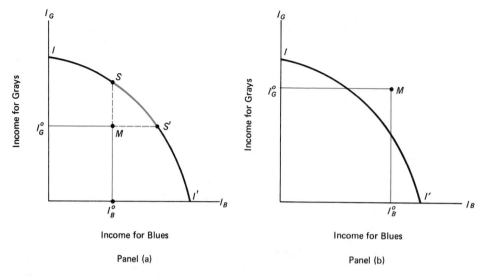

FIGURE 16.3 Confidence and Conflict. In Panel (a) the Blues anticipate that in the event of conflict their benefit, *on average,* will be equivalent to an income of I_B^o. The Grays similarly anticipate I_G^o. There is a region of mutual advantage MSS' achievable by a compromise agreement; the efficient solutions lie along the range SS'. In Panel (b) there is no possibility of a compromise solution.

In Panel (a) of Figure 16.3 the curve II' (like the similar curve in Figure 15.1 of the preceding chapter) shows the Social Opportunity Frontier—the income combinations attainable by two decision-makers.[6] We may think of the two parties here either as individuals or as groups: let us call them the Blues and the Grays. And "income" may stand for territory or for power in addition to, or in place of, ability to purchase consumption goods.

Suppose the Blues believe that in the event of conflict (taking into account the possibility of their losing as well as winning, and allowing for risk-aversion), *on average* their gain will be equivalent to an income of I_B^o. Let I_G^o be the corresponding average outcome anticipated by the Grays. Then, evidently, the roughly triangular area MSS' represents a "region of mutual advantage" wherein both parties can gain by compromise—assuming that a compromise settlement would be enforceable. An *efficient* solution would of course lie somewhere in the range SS' along the opportunity frontier.

Panel (b) represents a contrasting situation where each party has become more *confident* than before about the outcome of a clash. Here there is no region of mutual advantage, so no compromise settlement is possible. Of course, typically one side or the other is mistaken—over-optimistic about its chances of winning the struggle—or very likely both are. Nevertheless, in this situation a battle is inevitable since both contenders expect to do better by fighting than by settling.

[6]The analysis here is based in part upon Donald Wittman, "How a War Ends," *Journal of Conflict Resolution,* v. 23 (Dec. 1979) and David Friedman, "Many, Few, One: Social Harmony and the Shrunken Choice Set," *American Economic Review,* v. 70 (March 1980).

After having experienced the test of battle, one or both parties will very likely revise its attitude. This may not lead to a peaceful settlement, however; while the loser will probably be more willing than before to compromise, the winner may be less willing to do so. On the other hand, both sides will now have become somewhat impoverished by the struggle. So devoting additional resources to war becomes more and more painful, while there may be less and less left to gain from victory. Eventually, the war may end in a compromise—perhaps, though not necessarily, worse for both sides than what they could peacefully have attained in the first place.

Figure 16.3 highlighted the role of *confidence* as a source of conflict. Figure 16.4 illustrates the effect of *rivalry*. Panel (a) represents a strongly rivalrous situation; the shape of the II' curve shows that the interests of the two parties are sharply opposed. Here even relatively pessimistic anticipations I_B^o and I_G^o as to outcome of conflict may not lead to any compromise settlement. Panel (b) represents the opposite situation, where the two parties' interests are strongly complementary—each is highly useful to the other. Accordingly, even if each contender is quite optimistic about his chances in the event of conflict, a compromise settlement might still be preferred by both.

Finally, Figure 16.5 illustrates the role of antipathy (and its opposite, sympathy). In Panel (a) the two parties are antipathetic. For the Blues, Gray income I_G is a *bad* as indicated by the positively sloping indifference curve U_B^o through point M—and similarly for the Grays. The effect is to diminish the size of MSS', the region of mutual advantage, and make peaceful settlement less probable. In Panel (b) on the other hand, the parties are *sympathetic* to one another, making peaceful settlement more likely.

If agreements are not *enforceable*, two parties who otherwise could profit

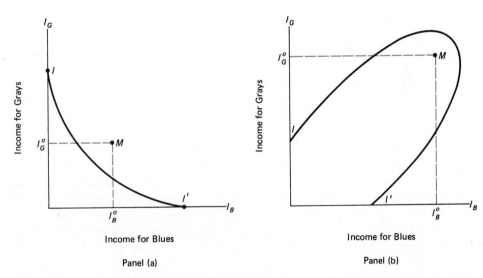

FIGURE 16.4 Rivalry and Conflict. In Panel (a) the two parties are strongly rivalrous, and a compromise settlement is unlikely. In Panel (b) their interests are highly complementary, making a compromise much easier to achieve.

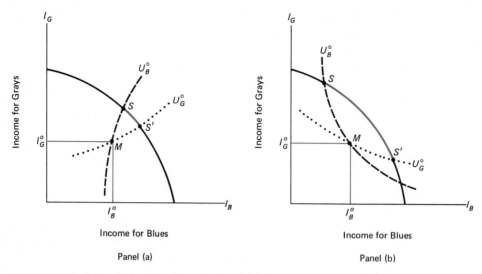

FIGURE 16.5 **Antipathy and Conflict.** In Panel (a) the parties are mutually antipathetic, which diminishes the region of mutual advantage *MSS'* and makes conflict more likely. In Panel (b) the parties are mutually sympathetic, making conflict less likely.

from cooperation may not be able to achieve a mutually advantageous settlement. Recall the Prisoners' Dilemma discussed in Chapter 10. While it is in the private interest of each prisoner to confess regardless of what the other does, the two would be better off if they both kept silent. They would surely agree to keep silent, *provided that each could guarantee living up to the agreement.* But, under the conditions of the Prisoners' Dilemma, such a guarantee is impossible.

There are two main ways of getting people to live up to agreements. First, through a neutral third party. A neutral judicial system to enforce private contracts is one of the main services that a government can provide. Second, some contracts may be *self-enforcing.* Two parties can so tie themselves to one another that it does not pay either to defect. Usually this happens when there is a profitable continuing relationship between them. If firm A has agreed to deliver materials to firm B, one reason for A not to cheat on quantity or quality—apart from the possibility of a lawsuit—may be the fear of permanently losing a valuable customer.

Enforceability of agreements is a matter of degree. Even if a judicial system stands behind contracts, going to court is expensive and judges are not infallible. As for "self-enforcing" agreements, they will be adhered to only so long as violating them remains unprofitable. So anyone who has made a deal must always be looking over his shoulder at the possibility that the other party will not carry out his share of the bargain. Furthermore, if he himself is just on the edge of deciding to renege, fear that the other party may be about to do the same is likely to provide the decisive push.

The real or seeming profitability of the conflict option raises very serious questions about the validity of Coase's Theorem (as discussed in the preceding chapter). That theorem says essentially that all mutually advantageous agree-

522

ments will be undertaken—and, by implication, adhered to. We saw above that Coase's Theorem appeared to "prove too much" in suggesting that monopoly would not permanently exist, that individuals would voluntarily contract with one another so as to internalize all externalities, etc. But what is much more drastic, the Coase Theorem is inconsistent with the persistence of war, crime, and politics! In fact, the Coase Theorem—with its partner, Adam Smith's Invisible Hand—is valid only under very ideal conditions. Certain of these conditions were already mentioned in the preceding chapter: e.g., well-defined property rights and absence of transaction costs. But more important, *individuals will be led by self-interest to serve others only to the extent that agreement appears, for each of them, to be more profitable than conflict.* Given the prevalence of antipathy, rivalry, and overconfidence plus the limited enforceability of compromise settlements, we can be quite sure that conflict (war, crime, and politics) will be with us for a long time.

Economists have just barely begun to analyze conflict. We can expect future research to look into such questions as (1) the advantages of offensive versus defensive strategies, (2) the circumstances that sometimes keep conflict limited rather than total, (3) the "production function" that converts resource inputs into chances for victory, (4) the additional issues raised by three-sided or even more complex struggles, and (5) the extent to which political developments like the size of nations or the balance of influence among social classes are explainable by coercive strength. But enough has been said to indicate that the *economics of conflict* is just as important as the *economics of exchange and markets.*

16.E
THE SCOPE OF GOVERNMENT

Perhaps the key scientific questions in political economy are: What are the forces determining the *types* of activities carried on through government, and the *scale* on which those activities are conducted? The economic approach suggests that observed activities reflect the goals and the relative strengths of the persons and groups participating in the day-to-day decisions of government, interacting according to the constitutional "rules of the game" in the political sphere.

16.E.1 ☐ Functions of Government

Standard statistical classifications of the expenditures of federal, state, and local government units in the United States do not always permit an entirely satisfactory breakdown by function. Table 16.1 is condensed from official data.

As a first step to understanding, we can categorize the various types of observed government activities under four main functions: (1) defense, (2) law, (3) production, and (4) redistribution.

1. *Defense:* The absolutely essential minimal function that government must provide for any society is protection against external and internal enemies. The data of Table 16.1 show that National Defense and International Relations accounted for about 20% of government general expenditures in

1971–72. To this should be added the bulk of expenses under the Police category; also, Interest on Public Debt in large part represents past military expenditures; and finally some share of Other might well be attributed to Defense. Overall, some 30% of U. S. government expenditures in fiscal 1979 can be regarded as accounted for by the Defense function.

2. *Law:* To operate at any level of effectiveness, members of a society cannot live completely at the whim of the governors. Rather, there must be some system of rights or property defining how individuals are permitted to act, alone or in association with others. The efficiency of a system of market exchange, in particular, depends (as we have seen) upon a well-defined structure of property rights. This system of rights, with correlative duties thus placed on others not to interfere with those rights, is *law.* Since law must be enforced to be useful, it cannot exist without government. (Hence the nullity of so-called *international law.*) The budgetary burden of the legal system (legislatures, courts, etc.) is not large, however. The costs constitute only some fractions of relatively small categories like Police and Financial Administration. (In early times, law was actually dispensed at a profit by royal courts, and fees for provision of justice served as an important source of government revenue.)

TABLE 16.1

Direct General Expenditures of All Governments by Function and Level of Government, Fiscal Year 1979 (millions of dollars)

FUNCTION	FEDERAL	STATE	LOCAL	TOTAL	PERCENT OF TOTAL
Total	$304,659	$124,554	$201,470	$630,683	100.0
National defense and international relations	128,529	—	—	128,529	20.3
Education	9,979	31,517	87,932	129,427	20.5
Highways	561	17,079	11,361	29,001	4.6
Public welfare	18,722	28,742	11,676	59,140	9.4
Hospitals	4,698	10,221	10,818	25,737	4.1
Health	4,235	3,565	3,614	11,414	1.8
Police	1,724	1,825	10,383	13,931	2.2
Natural resources	25,632	3,594	1,112	30,338	4.8
Housing and urban renewal	3,237	214	4,510	7,961	1.3
Air transportation	2,299	258	1,648	4,205	0.7
Water transport and terminals	1,797	304	741	2,842	0.5
Social insurance administration	2,292	1,799	7	4,098	0.6
Financial administration	4,808	5,300	8,512	18,621	3.0
Interest on general debt	48,768	5,790	7,197	61,755	9.8
Other*	47,378	14,346	41,960	103,684	16.4

Source: The Tax Foundation, *Facts and Figures on Government Finance,* 1981, p. 17.

*Includes postal service, space research and technology, correction, sewers, libraries, sanitation, fire, parking facilities, local parks, general (state-local) public buildings, and unallocable services.

Provision of a system of defense, and the administration of justice, are universally recognized as *essential* functions of government. Beyond this, however, governments may take a more or less activist role in guiding the economic performance of society—the production and distribution of goods and services.

3. *Production:* Government, as explained just above, is uniquely able to make the collective choices involved in the provision of *public goods*. In Table 16.1, the expenditures (apart from those already listed under Defense and Law) that contain important public-good elements include Education, Transportation, and Other (Space Research and Technology). Even on a fairly high estimate, the total of all expenditures going to the purchase of public goods other than Defense can only be around 30% of the aggregate of government spending.

Evidently, government is also in the business of providing a vast range of ordinary *private* goods. Postal Service, Social Insurance,[7] and Housing all represent goods that are essentially similar to commodities or services that are also provided privately—or surely would be so provided were it not (as in the case of the government's postal monopoly) illegal to do so. Health and Hospitals contain a small public-good component (preventing epidemics), but for the most part these expenditures also represent provision of a private good—personal medical care. Even Education (although counted above within the public-good category) is much more importantly a private than a public good; the benefits of governmental expenditures for education go *primarily* to the educated person, and only secondarily to the remainder of society.

Apart from the actual provision of public or private goods, modern governments affect the productive efficiency of the economy in a variety of important ways. The provision and control of *money* facilitates the process of exchange.[8] The *stabilization of economic activity*—prevention of depressions, inflations, etc.—is also generally recognized as an appropriate function of modern government.[9] Anti-monopoly activities of agencies like the Anti-trust Division of the Department of Justice, and the regulation of "natural monopolies" through governmental commissions, are designed to or can be defended as tending to improve efficiency in the allocation of resources.

Government policy toward monopoly provides an interesting test case for observing the interaction of politically powerful groups. To the extent

[7]Social Security and other social insurance arrangements are not included in the data of Table 16.1. The receipts and expenditures for these activities are regarded as going into or coming out of "trust funds" rather than the regular government accounts.

[8]It is an interesting issue in monetary theory whether the government role is inherent in the existence of money. Privately produced moneys, it might be argued, could serve as well as or better than government money.

[9]Unfortunately, it is easier to *recognize* this function than to perform it! Some observers wonder whether governmental attempts to stabilize the economy have made things worse instead of better.

that the political process tends (as remarked above) to give more weight to *producer* than to *consumer* interests, we might well doubt the effectiveness of government in controlling monopoly. And indeed, the charge has been made that regulatory agencies are often captured by the special interests they are supposed to be guarding against. On the federal level the Interstate Commerce Commission (regulating surface transportation), the Civil Aeronautics Board (regulating the airlines), and the Federal Communications Commission (regulating radio and television) have all been the targets of such charges. And in cases like the cartelization of many sectors of agricultural marketing (see Example 8.5), the fact that the aim of government action is higher prices for producers at the expense of consumers is scarcely a secret. On the other hand, whatever the wisdom of the "trust-busting" activities of the Department of Justice and the Federal Trade Commission, these agencies are generally regarded as independent of producer control. How the observed differences of behavior stem from the motivations, legal status, and incentives of the participants is a topic largely remaining to be explained.

4. *Redistribution:* An important activity of modern government is redistribution of income or wealth—in democratic countries at least, primarily from richer to poorer classes. In Table 16.1 the category of Public Welfare (9.4% of aggregate expenditures) is explicitly redistributive. But redistribution is also an important aspect of other categories, and indeed helps explain what might otherwise be regarded as anomalies. Consider the expenditures under the heading of Health and Hospitals. A typical procedure here is for government agencies to provide a relatively low quality of hospital or medical care, at zero price or at a very low price, to all who choose to use that service. But since the rich can afford and generally will prefer to buy somewhat better health care privately, only the poor choose the government service. The effect is a redistribution of income "in kind" to the poor. To greater or lesser degree, this analysis applies to public housing (all but the very poor will prefer private housing), to public education (the rich can afford private schools), to subsidized public transit (the rich travel by private car), etc.

EXAMPLE 16.5
Income Redistribution Through Government

For the year 1976 the Congressional Budget Office (CBO) attempted to summarize the distribution of family incomes before and after government taxes and budgetary expenditures. Their results are summarized in the Table. This Table indicates, for example, that the lowest 20% of families in 1976 initially received only 0.3% of aggregate family income, but redistribution through government taxes and transfers raised their share to 7.2%.

Redistribution of Family Incomes, 1976

| QUINTILE | PRE-TAX/ PRE-TRANSFER INCOMES | | NET TAX TRANSFER | POST-TAX/ POST-TRANSFER INCOMES | |
	Billions of Dollars	Percent	Billions of Dollars	Billions of Dollars	Percent
Lowest	$ 3.3	0.3%	$+ 71.8	$ 75.1	7.2
Second	76.3	7.2	+ 43.4	119.7	11.5
Third	173.7	16.3	− 1.1	172.6	16.6
Fourth	276.1	26.0	− 32.1	243.7	23.4
Highest	534.1	50.2	−104.4	429.7	41.4

In discussing these data, E. K. Browning and J. M. Browning[a] pointed out several significant facts. First, the true inequality of personal income distribution is not nearly so great as the Table suggests, because *family size* is much smaller in the low-income quintiles. In fact, the lowest 20% of families comprise only 13.8% of the population, while the highest 20% of families comprise 26% of the population. (The low-income "families" are often single persons whose bad economic position is due to ill-health, widowhood, etc.) Second, the CBO study counted only a fraction, around 20%, of the in-kind transfers made by government. In particular, such an important category as public education was omitted. A more complete tabulation would have further reduced the seeming inequality remaining in the "post-tax/post-transfer" columns. And third, the distressingly low figure for the "pre-tax/pre-transfer" incomes earned by the lowest quintile (0.3% of the total) is itself partly a result of the availability of government transfer income. In the case of the elderly, for example, it has been shown that older people have responded to government support by working less and saving less (see the discussion of Social Security in Chapter 14).

[a]Edgar K. Browning and Jacquelene M. Browning, *Public Finance and the Price System* (New York: Macmillan, 1979), pp. 203–205.

The governmental redistributive activity revealed by the preceding example suggests that the power of the vote is not as feeble as might have been inferred from the discussion in Section 16.B. In a one-person one-vote democracy, electoral strength will be distributed more equally than income. It then seems reasonable that the poor will be able to use the political process to convert some of their comparatively greater voting power into money income. And the higher the income bracket, the greater the weight of numbers and political power in the hands of those lower down on the ladder—hence, the more punitive the burden of fiscal redistribution that can be expected by those in that bracket.

Surprisingly, this argument is not ironclad. In a system of self-interested majority voting, and if we rule out political coalitions of both ends against the middle, the *median* voter—the one halfway up the wealth distribution—is in a position of exceptional power. By allying with those of less wealth, this voter can bring about a redistribution of wealth downward; by voting with those of greater wealth, a redistribution upward. If wealth is initially distributed unequally, there must be more wealth above the median voter than below. Thus, one might think, an inevitable tendency exists for the median citizen to vote with the poor against the rich. But a simple numerical example shows that such an outcome is not at all inevitable. Suppose that there is one rich voter R with wealth 300, one median voter M with wealth 200, and one poor voter P with wealth 100—i.e., a wealth distribution (300, 200, 100). Now, let M form a coalition with P. Then almost the best M can do for himself by political redistribution would be a revised wealth arrangement like (250, 249, 101). Here, of the 50 wealth units confiscated from R only 1 went to P, with M gaining the remaining 49. This seems quite profitable. Nevertheless, M might do better combining with R against P! Specifically, a voting coalition of M and R might achieve the revised distribution (301, 299, 0). Here the median voter gains 99 units going along with R, far better than the 49 won by lining up with P. This perhaps explains why throughout much of history government has often served to grind the faces of the poor in favor of those above them on the wealth scale. Just why democratic societies in modern times have generally engaged in governmental redistribution in favor of the poor is somewhat of an unresolved problem.

It ought to be remembered, also, that expenditures *on behalf of* the poor are not necessarily payments *to* the poor. In a program like federally funded job training, for example, the bulk of the actual payments may go to middle-class bureaucrats—specifically, to teachers and administrators. The benefits to poor trainees are "in kind," and may or may not translate into higher future cash incomes. Hence the interests of the poor and of the bureaucratic class in the redistributive process are intertwined.

16.E.2 ☐ Instruments of Government Policy

Government can carry out its functions either directly or indirectly. Given the objective of achieving a higher level of education of the population, for example, there are still policy choices to be made. Government might subsidize education (in the limit, make it free) thus *inducing* consumers to choose more education voluntarily. Or government might declare education compulsory, thus *forcing* consumers to buy more—or accept more, if free. Current practice in the United States is to have education both free and compulsory up to a certain school-leaving age, and optional (but still more or less subsidized) thereafter.

Perhaps an even more important policy choice is whether or not government is actually to *provide* the service. Education might be made free and compulsory, and yet provided entirely through a system of private schools. The government could reimburse private schools for students enrolled, setting standards and monitoring performance, without actually being in the business of hiring teachers, erecting buildings, etc.

At various times and places, a surprising variety of what we customarily think of as government-provided goods have actually been produced privately, sometimes at state expense, sometimes not. The bounty-hunters of the pioneer West tracked down criminals. Toll roads and canals have been private businesses. There are private arbitration courts today that reduce the need to use public justice. There is one single service that, one would suppose, *must* be provided by government itself if it is to remain government—defense. Yet even this service has at times been provided commercially, by firms supplying mercenary soldiers. (Experience on this score has been largely unfavorable, however; a mercenary chief strong enough to be useful in defense is all too inclined to take over the government himself.[10]) Still, *military research* today is largely produced privately, on government contract.

The interests of the bureaucracy, it is clear, lie in the larger scale of agency activity made possible by *direct* government provision of goods and services. The incentives of the other major actors on the political scene are mixed, however. The choice between direct and indirect instruments for carrying out government functions, like the scope of the functions themselves, remains a largely unexplored scientific question.

16.E.3 ☐ A Scientific Issue in Political Economy: Growth of Government

A striking phenomenon of modern times has been the steady growth of the government sector. Despite the hot political debates that have greeted the successive steps of government expansion, there is surprisingly little scientific understanding of the forces tending to bring it about.

The first and most obvious explanation is the increasing burden of the Defense function. As the technology of attack and destruction has improved so fantastically (nuclear bombs, intercontinental missiles, etc.), the complexity and cost of defense have grown correspondingly. But suppose we entirely exclude the Defense function. The scope of government has grown enormously in the non-defense sector as well.

[10]Machiavelli, *The Prince,* Chap. 12.

EXAMPLE 16.6 _____
Growth of Government

Various stages in the expansion of the overall government sector in the United States are shown in the following Table.

As may be seen, government expenditures have more than kept up with both the real growth of the economy and the inflation of prices, so as to constitute a steadily increasing fraction of GNP. While big jumps in expenditures have typically taken place in wartime, peacetime civilian expenditures as a percentage of GNP have also grown steadily.

DATE	TOTAL EXPENDITURES		CIVILIAN EXPENDITURES	
	$ Billions	Percent of GNP	$ Billions	Percent of GNP
1890	$ 0.8	6.5	$ 0.7	5.0
1902	1.5	7.3	1.2	5.8
1913	3.2	7.8	2.8	6.8
1922	9.3	12.6	7.9	10.7
1929	10.7	10.4	9.5	9.2
1940	17.6	17.6	15.5	15.5
1950	65.9	23.1	42.2	14.8
1960	136.1	27.0	84.4	16.7
1970	313.0	32.2	225.1	23.1

Source: R. A. Musgrave and P. B. Musgrave, *Public Finance in Theory and Practice* (New York: McGraw-Hill, 1973), p. 118.

Basically, there are two possible lines of explanation for the phenomenon of expansion of government. The first gives primary weight to the *voluntarist* or public-choice aspect of political decision. In this view, government has expanded in response to desires on the part of the community for the types of services government can best provide. The second approach emphasizes, in contrast, *changes in the balance of political power* permitting certain organized groups on the political scene to increase their exploitation of others through expanded government.

Voluntaristic explanations might run in terms of some or all of the following points: (1) Public goods, in contrast with private goods, might have income elasticity greater than unity (see Chapter 5). Then with rising national income over time, citizen-voters have desired more of the public goods that government characteristically provides. (2) With increasing wealth and population, the limited geographical space we inhabit has become more and more crowded. In our daily lives we are therefore increasingly imposing *externalities* (see Chapter 15) upon one another—hence the need for more government control of activities that could have safely been left private in a more dispersed and isolated society. (3) The technical efficiency of government may have grown relative to the private sector. With advances like computers it has become possible to conduct enterprises on a much larger scale than previously. Government, as the largest-scale enterprise in society, may have gained in relative effectiveness.

Explanations that run in terms of exploitation and political power, on the other hand, might point to considerations like the following. (1) The government bureaucracy, as it grows in numbers, becomes an increasingly potent political force. Wars and defense crises that require gigantic budgetary expansions leave in their wake a mass of officeholders, with sufficient political clout to resist budgetary contraction when the crises pass. (2) An important sociological development with consequences for the political structure has been the growth of the *educated class* in the population (say, those with college degrees). Educated persons are *relatively* better equipped to achieve status and power through government rather than in business. Legislators, bureaucrats, and other important actors on the political scene are themselves members of the educated class and inclined to be responsive to its interests, especially as the educated are much more politically active than the population at large. (3) A related point is that the extraordinary and continuing advances in ability to communicate with large audiences—due to improvements in printing, the spread of literacy, and of course radio and television—have made it increasingly possible to weld large numbers of people into exploitative political movements and pressure groups.

The degree of truth in each of these points, and the comparative explanatory values of the public-choice versus exploitation approaches, remain unsettled problems in political economy.

☐ SUMMARY OF CHAPTER 16

While market transactions are voluntary, the political sphere is characterized by involuntary interactions. The individuals who comprise the government are able, with the ultimate backing of force, to dictate to the rest of us.

The two polar models of government are the *service state* versus the *exploitation state*. The service state is a system of "public choice," in which citizen-consumers express their desires by voting. The exploitation state, in contrast, is a government whose rulers are in conflict with their subjects, seeking only to extract resources from them.

In an ideally democratic service state, competition for political leadership acts like competition in the marketplace. Just as competition for sales forces firms to satisfy consumers' desires, competition for office forces political parties to satisfy citizens' wishes.

Market competition has serious imperfections, but the imperfections of political competition are even more severe. Citizens vote only at relatively rare intervals; there are few political parties among which to choose (commonly, just two); and many issues are bundled together in the position of each candidate. Under majority rule, there is the very serious problem of adequate provision for minority desires. "Log-rolling" allows intense minority preferences on some issues to be exchanged for votes on other issues. In principle, log-rolling or even direct purchase of votes will lead to Pareto-optimal outcomes. Another source of imperfection is the fact that a voter has little motivation to incur the informational costs necessary to cast an intelligent ballot.

When it comes to public or collective goods, the *free-rider problem* limits the amounts that individuals will voluntarily provide. Government can overcome this limitation. Everyone might agree to a collective purchase when costs are to be shared via the tax system. Since it is costly to influence government policy, and the benefits are shared by many individuals, citizens face a similar free-rider problem in trying to get their way in a political system. Compact special interests have the advantage in forming pressure groups. This explains why democratic governments tend to favor producer interests at the expense of consumers.

The individuals comprising the government fall into a number of different categories, with differing motivations. One important category is the bureaucracy, the permanent (non-elected) personnel who actually implement political decisions. Bureaucrats are motivated to seek security of tenure in office, and to increase the size of their agencies.

Models of *conflict,* as between rulers and subjects, are only beginning to be studied by economists. Conflict is promoted by emotional antipathy, by rivalry for resources, by over-confidence in one's ability to deliver and bear up under punishment, and by lack of enforceability of agreements. Since in the real world all agreements are only imperfectly enforceable, Coase's Theorem (that all mutually advantageous bargains will be achieved) can be valid only to a limited extent. Hence we cannot expect the abolition of war, crime, and politics.

Among the key questions of political economy are the determinants of the types of activities conducted by government, and of the scale of such activities. The service-state explanation argues that government has a special advantage in providing public goods, and the traditional minimal functions of government—defense and justice—are indeed public goods. But present-day governments also supply a vast range of what are mainly private goods: postal services, housing, insurance, education, etc. Government also regulates the private economy in a variety of ways. Sometimes this may be in response to service-state motivations (prevention of depression), sometimes to help some groups exploit others (tariffs on imports). Redistribution of income or wealth is another important governmental activity with both public-good and exploitative aspects. Detailed scientific explanations of the nature and scope of government, and in particular of the seemingly irrepressible tendency of the modern state apparatus to grow in size and in influence over the private sector, remain largely unresolved problems for political economy.

☐ QUESTIONS FOR CHAPTER 16

MAINLY FOR REVIEW

*R1. Why is the "public choice" approach to the problem of political behavior particularly amenable to economic analysis? What other approaches are there?

*R2. What are some of the major obstacles preventing the expression of the "will of the people" through the political system? How are these analogous to, and how different from, the difficulties of the market system?

R3. How may *delegation* of decision-making power to political representatives lead to decisions diverging from the desires of constituents? Considering the corporation as a kind of political system, what protections and escape hatches do stockholders have that may not be available to members of the polity?

*R4. Under what circumstances does the "free rider" problem emerge? How valid is the assertion that all government is fundamentally a response to the free-rider problem?

R5. How do the goals and opportunities of bureaucrats differ from those of elected officials? How do they differ from those of managers of private firms?

*The answers to asterisked questions appear at the end of the book.

R6. How are the administrative decisions of a commissioner with a limited period of office likely to differ from those of a lifetime civil servant?

*R7. Would the fidelity of the political system to citizen desires be improved by any or all of the following: more frequent elections, more numerous legislatures, elected rather than appointed judges, the spoils system rather than the merit system in civil service? Comment.

*R8. Is a unanimous consent rule, in which dissident votes must be purchased, an ideal political system—apart from transaction costs? Does the process of "log-rolling" provide some approximation of this result? What are some objections to log-rolling?

R9. Under what political mechanisms or situations do majorities tend to exploit minorities? Under what mechanisms or situations is it the other way around?

R10. Show how emotional antipathy, rivalry for resources, and over-confidence all tend to promote conflict.

R11. In a situation where there would be a mutual gain from agreement, show how agreement might not be achieved in the absence of outside enforcement.

*R12. What are "self-enforcing agreements"? Give an example.

FOR FURTHER THOUGHT AND DISCUSSION

*T1. If votes could be bought for money, would *both* the rich and the poor be better off in accordance with the mutual advantage of trade? What is the objection to buying votes for money?

*T2. In market competition among firms, economic profit tends to be eliminated (the "zero-profit theorem" of Chapter 7). Does something analogous tend to occur in political competition between parties? Why or why not?

*T3. Which is more likely to gain legislative approval: a bill that would simply redistribute cash from the rich to the poor, or one to establish a bureaucracy to provide services to the poor? Explain.

*T4. Services that are *financed* by government need not actually be *produced* in the government sector. Give an example where government arranges with private enterprise for production of government-financed services. Give examples of activities paid for by the private sector but actually produced by government. Can you explain these developments?

T5. Why is there a risk that a regulatory agency may be "captured" by the industry it is intended to supervise?

*T6. Suppose there were a sudden unexpected increase in demand for a product now provided through the government sector. Would you expect any systematic differences in the price–quantity response as compared with a product provided through the private sector? What about the response to a decrease in demand? What about responses to increases or decreases in cost of production?

T7. Under a system that might be called "open corruption," government officials (including judges) could sell their decisions to the highest bidder. How bad would this be?

*T8. What explains the steady growth of the government sector relative to the private sector in the past century? Why was there a relative decline in the government sector during the era of industrialization in Great Britain?

ANSWERS

CHAPTER 1

R1. (a) Economics is a set of models or theories whose implications provide testable propositions about the real world. These models must stand or fall on the accuracy of their predictions. It is this use of evidence to judge theories that is scientific.

(b) Vegetables will be cheaper in season than out of season. People will seldom be observed throwing money away. Advertisers will claim that their products are better than competitors' products. To take a more extended example: sharply higher gasoline prices will tend to reduce auto travel generally, and also to lower average highway speeds (with a consequent reduction in accidents). It will also encourage sales of smaller cars, and thus lead Detroit to produce new models aiming at gas economy. In the longer run a trend to more compact cities will be observed. (Of course, all such predictions must be understood in an "other things equal" sense.)

(c) Certainly, economic science cannot predict everything. We have little or no idea as to causes of changes in tastes or social attitudes (the Protestant ethic versus "Consciousness III"), or as to determinants of ideological movements like fascism or Marxism or Christianity, or as to social trends like growth of government. And even important issues of a more narrowly defined "economic" nature, such as causes of business fluctuations, remain unresolved.

R2. (a) Behavior may be defined as rational either in terms of *method* of decision (the choice is made by calculating the costs and benefits of alternative actions) or in terms of *results* (the action chosen turns out to be well-suited for achieving one's goals).

(b) In terms of *method,* a prospective wagerer at roulette might calculate the odds and observe the behavior of the wheel before choosing a number. It would be irrational to place a bet on the basis of a dream or heavenly vision. In terms of *results,* it's probably irrational to bet at all.

(c) Aggregated over many individuals, a limited degree of individual rationality will show up as a tendency toward rational behavior for the group as a whole. Even if the rational element is small, it operates in a consistent and predictable direction.

R7. (a) In a market economy, self-interested individuals will devote their resources to satisfying others by providing desired goods and services. What others are willing to pay enables the sellers to earn higher income and so better satisfy their own desires.

(b)(c)(d) No. If their own income is not increased by serving others, self-interested individuals will not do so.

R9. (a) "Real" flow are flows of goods or services (e.g., lamb chops, labor). "Financial" flows are flows of general purchasing power (money). Each flow represents one side of a class of transaction. Goods or services are traded for general purchasing power.

(b) In the "product market," firms trade the goods and services that they produce to consumers for dollars. In the "factor market," consumers in their capacity as resource-owners trade their factor services to firms for dollars. The dollars that consumers can pay for goods and services must match what they receive for providing factor services. Similarly, the dollars that firms pay for factor services are those which they receive for the goods and services they produce.

T1. (a) Yes, *other things equal.* (If other things were not equal, a state or nation with capital punishment might also be found to have a high murder rate—if, for example, it was the high frequency of murder that led to the imposition of the death penalty in that jurisdiction.)

(b) Yes. Increasing this tax exemption lowers the cost of having children and so should result (other things equal) in an increase in the birth rate.

T2. If insurance companies refused to recognize "mental illness" as an insurable category of sickness, and if the government did not finance treatment under Medicare, doctors would be less motivated to diagnose patients' psychological problems as "disease." This would surely lower the reported incidence of "mental illness." Making medical treatment more costly would also induce potential patients to confront their problems rather than accept the dependent status of being "sick." Note that these predicted effects do *not* depend upon whether Dr. Szasz's theory about mental illness is in fact correct.

T5. The principle of the Invisible Hand applies to *market* interactions, which are voluntary and mutual in nature. Since the kinds of interactions mentioned in this question (crime, etc.) are not voluntary market exchanges, self-serving behavior may not benefit others.

T6. Drivers, being safer than before, would probably take a little less care to avoid accidents. Thus, *pedestrian* deaths might rise, though *driver* deaths would not.

T7. Dr. Johnson probably had in mind the Invisible Hand. Charles Baudelaire probably had in mind his publisher's refusing to give him a bigger advance on his royalties.

CHAPTER 2

R1. (a) Optimization. (b) Equilibrium. (c) Equilibrium. (d) Optimization.
(e) Equilibrium. (f) Optimization.

R3. The price of a good X is the amount of another good (usually money) that must be given up in order to acquire a unit of X. Consequently, price is a ratio of amounts, or a ratio of quantities (money/X).

R6. Yes. Shifting the supply curve up by $\$T$ leads to a solution at the intersection of the *gross* (of tax) supply curve with the original demand curve. Shifting the demand curve down by $\$T$ leads to a solution at the intersection of the *net* (of tax) demand curve with the original supply curve. As the only difference between gross and net supply or demand curves is a vertical displacement of $\$T$, the intersections take place at the same quantity. The intersection of the gross supply curve with the demand curve determines the gross price. The intersection of the net demand curve with the supply curve determines the net (of tax) price. But, of course, it is unnecessary to carry out both constructions; either suffices since the gross price and net price are related by $P^+ \equiv P^- + T$.

R7. (a) Both. (b) Raise price paid by consumers. (c), (d) Lower price received by sellers.

R9. (a) A meaningful price ceiling must be set *below* the equilibrium price, and a meaningful price floor must be set *above* the equilibrium price.
(b) Because trade is voluntary, it is the *smaller* of the desired transaction magnitudes (quantity supplied or quantity demanded) that determines the actual quantity traded. Price ceilings decrease the quantity that sellers are willing to offer. Price floors decrease the quantity that consumers wish to buy. Both decrease the actual quantity traded in the market.
(c) If a "meaningful" price floor, above the equilibrium level, is supported, sellers are able to complete some sales for which there are no demanders (apart from the supporting agency). Transactions then depend solely on the existence of supply at that price. If the floor price is above equilibrium, the quantity sold will increase. The supporting agency, however, will accumulate inventories.

R12. (a) May be true or false. (b) True. (c) False. (d) May be true or false. (e) True.
(f) May be true or false.

R13. The "better approximation" of Marginal Revenue assigns the per-unit incremental change in revenue, that takes place over a quantity interval, to the mid-point of the interval rather than to one or the other of the endpoints. Since *MR* varies from point to point over the entire interval, this procedure almost always provides a much more accurate estimate.

T1. (a) The tax would have a *small* effect on quantity exchanged in the market, a *small* effect on the gross price paid by buyers, but a *large* effect on net price to sellers. (The result here is seen more clearly if the demand curve is shifted down, rather than the supply curve up.)
(b) The steep supply curve means that suppliers are willing to offer even a slightly larger quantity only at a much higher price. Since the tax reduces quantity sold by lowering the *net* demand, the net price received by sellers falls sharply. The gross price paid by consumers rises, but only slightly, since the market quantity declines just slightly.

T3. (a) Since it would be more costly to operate automobiles, the demand curve for cars would shift to the left, leading to a fall in their price.

(b) The prices of big, heavy cars ("gas-guzzlers") would fall more.

T4. (a) A change in economic data occurs, affecting demand or supply (or both). The new supply–demand equilibrium is attained with no transactions taking place at "wrong" prices. In effect, the new equilibrium is arrived at instantaneously.

(b) In the real world, these conditions are never precisely met. But in a market where traders are well informed, the model may be a close approximation of reality.

T6. (a) Wherever the Roman armies marched, the demand for foodstuffs increased because of the addition of military demands to civilian demands. This increase in demand resulted in an increase in equilibrium price.

(b) Diocletian's edict set a price ceiling below the (new) equilibrium price. As a result, there must have been unsatisfied buyers. It is likely that Diocletian's armies made up a large portion of these unsatisfied buyers. So either efforts to evade the edict were successful or Diocletian's armies went hungry, unless indeed they simply confiscated the food they wanted. (See Jacob Burckhardt, *The Age of Constantine the Great* [New York: Pantheon, 1949], Chap. 2.)

T7. Average and marginal magnitudes are per-unit magnitudes. For income taxes, the appropriate per-unit dimensions are dollars per dollar. Because the units are the same in the numerator and the denominator, they cancel and the resulting dimension is a pure percentage.

T8. With such sparse data it is essential to use the "better approximation." At $Q = 0$, 3, 6 the Total Revenues are respectively $R = 0, 60, 72$. The upward variation from $Q = 3$ to $Q = 6$ provides an estimate of $(72 - 60)/3 = 4$ for the Marginal Revenue at $Q = 4\frac{1}{2}$. The downward variation from $Q = 3$ to $Q = 0$ provides an estimate of $(60 - 0)/3 = 20$ for the Marginal Revenue at $Q = 1\frac{1}{2}$. Interpolating, we obtain the approximation $MR = 12$ at $Q = 3$.

CHAPTER 3

R1. (a) violates the Axiom of Comparison. (b) expresses indifference, but does not violate the laws. (c) indicates *inconsistency,* and thus also violates the Axiom of Comparison.

R4. Utility is simply an indicator of preference ranking. Of two bundles, the fact that one is preferred indicates that its utility is higher.

R6. Since ordinal utility indicates only direction of preference, only the *signs* and not the quantitative increments of utility can be determined as amount consumed rises.

R8. (a) Ordinal. (b) Cardinal. (c) Interpersonal comparability.

T1. No.

T3. Placement in a horse race, or a tennis ladder, or a job seniority list. An interesting scientific example is a measure commonly used for *hardness,* based on the relation "scratches." Thus, diamond is harder than glass, and glass is harder than chalk, but this measure does not indicate *how much* harder.

T5. Any shape that is symmetrical across the 45° line. This would indicate, for example, that I am indifferent between the combination "His Income is $2000 while My Income is $1000" and the combination "My Income is $2000 while His Income is $1000."

T6. (a) No.

(b) The preference map would take the form of rays out of the origin. Along any single ray, representing a fixed *ratio* of "My Income" to "His Income," the individual would be equally happy. For such an individual the preference directions would be such that "My Income" is a good, while "His Income" is a bad.

CHAPTER 4

R3. (a) The budget line is the northeast boundary of an individual's market opportunity set. It is the locus of the achievable consumption bundles if the individual spends all of his income.

(b) The equation of the budget line is $I = P_x x + P_y y$.

(c) The slope of the budget line depends upon the relative prices of the goods X and Y. This slope will be $-P_x/P_y$.

R4. The optimum of the consumer is found geometrically as the point on the budget line touching the highest achievable indifference curve. If both goods are consumed, this will be an interior solution. If only one good is consumed (if the budget line touches the highest indifference curve at one axis), this will be a corner solution.

R6. (a) The Consumption Balance Equation is $MU_x/P_x = MU_y/P_y$. The Substitution Equivalence Equation is $MRS_C = MRS_E$ (or, slope of indifference curve = slope of budget line). The Consumption Balance Equation can be reduced to the Substitution Equivalence Equation, but not vice versa. This is because the CBE requires cardinal utility while the SEE requires only ordinal utility. (Cardinal utility implies ordinal utility, but not vice versa.)

(b) Both equations apply to interior solutions. At a corner solution an *inequality* will ordinarily hold, dictating spending all one's income on one of the commodities.

R10. (a) If the IEP has a positive slope, the Engel Curve for each good will have positive slope.

(b) The Engel Expenditure Curve for each good will have a positive slope, but this slope will not exceed unity (the slope of the 45° line).

(c) If X is an inferior good, the Engel Curve will have negative slope.

R13. If the Law of Demand holds, the PEP never curls back (toward the northwest).

R17. As long as a commodity X is a *good* (rather than a neuter or a bad), those receiving vouchers for purchase of X will consume at least the voucher equivalent. For those previously consuming less than this, the voucher will always increase consumption. For this reason, vouchers are particularly effective (relative to subsidies) in increasing consumption among persons who would otherwise have consumed little or none of a good.

T1. (a) An experiment could reveal the *maximum* amount of Y an individual might be willing to pay for a small increment of X. This would be an approximation of the MRS_C.

(b) No known experiment could reveal Marginal Utility.

T3. (a) In moving northwest, the PEP is entering regions of higher y but lower x. Since utility is increasing along the PEP, it must be that y is increasing fast enough to more than compensate for the decrease in x. But the amount of y it is possible to acquire is bounded by the horizontal line through the starting-point K. So this process can continue only over a limited range of the PEP—which must eventually turn northeast.

(b) This is impossible. Utility is increasing everywhere along the PEP, and the same starting-point cannot have both lower and higher utility.

T4. (a) An increase in P_x would tend to shift the IEP to the northwest.

(b) An increase in I would tend to displace the PEP toward the northeast (assuming X and Y are both normal superior goods).

T7. The pair of close substitutes is more likely to have a member that is an inferior good. The reason is that complements tend to be consumed together, while substitutes do not. Therefore, increased income is likely to result in increased consumption of both bread and butter (complements). But with increased income an individual is likely to consume less margarine, since he can now better afford the preferred (but more expensive) substitute—butter.

T8. Since usually only a limited fraction of income is spent on any single good X, the income effect (enrichment or impoverishment) due to a change in P_x will be relatively small.

T10. The market base price should *rise,* because increased quantities will be demanded. The effect will be to partially cancel the impact of the subsidy or voucher.

T12. (a) Coach travel is an inferior good here, since the purchased quantity of coach travel falls as income rises. Specifically, if income were to rise above $100, more first-class travel and less coach travel would be purchased.

(b) If the traveler's budget is so small that he can complete the trip *only* by traveling entirely in coach, then he will do so. If the traveler's budget permits the trip to be completed by traveling entirely in first-class, then only first-class travel will be purchased.

T13. (a) Yes.

(b) If the budget-line slope is exactly the same as the indifference-curve slope for the two perfect substitutes, then the individual does not care whether he consumes only one of the goods, or only the other good, or any mixture of the two.

T14. No, the two IEP curves cannot intersect. Assuming $P_y \equiv 1$ throughout, every point on the original IEP° curve represents an indifference-curve tangency with a budget line of slope $-P_x^\circ$. Every point on the new IEP' curve represents a tangency with a budget line of slope $-P_x'$. If the two IEP curves crossed, their point of intersection would have to be where an indifference curve is tangent to two budget lines of different slopes, which is impossible.

T15. Here $P_x = 120$ is the choke price for X; at that price, the quantity demanded falls to zero. For $P_x > 120$, the demand-curve equation given indicates a negative amount of X demanded, which we rule out as impossible. The correct demand equation, in the range where $P_x > 120$, is simply $x = 0$.

CHAPTER 5

R2. Such Engel Curves (of different steepness, but all being straight lines through the origin) depict the same *proportionate response* of changes in consumption to

540

changes in income. For such curves, greater steepness shows not greater income elasticity but rather that x/I is higher, i.e., that the commodity is absolutely more important in the consumer's budget.

R5. (a) "Elastic demand" means that the absolute value of the price elasticity of demand exceeds one. "Inelastic demand" means that the absolute value of the price elasticity of demand is less than one.

(b) For a linear demand curve, the elasticity at any point is the ratio of two slopes: the slope of a ray from the origin *to* that point on the curve, divided by the constant slope *along* the curve. For a nonlinear demand curve, the slope *along* the curve is interpreted as the slope of the tangent to the curve at that point.

R6. (a) Negative infinity. (b) Zero. (c) −1.

R9. Price elasticity is −1. Income elasticity is +1.

R10. Permitting the sale of coupons would benefit both the wealthy and the poor. The poor could sell coupons for dollars, shift their *income* constraint outward, and attain a more preferred position. The wealthy could buy coupons for dollars, shift their *ration* constraint upward, and also attain a more preferred position.

R12. This corresponds to the statement that the income index $\mathscr{E}$ is greater than the Laspeyres index of prices $\mathscr{L}_P$—which implies also that the Paasche index of quantities $\mathscr{P}_Q$ is greater than one. The statement is true.

T1. Assuming for simplicity just two goods X and Y, the equation that we want to prove can be written

$$\frac{P_x x}{I}\left(\frac{\Delta x}{\Delta I}\frac{I}{x}\right) + \frac{P_y y}{I}\left(\frac{\Delta y}{\Delta I}\frac{I}{y}\right) = 1$$

After cancellations:

$$\frac{P_x \Delta x + P_y \Delta y}{\Delta I} = 1$$

But since $I = P_x x + P_y y$, with P_x and P_y as constants, $\Delta I = P_x \Delta x + P_y \Delta y$. So the numerator and denominator of the fraction above are equal, proving that their ratio does indeed equal unity.

T2. (a) This argument is based upon the substitution effect of a price change and is valid. Indifference curves drawn for a commodity and its close substitute will have very little curvature. A small proportionate price decrease (a small tilt of the budget line) will then tend to result in a large proportionate increase in quantity (a large shift in the consumer's optimum).

(b) This argument is based upon the income effect of a price change and is valid, increasingly so as the good accounts for a bigger portion of the budget. A luxury is a commodity with a strong positive income effect. Since a price decrease tends to enrich the consumer, the income effect will strongly reinforce the substitution effect and so lead to a relatively large proportionate increase in quantity. However, if the luxury commodity accounts for very little of the budget, the enrichment will be small and so the income effect will be insubstantial.

(c) This argument is based upon the income effect of a price change, but is invalid. The argument asserts that, since the commodity accounts for a large portion of an individual's budget, a price decrease will have a large enriching effect and so will lead to a large increase in the quantity purchased. Up to this point the argument is correct, but what it implies is a large *absolute* increase in quantity. Since a large proportion of the consumer's budget is already being spent on this good, a large absolute increase in quantity does not generally imply the large *proportionate* increase required for high elasticity. (See Question R9 for the price elasticity of a commodity that accounts for 100% of the consumer's budget.)

(d) This argument is valid for a linear (or approximately linear) demand curve. Here the slope is the same at high or low prices, but at high prices there is a high ratio P/Q and at low prices a low ratio P/Q. Since elasticity equals the reciprocal of the slope times this ratio, the proposition follows. But if the slope is not constant—in particular, if it is high at high prices and low at low prices (as would be true for a constant-elasticity demand curve)—the proposition would not be valid.

T3. (a) At low incomes consumers are likely to be interested only in nutrition. High-quality and low-quality beef are good substitutes as far as nutrition is concerned. At high incomes other characteristics such as flavor become increasingly important to consumers. Here, low-quality beef is not a good substitute for high-quality beef. Higher indifference curves would therefore have greater curvature.

(b) Because high-quality beef is a luxury (it has a stronger positive income effect than low-quality beef), the price elasticity of demand for high-quality beef should be high relative to the price elasticity for low-quality beef.

T5. The secretary is mistaken. The prof would undoubtedly be *willing* to pay something more in total for three tickets than for two. But if the price is only $10, *he does not have to* pay more for three tickets than he would have paid for two at a price of $20 each. Looking at this another way, the $10 is the worth of a *third* ticket to the prof, not the worth of each of three tickets. (If the objection were valid, it would never make sense for a consumer to have an inelastic demand for a good.)

T6. This is indeed possible, though opinions may differ about how likely it is. Consumers seeking snob appeal gain utility from *exclusiveness.* At a high price, they are getting not only the commodity but also the exclusivity. The fact that the price is high guarantees that not many people can afford the commodity, and therefore makes "snob" consumers more willing to buy than at a low price. But if the exclusiveness were provided in some other way (as by the medieval Statute of Dress that made it illegal for the lower orders to wear upper-class clothes), presumably the Law of Demand would hold.

T7. This is very much like the previous question, but here the additional element gained by the consumer from the high-price product (or so he believes) is *quality.* There is of course nothing paradoxical if someone prefers high quality even at a high price over low quality at a low price. Again, if the quality were guaranteed in some other way than by high price (perhaps by a consumer organization's rating of the product), presumably the Law of Demand would hold—a high-quality product at a low price would be chosen over the *same* high-quality product at a high price.

T8. (a) The usual justification is that rationed commodities tend to be those that are "essential" to life or health. If ration allowances were exchangeable, rich people might end up with more than "their fair share" of these essential commodities. Note that this assumes that the poorer people who sell their allowances are foolish in giving up some "essentials" for non-essentials—or else possibly that poorer people have to be forced to remain in good working condition for the sake of the war effort, though they themselves might prefer otherwise!

(b) The adverse consequences include the loss of the gains from trade, plus the diversion of resources into black-market activities and the policing efforts required to minimize such activities.

T9. Consumption requires both income and time. A consumer will choose a most preferred position subject to both an income constraint and a time constraint. When relatively poor, the income constraint will tend to be binding. When relatively rich, the time constraint will tend to be binding. While "time-saving" devices in effect allow outward shifts of the time constraint, this has not occurred as rapidly as rising incomes have shifted out the income constraint. So the time constraint is increasingly the binding one upon individuals' consumption. Rich people simply do not have enough time to consume all the things they might enjoy and be able to pay for.

CHAPTER 6

R3. (a) Economic profit is the difference between revenues and economic costs, i.e., costs *inclusive* of implicit payments for self-supplied resources.

(b) Since owners receive profits, maximization of profit (owner wealth) is an appropriate goal for owners. Managers, if they are not also owners, have no claim on profits and so would be uninterested in maximizing profit. Managers might be interested in power, growth, stability, and a favorable corporate image as well as in larger salaries and more pleasant working conditions.

(c) Mechanisms tend to be developed by owners to impose their profit-maximizing goal upon managers. Lawsuits and proxy fights can punish managers who are not pursuing owners' goals. Similarly, profit-sharing and stock-option plans reward managers for pursuing owners' goals. These mechanisms are imperfect, though, so the likely result is that the firm will pursue some mixture of owner and manager goals.

R5. (a) Yes. At the vertical axis, AC is greater than or equal to MC, since AC allows for Fixed Costs while MC does not. As MC falls from its initial level along the vertical axis, it forces AC to be falling as well.

(b) No. By Proposition 2.2a, when AC is falling, MC lies below AC, but MC can be less than AC and still not be itself falling.

R7. A firm will make short-run adjustments to changes in economic conditions if such changes are viewed as temporary. A firm will make long-run adjustments to changes in economic conditions if such changes are viewed as permanent.

T1. Taking on additional traffic at a price lower than Average Cost would be financially advantageous if the price exceeds *Marginal* Cost. Even if AVC is only one-third of AC, Marginal Cost might not be low enough to warrant taking on the new traffic. (In fact, MC might even be above AC.)

T2. (a) If changing conditions are viewed as temporary, some factors may be held fixed in the face of a contraction of output to avoid the transaction costs incurred in selling the factors and then buying them back when conditions return to normal—or, for an expansion of output, to avoid the costs of buying factors and then selling them back. A similar result holds to the extent that the firm's operations involve *specializing* resources to the firm. Such specialized resources can only be sold at a low price to others, yet must be purchased at a high price. Then these resources may be held fixed during temporary changes in output.

(b) The factors that are held fixed are those which are highly specialized to the firm, or for which transaction costs are high.

T6. The short-run Marginal Cost is the additional cost of temporarily increasing output. Whether these costs are paid immediately (overtime wages, increased usage of power, etc.) or at a later time (deferred maintenance), they are all costs. The factory manager is confusing short-run costs with costs that must be *paid* immediately. They are not the same.

T8. (a) The Marginal Cost of providing service to more passengers when trains are running empty is quite low. Another passenger can be transported at very little additional cost. When trains are running full, however, the Marginal Cost of providing service is much higher. Additional trains must be run, or further unpleasant crowding imposed on passengers. Since Marginal Cost is very low in off-hours, the transit line should encourage off-hour business, not discourage it. The management consultant is confusing Marginal Cost with Average Cost.

(b) Commutation tickets will increase ridership at rush hours, but it is during these times that the trains are already running full. If the cost of running additional trains, or of imposing crowding on customers, is high then the transit line is likely to be worse off by selling commutation tickets. Discount tickets for *off-hour* riders, on the other hand, would likely increase revenues without a commensurate increase in cost. This type of discount would be a good idea.

CHAPTER 7

R1. Yes. Steepness and elasticity of supply, *at a given point,* must be inversely related.

R2. Whether the proposition (that doubling *all* inputs would always double output) is or is not true is arguable, but in any case it is not economically relevant. In the real world, it is never possible to double *all* relevant inputs.

R4. Where there are no "external" effects, the industry supply curve will be less steep than the firm supply curve but will have the same elasticity (the *proportionate* response of output to price will be the same).

R6. (a) In long-run equilibrium, the marginal firm is just on the borderline between staying in the industry and leaving. The value of its opportunities elsewhere practically equals what it can earn in this industry. Consequently, the economic profit of the marginal firm will be (only negligibly above) zero.

(b) Infra-marginal firms have access to some special resources particularly suited to producing in this industry. Other firms will bid for the right to use these special resources. When the infra-marginal firm charges itself the *opportunity cost*—what it could get by offering the special resources to these other bidders—it is also left with zero economic profit.

T1. True. A competitive firm will produce positive output only if Marginal Cost exceeds Average Variable Cost (in the short run) or Average Cost (in the long run). So AVC in the former case, or AC in the latter case, must be rising.

T4. No. All firms may be earning zero economic profit, and yet some may be able to survive even if product price falls. These will be the "infra-marginal" firms (see Question R6).

T6. (a) If all coupons were used initially, allowing resale would only redistribute coupons. Only if some coupons were initially unused would sale of coupons tend to raise the price of petroleum and elicit more supply.

(b) Salability, though, would cause a redistribution of coupons to those consumers having the highest demand prices for gasoline—at least as high as the sum of the product price and the price paid for a coupon.

(c) Without the sale of coupons, some buyers may receive little or no Consumer Surplus from their purchases of gasoline while others who would receive great Consumer Surplus may be unable to make purchases. Salability will allow those previously unable to make purchases to bid away the coupons from those currently receiving little Consumer Surplus from gasoline.

T8. No. The output from existing wells is based, even in the short run, upon a calculation of the price received for oil versus the cost of pumping. The higher the price, the more it pays to pump. In the longer run, the more it will pay to extend the life of an existing well by heating, flooding, re-drilling, etc.

T10. (a) By reversing the analysis pictured in Figure 7.10, it can be seen that Consumer Surplus will increase (rather than decrease) because of the lower price to consumers, and Producer Surplus will increase (rather than decrease) because of the higher price to sellers.

(b) No. A tax leads to inefficiency due to reduced exchange; a subsidy leads to inefficiency due to excessive exchange. Since the price received by sellers exceeds the price paid by consumers, there will be units produced and sold whose value to consumers does not cover the Marginal Cost of production. It may seem puzzling that Consumer Surplus and Producer Surplus both increase in this market and yet there is inefficiency. The explanation is that the subsidy here reduces Consumer Surplus and Producer Surplus elsewhere. Other industries must be taxed to finance the subsidy.

CHAPTER 8

R1. To maximize profit, a monopolist will set $MR = MC$. Since Marginal Cost is always positive, the monopolist will always produce where Marginal Revenue is positive. Using formula (8.5), $MR > 0$ implies $|\eta| > 1$.

R3. In comparison with pure competition, monopoly results in a smaller rate of output. Because less is produced and traded, some of the gains from specialization and trade are lost—the sum of Consumer Surplus and Producer Surplus is smaller.

R5. Owners of monopolies may not be any more interested in non-profit goals than owners of competitive firms, but reduced competitive pressure allows indulging such goals. As another matter, they may be less able to successfully impose the goal of profit maximization upon managers, since owners of monopolies cannot measure their managers' performance by looking at the performance of rival firms. Also, anti-trust policy may act as a threat. (If profits are too large, perhaps an anti-trust suit will be forthcoming.) Finally, many monopolies are regulated and so prevented from maximizing profits. For any of these reasons, monopolies may not pursue profits as vigorously as do competitive firms.

R7. In deriving the supply curve of the competitive industry, we assume that each separate firm will have set Marginal Cost equal to price. The height of the point on the supply curve therefore shows the Marginal Cost of each and every firm for that level of industry output. Consequently, that point on the supply curve also shows what the Marginal Cost would be if that industry were monopolized.

T1. Yes. An effective monopolist always operates in the range of elastic demand (see Question R1). But if demand is elastic, higher prices will have a big effect on quantity demanded.

T3. (a) At the simple monopoly optimum $MR = MC$, price exceeds Marginal Cost. A perfectly discriminating monopolist, on the other hand, will expand output until price *equals* Marginal Cost. A perfectly discriminating monopolist, then, might be expected to produce more than a simple monopolist. However, if the *income effect* is very strong, this conclusion may not hold. The discriminating monopolist extracts more income from consumers at each level of output, which tends to reduce demand for additional units.

(b) A market-segmentation monopolist will charge a price higher than the simple monopoly price to some market segments and so sell less in those segments, but will also charge a price lower than the simple monopoly price to the other segments and so sell more there. The total produced and sold by a market segmentation monopolist, then, may be more or less than that of a simple monopolist.

(c) While a multi-part pricing monopolist will charge a price higher than the simple monopoly price for small purchases, he will charge a price lower than the simple monopoly price for purchases beyond a certain size. Some customers will buy less because they purchase too little to receive the lower marginal price. Other customers will purchase enough to receive the lower marginal price and so will purchase more (in the absence of a strong income effect) than if faced with a single monopoly price. The multi-part pricing monopolist, therefore, also may or may not produce more than a simple monopolist.

T4. For a price-discriminating selling scheme to be effective, resale of the commodity must be difficult. Resale of services is more difficult than resale of manufactured goods.

T5. Many customers will lie about their age.

T6. One explanation: couples have better alternatives (closer substitutes for achieving thrills), so their demand is more elastic. Another explanation turns upon cost rather than demand considerations. Customers of such theaters like a degree of privacy, and so want a vacant seat on either side. The theater will then be undesirably crowded for singles once half the seats are taken, whereas couples can fill two-thirds of the seats before crowding becomes uncomfortable. In effect, 2 seats have to be provided for every singles customer, but only $1\frac{1}{2}$ seats per person for couples.

T10. Yes. Consider theft, for example. The marginal yield to the "industry" as a whole is probably less than that perceived by the individual competitive thief. One thief may steal on Tuesday what another thief had in mind filching on Wednesday. Also, any increase in the scale of thievery tends to raise the intensity of defensive actions by potential victims, thereby reducing the returns to thieves in the aggregate. A monopolized theft industry would take all this into account, and therefore engage in fewer (but more remunerative, on the average) crimes.

CHAPTER 9

R1. The greater the number of plants, the closer plants are on the average to customers, and so the smaller the transport losses incurred. This will lead to a larger aggregate demand for the product itself. Similarly, the greater the number of varieties, the more closely the available products match customer preferences, and so the smaller the satisfaction loss to consumers. Again this will lead to a larger aggregate demand.

R2. (a) While increased variety does raise the aggregate demand curve, it does so at a decreasing rate. Consequently, the *incremental* benefits to the monopoly firm from offering greater and greater variety are decreasing. On the other hand, the incremental cost of providing increased variety—in the text example, this is the fixed cost associated with each added plant—is ordinarily non-decreasing. There will be some point, then, where still greater variety raises cost more than it raises revenue.

   (b) If individuals' desires are for very similar products, there will be little benefit to the firm if it offers increased variety. And if there are large economies of scale, increased variety can only be offered at high cost. These two considerations may be powerful enough to induce the monopolist to offer only a single variety.

R6. Where a single attribute is desired by consumers, a monopolist will select that quality (amount of attribute per unit of product) which makes it possible to produce a chosen quantity of attribute at the lowest cost. While the monopolist will produce a smaller quantity of attribute than would a competitive industry, there is no reason to believe that the cost of producing this smaller quantity will be minimized when a lower-quality product is produced. In particular, if there is a single quality of product that provides attribute at lower cost of production throughout, this same quality of product would be offered either by a monopolist or a competitive industry.

R7. (a) A monopolist would obviously not suppress an invention that lowered costs. Nor, if consumers are fully informed, would it pay to suppress an invention that raised quality at a given cost. (The only possible exception would be if the invention somehow destroyed the monopoly.)

   (b) Consumers would not necessarily be better off. It is conceivable that adoption of a cost-reducing invention would lead the monopolist to produce a smaller amount than before, at a higher price. A similar result may come about for a quality-increasing invention.

T1. No, monopolistic competition emerges when consumers' tastes for different *varieties* provide each supplier with a degree of monopoly power over a "clientele" for its product. In contrast, if there is a single generally recognized *quality* attribute desired by all consumers, they will purchase from whichever firm offers this attribute at the lowest price. If there are many firms, each can survive only by offering the same price as the others, per unit of quality attribute. As price-taking suppliers of the single quality attribute, the firms are engaging in pure competition.

T3. The discussion of "Suppression of Inventions" (Section 9.E) showed that an invention lowering Total and Average Cost at every level of output *might* conceivably raise Marginal Cost in some ranges of output. If so, even for a competitive industry, a cost-reducing invention *might* reduce the quantity offered at some prices. (This could happen only over a limited range, and even so seems a rather unlikely possibility.) Since a quality-improving invention is logically equivalent to a cost-reducing invention (in terms of the cost of producing the attribute desired by consumers), a corresponding analysis applies: the invention *might* conceivably (though this seems improbable) be adverse to consumers' interests.

T4. Think of oranges as providing various amounts of a desired attribute, flavor. High-quality oranges contain more attribute than low-quality oranges. But it costs no more to ship a high-quality than a lower-quality orange. Then shipping costs *per unit of quality attribute* will be less if higher-quality oranges are shipped. Consequently, oranges shipped to distant locations tend to be of higher quality.

T5. The explanation seems to be that transportation itself (or the time that transport takes) degrades the quality of lobsters. If so, top-quality lobsters simply cannot be found except near the source. Oranges, in contrast, seem to retain their quality even when shipped long distances.

T6. This is similar to the situation with oranges. As a result of the tax, it becomes *relatively* cheaper than before to supply high-quality (high-mileage) gasoline. Some firms who previously found it more advantageous to produce a lower grade of gasoline are likely now to shift over to a better grade.

T8. No, this is not consistent with the analysis in the chapter. If consumers are interested only in the quality attribute (e.g., mileage), poorer consumers would tend to buy less mileage but there's no reason for them to buy a lower *grade* of gasoline. To the extent that the observation is correct, the explanation seems to be that purchase of higher-quality articles may yield a "luxury-good" attribute in the form of social distinction or prestige in addition to whatever material quality attribute the article contains. Chinchilla may not keep the wearer any warmer than squirrel, but there is something to be said for being seen in chinchilla.

T9. Since there is some tradeoff between quantity and quality, the program that restricted only the *number of acres planted* motivated farmers to enlarge output at the expense of quality. So in this period American tobacco farmers specialized in high-yield but low-quality varieties. The reformed program had exactly the opposite effect. Since the restriction was only upon the *number of pounds produced*, it paid farmers to make each pound of tobacco a more valuable product. So American farmers shifted over to high-quality strains of tobacco. See J. A. Seagraves, "The Life Cycle of the Flue-Cured Tobacco Program," Dept. of Economics and Business, North Carolina State Univ., Working Paper No. 34 (March 1983).

CHAPTER 10

R2. The "Prisoners' Dilemma" is a social interaction situation in which each participant is motivated to adopt a shortsightedly selfish strategy—with the result that all parties lose. The source of the difficulty is that an individual choosing a cooperative strategy has no way to induce or compel the others to do the same, so the unselfish player ends up worse off than the others. Evidently there is an unexploited mutual gain from exchange here, due to *inability to make binding agreements.*

R3. Monopolistic competition is a market structure in which each firm's product is differentiated from the others, but the relatively large number of firms rules out strategic behavior. In contrast, strategic behavior is the essence of oligopoly (competition among the few). Under oligopoly, products of the different firms may or may not be differentiated (the heterogeneous versus homogeneous cases).

R4. In the Nash solution of game theory, each party is doing the best he can *given* the strategies of the others. The Cournot solution for oligopoly similarly assumes that each firm adopts the best choice for its decision variable (price or quantity) *given* the choices made by the others.

R7. (a) If the demand curve is "kinked," the Marginal Revenue curve will have a vertical gap at the rate of output at which this kink exists. To maximize profit, the firm will set $MR = MC$. Assuming that MC initially cuts through the gap in MR, moderate changes in MC will still leave MC cutting through this gap in MR. As long as this is the case, the firm will not change its rate of output or price. Moderate shifts in the demand curve to the left or right may also leave MC cutting through the gap in MR—now at a greater or smaller rate of output. Again, price will tend to be rigid.

(b) One method of enforcing a collusive agreement is for "loyal" firms to match any price cut by a defecting firm, but to refrain from matching any price increase. This leads to each potential defector viewing its demand curve as kinked at the agreed level of prices.

T2. "Learning" on the part of the firms opens up many new possibilities and the final outcome is not easily predictable. Suppose first that at each output of the other firm, the "learned" duopolist produces more than the simple duopolist. If both firms "learn," the Reaction Curve of each will shift to the right relative to the Reaction Curves of simple duopolists. The consequence is that the outcome approaches the competitive solution—both firms are worse off than before! So they may "learn" by this to behave more cooperatively, holding back on output so as to approach the monopoly solution instead. But if one firm learns that the other is inclined to hold back, the first is tempted to "free ride" and produce more. So the final result is unclear.

T3. Yes. The kink would have a more extreme form under homogeneous oligopoly. A firm that raised its price, while other firms were keeping their prices constant, would lose *all* its business—so above the kink the demand curve would be flat (perfectly elastic). A firm that lowered price would find that other firms follow, so its demand below the kink would be no more elastic than the overall industry demand.

T5. (a) Table 10.5 shows that the symmetrical Collusive solution is not generally better than the Threat solution for *both* parties. If the threat can be made effective without having to be enforced very often, the "predatory price cutter" can do better than under collusion.

(b) Predatory price cutting is more likely to emerge where one firm is much more powerful or aggressive than the other, so that the threat is highly credible.

CHAPTER 11

R2. (a) For a monopolist in the product market, Marginal Revenue is always less than product price. Consequently, for such a monopolist mrp_a will always lie below (to the left of) vmp_a. For a competitor in the product market, Marginal Revenue equals product price. For such a competitor, mrp_a will be identical to vmp_a. So only for a monopolist in the product market will the mrp_a lie to the left of vmp_a.

(b) Whether the firm is a monopolist or a competitor in the product market, mrp_a is the firm's demand curve for factor A (within the relevant range of the curve).

R4. (a) Since mrp_a must be declining for $mrp_a = h_a$ to be an optimum, for a competitor in the product market it will never be rational *not* to be in the region of diminishing *marginal* returns (mp_a declining). For a monopolist in the product market, MR is also declining so it *may* be possible to achieve declining mrp_a even with rising mp_a.

(b) $mrp_a = h_a$ may hold in the region of diminishing marginal returns but rising *average* returns (where mp_a lies above ap_a). But then $h_a = mrp_a \equiv MR(mp_a) > MR(ap_a)$. Then for a competitive firm, $h_a > P(q/a)$, or $h_a a > Pq$. This means that the expenditure on factor A alone exceeds Total Revenue! So a competitive firm would *always* operate in the region of diminishing average returns.

(c) $mrp_a = h_a$ could never hold in the region of diminishing *total* returns. Here mp_a is negative and so mrp_a must also be negative. Since factor hire-price h_a can never be negative, a profit-maximizing firm would never hire so much factor as to be in the region of diminishing total returns.

R5. The conditions $mrp_a = h_a$ and $mrp_b = h_b$ imply that $mp_a/h_a = mp_b/h_b$. This equation states that an extra dollar spent on either factor A or factor B' will increase output by the same amount. Consequently, factor proportions are optimal. And $mrp_a/h_a = mrp_b/h_b = 1$ is also implied, which is equivalent to $MR/MC = 1$. Consequently, the scale of output is also optimal.

R6. (a) Yes. The slope of the output isoquant shows the rate at which factor B can be substituted for factor A while maintaining output. If one unit less of factor A is employed, the fall in output will be (approximately) mp_a. The number of units of factor B which must be hired to maintain output will be (approximately) mp_a/mp_b. The approximation approaches exactness for very small changes. So the absolute value of the slope at a point on the output isoquant is mp_a/mp_b.

(b) The absolute value of the slope along a cost isoquant is the rate at which factor B can be traded for factor A in the market—equal to h_a/h_b.

R8. No, because firms can enter or leave the industry. The entry–exit effect tends to make the industry's demand for a factor more elastic.

R9. (a) True. A drop in the hire-price of factor A will lead to an increase in the employment of factor A and so normally to an increase in output. If the demand curve for product is *inelastic*, this will induce a relatively large fall in product price. So the industry will respond to a fall in the hire-price with only a small increase in the employment of factor A (and a small increase in output). The demand curve for factor A will be steep and so tend to be inelastic.

(b) True. The weaker the operation of the Law of Diminishing Returns, the more gradual the decline in mp_a as more A is hired. When this decline is more gradual, firm demand curves for factor A and the resulting market demand curve will be relatively flat and so tend to be elastic.

(c) True. As the hire-price of factor A falls, more A will be hired and so the demand for complementary factors will increase. The more elastic the supply curves of factors complementary to factor A, the greater the increase in employment of these factors when the demand for them increases. The large increase in the quantity of complementary factors leads to a large upward shift in mrp_a and so to a relatively large increase in the quantity of factor A

employed. Consequently, each firm's demand curve (and so the market demand curve) for factor A will be flatter and so tend to be more elastic, the more elastic the supply of complementary factors.

T1. (a) See Examples 11.1 through 11.3.

(b) This is a question of fact. The Laws of Diminishing Returns appear to be founded upon certain very general physical aspects of the world. Note, however, that economists admit a range of exceptions when they say only that Marginal or Average or Total returns *eventually* diminish as employment of one factor increases relative to others. It is possible that in a practical situation the "eventual" point may not be reached, so that increasing returns apply in the relevant range.

T2. No. Here, the employer is not a price-taker. Consequently, there is no fixed relation between quantity employed and hire-price.

T4. (a) Even if two factors are anti-complementary, it is quite possible that each has positive Marginal Product. For each factor it is its *mp* that enters into $mrp \equiv MR(mp)$, to be compared with its hire-price h in making the employment decision.

(b) If interference is defined as a situation where hiring more of factor A reduces the *Total* Product tp_b of factor B (or, equivalently, the *Average* Product $ap_b \equiv q/b$), then output q must have fallen and so mp_a must be negative. This can never be rational.

T7. This chapter examines aspects of the *demand* for labor. Supply considerations (to be studied in the next chapter) also have a bearing upon whether wages are high or low. Demand for labor has been high in the U.S. as a result mainly of the presence of large amounts of complementary factors. In the early years these took the form of rich natural resources (fertile land, mineral wealth, navigable rivers). In more recent years, accumulations of complementary manufactured resources (machines, roads) have contributed to the demand for labor. Other possible sources of high demand for labor in the U.S. include rapid technological progress (see next question), relatively strong competition in product markets (so that *mrp* does not diverge very much from *vmp* for labor), and comparative absence of firms with effective monopsony power in the labor markets.

T8. Technological progress by definition tends to raise the *Average* Product of labor. It will tend to raise wages if the *Marginal* Product of labor increases. While the effects on Average Product and Marginal Product are usually parallel, there are exceptions. A "labor-saving" invention may raise the productivity of the first few workers employed so much that the Marginal Product for larger numbers falls. There is another line of causation, however, associated with the general enrichment that technological progress brings about. With higher wealth, there will be more demand for products involving labor of all types. So wages will tend to rise as a result of "revenue" considerations (see Question R1) even if the "productivity" considerations are affected adversely.

CHAPTER 12

R2. No. The supply curve can only bend backward if the income effect opposes the substitution effect. If leisure is an inferior good, the enrichment due to a wage increase would lead to less consumption of leisure (more supply of labor), thus *reinforcing* the substitution effect of the wage increase.

R3. At very low wage rates, few hours are being worked. A wage increase, multiplied by only a small number of hours, will have only a small enrichment effect compared to the substitution effect.

R4. The supply curve to a particular employment is likely to be much more elastic. Different employments of labor are probably, from the worker's point of view, close substitutes in his or her preference function. Then a relatively small change in the wage differential between two employments will induce a relatively large shift in labor supply from the less attractive to the more attractive employment.

R6. If the wage rate increases, so will the price of leisure, and the individual will tend to consume less leisure. Indeed, if the investment just leaves the individual as well off as before (on the same indifference curve), that person will surely work more, as shown in Figure 12.4. Here only the substitution effect of the wage increase is effective; the income effect is exactly cancelled by the income loss due to the cost of training. If the individual ends up on a higher indifference curve as a result of the investment, however, then there will be a net income effect which *may* lead to working less.

R8. Each is a source of productive services, and thus is a portion of society's real-capital.

R9. This relationship is $h_a = rP_A$. The hire-price of the factor is equal to the interest yield on the capital-value or purchase price of the factor. This is an *equilibrium* relation. The purchase price of the factor will be bid up or down until the relation holds.

R11. Economic rent is that portion of payment to a factor in excess of the amount required to call it into employment. Economic rent is a measure of the resource-owner's (seller's) net gain from trade in the factor market. It is, then, analogous to Producer Surplus which is a measure of the seller's net gain from trade in the product market.

T2. Most resources can be viewed as having some reservation uses. An obvious example is land. If not leased on the market, land could be used as a homesite, or a garden, or a private game reserve.

T4. (a) Such a change in taste would lead to an outward shift of the market supply curve of female labor. More labor would be offered at each wage rate.
(b) If males and females make up at least partially distinguishable types of labor, the outward shift in the supply of female labor would lead to a *decrease* in the equilibrium wage rate for female workers relative to male workers.

T5. As long as leisure is a normal good, rising per-capita *wealth* in the form of nonlabor income will lead to an increase in leisure and so to a decrease in the number of hours worked. Rising real *wages* embody both an income and a substitution effect. The pure substitution effect always implies a decrease in leisure and an increase in hours worked, but the income effect works in the opposite direction. Since hours worked have been steadily falling as real wages have risen, the pure substitution effect of rising real wages appears to have been overwhelmed by the sum of the two income effects: that due to rising per-capita wealth (property income), plus the income effect of rising real wages.

T6. (a) The preferred position S^* of the slave would be an all-leisure solution, assuming that leisure is always a good for him. The position M^* preferred by the master would be the all-work solution, so long as the slave's labor yields any positive Marginal Product.
(b) The master has two instruments to move the slave toward M^*. One is force;

the other, incentive payments or wages. It is likely that both will have a diminishing marginal effect. That is, additional units of either force or incentive payments will eventually motivate smaller and smaller increases in work. Consequently, it is likely that the master will choose a policy that includes both force and incentive payments to move the slave toward M^*.

(c) If additional units of incentive payments are *always* more effective than the first unit of force, the master would choose to use no force—which is equivalent to freeing the slave and paying wages. Otherwise, the master would choose to use some force.

T9. (a) The supply curve of land to *all* uses (including reservation uses) can be regarded as vertical, in the short run. But the supply of land to *market* uses will not be strictly vertical, even in the short run, since owners will have alternative reservation uses for their land. Both an income tax and a wealth tax on land would therefore affect market supply in the short run. A *wealth tax* normally leads to increased market supply, since owners will suffer impoverishment and will then cut down on their reservation uses of land (apart from the unlikely case that such uses are an inferior good). An *income tax* will, however, also have a strong substitution effect in the opposite direction, and this will probably dominate so that less land will be offered in the market for productive services. (For either type of tax there will also be a *long-run* adverse effect on market supply; the reduced returns will tend to induce owners not to maintain or develop land as a productive resource.)

(b) The effects on the supply of labor are entirely parallel. For labor, however, alternative (leisure) uses are probably much more important. Thus, a wealth tax upon labor capacity may have a significant effect in inducing more market supply of labor. And an income tax will have more equally countervailing income and substitution effects, with the final result indeterminate.

T10. If labor supply were more effectively cartelized in the United States, wages would tend to be higher. This seems unlikely, however. It may be that U.S. laborers are willing to work harder, which would tend to raise their wages. Probably most important, there is more educational and training investment ("human capital") bound up in typical U.S. workers, making them more productive.

T12. Wage rates are high in New York City mainly because in that area a very unusual combination of natural and manufactured resources (the harbor, buildings and streets, railroads and subways, etc.) raises workers' productivity. If not balanced by other considerations, workers would flow in from the rest of the country to take advantage of these high wages. As they do so, however, crowding of the New York area tends to raise the cost of living there until the net advantage of such movement disappears and the population stabilizes.

CHAPTER 13

R2. (a) It does not follow. Mutually beneficial trade can occur as long as their MRS_C's differ at their endowed positions (or at their Crusoe optimum positions, if production is possible).

(b) If individuals have identical preferences and identical endowments in a world of pure exchange, each individual's MRS_C will be the same and no mutually beneficial trade can occur.

(c) Similarly, if they have identical preferences and identical production opportunities, each individual's MRS_C at the Crusoe optimum will be the same and no mutually beneficial trade can occur.

R3. (a) Asymmetrical Production-Possibility Curves will tend to lead to specialization in production. (Another possibility would be a range of increasing returns.) An individual who is relatively well-suited to producing one good will tend to specialize in production of that good. Symmetrical indifference curves tend to lead to diversification in consumption.

(b) Yes. In the absence of trade an individual's degrees of specialization in production and in consumption would have to be identical. Trade allows the simultaneous existence of productive specialization and consumptive diversification.

R6. In a world of production and exchange (assuming interior solutions), at the productive optimum each individual must be producing at a point along his Production-Possibility Curve such that his MRS_T equals the ratio of market prices. Similarly, at the consumptive optimum each individual's MRS_C must equal the ratio of market prices. Additionally, for each good, the sum over all individuals of the produced quantities must equal the sum of the consumed quantities.

R8. The intersection of the full demand and supply curves determines the point at which the total quantity desired for consumption just equals the total quantity available for consumption. The intersection of the transaction demand and supply curves determines the point at which the quantity desired in exchange equals the quantity offered for exchange. Since the two pairs of curves differ only by the *non-traded* amounts of the good (endowed and self-consumed quantities in pure exchange, or produced and self-consumed quantities in a world of production), the price that brings desired transaction quantities into equilibrium must also bring desired full quantities into equilibrium.

R11. (a) Yes, but only in a very special case. Autarky will occur in costless exchange if, for every individual, the ratio of market prices exactly equals the MRS_C and MRS_T at his or her Crusoe solution.

(b) Transaction costs create a spread between the gross and net price ratios. Any time an individual's MRS_C and MRS_T at the Crusoe solution fall inside this spread, the individual will choose an autarky solution (the Crusoe solution). The higher the transaction costs, the greater this spread and the more likely the autarky solution.

(c) Both payroll taxes and sales taxes can be viewed as transaction costs. Each type of tax creates a spread between the buyer's (gross) price and the seller's (net) price for goods and services traded in the market. But neither tax bears upon *self-supplied* goods and services. The increasing weight of payroll and sales taxes, by increasing the spread between buy and sell prices, raises the attractiveness and likelihood of self-supply (autarky) solutions as exemplified by the "do-it-yourself" trend.

R14. A command economy could avoid transaction costs by dispensing with markets, but it might incur larger enforcement costs than transaction costs saved. While market economies must use resources to integrate individual decisions, command economies must use resources to enforce central decisions. At least as important, the commanders would require an enormous input of information if the economy is to function rationally—information automatically provided by price signals in market economies. Most important of all, what the command economy will aim at is "efficiency" in carrying out the desires of the commanders, which may be quite different from the desires of consumers.

T2. A tax on *consumption* will reduce the incentive to acquire the taxed good either by production or by exchange. There will be less consumption and less production, whether for self-supply or for the market. A tax on *production* will have quite similar effects. A tax on *exchange*, in contrast, will tend to diminish production for the market but to increase production for self-supply. On balance, consumption of the good will also be less since some of the cost-reducing advantages of specialization will have been lost.

T3. Diminishing MRS_T is a reflection of the general law of diminishing returns that applies to all *productive* activities. Ideally, exchange does not involve any sacrifice of resources and so is not subject to diminishing returns. (However, with *costly* exchange, diminishing returns might be expected to apply.)

T5. Clearly, at least one of the two parties must be better off, since there is more of C and no less of Y available. But i (the seller of C) might end up worse off. If the demand for corn is inelastic, in trying to sell more, i will get less revenue in Y-units. More surprisingly, j (the buyer of C) might alternatively end up worse off—if Y is an inferior good for i. (Work this out!)

T6. Some markets have disappeared mainly because of reduction in demand. Leeches are no longer sold to physicians, since bleeding has lost favor as a medical practice. Other markets have disappeared because supply has become excessively costly. An example might be the market for handmade shoes. One historically important market that has disappeared, mainly because of higher *transaction costs* (in the form of legal penalties), is the international slave trade.

T8. (a) Integration might be achieved by commands of a central authority. Or by mutual love and helpfulness, as within a family. Or even by instinct (see the next question).
(b) Barter markets can and do function without the use of money.

T9. A Martian observer, unfamiliar with the mental limitations of flowers and bees, might indeed fail to appreciate the difference as compared with human exchange. Perhaps we're kidding ourselves, but we like to think that our exchanges are the result of *choice*. Presumably, the behavior of the bees is governed entirely by blind instinct, while the flowers are even farther from having any choice as to whether or not to offer their nectar to bees.

T12. Where both ration coupons and cash are required for trade, traders must maintain inventories of coupons as well as cash. In addition, traders must transport, authenticate, and physically transfer ration coupons as well as cash. If coupons can be bought and sold, there is also the cost of the coupon market. If coupons cannot be bought and sold, there are the costs of enforcing (and the costs of evading) the restrictions on the sale of coupons.

T13. All these qualities reduce the cost of using money as medium of exchange or as store of value. A somewhat less obvious but very important quality, illustrated by the prisoner-of-war example, is that the monetary commodity should not also be a consumption good. And, of course, the money should be cheap to produce.

CHAPTER 14

R2. (b) is correct. The ratio P_0/P_1 is the rate at which current consumption claims can be traded for one-year future consumption claims. If a current consumption claim is foregone, the market will pay back that claim plus interest next year. So

$P_0/P_1 \equiv 1 + r$. Consequently, $r \equiv (P_0/P_1) - 1$. The annual rate of interest is the *premium* on the relative value of current over one-year future consumption claims.

R4. Investment must always equal zero in a world of pure exchange. So, at equilibrium, aggregate saving equals aggregate investment at zero.

R5. At equilibrium in a productive situation, aggregate saving equals aggregate investment. It is also true that aggregate borrowing equals aggregate lending, but the total of borrowing or lending will generally be less than the total of saving or investment.

R7. (a) The Present-Value Rule directs decision-makers to adopt any incremental project for which the Present Value is positive, and to reject projects for which Present Value is negative.

(b) As long as the Separation Theorem holds, productive optimization is equivalent to wealth maximization. Since the Present-Value Rule is a wealth-maximizing rule, decision-makers will then be led to the productive optimum. If the Separation Theorem does not hold, however, wealth maximization and productive optimization are not identical. Here, not only wealth but its distribution over time becomes important, and so the Present-Value Rule will not necessarily lead to a productive optimum.

T2. At equilibrium it must be true that—even though saving need not equal investment for any individual—both actual and desired saving equal actual and desired investment in the aggregate. If this were not the case, the interest rate would adjust to bring about the equality. If a floor or ceiling were placed upon the interest rate, it will still be true that *actual* aggregate saving equals *actual* investment. Here, the smaller of desired aggregate saving and desired aggregate investment will determine the actual quantity of saving and investment. It will not be true, in general, that *desired* aggregate saving equals *desired* aggregate investment at the "frozen" market interest rate.

T3. (a) Because time-productivity will be relatively great in such a newly settled country, the real interest rate will tend to be high.

(b) The more isolated such a country is, the higher its real interest rate will be. Close contact with the rest of the world will lead to an inflow of resources which will increase total investment and decrease the real rate of interest in the new country.

T4. If little investment is taking place because of low time-productivity, real interest rates will be low. If little investment is taking place because of high time-preference, interest rates will be high.

T6. (a) Negative rates of interest are not impossible. As equation (14.1) indicates, all that is required is that future claims exchange at a premium against current claims ($P_0 < P_1$). Negative interest rates are rarely observed, however. In most situations there are attractive investment opportunities which increase the investment demand for current funds, while time-preference (impatience) raises the consumptive demand for current funds. The combination assures that current funds will almost always exchange at a premium against future funds.

(b) Yes. In equation (14.1"), since P_0/P_1 cannot be less than zero, r cannot fall below -1. In terms of percentages, the interest rate cannot be less than -100%.

T8. One does not find the present worth of a stream of payments by adding up the simple total of the interest-plus-principal installments over the years. This fails to allow for the fact that, due to the force of interest, a future payment is worth less today. In fact, at $7\frac{3}{4}\%$ a dollar payment deferred 27 years is worth today only about 13 cents. At $7\frac{3}{4}\%$ interest, the payments required by the two-year contract ($392.50 one year from now, and an equal amount two years from now) have a present worth of $702.34. But the 27 annual payments (of $39.81 each) of the other contract have a present worth of only $445.21! So the consumer advice provided was seriously off the mark. (Note that the quoted "price" of the appliances is irrelevant for these calculations; only the actual cash payments matter.)

CHAPTER 15

R2. The contract curve of the Edgeworth box diagram shows all those allocations from which no mutually beneficial trade can occur. Consequently, the utilities of the two individuals at a point on the contract curve become the coordinates for a point on the utility Social Opportunity Frontier.

R3. (a) A "social optimum" can only be defined in terms of a social criterion. Given a social criterion, the "social optimum" is simply that allocation which best achieves the criterion. Currently, there seems to be no agreement as to a social criterion, and so the term "social optimum" lacks agreed meaning. For example, some people regard unlimited abortion as social progress, others as social calamity.

(b) Efficiency seems a valid goal, but there are many reasons why it should not be the only element in a social criterion. For one thing, considerations of equity may indicate some sacrifice of efficiency. Also, efficiency is based upon the satisfaction of individual wants as the measure of well-being. It might be argued that individuals are poor judges of what will actually benefit them, or that wants are not autonomous but really socially determined, or that supra-individualistic policy goals (liberty, justice, community) are also important.

R5. (a) The efficiency conditions are three. First, $MRSC_{XY}^{j} = P_X = MRSC_{XY}^{k}$, so goods are allocated efficiently between consumers. Second, $MRSR_{al}^{j} = h_a = MRSR_{al}^{k}$, so reservation uses of resources are allocated efficiently between resource-owners. Third, $vmp_a^{f} = h_a = vmp_a^{g}$, so resource services are used efficiently by firms.

(b) These conditions could in principle be achieved without the market process. Efficient allocation might be directly imposed by a dictator.

R7. (a) The product-market monopolist and the factor-market monopsonist both violate the efficiency condition $vmp_a = h_a$. The product-market monopolist sets $h_a = mrp_a < vmp_a$. The factor-market monopsonist sets mrp_a (which may equal vmp_a) $= mfc_a > h_a$. That they both produce "too little" follows, since in either case $vmp_a > h_a$. This causes an efficiency loss because these firms could, by producing more, convert units of resource A into a larger product value than competitive firms satisfying the condition $vmp_a = h_a$.

(b) Yes, it follows that "too much" of resource A is used by competitive firms, and that "too much" A is retained for reservation uses that could more efficiently be devoted to market employment.

R10. (a) This efficiency condition is $MC_Z^{f} = MRSC_{ZY}^{j} + MRSC_{ZY}^{k}$, i.e., the Marginal Cost of providing the public good Z must equal the sum of each consumer's marginal valuation of the public good (Marginal Rate of Substitution in Consumption between the public and private goods).

(b) For a public good, since *every* consumer can receive the same unit, the vertical summation of individual demand curves for a public good shows the social marginal valuation. For a private good, only one consumer receives each unit—so the social marginal valuation of the private good is simply the marginal valuation of the consumer receiving the marginal unit. It is, however, incorrect to view the vertical summation of individual demand curves for a public good as a *demand curve* for the public good. This vertical summation does *not* indicate the quantity that would be purchased at any price; all it shows is the social marginal valuation of the public good.

R11. (a) The private supply of public goods is limited, first, by the difficulty and cost of exclusion. Non-payers would have to be excluded for private provision to be feasible, and this may be impossible or quite costly. Where exclusion costs are sufficiently low a private firm may provide a public good, but will still not likely provide an efficient quantity. For efficient provision, firms would have to charge different prices to different individuals. Such price discrimination might be illegal or simply too costly.

(b) Public provision *may* result in a more nearly optimal quantity, but this depends upon the forces determining governmental decisions (to be studied in the next chapter). Where exclusion is impossible or very costly, private provision is unlikely, and so public provision may be inevitable.

T1. The Duke has not read the text carefully enough. If the Duchess were initially endowed with a property right in her own life, a Pareto-preferred movement toward an efficient solution would have to be *mutually* beneficial. It seems unlikely that the Duke could have paid enough to have the Duchess agree to her own death. If the Duke initially possessed the right to take the Duchess's life, on the other hand, his argument would be valid on efficiency grounds. Even then, however, he was not necessarily "justified" in terms of moral criteria.

T2. Definitely false. First of all, conventional national income measures fail to allow for a whole variety of sources of utility and disutility: for example, homemakers' services are not counted, nor is the value of leisure, nor degradation of the environment as a negative element. But the statement would not be true even if there were a perfect national income measure. Monopolization of a good, for example, might raise the market value of national income while reducing efficiency.

T4. Property rights will be ill-defined when laws or court rulings are ambiguous and where legal precedents are conflicting or in a state of flux. Also, if it is costly to learn about one's rights, subjective uncertainty may persist even if the underlying legal theory is settled. The costs of transacting (negotiating and enforcing contracts) will tend to be high when multilateral contracting is required, or when individuals have incentives to behave strategically in order to capture more of the gains from an agreement. Some potential trades are hampered by the difficulty of describing the good or service in advance, or of measuring delivery performance thereafter. For example, contracts for labor service cannot generally guarantee in advance how devotedly the worker will perform, and this may even be hard to measure afterward. Another example is the used-car business, where prior determination of quality is notoriously difficult and where writing a level of agreed quality into the contract is almost impossible.

T6. True, since market reallocations of resources must be mutually beneficial. A dictator, in contrast, might achieve a Pareto-*efficient* outcome that was not Pareto-*preferred* to the original situation.

T7. Such a ban is certainly inefficient. The hepatitis problem is not a sufficient reason for banning the market in blood, since buyers are at liberty to use whatever method they deem appropriate in screening commercial donors. (As might have been anticipated, the prohibition of blood sales has caused dangerous blood "shortages.")

T8. (a) Yes, the analogy is sound. Laws banning polygyny reduce the demand for wife-services. Since only women can provide those services, the laws work to the disadvantage of women in general. (For exceptions, see below.)

(b) Women in general lose, and especially those who would rather be a multiple wife of a desirable husband than remain unmarried or be an only wife of a less desirable spouse. Those men who would have been willing and able to acquire multiple wives also lose. The gainers from monogamy laws include women who are exceptionally desirable wives, assuming they prefer to be the sole wife. If polygyny were legal, any such woman could still contract with her husband to be the sole wife, but might have to pay a high price for that privilege. But the biggest gainers from the monogamy laws are undoubtedly those men who would not otherwise have been able to obtain wives.

(c) Monogamy laws cannot be defended in terms of efficiency.

(d) Monogamy laws tend to *increase equality among men*, since males who are less attractive husbands have better chances of acquiring wives. They probably *increase inequality among women*, however, since they improve the ability of more-desirable wives to monopolize the best husbands.

CHAPTER 16

R1. The public-choice approach views politics as a kind of exchange process. Citizens in a sense shop for that government which provides them the largest increase in welfare. Political parties compete to become the government and so to capture the rewards of being in power. Since utility maximization, exchange, and competition are all involved, this approach is particularly amenable to economic analysis. An alternative approach views politics as a conflict process, in which some individuals and groups are attempting to exploit others.

R2. The imperfections of the democratic political system, as a mechanism for serving citizen desires, are somewhat analogous to the imperfections of the market—but are, often, even more pervasive. In the political system citizens almost never make choices directly on substantive issues; actual decisions are made by imperfectly controllable delegates. Second, citizens have only a very narrow range of choice even of delegates. They must select from a very limited number of candidates (i.e., political competition is highly imperfect) at widely separated election intervals, whereas in the market individuals may select almost continuously from a vast menu of choices. Third, a democratic political system whose decisions are based upon some form of majority rule must always over-ride minority desires. In the market process, even though most people consume Chevys, the minority may still consume Fords. Fourth, the cost of acquiring information is much higher for political choices.

R4. (a) A free-rider problem in the provision of goods will tend to arise whenever it is difficult to exclude non-payers from the benefits of group action—as when public goods are provided even to those who do not contribute to defray the costs.

(b) Not very valid. While much of government activity appears to be concerned with the provision of public goods—defense, law, and redistribution all can be viewed as having public-good characteristics—governments are also heavily involved with the provision of private goods. And to the extent that the "exploitation" model is valid, government may not be interested in serving the citizens at all.

R7. More frequent elections, more numerous legislatures, and elected judges would all give citizens the *potential* of more control over government officials. The more frequent are elections and the more numerous the legislatures, though, the less important is any single election and so the less informed will voters typically be. So it is not clear whether or not any of these proposals would actually improve the fidelity of the political system to citizen desires. Replacing the merit system in civil service by the spoils system gives citizens some control (though indirect) over bureaucrats. The spoils system would therefore make the governmental mechanism more accountable to citizen desires, but may reduce the quality of personnel in government.

R8. (a) Unanimous consent, involving the purchase of dissident votes, would always result in decisions that improve the welfare of every voter—Pareto-preferred moves. In terms of Pareto-efficiency, this would be an ideal political system.

(b) Log-rolling allows voters to trade votes on one issue for votes on another issue, and so would tend indeed to lead to Pareto-preferred outcomes—a series of decisions which together leave everyone better off. The objections to log-rolling are due primarily to the fact that *delegates,* not citizens, actually vote on policies. Because delegates vote, pressure groups with a strongly concentrated stake in a particular issue will be able to influence delegate votes unduly—in extreme cases, log-rolling might represent outright bribery.

R12. An agreement is "self-enforcing" when neither party to the agreement can gain by defecting. For example, a doctor and his patient might have invested significant effort in getting to know one another. In order to maintain the relationship the patient may pay his bills and the doctor may provide good service even if legal enforcement were lacking.

T1. Any voluntary trade is mutually beneficial. So if the poor traded votes to the rich for money, both would gain in comparison with the initial situation. Objections to this practice are probably based on objections to the initial situation, in which the rich have more money to begin with.

T2. Yes, there is a certain tendency in this direction. A political party in office might "profit" by simply looting the taxpayers, or more subtly by carrying out ideological programs in opposition to voters' desires. The potential competition of other parties limits how far a party in power can go in this direction. But political competition is a much weaker force than economic competition (see Question R2), and so "political profit" may not be driven to zero.

T3. Cash redistributions are not unknown. Social Security comes close to falling into this category, being a redistribution from the working age-group to the retired age-group. But that politicians prefer to establish service programs to "help" the poor (by health care, job training, education, etc.) has become increasingly evident in recent years. The advantage to legislators of being in on the ground floor when a large new bureaucracy is established to staff a service program (jobs to political supporters) is obvious.

T4. (a) Government construction is a service very often provided by private suppliers, rather than by government employees. Perhaps the irregular extent and timing of construction work does not fit in so well with the security of employment tenure which is typical of government service. The political influence of private construction interests, in heading off competition from the government sector, also plays a role.

(b) Private customers pay (apart from possible elements of subsidy) for government-provided services like the post office, hospitals, and (in many countries) railroad, telephone, etc. The explanation is not well understood. Once a service has been provided by government, a bureaucratic constituency develops tending to perpetuate that situation. So if first historical provision of telephone service, for example, happened to be by a government agency, it is likely to remain that way.

T6. Viewing government in a public-choice framework, changes in demand or costs should have the same qualitative effects upon price and output for a governmentally provided good as for a privately provided good. The strength of the effects, however, will differ. Bureaucrats tend to have an interest in larger output and so in keeping prices low to users. With an increase in demand, therefore, government provision will tend to result in a greater increase in quantity and a smaller increase in price than in the case of private provision. For a decrease in demand, government provision will probably result in a smaller decrease in quantity and a larger fall in price than private provision. Analogous conclusions apply for changes in costs.

T8. (a) Public-choice explanations look for reasons why voters would prefer larger government. For example, a high income elasticity of demand for government-provided goods coupled with rising incomes would generate increases in the demand for such goods. Non-voluntarist explanations might look for shifts in *political power* toward those who prefer larger governments. For example, the enlargement of bureaucracy in wartime might so increase the relative political power of bureaucrats as to preclude a return to a smaller level of government thereafter.

(b) Here again, there are various explanations. A public-choice explanation might be that the new factory-provided private goods became cheaper relative to government-provided goods, and so the private sector grew in response to consumer-citizen desires. A conflict-model explanation might be that the newly rich merchant class had become sufficiently powerful to throw off the burden of a government dominated by the old landed aristocracy.

INDEX OF NAMES

Robins, P. K., 372
Rose, L., 387
Rottenberg, Simon, 382

Sahlins, Marshall, 436
Salop, S. C., 309
Scherer, Joseph, 381
Scully, Gerald W., 349
Seagraves, James A., 383
Seers, Dudley, 163
Shubik, M., 296
Siegel, S., 299
Silberberg, E., 511
Simon, Julian L., 64, 305
Singer, S. Fred, 265
Sinquefield, Rex A., 461–62, 467
Slutsky, Eugen, 164–65
Smith, Adam, 10, 13, 14
Smith R. T., 51
Smith, Vernon L., 419
Sobell, L. C., 111–12
Sobell, M. B., 111–12
Spitzer, Matthew L., 490–91
Stein, J. P., 463

Stigler, George J., 208, 217, 227, 251, 304–5, 516
Szasz, T. S., 21

Taubman, P., 458
Thales, 7
Tinic, S. M., 246
Toda, M., 74
Tuckman, H. P., 460
Tuma, N. B., 372
Tyrrell, T., 134

Wales, T. J., 139
Weber, E. H., 65
Weinstein, Arnold A., 58–59
Welch, Finis, 73
Westfield, Fred M., 189
Wise, Donald E., 374
Wohl, M., 129–30
Wolfe, L. L., 48
Worcester, D. A., Jr., 251

Zeckhauser, R., 514

INDEX OF TOPICS

Wants (*see* Preference)
War (*see* Conflict)
Water-diamond paradox, 219–21
Water law, 492
Wealth, 448–49 (*see also* Income)
Weber-Fechner Law, 65
"Welfare" (income maintenance),
    366–72
Welfare, social (*see* Social welfare
    function)

Welfare economics, 474, 500–02
Windfall gains and losses, 49–50
Wolfram, 210–11

Yields (*see* Interest and interest rates)

Zero-Profit Theorem, 215–17
Zero-sum game, 293

For Emma and Hannah